ISBN-13: 9781797567617

Contents

List of Tables

List of Figures

Chapter 1. Introduction, Purpose and Scope

1.1 Introduction

This book describes solution architecture as a value-adding information technology consulting service. Solution architecture is concerned with the design and definition of (information technology) solutions so they can be subsequently implemented, used, operated and supported securely and efficiently. The solution exists to operate business processes in order to achieve business objectives, meet a business need and deliver business value. Solution architecture is concerned with engaging with the originating business function looking for the solution to create a solution vision and design a solution that meet their needs, subject to a range of constraints such as cost and affordability, time to deliver and organisational standards. The solution must exist as a coherent whole.

Solutions must be designed consistently across the solution landscape and make optimum use of appropriate technologies.

Solution architecture must focus on creating usable and useful solutions. Solution architecture must have a standard reliable approach to business engagements and the design of solution that emerge from them.

Solution architecture must work collaboratively with other information technology functions – other architecture roles, business analysis and service management – to ensure continuity along the solution delivery journey.

Effective solution architecture means:

- Having a depth and breadth of solution delivery and technical experience to be able to identify solution design options quickly

- Being able to understand the detail of the solution while maintaining a view of the wider (and higher) context of the business need for the solution and being able to explain both these views of sets of information

- Being able to communicate effectively with all parties – technical and business – involved in the solution design and delivery journey, assist with decision-making, be realistic and make appropriate compromises and design choices in order to create the best solution design

- Being able to apply technology appropriately and with selective innovation (and the desire to constantly acquire new knowledge and ways of applying technology)

- Being involved in the solution delivery journey along its entire length

- Being able to be the solution advocate and subject matter expert

A solution is almost never just a custom-developed software component. The complete span of a solution consists of many components that must be designed and delivered in order to create a usable and operable solution. These solution components can consist acquired or developed software, new and changed existing business processes, data migrations and new data loads, organisation changes, infrastructure, service management processes, maintenance and support services, initial period of hypercare and others.

This book has a number of themes:

- The need for solution architecture to concern itself with the full breadth and depth of the solution

- The way in which solution architecture can contribute to ensuring the success of solution delivery

- Solution architecture is or has the potential to be a value-adding information technology consulting service

- That solution architecture should be involved during the solution delivery journey

- The need for solution architecture to have skills in other information technology areas such as data architecture, security and external solution component acquisition

- The importance for solution architecture to work closely with other information technology functions such as business analysis, solution delivery, other information technology architecture functions and service management

- The need for solution architecture to be able to engage flexibly and in different ways with the business function where the need for a solution originates to offer consulting and value-adding services to the business organisation

- The importance of data in solution architecture and design

- The way in which the solution architecture function can structure itself to be able to provide such value

- The need for solution architecture to be aware of and be able to respond to information technology and business trends and changes

The purposes of this book are:

- To articulate a vision for solution architecture

- To express a complete end-to-end solution design approach, from initial idea to steady state solution operation

- To describe the process by which solution designs are created

- To describe the wider context of solution architecture and solution design within the information technology function and the business, including how solution architecture can assist with addressing the issue of solution delivery failure

- To create an understanding of the actual scope of solutions

- To describe the importance of solution architecture in the successful delivery of operable, useful, usable, maintainable and supportable solutions

- To detail a set of solution architecture engagements where the solution architect can work with the business in a variety of ways to create designs to resolve problems or address challenges of opportunities

- To examine specific solution architecture areas of concern such as data architecture, security or digital transformation

- To define the concept of a Solution Architecture Centre of Excellence and to describe its possible structure and operation

- To identify existing well-defined and well-proven frameworks, standards and approaches that can be successfully applied to solution architecture

The book is not about specific technologies that are included in solutions. There are simply too many technologies to cover across the span of an information technology solution. Those technologies are constantly changing. The way in which those technologies are implemented and deployed is also changing. An increasing number of the application components of solutions consists of acquired products or services rather than developed software. The span of any book on solution architecture can be located along two dimensions: its technology and solution emphasis ranging from narrow to broad and its engagement emphasis from an internally-focussed technical approach to a wider consulting one. This book is very definitely located in the domain that is the combination of broad solution and consulting areas.

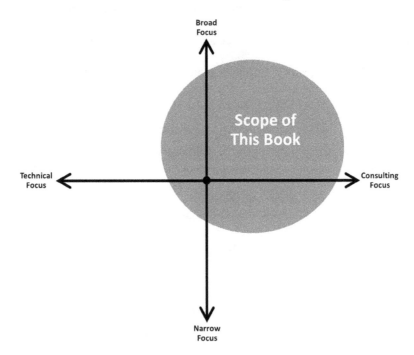

Figure 1 – Solution Architecture Focus of the Book

1.2 Who This Book Is Aimed At

This book is aimed at a variety of potential readers:

- Existing solution architects who want to have a more theoretical and a broader understanding of their role

- Existing or new managers of solution architecture functions who want to create a high-performing practice within their organisations and who want to articulate the benefits and value solution architect can contribute both to the information technology function and the wider business and the potential it can offer to the business organisation

- Mangers of information technology functions who want to understand what solution architecture is, where it fits into the wider architecture context and disciplines and solution delivery and operation and the value it can contribute to both the information technology function and the wider business

- Other information technology architects who want to understand how the architecture disciplines can work together to deliver value

- Business analysts and managers of business analysis functions who want to understand how they can work more closely with the solution architecture function in order to provide the business with a better overall solution analysis, design and delivery service

- Other information technology personnel who are interested in moving into solution architecture and who want to understand what it is

- Consulting organisations and individuals who want to develop and offer value-adding solution architecture services

- Students who are interested in understanding the principles of solution architecture and solution design from a business-oriented viewpoint

1.3 Terminology

In this book, solution architecture means the function and the process that creates solution designs. Solution designs are the specification for solutions. These designs can be at various levels of detail.

The phrases solution architect and solution designer have the same meaning. This is the role that creates solution designs and participates in business engagements that resolve problems or address challenges and opportunities.

1.4 Structure and Contents of This Book

I have numbered the chapters and sections of this book to allow them to be referred easily. While this may seem cumbersome it makes for easy identification of and cross-referencing between sections and avoids duplication of information.

In summary the structure of this book is illustrated below.

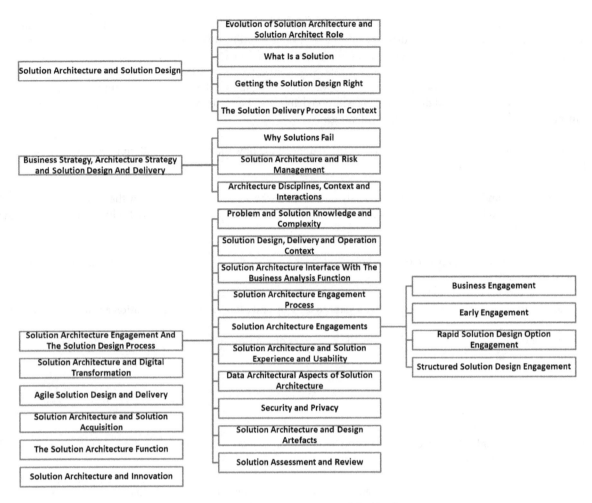

Figure 2 – Summary Structure of this Book

This structure is:

- Solution Architecture and Solution Design — Chapter 2 on page 25 - Summarises the capabilities of solution architecture and provides a context for solution design

  - Evolution of Solution Architecture and Solution Architect Role — Section 2.3 on page 30 - Briefly provides background information to the evolution of the solution architect role

  - What Is a Solution — Section 2.4 on page 33 - Defines what exact a complete solution consists of, the true cost of a solution, the solution boundaries and options and the underlying need for organisational change

  - Getting the Solution Design Right — Section 2.5 on page 50 - What is involved in getting the solution design right

  - The Solution Delivery Process in Context — Section 2.6 on page 50 - What is involved in delivering the solution

- Business Strategy, Architecture Strategy and Solution Design And Delivery — Chapter 3 on page 57 - Contains details on where solution architecture fits into the organisation's over strategy

  - Why Solutions Fail — Section 3.1 on page 57 - Describes how the delivery of solutions fail and how solution architecture can mitigate against solution failure

Review	validating a solution design
• Solution Architecture and Digital Transformation	Chapter 5 on page 391 - Describes the contribution solution architecture can make to designing solutions that achieve digital transformation
• Agile Solution Design and Delivery	Chapter 6 on page 422 - Outlines an iterative and flexible approach to solution design and delivery
• Solution Architecture and Solution Acquisition	Chapter 7 on page 447 - Details the approach to the procurement of packaged solution components
• The Solution Architecture Function	Chapter 8 on page 472 - Contains information on the structure of the solution architecture function, defines a solution architecture capability model, introduces the concept of the Solution Architecture of Excellence and highlights potential issues that can arise with the solution architecture function
o Solution Architecture Skills, Capabilities and Experience	Section 8.2 on page 472 - Describes a set of skills that are required for a solution architect and defines a capability model
o Solution Architecture Function	Section 8.3 on page 487 - Discusses the structure of the solution architecture function
o Solution Architecture Tools	Section 8.3.5 on page 511 - Outlines various tools and techniques that can be used by solution architects
• Solution Architecture and Innovation	Chapter 9 on page 534 - Describes how the solution architecture function can assist the organisation with solution and technology innovation

1.5 Checklists

This book contains a lot of information in the form of tables and lists. While densely-presented material in this format may be more difficult to read than narrative text, this information can be applied in the form of checklists. These can be used during different stages of the business engagement and solution design processes. The following table lists some of these checklists.

Section	Checklist	Description
Section 2.4.2 on page 33	Scope of Complete Solution	List of component types of solution
Section 3.1 on page 57	Challenge Reasons	List of reasons why solution delivery projects are challenged
	Success Factors	List of factors that lead to successful solution delivery
Section 3.2 on page 71	Solution Risk Factors	List of risks associated with solution design
Section 3.3.3 on page 81	IT Architecture Principles	List of principles underpinning solution architecture
Section 3.3.4 on page 83	Problems with IT Architecture Operation	List of problems that can occur with the operation of IT architecture functions
Section 4.2.2 on page 100	Complexity Factors	List of factors that affect solution complexity and method for assessing the complexity of a solution
Section 4.3 on page 112	Solution Delivery Stages	List of stages involved in the delivery of a solution
	Solution Delivery Artefacts	List of artefacts that can be created during the delivery of a solution

Section 4.4.2	Lessons Learned from System Implementation	List of lessons learned when implementing large systems
	Causes Of Waste	Causes of waste in business process design and operation
	Business Process Design Success Factors	List of factors that lead to successful business process design
	Business Process Design Standards and Approaches	List of standards to use when designing business processes
Section 4.6.1.1	Factors Driving the Need for a Business Engagement	List of reasons that give rise to the need for a solution architecture engagement with the business
	Architecture Engagement Extended Factors	List of factors that govern the scope of the solution architecture engagement with the business
Section 4.6.1.3 on page 167	Business Engagement High Level Activities	List of stages in the solution architecture engagement with the business
Section 4.6.1.6.1 on page 183	Business Vision Factors	List of factors to be considered when developing the initial business vision
Section 4.6.1.6.3 on page 188	Business Domain Principles	List of current and target application and system, business process, organisation and structure and locations and offices principles
Section 4.6.1.7.4 on page 199	Cost Estimation Process	List of steps involved in creating a solution cost estimate
Section 4.6.1.9.2 on page 209	Factors Affecting Application And Data Organisation	List of factors to use when analysing and defining the business application and data structures
Section 4.6.1.10.1 on page 213	Product and Service Evaluation And Selection	List of factors to use when evaluating products and services
Section 4.6.1.11.1 on page 221	Activities to Design Infrastructure Model Architecture	List of steps to perform when designing the business infrastructure architecture
Section 4.6.2 on page 226	Steps in Solution Design Process	List of steps to following in the solution design process
Section 4.6.4.7 on page 251	Resolution Options	List of options to evaluate the available resolution options
	Solution Quality Factors	List of solution quality and operational factors
Section 4.6.5 on page 257	Rapid Solution Design Steps	List of steps to follow when creating an initial high-level solution design
Section 4.6.6 on page 276	Solution Design Activities Across Solution Views	List of steps to follow and information to gather when creating a detailed solution design
Section 4.7 on page 311	Solution Usability Factors	List of factors to consider when assessing the usability of a solution
	Solution Usability Standards	List of standards and methodologies developed for solution usability
Section 4.8.1 on page 321	Solution Data Management Framework	List of data management framework components that can be used to validate the data aspects of a solution
Section 4.8.2 on page 326	Components in Solution Data Landscape	List of possible component types and their interactions in a solution data landscape
Section 4.8.4 on page 337	Data Lifecycle Stages	Set of stages in the data lifecycle
Section 4.8.5 on page 339	Data Integration Types and Solution Components	List of data integration option, components and interactions
Section 4.9.1 on page 352	Solution Security Controls	List of security controls to use the check the security of a solution
	Security Standards	List of security standards and frameworks

Section 4.9.2.3 on page 366	Privacy and Personal Data Related Processes and Impact on Solution Design	List of data privacy processes that apply to personal data and how they will impact solution design
Section 4.10 on page 377	Solution Design Table of Contents	Table of contents of a solution design artefact
Section 4.11.1 on page 381	Solution Benefits Review Checklist	Checklist of potential solution benefits
Section 4.11.2 on page 383	Solution Design Review Checklist	Checklist of design factors to be used in solution design reviews
Section 5.3 on page 399	Digital Target Architecture Components	List of components of a digital reference architecture
Section 5.4.3 on page 418	Digital Solution Common Characteristics and Principles	Set of principles to consider when designing solutions with a digital focus
Section 6.3 on page 426	Agile Solution Design and Delivery Principles	List of solution design principles to apply when using an agile approach
Section 6.4 on page 427	Agile Approach Suitability Checklist	Checklist of questions to assess if a solution is suitable for an agile process
	Key Principles of Iterative Agile Approach	Set of principles to apply when using an agile solution design and delivery approach
Section 6.5 on page 431	Control Components of Agile Process	Set of controls to use when following an agile solution design and delivery approach
Section 6.7.2 on page 438	Agile Feasibility Analysis and Study Checklists	Checklists on the initial study and feasibility plan
Section 7.1 on page 447	Solution Architecture and Solution Acquisition Approaches	List of standards and methodologies that can be applied for solution procurement
	Aspects of a Solution or Service	List of characteristics of a solution or service being procured
Section 7.1.1 on page 452	Sourcing Phases and Activities	Set of activities to be performed when sourcing a solution
Section 7.1.1.1 on page 454	Solution Architecture Activities During Initiation/Transition and Service Delivery Phases	Set of activities to be performed when transitioning to a newly acquired product or service
Section 7.1.1.2 on page 459	Solution Architecture Activities During Ongoing Service Phase	Set of activities to be performed during the life of an acquired product or service
Section 7.1.2 on page 466	Service Organisation Controls Structure	Set of controls to be applied to an organisation providing a service
Section 8.2 on page 472	Solution Architect Skills, Capabilities and Experience	Checklist of solution architecture skills and capabilities
Section 8.3.2 on page 489	Solution Architecture Function Structure	Set of capabilities of a solution architecture function
Section 8.3.3 on page 492	Solution Architecture Centre Of Excellence (SACOE) Functions	Set of capabilities of a solution architecture centre of excellence
	Solution Architecture Knowledge and Skills	Checklist for assessing the skills, experience, knowledge and capabilities of solution architects
Section 8.3.5.1 on page 512	Solution Architecture Design Tools	List of architecture design tools
Section 8.3.5.2 on page 528	IT Architecture Frameworks, Methodologies and Description Languages	List of architecture standards, methodologies and design languages
Chapter 9 on page 534	Areas To Look For Innovation	List of potential areas where to look for and apply innovation

Table 1 – Solution Architecture-Related Checklists Contained in the Book

Chapter 2. Solution Architecture and Solution Design

2.1 Introduction

Solution architecture and design is concerned with the definition and description of new (Information Technology) solution designs to resolve problems or address opportunities through engagement with the business. The solution may or may not include a technology component. For example, the optimum solution could involve just business process and organisation changes.

Generally there are many potential resolutions to a problem with varying degrees of suitability and cost. All solutions are subject to constraints. The solution constraints need to be included in the solution design process.

These resolutions can be standard solutions where the knowledge – problem knowledge and solution knowledge - required to create the design is known and available or new and innovative where there are knowledge gaps that must be identified and completed.

Solution architecture requires a (changing) combination of technical, leadership, interpersonal skills, experience, analysis, appropriate creativity, reflection and intuition applied in a structured manner to derive the most suitable solution.

Solution architecture involves a number of overlapping foundational capabilities, sets of knowledge and areas of interaction and involvement with other areas of the organisation.

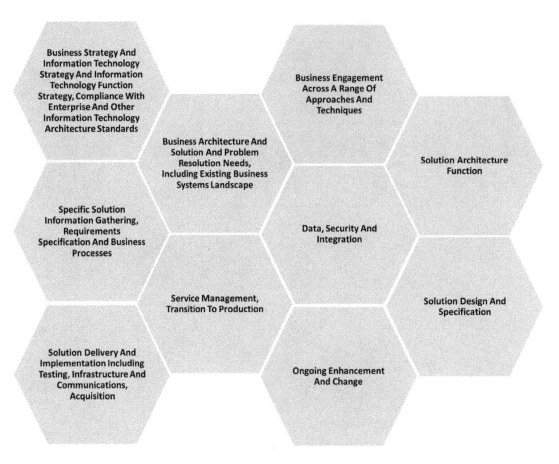

Figure 3 – Overlapping Solution Architecture Capabilities and Areas of Solution Involvement and Knowledge

These overlapping foundational capabilities are listed in the table below.

Solution Architecture Capabilities	Description
Business Strategy And Information Technology Strategy And Information Technology Function Strategy, Compliance With Enterprise And Other Information Technology Architecture Standards	The organisation will have an overall business strategy and underpinning objectives. The organisation's information technology strategy will follow from this as a means of achieving the business strategy and objectives. The information technology function will have its own internal strategy that will detail how it will structure and organise itself to deliver the organisation's overall information technology strategy. The solution architecture function must have an understanding of this organisation context within which solutions will operate. The information technology function will define a set of technology standards in the areas of enterprise, security, data and service architectures that solutions must comply with. The solution architecture function must understand these core technology standards.
Business Architecture And Solution And Problem Resolution Needs, Including Existing Business Systems Landscape	Solutions must be designed to operate in a business context. Solutions consist of more than just software components. There is a greater solution operational environment that includes integration across a number of elements, organisation change, data migration, service introduction, maintenance and support, training and documentation and other areas. The solution architect must design solutions with this larger perspective in mind.
Business Engagement Across A Range Of Approaches And Techniques	The nature of the solution required by the originating and requesting business function can take several forms, from a standard solution specification to a consulting engagement that refines and defines a problem to be resolved or a challenge or opportunity to be addressed. Also, not all solutions proceed to implementation. The solution architecture function must possess the necessary

Solution Architecture Capabilities	Description
	engagement skills and techniques to handle these different assignment types.
Solution Architecture Function	The solution architecture function needs to have three central areas of work 1. *External* – making the skills and capabilities of the function known to the wider business, handling requests from business functions for consulting and solution design engagements, managing the progress and the quality of the work done and any deliverables created, handling and resolving issues and establishing and maintaining relationships. The management can also advertise the work of the function and conduct regular showcase events where new technologies and technical capabilities that might be of potential use are demonstrated to the business. 2. *Internal* – developing and managing the team, allocating work, overseeing quality reviews, providing assistance with business engagement, recruiting, training and mentoring the team and managing talent and succession. 3. *Other Information Technology Functions* – developing and maintaining relationships with information technology management, other architecture functions, business analysis, solution delivery and service management.
Specific Solution Information Gathering, Requirements Specification And Business Processes	The solution business stakeholders will provide details on some of the solution requirements. The solution architect must be able to work with the business analysis function define the full set of solution requirements, including operational and quality ones. The solution architect must understand the underlying existing and new business processes that the solution aims to enable and operate.
Solution Design And Specification	The solution architect must be able to specify the design of the complete solution that includes all the areas that must be worked on to create a full operable, usable, maintainable and supportable solution. The solution architect must have the necessary technical skills to define the technology aspects of the solution in sufficient detail to allow the design to be implemented.
Data, Security And Integration	Data across all its dimensions of generation, transportation, processing and retention breathes life into the solution. The solution architect must specify the solution data landscape in sufficient detail to ensure that the solution can work and handle the required data interactions and volumes. The solution and its data must be secure across all its components. The solution will be required to integrate with other components, other systems and solutions and other entities. The solution architect must understand and describe this integration environment.
Solution Delivery And Implementation Including Testing, Infrastructure And Communications, Acquisition	The solution architecture function must provide solution leadership and solution subject matter expertise as the solution and its individual components are implemented and integrated. This includes working to define the necessary infrastructure and acquire the necessary external products and services.
Service Management, Transition To Production	The solution must be transitioned to production. The necessary service management processes must be put in place to allow this. The solution architecture function must work with service management early during solution design to ensure this work is understood and specified.
Ongoing Enhancement And Change	After the solution is operational, it will be subject to ongoing requests for enhancements and fixes. The solution architecture function can provide solution leadership and solution subject matter expertise to assist with this.

Table 2 – Overlapping Solution Architecture Capabilities and Areas of Solution Involvement and Knowledge

Solution architecture needs to be an operational and transactional function within information technology. It needs to be capable to doing work and achieving results and value to the organisation. It is a doing as well as a thinking function.

Solutions are designed, delivered and operated on these foundational pillars. Chapter 8 on page 472 looks at the structure of the solution architecture function and the capabilities of a solution architect in more detail needed to achieve this.

The purpose of the solution architecture deliverable – the solution design – is to enable the solution to be implemented and operated. The design is a specification of an IT-oriented solution whose purpose is to realise a defined set of end states and generate a set of outputs. The solution is intended to operate in a defined environment. The solution is designed to satisfy a set of requirements and to meet a set of expectations. The solution and its design are subject to a variety of environment-specific constraints and limitations.

The means by which the design is arrived at is not necessarily straightforward and linear. The design process may involve different engagements with the business and business stakeholders as the problem being resolved or the challenge being addressed is expanded on, clarified and ultimately defined to a sufficiently detailed extent that it can be passed to delivery.

Solutions are typically described and defined in the context of individual solution delivery projects. That is, solutions are implemented individually by separate projects or as a collection of solutions implemented as a programme. The solution is intrinsically concerned with solving one problem.

The high-level context of an individual solution design incorporates the aspects of:

- The functionality of the solution – what is how and how the functionality is to be delivered and operated, how it is implemented and subsequently supported and maintained

- How the solution appears to users, how users access and interact with and use it

- The operating landscape of the solution in terms of the business processes, organisation structures and users (and its external users, if relevant)

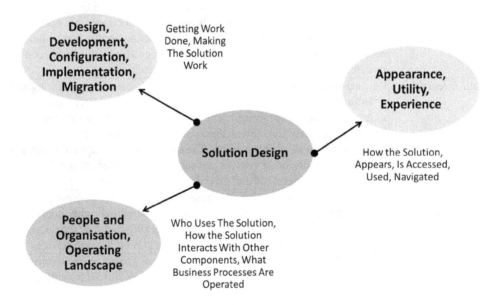

Figure 4 – High Level Context of Solution Design

However, the solution architecture practice or function within an organisation must be able to co-ordinate and manage the creation of multiple solutions designs that work in an integrated business and information technology organisation context. The individual solution designs create by the members of the solution architecture team must maximise the use of organisation technical resources and comply with organisation standards. One of the key roles of the solution architecture function and the individual solution architects is to avoid the creation of multiple point solutions with little commonality and reuse that increase long-term information technology costs for the organisation.

The theory and practice of project management is mature, well-proven and clearly defined. The benefits of project management are understood and appreciated. The necessary costs of a project management overhead to a delivery project are accepted. Likewise, business analysis is reasonably well-defined, though not to the same extent as project management. Business analysts tend to be siloed into the requirements gathering phase of solution delivery. Solution architecture is as not well-defined or understood as these other practices.

The project is the temporary engagement to get the solution operational. The solution will endure long after its delivery project has come to an end. The solution will continue to be used and to incur ongoing costs in terms of its operation, support and maintenance. Problems with and inefficiencies in the solution will have long-term consequences.

2.2 Solution Architecture – A Lesson From History

In Book 1, Chapter 2 of *The Fundamental Principles Of Architecture*[1], Vitruvius gives the core principles of architecture as:

> *Architectura autem constat ex ordinatione et ex dispositione et eurythmia et symmetria et decore et distributione.*

> *Architecture depends on Order, Arrangement, Eurythmy, Symmetry, Propriety, and Economy.*

He then expands on each of these principles to describe a more detailed framework and set of values for architectural designs. This expansion can be described as follows:

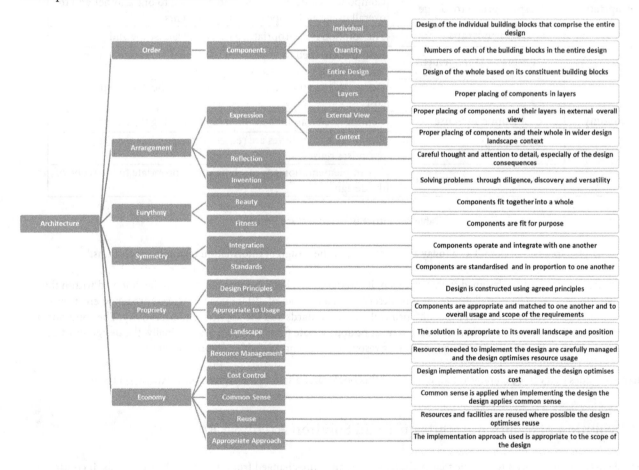

Figure 5 – Vitruvius' Architecture Principles

---

[1] *Ten Books on Architecture* Marcus Vitruvius Pollio, http://www.gutenberg.org/files/20239/20239-h/20239-h.htm

These expanded principles are:

Order	Components	Individual	Design of the individual building blocks that comprise the entire design
		Quantity	Numbers of each of the building blocks in the entire design
		Entire Design	Design of the whole based on its constituent building blocks
Arrangement	Expression	Layers	Proper placing of components in layers
		External View	Proper placing of components and their layers in external overall view
		Context	Proper placing of components and their whole in wider design landscape context
	Reflection		Careful thought and attention to detail, especially of the design consequences
	Invention		Solving problems through diligence, discovery and versatility
Eurythmy	Beauty		Components fit together into a whole
	Fitness		Components are fit for purpose
Symmetry	Integration		Components operate and integrate with one another
	Standards		Components are standardised and in proportion to one another
Propriety	Design Principles		Design is constructed using agreed principles
	Appropriate to Usage		Components are appropriate and matched to one another and to overall usage and scope of the requirements
	Landscape		The solution is appropriate to its overall landscape and position
Economy	Resource Management		Resources needed to implement the design are carefully managed and the design optimises resource usage
	Cost Control		Design implementation costs are managed the design optimises cost
	Common Sense		Common sense is applied when implementing the design
	Reuse		Resources and facilities are reused where possible the design optimises reuse
	Appropriate Approach		The implementation approach used is appropriate to the scope of the design

Table 3 – Vitruvius' Architecture Principles

These principles are just as relevant and today and applicable to the design of information technology solutions.

The overall solution must be designed in the context of its components. Each component needs to be designed within the overall solution setting. The overall design must be described in a number of different views. The approach to creating a design involves both the application of thought, principles and standards and the application of creativity. The components of the design must fit and worth together. The design must be appropriate to its intended usage. Finally, the design must be created to be implemented cost effectively, optimising resource usage and available component reuse.

These are values that can be employed today. Much of this book can be said to follow from and expand on them.

2.3 Evolution of Solution Architecture and Solution Architect Role

The role of the solution architect is one that evolved as IT architecture changed from the early 1990s onwards. It continues to evolve in the light of the major technology deployment changes that have occurred since then: from mainframe to client server to N-tier models to web-based models to service orientation, XaaS patterns and digital transformation.

Prior to the advent of client/server architecture and subsequent N-tier, distributed, service oriented, public-facing solution and cloud architectures and the solutions deployed on them, there was effectively only one mainframe-based IT architecture that evolved from or were similar to IBM System/360 and System/370 hardware (and from these all the way to the current zEnterprise systems) and the various operating systems (OS/VS1, MVS/370, VM/SP, MVS/XA, VM/XA, MVS/ESA VM/ESA up to the current zOS operating system) that ran on this hardware and provided the core work management, data management and communications management facilities.

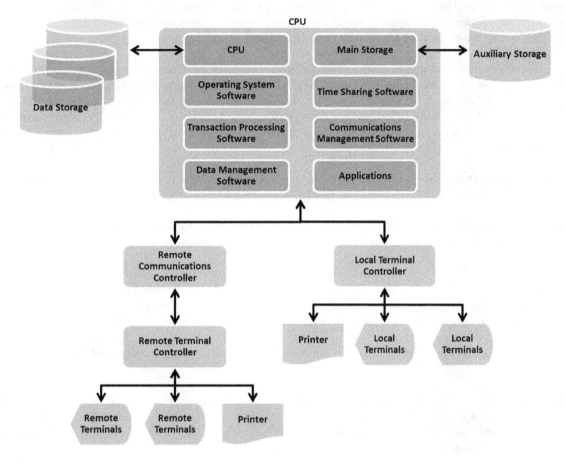

Figure 6 – High-Level Logical Mainframe IT Architecture

In the context of this computing model, the platform was the IT architecture. The platform was homogenous, monolithic and centralised. The IT architecture was effectively given and unvarying. All of the IT landscape was under the control of the central platform. There was a master/slave relationship between the mainframe and attached components. The issues regarding the design of solutions related to implementation factors such as batch or online processing or a combination of both in a suite of applications, choice of development language (from a limited set), use of transaction processing facility as an application development and deployment framework, the method of data storage and the functionality to be delivered.

In parallel to the relative lack of complexity in the IT landscape, concepts such as workflow and business process management and design were very new and seldom applied.

In this context, the core solution design role was performed by the systems analysis function that was involved in the analysis, design and assisted with the subsequent implementation and transfer to operation of information system solutions. The systems analyst was both business-facing, working with the business function to understand their requirements and IT-facing, designing IT solutions and working with developers to implement them and participating in their development and testing. The work of the systems analyst was divided into two parts: systems analysis and systems design. Systems analysis involves gathering information on how the work targeted for the proposed solution is being performed, what problems occur and the options for the resolution. Systems design involves design the solution to replace or complement the existing work processes. The Structured Systems Analysis and Design Methodology (SSADM) briefly described in section 8.3.5.1.1 on page 516 was typically used in systems analysis.

The move from a centralised mainframe platform to one incorporating distributed and heterogeneous system components requiring application and data integration gave rise to the need for a solution architect role to design solutions that incorporated multiple components across this more diverse IT topography.

The systems analyst role split into separate roles: the business analysis that performed the business facing role and the solution architect that performed the solution design role. While the systems analyst role continues in many incarnations it does not have the same broad spread of activities that it had in the past.

The loss of the systems analyst role as a function that worked across analysing business requirements, designing solutions to meet those requirements and subsequently on the development and implementation of those solutions means that this broad view is all too frequently absent from the current analysis and design processes. The platform nature of the mainframe-based IT architecture for which solutions were designed and on which they were deployed and operated allowed for one role to encompass the full scope of the solution journey. The complexity and heterogeneity of current IT architectures means that this is more difficult.

The existence of separate functions means that there are handoffs between functions of information related to solution design rather than the previous continuity. This issue is discussed more in section 2.6 on page 50.

The functional specification artefact that was produced by the systems analyst that specified the detailed design and operation of the solution has now also almost disappeared from the current solution design process and the associated set of artefacts now produced.

The current process frequently involves multiple handoffs and associated artefacts are passed between the separate roles, from the business requirements specification produced by the business analyst to the solution design produced by the solution architect to the technical design produced by the technical architect or the technical team lead.

The topic of the interface between the business analysis and solution architecture functions is covered in more detail in section 4.4 on page 124.

The concept of the platform as the IT architecture for the organisation is discussed further in Chapter 5 on page 391 where the future of solution architecture in the context of organisation digital transformation is examined. The question of whether the digital framework to support the digital organisation represents a new platform that reduces or removes the need for solution architecture is considered.

The monolithic centralised IT architecture meant that changes and new solutions were introduced slowly and expensively. It was inflexible in responding quickly to business needs. The only data that was available was that obtained or presented through reports.

This monolithic IT architecture has been replaced in many organisations by monolithic applications – large, apparently all-encompassing systems such as ERP – that have the same characteristics of being inflexible, unyielding, slow and expensive to change as large centralised systems.

This monumental approach to IT systems and the design of solutions that operate within this uniform and rigid context has led in the past and continues to lead to the growth of Shadow IT. This is addressed further in section 3.3.5 on page 86.

The digital platform referred to in Chapter 5 on page 391 needs to avoid becoming another such monolithic information technology system.

The solution architecture function could look to restore the depth and breadth of the systems analyst role in the way it approaches being involved both in working with the business to define a solution and in subsequent solution delivery.

2.4 What Is a Solution?

2.4.1 Introduction

An (Information Technology) solution is a *Resolver*, a *Provider* or an *Enabler*. It fixes an existing set of problems. It provides a new set of functions. It enables the consumers of the solutions to work in different ways to operate business processes and provide new products and services or to provide existing products and services differently or take advantage of a new opportunity.

The need for a solution arises because of one (or more) of the following occurs:

- There is an opportunity I want to take advantage of
- I have received a directive or need to respond to a new regulation
- I want to be able to do what I am currently unable to do
- I cannot do what I want
- I need to be able to do something
- The current solution is too manual, inefficient, costly to operate or not scalable or needs to be replaced or upgraded because it uses unsupported technology

An originator will identify the need for a solution. Solution architecture must then work with the originator to provide a usable response to the solution need. The resulting business solutions should be must haves rather than nice to haves in terms of functionality and the requirements that are delivered.

2.4.2 Scope of Complete Solution

The complete solution required is rarely, if ever, just a collection of software components. The whole solution comprises the entire set of components needed to operate the business processes associated with delivering the service for which the solution has been designed. Ultimately, a successful solution requires the interoperation of all these components and that the components are properly designed and implemented.

Any complete solution will consist of zero or more instances of the following components types:

Component Type	Description
Changes to Existing Systems	Existing software components, either custom-developed applications or products sourced from external suppliers, both installed on the organisation's IT infrastructure or hosted externally, and configured or customised, may need to be changed in some way to accommodate the requirements of the new solution. The affected applications will need to be identified and the nature of the changes required will need to be described. These will need to be tested during their implementation and the results of the testing actioned as required.
New Custom Developed Applications	New software components will need to be developed. The list of these components will need to be identified. This may include the development of prototypes to validate their functionality and/or their appearance and navigation. These will need to be tested during their implementation and the results of the testing actioned as required.

Component Type	Description
Information Storage Facilities	The various application components will generate data at different rates that will need to be stored for various intervals. This includes interim data storage, operational data storage and derived data storage for reporting and analysis. The volume of data to be stored and the types of storage required to deliver the required access times will need to be quantified.
Acquired, Configured and Customised Software Products	New software products that are intended to be installed on the organisation's information technology infrastructure will need to be acquired and then configured or customised. The products required by the solution will need to be ascertained and the nature of the configuration or customisation will need to be defined. These will need to be tested during their implementation and the results of the testing actioned as required.
System Integrations/ Data Transfers/ Exchanges	Data may be supplied to or exchanged between solution components. These integrations, transfers or exchanges can take many forms, from file transfer to messages exchanged using a message queueing facility to data supplied by an application programming interface to data exchanged via a mailbox to email integration. The precise method by which the data integrations, data transformations, transfers or exchanges take place should be listed. The content and format of the data being exchanged, the protocols to be used and the security to be applied should be defined. If the infrastructural applications required to perform the data integrations, transfers or exchanges are new then they should be listed as a member of Acquired and Customised Software Products. If existing facilities are being used, their reuse should be stated. These will need to be tested during their implementation.
Changes to Existing Business Processes	Existing business processes may need to be changed to take advantage of or in response to the new solution. These business processes should be listed with a description of the changes required.
New Business Processes	New business processes may need to be defined to allow the solution to be operated. These processes should be identified.
Organisational Changes	The organisation may need to be changed. New roles and staff may need to be created. Existing roles and staff may need to be changed. New offices and facilities may need to be acquired. Existing offices, locations and facilities may need to be changed.
Reporting and Analysis Facilities	All applications generate new data and use existing data. The solution will typically need facilities to report on this data, to report on the operation and use of the solution itself and will need facilities to analyse data. The organisation may have an existing report and analysis set of tools that can be reused. Solution data stores are typically operational and do not store historical time-oriented data. The reporting and analysis component may require a data warehouse. The definition of reporting and analysis is frequently either an afterthought in solution design, dropped from solution delivery because of schedule and cost pressures or is specified in a non-integrated way using solution-specific tools. These will need to be tested during their implementation.
Existing Data Conversions/ Migrations	Data from existing application components may need to be migrated to the new platforms to avoid data loss and to make the new system usable. The migration activities may include data reformatting, mapping to new data structures, data enrichment and data cleansing.

Component Type	Description
	These will need to be validated.
New Data Loads	New data loads may be required to populate some of the data structures of the new solution to make the new system usable. These will need to be validated.
Training and Documentation	Internal users and external partner and service provider users may need to be trained in the operation and use of the solution and its business processes. Training documentation and other material may be required.
Central, Distributed and Communications Infrastructure	The solution may require additional communications infrastructure to, for example, enable external access by mobile users from within the organisation or by external users or service providers or to access externally hosted components. It may also require such infrastructure for new locations to be defined as part of the solution. This may also require additional security infrastructure to support these new accesses.
Sets of Installation and Implementation Services	Some of the solution components may require externally provided installation and implementation services to install, configure or customise these components.
Cutover/ Transfer to Production And Support	The solution will need to be transitioned to support. The support function will need to be trained in providing first line support. Second and third level support arrangements will need to be put in place for the operational solution components. The operational and organisational readiness for the solution may need to be assessed and any issues resolved so the organisation is prepared and capable of taking on the solution. There may be an operational acceptance testing phase where the operability and supportability of the solution is verified and any issues identified during such testing are addressed.
Operational Functions and Processes	Processes may need to be defined relating to the operation of the solution and housekeeping functions to be performed. These functions may need to be configured and tested. These can include: • Monitoring, alerting and event management including the configuration of alerts and rules for the handling • Backup and recovery • Business continuity and availability • Capacity planning and management
Parallel Runs	The existing and new solutions may need to be run in parallel for an interval. The results of the parallel runs may need to be compared.
Enhanced Support/ Hypercare	After the solution has gone live, an initial period of enhanced support or hypercare may be needed where problems receive special attention to ensure they are resolved quickly. This may require special arrangements with suppliers.
Sets of Maintenance, Service Management and Support Services	The components of the solution will need to be supported and maintained. Agreements may need to be put in place with suppliers of these services.
Application Hosting and Management Services	Elements of the solution may be hosted externally or provided entirely as an outsourced service. These elements will need to be established. Infrastructure may be needed to enable secure communications and the exchange of data between these external components.

Table 4 – Components of Complete Solution

This is just one view of the components of a solution. Other categorisations and breakdowns are possible. Testing could be specified as a separate component rather than being allocated as an activity associated with each applicable component. This is the itemisation approach used in this book as a way of defining the scope of a solution.

So, while not all solutions will have all these component types, all solutions will have at least some of them. Each of these component types and the individual components within each type give rise to work and cost. Omitting them from the solution scope (and therefore from the solution design) does not mean that they are not required or should not or will not be part of the solution as ultimately implemented. In some cases, their omission can be regarded as a form of strategic misrepresentation where the person or group responsible for the solution does not want to represent the actual solution scope or cost or resources or time required, at least during the initial solution approval and agreement stages. This, the design work of the solution architect is not allowed to encompass the complete solution.

The solution design therefore needs to include the full scope of the solution. It does not have to include all the components in a fully defined state. But it needs to include them to such an extent and level of detail so they are known about and included in subsequent time and resource planning and cost estimates.

Figure 7 – Scope of Complete Solution

One further advantage of this complete, end-to-end view is that the solution as a whole is visible to all. Where the solution is broken down into individual components, the individuals involved just see and focus on their areas of expertise. The individuals design the components as isolated items. The can lead to poor overall performance, throughput, operation, usability and consumer experience. No one is responsible for the integrity of the solution in its entirety. This end-to-end view means that the solution is designed and implemented as a whole from the start. The impact of a decision to delay or remove functionality from a component can be seen in terms of the effect it has on the entire solution. The solution is considered as the sum of its components operating together. The solution is viewed as an organised set of interconnected components.[2]

---

[2] The end-to-end entire solution view is similar to the concepts of internal and external integrity introduced in ***The Power of Product Integrity*** Kim B. Clark and Takahiro Fujimoto https://hbr.org/1990/11/the-power-of-product-integrity . External integrity means that the entirety of the solution represents a balance of form, function, usability and reliability that consumers want. Internal integrity means that the solution's components operate together as a complete whole.

> *Product integrity has both an internal and an external dimension. Internal integrity refers to the consistency between a product's function and its structure: the parts fit smoothly, the components match and work well together, the layout maximizes the available space. Organizationally, internal integrity is achieved mainly through cross-functional coordination within the company and with suppliers.*

Omitting solution elements such as, for example, process and organisation changes from the solution design does not remove them from the scope of the solution that is ultimately required. They are still needed in order to create a fully operational solution. They do not go away just because they have been ignored. More likely, they will be added later during solution delivery, either explicitly or implicitly as a form of shadow project work or as a change request, where they will add ostensibly unforeseen (but not unforeseeable) cost, time and resources to the project. In reality, this is not a change but the correction of an omission.

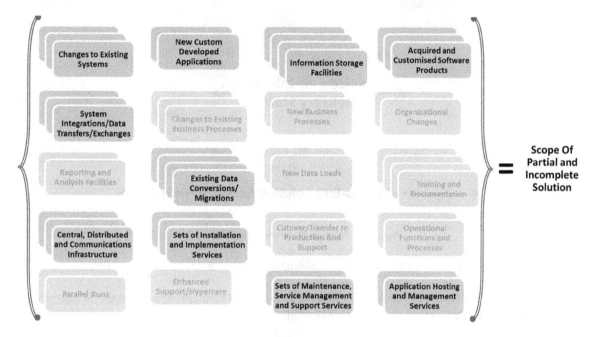

Figure 8 – Scope of Partial and Incomplete Solution

An all too frequent occurrence is the descoping of the solution and its components during its implementation project. Because of pressures on budget, schedule or resources, components of the solution or functionality within components are removed from its scope in order to reduce those pressures. This descoping removes functionality that is needed for the solution to work fully. The implementation of these components is deferred to (a sometimes non-specific or even non-existent) future stage. The result is a partially completed solution with manual workarounds and its associated inefficiencies and extra cost and with a backlog of rework. For example, the delivery of reporting and analysis facilities and the associated data infrastructure is one that is commonly deferred.

Solution delivery too often takes a ***middle-to-middle*** rather than an ***end-to-end*** view of what needs to be implemented in order to create a fully operational solution. Solution delivery assumes that the components outside the middle-to-middle solution delivery scope will be implemented by others. These components can be regarded as solution negative externalities[3]. These are costs that the solution delivery imposes on others because of the limited solution scope it chooses to implement.

External integrity refers to the consistency between a product's performance and customers' expectations. ... external integrity is critical to a new product's competitiveness. Yet for the most part, external integrity is an underexploited opportunity. Companies assign responsibility for anticipating what customers will want to one or more functional groups (the product planners in marketing, for example, or the testers in product engineering). But they give little or no attention to integrating a clear sense of customer expectations into the work of the product development organization as a whole.

The article is derived from a larger publication ***Product Development in the World Auto Industry***, KIM B. CLARK, W. BRUCE CHEW, TAKAHIRO FUJIMOTO - https://pdfs.semanticscholar.org/90f2/15d9f0c0e49e3ea2a366b8b06de3b81d094f.pdf.
[3] See:
https://en.wikipedia.org/wiki/Externality.

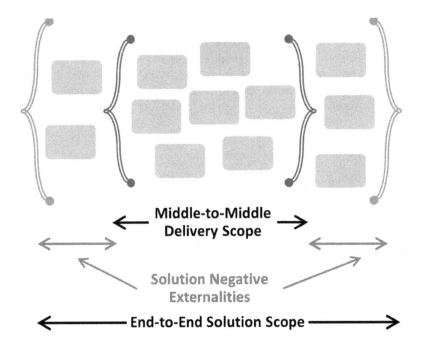

Figure 9 – Solution Delivery Externalities

Be aware of and beware of solution externalities. These are hidden solution delivery costs and responsibilities.

The relative size and contribution to the overall project scope of each of the solution component types will depend on the profile of the project. So, the impact of the omission of some components will therefore depend, at least indirectly, on their size.

Organisational Changes	System Integrations/ Data Transfers/ Exchanges	New Custom Developed Applications	Information Storage Facilities
Operational Functions and Processes	Reporting and Analysis Facilities	Cutover/ Transfer to Production	Central, Distributed and Communications Infrastructure
Training and Documentation	Changes to Existing Business Processes	Existing Data Conversions/ Migrations	New Data Loads
		Acquired and Customised Software Products	Sets of Maintenance, Service Management and Support Services / Sets of Installation and Implementation Services
Changes to Existing Systems	Application Hosting and Management Services	Parallel Runs	New Business Processes

Likely scope of complete solution

Organisational Changes	System Integrations/ Data Transfers/ Exchanges	New Custom Developed Applications	Information Storage Facilities
Operational Functions and Processes	Reporting and Analysis Facilities	Cutover/ Transfer to Production	Central, Distributed and Communications Infrastructure
Training and Documentation	Changes to Existing Business Processes	Existing Data Conversions/ Migrations	New Data Loads
		Acquired and Customised Software Products	Sets of Maintenance, Service Management and Support Services / Sets of Installation and Implementation Services
Changes to Existing Systems	Application Hosting and Management Services	Parallel Runs	New Business Processes

If elements of the solution scope are omitted then the solution design will not be complete

Figure 10 – Omission of Components from Solution Design Scope

The omission of components from the solution design can be viewed as red flags, indicating the potential for future problems.

The solution can only really be regarded as delivered and operational when all the required components have been delivered successfully and that they work. The solution is only complete when all its constituent components are operational. The implementation of the individual components must converge at some point during the solution delivery phases.

Figure 11 – Convergence of Solution Components to Create Complete Operational Solution

Once this convergence of solution components is understood then informed decisions can be made about the staging of the components and their constituent elements along the following lines:

Figure 12 – Staged Delivery of Solution Components

It is an inconvenient truth that complete and accurate information is rarely available. So, decisions such as the scheduling of solution component delivery and functionality to be included within solution components within a phased delivery be made on the available information.

The topic of solution delivery are discussed further in section 4.3 on page 112 and Chapter 6 on page 422.

2.4.3 Solutions and Organisation Change

Every solution involves internal organisation change. These changes typically occur across one or more of six core domains.

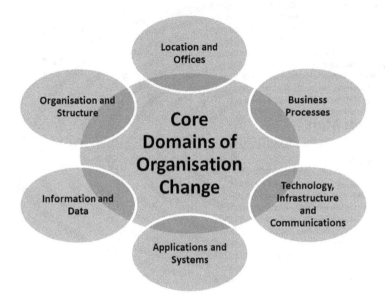

Figure 13 – Organisation Core Change Domains

These six core change domains are divided into two groups: those relating to the business and those relating to information technology

- *Business-Oriented Change* Areas

  - *Location and Offices* – existing and new locations and facilities of the organisation, their types and functions and the principles that govern the selection of new locations
  - *Business Processes* – current and future business process definitions, requirements, characteristics, performance
  - *Organisation and Structure* – organisation resources and arrangement, business unit, function and team structures and composition, relationships, reporting and management, roles and skills

- *Technology-Oriented Change* Areas

  - *Technology, Infrastructure and Communications* – current and future technical infrastructure including security, constraints, standards, technology trends, characteristics, performance requirements
  - *Applications and Systems* – current and future applications and systems, characteristics, constraints, assumptions, requirements, design principles, interface standards, connectivity to business processes
  - *Information and Data* – data and information architecture, data integration, master and reference data, data access and management, data security and privacy

These six core change domains affect the organisation or business function where the solution will be operated. There is a seventh change domain for changes that occur outside the organisation such as the external business landscape that the solution must react to or solution users who are located outside the organisation.

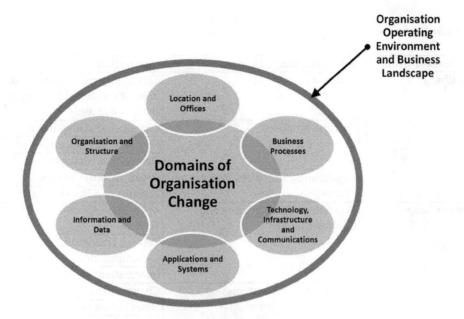

Figure 14 – Extended Organisation Change Domain

While the organisation generally has control around internal changes and the reaction to them, externally-facing changes and the response to them are more difficult to anticipate, control and manage.

The topic of the organisation changes cause by the introduction of solutions is covered in more detail in section 4.6.4.8 on page 253.

2.4.4 Solution Components and Organisation Change

The generic component types of which every solution is composed can be allocated across these six change domains.

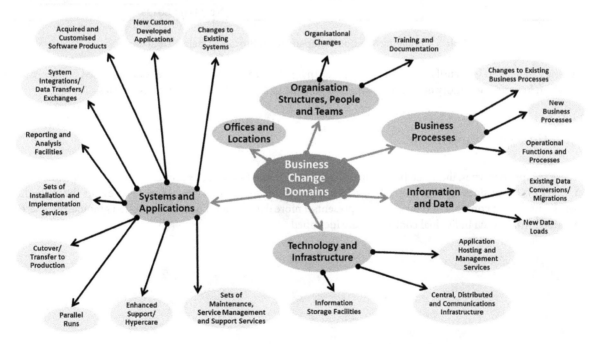

Figure 15 – Solution Components Mapped to Organisation Change Domains

The information in this diagram is:

Business Change Domain Group	Business Change Domain	Description
Business-Oriented Change	Location and Offices	This is not explicitly included. It is implicitly included in the organisation changes domain.
	Business Processes	Changes to Existing Business Processes
		New Business Processes
		Operational Functions and Processes
	Organisation Structures, People and Teams	Organisational Changes
		Training and Documentation
Technology-Oriented Change	Technology, Infrastructure and Communications	Application Hosting and Management Services
		Central, Distributed and Communications Infrastructure
		Information Storage Facilities
	Applications and Systems	Changes to Existing Systems
		New Custom Developed Applications
		Acquired and Customised Software Products
		System Integrations/ Data Transfers/ Exchanges
		Reporting and Analysis Facilities
		Sets of Installation and Implementation Services
		Cutover/ Transfer to Production
		Parallel Runs
		Enhanced Support/ Hypercare
		Sets of Maintenance, Service Management and Support Services
	Information and Data	Existing Data Conversions/ Migrations
		New Data Loads

Table 5 – Mapping Solution Components to Business Change Domains

This mapping can be used to identify the business domains that will be most affected by the solution based on its profile in terms of its number and complexity of its constituent components in each of the component categories.

2.4.5 Solution Decomposition

Within these component types, there can be multiple lower levels. In the following example, Level 0 represents the entire solution. Level 1 is the business change domain. Level 3 is the solution component type. Level 4 represents the individual components within each component type. Level 4 represents a more detailed level of solution design granularity where the items contained within each individual component are identified.

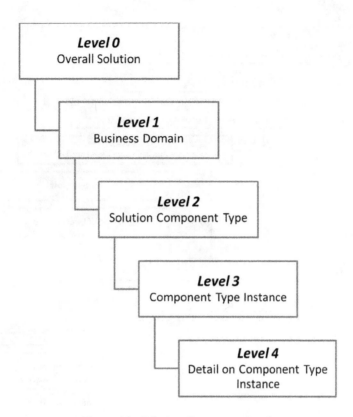

Figure 16 – Solution Component Levels

For example, the following component types are at level 3:

- Changes to Existing Business Processes
- New Business Processes
- Operational Functions and Processes

The level 4 breakdown for these would be the individual business processes affected.

The component type Organisational Changes is at level 2. The level 3 detail breakdown could be:

- Personnel Changes
- Organisation Structure Changes
- Location and Office Changes

In this example, level 4 could list the individual personnel and organisation changes.

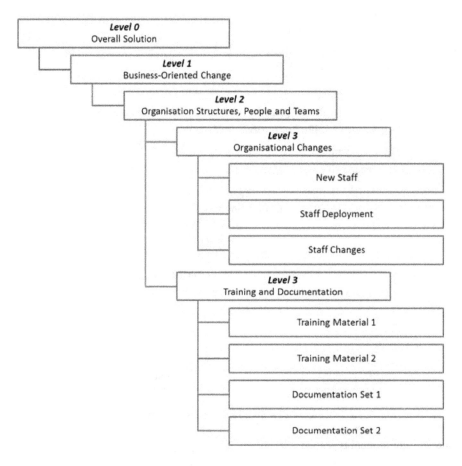

Figure 17 – Sample Level 1 to Level 4 Solution Breakdown

The greater the level of detail that is contained in the solution design allows greater certainty about the design and its cost and resource and time requirements. As the design is elaborated more detail can be added. Initially, the solution design to level 3 is generally sufficient to understand the full scope of the solution and thus the accuracy of the implementation cost, time and resource estimate.

This level approach is similar to and can be used to create a solution delivery work breakdown structure that can in turn be used for project planning and its related estimation and resource planning. This means that the solution delivery plan is explicitly linked to the solution design structure.

2.4.6 Solution Cost

Each of the components of the solution will give rise to a cost, either directly or indirectly. The real solution delivery costs are the costs of all the components required to make the solution operational and to keep it operational thereafter.

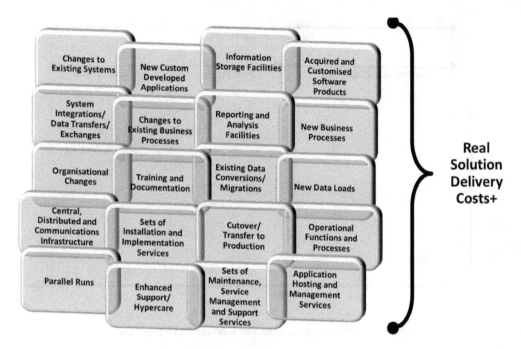

Figure 18 – Solution Components Contributing to Solution Delivery and Operation Costs

Throughout the lifetime of the solution, these components will give rise to costs and resource requirements. If the true lifetime costs of the solution are to be known, then the true solution scope must be accepted.

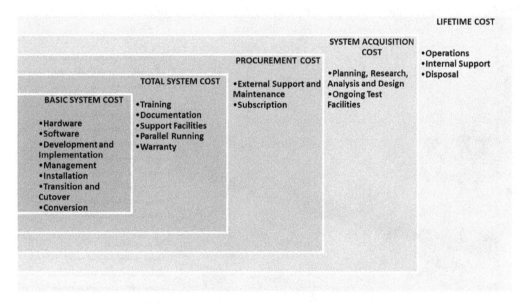

Figure 19 – Total Solution Lifetime Costs

Depending on the duration of the life of the solution, its operating costs can be or the order 1-3 times the cost of acquisition. The total cost of ownership of the solution – the sum of the initial and ongoing costs – needs to be less than the benefits the organisation derives from the solution – either through savings, cost avoidance, additional revenue generated or compliance with regulations. If the cost estimates are incorrect then the cost benefit justification for the solution will also be flawed.

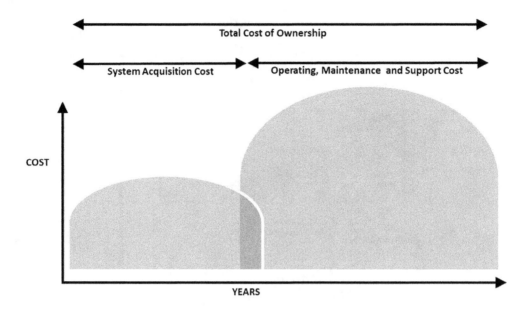

Figure 20 – Solution Acquisition and Lifetime Operating Costs

Getting the solution design right and getting the right solution implemented contributes both to the success of the solution delivery project and the long-term cost-effectiveness of the operation of the solution.

Each solution component contributes to the overall lifetime cost profile of the solution. Over time, these costs can be substantial. The following diagram shows a sample cost profile of the components of a solution over its life.

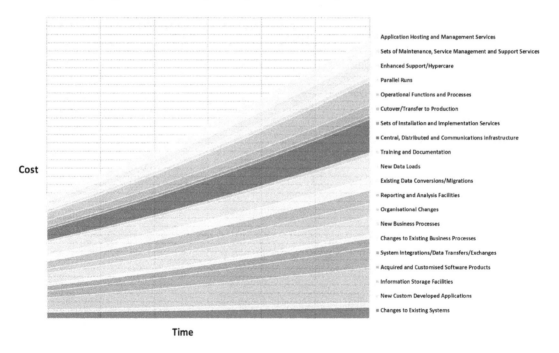

Figure 21 – Sample Solution Lifetime Cumulative Cost Profile

A sufficiently detailed solution design that includes all of the components of the solution will allow the cost of the solution delivery project to be estimated. It provides complete visibility of the solution costs. If all the components of the required solution are known, then the solution implementation and operational cost can be quantified accurately.

The absence of knowledge about the full scope of the solution will mean that the cost, resource and time estimates for the delivery of the solution will not be accurate or reliable.

Solution delivery success is commonly assessed with respect to the money, resource and time allocated to the project and how the project performed against these assigned resource budgets. This is discussed in section 3.1 on page 57. If the solution design is incomplete or if the estimates omit elements of the solution design in order to make the project costs appear lower, then the solution delivery project will be deemed to have failed to some extent. In reality, this failure is largely artificial. The project resource requirements were knowable but either this knowledge was not acquired or allowed to be acquired during the design process or it was excluded from the estimation process.

There are many reasons for poor solution delivery resources estimates. Many of these relate to using incomplete information to create those estimates, either deliberately or by not using enough rigour in the estimation process.

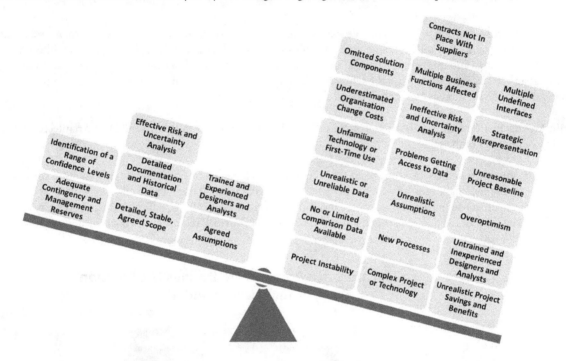

Figure 22 – Sources of Good and Poor Solution Delivery Estimates

Sources of Good Solution Delivery Estimates	Sources of Poor Solution Delivery Estimates
Effective Risk and Uncertainty Analysis	Contracts Not In Place With Suppliers
Identification of a Range of Confidence Levels	Omitted Solution Components
Identification of a Range of Confidence Levels	Multiple Business Functions Affected
Trained and Experienced Designers and Analysts	Multiple Undefined Interfaces
Adequate Contingency and Management Reserves	Underestimated Organisation Change Costs
Detailed, Stable, Agreed Scope	Ineffective Risk and Uncertainty Analysis
Agreed Assumptions	Strategic Misrepresentation
	Unfamiliar Technology or First-Time Use
	Problems Getting Access to Data
	Unreasonable Project Baseline
	Unrealistic or Unreliable Data
	Unrealistic Assumptions
	Over optimism
	No or Limited Comparison Data Available
	New Processes
	Untrained and Inexperienced Designers and Analysts
	Project Instability
	Complex Project or Technology

Sources of Good Solution Delivery Estimates	Sources of Poor Solution Delivery Estimates
	Unrealistic Project Savings and Benefit

Table 6 – Sources of Good and Poor Solution Delivery Estimates

Sufficient knowledge is a safeguard against poor project estimates.

Some of these reasons are related to the subject of solution complexity. Identifying and quantifying solution complexity is discussed further in section 4.2.2 on page 100.

2.4.7 Solution Options, Boundaries and Constraints

As stated above, there will always be many possible solution options to a business requirement or problem. All solutions are subject to sets of constraints that will limit and restrict the ultimate solution design options. The solution architect must be aware of these constraints and must clearly and plainly state them in any solution design artefacts so their part in the solution design process and the effects they have on the solution design options are explicitly understood by all. These constraints form boundaries to the solution design that is created during the design process.

Enterprise Architecture (and the related IT architecture disciplines of Security Architecture and Data Architecture) defines the technical boundaries of the solution.

Solution Architecture then defines the scope boundary of the solution based on business and implementation constraints. One of the objectives (and challenges) of solution architecture is to take an often fragmented and incomplete set of requirements and to create an integrated and coherent solution based on these, filling-in the blanks during the solution design process. The topic of requirements and the sparsity of business-provided requirements is detailed in section 4.4 on page 124.

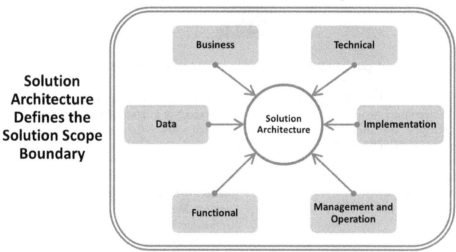

Figure 23 – Solution Design Boundaries

Constraints can be defined as *Core* – these are concerned with essential solution attributes - or *Extended* – these are concerned with solution implementation and operation.

In simple terms, the Core constraints can be grouped into four sets:

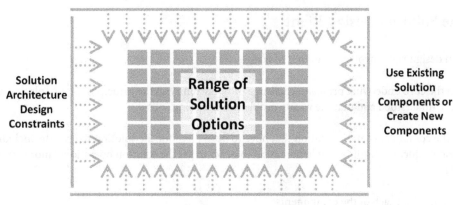

Figure 24 – Solution Design Constraints

Solution Constraint	Description
Enterprise and Other IT Architecture Constraints	These constraints relate to organisation enterprise and other architecture standards such as what packages, tools and platforms may or may not be used, what devices the solution can be accessed from and how security and privacy should be implemented. IT architecture functions such as Enterprise Architecture, Security Architecture and Data Architecture should define standards and approaches in these areas. These standards should be complied with (or explicit derogations obtained for any deviations from those standards).
Solution Architecture Design Constraints	The solution design process will uncover constraints based on requirements that have been explicitly articulated or have been identified during design. This topic of requirements in the context of solution design covered in more detail in section 4.4 on page 124.
Use Existing Solution Components or Create New Components, Cost, Time, Resources, Business Constraints	There may be the opportunity to reuse existing components when implementing the solution. The reuse can be partial or complete. Partial reuse involves reworking the existing components. Reuse can be more complex and time-consuming than implementing new components. There can be an unwarranted confidence in the level of reuse that is possible that will cause problems during subsequent solution implementation. Reuse options need to be validated before they are included in the solution design.
Degree of Automation of Solution	The solution can be automated to a lesser or greater extent. Greater automation involves greater complexity, implementation cost and validation. Automation offers advantages in terms of elimination of manual support and operations effort. Automation needs to focus on processes and their decisions and how to make them consistent, repeatable and autonomous and be able to be performed in real time.

Table 7 – Solution Design Constraints

The solution should be designed according to common principles developed and maintained by the solution architecture function. Section 5.4.3 on page 418 lists principles that can be applied when designing digital solutions. These can be applied more generally. Section 4.11.2 on page 383 lists the principles that can be applied when reviewing a solution for completeness. The solution should be designed with these review principles in mind.

The solution will have quality requirements and characteristics. These are described on section 4.6.4.7 on page 251.

2.5 Getting the Solution Design Right

Getting the solution design right involves a number of factors:

- Understanding the core underlying problem, challenge or opportunity so the principles of the solution addresses what is really needed are understood and that the wrong problem is not being solved

- Identifying all the components of the solution that have to be in place for the solution to operate, including options to bypass components during the initial implementation in order to get the solution operational more quickly but that are implemented later

- Defining the scope of the each of the components

- Identifying the correct design option for each of these components

However, getting the design right is one part of answer. The second part is getting the solution implemented successfully. This means avoiding making incorrect decisions on solution delivery phasing, resource allocation, the removal of necessary components to meet constraints, making unnecessary changes or leaving the design ambiguous so sub-optimal decisions are made.

The convergence of all these solution dynamics can be very difficult. Section 3.1 on page 57 examines why solution delivery failure occurs so frequently.

2.6 The Solution Delivery Process in Context

The solution delivery journey, from initial concept to operational, usable and used solution, is often difficult. It can involve ups and downs, compromises and concessions until an operational solution steady state has been accomplished.

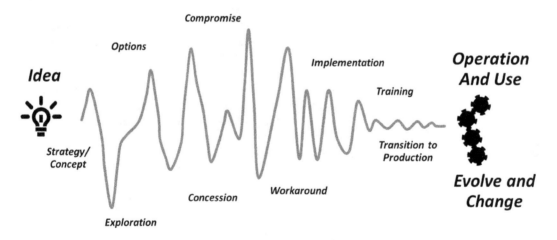

Figure 25 – Solution Delivery Journey

The solution architect must persevere during this process, focussing on the objective of creating a complete design and then subsequently assisting with its implementation.

One objective of the IT function is to act as a lens, focussing business needs onto solutions whose components are acquired or developed, implemented and transitioned to operations. The solution design process must assist in maintaining this focus. The solution architecture function needs to have the capability to achieve this. Solution architecture is (or should be – see section 3.3.5 on page 86 for information on Shadow IT) the primary means by which new solutions are introduced into the organisation. The selected solutions, either internal or external, must comply with the organisation's overall IT architecture standards.

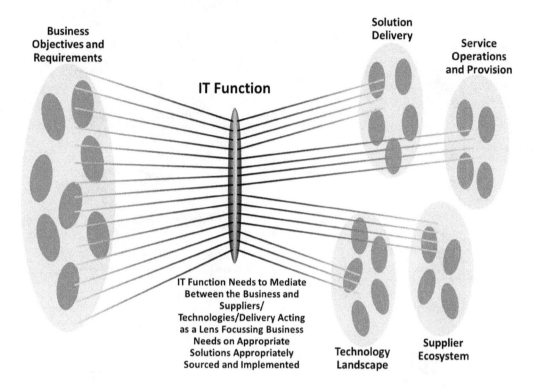

Figure 26 – IT Function as a Lens Focussing Business Needs On To Solutions

Achieving the objective of the IT function focussing business needs onto solution requires that the IT function be the trusted advisor to the business.

The end-to-end solution delivery process involves multiple partially overlapping individual journeys across different disciplines. Each of these journeys does not span the entire length of the journey from initial concept or identification of the need for a solution to that solution being completely operational and used.

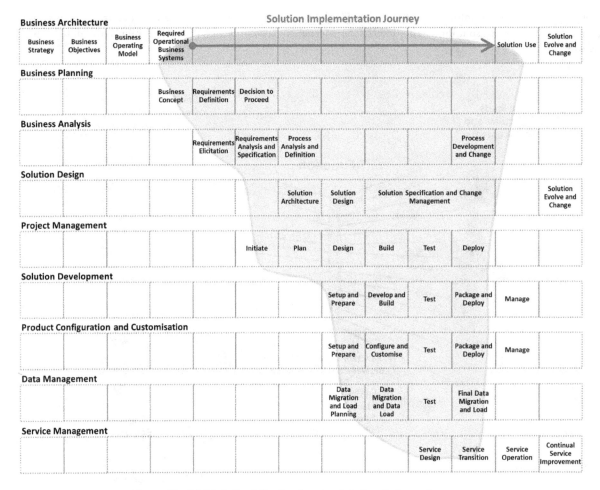

Figure 27 – Multiple Partially Overlapping Solution Delivery Journeys

The solution delivery journey can be viewed as an iceberg with many overlapping activities hidden below the apparently simple requirement to move from the set of solutions required to operate the organisation and achieve the business objectives to those solutions being operational, usable and in use. There evolution of the solution concept can occur earlier than shown in this diagram – see section 4.6.4 on page 235 for more information on an early engagement process and section 4.6.5 on page 257 for a rapid solution concept definition engagement.

The aim of the solution design process is to create solution designs that meet the needs of the solution user population. The solution design process is one part of the overall solution delivery process.

The solution journey therefore both starts with and ends with the solution consumer.

The high-level sets of steps for each of these journeys are listed below.

Discipline	Journey Step
Business Architecture	Business Strategy
	Business Objectives
	Business Operating Model
	Business Processes
	Required Operational Business Systems
Business Planning	Business Concept
	Initial Discovery
	Requirements Elicitation
	Decision to Proceed

Discipline	Journey Step
Business Analysis	Requirements Elicitation Requirements Analysis, Consolidation and Documentation Process Analysis and Definition Requirements Management
Solution Design	Solution Architecture - Business, Application, Data, Security, Infrastructure Solution Design Solution Specification and Change Management
Project Management	Initiate Plan Design Build Test Deploy
Solution Development	Setup and Prepare Develop and Build Test Package and Deploy Manage
Product Configuration and Customisation	Setup and Prepare Configure and Customise Test Package and Deploy Manage
Data Management	Data Migration and Load Planning Data Migration and Data Load Test Final Data Migration and Load
Service Management	Service Design Service Transition Service Operation Continual Service Improvement

Table 8 – High-Level Steps of Individual Discipline Solution Delivery Journeys

Not all disciplines are involved in the delivery of all solutions. For example, the involvement of the Business Architecture area tends to intermittent and based on specific engagements. Most organisations will not have a Business Architecture function or capability. Where the need for such an engagement arises, it tends to be outsourced to a consulting service provider. Most of the other disciplines will be involved in most solutions. This list of disciplines is high-level and does not explicitly reference ones such as testing, infrastructure, security, procurement, product configuration and others.

The overall high-level solution delivery journey is:

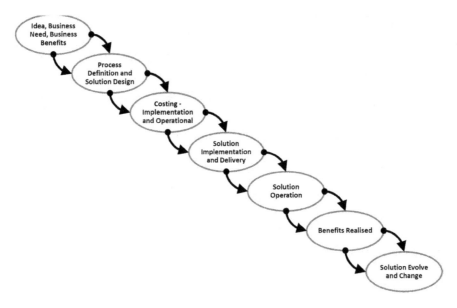

Figure 28 – Overall Solution Delivery Journey

The steps in this journey are:

- Idea, Business Need, Business Benefits
- Process Definition and Solution Design
- Costing -Implementation and Operational
- Solution Implementation and Delivery
- Solution Operation
- Benefits Realised
- Solution Evolve and Change

For a wide variety of reasons, solutions often fail to achieve the benefits expected or promised (see section 3.1 on page 57 for more information on solution delivery failures).

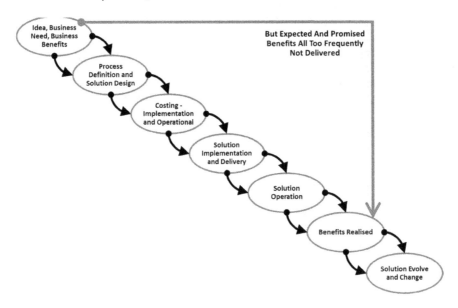

Figure 29 – Solution Delivery Failure

One of the reasons for this failure is that there are multiple handoffs between isolated and insulated teams during the solution delivery process. This leads to an accumulation of information losses that means that what get implemented is not what is needed to allow the benefits to be realised.

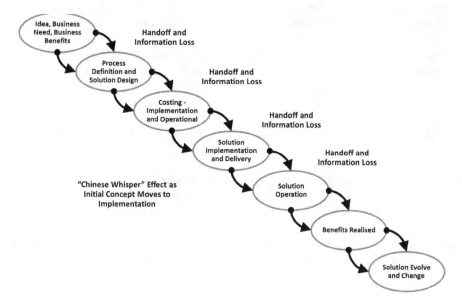

Figure 30 – Information Loss Due to Multiple Handoffs During Solution Delivery

All too often the work done on the solution is passed from one architecture discipline to the next with a poor and imperfect handoff. Each discipline operates in an isolated silo. The implementation of the solution is not seen as a continuum. There is no end-to-end view across all disciplines. Even the project management discipline which is tasked with the delivery of the solution does not see the complete span of the solution.

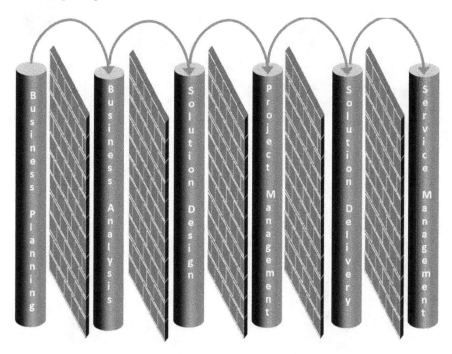

Figure 31 – Siloed Operation of Solution Delivery Disciplines

The siloed arrangement within the solution delivery journey is replicated within the communications between the individual IT architecture functions as discussed on page 79.

These siloed structures tend to be characterised by some or all of the following

- Closed, internally focussed groups with their own culture and language that discourage outsider involvement
- Individuals with the siloed functions see themselves as belonging to and identify with the group rather than the wider organisation
- The siloes do not see themselves as responsible for organisational problems and failure to perform and deliver
- The silos measure their performance and set performance expectations using internal metrics that reinforce siloed behaviour
- Top-down management structure with control-based behaviours and attitudes to team members

The topic of the solution architecture function and the issues that can arise with a poorly structured function is addressed in section 8.3.4 on page 504.

Every organisation will have a solution delivery project management process such PRINCE2, PMBOK or another. The solution architect must work within this framework and be supported by it. Section 3.1 on page 57 contains more information on the issues that arise during solution delivery and how solution architecture can work to address these.

Section 4.3 on page 112 describes solution design in a wider solution delivery context. Chapter 6 on page 422 contains details on the application of an agile delivery method to solution design and subsequent implementation.

Chapter 3. Business Strategy, Architecture Strategy and Solution Design and Delivery

3.1 Why Solutions Fail

This information provides a solution architecture perspective on why solution delivery fails. Getting the architecture and design right puts the solution delivery project on a solid foundation and maximises the likelihood of success. The delivery estimates use a realistic solution scope with all factors included. Getting the solution architecture and design wrong puts the solution delivery project on an unstable foundation and negatively impacts on the deliverability of the solution and the probability of success of the solution delivery project.

It is a reasonable statement that in the minds of many people failure is synonymous with information technology projects. While this perception is an exaggeration, the outcomes of many IT solution delivery projects represent failures to at least some extent.

It is also often true that solution delivery failure is attributed to project management failure such as the quality, skill and experience of the project manager or the misapplication or lack of application of a project management methodology. However, the most effective project management will not make an undeliverable, unworkable, unusable solution deliverable, workable or usable.

The solution architect should concern himself or herself with the ultimate success of the project to deliver the designed solution. There are several organisation characteristics that negatively affect this:

- As described in section 2.6 on page 50 the solution delivery process can be siloed with multiple hand-offs, including that from solution architecture to project management and solution delivery

- The solution design produced by the solution architect does not or is not allowed to include the full scope of the solution

These are not mutually exclusive and regularly occur together.

The goal of the solution delivery project is to successfully implement the right solution. This is a combination getting the solution design right and then implementing this design successfully. The two areas are connected: the right solution design includes identifying all the solution components that comprise solution delivery. The delivery project can then implement these.

There is little, if any, merit in initiating a delivery project to implement a solution if the scope of that solution is not well-defined. Any scope definition work needs to be moved to a separate activity focussed on just that purpose so that when solution implementation starts, its scale and extent are well-defined and accepted or the uncertainly of the solution design needs to be accepted and embedded into the delivery project such as in an agile process. The topic of agile solution delivery is discussed further in Chapter 6 on page 422.

Solution Identification and Design

		Wrong	Right
Solution Delivery	**Unsuccessful**	*Wrong Solution Unsuccessfully Implemented*	*Right Solution Unsuccessfully Implemented*
	Successful	*Wrong Solution Successfully Implemented*	*Right Solution Successfully Implemented*

Figure 32 – Goal of Solution Delivery – the Right Solution Implemented Successfully

It is a continuing truth that the combination of the successful delivery of the right solution still occurs infrequently.

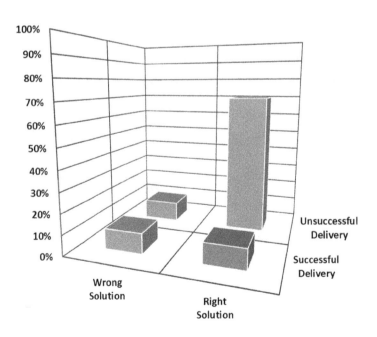

Figure 33 – Right Solution Delivered Successfully is in the Minority of all Solution Delivery Outcomes

This section is not intended to be a comprehensive review of project management literature. It is intended to illustrate how good solution design contributes to solution delivery success and reduces the prospects of solution delivery failure.

Section 4.4.2 on page 134 which describes the importance of business processes (and organisation change) to solution success can be referred to when reading this section. The solution ultimately exists to implement the business process.

Also, the problem of Shadow IT referred to 3.3.5 on page 86 can be viewed as another form of solution delivery failure where the business function sources the solution externally rather than from the internal IT function and without the knowledge or involvement of the IT function. Secondly, many business-acquired solutions whose delivery was challenged do not appear in any project failure statistics.

Over two decades has passed since the first Standish Group CHAOS report[4] on the state of delivery of information technology projects was published. The results from this study are well known and often quoted:

> *… staggering 31.1% of projects will be cancelled before they ever get completed. Further results indicate 52.7% of projects will cost 189% of their original estimates.*

> *On the success side, the average is only 16.2% for software projects that are completed on- time and on-budget.*

Solution delivery success and failure are not binary options: there is a domain of outcomes between complete success and complete failure. There are many reasons why the implementation of a solution may be regarded as less than successful. These reasons are not exclusive: the delivery of a solution can demonstrate more than one of these characteristics. Also, they are not binary factors: each of these solution deficiency issues can be more or less serious, representing a greater or lesser level of solution delivery non-performance with respect to that factor.

The CHAOS reports classify projects outcomes according to three categories:

1. *Success* - The project is completed on time and on budget, offering all features and functions as initially specified.
2. *Challenged* –The project is completed and operational but over budget and over the time estimate and offers fewer features and functions than originally specified.
3. *Impaired* - The project is cancelled at some point during the development cycle

The following diagram shows a simple model of solution success and failure.

---

[4] See *The CHAOS Report 1994*:
https://www.standishgroup.com/sample_research_files/chaos_report_1994.pdf
There have been many comments on this and subsequent reports questioning their categorisation of project success and failure and the calculation of the proportion of projects that fall into each category. For example, see:
- *How Large Are Software Cost Overruns? A Review of the 1994 CHAOS Report* - http://www.umsl.edu/~sauterv/analysis/Standish/standish-IST.pdf
- *The Rise and Fall of the Chaos Report Figures* - https://www.cs.vu.nl/~x/the_rise_and_fall_of_the_chaos_report_figures.pdf
However, for the purpose of this analysis, the Standish Group numbers are assumed to be valid.

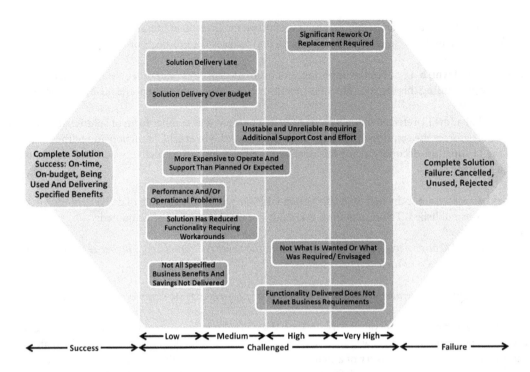

Figure 34 – Field of Solution Delivery Project Success and Failure

These are not point reasons for solution delivery challenge or failure. Each of these reasons can occupy a band of impacts of just how challenged the delivery was from Low to Very High.

The challenged solution delivery reasons are:

Challenge Reason	Likely Impact Range of Challenge	Description
Significant Rework Or Replacement Required	High to Very High	Elements of the solution as delivered need to be replaced or significantly reworked to operate as planned or needed.
Solution Delivery Late	Low to Medium	The solution exceeded its original budget.
Solution Delivery Over Budget	Low to Medium	The solution exceeded its schedule.
Unstable and Unreliable Requiring Additional Support Cost and Effort	Medium to Very High	The solution does not work as automatically and without intervention as expected or designed or is unstable or unreliable and requires a degree of manual support work.
More Expensive to Operate And Support Than Planned Or Expected	Low to High	The solution works but the effort and cost to support and operate it is greater than planned.
Performance And/Or Operational Problems	Low to Medium	The solution does not have the required throughput or response times as expected or designed. The span of this challenge is generally low to medium but in extreme circumstances, the impact can be high.
Solution Has Reduced Functionality Requiring Workarounds	Low to Medium	Some of the initially designed functionality was omitted from the delivered solution requiring additional manual effort and work outside the core solution components.
Not What Is Wanted Or What Was Required/ Envisaged	High to Very High	The delivered solution is not what the business wanted or expected or does not fulfil their needs.

Not All Specified Business Benefits And Savings Not Delivered	Low to Medium	Some of the expected benefits have not been realised.
Functionality Delivered Does Not Meet Business Requirements	Medium to Very High	Some of the functionality contained in the solution does not work exactly as the solution consumer expected or wanted.

Table 9 – Field of Solution Delivery Project Success and Failure

At its simplest, the challenged domain includes solutions that are characterised by *less* for *more* of:

- *Cost More* – the original budget was exceeded or other unanticipated costs arose

- *More Time* – the original schedule was exceeded which means the business were late in having access to the solution

- *Delivered Less* – the original scope was reduced, making the solution less usable or requiring additional unplanned for effort or the solution takes longer to use or the solution does not meet the expectations of the target solution consumers

- *Achieved Less* – the solution does not deliver the expected benefits and savings or the solution is less widely used that expected or planned

Lost functionality is only really an issue if its absence leads to a problem in terms of work not done or work done elsewhere that takes more time or costs most. Loss of unnecessary functionality is not a problem. This relates to unnecessary solution complexity described in section 4.2.2 on page 100.

So-called challenged projects can be characterised as delivering *less* – less functionality, fewer benefits, less usability, less usefulness – *for more* – more time and more money. The degree of the combination of how much less for how much more can be regarded as the total operational solution deficit.

There is no easy formula to determine the total solution deficit, such as:

$$\left(1 - \frac{(Planned\ Cost\ and\ Time - Achieved\ Cost\ and\ Time)}{Planned\ Cost\ and\ Time}\right) x\ Cost\ and\ Time\ Weight$$
$$+$$
$$\left(1 - \frac{Planned\ Functionality\ Benefits\ Usage - Achieved\ Functionality\ Benefits\ Usage)}{Planned\ Functionality\ Benefits\ Usage}\right) x\ Functionality\ Benefits\ Usage\ Weight$$

Such attempts at creating an arithmetic of solution delivery failure are, at best, superficial and simplistic.

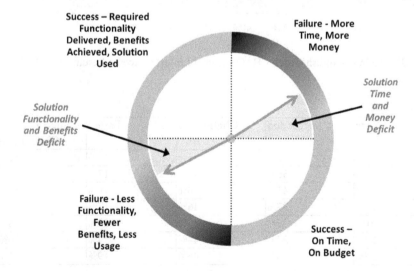

Figure 35 – Operational Solution Deficit – Degrees of Less for More

These *less for more* factors overlap. If the delivery of the solution took longer, this will mean that the solution delivery team were working longer incurring more cost than budgets. If the solution delivered less and thus either did not generate the expected savings or benefits (see section 4.11.1 on page 381) or required manual workarounds or both this would also increase the effective solution delivery and operations cost.

So, solution delivery success means avoiding these *less for more* characteristics. One way this can be achieved is to know as much as possible of what is needed up-front, so the real effort, time and cost can be quantified.

Since the original Standish Group CHAOS report, there have been several follow-up Standish reports[5], each reporting different levels of project success, challenge or impairment. The following summarises the results of their analyses from 1994 to 2015.

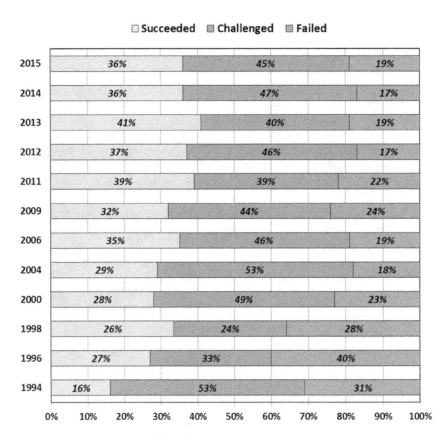

Figure 36 – Standish Group CHAOS Report Project Outcome Results 1994-2015

The data in the chart is:

Year	Succeeded	Challenged	Failed	Succeeded or Challenged
2015	36%	45%	19%	81%
2014	36%	47%	17%	83%
2013	41%	40%	19%	81%
2012	37%	46%	17%	83%
2011	39%	39%	22%	78%
2009	32%	44%	24%	76%
2006	35%	46%	19%	81%

---

[5] For example, see the CHAOS Report 2015:
https://www.standishgroup.com/sample_research_files/CHAOSReport2015-Final.pdf

Year	Succeeded	Challenged	Failed	Succeeded or Challenged
2004	29%	53%	18%	82%
2000	28%	49%	23%	77%
1998	26%	24%	28%	50%
1996	27%	33%	40%	60%
1994	16%	53%	31%	69%

Table 10 – Standish Group CHAOS Report Project Outcome Results 1994-2015

According to these Standish Group figures, between 1994 and 2015, the relative proportions of projects that succeeded and those that failed have effectively been transposed. Successful projects increased in proportion from 16% to 36% while failed projects fell from 31% to 19%.

The information from the Standish Group is presented here without detailed analysis. This is beyond the scope of this book. It is not clear if project success is assessed against the original project timescale, budget and functionality or against a replanned project with the original scope having been changed.

Also, the degree by which a project is challenged can be very small or very large due to one of more factors with varying degrees of severity as discussed above.

There have been other more recent analyses of project failure that generate similar outcomes[6]. The analysis by Brenda in 1999 Whittaker was based on a survey of 176 projects in Canada. It defined project failure as:

> *Project failure was defined in three ways: overrunning its budget by 30 per cent or more; overrunning its schedule by 30 per cent or more; or failing to demonstrate the planned benefits. Of these, failure by overrunning schedule was by far the most common. A total of 87 per cent of failed projects exceeded their initial schedule estimates by 30 per cent or more. This compares to 56 per cent of failed projects that exceeded their estimated budget by the same amount, and 45 per cent of failed projects which failed to produce the expected benefits*

It identified a hierarchy of project failure causes based on three core sets of reasons:

1. Poor project planning
2. A weak business case
3. Lack of senior management involvement and support

The following table summarises the hierarchy of causes identified in this paper:

Component Type	Description	Description
Poor project planning (specifically, risks were not addressed or the project plan was weak).	Risks were not addressed as part of the project planning process.	Slippage from the schedule
		Change in scope of technology, functionality or business case
		Cost overruns associated with one or more project components
		Change in any key individuals such as the business sponsor, project manager or vendor manager
	The plan was weak	Incorrectly estimated activity durations

---

[6] For some examples, see:

- ***Lessons for IT Project Manager Efficacy: A Review of the Literature Associated with Project Success*** Chuck Millhollan, Michelle Kaarst-Brown - https://journals.sagepub.com/doi/abs/10.1177/875697281604700507?journalCode=pmxa
- ***What went wrong? Unsuccessful information technology projects*** Brenda Whittaker (1999) Information Management & Computer Security. Vol. 7, No. 1 pp. 23-29. http://cs.mvnu.edu/twiki/pub/Main/SoftwareEngineering2010/What_went_wrong.pdf
- ***Six Reasons for Software Project Failure*** Barry Boehm, (2002) IEEE Software, September/October, pp. 97.

Component Type	Description	Description
		Incorrect assumptions regarding resource availability
		Inadequate assignment of activity accountabilities
		Missing or incomplete review and approval activities
The business case for the project was weak in several areas or missing several components	Business and operational changes needed to deliver the benefits	
	Clearly understood deliverables	
	Quantified costs and benefits	
	Overall scope of project	
A lack of management involvement and support.		
Custom-developed applications were associated with serious budget and schedule overruns.		
Budget and schedule overruns	Risks were not addressed in several areas	
	The project manager did not have the required skills or expertise	
	Project progress was not monitored and corrective action was not initiated	
	The experience, authority and stature of the project manager were inconsistent with the nature, scope and risks of the project	

Table 11 – Causes of Project Failure from *What went wrong? Unsuccessful information technology projects*

The paper by Barry Boehm lists the following six reasons for project failure:

1. Incomplete requirements
2. Lack of user involvement
3. Lack of resources
4. Unrealistic expectations
5. Lack of executive support
6. Changing requirements and specifications

The more recent work by Alexander Budzier and Bent Flyvbjerg[7] of the BT Centre for Major Programme Management at the Saïd Business School in the University of Oxford[8] which has an academic rather than a commercial basis shows comparable results. This analysis differs from the Standish Group as it looks at variance from planned budget and schedule and analyses the proportion by which the actual varies from the initially planned or budgeted time or amount: (Actual Budget/Schedule – Forecast Budget/Schedule) Forecast Budget/Schedule.

> *Our first statistical approximation of the collected sample has shown that on average ICT projects perform reasonably well – +27% cost overrun, +55% schedule overrun in three out of four projects. Apart from the risk of getting the budget cut a very high risk exists that a project turns into a Black Swan. One in six projects (17%) with cost overruns of nearly +200% and schedule slippage of nearly 70%.*

The Budzier and Flyvbjerg analysis was produced in 2011. It states that 75% of projects experienced significant budget and schedule overruns. The Standish Group proportion of challenged projects for 2011 was just 39%.

The Budzier and Flyvbjerg analysis does not include details on the benefits shortfall of these projects that experienced cost and budget overruns.

---

[7] See:

- *Double Whammy – How ICT Projects are Fooled by Randomness and Screwed by Political Intent* - https://arxiv.org/ftp/arxiv/papers/1304/1304.4590.pdf
- *Why Your IT Project May Be Riskier Than You Think* - https://hbr.org/2011/09/why-your-it-project-may-be-riskier-than-you-think
- *Quality Control and Due Diligence in Project Management: Getting Decisions Right by Taking the Outside View* - https://arxiv.org/ftp/arxiv/papers/1302/1302.2544.pdf

[8] See:
https://www.sbs.ox.ac.uk/

The CHAOS reports include a top ten factors that they say can be used to assess the likelihood of the success or failure of a project. These factors have changed over time. Each of these success factors is assigned a score with the total summing to 100. Their weightings and titles have changed over time. I have grouped similar success factors over time in the following table and so any errors in this grouping are mine.

Success Factor	1994	1999	2000	2015
	Factor Importance Score			
User Involvement	19	20	16	15
Executive Management Support/ Executive Sponsorship	16	15	18	15
Emotional Maturity (Managing Expectations, Gaining Consensus)				15
Optimisation (Clarify Objective, Divide Larger Projects Into Multiple Smaller Projects)				15
Clear Statement of Requirements	15			
Firm Basic Requirements		5	6	
Clear Vision and Objectives/Clear Business Objectives	3	15	12	4
Proper Planning	11	5		
Reliable Estimates			5	
Realistic Expectations	10			
Smaller Project Milestones	9	10		
Minimised Scope			10	
Modest Execution				6
Standard Software Infrastructure			8	
Standard Architecture				8
Formal Methodology			6	
Agile Process				7
Competent Staff/Skilled Resources	8	5		10
Experienced Project Manager/Project Management Expertise		15	14	5
Ownership	6	5		
Hard-Working, Focused Staff	3			
Other		5	5	
Total Success Factor Score	100	100	100	100

Table 12 – Standish Group Project Success Factors Over Time

To assess the probability that the project will be a success, the project is scored with respect to the success factors. The higher the score, the greater will be the chance of success. The lower the score, the greater will be the chance of some of project failure.

According to the Standish Group, the two most important success factors that are common to all their analyses are:

- User Involvement
- Executive Management Support/ Executive Sponsorship

It is interesting to note that the design of the solution is not explicitly mentioned in any of these factors. It may be subsumed into those factors that related to requirements and objectives.

Other overlapping important success factors that have been assigned different names over time are:

- Emotional Maturity (Managing Expectations, Gaining Consensus)
- Optimisation (Clarify Objective, Divide Larger Projects Into Multiple Smaller Projects)
- Clear Statement of Requirements
- Proper Planning
- Realistic Expectations

- Smaller Project Milestones

The analyses performed by Budzier and Flyvbjerg identified seven organisational challenges (these are no scored) that exist before a project starts (what they call organisational a priori challenges) that are associated with troubled projects. These are:

Organisational Challenge	Scope of Impact
Political bias and ineffective project sponsorship	Business
Ineffective governance structure	Business, IT
Unclear goals and business cases and success criteria	Business
Competing and shifting criteria	Business
Lack of risk management	Governance, IT
Big Bang approaches	Business, IT
No user involvement	Business, IT

Table 13 – Budzier and Flyvbjerg Project Organisational Challenges

These studies all tend to focus on the narrow aspects of software projects rather than on the wider aspects of a complete solution encompassing all the components of the types listed in section 2.4.2, including but not limited to developed or acquired and customised software.

These also tend to focus on project management failures as the root cause of the project failure. They do not consider the wider aspects such as the incompleteness of the solution design targeted for delivery by the project or the fundamental undeliverability of the solution as a cause. They start with the assumption that the project has been given a fundamentally sound and deliverable solution design and scope and that it is the delivery that goes wrong.

Again, the fundamental issue of the implementability of the solution is not explicitly considered.

An effective solution architecture function and a good solution design process that produces detailed, high-quality solution designs and identifies the complete scope of the solution will address many of these challenges and increase the likelihood of successful solution delivery and use. Good solution design means being aware of all the options and selecting the most appropriate one subject to all constraints. It means avoiding all the conscious and unconscious biases that lead to bad solutions.

A solution design process that identifies the end-to-end scope of the solution means the solution delivery project starts with an awareness of the effort, risks, scope and costs involved. The following table summarises how a solution design process can maximise the Standish Group solution delivery success factors. Again, I have grouped similar success factors.

Success Factor	Solution Design Contribution
User Involvement	A comprehensive solution design with all the scope elements identified will require user engagement. An effective user engagement process (such as those identified in section 4.6 on page 161) will both gather information and get the target business users involved. The business will contribute to the solution design and be able to see and understand the real solution scope. This will allow informed decisions to be made on what must be included and what can be excluded or deferred.
Executive Management Support/ Executive Sponsorship	A solution engagement process will demonstrate management support for the solution. Detailed knowledge of the real project scope will allow management to understand what they are sponsoring and to decide if the project is worthwhile.
Emotional Maturity (Managing Expectations, Gaining Consensus)	Knowing the full and realistic extent of the project, derived from the solution design, will allow expectations on what can be delivered and what is involved in getting an operational solution to be managed.
Optimisation (Clarify Objective, Divide Larger Projects Into Multiple Smaller Projects)	Knowing the components of the entire solution will allow their delivery to be allocated to different solution delivery stages or separate delivery projects by decision grounded in facts.
Clear Statement of Requirements	The engagement process will both define requirements and embed these in the

Success Factor	Solution Design Contribution
Firm Basic Requirements	context of a complete solution. The requirements and their delivery are shown together. The entire solution can be seen and understood.
Clear Vision and Objectives/Clear Business Objectives	
Proper Planning	Knowing the actual scope of the required full solution means that a plan to achieve that includes all elements it can be developed. Evidence-based decisions can then be made on the sequencing of solution delivery activities and the exclusion or postponement of components.
Reliable Estimates	
Realistic Expectations	
Smaller Project Milestones	
Minimised Scope	
Modest Execution	
Standard Software Infrastructure	The solution design will identify the components of the solution, including the software components, either acquired and configured/customised or developed. This will provide full visibility on what is required. These components can be delivered using standard components where they are available within the organisation's enterprise architecture or where they can be acquired.
Standard Architecture	
Formal Methodology	
Agile Process	
Competent Staff/Skilled Resources	
Experienced Project Manager/Project Management Expertise	A good project manager will seek to understand the full scope of the solution in order to create a realistic and achievable delivery plan that includes the necessary time, budget and resources. The project manager can then make rational decisions on phasing and scoping.
Ownership	
Hard-Working, Focused Staff	
Other	

Table 14 – Solution Architecture Contribution to the Standish Group Solution Delivery Success Factors

The following table summarises how a solution design process can address the organisational challenges expressed by Budzier and Flyvbjerg.

Organisational Challenge	Solution Design Contribution
Political bias and ineffective project sponsorship	An effective and working solution design process should allow informed solution delivery sponsorship because the sponsors will have greater confidence in the deliverability of the solution.
Ineffective governance structure	Knowing the actual and required scope of the solution should allow the required governance to be defined and put in place.
Unclear goals and business cases and success criteria	The solution design engagement process will clarify the solution goals and link business objectives to solution components. The engagement process will involve the business users so they understand the solution design process and participate in the solution design process.
Competing and shifting criteria	An honest and complete solution design will present the business with what is needed to achieve the required aims.
Lack of risk management	A comprehensive solution design will allow risks to be identified and mitigating and circumventing actions taken.
Big Bang approaches	Knowing the actual scope of the required full solution means that a plan to achieve that includes all elements it can be developed. Evidence-based decisions can then be made on the sequencing and phasing of solution delivery activities and the exclusion or postponement of components. Knowledge-based actions can be performed on what to do to balance delivery.
No user involvement	A comprehensive solution design with all the scope elements identified will require user engagement. An effective user engagement process (such as those identified in section 4.6 on page 161) will both gather information and get the target business users involved. The business will contribute to the solution design and be able to see and understand the real solution scope. This will allow informed decisions to be made on what must be included and what can be excluded or deferred.

Table 15 – Solution Architecture Contribution to Budzier and Flyvbjerg Organisational Challenges

Good solution design is not the answer to all project failures and challenges. It can only go so far. It cannot protect the organisation against other causes. Many of the reasons why solution delivery fails, either fully or partially, are due to circumstances such as organisation or individual cognitive or other biases and other influences such as groupthink. Good solution design cannot stop these. It may reduce their possibility or lessen their impact. Being aware of these biases and other influences can alleviate their consequences.

Some of the causes of poor organisation decision-making are:

- *Cognitive Bias* – Poor or inaccurate judgements, illogical interpretations and decisions, characterised by patterns of behaviour
- *Strategic Misrepresentation* – Deliberate misrepresentation in budgeting caused by distorted incentives
- *Planning Fallacy* – Systematic tendency to underestimate how long it will take to complete a task even when there is past experience of similar tasks over-running
- *Optimism Bias* – Systematic tendency to be overly optimistic about the outcome of actions
- *Focalism* – Systematic tendency to become inwardly focussed and to lose situational awareness and appreciation of wider context and display characteristics of cognitive tunnelling during times of stress
- *Groupthink* – The need for agreement, accord and compliance within the group results in a flawed, illogical and inhibited decision-making processes and decisions

Figure 37 – Factors Affecting Good Solution Delivery Decisions

These factors can manifest themselves at times of solution delivery stress where the delivery project is experiencing pressure and strain due to previous poor decisions.

There are many classifications and types of cognitive bias. They can be very difficult to avoid because of their embedded nature in people's personalities and their emotional and irrational basis. Cognitive biases are very real and can have damaging effects. They can be grouped in a number of categories:

- **Decision-Making and Behavioural Biases** - affecting belief formation and business decisions
- **Probability and Belief Biases** - affecting way in which information is gathered and assessed
- **Attributional Biases** - affecting the determination what was responsible for an event or action

Some of the common decision-making and behavioural biases include:

- *Anchoring* – Relying too heavily on one piece of information when making a decision
- *Attention Bias* – Assigning greater weight to apparently dominant factors
- *Bandwagon* – Believing things because many others, believe the same
- *Blind Spot* – Seeing oneself as less biased than others
- *Confirmation Bias* – Interpreting information so as to that confirms preconceptions
- *Exposure Effect* – Greater preferences just because of familiarity
- *Focusing Effect* – Placing too much importance on one aspect
- *Hyperbolic Discounting* – Strong preference for immediate payoffs relative to later ones
- *Information Bias* – Looking for information even when it cannot affect action
- *Irrational Escalation* – Justifying increased investment based on the cumulative prior investment despite new evidence suggesting that the decision was wrong
- *Negativity Bias* – Paying more attention and giving more weight to the negative rather than the positive
- *Omission Bias* – Viewing a harmful action as worse than an equally harmful omission or inaction
- *Semmelweis Effect* – Rejecting new evidence that contradicts an established paradigm
- *Sunk Cost Effect* – Assigning a higher value to disposal/loss compared with cost of acquisition
- *Wishful Thinking* – Making decisions based to what is pleasing to imagine instead basing decisions on evidence and rationality
- *Zero-Risk Bias* – Looking to reduce a small risk to zero rather than a greater reduction of a larger risk

Some of the common probability and belief biases include:

- *Ambiguity Effect* – Selecting an option for which the probability of a favourable outcome is known over an option for which the probability of a favourable outcome is unknown
- *Attentional Bias* – Failure to examine all possible outcomes when making a judgment
- *Availability Cascade* – Belief gaining plausibility through increasing repetition
- *Clustering* – Perceiving patterns where none exist
- *Optimism Bias* – Judging future events in a more positive light than is warranted by actual experience
- *Ostrich Effect* – Avoidance of risk or the negative by pretending they do not exist
- *Overconfidence Effect* – Excessive or inflated belief one's performance, ability
- *Serial Position Effect* – Assigning greater weight to initial or recent events more than subsequent or later events
- *Subadditivity Effect* – Assigning a lower probability to the whole than the probabilities of the parts
- *Subjective Validation* – Considering information to be correct if it has any personal meaning or significance
- *Valence Effect* – Overestimating the likelihood of positive rather than negative outcomes

Some the common attributional biases include:

- *Dunning–Kruger Effect* – Where skilled underrate their abilities and unskilled overrate their abilities
- *False Consensus Effect* – Overestimation of agreement
- *System Justification* – Defending the status quo

Strategic misrepresentation is the deliberate misrepresentation in planning and budgeting caused by issues such as distorted incentives. It is often a response to how organisations structure rewards and motivate individuals and groups. It is characterised by:

- Deliberately underestimating costs to gain acceptance with understanding that costs will increase
- Not willing to face reality of high costs
- Overstatement or understatement of requirements
- Inclusion of ideology into planning

The underlying rewards system and processes need to be redesigned to eliminate this.

Groupthink is the need for agreement, accord and compliance within the group. It results in a flawed, illogical and inhibited decision-making processes and decisions. It happens when the group becomes dominated by small number of or single individual who forces their beliefs on the group. There is a tendency for consensus and agreement and the desire to minimise contention which means alternatives are not fully evaluated. The group isolates itself from information on alternatives. Disagreement and dissent within the group are quashed or concealed through self-censorship

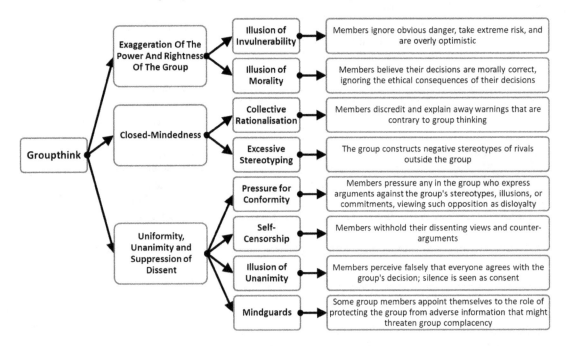

Figure 38 – Characteristics of Groupthink

Having written all of the above regarding the causes of solution delivery failures and challenges, there is one school of thought that states that this concern with and focus on delivering information technology solutions on time and on budget is wrong. It states that the more important objective is to deliver solutions that enable the organisation to transform its operations. Some organisations have excelled at transformation and at creating entire new industries. Information technology systems are of necessity new, untried and will involve trial-and-error to get right.

This provocative view is worth considering. But most solutions are delivered by more conventional organisations that have an existing set of operations and an existing heterogeneous information technology landscape that needs to be maintained and kept usable while new solutions are implemented. These organisations have limited resources that must be spent wisely. They have a limited capacity to handle change and so must select their changes carefully. They have a limited time in which to accomplish these changes. Finally, solution conception and design are the areas where new, untested and unproven ideas are explored. Solution delivery should be a more matter-of-fact and routine process unless, in the case of an agile approach, there is an element of discovery in this. Once the solution design is known, its implementation should have limited tentative, explorational and experimental characteristics unless it is a pure research and development initiative. Some of the underlying technologies may be new but this novelty can be allowed for. The complete solution is always much more than the sum of its pure technology components.

Solution delivery failure is at least partially a failure of understanding the actual scope of the solution and failure to put structures in place to achieve that delivery.

It is not really possible to create a plan to implement a solution if the complete scope of the work required in not known, understood and accepted.

Similarly, the best project management practices will not make a poor solution design implementable, operable, usable, supportable and maintainable. At best it will make the process for realising the deficiencies of the solution design and the need for their remediation slightly less painful and unpleasant.

3.1.1 The Business Value of Solution Architecture

The corollary to the previous section on solution delivery failure is what causes or influences solution delivery success.

The 2009 paper ***Business Value of Solution Architecture***[9] attempted to answer this question. The authors note:

> *In the literature, project management, analysis & design and software development and testing, attract a lot of attention and many methods and approaches have been devised for these activities.*
> *…*
> *None of these approaches recognizes explicitly the role of solution architecture, …*

The paper examined 49 custom software delivery projects. About half of the projects related to software being developed for companies in the financial sector. The remaining applied to other types such as industrial and public sector. There were a range of project types from transformation, merger and acquisition, single function integration and lifetime extension.

Some of the authors' key conclusions regarding the business benefits of solution architecture are:

> *The presence of an architecture governance process is significantly correlated with a lower expected value of budget overrun, compared to a situation where there is no architecture governance process in the customer's organization present. The difference in expected value is 19%.*

> *The presence of an architect during the calculation of the technical price is significantly correlated with a lower variance of the actual project budget, compared to a situation when there is no architect present during technical price calculation. The difference in the standard deviation of the project budget overrun percentage is 21% (13% versus 34%)*

> *The presence of a high-quality project architecture correlates with a decrease in time overrun of the project, compared to a situation where there is a medium or poor quality project architecture present. The difference in overrun is 55% (71% overrun versus 16% overrun).*

> *Usage of solution architecture is correlated with a significant increase in customer satisfaction.*

So, the involvement of high-quality solution architects in the solution design and delivery process resulted in:

1. 19% lower budget overspend

2. 21% small variance between actual and budgeted expenditure

3. 55% lower schedule overrun

4. Increased overall solution consumer satisfaction

The results of the analysis in this paper demonstrate that a high-performing solution architecture function can produce significant business value.

3.2 Solution Architecture and Risk Management

---

[9] Raymond Slot, Guido Dedene, and Rik Maes, https://onderzoek.hu.nl/~/media/sharepoint/Lectoraat%20Architectuur%20voor%20Digitale%20Informatiesystemen/2009/Business%20Value%20of%20Solution%20Architecture.pdf

The previous section on solution delivery failures analysed some of the reasons for these failures and described how an end-to-end approach to solution design will mitigate against the causes of failure.

A comprehensive view of the real scope of a solution that addresses all its components contributes to the management of risks during solution delivery.

There are many risks that arise when implementing new solutions, especially ones that are large, complex and that touch many parts of the organisation, as well as digital solutions that touch parties external to the organisation, such as:

- Product customisation
- Product functionality
- Product quality
- Vendor capability
- Solution complexity
- Solution delivery team
- Management

Risks are uncertain events that may occur with a probability that may or may not be known. If they occur, they will have negative effect on the solution.

Solution architecture can assist with solution delivery risk management in two ways:

1. **Passively** – by defining all the components of the overall solution so their risks and by defining individual components that have a low risk

2. **Actively** – by assisting with assessing the solution risks across all its components

The risks associated with a product or hosted or outsourced service will generally (but not always) be lower than a development option. Product vendors tend to be specialists with more experience. The product already exists and is readily available. It is in use by other customers and proven (or should be). These customers can be consulted. The vendor is responsible for product support. The product is enhanced and maintained by the vendor and new functionality is typically provided as part of maintenance and support agreement.

A product can always be changed and enhanced to suit the exact requirements of the organisation. The extent of the changes applied affects the overall solution risk along the scale, from low to very high:

- **Standard** – functionality included as standard or that can be configured by business users
- **Configuration** – features and functions that can be added using configuration tools
- **Customisation** – features and functions not provided by the vendor
- **Code Change, Developed Modules** – code changes to the product

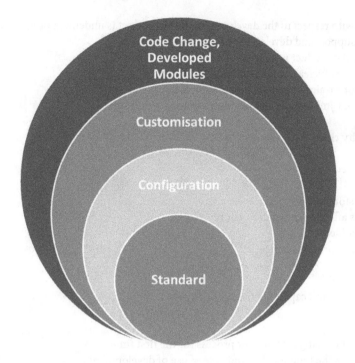

Figure 39 – Scale and Complexity of Product Changes and Enhancements

More complex changes involve reimplementation and testing after the product has been upgraded or new releases of the underlying base product have been applied. This is especially true of hosted or cloud-based multi-tenant solutions. Also, the scheduling of changes on these platforms may be outside the control of the organisation. These involve cost and risk throughout the life of the solution and delay subsequent upgrades.

There is a range of risks associated with the standard functionality provided (or supposed to be provided) by a product:

- Business requirements are not clearly articulated and subject to change
- Vendor does not understand the requirements of the business
- Business does not understand the functionality of the product
- Business cannot define the configuration and customisation changes required
- Vendor misrepresents the functionality of the product
- Product is not accepted by business users
- Product requires too much customisation to meet the business requirements
- Product cannot be configured or customised to meet the business requirements
- Product may be too complex to change to suit the needs of the business
- Product cannot interface with external systems
- Legacy data cannot be migrated to the product
- Product is not easily usable
- Product is unstable
- Product is not scalable
- Product is not secure

There are product technology risks associated with its underlying technology:

- The underlying technology is too old
- The underlying technology is too new
- The product or the technology may not meet the required performance or operations requirements

There are risks associated with vendor and their ability to supply and support the product:

- The product is new to the vendor

- The vendor's direction with respect to the development of the product is undefined or uncertain
- The vendor's ability to support and develop the product are unclear
- The technical quality of the product is poor
- The vendor may not have sufficient implementation skills
- The quality of the vendor's training and documentation is poor
- The vendor's contract may impose onerous or unsatisfactory conditions

There are solution complexity risks:

- Range of technologies used
- Hardware limitations
- Process for applying customisations
- Number of components affecting integration effort
- Large number of stakeholders
- Organisation and business process change
- Scale of solution

There are solution delivery team and capability risks:

- Mixed skills of team
- Incorporating a new method, language, tool or process for the first time
- Optimistic assumptions on the functionality and ease of use of development tools
- Optimistic assumptions on productivity
- Geographically dispersed team making communication and coordination more difficult

There are management risks:

- Management is dictating an unrealistic schedule
- Not handling creeping requirements and change proactively
- Inadequate quality control, causing delays in fixing unexpected defects
- Unanticipated risks associated with package software upgrades and lack of support

The solution architect should take a proactive to identifying risks during the solution design process and also during subsequent solution delivery. Solution design risks can be avoided or mitigated through greater solution knowledge (see section 4.2.1 on page 95). This involves:

- Identifying the known solution design risks and their potential impact on solution delivery, implementation and operation
- Assessing the probability that each risk will occur – beware of assigning pseudo-scientific evaluations of risk probability
- Estimating the potential negative impact if the event associated with the risk occurs
- Calculating a risk reserve that should be included in the solution delivery resource estimates to allow for risk
- Highlighting the high-priority risks and leading the development of plans to handle then
- Ensuring the that risks are recognised and managed

Risks are associated with the solution knowledge unknowns, both the known unknowns and the unknown unknowns.

The assessment of the impact and probability of occurrence of risks can be subjective. One person's view of a risk, probability of its occurrence and estimate of impact will be different from another's.

Solution components will have options. Each option will have a different set of risks. These will need to be balanced against the cost of these options. Solution architects need to be proactive in identifying risks and need to show leadership in how they are evaluated and managed.

3.3 Architecture Disciplines, Context and Interactions

3.3.1 Introduction

There are multiple overlapping logical information technology architecture disciplines that comprise the full spectrum of IT architecture. Not all organisations will have all roles. Also, these roles can be combined.

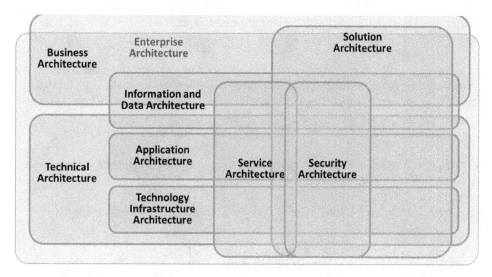

Figure 40 – IT Architecture Disciplines

In summary, the objectives of these IT architecture roles are:

- *Enterprise Architecture* – this defines, maintains, manages and updates the overall set of information technology standards, policies, principles and direction within which the organisation's IT systems are sourced, implemented and operated.

- *Business Architecture* – this is concerned with a structured approach to analysing the operation of an existing business function or entire organisation with a view to improving its operations or developing a new business function, with a strong focus on processes and technology.

- *Information and Data Architecture* – the defines the organisation's standards for the management of data and data-related technologies across the organisation across data types and sources including data management and governance, data quality, data operations and reference and master data management and through its lifecycle.

- *Technical Architecture* – this is concerned with translating functional solution design architectures into technology-specific detailed implementation-oriented specifications and solution delivery documentation so the software components of a solution can be built, acting as a bridge between solution architecture and the delivery function and designing new delivery approaches.

- *Application Architecture* – this is concerned with defining and managing the organisation's portfolio of information technology applications, their integrations, interactions and data exchanges between applications and the flow of data into and out of applications. It aims to ensure that the application portfolio meets the current and planned future needs of the organisation.

- *Technology Infrastructure Architecture* – this defines and manages the organisation information technology infrastructure across the computing, storage and communications landscape. It ensures that the infrastructure is able to meet the current and planned future needs of the organisation.

- *Service Architecture* – this is concerned with defining and maintaining the organisation's service management and service operations framework for the operational information technology applications and infrastructure including support, new releases and changes, capacity and performance, events and alerts, service levels, continuity, resilience and availability.

- *Security Architecture* – this defines, maintains, enforces and manages the architecture and set of facilities and tools to protect and defend the organisation's information technology hardware, software and data assets from attacks, threats and vulnerabilities that can lead to theft, damage and disruption, both from within and from outside the organisation.

- *Solution Architecture* – this is concerned with the definition and description of new (Information Technology) solution designs to resolve problems or address opportunities.

These information technology architecture disciplines all have one factor in common: they are concerned (or need to be concerned) with providing the business with an operational, functional information technology unit that provides a set of usable business applications and related supporting applications and processes that enable the business to work.

The IT architecture disciplines should and can contribute to the success of the business in two ways:

1. By taking the needs of the business for business systems and supporting and enabling technologies into an information technology infrastructure and a portfolio of business solutions

2. By identifying potential uses for new technologies to enable the business to operate more effectively

Figure 41 – IT Architecture Two-Way Contribution to the Business

The topic of solution architecture's potential to contribute to information technology and business innovation is covered in Chapter 9 on page 534.

IT architecture in general should both enable the business respond to and realise changes in response to external and internal pressures and should identify business opportunities in technology trends and occasions for changes and greater efficiencies.

IT architecture needs to be able to contribute to the development of business strategy and to be trusted to be able to make a contribution. That trust has to be proven and earned.

The IT architecture functions need to be involved along the entire business application portfolio solution journey.

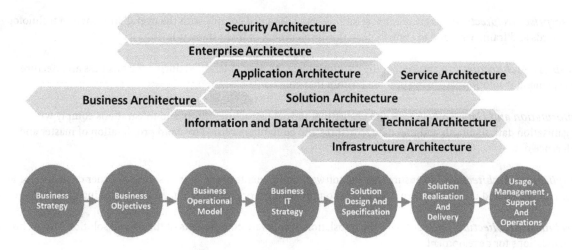

Figure 42 – IT Architecture Discipline Involvement Throughout Solution Portfolio Delivery

The separate IT architecture disciplines are (or should be) involved in the spectrum of activities concerned with the translation of business strategy and objectives into an integrated portfolio of IT solutions. All too commonly, the complex and fragmented operational IT architecture disciplines and their multiple separate views and handoffs between them contribute to the problems between business and IT.

Design guidance will be needed throughout the solution delivery and implementation process. The solution architect should take on the role of solution subject matter expert and provide this solution leadership.

The IT architecture disciplines need to work with one another in order to provide an effective service to the IT function and to the wider business organisation. The business organisation needs a portfolio of business applications as well as a set of infrastructural applications to support its business operations. The IT architecture disciplines play a crucial role in guaranteeing that this happens effectively, efficiently and in a timely and cost-effective manner.

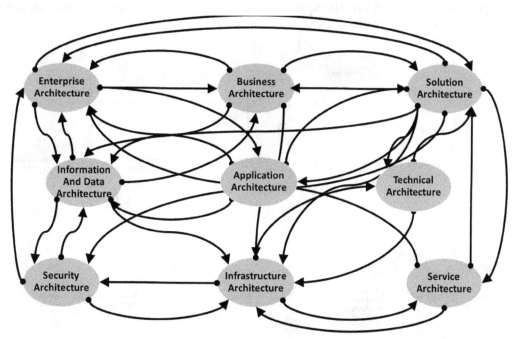

Figure 43 – Interactions Between IT Architecture Disciplines

In particular, the solution architecture function needs to interact with the other IT architecture disciplines in order to deliver complete solution designs:

- *Enterprise Architecture* – to ensure that solutions being designed comply with the overall information technology standards and framework and to contribute to the development of these standards

- *Business Architecture* – to ensure that the solutions meet the needs identified during the business architecture engagement, if solutions are being designed within that context

- *Information and Data Architecture* – to ensure that the data structures, flows and integrations comply with organisation data standards and that data structures and content are reused to avoid proliferation of master and reference data

- *Application Architecture* – to ensure that the software components of the overall solution, either developed or acquired and configured and customised, are designed to comply with the organisation's application and integration standards

- *Technical Architecture* – to assist with the translation of software components of the overall solution into technical specifications for development

- *Security Architecture* – to ensure that the overall solution and its components and interactions comply with the organisation's security standards

- *Infrastructure Architecture* – to ensure that the infrastructural components – hardware, communications and infrastructural software elements - of the overall solution fit with the organisation's infrastructure and that infrastructure components are reused and standardised as much as possible

- *Service Architecture* – to ensure that the solution design includes and complies with service management standards

Additionally, the solution architecture function must interface directly with the business and with the business analysis function during the solution design process.

The solution architecture function is the glue that joins all these elements together – business, business analysis, other IT architecture disciplines and the teams involved in the delivery of the various solution components – to create usable and used solutions designs that are translated into operable and usable solutions.

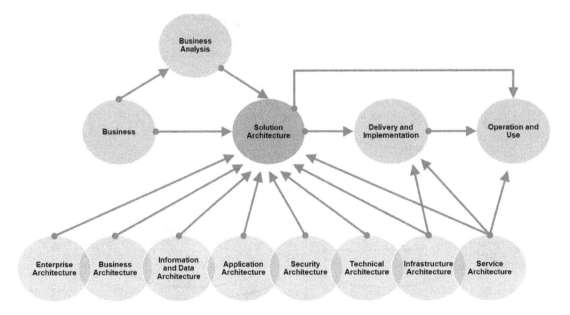

Figure 44 – Solution Architecture – Bringing It All Together

Solution architecture both works directly with the business organisation and the business analysis function to understand the requirements for and the background of the desired solution. Solution architecture then incorporates the standards developed by the other architecture areas into the solution design. Solution architecture subsequently works with the solution delivery and implementation teams as the solution design is translated into reality.

All too frequently, the information technology architecture disciplines operate in a self-contained, disintegrated and siloed manner with no overall management, separate and inconsistent approaches to work and limited communications between one another. The individual architecture practices throw work over the wall at one another with poor handoffs and no overall strategy

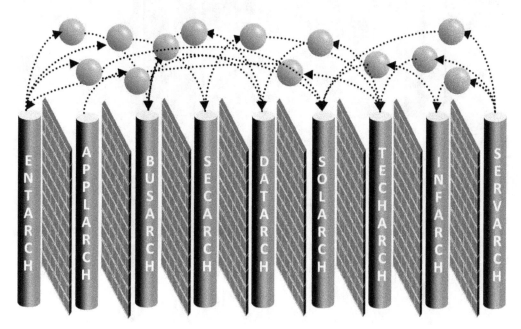

Figure 45 – Siloed Operation of Information Architecture Disciplines

There is deficient or absent cooperation between the architecture areas. Frequently there are adversarial relationships between disciplines that are characterised by infighting. This leads to an overall lack of efficiency and effectiveness across the IT architectures. In turn, this contributes to poor perception of the IT function by business.

Unfortunately, the siloed operations within the IT architecture disciplines is regularly replicated in the overall solution delivery process, as discussed in section 2.6.

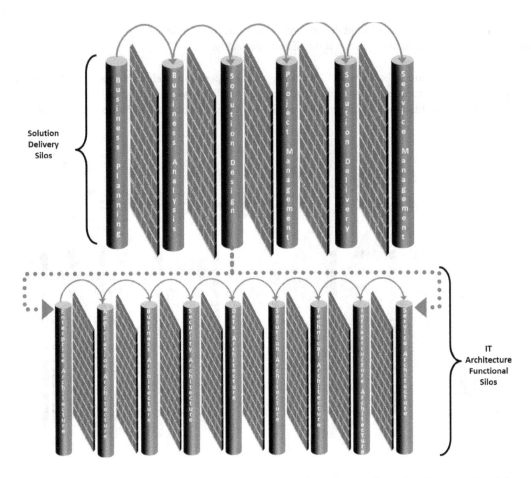

Figure 46 – Nesting of Siloed Operations Within Solution Delivery and Within IT Architecture Disciplines

This nesting of functions whose operations are separated from one another contributes to complexity in solution delivery and to increased chance of solution failure.

3.3.2 Run the Business and Change the Business

Organisations in general and the information technology function in particular need to be good at two general sets of skills, each divided into a doing and a managing the doing portion.

- *Run the Business (RTB)* – business as usual operations
  - o Doing – Run The Business
  - o Managing The Doing – Run The Business

- *Change the Business (CTB)* – changing existing operations to survive, compete, grow or expand
  - o Doing – Change the Business
  - o Managing The Doing – Change The Business

Not all these activities are of equal weight or importance to the IT function. Run The Business work will always dominate IT resources.

Figure 47 – Balance Between Run the Business and Change the Business Activities

These information technology architecture disciplines have both RTB and CTB dimensions to a greater or lesser extent.

The actual or perceived organisation run/change profile and what it really is may be different. There may be unnoticed latent demand for solutions that is not recognised or is ignored. This can be one source of shadow IT described in section 3.3.5 on page 86.

Solution architecture and the solution designs it develops and creates generally introduce changes to existing processes, organisation structures, solutions, applications, technology, infrastructure and structures. These solutions are a way of introducing innovation and change into the organisation. The solution architecture function resides largely in the Change the Business portion of the IT function.

The extent of the need for an effective solution architecture function depends on the size of the Change the Business workload. The solution architecture can deliver value after solutions have been implemented when those solutions need to be enhanced and modified. If the organisation does not envisage the need for many new solutions or changes to existing solutions, the need for and the corresponding size of the solution architecture function will be small.

The organisation needs to be honest about its need for solution architecture.

3.3.3 IT Architecture Principles

The IT architecture disciplines in general and solution architecture in particular should define a set of overlapping and sometimes contradictory principles that underpins its operation.

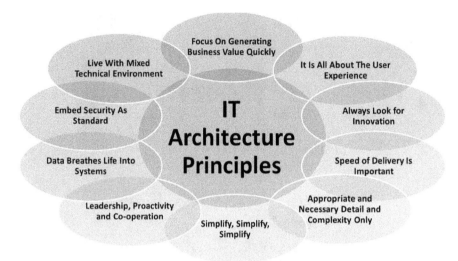

Figure 48 – IT Architecture Principles

These principles are:

- *Focus On Generating Business Value Quickly* – speed of delivery of solutions to allow the business respond to changes and to take advantage of new opportunities quickly is important. Subject to the constraints of knowing the scope of the solution, enable the business stakeholders make informed decisions on the options to achieve results quickly, understanding the consequences and implications.

- *It Is All About The User Experience* – there can be two types of solution consumer: the internal organisation user and the external organisation customer user. The latter may experience the solution directly or indirectly by interacting with internal users. Solutions exist to be usable, useful and to be used. People are always part of the operation and use of any solution. Solution usability contributes to the long-term success of a solution. Users experience the complete operational solution across its entire scope and experience its functional and quality properties and the underlying business processes.

- *Always Look for Innovation* – the solution architect should always take the larger architectural view of any solution and seek to improve and add value through appropriate innovation.

- *Speed of Delivery Is Important* – the solution architect should structure the solution design to allow components be implemented in parallel. The solution architect should structure and schedule the design work to optimise the use of the delivery teams, keeping the delivery engine occupied and optimally engaged.

- *Appropriate and Necessary Detail and Complexity Only* – necessary complexity is good. Unnecessary complexity is not. This has two applications: including only necessary and useful detail during the solution concept and exploration stage and removing unnecessary complexity from the ultimate solution design.

- *Simplify, Simplify, Simplify* – keep solution designs as simple as possible. Question solution designs and eliminate redundant or superfluous elements. Use common standards and infrastructural application components as much as is practical.

- *Leadership, Proactivity and Co-operation* – demonstrate solution leadership to the business functions. Respond to the concerns and issues of the business functions rather than waiting passively to be asked to contribute. Understand the concerns of the business and their need for usable business solutions.

- *Data Breathes Life Into Systems* – remember that the movement of data – data input, data processing and transformation, data outputs, data access, data reporting and analysis and data integrations – are at the heart of business applications. Data breathes life into solutions. Data quality, speed and ease of data access and data throughput have to be central to any solution design.

- *Embed Security As Standard* – security cannot be an afterthought, considered after the solution has been designed and retrofitted to the solution environment. Security needs to be embedded in all components of the solution and at all stages in the processing pipeline, especially at the periphery. There needs to be a common set of security standards and associated hardware and software infrastructure to support solution security across the entire landscape.

- *Live With Mixed Technical Environment* – while an entirely homogenous hardware and software environment is a desirable target, it is very difficult, expensive and time-consuming to achieve. All but the youngest organisations will have a legacy of mixed information technology solutions. While it is possible to reduce the amount of heterogeneity in the information landscape, its complete elimination is not realistic or achievable. The benefits of simplicity in the information technology environment are long-term and largely of direct benefit to the IT function in terms of reduced support and operating costs. The wider business organisation will see those benefits only indirectly. Too much effort spent on simplification of the information technology environment means fewer resources are available to work on business solutions. The IT function should not let itself become obsessed with simplification at the expense of other business-oriented work. Environment simplification can be contributed to by investment in infrastructural solutions – such as data interface, data integration and exchange – that can be used commonly across multiple solutions.

3.3.4 Problems with IT Architecture Operation

The unhappy reality is that the operation and interoperation of the set of IT architecture disciplines and the groups that perform those functions can be characterised by many of the following failings, flaws and deficiencies.

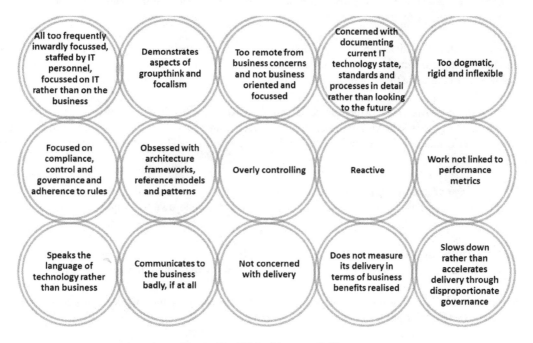

Figure 49 – IT Architecture Failings

- *All Too Frequently Inwardly Focussed, Staffed By IT Personnel, Focussed On IT Rather Than On the Business* – the architecture functions, including business architecture (which is not a widely practiced discipline), even though they provide a service to the business do not second business representatives to them to gain business experience and knowledge.

- *Demonstrates Aspects of Groupthink and Focalism* – groupthink and focalism occur where the group becomes inwardly focussed and does not learn or believe that it can learn from anyone outside the group. The group becomes dominated by small number or a single individual who force their beliefs on the group. This leads to decisions being made not based on wider concerns and information. The result is cognitive tunnelling where the group disregards external evidence and pursues its own initiatives irrespective of the damage they cause or the resources they waste.

- *Too Remote From Business Concerns and Not Business Oriented and Focussed* – the IT architecture disciplines do not ground their work in the context of business needs and business operations. Their work is internally focussed on technologies rather than addressing the wants of the business.

- *Concerned With Documenting Current IT Technology State, Standards and Processes in Detail Rather Than Looking to the Future* – IT architecture, especially enterprise architecture, is overly concerned with detailing and recording the current IT systems and platforms rather than looking to define a target future state that addresses more effectively business needs. The current state needs only enough information to allow its deficiencies and problems to be identified. It is only important insofar as it contributes value to the future.

- *Too Dogmatic, Rigid and Inflexible* – the IT disciplines do not respond and react flexibly to business needs. They concentrate on the internals of their practices.

- *Focused on Compliance, Control and Governance and Adherence to Rules* – the IT architecture practices value compliance with their internal rules and on governance standards to the detriment of service delivery.

- *Obsessed with Architecture Frameworks, Reference Models and Patterns* – IT architecture, especially enterprise architecture, looks at architecture frameworks as ends in themselves rather than as a means of adding value and delivering a service. The merit and value of architecture patterns and their applicability to real world business concerns and issues tend to be overestimated.

- *Overly Controlling* – the IT architecture disciplines seek to impose controls that they view as important and relevant but which are driven only by internal concerns.

- *Reactive* – the IT architecture disciplines react to business needs and business changes rather than seeking to be proactive in identifying problems and opportunities, either internally with their own operations or externally with the business, especially in the value that can be derived from exploiting new technologies.

- *Work Not Linked To Performance Metrics* – the IT architecture functions do not measure the value of the work they do and the results, if any, they achieve and the outcomes they generate. There is no assessment or evaluation framework with constituent performance or results indicators that links the costs of the IT architecture functions to the value realised.

- *Speaks the Language of Technology Rather Than Business* – the IT architecture disciplines communicate with the business using the language of IT. They do not speak to the business in their own language or see to express themselves in that way.

- *Communicates To the Business Badly, If At All* – the IT architecture functions do not regularly communicate what they do, what their role in the overall organisation it and what benefits and values they provide to the organisation.

- *Not Concerned With Delivery* – the IT architecture disciplines do not relate their work to the delivery of operable, usable, efficient, effective solutions and services to the business.

- *Does Not Measure Its Delivery In Terms of Business Benefits Realised* – the IT architecture functions do not understand the benefits that are realised from the work they do and the contribution they make either to the IT function or the overall business organisation. They do not have a benefits realisation measurement structure or framework.

- *Slows Down Rather Than Accelerates Delivery through Disproportionate Governance* – a far too common consequence of the operation of the IT architecture disciplines is that solution delivery is slowed down. For example, the introduction of new technologies that would contribute to business success is frequently prevented or stalled. Failure to comply with architecture governance standards, whose value have not been established or proven, is used as an excuse to inhibit change.

These failings within the IT architecture functions lead to failings in the relationship the business organisation has with the IT function. IT architecture does not provide technology leadership to either the IT function or the business organisation. The business does not seek out the services of the IT architecture disciplines for advice or technology consulting services. The business organisation wants a flexible IT function that enables it respond quickly to business needs and changes. The IT function responds slowly and provides a poor overall service to the business.

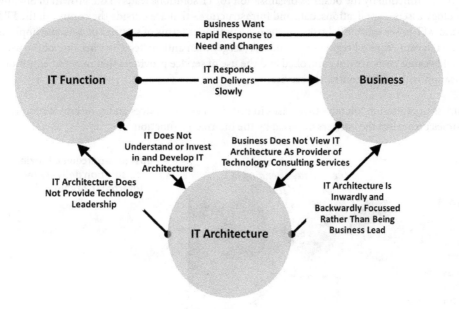

Figure 50 – IT and Business Relationship Failings

The consequence of these failings is that the business organisation bypasses the IT function and acquires information technology solutions and services directly from external service providers. Given the increasingly pervasive availability of externally hosted solutions requiring no central information technology infrastructure, this has become a very easy and progressively more common route for the business to take.

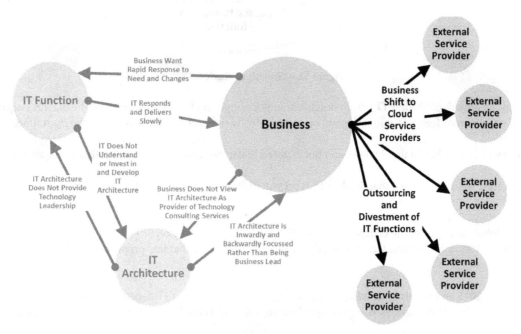

Figure 51 – Consequences of Failing Business and IT Relationship

The business organisation also bypasses the internal IT function by outsourcing the provision of IT services to external service providers.

3.3.5 Shadow IT

This bypassing of the IT function by the business organisation for IT solutions leads to the growth of Shadow IT – information technology assets – applications, data and infrastructure - that are outside the control of the IT function. In the medium term, Shadow IT poses substantial risks for the organisation is terms of security of data and applications, lack of compliance with the relevant required regulatory standards, larger than anticipated costs because of the use of subscription-based payments and because costs are not controlled and the use of service providers that may not continue in business, leaving the organisation without the contracted service.

However, the business organisation tolerates these risks in order to get the services and solutions it requires from external sources when it comes up against the barriers imposed by the internal IT function.

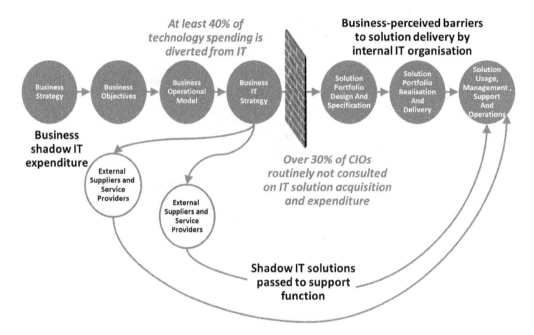

Figure 52 – Growth of Shadow IT

The size of and the growth of Shadow IT within organisation is a symptom of an IT function that the business organisation does not trust or rely on or feels it is able to depend on to provide the right set of solutions within the right time.

Because Shadow IT is just that, in the shadows and not exposed to detailed analysis, its size is difficult to quantify.

In 2017, the Everest Group estimated that Shadow IT represented 50% of more of the total IT spending of large organisations.[10]

In 2013, CEB Global (now part of the Gartner Group) estimated that the proportion of IT spending outside the IT function was of the order of 40%.[11] In the same CEB survey, the IT function estimated that this proportion of the IT spend was only 20%.

Cisco published in 2015 an analysis of cloud application usage that indicated that IT departments estimated their organisations were using 51 cloud services on average while in reality 730 cloud services were being used, a difference of 15

---

[10] See:
https://www.everestgrp.com/2017-04-eliminate-enterprise-shadow-sherpas-blue-shirts-39459.html/
https://www.cio.com/article/3188726/it-industry/how-to-eliminate-enterprise-shadow-it.html
[11] See:
https://www.forbes.com/sites/tomgroenfeldt/2013/12/02/40-percent-of-it-spending-is-outside-cio-control/

times.[12] Cisco also estimates that the difference between the IT department's understanding and the reality in terms of usage of cloud services grew from a multiplier of 7 to 10 to 15 in one year. This demonstrates what was written earlier about the easy availability of cloud-based solutions.

In 2015, Logicalis conducted a survey of over 400 global CIOs. 90% said there were sometimes bypassed the business. 31% of CIOs said they were routinely bypassed when the business was making IT buying decisions.[13]

CipherCloud published a report on cloud adoption[14] in which they identified issues with the use of unsanctioned cloud applications:

86% of cloud applications used by enterprises are unsanctioned "Shadow IT"

Our study found that enterprises vastly underestimate the extent of Shadow IT cloud applications used by their organizations. Various media sources claim 10% to 50% of cloud applications are not visible to IT. Our statistics show that on average 86% of cloud applications are unsanctioned. For example, a major US enterprise estimated 10–15 file sharing applications were in use, but discovered almost 70.

The CipherCloud report also identifies a lack of knowledge of the extent of such Shadow IT usage in organisations:

Enterprises Underestimate the Extent of Shadow IT

We all know that the use of Shadow IT within businesses is exploding, but few enterprises have been able to accurately assess the extent of the problem. Self-reported surveys of the percent of enterprises using cloud services range from as low as 19%1 to 50%—clearly ignoring Shadow IT. Other surveys have shown as many as 80%1 of end-users admitting to using unsanctioned applications, but without any measurements of actual usage.

The Cloud Security Alliance published a report[15] in January 2015 on the adoption of cloud applications by organisations. In this report, they noted:

Employees are more empowered than ever before to find and use cloud applications, often with limited or no involvement from the IT department, creating what's called "shadow IT." Despite the benefits of cloud computing, companies face numerous challenges including the security and compliance of corporate data, managing employee-led cloud usage, and even the development of necessary skills needed in the cloud era. By understanding the cloud adoption practices and potential risks, companies can better position themselves to be successful in their transition to the cloud.

The concerns raised by survey respondents in relation to cloud applications and Shadow IT were:

The survey respondents' primary concerns about Shadow IT are:

- *Security of corporate data in the cloud (49 percent)*
- *Potential compliance violations (25 percent)*
- *The ability to enforce policies (19 percent)*

---

[12] See:
https://blogs.cisco.com/cloud/shadow-it-and-the-cio-dilemma
https://blogs.cisco.com/cloud/shadow-it-rampant-pervasive-and-explosive
[13] See:
https://www.logicalis.com/news/cios-line-up-to-transform-it-in-response-to-the-shadow-it-phenomenon/
https://www.logicalis.com/globalassets/group/cio-survey/cio-survey-2015_final3.pdf
[14] Cloud Adoption & Risk Report in North America & Europe - 2014 Trends Published by CipherCloud in February 2015
http://pages.ciphercloud.com/rs/ciphercloud/images/CipherCloud-Cloud-Adoption-and-Risk-Report.pdf
[15] Cloud Adoption Practices & Priorities Survey Report Published by the Cloud Security Alliance.
https://downloads.cloudsecurityalliance.org/initiatives/surveys/capp/Cloud_Adoption_Practices_Priorities_Survey_Final.pdf

- *Redundant services creating inefficiency (8 percent)*

They also identified a lack of knowledge about the use of cloud applications:

> *Only 8 percent of companies know the scope of shadow IT at their organizations, and an overwhelming majority (72 percent) of companies surveyed said they did not know the scope of shadow IT but wanted to know. This number is even higher for enterprises with more than 5,000 employees at 80 percent. Globally, 71 percent of respondents were somewhat to very concerned over shadow IT. There are some stark geographic differences, with 85 percent of APAC respondents concerned versus just 66 percent and 68 percent of their Americas and European counterparts, respectively.*

This range of survey and other information illustrates the scope and concerns about Shadow IT, especially in the era of cloud applications.

The extent of the problem of Shadow IT and the bypassing of the internal IT function may be masked by IT outsourcing which may be notionally counted as a central IT spend. Some IT outsourcing activities are caused by the business organisation bypassing the IT function when acquiring IT services.

Shadow IT has existed since there was a centralised IT function. The original PC was effectively a form of Shadow IT, reacting against the inflexibility, slowness and lack of access to information by providing end-user direct access to information processing facilities.

Shadow IT in the form of end-user computing (EUC) – applications typically developed using tools such as Excel and Access – existed long before cloud applications became pervasively available and still continues to exist. These applications are typically developed without any formal analysis, design and testing. They evolve from the simple to the complex and become important to the daily operations of a business function or an organisation. They are contributed to by many people over time. They are not formally supported or documented. The well-proven risks that are associated with these EUC applications are now being transferred to cloud-based Shadow IT applications.

There are many reports of substantial losses being attributed to EUC applications, especially Excel. The following table lists a small number of these.

Publication	Details	Estimated Amount of Loss
https://www.reuters.com/article/us-solarcity-lazard-idUSKCN11635K	Lazard Ltd (LAZ.N), the investment bank that advised SolarCity Corp SCTY.O on its $2.6 billion sale to Tesla Motors Inc (TSLA.O), made an error in its analysis that discounted the value of the U.S. solar energy company by $400 million, a regulatory filing by Tesla showed on Wednesday.	$400 million
http://ww2.cfo.com/spreadsheets/2014/10/spreadsheet-error-costs-tibco-shareholders-100m/	Tibco Software shareholders will be getting $100 million less than originally anticipated from the company's more than $4 billion sale to Vista Equity Partners as a result of a spreadsheet error that overstated Tibco's equity value. According to a regulatory filing, Goldman Sachs, which is advising Tibco on the deal, used the spreadsheet in calculating that Tibco's implied equity value was about $4.2 billion. The merger agreement, reflecting that number, was announced Sept. 29.	$100 million
http://calleam.com/WTPF/?p=5517	Sometimes the mightiest of the mighty is humbled by the meekest of the meek. Microsoft Excel may not be the most grandiose software tool in the market, but it's amazing capabilities mean that it is one of the most widely used there is. As those of us who are regularly users know, there is however a dark side to the mathematical marvel that Excel has become. As you are absorbed into the wizardly magic of its number crunching capabilities, it is all too easy to make a mistake,	Approximately $6B

Publication	Details	Estimated Amount of Loss
	and, once your formulas are wrong, it be can be very hard to see that you have gone wrong. J.P. Morgan Chase, one of the world's most mighty banking and financial services firms, is one organization that has learned the risks of Excel the hard way. In an incident that drew worldwide attention, J.P. Morgan lost billions of dollars in the so called "London Whale" incident. The London Whale was a trader based in J.P. Morgan's London Chief Investment Office (CIO). He had earned his nickname because of the magnitude of the trading bets he was making. It is said that his bets were so large his actions alone could move a market. Despite his undeniable power, things went seriously wrong between Apr and Jun 2012 and a poorly positioned trade resulted in losses that eventually totalled up into the billions of dollars. According to available reports, the part of the CIO office involved was responsible for managing the bank's financial risk using complex financial hedging strategies in the derivatives markets. To support the operations J.P. Morgan had developed a "Synthetic Credit Value at Risk (VaR) Model" that helped them understand the level of risk they were exposed to and hence make decisions about what trades they should be making and when. The tool had been developed in-house in 2011 and was built using a series of Excel spreadsheets. According to J.P. Morgan's own report to their shareholders that was published following the disaster, the spreadsheets "had to be completed manually, by a process of copying and pasting data from one spreadsheet to another". To pick what appears to be an appropriate word in this particular case: YIKES! Immediately any serious user of Excel would know that relying on copy and paste is risky business. One minor slip and the data you have isn't what you thought it was. One accidental move and you can wipe out the embedded formulas without realizing what you've done. Relying on copy and paste in a tool that supported billion dollar transactions seems unfathomable to me.	
https://www.sec.gov/news/press/2011/2011-37.htm	Feb. 3, 2011 – The Securities and Exchange Commission today charged three AXA Rosenberg entities with securities fraud for concealing a significant error in the computer code of the quantitative investment model that they use to manage client assets. The error caused $217 million in investor losses. AXA Rosenberg Group LLC (ARG), AXA Rosenberg Investment Management LLC (ARIM), and Barr Rosenberg Research Center LLC (BRRC) have agreed to settle the SEC's charges by paying $217 million to harmed clients plus a $25 million penalty, and hiring an independent consultant with expertise in quantitative investment techniques who will review disclosures and enhance the role of compliance personnel.	$232 million
https://www.theglobeandmail.com/report-on-business/human-error-costs-transalta-24-million-on-contract-bids/article18285651/	A slip of the hand in a computer spreadsheet for bidding on electricity transmission contracts in New York will cost TransAlta Corp. $24-million (U.S.), wiping out 10 per cent of the company's profit this year.	$24 million

Table 16 – Errors in End User Computing Applications Leading to Financial Losses

Many companies have suffered and continue to suffer very substantial financial losses due to errors and misuse of computer applications, mainly Excel-based, developed by end users.

Chartis Research[16] produced in July 2016[17] an analysis of the risks of such EUC applications to financial services organisations in which they stated:

> *Chartis estimates that the current End User Computing (EUC) Value at Risk (VaR) for the largest 50 FIs (Financial Institutions) is $12.1 billion (bn) (at a confidence interval of 97.5%, over a one-year period). The estimated annual average VaR for large FIs is $285 million (m) per institution. The results of our methodology applied to publicly disclosed loss events gave an estimate of the VaR that large FIs are exposed to, though it does not take into account secondary effects such as regulatory fines, reputational damage, loss of customers etc. Chartis believes there is a strong qualitative argument that the potential secondary impact of EUC risk is significantly larger than the direct losses covered in this paper.*

The problem of the business bypassing the central IT function is getting worse. The failure of IT architecture to engage with business requirements is one cause of this. This leads to a fragmented IT solution landscape that is characterised by problems such as:

- High variability and lack of standardisation across business units, driven by changes in business strategy, governance, organisation and process

- Inconsistent data definitions, multiple databases, releases and configurations which result in duplication of licenses, duplicate and inconsistent information, complexity in testing, no single version of the truth and no control of master and reference data

- Multiple vendors, multiple instances and versions which add complexity in procurement, development and release management, resulting in higher costs and longer time to market

- Multiple operating environments, multiple hardware vendors and types, leading to higher maintenance and personnel costs, greater instability and time-to-fix

- No control of costs

- No control of risks associated with failure to comply with relevant regulations

- No control of risks associated with failure of external service providers

- No control of risks relating to data privacy and data protection

It may simply a matter of time before a similar set of stories regarding EUC applications starts to emerge for cloud-based applications.

The EUC Shadow IT problem has not been resolved. So, the cloud application Shadow IT may not also be resolved easily.

The solution architecture function can at least seek to minimise both its use and the likelihood and impact of problems by engaging with the business function earlier to identify the need for solutions.

---

[16] See:
http://www.chartis-research.com/
[17] Quantification of End User Computing Risk in Financial Services
http://www.clusterseven.com/wp-content/uploads/2016/07/Quantification-of-EUC-Risk-Final.pdf

Chapter 4. Solution Architecture Engagement and the Solution Design Process

4.1 Introduction

This chapter contains details on solution architecture and the solution design processes across a range of business engagement types. It discusses how solution architecture fits into the overall organisation and the information technology function. It discusses the topics of:

- Problem and solution knowledge and complexity

- The solution design and delivery process

- How the solution architecture function needs to interface with the business analysis function, especially in relation to requirements gathering and business process analysis

- The ways in which the solution architecture function can engage with the business to design solutions to resolve problems or address opportunities, including describing a number of detailed engagement processes that can be used at different stages of solution design

- The importance of solution usability and the solution consumers' experience of the solution

- The need to take data architecture view of the solution from the initial stages of solution design and the approaches and frameworks that can be used to make this easier

- The necessity to consider solution security and privacy

- The artefacts that can be created during the various engagement and design processes

- The process for validating solution designs

Solution architecture and solution design needs to operate in a wider organisational context. At this high level, this context is:

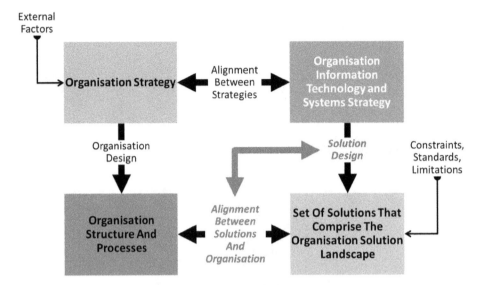

Figure 53 – Solution Design in an Outline Organisation Framework

This is a generic representation. It will be different for individual organisations and businesses, such as those operating in the public and private sectors. The organisation defines its strategy, informed by external factors such as its operating environment, business pressures, drivers for change and the legal and regulatory framework to which it is subject. The organisation then defines its structure and processes to achieve the strategy. The organisation then creates its overall information technology strategy with the help of the IT function. The organisation strategy and IT strategy need to be synchronised so the latter assists with the achievement of the former. The IT strategy leads the design, delivery and operation of the portfolio of solutions needed to run the organisation. These solutions must harmonise with the organisation structure and the operational business processes.

The Solution Architecture and Design function needs to be involved both in the design of the required business solutions and in making certain that the solutions are what the business really needs to operate the business processes.

The following diagram illustrates in more detail the components and their linkages needed to make sure than the business gets solutions that meet their needs to achieve business and information technology alignment

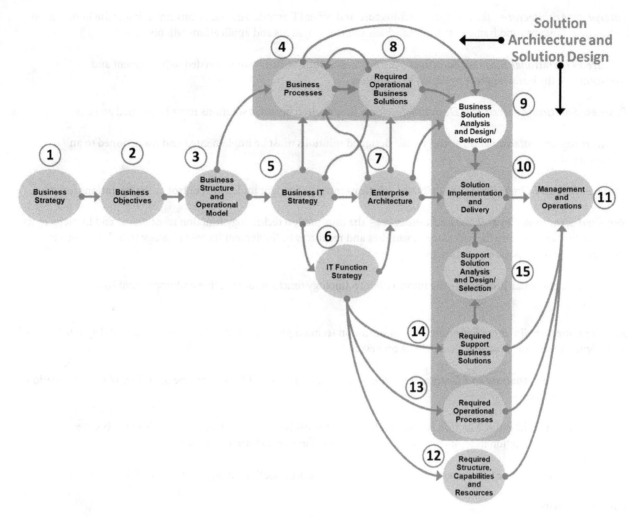

Figure 54 – Organisation Context of Solution Architecture

The numbered elements of the diagram above are:

1. ***Business Strategy*** – the business or organisation must create an overall strategy for its operations defining what it does and what it seeks to achieve. The business strategy provides the context in which all other activities take place.

2. ***Business Objectives*** – the business strategy is translated into a number of objectives that must be achieved in order to realise the business strategy.

3. ***Business Structure and Operational Model*** – an organisational structure and operating needs to be defined in order to achieve the defined set of objectives.

4. ***Business Processes*** – the operational business processes needed to actualise the achievement of the defined objectives must be defined and implemented.

5. ***Business IT Strategy*** – the organisation needs to define an overall information technology strategy that encompasses the solutions, systems and applications needed to operate the business processes.

6. ***IT Function Strategy*** – the organisation's information technology function must define its own strategy to achieve the wider organisation's business IT strategy. This must include the information technology function structures and business processes.

7. *Enterprise Architecture* – the enterprise architecture and other IT architecture functions must define the information technology standards and frameworks within which solutions, systems and applications will operate.

8. *Required Operational Business Solutions* – the business solutions and systems needed to implement and operationalise the business processes must be identified.

9. *Business Solution Analysis and Design/Selection* – the required business solutions must be defined and designed.

10. *Solution Implementation and Delivery* – the designed solutions must be implemented and transitioned to an operational state.

11. *Management and Operations* – the delivered solutions must be brought under the control of the operations function.

12. *Required Structure, Capabilities and Resources* – the information technology function must define and implement its own structure and acquire the necessary capabilities and resources to implement its own strategy in order in turn to implement the organisation's IT strategy.

13. **Required Operational Processes** – the information technology function must define and implement its internal processes.

14. *Required Support Business Solutions* – the information technology function must define solutions and systems needed to implement and operationalise the business processes

15. *Support Solution Analysis and Design/Selection* – the solutions required to support the operation of the information technology function

An effective solution architecture function and solution design process is needed to ensure the needs of the business are responded to by the IT function in terms of providing a portfolio of usable and useful solutions.

As mentioned above, there are three interrelated strategies using the organisation change domain model discussed earlier:

1. Business Strategy
   - Defines the strategic goals, imperatives and initiatives to direct the business
   - Business strategy is the principal driver of IT strategy
   - IT strategy is developed to support the business strategy
   - IT can also provide opportunities to reshape the business strategy

2. Organisation IT Strategy
   - Defines the strategic direction of information technology within the organisation required to support and achieve business strategy.

3. IT Business Function Strategy
   - Defines the strategic direction of the IT function to develop, deploy, operate, manage and support the IT systems needed by the business
   - Includes processes and supporting technology

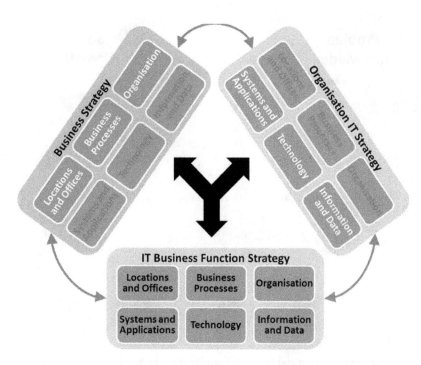

Figure 55 – Interrelated Strategies – Business Strategy, Overall Organisation IT Strategy and Internal IT Function Strategy

4.2 Problem and Solution Knowledge and Complexity

4.2.1 Problem and Solution Knowledge

One aspect of the solution design process is the acquisition of knowledge: knowledge about the problem being solved and knowledge about the solution options. This knowledge is an input to the solution design process.

The purpose of gathering knowledge is to gain insight and make decisions. You need a systematic, structured and measurable approach to decision making. Decision making that follows a systematic approach is more productive and results in better decisions.

A structured decision-making approach is characterised by:

- Appropriate and sufficient problem analysis
- Definition of evaluation factors
- Identification of alternative options and solutions
- Identification and evaluation of likely positive consequences of solutions
- Identification and evaluation of likely negative consequences of solutions

You need to avoid factors that cause ineffective decision making such as:

- The real decision maker is not known or unavailable
- There are multiple, possibly conflicting, decision makers
- Objectives cannot be plainly identified and clarified
- There are trade-offs to be agreed
- The key uncertainties cannot be understood
- The available and viable options cannot be agreed
- The measures of value cannot be agreed

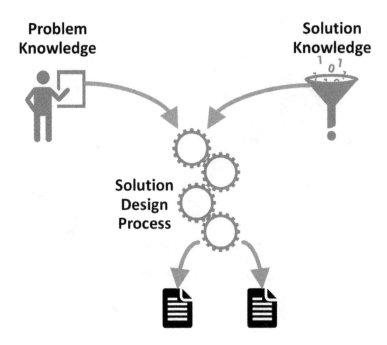

Figure 56 – Problem and Solution Knowledge in the Solution Design Process

The amount of already known knowledge about the problem being resolved through the design of a solution and the amount of knowledge that must be acquired governs the complexity of the solution design process.

The solution design process acquires and uses knowledge about the problem and the solution to create one or more implementable and usable solution options.

Solutions can, simplistically, grouped into one of four categories based on a combination of the amount of problem knowledge known and the amount of solution knowledge known.

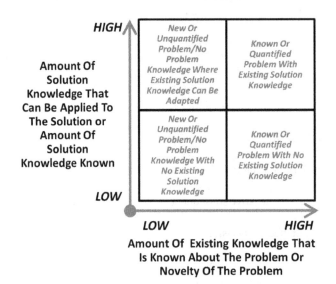

Figure 57 – Problem and Solution Knowledge and Solution Design Complexity

This leads to four very broad categories of problem and solution knowledge and the associated solution design complexity:

1. *New Or Unquantified Problem/No Problem Knowledge With No Existing Solution Knowledge* – where the existing knowledge both about the problem and its resolution are low

2. *Known Or Quantified Problem With No Existing Solution Knowledge* – where the problem is largely known but the resolution options are not

3. *New Or Unquantified Problem/No Problem Knowledge Where Existing Solution Knowledge Can Be Adapted* – where the knowledge about the problem is low but where there is existing solution knowledge based on the resolution of generally similar problems

4. *Known Or Quantified Problem With Existing Solution Knowledge* – where the existing knowledge about the problem and its resolution are both high

The category of problem and resolution knowledge can be used to determine the approach to defining a resolution and an associated implementing solution.

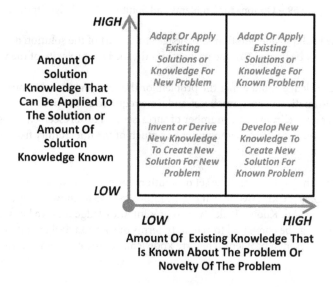

Figure 58 – Problem and Solution Knowledge and Solution Design Options

There are four broad categories of resolution determination approach linked to the categories of knowledge:

1. *Invent or Derive New Knowledge To Create New Solution For New Problem* – where the existing knowledge both about the problem and its resolution are low, the solution approach will involve inventing or deriving new solution design knowledge to the new problem.

2. *Develop New Knowledge To Create New Solution For Known Problem* – where the problem is largely known but the resolution options are not, new solution knowledge must be developed to create a new solution design for a known problem.

3. *Adapt Or Apply Existing Solutions or Knowledge For New Problem* – where the knowledge about the problem is low but where there is existing solution knowledge based on the resolution of generally similar problems, the solution approach will involve adapting or applying existing solution design knowledge to the new problem.

4. *Adapt Or Apply Existing Solutions or Knowledge For Known Problem* – where the existing knowledge about the problem and its resolution are both high, the solution approach will involve adapting or applying existing solution design knowledge to the problem.

This mapping is shown in the diagram below.

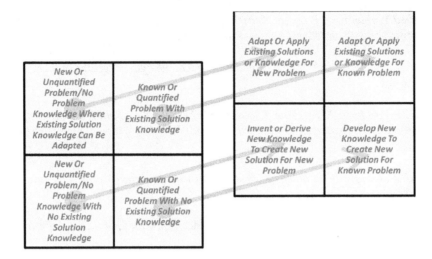

Figure 59 – Options for Problems and Solution Knowledge Options

Understanding the extent of the problem and solution knowledge at the start of the solution design process allows you understand the likely effort that will be involved in the process and the likely complexity of the work.

Solution unknowns – gaps in knowledge about either the problem or the solution - are the source of potential problems during solution delivery, from estimation of cost, resources and time required to the performance of the work. One goal of solution design is to minimise or even eliminate the number of surprises and unforeseen circumstances and events that occur after the design is complete. It is concerned with removing the as much of the uncertainty from the solution design as is possible, subject to time and resource constraints.

Potential knowledge – both about the problem and the set of solution options – must be converted into actual knowledge. Simplistically, potential knowledge is the knowledge that can be known. Known Knowns represent knowledge that can be and is known – potential converted to actual. Known Unknowns represent knowledge that we know that we do not know – potential that can at some future stage be converted to actual. In terms of solution design and ultimately the delivery of the solution, Unknown Unknowns represent a problem. They are knowledge of the problem and the solution that we do not know about.

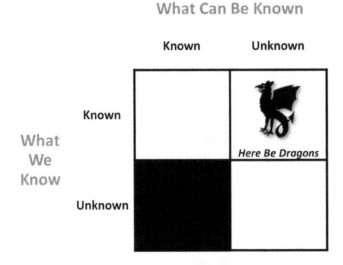

Figure 60 – Problem and Solution Knowns and Unknowns

The solution design process is concerned with maximising the Known Knowns and minimising the other areas of unknown knowledge through exploration, investigation and analysis. It is about taming the solution knowledge dragons. The more that is known about the solution design the fewer the problems relating to scope and changes and associated cost, time and resource increase will occur later in solution implementation.

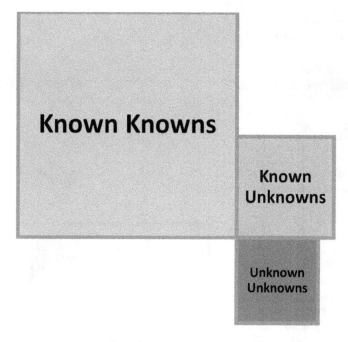

Figure 61 – Maximising the Solution Knowns and Minimising the Unknowns

Greater certainty about the problem being resolved and the design of the solution required to resolve it leads to more exactness in the estimate of resources, time and cost required to implement the solution.

The need to acquire knowledge and thus remove uncertainty cannot be used as an excuse for lack of progress towards creating a solution design. The rapid solution design engagement process described in section4.6.5 on page 257 can be used to create broad solution concept options quickly.

The high-level set of steps to identify solution options and to create a conceptual architecture is illustrated below.

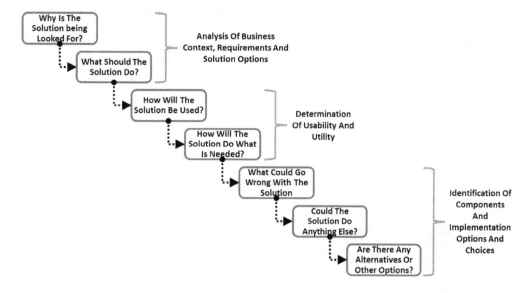

Figure 62 – Solution Option Definition Steps

The fundamental questions to be asked are:

- Why Is The Solution being Looked For?
- What Should The Solution Do?
- How Will The Solution Be Used?
- How Will The Solution Do What Is Needed?
- What Could Go Wrong With The Solution
- Could The Solution Do Anything Else?
- Are There Any Alternatives Or Other Options?

4.2.2 Solution Complexity

The likely complexity of the solution design process is partially related to the state of the problem and solution knowledge. This can be represented as a solution design complexity heatmap.

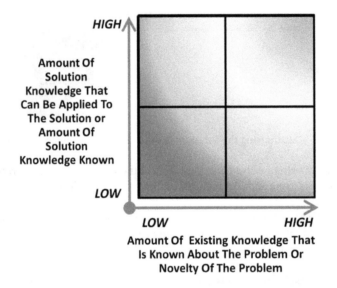

Figure 63 – Solution Design Complexity Heatmap

The red areas indicate areas of potentially high complexity. The green areas indicate areas of potentially low complexity. However, the problem/solution knowledge gap is just one aspect of complexity in the solution design process and in the solution design created.

The solution is likely to be complex system if the problem to be resolved or the way which the problem can be resolved comprises many components that can interact with one other in many different ways. Having many components in itself does not lead to complexity. The complexity of the solution arises when those components have many relationships, dependencies and interactions. [18]

---

[18] The eponymous Gall's Law should be borne in mind. See page 52 of *SYSTEMANTICS: How Systems Really Work and How They Fail* ISBN 978-0812906745 by John Gall:

> *A Complex System That Works Is Invariably Found To Have Evolved From A Simple System That Works.*

> *The parallel proposition also appears to be true:*

>> *A Complex System Designed From Scratch Never Works And Cannot Be Patched Up To Make It Work. You Have To Start Over, Beginning With A Working Simple System.*

Gall's short book is an entertaining read if somewhat cynical and facetious. This law is not necessarily a formal statement about complexity but it is worth remembering.

Complexity arises and needs to be addressed and managed in a number of areas in the solution design process:

1. The complexity of the solution required to resolve the problem, its number of components and its interactions – the solution's intrinsic complexity
2. Complexity in arriving at the solution design option or options based on the amount of knowledge required and the knowability of this knowledge
3. Complexity in the way the solution is interacted with and the ways in which the solution can or will be used – this can be regarded as uncontrollable usage complexity

Complexity can be very enticing. Complexity makes solutions interesting and captivating. Solution architects must work hard to avoid the fascination of complexity.

Usage complexity can be reduced by actions such as limiting the number of users and reducing the available functionality to limit the actions that solution users can perform.

Usage complexity can arise in situations where there is substantial latent demand for the solution. This is demand that does not currently manifest itself but becomes apparent when the solution is made available.

Such latent demand frequently occurs when solutions are implemented that are deployed to a user population outside the organisation. The internal organisation user population is reasonably easy to know and control. It is considerably more difficult to control external users. There can be uncertainty and unpredictability about their interactions with the solution.

The solution designer needs to ensure that the designed solution is only as complex as it needs to be to resolve the problem and not any more complex but not any less[19]. Complexity and richness of features can be very seductive. Simplification and removing unnecessary complexity in the solution design is one of the tasks of the solution designer.[20] Necessary complexity is what remains when unnecessary complexity has been removed. Necessary complexity can only be removed when the solution functionality that leads to that complexity is explicitly removed.

The analogy of a waterbed can be used when discussing necessary and unnecessary complexity. Water is incompressible so pressing down on one part of the waterbed will cause it to rise elsewhere. So, as with the waterbed, attempts to eliminate

---

[19] There is a strong theoretical basis to the concept of solution complexity. In his book *An Introduction to Cybernetics* http://pespmc1.vub.ac.be/books/IntroCyb.pdf, W Ross Ahsby introduced his *Law Of Requisite Variety* (page 206). Essentially the system as a regulator requires an equivalent amount of variety (processing functionality) as the information or signals it must handle. That is, the solution must as a complex as the streams of information, inputs and actions it is designed to handle. This is further elaborated by Roger C. Conant and W. Ross Ashby in their *Good Regulator* theorem - http://pespmc1.vub.ac.be/books/Conant_Ashby.pdf - which states that "*every good regulator of a system must be a model of that system*". That is, there should be a mapping from the states of the system being handled to the states of the solution that handles that system. When applied to solution architecture, this approach views the solution as a receiver and processor of signals – data exchanges, integrations, inputs and requests for functions to be performed. The solution must have sufficient complexity to handle and process the range of signals it is expected to accommodate. From this it can be inferred that complexity can be avoided by simplifying the amount of processing expected to be performed by the system.

[20] The often-quoted figures from Jim Johnson of the Standish Group on product features not used is worth considering. See. *ROI: It's your job. Proceedings of the Third International Conference on Extreme Programming and Flexible Processes in Software Engineering (XP 2002)*, Alghero, Sardinia, Italy. He claimed that 46% of product features implemented were never used.

	Features Used
Never	45%
Rarely	19%
Sometimes	16%
Often	13%
Always	7%

The analysis was based on just four internally developed software solutions and so the analysis may not be widely applicable. However, it represents a warning to always question and avoid complexity.

necessary complexity in one area of the solution will cause additional compensating complexity to occur or be needed elsewhere.

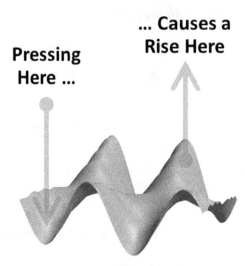

Figure 64 – The Waterbed Analogy of Necessary Solution Complexity

There is a related area of complexity in the wider solution delivery process. This relates to the complexity of the project to implement the solution. A complex solution design will invariably lead to a complex solution delivery process. This complexity can be further increased by delivery factors such as:

- Skill level of solution delivery team
- Number of organisation locations affected by the solution
- Skill and experience of suppliers, if third parties are being used
- Newness of technologies included in the solution
- Involvement of third-parties in the delivery of the solution and the nature of the organisation's relationships with those third parties

There is a detailed list of complexity factors later in this section.

These factors can be outside the core solution design. But they can be included in or at least adverted to in the solution design.

Factors that are commonly included in an assessment of the complexity of the solution delivery projects such as:

- Amount of work performed by and expected throughput of the system – number of transactions, complexity of transactions
- Number of people that will use the solution
- Security, performance, reliability and availability requirements
- Volume of data to be migrated or initially loaded to make the solution usable
- Volume of data to be stored and processed
- Complexity in the data structures and the relationships between data elements

are not purely delivery related. These can and should be included in the solution design.

Complexity accumulates and is magnified across these contributing factors. The complexity adds to the riskiness associated with solution implementation. Taking an end-to-end solution delivery view means that the complexity that has accumulated across the entire path and its consequent risks can be understood.

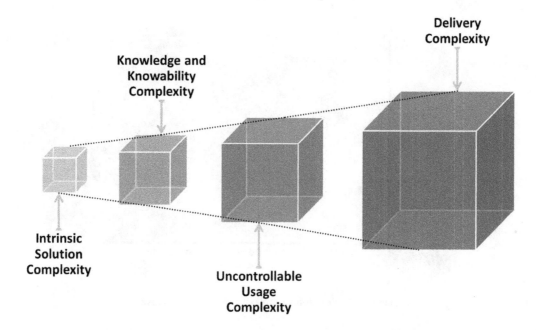

Figure 65 – Accumulating Solution Complexity

Knowing the likely complexity of the solution allows an informed decision to be made on the solution design effort and the number and skills and experience levels of the resources required. Solutions of low complexity require few resources and can be assigned to solution designers who are starting to gain experience. Highly complex solutions, even after unnecessary complexity has been removed, involve greater risk along the solution design and implementation journey. This complexity needs to be understood and managed.

However, estimating the complexity requires some initial assessment of the both the state of problem and solution knowledge and of the number and complexity of the components and their interactions of the solution.

In general, complex problems require complex solutions. Simple solutions will not work. Similarly, simple problems do not require and should not be given complex solutions.

		Solution	
		Simple	**Complex**
Problem	**Simple**	Simple problems have simple solutions	Simple problems *do not have* complex solutions
	Complex	Complex problems *do not have* simple solutions	Complex problems have complex solutions

Figure 66 – Simple and Complex Problems and Solutions

A further aspect of complex solutions is that they can take a long time to implement. Frequently solutions need to be deployed, operable and usable quickly to take advantage of a changing business environment.

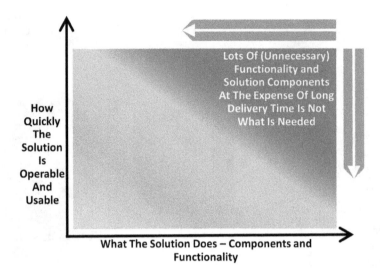

Figure 67 – Solution Complexity and Time to Deliver

Complexity is the enemy of speed and dynamism. Reducing complexity reduces the time to get the solution operational. However, speed and dynamism of solution delivery are themselves not without major risks:

- Higher operational costs due to manual workaround, poorly integrated solution components, poor data quality
- Unstable solution that is prone to errors and failures, leading to poor user experience, reputational damage and the possible rejection of the solution
- Necessary components missing – the solution as implemented does not include functionality that is needed to make the solution usable
- Cannot scale to handle volumes – the solution worked for small volumes of activity and data but cannot scale in a production environment leading to delays, higher support costs, manual effort and rejection of the solution
- Insecure – the solution has security gaps and flaws
- Not accepted by target user population – the solution is rejected by the users for who it is intended
- Wrong solution – the solution is simply not what is needed or envisaged
- Cost of rework - the solution problems must be resolved through rework, requiring more time and cost

There is no simple answer to the question of what complexity is necessary. There is no magic bullet to kill the problem. It requires analysis and thought. If the scope of the required solution is not understood then the risks cannot be understood. Getting the solution wrong can be expensive.

Solution complexity is frequently assessed as a weighting factor, when creating solution delivery estimates. The overall weighting is calculated based on scores assigned to individual factors such as:

Complexity Factor Group	Complexity Factor	Reverse Weighting	Weighting/ Importance	Simple/Few/Low/Yes/Not Applicable To Complex/Large/High/No
Operational Factors	Operational Security Requirements			
	Privacy and Confidentiality Of Data Being Processed			
	Operational Performance And Throughput Requirements			
	Operational Reliability And Availability Requirements			
	Amount Of On-Premises Infrastructure Required			

Complexity Factor Group	Complexity Factor	Reverse Weighting	Weighting/ Importance	Simple/Few/Low/Yes/Not Applicable To Complex/Large/High/No
	Volume Of Data Being Processed			
	Volume and Variability of Workload To Be Processed			
	Number Of Different Types Of Transactions To Be Processed			
	Number Of Internal Solution Consumers			
	Number Of External Solution Consumers			
Technical Factors	Number Of Technologies Included In The Overall Solution			
	Number Of Solution Components			
	Number Of Solutions Integrations And Interfaces			
	Number Of Application Tiers			
	Technologies Already Part Of The Organisation's Enterprise Architecture			
	Availability Of Skills And Experience In Technologies	Y		
	Amount Of Custom Development			
	Development Platform Productivity			
	Amount And Complexity Of Data To Be Loaded Or Migrated			
	Reuse Of Existing Custom Components			
Business Factors	Overall Business Project Size			
	Number Of Business Functions Or Areas That Will Use The Solution			
	Number And Complexity Of Underlying Business Processes			
	Familiarity Of The It Function With The Business Functions Or Areas	Y		
	Availability Of Business Resources To Work On The Solution	Y		
	Number Of Locations Of Business Functions			
	Number Of Existing Solution Components Being Replaced			
	Organisation Change Requirements			
Product Factors	Number Of Products and Services Required To Deliver The Solution			
	Number Of Separate Suppliers Involved In The Delivery Of The Product(s) and Service(s)			
	Maturity Of The Product(s) and Service(s)	Y		
	Supplier Proven Skills And Experience In Implementing Products and Services	Y		
	Products and Services Are Being Provided By Existing Suppliers To The Organisation	Y		
	Number Of Supplier Offshore Locations Involved In The Delivery Of The Product(s) and Service(s)			
	Degree Of Configuration Of Product(s) and Service(s)			
	Degree Of Customisation Of The Of Product(s)			

Complexity Factor Group	Complexity Factor	Reverse Weighting	Weighting/ Importance	Simple/Few/Low/Yes/Not Applicable To Complex/Large/High/No
	and Service(s)			
	Number Of Personnel From Supplier Involved In The Product and Service Delivery			
	Complexity Of Outsourcing Relationship, If Applicable, To The Delivery Of The Product(s) and Service(s)			
	Amount Of New Technology Introduced By The Product(s) and Service(s)			
Project Factors	Fixed Project Implementation Deadline			
	Expected Project Duration			
	Overall Solution Delivery Project Size			
	Number Of Outsourcing Arrangements Included In The Overall Solution			
	Number Of Externally Hosted Components Included In The Overall Solution			
	Size Of Implementation Project Team			
	Multiple Language Requirements			
	Number Of Jurisdictions In Which The Solution Will Operate			
Skill and Experience Factors	Project Manager Skills And Experience	Y		
	Implementation Team Skills And Experience	Y		

Table 17 – Solution Complexity Factors

Individual factor scores are assigned in a range of 1 to 10 on the scale where 1 represents *Simple/Few/Low/Yes/Not Applicable* to 10 representing *Complex/Large/High/No*.

The Reverse Weighting column indicates that the score is reversed: 10 means a very low contribution to the overall complexity and 1 means a very high complexity score. For example, the complexity factor *Number of separate suppliers involved in the delivery of the product(s)* is rated from 1 to 10 where 1 means a single supplier and 10 means a very large number of suppliers. Where the rating of the complexity factor *Maturity of the product(s)* which has a reverse rating flag is 1, it means it is an immature product and a score of 10 means it is very mature.

The calculated weighting is used as an uplift to the base resource estimates.

It is also used to identify high-risk solution delivery projects that require a higher degree of governance.

These are not so much solution complexity factors as solution implementation and organisation and project complexity factors.

Using an approach such as this can give a false sense of comfort that the solution complexity has been understood, captured and catered for and a misleading rigour to the complexity score. Solution delivery complexity is non-linear rather than linear. A higher complexity score indicates that the solution delivery is much more complex. A score of the 75th percentile does not mean the solution delivery complexity is 50% greater than that of a 50th percentile score. It is more likely to be 70% more complex. The reasoning here is that the amount by which the estimated resources should be increased to cater for solution complexity must start to taper off. There is only so much complexity that the delivery of a solution can handle and only so many resources that can be added to the solution delivery resources before the project cannot absorb any more.

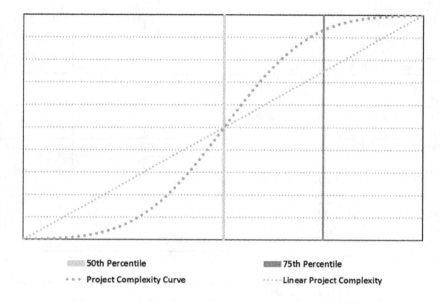

Figure 68 – Non-Linear Nature of Solution Delivery Complexity

However, the exact nature of the non-linearity is not obvious. In reality the complexity curve will be like:

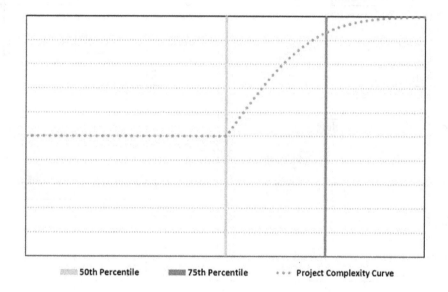

Figure 69 – Adjusted Complexity Curve

A notional reduction in complexity will not lead to a reduction in the effort and resources required to deliver the solution. The solution will always require a basic amount of resources to implement. Complexity adds to these.

The applicability of the weightings assigned to the complexity factors is unvalidated. The values assigned to the weights are similarly not formally established. Also, complexity factors and weightings are interrelated and this relationship is not represented in the overall complexity score. For example, the experience of the project manager assigned to a small project is much less important that that person's experience if the project is very large.

In some cases, these complexity factors reflect the solution implementation causes of failure listed in section 3.1 on page 57.

The following table contains an example of the application of this complexity model.

Complexity Factor Group	Complexity Factor	Reverse Weighting	Weighting/ Importance	Unweighted Score	Weighted Score
Operational Factors	Operational Security Requirements		VH	6	9
	Privacy and Confidentiality Of Data Being Processed		VH	7	10.5
	Operational Performance And Throughput Requirements		H	4	5
	Operational Reliability And Availability Requirements		H	6	7.5
	Amount Of On-Premises Infrastructure Required		M	3	3
	Volume Of Data Being Processed		H	5	6.25
	Volume and Variability of Workload To Be Processed		H	4	5
	Number Of Different Types Of Transactions To Be Processed		M	6	6
	Number Of Internal Solution Consumers		M	5	5
	Number Of External Solution Consumers		VH	6	9
Technical Factors	Number Of Technologies Included In The Overall Solution		H	7	8.75
	Number Of Solution Components		H	7	8.75
	Number Of Solutions Integrations And Interfaces		H	7	8.75
	Number Of Application Tiers		L	5	3.75
	Technologies Already Part Of The Organisation's Enterprise Architecture		M	4	4
	Availability Of Skills And Experience In Technologies	Y	M	8	8
	Amount Of Custom Development		H	6	7.5
	Development Platform Productivity		M	5	5
	Amount And Complexity Of Data To Be Loaded Or Migrated		H	7	8.75
	Reuse Of Existing Custom Components		M	5	5
Business Factors	Overall Business Project Size		VH	7	10.5
	Number Of Business Functions Or Areas That Will Use The Solution		H	2	2.5
	Number And Complexity Of Underlying Business Processes		H	6	7.5
	Familiarity Of The It Function With The Business Functions Or Areas	Y	M	8	8
	Availability Of Business Resources To Work On The Solution	Y	M	7	7
	Number Of Locations Of Business Functions		H	4	5
	Number Of Existing Solution Components Being Replaced		M	6	6
	Organisation Change Requirements		H	5	6.25
Product Factors	Number Of Products and Services Required To Deliver The Solution		M	6	6
	Number Of Separate Suppliers Involved In The Delivery Of The Product(s) and Service(s)		H	4	5
	Maturity Of The Product(s) and Service(s)	Y	H	7	8.75
	Supplier Proven Skills And Experience In Implementing Products and Services	Y	M	9	9

Complexity Factor Group	Complexity Factor	Reverse Weighting	Weighting/ Importance	Unweighted Score	Weighted Score
	Products and Services Are Being Provided By Existing Suppliers To The Organisation	Y	L	8	6
	Number Of Supplier Offshore Locations Involved In The Delivery Of The Product(s) and Service(s)		H	5	6.25
	Degree Of Configuration Of Product(s) and Service(s)		M	7	7
	Degree Of Customisation Of The Of Product(s) and Service(s)		H	7	8.75
	Number Of Personnel From Supplier Involved In The Product and Service Delivery		H	5	6.25
	Complexity Of Outsourcing Relationship, If Applicable, To The Delivery Of The Product(s) and Service(s)		M	1	1
	Amount Of New Technology Introduced By The Product(s) and Service(s)		M	1	1
Project Factors	Fixed Project Implementation Deadline		VH	1	1.5
	Expected Project Duration		VH	4	6
	Overall Solution Delivery Project Size		VH	6	9
	Number Of Outsourcing Arrangements Included In The Overall Solution		VH	1	1.5
	Number Of Externally Hosted Components Included In The Overall Solution		H	7	8.75
	Size Of Implementation Project Team		H	6	7.5
	Multiple Language Requirements		H	1	1.25
	Number Of Jurisdictions In Which The Solution Will Operate		H	8	10
Skill and Experience Factors	Project Manager Skills And Experience	Y	H	8	10
	Implementation Team Skills And Experience	Y	H	8	10
Score				264	317.75

Table 18 – Sample Solution Complexity Scores

The example solution delivery has a weighted score of 317.75. Based on the assumption that complexity is non-linear and a higher than average complexity score indicates a proportionally higher complexity, this project would be assigned a complexity uplift of 1.23 to the initial project resource estimates. This assumes that the resource estimates did not already, either implicitly or explicitly, account for solution delivery complexity.

The following shows where this complexity score is located on the proposed non-linear solution complexity curve.

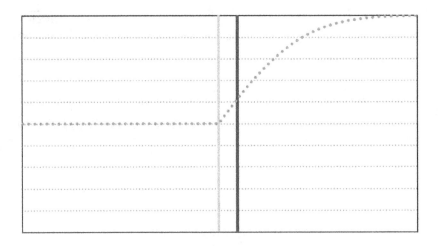

■ Sample Solution Complexity ▥ 50th Percentile

Figure 70 – Sample Solution Complexity Score on Solution Complexity Curve

Using this approach, the following complexity score would lead to the following resource uplifts.

Complexity Score	Possible Resource Uplift
300	1.06
350	1.44
400	1.73
450	1.89
500	1.97

Table 19 – Complexity Scores and Resource Uplifts

This is not a precise complexity determination method. It illustrates a type of approach regularly used but one which has flaws, such as:

- The values assigned to the weights that reflect the importance of a complexity factor are not formally derived.

- The same weighting is applied to all complexity factors with the same importance.

- The validity of the complexity factors and their contribution to the overall complexity of the solution has not been determined.

- The complexity scores assigned to each complexity factor are subjective and do not have a defined objectively defined scale.

- The relationship between risk factors is not reflected in the model.

- In deriving the final complexity score, each individual weighted score is added without any account being taken of the spread of scores. A low overall score could be the result of the sum of a small number of very high-risk factors combined with a large number of very low risk factors. The small number of high-risk factors would indicate the solution delivery had some inherent major risks that would be masked in the final score.

- Not all factors apply to all solutions. Assigning these factors a zero score would falsely underestimate the complexity of the solution measured against the applicable complexity factors.

It could be possible to create a solution complexity dashboard along the following lines. This example contains the following numbered sections:

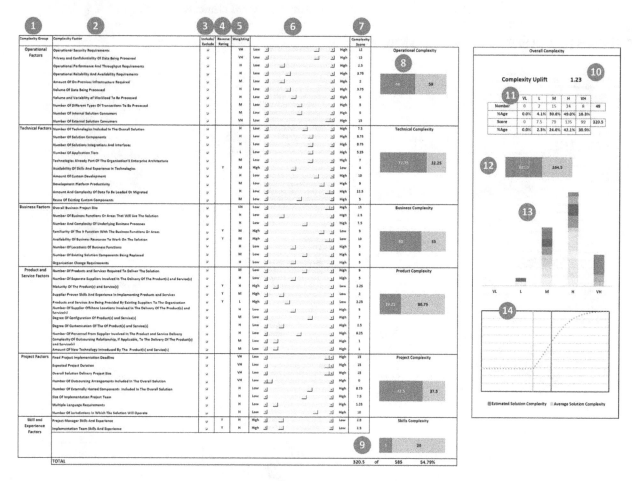

Figure 71 – Sample Solution Complexity Dashboard

The numbered elements of this are:

Number	Description
1	This shows the complexity factor groups.
2	This shows the individual complexity factors.
3	This allows individual complexity factors to be included or excluded from the derivation of the overall solution complexity.
4	This indicates if the score for the factor is reversed.
5	This is the weighting applied to the factor based on the scale of VL, L, M, H and VH.
6	This allows the individual complexity factor to be assigned a value.
7	This is the weighted score of the complexity factor.
8	The shows the relative value of the group of complexity factors.
9	This shows the overall complexity score against the available score.
10	This shows the estimated uplift that should be applied to the estimated based on the derived complexity of the solution.
11	This shows the number and percentage of solution complexity factors across the different weightings. It also shows the scores and their percentage of the overall score for each weighting category.
12	This shows the overall solution complexity score.
13	This charts the range of scores assigned to complexity factor based on their weighting where green indicates a low score and red a high score. In this example, there is a disproportionate number of factors with a weighting of very high assigned a high score.

| 14 | This shows where the overall solution complexity lies on the solution complexity curve. |

Table 20 – Sample Solution Complexity Dashboard Elements

The following diagram shows this sample complexity dashboard with some of the factors excluded.

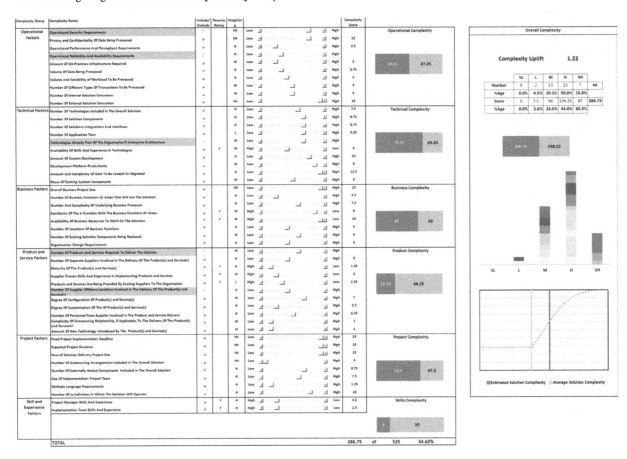

Figure 72 – Solution Complexity Dashboard With Not Applicable Complexity Factors

The solution architect cannot design solution in isolation without being aware of the implications of its subsequent delivery. Inherent unnecessary complexity must be avoided. The solution architect does not have control of the wider environment in which the solution will be delivered and that may be a source of additional complexity. But the solution architect can try to influence this by indicating where solution delivery problems may arise due to complexity so mitigation actions can be taken. The complexity factors can be used to assess and select solution options. The goal is, as always, no surprises.

4.3 Solution Design, Delivery and Operation Context

Every organisation will have a solution delivery process based on project management standards such as PRINCE2[21] or PMBOK[22] or a local variant of one of these. This process may be based on a locally developed variant of one of these standards. Note that the project management process does not necessarily imply a specific approach to the implementation of solution components, such as agile or waterfall. Chapter 6 on page 422 discusses the topic of solution delivery and the use of agile delivery processes in more detail.

---

[21] See:
https://www.axelos.com/best-practice-solutions/prince2
[22] See:
https://www.pmi.org/pmbok-guide-standards

The solution design process works within the wider organisational and operational solution delivery and operation context. The objective of solution architecture and of the solution design process is to create deliverable designs that are implemented, become operational and generate the expected business benefits and value.

Unless there is a strong solution delivery process with associated effective governance, there is little merit in having an effective solution design process.

The core dimension of any solution delivery process is the set of phases that are followed sequentially from start to end. These phases typically take the form of the following:

- Concept
- Initiate
- Plan
- Design
- Build
- Test
- Deploy
- Operate

These phases are not necessarily sequential. However, ultimately, the solution delivery process must deliver an operational solution. The phases can be iterated.

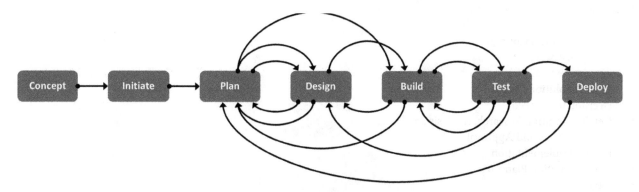

Figure 73 – Iterated Solution Delivery Phases

This high-level set of solution delivery stages could be expanded to include a more detailed set of steps.

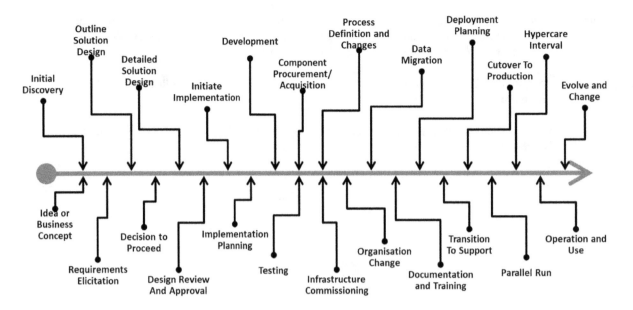

Figure 74 – Expanded Set of Solution Delivery Steps

These solution delivery steps are:

- Idea or Business Concept
- Initial Discovery
- Requirements Elicitation
- Outline Solution Design
- Decision to Proceed
- Detailed Solution Research, Analysis and Design
- Design Review and Approval
- Initiate Implementation
- Implementation Planning
- Development
- Testing
- Component Procurement/ Acquisition
- Component Installation, Configuration and Customisation
- Data Interfaces and Exchanges
- Process Definition and Changes
- Organisation Change
- Infrastructure Commissioning
- Data Migration, Load and Validation
- Documentation and Training
- Deployment Planning
- Transition To Support
- Cutover To Production
- Parallel Run
- Hypercare Interval
- Operation and Use
- Evolve and Change

These solution delivery steps are not necessarily sequential and linear. They can be reordered, repeated in greater levels of detail and performed in parallel. They represent activities to be performed and work to be done. How and when this happens can be defined during detailed delivery planning.

There may (and should) be gates at the end of each of these stages where the validity of the solution progressing to the next stage should be assessed and a decision made. Even if the solution is sufficiently worthwhile to progress, the quality of the work may not be sufficient to merit its advancement until it is reworked to an appropriate standard. The gate and review process ensures that the solution delivery work remains on track.

This generic solution delivery process can be expanded to add a second dimension of the solution delivery role involved in solution delivery stages. The following shows this expanded solution delivery process with a view of the possible artefacts that could be created as the solution delivery process proceeds. The precise set of artefacts to be produced based on work done and outcomes and results achieved, whether the artefacts are actually produced and when and who produces them will vary across organisations.

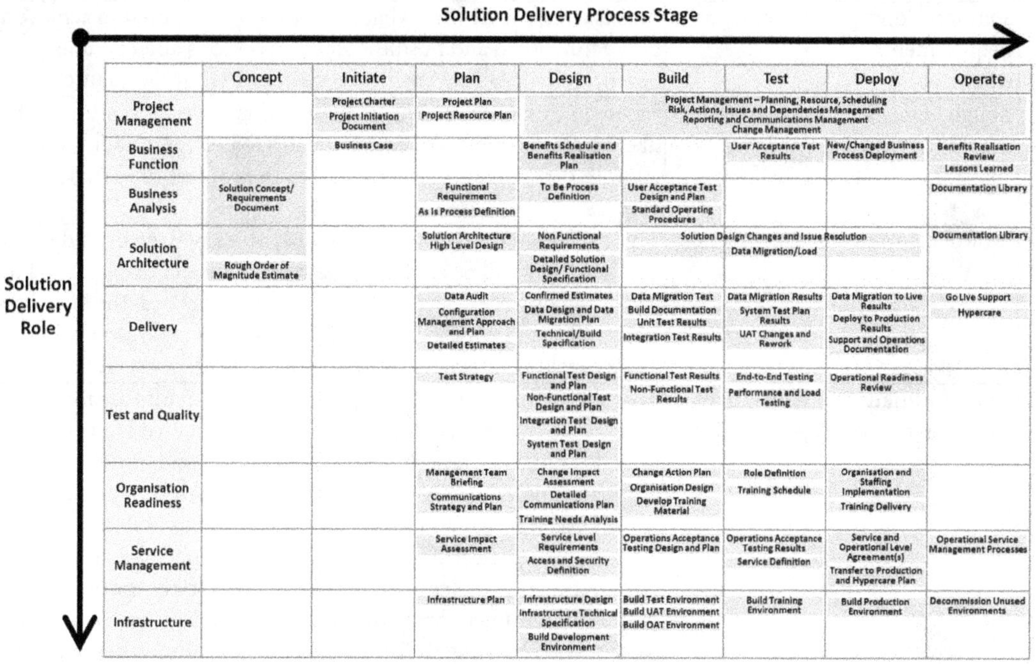

Solution Delivery Process Stage

Solution Delivery Role	Concept	Initiate	Plan	Design	Build	Test	Deploy	Operate
Project Management		Project Charter; Project Initiation Document	Project Plan; Project Resource Plan	Project Management – Planning, Resource, Scheduling Risk, Actions, Issues and Dependencies Management; Reporting and Communications Management; Change Management				
Business Function		Business Case		Benefits Schedule and Benefits Realisation Plan		User Acceptance Test Results	New/Changed Business Process Deployment	Benefits Realisation Review; Lessons Learned
Business Analysis	Solution Concept/ Requirements Document		Functional Requirements; As Is Process Definition	To Be Process Definition	User Acceptance Test Design and Plan; Standard Operating Procedures			Documentation Library
Solution Architecture	Rough Order of Magnitude Estimate		Solution Architecture High Level Design	Non Functional Requirements; Detailed Solution Design/ Functional Specification	Solution Design Changes and Issue Resolution; Data Migration/Load			Documentation Library
Delivery			Data Audit; Configuration Management Approach and Plan; Detailed Estimates	Confirmed Estimates; Data Design and Data Migration Plan; Technical/Build Specification	Data Migration Test; Build Documentation; Unit Test Results; Integration Test Results	Data Migration Results; System Test Plan Results; UAT Changes and Rework	Data Migration to Live Results; Deploy to Production Results; Support and Operations Documentation	Go Live Support; Hypercare
Test and Quality			Test Strategy	Functional Test Design and Plan; Non-Functional Test Design and Plan; Integration Test Design and Plan; System Test Design and Plan	Functional Test Results; Non-Functional Test Results	End-to-End Testing; Performance and Load Testing	Operational Readiness Review	
Organisation Readiness			Management Team Briefing; Communications Strategy and Plan; Training Needs Analysis	Change Impact Assessment; Detailed Communications Plan	Change Action Plan; Organisation Design; Develop Training Material	Role Definition; Training Schedule	Organisation and Staffing Implementation; Training Delivery	
Service Management			Service Impact Assessment	Service Level Requirements; Access and Security Definition	Operations Acceptance Testing Design and Plan	Operations Acceptance Testing Results; Service Definition	Service and Operational Level Agreement(s); Transfer to Production and Hypercare Plan	Operational Service Management Processes
Infrastructure			Infrastructure Plan	Infrastructure Design; Infrastructure Technical Specification; Build Development Environment	Build Test Environment; Build UAT Environment; Build OAT Environment	Build Training Environment	Build Production Environment	Decommission Unused Environments

Figure 75 – Solution Delivery Process with Solution Delivery Phase and Role Dimensions

The possible list of artefacts to be created is listed in the table below. This is a very comprehensive (and time consuming to produce) set of artefacts. It includes both documentation and other items such as environments that are delivered during the solution delivery process. Documentation artefacts are designed to serve three main functions:

1. To contain a record that the work that generated the artefact was done to a sufficient rigour and level of detail

2. To create a set of information that can be passed to subsequent delivery stages and other members of the solution delivery team

3. To create a store of solution delivery knowledge that can be used in subsequent work such as support, solution enhancement and evolution and other solution design work

All of these artefacts proceed from the solution architecture work at the start of solution delivery and from the solution design created and revised throughout the delivery effort. The solution design must be able to support the creation of these artefacts. It must provide a sufficiently firm foundation to enable this to happen. Solution architecture must be involved throughput the solution delivery process. The siloed nature of solution delivery with multiple handoffs described in section 2.6 on page 50 must be avoided.

Document artefacts must serve a purpose. There is no merit in creating large volumes of documentation unless they service a function. These are logical artefacts are can be combined. Behind each of these artefacts is a substantial set of work. The artefacts can be repeated for different component of the solution.

The approach to solution delivery and the set of artefacts to be created must be agreed during the planning stages.

These are specific solution delivery artefacts. In addition, there will be other artefacts created during the delivery project relating to its management such as status reports, communications, documentation from meetings, changes requests and record of change management activities.

Stage	Artefact	Type	Description
Concept	Solution Concept/ Requirements Document	Document	This is a high-level view what the solution is required to achieve and of the functional and business solution options and contains a description of the key business requirements for the solution.
	Rough Order of Magnitude Estimate	Document	Based on the solution concept design, this is a rough estimate of the likely resource, time and cost estimates to deliver the solution. This allows a decision to be made whether to progress the solution delivery process.
Initiate	Project Charter	Document	This is a broad statement of the scope, objectives, goals of the project and how they will be achieved, the reason for and the value to be generated by the project, what is and is not in scope, the high-level risks and their proposed mitigations, the roles and responsibilities of those involved in the project and identifies the key stakeholders.
	Project Initiation Document	Document	This acts as a reference to the project throughout its life for the members of the project team. It defines the detailed scope of the project, contains a description of the solution and its delivery approach and defines what is and is not in scope. It describes the project background and why the project is being undertaken. It describes the project structure, project team and roles, organisation and governance and control approach. It describes the approach to project communications, finance, change and risk management, quality and reporting. It lists known assumptions, dependencies, constraints, issues and risks. It contains the initial solution delivery plan.
	Business Case	Document	This defines the justification for the solution delivery project. It defines the expected benefits, describes how they will be achieved and measured, quantifies their value and lists the solution delivery costs. It outlines the alternatives considered and the benefits and values each option would have been expected to achieve.
Plan	Project Plan	Document	This defines the project activities and tasks, their schedule, the resources that will perform them and the dependencies between the activities.
	Project Resource Plan	Document	This is effectively a bill of materials for the project and defines how the people resources assigned to the project will be managed. It defines the amount and types of effort, the roles and responsibilities for each type of effort, equipment and other materials needed to deliver the solution.
	Functional Requirements	Document	These are the requirements that define what the solution must do and the functionality and features it must include.
	As Is Process Definition	Document	This describes the current processes in use in the pre-solution landscape of the business functions that will use the solution.
	Solution Architecture High Level Design		This is a high-level solution architecture that could be produced using the rapid engagement process described in section 4.6.5 on page 257. This contains an initial view of the solution design options and describes the scope of the required solution.

Stage	Artefact	Type	Description

	Data Audit	Document	The objectives of the data audit are to understand the current data management systems, structures and data processes that are to be included in and migrated to the solution. It can contain some or all of:
			
			• *Data landscape view* - describes the entities and functional units within and outside the organisation with which the organisation interacts and to describe the interactions in terms of data flows
			• *Data supply chain view* - describes the in-bound and out-bound data paths within and outside the organisations in terms of the applications and the data that flows along the data paths
			• *Data model view* - data specifications that reflect data requirements and designs and defines the critical data produced and consumed across the organisation
			• *Data lifecycle view* – view of data across its life from creation to deletion
			• *Current information and data architecture and data strategy view* - review of current information and data architecture and implementation and operational under the key component areas of:
			   o Data Governance
			   o Data Architecture
			   o Data Modelling and Design
			   o Data Storage and Operations
			   o Data Security
			   o Data Quality
			   o Data Integration and Interoperability
			   o Reference and Master Data
			   o Data Warehousing and Business Intelligence
			   o Documents and Content
			   o Metadata
			• *Current data management view* - quantify the relative importance and current state of implementation and operation of data management components and functional elements

	Configuration Management Approach and Plan	Document	This describes the approach to managing the configuration of the solution development and delivery environment. It defines naming and control scheme, tools, approach to change management and backup and recovery.
	Detailed Estimates	Document	This will contain an initial view of the detailed time, cost and resource estimates for the delivery of the solution.
	Test Strategy	Document	This will describe the high-level approach to testing the overall solution to achieve the testing objectives, the types of tests and the test entry and exit criteria across the testing phases of unit testing, integration testing, system testing, user acceptance testing and operations acceptance testing.
	Management Team Briefing	Document/ Meeting	This will present the initial results of the solution design work including business need, requirements, solution design overview, delivery estimates.
	Communications Strategy and Plan	Document	This will describe the approach to communications during solution delivery across the core and extended project teams, with business stakeholders and with the wider organisation likely to be impacted by the solution.
	Service Impact Assessment	Document	This will contain an assessment of the impact of the introduction of the new services contained in the solution. It will identify the existing

Stage	Artefact	Type	Description
			services impacted and the new services being introduced. It will describe how the services will be introduced and how the services will be managed and administered.
	Infrastructure Plan	Document	This will contain the plan for the infrastructure required by the solution and by the solution delivery project for the duration of its implementation.
Design	Benefits Schedule and Benefits Realisation Plan	Document	This will describe the benefits that the solution will deliver, what has to be done to realise them, how this will be achieved and assessed in order to maximise the value derived from the solution delivery. Section 4.11.1 on page 381 contains more details on solution benefits assessment.
	To Be Process Definition	Document	This will contain a description of the changes to existing business processes and the new business processes required to use and operate the solution. Section 4.4.2 on page 134 contains more details on business process analysis and definition.
	Non-Functional Requirements	Document	This will define the operational service and non-functional requirements of the solution. Section 4.6.4.7 on page 251 contains more details on the types of solution quality factors to be defined here.
	Detailed Solution Design/ Functional Specification	Document	This will contain a detailed design of the entire solution across all the solution components. This is intended to be a specification for all subsequent solution implementation and delivery work.
	Confirmed Estimates	Document	This contains a review and an update of the previous delivery estimates based on additional information produced during the Design phase.
	Data Design and Data Migration Plan	Document	This contains a detailed design of the static and dynamic data elements of the solution components including data integrations, transfers and exchanges. Section 4.8 on page 321 contains more details on data aspects of solution architecture and design.
	Technical/Build Specification	Document	This is created by those involved in creating the application components of the overall solution. They will translate the solution design into technical build documents for both developed components and packaged or hosted components that are being configured and customised. It will also contain the technical build details for data integration, either their implementation using existing data integration capability or custom data integrations.
	Functional Test Design and Plan	Document	This will define the test cases for those solution components that are providing functionality and will define the approach to the tests. The scope of the testing will include: • The functionality being validated during testing • The data to be used during tests • The specification of the expected outputs from the tests • The execution of the tests and the recording of the functionality experienced and the outputs generated • Comparison of the expected and actual functionality and outputs
	Non-Functional Test Design and Plan	Document	This will define the set of tests to be performed to validate the operational characteristics of the solution and its components to ensure it meets business expectations. It can include testing across all the solution's quality attributes (see section 4.6.4.7 on page 251). Some of the most important characteristics to be validated are:

Stage	Artefact	Type	Description
			<ul><li>Performance and load including stress</li><li>Response time and throughput</li><li>Capacity and growth</li><li>Security</li><li>Recoverability</li></ul>
	Integration Test Design and Plan	Document	This will define how individual functional components are tested together. The scope of the integration test and the components to be tested must be defined. Integration testing can be complex if there are many components to be tested together. The number of combinations can be large. Risk-based testing can be used to identify the most commonly used integrations and sequences that should be tested to a greater degree than others.
	System Test Design and Plan	Document	This describes the testing approach that will be used to validate that the application meets the defined business requirements. This should define a comprehensive set of overall application testing scenarios.
	Change Impact Assessment	Document	This will contain an assessment of the impact of standards, organisation – structure, reporting, training, process and measurement changes the solution will give rise to. Measurement changes may arise because of possible changes in the way performance and processes.
	Detailed Communications Plan	Document	This will define how communications are handled throughout the solution delivery project across all affected functions and levels of the organisation. It will define the messages to be articulated, the method and frequency by which they are communication and how feedback is to be handled.
	Training Needs Analysis	Document	This will define the solution training required across all functions affected by the solution including business users, system managers and administrators, support and service management.
	Service Level Requirements	Document	This will specify the solution service levels across the area of availability, performance, throughput, support including incident and problem management, release management and backup, recovery and business continuity.
	Access and Security Definition	Document	This will define who has what access to the various components of the solution and how application and data security including encryption in transit and at rest and authentication is to be handled,
	Infrastructure Design	Document	This will define the solution infrastructure across all technology areas: processing, storage, communications including infrastructural applications such as authentication, backup, recovery and business continuity.
	Infrastructure Technical Specification	Document	This will contain the detailed infrastructural build documentation.
	Build Development Environment	Technology	The solution development environment is built according to the Infrastructure Technical Specification. Where the development environment is hosted externally this will involve its configuration.
Build	User Acceptance Test Design and Plan	Document	This will document the approach to user testing and the support to be provided. It will define the test cases, the data to be used and the expected results.
	Standard Operating Procedures	Document	This will detail the operating procedures associated with the support, operation and use of the solution.
	Solution Design	Document	This will contain a log of any solution design changes raised, their

Stage	Artefact	Type	Description
	Changes and Issue Resolution		results and details on the resolution of issues that arose during solution delivery. This occurs throughout the Build, Test and Deploy solution delivery phases. The solution architect needs to be involved throughout delivery.
	Data Migration/Load	Data	The data to be loaded or migrated will be copied to the development environment. This step will be repeated for the various environments as they are built and for the various sets of data to be migrated or loaded. This occurs throughout the Build, Test and Deploy solution delivery phases.
	Data Migration Test	Document	This will document the results of the various data migration and load trial runs.
	Build Documentation	Document	This will document the work done on the development environment. This artefact will be repeated for the other environments being built.

Where the infrastructure is being hosted externally, this will describe its provisioning and configuration. |
	Unit Test Results	Document	This will contain the results of the unit tests.
	Integration Test Results	Document	This will contain the results of the unit tests and identifies any issues to be resolved. The tests may be repeated after the issues uncovered have been fixed.
	Functional Test Results	Document	This will contain the results of the functional tests and identifies any issues to be resolved. The tests may be repeated after the issues uncovered have been fixed.
	Non-Functional Test Results	Document	This will contain the results of the non-functional tests and identifies any issues to be resolved. The tests may be repeated after the issues uncovered have been fixed.
	Change Action Plan	Document	This will describe how organisation changes are to be implemented.
	Organisation Design	Document	This will specify the design of the new and changed organisation structures being implemented as part of the overall solution design.
	Develop Training Material	Training Material	This will consist of training material that will be used to train all those involved in the solution: business users, support and service management.
	Operations Acceptance Testing (OAT) Design and Plan	Document	This will document the approach to validating that the new services associated with the solution are capable of being introduced, operated, supported and maintained. The scope will include:

• Infrastructure has capacity to accommodate the new services
• Services can be monitored and event and alert management policies and procedures are in place
• Services comply with business continuity standards
• There is no single point of failure within the infrastructure to deliver the availability requirements
• Services can be backed-up and recovered to meet the solution requirements
• Any batch or scheduled processes can be run automatically without the need for manual intervention
• Services comply with security standards
• The solution can be handed-over to support
• Procedures for handling and recovering from errors have been defined
• Required data archival procedures are in place
• Any new roles and responsibilities have been defined, agreed and staffed
• User access management policies and procedures have been |

Stage	Artefact	Type	Description
			defined • The services have been benchmarked for performance and throughput • Service level and operating level agreements are in place • Any required enduring test environments are in place
	Build Test Environment	Technology	The test environment will be built according to the build standards.
	Build UAT Environment	Technology	The UAT environment will be built according to the build standards.
	Build OAT Environment	Technology	The OAT environment will be built according to the build standards.
Test	User Acceptance Test Results	Document	This documents the results of the user acceptance tests and identifies any issues to be resolved. The tests may be repeated after the issues uncovered have been fixed.
	Data Migration Results	Document	This will document the results of the data load and migration including any issues that arose and how they were resolved and any changes made to the data migration and load processes.
	System Test Plan Results	Document	This will contain the results of the system tests and identifies any issues to be resolved. The tests may be repeated after the issues uncovered have been fixed.
	UAT Changes and Rework	Technology	Changes identified during user testing and approved will be implemented.
	End-to-End Testing	Document	This documents the results of end-to-end solution testing across the solution landscape.
	Performance and Load Testing	Document	This documents the results of performance and loading testing.
	Role Definition	Document	The details of the new roles and any changes to existing roles in the business functions impacted by the solution will be defined.
	Training Schedule	Document	This will define the training to be provided to all users impacted by the solution.
	Operations Acceptance Testing Results	Document	This documents the results of operations acceptance testing.
	Service Definition	Document	This will define the new services being introduced by the solution.
	Build Training Environment	Technology	If needed, a training environment will be built.
Deploy	New/Changed Business Process Deployment	Document	The new and changed existing business processes will be implemented in their production environments.
	Data Migration to Live Results	Document	The results of the data migration and load into the production environment will be documented
	Deploy to Production Results	Document	This will document the results of the solution components being deployed to the production environment.
	Support and Operations Documentation	Document	This will contain the information needed to support the solution in its production environment.
	Operational Readiness Review	Document	This will contain an assessment of the organisation to accept the solution.
	Organisation and Staffing Implementation	Document	The documents the results of the implementation of the organisation and personnel changes required to put the solution into production.
	Training Delivery	Document	The records the delivery of the training and any feedback received.
	Service and Operational Level	Document	The Operational Level Agreement (SLA) is the foundation governance and formal operating document for the services being

Stage	Artefact	Type	Description
	Agreement(s)		provided. It defined the end-to-end service performance principles, activities, objectives and measurements. The Service Level Agreement (SLA) is the formal agreement relating to the management and operation of the services. It defines the meaning of all aspects of the service and the roles and responsibilities of all stakeholders, how service delivery is measured and what actions are to be taken in the event of service delivery failures. In the case of externally hosted applications or services the OLA and SLA are very important documents.
	Transfer to Production and Hypercare Plan	Document	This documents the procedures for putting the solution into production and for any initial period of intensive support.
	Build Production Environment	Document	This documents the results of the building of the production environment
Operate	Benefits Realisation Review	Document	This documents the results of a review of the status of the benefits that were meant to have been achieved by the project. This should include an assessment of the actual amount spent of the delivery of the solution and a comparison against the original budget.
	Lessons Learned	Document	This documents the lessons learned during solution delivery.
	Business Analysis Documentation Library	Document	This collects the various artefacts created by the business analysis function during solution delivery, indexes them and stores them in a defined location
	Solution Design Documentation Library	Document	This collects the various artefacts created by the solution architecture function during solution delivery, indexes them and stores them in a defined location
	Go Live Support	Service	This is the set of support services provided during and after the solution goes live.
	Hypercare	Service	This is the set of intensive support services provided during the interval after the solution first goes live.
	Operational Service Management Processes	Document	These are the support processes across the range of service management activities,
	Decommission Unused Environments	Technology	After the solution is fully operational, any unneeded environments will be decommissioned.

Table 21 – Set of Solution Delivery Artefacts

The solution delivery process starts in the top left of this view and moves out through the project phases and down through the delivery roles as the project proceeds. Section 4.6.3 on page 234 locates different solution design engagement types within this overall solution delivery process framework.

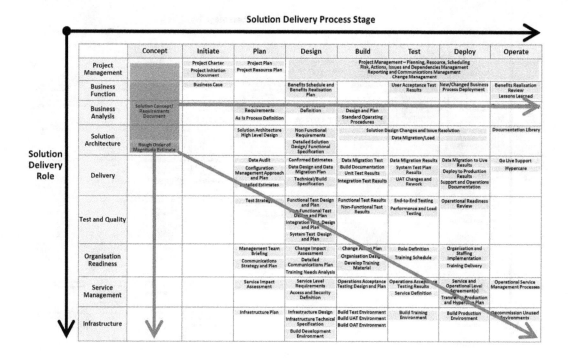

Figure 76 – Progress of Solution Delivery Through Phases and Roles

The solution architecture function needs to be involved at the earliest stage of solution design when the concept of the solution is being explored. At this early exploration and investigation point, the solution architecture function needs to have the tools, techniques and experience to offer consulting services to the business function. The solution idea needs to be examined and validated quickly and to just a sufficient level of detail as to allow an educated decision to be made to continue or not

However, for this approach to solution engagement to be effective the solution architecture must be enabled to operate in this way. The business must accept and trust that the solution architecture function has the necessary capabilities. The governance of the overall solution delivery process must support this mode of operation.

The foundational activities that lead to successful solution delivery project occur in the top left quadrant of the solution delivery domain.

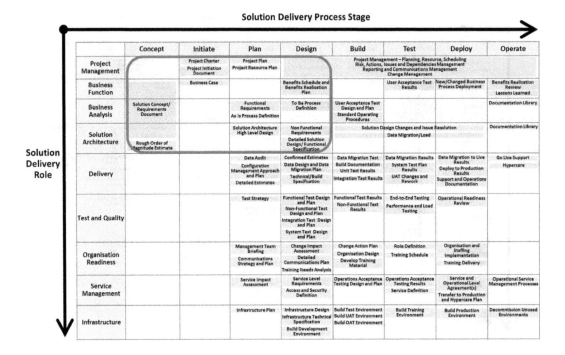

Figure 77 – Foundational Solution Delivery Activities

Focussing on these solution delivery stages and activities will ensure that the solution delivery foundations are sound.

4.4 Solution Architecture Interface with the Business Analysis Function, Requirements Gathering and Process Analysis

In the traditional solution design and delivery journey, requirements are gathered by the business analysis function during requirements gathering workshops organised with business representatives. Analysis is used to gather information and requirements. Analysis does not solve problems or deliver solutions. It is an important step in solution design. The analysis function interfaces between the business and the solution architecture function.

In many cases the requirements gathered by business analysts are handed-off to the solution architecture function as described in section 2.6 on page 50. This frequent lack of continuity in the solution design journey can contribute to solution failure.

A detailed discussion of requirements gathering and management and the role of business analysis are not within the scope of this book.

The ideal set of solution requirements should have three essential characteristics:

1. They should be well-formed – SMART (Specific, Measurable, Achievable, Realistic, Traceable). They should have the following features

    - Complete
    - Correct
    - Feasible
    - Implementation Independent
    - Necessary
    - Singular
    - Traceable

- Unambiguous
- Verifiable

2. The needs and constraints of stakeholders should be complete and consistent.

- Complete

  o Embodies a complete set of needs and constraints from stakeholders, external interfacing systems and enabling and supporting systems
  o Contains a complete set of business processes

- Consistent

  o Requirements do not contradict one another
  o Requirements are not repeated
  o The same terms are used for the same meaning across all requirements

3. The solution design should be complete and consistent with respect to stakeholders' expectations and should describe a realistic and feasible solution that meets the stakeholders expectations and constraints

- Complete

  o Addresses the complete set of expectations and constraints

- Consistent

  o Requirements do not contradict one another
  o Requirements are not repeated
  o The same terms are used for the same meaning across all requirements
  o Aligned and consistent with solution components

- Realistic and Feasible

  o The requirements can be fulfilled by a solution that can be acquired or developed within implementation constraints such as cost, schedule, technical, legal and regulatory

- Bounded

  o The solution does not go beyond what is necessary to satisfy solution consumer needs

Because business stakeholder requirements both flow directly into solution design and frequently represent only a subset of the actual solution requirements, the requirements gathering activities need to be fully integrated within the solution design process and not be a parallel or external activity.

As discussed in section 2.3 on page 30 the business analyst role evolved (or more correctly devolved) from the earlier systems analyst role.

There are a number of myths about requirements and the requirements gathering process:

- Requirements gathered from business users and business stakeholders through requirements gathering meetings and workshops define the scope and functionality of the solution

- In order to define the solution, all that is needed is business requirements

- Requirements change

It is unreasonable to expect that business stakeholders in a potential solution can articulate a set of complete, fully-developed and consistent requirements through part-time involvement in a few requirements gathering exercises.

The wider view of requirements includes the following different classifications:

- *Overall Business and Solution Requirements* – these are underpinning requirements that describe the need for and drivers of the requirements, the objectives that must be achieved, the key stakeholders that must be and the benefits that must be realised

- *Functional Requirements* – these describe what the solution must do, what processing it will perform, what results it will generate

- *Operational and Quality Requirements* – these describe properties and attributes the solution and its operation must have. They can include areas such as:

    o   Look, Feel and Navigation
    o   Usability
    o   Capacity, Performance, Throughput and Response Times
    o   Operational and Environmental
    o   Maintenance and Support
    o   Security
    o   Regulatory, Legal and Compliance

- *Design Constraint Requirements* – the solution may be constrained to operate in a specific environment or use certain tools or products

- *Implementation Requirements* – these relate to constraints how the solution must be delivered in terms of time, cost, resources, available personnel and levels of skills and experience and facilities needed during solution implementation

- *Delivery Requirements* – these relate to how the solution must be implemented and how it must operate in the current existing solution landscape – what integrations must be implemented, what data must be reused

It is not requirements that change during solution delivery. It is that latent requirements that were not identified or were ignored become apparent or unavoidable during implementation. Undiscovered and unarticulated requirements then impact solution components leading to additional downstream changes which affect the implementation project

Even with an effective elicitation approach, requirements elicited from business stakeholders tend to be:

- Sparse and disconnected
- Isolated and disintegrated statements
- Inconsistent
- Incomplete
- Disjointed
- Conflicting
- Uncosted
- Unprioritised
- At different levels of detail

The requirements are representations of specific points of functionality that rarely aggregate into a defined solution. The reality is that what is gathered during requirements workshops, meetings, interviews, questionnaires and other activities are not solution requirements but business stakeholder requirements. These must be translated into solution requirements which is turn must be translated into a realistic and implementation solution design. These business stakeholder requirements are one source of solution requirements.

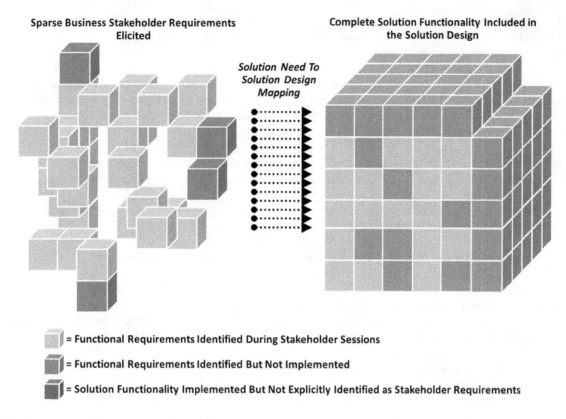

Sparse Business Stakeholder Requirements Elicited

Complete Solution Functionality Included in the Solution Design

Solution Need To Solution Design Mapping

▢ = Functional Requirements Identified During Stakeholder Sessions

▢ = Functional Requirements Identified But Not Implemented

▢ = Solution Functionality Implemented But Not Explicitly Identified as Stakeholder Requirements

Figure 78 – Sparse Business Stakeholder Requirements and the Complete Set of Solution Requirements

This diagram shows the three types of requirements that arise during the process:

1. Business stakeholder requirements and the associated functionality required to deliver them that were identified during requirements gathering that are included in the solution design.

2. Business stakeholder requirements that were identified during requirements gathering that are omitted from the solution design after review and evaluation of solution implementation options.

3. Additional solution requirements identified during the Solution Requirements Collection and Specification (see section 4.6.2 on page 226) stage of the solution design process where all the solution components are identified. These requirements are not expressed by business stakeholders during any requirements gathering process.

Business stakeholder requirements can be excluded from the complete solution design because they cannot be implemented or are too expensive or time consuming to deliver for the benefits they provide. This needs to be done after discussions with and the agreement of the business stakeholders.

Requirements gathering should not be part of any solution delivery project but be the subject of an analysis and solution architecture and design exercise prior to any delivery project. The project to deliver the solution cannot be estimated until the solution design is complete, unless a more agile approach is being followed where uncertainty is tolerated and resolved during delivery.

The solution design is always much greater than the sum of the functionality implied by the elicited business stakeholder requirements. Business stakeholder requirements are just one input into a fully developed solution design. The generalised solution design process described in section 4.6.2 on page 226 has business requirements being gather in the context of a Conceptual Solution Architecture (CSA). This can be created using elements of the rapid solution design process outlined in section 4.6.5 on page 257. The CSA is essentially a solution hypothesis that can be validated, refined, modified, expanded on or even rejected during consultations with the business.

The CSA focusses on the core functional and system components of the solution. The CSA provides a framework for identifying solution requirements across the solution landscape. It also assists with compiling business stakeholder requirements as requirements can be elicited within the context of the complete end-to-end solution concept.

This structured approach to gathering requirements in the context of indicative solution architecture yields greater results than standalone requirements gathering. The analysis and architecture functions need to work together to transform business stakeholder requirements into solution requirements. Architecture synthesises and actualises overall solution design and options from business stakeholder requirements and other constraints.

Taking this approach means the solution implementability, operability, usability, maintainability and supportability can be quantified in advance. It is only after the solution design is defined and agreed that the implementation project can be started.

Rather than operating separately, the business analysis and solution architecture functions need to work together during the solution design process. The interface between the two functions must become a collaboration.

The solution does not deliver requirements. The solution encompasses multiple interoperating elements that provide functionality that enable business processes that allow requirements to be complied with.

The solution has functional (and other) requirements that must be delivered in order to be deemed to be complete. As stated above, the requirements identified during any business requirements elicitation process will only ever be a sparse and fragmented representation of what the full set of solution requirements that constitute a complete solution

One of the objectives of the solution design process is to minimise the Solution Space – the size and complexity of the solution and therefore its cost, time, resources and risk to implement - while maximising the size of Requirements Spaces encompassed by that solution. There will be two Requirements Spaces – that contained in the business stakeholder requirements and that contained in the wider solution requirements not explicitly defined as requirements by the business stakeholders.

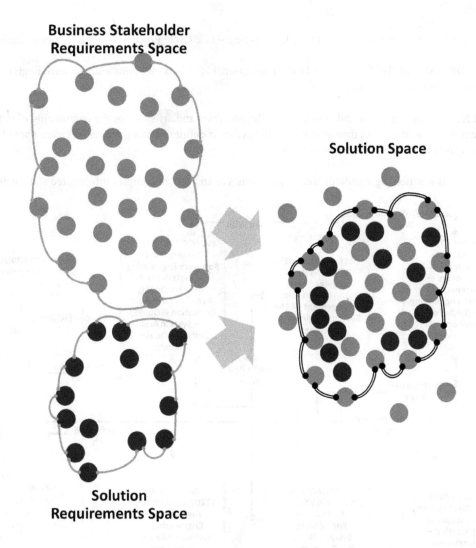

Figure 79 – Mapping the Requirements Space to the Solution Space

Decisions must be made on what can be included and what cannot be included in the solution. The delivery can be phased and prioritised to maintain solution implementation momentum. Solution design is concerned with finding an optimal Solution Space. There may be many Solution Space options. The solution architect needs to focus on finding the most viable ones quickly and the deciding on the one(s) to pursue.

This relates to the Bounded attribute of a requirement described at the start of this section.

4.4.1 Requirements Engineering

It is outside the scope of this book to describe in detail the area of requirements engineering. It is mentioned briefly here to provide background information on the topic, given the traditional importance of requirements elicitation in the solution design process.

There is a large amount of material available on the subject of requirements engineering. For example, there have been several revisions of ISO/IEEE standards that have evolved and developed overtime:

• IEEE Standard 830-1998 IEEE Recommended Practice for Software Requirements Specifications[23]

---

[23] see:

- ISO/IEC/IEEE 29148:2011 Systems and Software Engineering – Life Cycle Processes – Requirements Engineering[24]

- IEEE 29148-2018 - ISO/IEC/IEEE Approved Draft International Standard - Systems and Software Engineering -- Life Cycle Processes --Requirements Engineering[25]

The ISO/IEC/IEEE 29148 standard is intended to describe the processes and artefacts for the engineering of requirements for systems, software products and services throughout their life cycles. It defines what a good requirement should look like and lists their attributes and characteristics of requirements.

The wider requirements engineering standards landscape consists of an array of complex interrelated standards:

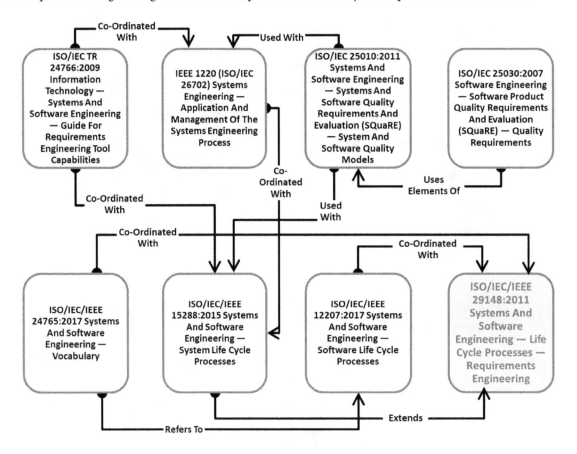

Figure 80 – Wider Requirements Engineering Landscape

The wider requirements engineering landscape consists of the following standards:

- ISO/IEC TR 24766:2009 Information Technology — Systems And Software Engineering — Guide For Requirements Engineering Tool Capabilities[26]

---

https://standards.ieee.org/standard/830-1998.html . This was replaced by ISO/IEC/IEEE 29148:2011.

[24] See:
https://standards.ieee.org/standard/29148-2011.html
[25] See:
https://standards.ieee.org/standard/29148-2018.html
[26] See:
https://www.iso.org/standard/51041.html

- IEEE 1220 (ISO/IEC 26702) Systems Engineering — Application And Management Of The Systems Engineering Process[27]

- ISO/IEC 25010:2011 Systems And Software Engineering — Systems And Software Quality Requirements And Evaluation (SQuaRE) — System And Software Quality Models[28]

- ISO/IEC 25030:2007 Software Engineering — Software Product Quality Requirements And Evaluation (SQuaRE) — Quality Requirements[29]

- ISO/IEC/IEEE 24765:2017 Systems And Software Engineering — Vocabulary[30]

- ISO/IEC/IEEE 15288:2015 Systems And Software Engineering — System Life Cycle Processes[31]

- ISO/IEC/IEEE 12207:2017 Systems And Software Engineering — Software Life Cycle Processes[32]

The ISO/IEC/IEEE 29148:2011 standard includes five deliverables:

1. Stakeholder Requirements Specification (StRS) document
2. System Requirements Specification (SyRS) document
3. Software Requirements Specification (SRS) document
4. System Operational Concept (OpsCon) document
5. Concept of Operations (ConOps) document

The contents of these documents are listed below.

The scope of the Stakeholder Requirements Specification (StRS) document is:

- Business Purpose
- Business Scope
- Business Overview
- Stakeholders
- Business Environment
- Goal And Objective
- Business Model
- Information Environment
- Business Processes
- Business Operational Policies And Rules
- Business Operational Constraints
- Business Operation Modes
- Business Operational Quality
- Business Structure
- User Requirements
- Operational Concept

---

[27] See:
https://www.iso.org/standard/43693.html
[28] See:
https://www.iso.org/standard/35733.html
[29] See:
https://www.iso.org/standard/35755.html
[30] See:
https://www.iso.org/standard/71952.html
[31] See:
https://www.iso.org/standard/63711.html
[32] See:
https://www.iso.org/standard/63712.html

- o Operational Policies And Constraints
- o Description Of The Proposed System
- o Modes Of System Operation
- o User Classes And Other Involved Personnel
- o Support Environment
- Operational Scenarios
- Project Constraints

The scope of the System Requirements Specification (SyRS) document is:

- System Purpose
- System Scope
- System Overview
  - o System Context
  - o System Functions
  - o User Characteristics
- Functional Requirements
- Usability Requirements
- Performance Requirements
- System Interfaces
- System Operations
  - o Human System Integration Requirements
  - o Maintainability
  - o Reliability
- System Modes And States
- Physical Characteristics
  - o Physical Requirements
  - o Adaptability Requirements
- Environmental Conditions
- System Security
- Information Management
- Policies And Regulations
- System Life Cycle Sustainment
- Packaging, Handling, Shipping And Transportation
- Verification
- Assumptions And Dependencies

The scope of the Software Requirements Specification (SRS) document is:

- Purpose
- Scope
- Product Perspective
  - o System Interfaces
  - o User Interfaces
  - o Hardware Interfaces
  - o Software Interfaces
  - o Communications Interfaces
  - o Memory Constraints
  - o Operations
  - o Site Adaptation Requirements
- Product Functions
- Product Functions
- Product Functions
- Assumptions And Dependencies
- Apportioning Of Requirements
- Specific Requirements

- External Interfaces
- Functions
- Usability Requirements
- Performance Requirements
- Logical Database Requirements
- Design Constraints
- Standards Compliance
- Software System Attributes
- Verification
- Supporting Information

The scope of the System Operational Concept (OpsCon) document is:

- Scope
  - Scope
  - Document Overview
  - System Overview
- Referenced Documents
- Current System Or Situation
  - Background, Objectives, And Scope
  - Operational Policies And Constraints
  - Description Of The Current System Or Situation
  - Modes Of Operation For The Current System Or Situation
  - User Classes And Other Involved Personnel
    - Organisational Structure
    - Profiles Of User Classes
    - Interactions Among User Classes
    - Other Involved Personnel
  - Support Environment
- Justification For And Nature Of Changes
  - Justification For Changes
  - Description Of Desired Changes
  - Priorities Among Changes
  - Changes Considered But Not Included
  - Assumptions And Constraints
- Concepts For The Proposed System
  - Background, Objectives, And Scope
  - Operational Policies And Constraints
  - Description Of The Proposed System
  - Modes Of Operation
  - User Classes And Other Involved Personnel
    - Organisational Structure
    - Profiles Of User Classes
    - Interactions Among User Classes
    - Other Involved Personnel
  - Support Environment
- Operational Scenarios
- Summary Of Impacts
  - Operational Impacts
  - Organisational Impacts
  - Impacts During Development
- Analysis Of The Proposed System
  - Benefits
  - Disadvantages And Limitations
  - Alternatives Considered

The scope of the Concept of Operations (ConOps) document is:

- Purpose
- Scope
- Strategic Plan
- Effectiveness
- Overall Operation
    - Context
    - Systems
    - Organisational Unit
- Governance
    - Governance Policies
    - Organisation
    - Investment Plan
    - Information Asset Management
    - Security
    - Business Continuity Plan
    - Compliance

These deliverables are very detailed, comprehensive and time-consuming to produce. The extent and level of detail is appropriate only to large and complex software product solutions. It is also not always possible to create these deliverables at the requirements gathering phase. Most organisations simply do not have the resources to adopt and put into practise these standards.

Elements of them could be incorporated into standard requirements artefacts produced during most solution delivery projects,

These represent a highly complex set of standards that have a limited applicability to the business world. They may have some relevance to organisations developing very complicated automation and process control systems and software products for certain (highly regulated) industries and applications such as airlines and aerospace, petro-chemical, pharmaceutical, power stations, medical devices and military. Outside these particular areas, they are of limited if any value and use. Understanding, applying and keeping current with these standards represents a substantial overhead for any organisation whose effort would have to be justified.

Finally, these standards focus largely on the software development process. A business or any other information technology solution consists of much more than just software.

In common with many other information technology practice areas, there has been an initiative to create a Body of Knowledge, in this case the REBOK (Requirements Engineering Body Of Knowledge). This has been led by JISA (Japan Information Technology Services Association)[33]. Some time ago, JISA initiated a RE WG (Requirements Engineering Working Group) that has evolved to create the REBOK. Unfortunately, the REBOK is currently only available in Japanese[34].

4.4.2 Business Processes

As discussed in section 4.1 on page 91, solutions exist to allow business processes to operate. The business organisation develops, implements and operates business processes. Solutions enable these business processes. So, solutions should be designed with respect to the processes they will implement. Similarly, the business must take account of the capabilities of software components, especially acquired products, either on-premises or hosted, when designing processes. While products

---

[33] See:
https://www.jisa.or.jp/
[34] See:
http://www.re-bok.org/ and https://www.jisa.or.jp/publication/tabid/272/pdid/Rebok2014/Default.aspx

can be customised to suits the needs of the business such customisation is risky (see section 3.2 on page 71), it is almost always better to adapt processes to the capability of the product.

Processes impact solution design and solution operation is several ways:

- New business processes may need to be defined that describe how the business function should use the solution
- Existing business processes may need to be changed
- Both the new and existing processes should be optimised in a way that the number of activities and the number of roles involved (and their associated handoffs) are kept to a minimum
- Decisions may be made about the scope of solution, the components to be implemented and the functionality provided by those components that necessitate work being done outside the scope of the solution, such as manual workarounds

You cannot ignore the process dimension when defining the full set of components that comprise the solution.

There is a hierarchy from information technology infrastructure, platforms, the solutions implemented on those platforms, the functionality those solutions deliver, business processes that use those functions and the results, outcomes achieved and value generated for the organisation.

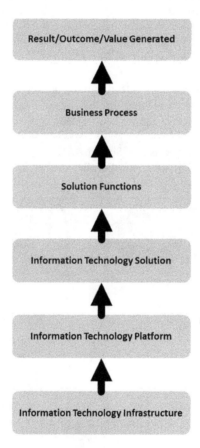

Figure 81 – Hierarchy of Information Technology, Business Processes and Value Achieved

The solutions enable business processes to operate. So, the solution design must be aware of the business processes whose execution it has to enable.

Business process analysis and design is typically performed by business analysts or business process analysts within the business analysis function. It is common for the business process analysis function to be separate from the business analysis function. This splitting of functions that are important to the complete design of the overall solution leads to further loss of information and detail.

The business function looking for the solution must define or be guided and directed through and assisted with the definition of the new business processes and the changes to existing business processes that the solution and its components will operate. This is one of the reasons why the rapid solution design process described in section 4.6.5 on page 257 has as one of its core elements the identification of the inventory of business processes enabled and impacted by the solution. This provides a context for subsequent detailed process design work. It means the solution design work does not get bogged down in process details before the overall background is understood and before identifying what the affected processes are and how they relate to one another

As with business analysis and requirements engineering, a full description of business process analysis approaches and techniques is outside the scope of this book. However, given the importance of business processes to the solution design process, I have included some relevant details on the topic here.

Neither the solution architecture nor the business analysis functions should develop business processes. They can help with their design or redesign. But the business must originate and own the business processes.

The topic of business processes and that of organisational change are linked. Business change, especially when associated with new solutions, can be inevitable. An organisational change process addresses an essential element of business change associated with the implementation of new solution - the people working in the organisation. Effective deployment of solutions and realisation of business results requires active management of the people issues. The organisational change process starts with understanding the objective of and reason for the business changes and the role that other causes of and enablers of change in the technology and process areas play.

The failure to manage the business change and human side of solution delivery is a major contributor to the reasons solutions and initiatives fail. Organisation managers can be all too commonly focussed on tactical and operational issues and do not have the time to consider organisational changes in the necessary detail.

In an unpublished survey conducted by ARIS, now part of Software AG[35] on what lessons were learned from the implementation of large information technology solutions, the following results were obtained:

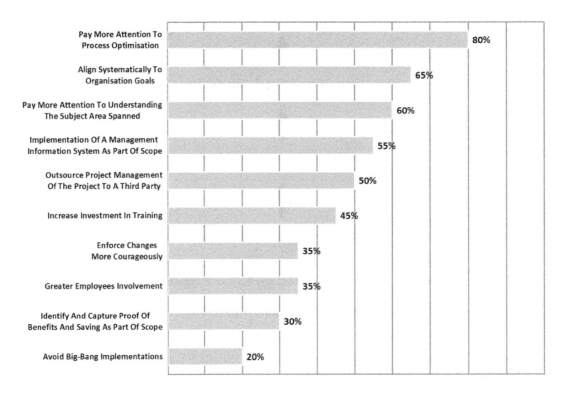

---

[35] See:
https://www.softwareag.com/nl/products/aris_alfabet/bpa/default.html

Figure 82 – Lessons Learned from Large Solutions Implementations

The importance of these various factors was:

Lesson	Importance
Pay More Attention To Process Optimisation	80%
Align Systematically To Organisation Goals	65%
Pay More Attention To Understanding The Subject Area Spanned	60%
Implementation Of A Management Information System As Part Of Scope	55%
Outsource Project Management Of The Project To A Third Party	50%
Increase Investment In Training	45%
Greater Employees Involvement	35%
Enforce Changes More Courageously	35%
Identify And Capture Proof Of Benefits And Saving As Part Of Scope	30%
Avoid Big-Bang Implementations	20%

Table 22 – Lessons Learned from Large Solutions Implementations

The need for business process optimisation was assigned the highest importance. The principles for process optimisation include:

- Design around Customer Interactions
- Design around Value-Adding Activities
- Introduce Parallel Processing Where Possible
- Identify and Handle Exceptions Separately
- Minimise Handoffs
- Perform Work Where it Makes the Most Sense
- Provide a Single Point of Contact
- Create a Separate Process for Each Cluster
- Ensure a Continuous Flow
- Reduce Batch Size
- Bring Downstream Information Needs Upstream
- Capture Information Once at the Source and Share It
- Involve as Few as Possible
- Redesign, then Automate
- Ensure Quality at the Beginning
- Standardise Processes
- Use Co-located or Networked Teams for Complex Issues

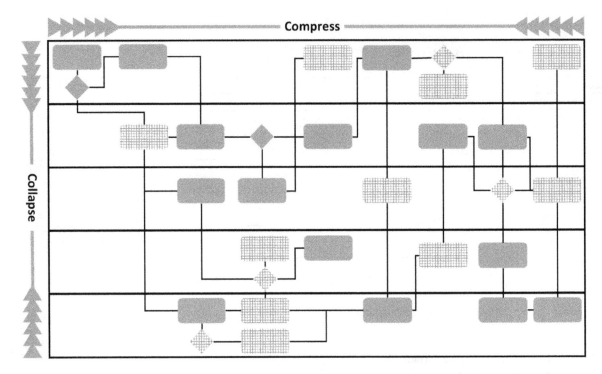

Figure 83 – Process Optimisation Through Compression of Steps and Collapse of Handoffs

Processes should be optimised through:

- **Compression** – reduce unnecessary/non-value-adding steps and combine and automate steps
- **Collapse** – eliminate unnecessary handoffs and involvement by unnecessary roles

Process optimisation is similar to identifying and eliminating unnecessary complexity in solution design that is discussed in section 4.2 on page 95.

One dimension of optimisation is the elimination of waste within processes. The original concept of process waste came from the Lean Manufacturing.

The original Lean Manufacturing listed seven causes of waste:

1. **Overproduction** - manufacturing an item before it is actually required
2. **Waiting** - whenever goods are not moving or being processed
3. **Transport** - moving products between processes is a cost which adds no value to the product
4. **Inventory** – excess work in progress (WIP) cases by overproduction and waiting
5. **Unnecessary / Excess Motion** - people or equipment moving or walking more than is required to perform the processing
6. **Over/Inappropriate Processing** - using expensive resources where simpler ones would be sufficient
7. **Defects** - resulting in rework or scrap or the need for excessive quality control

Over time additional causes of waste were added:

8. **Wrong Product** - manufacturing goods or services that do not meet customer demand or specifications
9. **People Unmatched to Role** - waste of unused human talent/underutilising capabilities and skills and allocating tasks to people with insufficient training to do the work
10. **Inadequate Performance Measurement** - working to the wrong performance metrics or to no metrics
11. **Uninvolved Personnel** - not using staff fully by not allowing them to contribute ideas and suggestions and be part of participative management

12. *Inadequate Technology* - improper use of information technology - inadequate or poorly performing systems requiring manual workarounds, systems that deliver poor response times, systems or the underlying data that are unreliable or inadequate training in the use of systems

The identification of waste in business processes can be applied as listed in the following table.

Cause Of Waste	Business Process Approach to Eliminating Waste
1. Overproduction	• Process work as it arises
2. Waiting	• Reduce delays as work waits to be processed • Reduce linear processing and include as much parallelism as possible
3. Transport	• Reduce number of steps and movement and delays • Ensure work in performed in the optimum location • Reorganise work processing to optimise locations
4. Inventory	• Eliminate batching of work rather and move individual cases through the process
5. Unnecessary / Excess Motion	• Reduce unnecessary handoffs • Reduce fragmentation of work • Reduce the need to search for information
6. Over/Inappropriate Processing	• Reduce unnecessary variation in work types • Reduce the application of unnecessary steps to work • Do not delay simple work with steps that only need to be applied to complex work • Reduce non-value adding steps • Eliminate unnecessary checks and controls
7. Defects	• Reduce the need for inspection by automating quality checks and identifying errors as early in the process as possible • Do not allow work to start until necessary pre-requisites are available
8. Wrong Product	• Organise work around processes rather than processes around work and focus
9. People Unmatched to Role	• Ensure people are adequately and continuously trained • Structure work around required functional competencies
10. Inadequate Performance Measurement	• Design process metrics to allow process efficiency to be measured • Implement process data collection, reporting and analysis • Take decisions on process metrics
11. Uninvolved Personnel	• Delegate decision-making and empower people to complete work • Encourage, support and reward new ideas • Encourage feedback from those performing the work
12. Inadequate Technology	• Ensure people has access to the necessary technology to allow work to be done efficiently • Use technology to automate business processes • Optimise technology • Build knowledge-base and documentation into technology

Table 23 – Applying Waste Elimination Principles to Process Optimisation

A business process can be defined as the set of activities that is triggered by one or more events or statuses, requiring one or more inputs and performed in structured outcome-dependent order or sequence to generate one or more outputs or results and influence one or more outcomes.

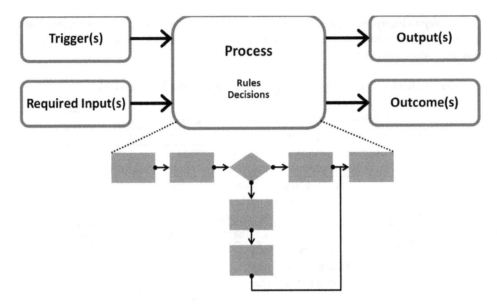

Figure 84 – Generic Representation of a Process

The individual activities within the process concerned with making decisions and generating outputs. The process is the self-contained unit that completes a given task. The process can consist of sub-processes and/or activities. The process and its constituent activities, stages and steps can be decomposed into a number of levels of detail, down to the individual atomic level.

Process analysis and design is concerned with optimising an existing or new process and focussing on efficiency and adding value. The process is primarily concerned with its results and outputs.

A process activity and sequence view is useful for identifying opportunities for efficiencies, resource optimisation, monitoring progress, collecting volumetric information and detecting problems, duplicated effort, bottlenecks, resource constraints and non value-adding activities such as waste and the opportunity for process compression/collapse described earlier.

An organisation can be viewed as an assembly of processes that co-ordinate activities to design, develop, produce, market, sell and deliver products and services to its consumers and provide subsequent support and other services. These are the core value-adding activities. There are many supporting processes and activities. Core value-adding processes and their activities are grouped into primary process groups. Each primary process group contains one or more value-adding process activity sets as well as management and supporting processes.

The process activity set is the set of activities performed to respond to a business event. These can be sub-divided until the Fundamental Business Process Activity Set level is reached.

Processes can be analysed and decomposed to varying levels of detail and granularity.

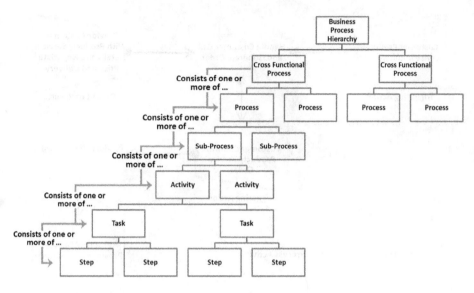

Figure 85 – Process Decomposition

The decomposition of the sample customer process for buying a product or service described section 4.6.5.11 on page 272 could be represented as follows:

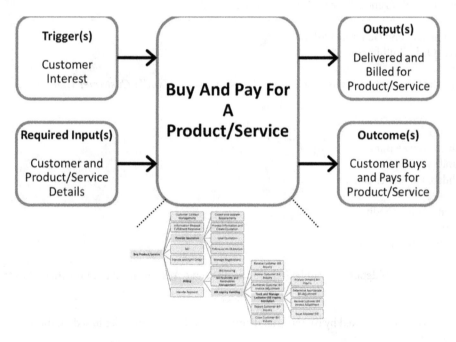

Figure 86 – Process Decomposition Example

The Fundamental Business Process Activity Set can be viewed as the lowest level of business activity that is performed by a single person within the organisation either entirely manually or with system support and Is generally performed by that person within a single session. These Fundamental Business Process Activity Sets are at the core of business analysis and design in the context of solution architecture and design. You should identify the minimum set of Fundamental Business Process Activity Sets that comprise the business process. The Fundamental Business Process Activity Sets for this buying a product or service example can be viewed as:

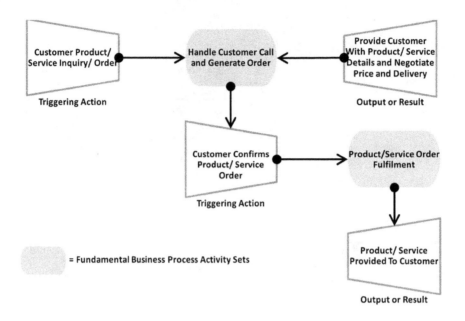

Figure 87 – Identification of Fundamental Business Process Activity Sets

There are two Fundamental Business Process Activity Sets here:

1. Handle Customer Call and Generate Order
2. Product/Service Order Fulfilment

Each of these process activity sets will consist of multiple tasks and steps. ***Handle Customer Call and Generate Order*** could include the following steps

- Respond to Customer
- Identify Product/Service Bundle
- Check Availability
- Take and Validate Customer Details
- Agree Price
- Process Payment/Agree Credit
- Handle Exceptions
- Agree Delivery/Provision Schedule

This decomposition and level of detail may not be required at this stage. We just need to know that it has to be and can be done later.

Activities within processes can be linked by routers that direct flow and maintain order based on the values of output(s) and the status of outcome(s).

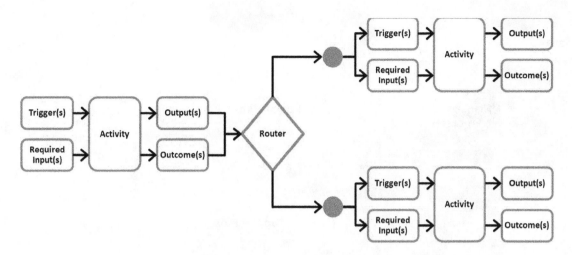

Figure 88 – Activity Linkage within Processes

Decisions are the results of (activities and tasks within) business processes. Business processes define the paths to these results. A business rule defines how inputs are processed to perform actions and make decisions. Business rules (should) describe and contain the intelligence and decision making of the organisation. The linkage between process inputs, business rules, actions, decisions and results is shown below.

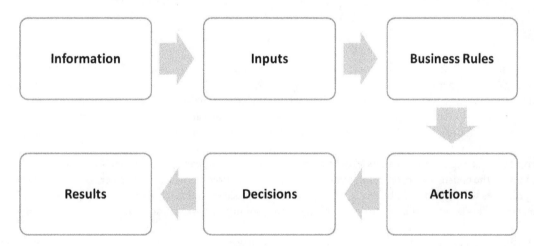

Figure 89 – Process Inputs, Rules, Actions, Decisions and Results

Processes generate results by applying business rules. These results can be actions performed or decisions made.

Processes do not achieve outcomes. An outcome is the desired consequence of a successfully executed process. Examples of outcomes include:

- Increased sales
- Higher sales conversion rate
- Increased revenue
- Increased profit
- Improved cashflow
- Improved customer satisfaction

The process can influence the achievement of these outcomes through characteristics such as stream-lined operation, speed and accuracy of response, better process consumer experience and flexibility.

When recognising the processes impacted by a solution, these will occur in three groups:

1. Primary
2. Support
3. Management

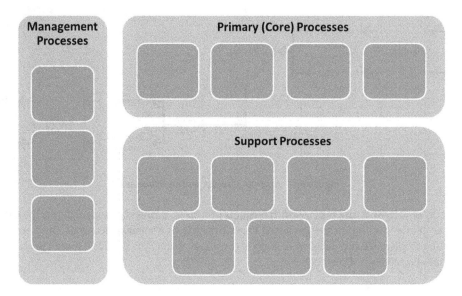

Figure 90 – Process Groups

Primary processes are end-to-end, cross-functional processes which directly deliver value. They represent the essential activities an organisation performs to fulfil its business objectives. These primary processes make up the value chain where each step adds value to the preceding step as measured by its contribution to the creation or delivery of a product or service, ultimately delivering value to the organisation. Primary processes can move across business functions, across departments or even between organisations (such as business partners) and provide a complete end-to-end view of value creation.

All too commonly, the organisation sees its structure vertically and in a compartmentalised view and does not take a cross-functional view of the end-to-end process that cross these vertical functions. This absence of a cross-functional view leads to inefficient processes with additional non-value adding steps, unnecessary handoffs and delays while work move between vertical functions. This is very similar to the issue of silos within solution delivery described in section 2.6 on page 50.

Changing business process operations to take a cross-functional view eliminates waste and inefficiencies associated with work moving through these organisational silos.

Support processes assist primary processes by performing activities such as managing resources and/or infrastructure required by primary processes. The differentiator between primary and support processes is that support processes do not directly deliver value. This does not mean that they are unimportant to an organisation. Support processes include information technology management, facilities or capacity management and human resource management. Support processes are generally associated with functional areas but can and often do cross functional boundaries.

Management processes are used to measure, monitor and control business activities and the performance of primary and support processes. They ensure that a primary or supporting process meets operational, financial, regulatory and legal targets. Again, they do not directly add value. They are necessary in order to ensure the organisation operates effectively and efficiently. They can identify process bottlenecks and constraints and the need or opportunity for process improvement. Many organisations do not have well defined management processes. Effective process management requires measurement and the ability to analyse the process measures collected. Business process measurement and monitoring provides critical feedback on process design, performance and compliance. It is necessary to measure process performance in terms of a variety of possible metrics related to how well the process meets its stated goals.

The following table lists the sample primary and support processes for buying a product or service described on page 273:

Phase	Step	Primary Processes	Secondary Processes
Research/ Consider	Look For Information/ Awareness and Interest Generated	• Manage Contact	• Record, Track, Analyse and Report on Customer Contacts • Manage Information Content and Access
Inquire/ Evaluate	Look For Details on Specific Product/ Service/ Offer	• Respond to Customer and Issue and Distribute Marketing Collateral • Qualify Customer	• Track Leads • Manage Prospect
	Receive, Evaluate Offer, Negotiate and Compare	• Negotiate Sales/Contract • Acquire Customer Data • Cross/Up Selling • Develop Sales Proposal	• Manage Sales Accounts
Decide/ Negotiate	Decide To Buy Product/ Service		
Buy/Subscribe	Buy/ Subscribe and Receive Product/ Service	• Determine Customer Order Feasibility • Authorise Credit • Complete Customer Order • Issue Customer Orders • Fulfil Order	• Track and Manage Customer Order Handling • Report Customer Order Handling • Manage Inventory • Manage Deliveries
Use/ Bill and Pay/ Change/ Upgrade/ Complain/ Report Fault/ Leave	Receive and Pay Usage Statements and Bills, Pay Bill	• Apply Pricing, Discounting, Adjustments and Rebates • Create Customer Bill • Produce and Distribute Bill	• Collect Billing Information • Manage Customer Billing • Manage Customer Payments • Manage Customer Debt Collection
	Query Usage Statement and Bill	• Receive and Handle Inquiry • Track Inquiry to Completion • Respond to Query	• Record, Track, Analyse and Report on Customer Contacts
	Report Fault/ Complain	• Receive and Handle Fault Report/Complaint • Track Fault Report/Complaint to Completion • Respond to Fault Report/Complaint	• Record, Track, Analyse and Report on Customer Contacts
	Upgrade/ Buy Additional Product/ Service/ Respond to Offer	• Manage Contact • Negotiate Sales/Contract • Cross/Up Selling • Develop Sales Proposal	• Build Customer Insight • Analyse and Manage Customer Risk • Personalise Customer Profile for Retention and Loyalty • Validate Customer Satisfaction • Manage Information Content and Access
	Renew, Evaluate Alternatives and Negotiate	• Negotiate Sales/Contract • Cross/Up Selling	
	Decide to Leave/ Cancel	• Manage Termination	

Phase	Step	Primary Processes	Secondary Processes
	Service		
	Accept Counteroffer		

Table 24 – Primary and Support Processes Example

The design of the solution may need to encompass the design of the processes that the solution will impact or enable or require. Very frequently, the process design work associated with the design of a new solution is the first time the entire end-to-end business process will have been documented or attempted to be documented. The business analysis function will assist the business function in doing this work as part of the inclusive solution design work.

Focus on the design of how end-to-end work occurs in order to deliver value. Document the sequence of activities, including the design of what work is performed, at what time, in what location, by what process actors using what rules.

The high-level process analysis steps are shown below

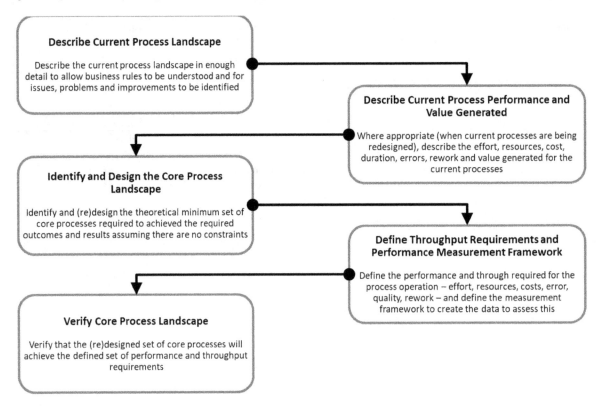

Figure 91 – Business Process Analysis High-Level Steps

Step	Description
Describe Current Process Landscape	Describe the current process landscape in enough detail to allow business rules to be understood and for issues, problems and improvements to be identified.
Describe Current Process Performance and Value Generated	Where appropriate (when current processes are being redesigned), describe the effort, resources, cost, duration, errors, rework and value generated for the current processes.
Identify and Design the Core Process Landscape	Identify and (re)design the theoretical minimum set of core processes required to achieve the required outcomes and results assuming there are no constraints.
Define Throughput Requirements and Performance Measurement Framework	Define the performance and through required for the process operation – effort, resources, costs, error, quality, rework – and define the measurement framework to create the data to assess this.
Verify Core Process Landscape	Verify that the (re)designed set of core processes will achieve the defined set of performance and throughput requirements.

Table 25 – Business Process Analysis High-Level Steps

The structure of the information to be gathered during process analysis is:

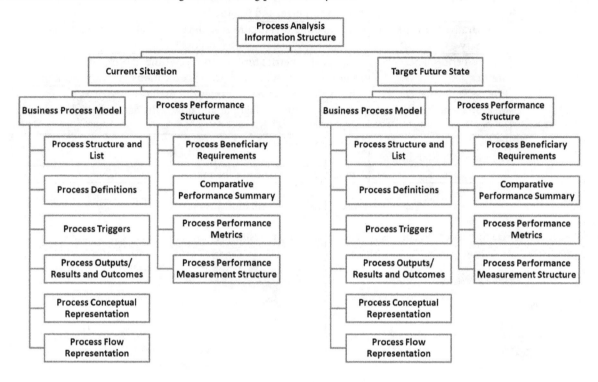

Figure 92 – Process Analysis Information Structure

This shows information being collected for current and new processes. If existing processes are not being analysed them this side of the analysis can be omitted. The details of this information structure are listed in the table below.

Analysis Group	Analysis Item	Description
Business Process Model	Process Structure and List	List the process hierarchy: major process groups and key processes within each group. There will be two types of processes: 1. Delivery processes 2. Management and support processes that are concerned with the internal management and operation of the business function
	Process Definitions	Create high-level descriptions for the major process groups and key processes within each group.
	Pre-Conditions	Detail what must have happened before the process can start.
	Pre-Requisites	What must be in place before the process can start.
	Inputs	What the process needs to operate.
	Dependencies	What the process is dependent on.
	Process Triggers	Detail what causes each of the key processes to be initiated.
	Processing	What the process does.
	Process Outcomes/ Results	Detail the outcomes, deliverables and results of the key processes.
	Process Conceptual Representation	Conceptual representations are actor/entity-based pictures that communicate at a high level how a business process works.
	Process Flow Representation	These are standard business process flows, typically represented as cross-functional diagrams.
	Timelines	What are the expected process times.
	Roles and Responsibilities	Who is involved in the process.

Analysis Group	Analysis Item	Description
	Skills and Capabilities	What skills are required of the process participants.
Process Performance Structure	Process Beneficiary Requirements	What are the requirements of each of the main beneficiaries (such as customers) want from the process, both in terms of performance (time to compete) and results.
	Comparative Performance Summary	What do other organisations achieve for similar processes to similar beneficiaries illustrating what is possible.
	Process Performance Metrics	What are the metrics for the processes: time to complete, cost, resources, steps, number of process executions, errors, rework.
	Process Performance Measurement Structure	What is the measurement framework used to assess process performance and throughput and how is the data collected, analysed and presented.
Other	Issues Identified/Outstanding	Any issues not clarified.
	Assumptions	Any assumptions made in the process design.

Table 26 – Process Analysis Information Structure

The factors that increase the success of business process design and redesign are:

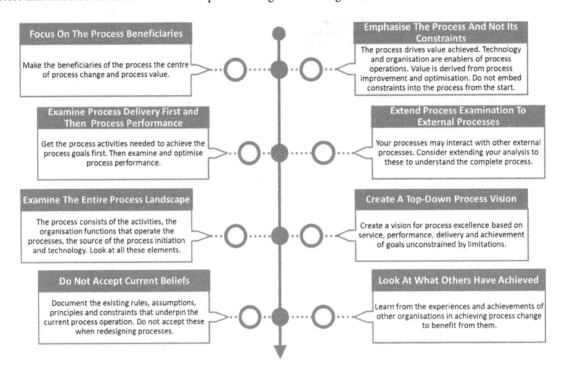

Figure 93 – Business Process Design Success Factors

These success factors are:

Factor	Description
Focus On The Process Beneficiaries	Make the beneficiaries of the process the centre of process change and process value.
Emphasise The Process And Not Its Constraints	The process drives value achieved. Technology and organisation are enablers of process operations. Value is derived from process improvement and optimisation. Do not embed constraints into the process from the start.
Examine Process Delivery First and Then Process Performance	Get the process activities needed to achieve the process goals first. Then examine and optimise process performance.

Factor	Description
Extend Process Examination To External Processes	Your processes may interact with other external processes. Consider extending your analysis to these to understand the complete process.
Examine The Entire Process Landscape	The process consists of the activities, the organisation functions that operate the processes, the source of the process initiation and technology. Look at all these elements.
Create A Top-Down Process Vision	Create a vision for process excellence based on service, performance, delivery and achievement of goals unconstrained by limitations.
Do Not Accept Current Beliefs	Document the existing rules, assumptions, principles and constraints that underpin the current process operation. Do not accept these when redesigning processes.
Look At What Others Have Achieved	Learn from the experiences and achievements of other organisations in achieving process change to benefit from them.

Table 27 – Business Process Design Success Factors

The objective of this work is to define what the organisation wants the process to be and answers the what, when, where, who and how questions of how end-to-end work is executed. This contributes to the solution design.

The process design work should ensure that the proper management controls and metrics are in place for compliance and performance measurement of process operation.

Understanding the process typically involves process modelling and an assessment of the environmental factors which enable and constrain the process. A model is rarely a complete and full representation of the actual process. The objective is to create a representation of the process that describes it accurately and sufficiently for the task at hand to assist with:

- Understanding the business process through the creation of the model
- Creating a visible representation and establishing a commonly shared perspective
- Analysing process performance and defining and validating changes

The To-Be model is an expression of the desired target process state and specifies the requirements for the supporting resources that enable effective business operations. There is a range of process design, modelling and notational standards and techniques – see section 8.3.5.1.2 on page 518 for information on the Archimate language and section 4.4.2.1 on page 151 for an outline of the BPMN standard. These process modelling approaches provide a language for describing and communicating as-is and to-be process information. Like all new languages they must be learned and understood.

There are a number of benefits to using a standards-based approach including:

- A common symbology, language and technique which facilitate communication and understanding
- Standards-based models provide common and consistently defined processes definitions which eases the process of design, analysis and measurement and facilitates model reuse
- An ability to leverage modelling tools based on common standards and notations
- An ability to import and export models created in various tools for reuse in other tools
- Some tool vendors are leveraging standards and notations for developing the ability to be exported from a modelling notation to an execution language (for example BPMN to BPEL – WS-BPEL)

The principles of business process analysis and design are:

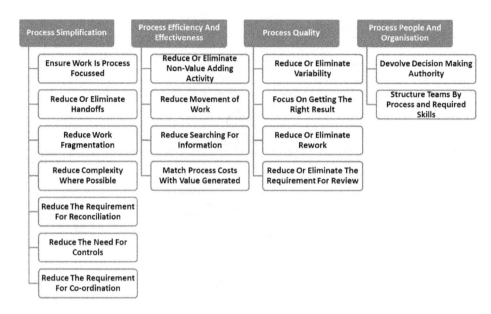

Figure 94 – Business Process Design Standards and Approaches – Part 1

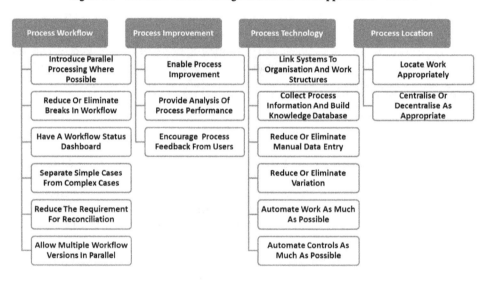

Figure 95 – Business Process Design Standards and Approaches – Part 2

Process Design Standard and Approach Group	Process Design Standard and Approach Area
Process Simplification	Ensure Work Is Process Focussed Reduce Or Eliminate Handoffs Reduce Work Fragmentation Reduce Complexity Where Possible Reduce The Requirement For Reconciliation Reduce The Need For Controls Reduce The Requirement For Co-ordination
Process Efficiency And Effectiveness	Reduce Or Eliminate Non-Value Adding Activity Reduce Movement of Work Reduce Searching For Information Match Process Costs With Value Generated
Process Quality	Reduce Or Eliminate Variability Focus On Getting The Right Result Reduce Or Eliminate Rework

Process Design Standard and Approach Group	Process Design Standard and Approach Area
	Reduce Or Eliminate The Requirement For Review
Process People And Organisation	Devolve Decision Making Authority
	Structure Teams By Process and Required Skills
Process Workflow	Introduce Parallel Processing Where Possible
	Reduce Or Eliminate Breaks In Workflow
	Have A Workflow Status Dashboard
	Separate Simple Cases From Complex Cases
	Reduce The Requirement For Reconciliation
	Allow Multiple Workflow Versions In Parallel
Process Improvement	Enable Process Improvement
	Provide Analysis Of Process Performance
	Encourage Process Feedback From Users
Process Technology	Link Systems To Organisation And Work Structures
	Collect Process Information And Build Knowledge Database
	Reduce Or Eliminate Manual Data Entry
	Reduce Or Eliminate Variation
	Automate Work As Much As Possible
	Automate Controls As Much As Possible
Process Location	Locate Work Appropriately
	Centralise Or Decentralise As Appropriate

Table 28 – Business Process Design Standards and Approaches

4.4.2.1 Business Process Modelling Notation (BPMN)

This section contains a brief introduction to BPMN.

BPMN[36] is a reasonably widely used and supported standard for business process modelling. One advantage of using BPMN is that you can output BPMN to Business Process Execution Language (BPEL – WS-BPEL[37]). This is a standard executable language for specifying interactions with Web Services.

Like Archimate (see section 8.3.5.1.2 on page 518), BPMN is an inflected language where a basis set of code symbols are modified by the addition of extra codes to indicate a specific purpose or meaning.

BPMN is not an:

- Organisation structure design language
- Data model and data flow design language but it does contain some data modelling elements
- System functional flow design language

BPMN can be used to show cross-functional process flow. The Pool represents major participants in a process with separate pools for different organisations or major business units. The Lane is contained within pools. You organise and categorise process activities within a pool according to function or role. All BPMN diagram elements are placed within swim lanes and pools.

---

[36] See https://www.omg.org/bpmn/ and https://www.omg.org/spec/BPMN/2.0/About-BPMN/ for more details on BPMN.
[37] See https://www.oasis-open.org/committees/download.php/23964/wsbpel-v2.0-primer.htm and http://docs.oasis-open.org/wsbpel/2.0/OS/wsbpel-v2.0-OS.html for more details on BPEL

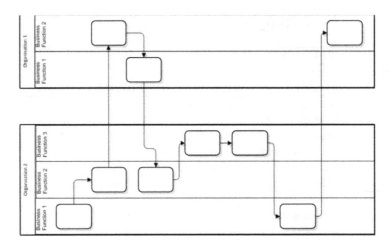

Figure 96 – BPMN Pools and Lanes

Schematically, the basic structure of BPMN is

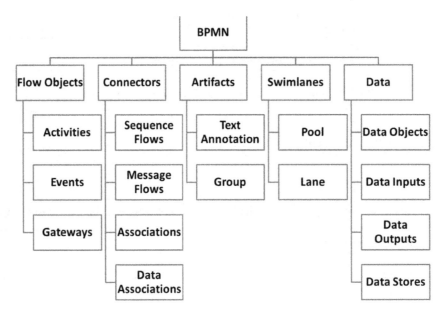

Figure 97 – BPMN Structure

Flow Objects are grouped as follows:

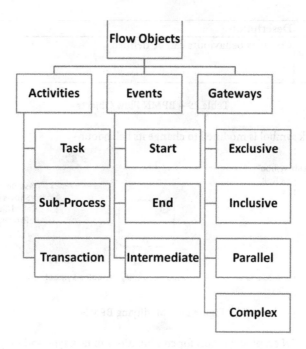

Figure 98 – BPMN Flow Objects

Flow Objects define the flow of the process.

Flow Object	Symbol	Description
Task		Unit of work
Sub-Process		A set of self-contained activities collapsed within process representation for ease of understanding
Transaction		A sub-process that must be completed or undone if not completed
Start		Acts as a trigger for a process/sub-process and takes an input only
End		Represents the result of a process/sub-process and generates an output only
Intermediate		Represents something that happens between the start and end events
Exclusive		Where the sequence slow can take only one of two or more alternative paths
Inclusive		Where the sequence slow can take one, more than one or all of two or more alternative paths and results from paths must be subsequently merged
Parallel		Multiple parallel paths are defined

Flow Object	Symbol	Description
Complex	✳	Complex behaviours can be defined

Table 29 – BPMN Flow Objects

The following shows how the task symbol is modified to change its behaviour

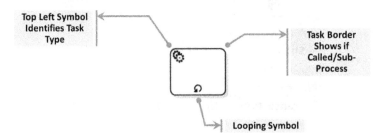

Figure 99 – Modifying BPMN

The following table shows the BPMN graphic symbols for combinations of task type and loop type.

	No Loop	Simple Loop	Multiple in Parallel	Multiple in Sequence
Simple/Not Specified		↺	|||	≡
Service	⚙	⚙ ↺	⚙ |||	⚙ ≡
Send	▼	▼ ↺	▼ |||	▼ ≡
Receive	▽	▽ ↺	▽ |||	▽ ≡
User	👤	👤 ↺	👤 |||	👤 ≡
Script	📜	📜 ↺	📜 |||	📜 ≡

	No Loop	Simple Loop	Multiple in Parallel	Multiple in Sequence
Manual				
Business Rule				

Table 30 – BPMN Graphics for Combinations of Task Type and Loop Type

The following table shows the BPMN graphics for sub-processes.

	Embedded Sub-Process	Embedded Transaction Sub-Process	Embedded Sub-Process Triggered by Event	Embedded Called Sub-Process
No Event Specified				
Message				
Error				
Escalation				
Compensation (Backout of Transaction)				
Conditional				
Signal				

	Embedded Sub-Process	Embedded Transaction Sub-Process	Embedded Sub-Process Triggered by Event	Embedded Called Sub-Process
Multiple		(multiple event sub-process graphic)	(multiple event-triggered sub-process graphic)	
Timer		(timer event sub-process graphic)	(timer event-triggered sub-process graphic)	
Multiple in Parallel		(multiple-in-parallel event sub-process graphic)	(multiple-in-parallel event-triggered sub-process graphic)	

Table 31 – BPMN Graphics for Sub-Processes

BPMN events can be modified using a variety of symbols.

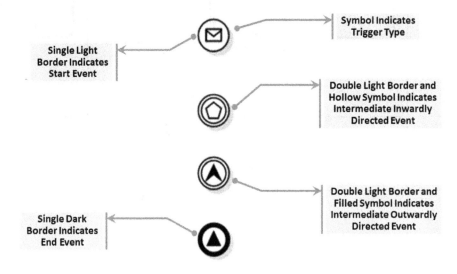

Figure 100 – BPMN Event Modification

The following table shows event modifications available:

	Start	Intermediate (Inward Direction "Catching")	Intermediate (Outward Direction "Throwing")	End
No Trigger	◯	◎		◉
Message	✉	✉	✉	✉
Timer	🕐	🕐		
Conditional	▤	▤		

	Start	Intermediate (Inward Direction "Catching")	Intermediate (Outward Direction "Throwing")	End
Signal	△	△	▲	▲
Multiple	⬠	⬠	⬟	⬟
Multiple in Parallel	✛	✛		
Error	⚡	⚡		⚡
Escalation	⌃	⌃	⌃	⌃
Compensation (Backout of Transaction)	◀◀	◀◀	◀◀	◀◀
Link		⇨	➡	
Cancel				✗
Terminate				●

Table 32 – BPMN Event Modifications

Gateways in BPMN control the execution of the process. They represent decisions/branching (exclusive, inclusive, and complex), merging, forking and joining. Parallel gateways synchronise/combine and create parallel flows. Event-based gateways represent a branching point in the process where the alternative paths that follow the gateway are based on events that occur.

Inclusive (AND)	◇○
Exclusive (OR)	◇✗ or ◇
Complex	◇✳
Parallel	◇✛
Exclusive Event	◇⬠
Start Exclusive Event	◇⬠
Start Parallel Event	◇✛

Table 33 – BPMN Gateway Symbols

BPMN allows the modelling of items (physical or information items) that are created, manipulated and used during the execution of a process such as data inputs, data outputs, persistent data stores and collections of data.

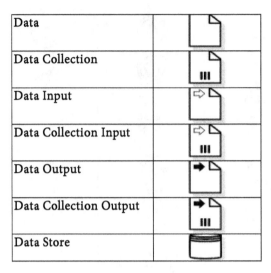

Table 34 – BPMN Data Symbols

As a process representation language BPMN offers the opportunity for great rigour and exactness. However, that level of detailed information has to be captured about the process. This can be time-consuming and complex. Also, the language has to be understood by all those participating in the process design activity. This includes business participants whose involvement is most likely temporary and part time. It is not reasonable to expect them to learn full BPMN language.

The rigour of BPMN is necessary when you are publishing process to a BPEL where it will be executed. For simple process analysis, definition and description, the full BPMN language is perhaps less useful.

4.5 Solution Architecture Engagement Process

The solution architecture function needs to have a number of engagement models and approaches available in its toolbox to assist the business with designing solutions to meet its needs. The purposes of having defined engagement models are:

- They provide certainty about the purpose, scope, duration and outputs for the business

- Having separate engagement models provides the flexibility to allow the needs of the business to be met at any stage of the solution journey

- They maximise reuse and repeatability

- They ensure that quality deliverables are produced

- They ensure the work done is comprehensive

- They increase the confidence of the business that the solution architecture function will provide a quality service

These engagements can occur at different stages in the solution design journey, from the business looking for a concept to be explored or the business looking for a consulting exercise on the solution needs of a business function or for a solution to be designed to different levels of detail to understand its likely delivery cost, time and resources.

The following sections describe in detail a number of different engagement types. These can occur in the context of a solution delivery project or can occur separately from or prior to any decision to implement the solution design.

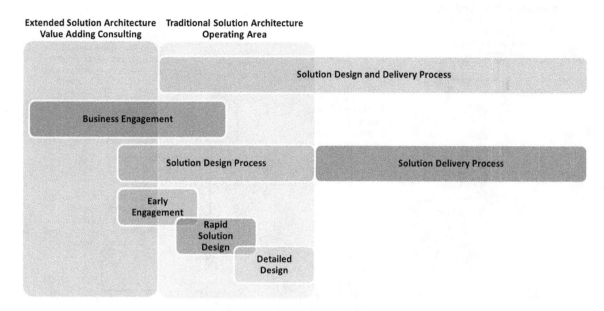

Figure 101 – Solution Architecture Engagement Models

These engagement types are:

- ***Business Engagement*** – this is a formal business consulting assignment designed to take place before the idea of implementing one or more new solutions has been formalised. It aims to take a broad business concern, opportunity or problem and define new business structures and associated information technology and business processes to realise a potential resolution. This engagement is designed to take place before any formal solution delivery project is initiated. Such a project cannot be defined until the objectives of the project can be defined to a sufficient extent and in sufficient detail that it can be termed a project. This is a non-traditional solution architecture engagement but one which potentially offers real value to the organisation. This is described in section 4.6.1 on page 161.

- ***Solution Design Process*** – this is a formal process for iteratively creating a solution design that can use elements and techniques of the following engagement types to progress the design process:

  - ***Early Engagement*** – this is a consulting-type engagement where the problem to be resolved or the opportunity to be addressed is uncertain. There is some overlap in this type of engagement and that of the business engagement. The latter is broader in that it is looking to design the structure of the business function (including any information technology and solution landscape). The former is more focussed on addressing a specific but currently undefined potential solution area. This is described in section 4.6.4 on page 235.

  - ***Rapid Solution Design*** – this is concerned with providing a quick solution scoping result for a reasonably well-defined solution requirement. This allows for an informed decision to be made quickly to proceed or not to proceed to a more detailed solution design stage. This is described in section 4.6.5 on page 257.

  - ***Detailed Design*** – this describes a formal structured approach for defining the detail of a solution. This is described in section 4.6.6 on page 276.

These different engagements are designed to handle different business requests in terms of how specific and known the problem or opportunity is and how detailed the response required is.

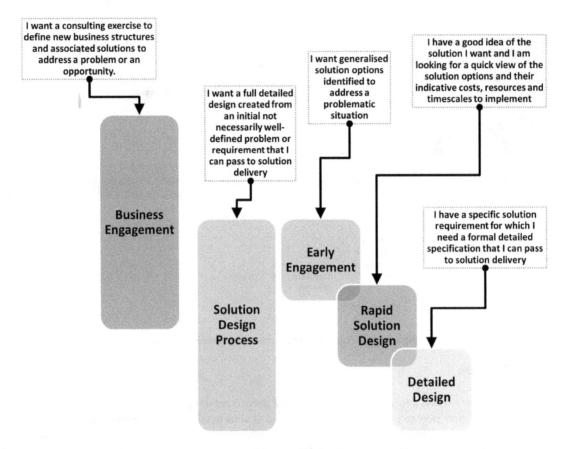

Figure 102 – Mapping Business Need to Engagement Types

In terms of the specificity of the business request, the level of detail of the output required and the duration, the engagement mapping is listed in the table below.

Business Request	Level of Specificity of Business Request	Level of Solution Detail Required	Likely Duration	Engagement Type
I have a good idea of the solution I want and I am looking for a quick view of the solution options and their indicative costs, resources and timescales to implement.	High	Low to Medium	Short	Rapid Solution Design
I want a full detailed design created from an initial not necessarily well-defined problem or requirement that I can pass to solution delivery	Low	High	Medium	Solution Design Process
I have a specific solution requirement for which I need a formal detailed specification that I can pass to solution delivery	High	High	Short to Medium	Detailed Design
I want generalised solution options identified to address a problematic situation.	Low	Low to Medium	Medium	Early Engagement
I want a consulting exercise to define new business structures and associated with solutions to address a problem or an opportunity.	Very Low	Medium to High	Medium to Long	Business Engagement

Table 35 – Mapping Business Need to Engagement Types

4.6 Solution Architecture Engagements

4.6.1 Business Engagement

4.6.1.1 Introduction

The business engagement is concerned with analysing the structure and operations of a business function and creating a target business architecture that includes identifying business solutions.

This is a potentially complex engagement as it may involve the solution architecture function operating outside its traditional comfort zone.

The objective is to create a realistic, achievable, implementable and operable target business solution architecture to achieve the desired business solution targets, supported by information gathered and analysed.

This is not an exact engagement with an easily defined and understood extent and duration. It has an essential investigative and exploratory aspect that means it has to have a necessary latitude. This is not an excuse for excessive analysis without reaching a conclusion. The goal of this and the other engagements described here is to produce results and answers within a reasonable time to allow decisions to be made based on evidence.

This engagement is an example of the solution architect offering true business consulting services and being able to offer value to the business. The engagement can be performed entirely by solution architecture or the solution architecture function can be part of a wider engagement team. It is intended to describe a structured and focussed engagement. It is suited to situations where detail and implementation structure and framework are required.

This engagement contains a comprehensive and generalised set of components from which the details and scope of a specific engagement can be defined. This can be used to create a customised engagement from this menu of options to suit the specific needs of the business request.

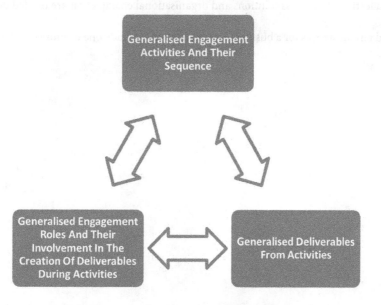

Figure 103 – Generalised Business Engagement Structure

The engagement menu consists of the following groups of items:

- *Generalised Engagement Activities And Their Sequence* –complete set of possible activities and their groups and sequence and flow through the engagement from which the specific engagement can be created

- *Generalised Deliverables From Activities* – complete set of possible deliverables from the possible set of activities

- *Generalised Engagement Roles And Their Involvement In The Creation Of Deliverables During Activities* – identification of possible roles and their involvement in the possible set of activities and the generation of the possible set of deliverables

These are used to create a customised path through the architecture engagement process involves agreeing activities to be performed, deliverables from the engagement and participating roles.

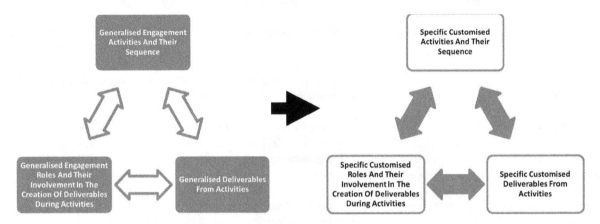

Figure 104 – Creating Customised Set of Activities, Roles and Deliverables

The engagement is a structured approach to analysing the operation of an existing business function with a view to improving its operations or developing a new business function, with a strong focus on solution, processes and technology.

Business architecture is not specifically concerned with a set of business requirements. It is about a taking a wider, broader and higher view of the collection of business solutions and organisational changes that are needed deliver business objectives.

The business reasons and circumstances for a business engagement can include one or more of the following factors.

Figure 105 – Possible Factors Driving the Need for a Business Engagement

These possible factors are:

- Globalisation
- Need for Transparency
- Service Focus and Customer Expectations
- Challenging Economic Circumstances
- Acquisition, Consolidation or Divestment of Operations
- Increased Regulation
- Business and Technology Changes and New Opportunities
- Mobile and Social Computing Changes and Opportunities
- Competition
- New Business Models
- Increased Pace of Change
- Problems with Existing Operations
- Inability to Scale Current Operations
- Change to Outsourcing Operations
- Move to Different Jurisdictions

The engagement is about identifying the changes required to the core domains described in section 2.4.3 to respond to the business changes. It defines a target architecture and a path to transition to or transformation into it across the core business domains.

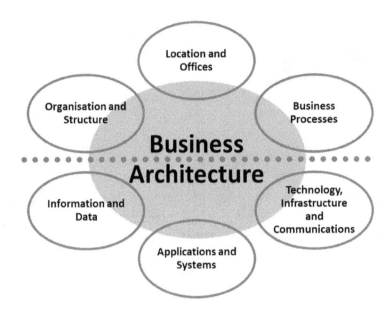

Figure 106 – Business Engagement Change Domains

The change domains can be divided into two groups:

1. *Above The Line* - Concerned with the organisation or the business function

2. *Below The Line* - Concerned with the technology and infrastructure that underpins and enables the operation of the organisation or the business function

These domains are internal to the organisation and the business function that is the subject of the engagement and, as such, are within the direct control of the business function.

There are two extended domain areas that also need to be considered:

1. *Organisation Operating Environment and Business Landscape* – this is external to the organisation. It consists of the organisation's customers, partners, suppliers and other external parties. The organisation has limited control over these external parties. If the organisation is deploying solutions that are to be used by these parties, the organisation will have limited control over how those solutions are used. This adds to the complexity of the design of such solutions.

2. *Overall Organisation Business Strategy* – this defines how the organisation as a whole operates and constrains the options available within the architecture engagement.

The business strategy will be underpinned by a number of factors such as those listed below. These factors will both constrain and direct the architecture engagement.

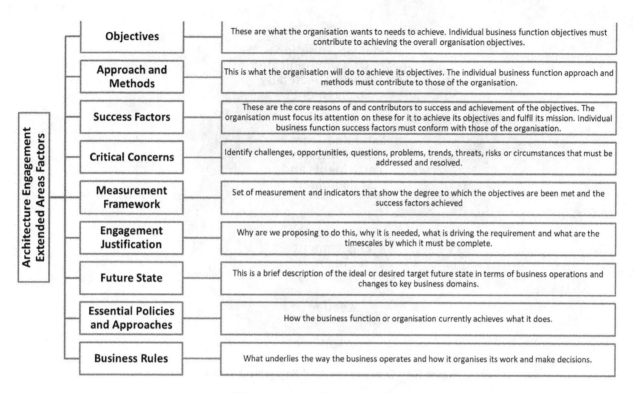

Figure 107 – Architecture Engagement Extended Factors

These factors are listed in the table below.

Extended Factor	Description
Objectives	These are what the organisation wants to or needs to achieve. Individual business function objectives must contribute to achieving the overall organisation objectives.
Approach and Methods	This is what the organisation will do to achieve its objectives. The individual business function approach and methods must contribute to those of the organisation.
Success Factors	These are the core reasons of and contributors to success and achievement of the objectives. The organisation must focus its attention on these for it to achieve its objectives and fulfil its mission. Individual business function success factors must conform to those of the organisation.
Critical Concerns	Identify challenges, opportunities, questions, problems, trends, threats, risks or circumstances that must be addressed and resolved.
Measurement Framework	Set of measurement and indicators that show the degree to which the objectives are been met and the success factors achieved
Engagement Justification	Why are we proposing to do this, why it is needed, what is driving the requirement and what are the timescales by which it must be complete.
Future State	This is a brief description of the ideal or desired target future state in terms of business operations and changes to key business domains.
Essential Policies and Approaches	How the business function or organisation currently achieves what it does.
Business Rules	What underlies the way the business operates and how it organises its work and make decisions.

Table 36 – Architecture Engagement Extended Factors

The expected scope and goals of the engagement needs to be agreed and understood before commencement. The scope can change during the engagement.

Figure 108 – Core and Extended Engagement Teams

There will be core and extended teams involved in and participating in the engagement.

- *Leader* – this role will both manage the engagement and take a lead role in its delivery. This is not a project management role. It is a consulting position. This person needs to have the skills and experience to represent the work of the team to the wider set of participants and stakeholders as well as the ability to manage the team that performs the work, provide leadership and mentoring and to validate the work done, the results generated, the conclusions reached and the recommendations made. The leader must become a temporary expert in the subject area. The leader must be able to bridge the business and information technology areas of knowledge and work.

- *Core Engagement Team* – this consists of both information technology and business participants. Business experts who understand the operation of the current function, if relevant, and the business problem, challenge or opportunity being analysed. The team will need to have the required experience in analysis, research and design and in the various techniques to be used in the engagement.

- *Extended Team – Direct Business Participants and Stakeholders* – the members of the extended team will be involved in meetings, workshops, interviews and other information gathering, assessment and validation activities.

- *Wider Organisation – Aware Of, Communicated About And Affected By Engagement* – the wider organisation will be aware of the engagement and may have concerns about its scope and impact. This will be especially true if the engagement is controversial. The work will not take place in isolation. The purpose and scope of the engagement should be communicated as necessary to the affected or concerned elements of the wider organisation to stop unfounded reports and stories spreading.

There may be other temporary participants such as developers if prototypes are being developed or specialists for the provision of specific services or knowledge.

4.6.1.2 Workshops

The engagement will involve a number of workshops. These can an effective and necessary information gathering tool as part of the architecture engagement. The effectiveness of workshops needs to be optimised with careful preparation, planning and delivery and post-workshop communications.

Workshops involve the core engagement team presenting to and learning from the extended business team and the wider organisation. They have two sets of purposes:

1. *Primary* – achieve the stated objective, gather and confirm information

2. *Secondary* – build team, get acceptance and buy-in from extended team and wider organisation, identify potential organisation and personnel problems and hidden agendas, assist with communication and control the message, assist with making decisions, uncover conflicts

The following is a list of common workshop activities:

*   Define and communicate objectives
*   Identify and profile extended and wider team participants
*   Allocate roles to core team participants
*   Define schedule, timescale and duration
*   Deal with issues such as facilities and equipment
*   Prepare, review, agree and distribute inputs
*   Create tables of contents of target deliverables
*   Prepare, review, agree set of topics to be covered and presentation material
*   Document results and circulate for review and feedback

4.6.1.3 High Level Activities and Their Logical Sequence

The menu of activities for the business engagement and their logical sequence is illustrated below.

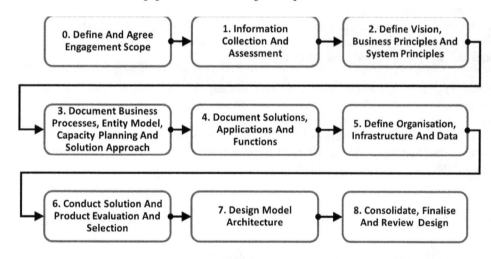

Figure 109 – Business Engagement High Level Activities and Their Logical Sequence

These high level activities are:

0. Define And Agree Engagement Scope
1. Information Collection And Assessment
2. Define Vision, Business Principles And System Principles
3. Document Business Processes, Entity Model, Capacity Planning And Solution Approach
4. Document Solutions, Applications And Functions
5. Define Organisation, Infrastructure And Data

6. Conduct Solution And Product Evaluation And Selection
7. Design Model Architecture
8. Consolidate, Finalise And Review Design

These activities do not have to be performed sequentially and linearly. The order can be agreed at the start of the engagement to suit the available resources and time, the scope of the engagement and the level of detail required.

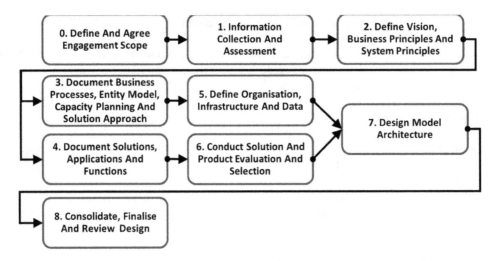

Figure 110 – Business Engagement Activity Sequencing

Some of the steps can be iterated and repeated to increasing levels of detail but there should not be too many iterations.

The information gathering and analysis activities need to be time-limited. Activities can occur in parallel by different sub-teams to optimise elapsed time and the work schedule.

Always check for previously collected information and inventories of material to avoid duplication of effort. Analysis paralysis needs to be avoided. The purpose is to move to a conclusion and set of solution and architecture options quickly. The reason for documenting the current state is to provide a basis for, a context and a justification of the definition of the desired target state and set of solution and architecture options.

Section 4.2.1 on page 95 contains some notes on the decision leadership that the solution architect needs to demonstrate during the design process.

The next sections describe these activities and their logical steps in more detail. These steps can be combined or expanded as required depending on the complexity of the engagement and the amount of information and analysis required. In many cases, these are logical steps. They can be mapped to a different set of physical steps.

4.6.1.4 Business Engagement Activity 0. Define And Agree Engagement Scope

The possible steps for activity *Define And Agree Engagement Scope* are:

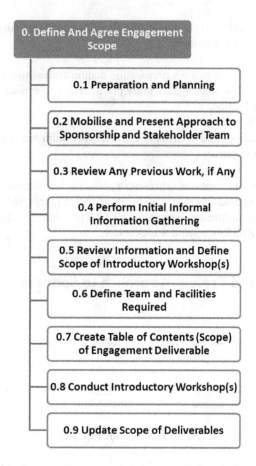

Figure 111 – Steps Within Business Engagement Activity *0. Define And Agree Engagement Scope*

These steps are documented in more detail below:

> 0.1 Preparation and Planning
> 0.2 Mobilise and Present Approach to Sponsorship and Stakeholder Team
> 0.3 Review Any Previous Work, if Any
> 0.4 Perform Initial Informal Information Gathering
> 0.5 Review Information and Define Scope of Introductory Workshop(s)
> 0.6 Define Team and Facilities Required
> 0.7 Create Table of Contents (Scope) of Engagement Deliverable
> 0.8 Conduct Introductory Workshop(s)
> 0.9 Update Scope of Deliverables

4.6.1.4.1 Step 0.1 Preparation and Planning

This step involves preparing for the engagement scoping activity. One-to-one meetings will be held with the engagement sponsors and the business experts on the problem or issue being investigated. Background research on the topic can be conducted.

The key business participants can be identified and their time can be formally allocated to the engagement.

The purpose of this step is to create material to present at the initial mobilisation sessions. This material can then be refined and updated during the remaining steps in this activity.

The generic approach and its activities and steps should be described. The proposed customisation of the general approach to suit the specific requirements should be documented.

It is important to be prepared for such meetings. Such preparation demonstrates interest in the topic and generates the confidence of the business participants. The meetings are more productive. The approach should be reviewed with the sponsors in advance of the initial mobilisation.

Create an initial schedule for the workshops and information gathering sessions based on the initial understanding of the central requirements and information required.

You should decide on the approach to capturing and representing visually the information collected at this early stage of the engagement. A standard approach or approaches means all the information is represented in the same way. You could an enterprise modelling approach such as Archimate (see section 8.3.5.1.2 on page 518). This would require all parties involved in the engagement to understand the Archimate symbol vocabulary.

4.6.1.4.2 Step 0.2 Mobilise and Present Approach to Sponsorship, Stakeholder and Core Project Team

This step is the start of the continuous communication process during the engagement and so it sets the tone for the remainder of the engagement.

Ensure that the individuals in the business who sponsoring the engagement and the stakeholders involved in the business area covered by the engagement are known and agreed and that their participation has been confirmed.

Gather information about the expected scope of, the reason for, the expected schedule of and the required deliverables from the engagement from the sponsor.

Prepare and review the material to present to the team created in the previous step. This includes:

- The reason why the engagement is taking place
- The scope and objectives
- The generic set of steps presented in this section
- The proposed adaptation of the generic approach to suit the engagement
- Indicative work plan and schedule
- Indicative team roles and responsibilities
- Indicative engagement outputs and deliverables such as the table of contents of the report to be produced
- Allocation of resources and facilities
- Approach to communications within the team and between the team and the business participants
- Approach to quality assurance and the review of material before it is presented externally
- Workshop and meeting approach and indicative schedule

This is a mobilisation session. It should present a plan for a plan rather than a fully articulated plan.

The engagement is a consulting, exploratory and learning activity. Not everything can or will be known initially.

4.6.1.4.3 Step 0.3 Review Any Previous Work, if Any

The business function may have conduced previous similar engagements relating to the problem or issue under consideration. If it exists, this material should be identified and reviewed. It may inform how the current engagement should proceed and how problems that previously arose can be addressed. For example, the business may have engaged the services of an external consultancy to review operations, perform an audit or identify gaps between what is being done and the best practises implemented by other organisations.

Determine if any of this material is useful and relevant and can be reused or incorporated into the current engagement.

Understand the issues identified during these previous exercises. Review how their recommendations were implemented or attempted to be implemented, if at all. Identify the reasons, if any, for the partial or incomplete realisation.

4.6.1.4.4 Step 0.4 Perform Initial Informal Information Gathering

Before the formal introductory workshops described later in this activity, conduct informal and preparatory individual meetings with key business experts and the engagement sponsors and stakeholders.

Understand their vision and objectives for both the engagement that the target architecture that will be produced from it. Ascertain the key underlying issues they are looking to resolve or the opportunity they are looking to address. Confirm their level of commitment – how much effort are they and their teams able and willing to devote to the engagement.

Where possible, relevant and useful, walk the floor of the current operation or business function and observe the work being performed. Understand how work currently gets done if the engagement relates to changing an existing business function or operation.

Document the organisation structure, the key people, their roles, reporting structure, experience, levels of skills.

Understand the state of the current business processes and review any existing process documentation. If there is no inventory of business processes or the processes are not documented, omit this from the initial information gathering as the effort could be too substantial at this stage.

Present the previously created draft workshop schedule. Agree the workshop participants. Understand the personalities involved and any likely objections and resistance to the engagement process and to any recommendations for change that may come from it as a result of creating a target architecture.

4.6.1.4.5 Step 0.5 Review Information and Define Scope of Introductory Workshop(s)

Review the results of the informal meetings and information gathered in the business area and previous engagement. Define the scope of the introductory workshop(s) for the project team.

The purpose of the introductory workshop is intended to present the engagement to those participants who will be contributing to information gathering and analysis, issue analysis, research and identification of resolution options.

These introductory workshop(s) need to be prepared carefully to demonstrate professionalism and seriousness of the engagement.

The following table contains a list of possible topics to cover in the workshop.

Area	Topics
Scope	• Business functions involved in the engagement • Locations and jurisdictions involved in the work delivery • Sets of products and services being provided • Business processes, business rules • Facilities, systems and applications used or that support service delivery
Why The Engagement	• Why the engagement is taking place, what issues, challenges, needs are driving the engagement – poor performance, service, loss of business, new regulations? • What is likely to happen if no action is taken? • What benefits are likely to accrue?

Area	Topics
Indication Of Changes	• What are the likely changes across the core business areas?
Aims	• Business aims • Success factors
Stakeholders	• Who needs to be involved?
Measurement Framework	• Key performance indicators across dimensions of: • Service and product delivery – cost, time, quality, volume • Financial – input costs, cost of product and service delivery, return • Customer (external party) view – satisfaction, retention • Organisation – ability to adopt changes and apply new ways of operating • How will we know if we have been successful?
Future Vision	• What does the future look like?
Limitations	• What will constrain the range of solution options: • Cost • Time • Resources • Extent of changes required • Availability of technology
Obstacles	• What are the challenges, problems and issues we need to overcome in order to complete our methods and achieve the future vision?
The Team And Schedule	• Who will be involved in doing the work? • Who will contribute to the work? • Who will review the work? • How will the core and extended teams operate? • How long will it take? • What are we going to produce?
Ground Rules	• What are the ground rules for the work: • Communications – what is the message? How do we communicate? How will we be communicated with? Who communicates outside the team? • Reporting - who reports to whom? • Review and quality – what is the process for checking and validating analyses and results?

Table 37 – Introductory Workshop Topics

4.6.1.4.6 Step 0.6 Define Team and Facilities Required

This step involves the following activities:

• Determine the required competencies/skills/experience of core team

• Create engagement delivery standards and templates.

• Agree and document communication process

• Agree and document work delivery process including artefact creation and review

• Acquire facilities

• Conduct team building and introductory round table session

This team building and introductory round table session will include:

- Describe engagement, its objectives and deliverables
- Describe the known work programme and schedule
- Describe the planned work delivery process
- Describe the participants, stakeholders, organisation structure
- Define team roles, relationships and structures
- Understand team members' experience and knowledge
- Define internal and external communication processes
- Define principles of operation such as:
  o Document all interactions with extended team to avoid confusion and doubt later
  o Information gathering needs to be timeboxed
- Define work delivery standards, performance, accountability and processes
- Detail internal and external meeting schedule including daily stand-ups
- Detail the team decision-making process
- Describe the boundaries:
  o Between groups within the engagement team
  o Between external stakeholders and participants
- Document team charter

4.6.1.4.7 Step 0.7 Create Table of Contents (Scope) of Engagement Deliverable

This step involves creating an initial draft table of contents of the analysis and report that will be generated from the business architecture engagement.

The table of contents is effectively a high-level work breakdown structure for the set of activities needed to create the deliverable.

The engagement should aim to generate a comprehensive deliverable that describes where the business function or organisation wants to be and how this can be achieved. It does not have to be lengthy. It can be supported and supplemented by the other artefacts created during the engagement.

The table of contents could consist of:

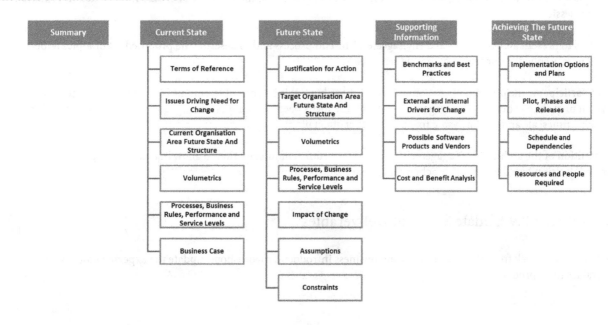

Figure 112 – Sample Table of Contents for Architecture Engagement Main Deliverable

The possible chapters and sections are:

Chapter	Section
Summary	
Current State	• Terms of Reference • Issues Driving Need for Change • Current Organisation Area Future State And Structure • Volumetrics • Processes, Business Rules, Performance and Service Levels • Business Case
Future State	• Justification for Action • Target Organisation Area Future State And Structure • Volumetrics • Processes, Business Rules, Performance and Service Levels • Impact of Change • Assumptions • Constraints
Supporting Information	• Benchmarks and Best Practices • External and Internal Drivers for Change • Possible Software Products and Vendors • Cost and Benefit Analysis
Supporting Information	• Implementation Options and Plans • Pilot, Phases and Releases • Schedule and Dependencies • Resources and People Required

Table 38 – Sample Table of Contents for Architecture Engagement Main Deliverable

4.6.1.4.8 Step 0.8 Conduct Introductory Workshop(s)

The introductory workshops with the business participants are aimed at initiating the project and setting expectations. These are designed to introduce the engagement based on the scope agreed with the sponsor. There are not detailed information collection sessions.

The aim is to present an overview of the envisaged end-to-end process and to describe the proposed set of topics to be covered in subsequent information gathering sessions.

It gives participants the opportunity to comment and contribute. It is important to emphasise that the approach and workplan may change during the engagement and that the focus needs to be on producing quality deliverables within a reasonable timescale and not analysing to a minute level of detail.

The intention of the architecture engagement is to produce sufficient information to allow business management to make an informed decision based on the likely achievable and realistic options.

4.6.1.4.9 Step 0.9 Update Scope of Deliverables

Based on the feedback from the various team and business introductory workshops, update the expected scope of the deliverables to be produced.

4.6.1.5 Business Engagement Activity 1. Information Collection And Assessment

The possible steps for activity *Information Collection And Assessment* are:

Figure 113 – Steps Within Business Engagement Activity *1. Information Collection And Assessment*

These steps are documented in more detail below:

  1.1 Current Business Review
  1.2 Assess Customer (Or External Party) Perceptions
  1.3 Review Current Industry Best Practices And Technology Changes
  1.4 Analyse Current Business Systems
  1.5 Analyse Available Solutions And Products

4.6.1.5.1 Step 1.1 Current Business Review

This step involves gathering information on the structure and operation of existing organisation or function operations including locations, if this is relevant.

The objective is to have sufficient information on current operations and business processes to understand any performance and operational issues. The existing business processes should be identified and documented at a high-level, if process documentation does not already exist. The purpose here is not to create process documentation but to understand the operation of the processes.

The organisation or function structure, locations and its interactions with internal and external parties should be defined.

Create a model for the existing structure of the function. For each unit within the structure of the function, if relevant, and for the function itself, identify the following:

- Roles, positions, levels/grades, functions, responsibilities, key personnel
- Decision making processes
- Work groups, work organisation, work types, work allocation and distribution, work volumes
- Business processes operated, level and currency of documentation
- Performance, throughput, service levels, monitoring and reporting
- Technology used and staff opinion of technology
- Relationships between work groups and functions
- Interactions with other business functions
- Interactions with external product or service delivery partners
- Staff engagement, staff awareness of issues
- Issues and problems
- Any existing planned changes, their reason and status

Examine the support processes and the associated solutions:

- Work allocation and planning systems - How is work allocated, recorded and workload planned for
- Learning management - Examine staff training processes and approaches and how are business processes linked to training and skills and experience
- Time recording and management
- Performance recognition and reward - How are good staff performance identified, recognised and rewarded and how is poor performance handled
- Personnel development and talent management - What is the approach to staff development and progression
- Staff communications - Evaluate how staff are communicated with and how information is disseminated

If relevant, document each business or function location that comes under the scope of the engagement. Define the location type: office, distribution, storage, service, sales. Describe details about the location including size, number of staff, facilities.

Look at the business processes that govern how work is performed and their business rules. This involves documenting existing business processes and associated rules at a high-level. The detail may (or may not) come later but only if it is relevant and useful to the engagement. It is also not concerned with redesigning existing processes. This may also come later.

Identify core business processes categories or groups of processes that contribute to the performance of the same types of work. Document the major processes within each process category or group. This should include:

- What causes the process to be initiated?
- What information is required and where does it come from?
- What are the outcomes of the process?
- What are the key metrics about each process: time to complete, errors and rework, cost, resources and skills required, systems used?
- How is process performance recorded and reported on?
- What rules and decision-making are applied to process operations?
- What restrictions, limitations and implied assumptions are applied to each process?
- Where are the manual steps and handoffs?
- What process documentation exists and how does it differ from the actual process as performed?

For each process category, answer the following questions:

- What work areas do not map to existing defined business processes?

- What processes are shared between or performed at multiple locations?

- What processes rely on external involvement and what is that involvement?

- Where are processes and rules automated?

Review and create an inventory of all systems and applications that are used to perform or support the performance of work including:

- Core business applications
- Office support systems
- Reporting applications
- Analysis applications
- Data structures
- Level of automation
- Manual workarounds used with business applications
- Documentation and its currency for each application
- Staff satisfaction with each application

4.6.1.5.2 Step 1.2 Assess Customer (Or External Party) Perceptions

If the business function that is the subject of the architecture engagement is involved in the provision of products and services to customers or external parties (such as partners, suppliers or regulators), identify some representative customers (or external parties) that interact with the business function and that agree to be contacted to discuss their interactions and experiences. For each of these look to gather details on the following:

- Products or services used or acquired
- How much, how frequently
- Alternatives evaluated – both supplier and products or services
- Experiences of interactions and level of satisfaction
- Experiences of products or services and level of satisfaction
- Overall perception of organisation or business function
- Overall satisfaction
- Importance of organisation to customer
- Desired performance
- Views of how the organisation or business function should change or can improve
- Views of how the products or services should change or can improve

The purpose here is to understand how the organisation and its products and services are perceived:

- What products and services are used by the customer?
- How are the products and services are used in customers' businesses?
- What business issues do these customer face in using the products and services?
- How do the products and services enable customers' businesses succeed?
- What do customers like?
- What do customers not like?

The goal is to understand what your customers (external parties) want, how they perceive you and what you are capable of. Customers (external parties) generally want the organisation to demonstrate a mix of one, two or three core values:

1. *Understanding and Closeness (Enhancement)* – demonstrate and act on customer knowledge and offer customised products and services to meet those exact needs

2. *Product and Service Operational Excellence (Efficiency/Utility)* – provide reliable, convenient, easy-to-use, cost-effective, value for money products and services

3. *Product and Service Innovation and Leadership (Transformational)* – offer products and services that are better, more innovative, technologically advanced than others

Figure 114 – What Customers Want

Identify the issues customers (external parties) encounter during business interactions:

- Access to information
- Quality of information
- Access to person
- Speed and quality of response
- Provision of response
- Ease of ordering products and services
- Order status
- Product and service delivery
- Product and service utility
- Price, billing
- Accuracy and rework
- Query and error handling and resolution

Use the previously identified process groups to identify the points where these issues and problems arise.

4.6.1.5.3 Step 1.3 Review Current Industry Best Practices And Technology Changes

The objective of this step is to understand how comparable organisations achieve better performance.

Review best practices within the industry area in which the organisation or business function operates and identify other organisations that excel in similar areas.

Review what other competing organisations use and how their performance compares.

Review business trends.

Review solutions and technologies that are available to support operation and their providers.

Review technology trends affecting these solutions and technologies and the business trends.

This should involve:

- Reviewing organisations offering similar products and services

- Review organisations that excel in specific areas and that do not necessarily offer similar products and services

These areas can include some or all of:

- Customer service
- Brand development
- Innovation
- Cost reduction
- Sales
- Similar complexity of operation, products or services
- Supply chain management
- Efficiency, performance, throughput for numbers of staff
- Quality control, errors
- Use of technology
- Use of resources
- Organisation structure

Look for excellence in the previously identified core process categories. Identify how that excellence is achieved and what the previous state was, if possible. Examine the what – results and outcomes achieved – and the how. Use the information to identify possible new approaches and options to operate the core processes.

There are many possible source of best practice information such as:

- Search of publications and articles
- Industry experts
- Consulting organisations
- Direct contacts
- Industry groups
- Supplier experience
- Relevant industry associations
- Employees' previous experience
- Customers' (external party) experience with other organisations

You could consider using services of professional survey organisation if time and budget allow and if the scope of the work justifies it.

Classify the results of the best practice analysis using the previously identified process categories and other analysis factors:

- Customer service
- Brand development
- Innovation
- Cost reduction
- Sales
- Similar complexity of operation, products or services
- Supply chain management
- Efficiency, performance, throughput for numbers of staff
- Quality control, errors
- Use of technology including externally hosted solutions
- Use of resources
- Organisation structure

Identify those organisations that achieve more and determine the gaps between the two organisations.

Quantify the differences and describe the reasons for the difference.

For the technology trends review, determine what new technologies are available and how commercially available these new technologies are.

How can these new technologies be applied within the organisation?

How are other organisations using new technologies?

Who are the vendors offering these new technologies?

4.6.1.5.4 Step 1.4 Analyse Current Business Systems

Examine the business system and technology landscape, data and communications infrastructure of the organisation, including externally used solutions.

Determine the major data stores:

- Subject area(s)
- Underlying applications
- Data source(s)
- Data types and formats
- Size, amount of data, number of transactions
- Technology and its currency
- Data quality issues
- Value and utility to the business
- Year of implementation, year of last major upgrade/update

Create logical entity diagram(s) that identify key data topics or classes. Data topics are logical groups of data that relate to the same subject. Document the high-level contents of each data topic. Identify relationships and linkages between data topics. This is useful in understanding the data topic landscape and connections.

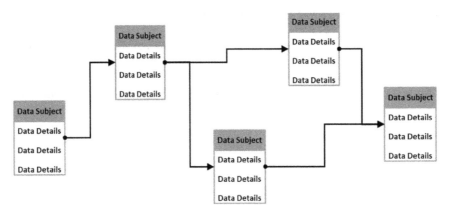

Figure 115 – Data Relationship Diagram

Create an inventory of solutions and applications that are in use. Describe their technology basis – product/custom-developed, software used, technical infrastructure.

Detail the core functions provided by the systems and applications. Link the solutions and applications and their functions to the core process categories and their constituent processes.

Describe the state of these systems and applications in terms of:

- Fitness for purpose and suitability for current business operations
- Value to the business
- Manual workarounds and manual handoffs to other systems
- Ease of use and usefulness
- Goodness of fit for planned and known future business changes
- Efficiency of operations
- User experiences of the system
- Level and currency of documentation and training material
- Volume of work, number of users, number of transactions
- Year of implementation, year of last major upgrade/update
- Internal or hosted

Evaluate the technical state of the solutions and applications in terms of:

- Reliability
- Availability
- Compliance with technical standards
- Compliance with data regulations
- Flexibility and ease of modification
- Vendor plans for packaged applications
- Version in use and current versions supported by vendor
- Issues with technical infrastructures - for example, operating system and database versions
- Cost of operations, support and maintenance
- Fitness and appropriateness as a platform for future developments
- Compliance with organisation IT architecture standards

Create a diagram showing the communications infrastructural components, including any network, and their relationships. Identify major elements of the infrastructure including:

- External hosting and communications links
- Internal infrastructure – server operating systems, databases
- Security
- Application access
- User access devices

Based on the review of business solutions and applications, create a four-state classification based on two factors:

1. Value to the business
2. State of application and underlying technology and vendor

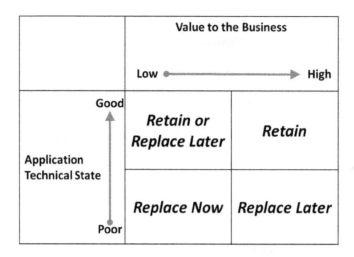

Figure 116 – Business Solution Classification

The extremes of the combinations of the two classifications are:

1. Application Technical State *Poor* Value to the Business *Low* = Replace Now - These applications need to be replaced or retired and their data converted to new platforms.

2. Application Technical State *Good* Value to the Business *Low* = Retain or Replace Later - These applications may be considered for replacement in the future or may be retained depending on the target business architecture, the associated technology architecture and the systems needs to support its operation.

3. Application Technical State *Poor* Value to the Business *High* = Replace Later - These applications should be flagged for replacement in the future.

4. Application Technical State *Good* Value to the Business *High* = Retain - These applications should be retained unless there are better options readily available that can be implemented easily and quickly with minimum disruption.

In reality, business solutions will not fit neatly into the extreme ends of the two classification ranges and so some judgement will be required regarding the positioning those applications.

4.6.1.5.5 Step 1.5 Analyse Available Solutions And Products

The objective of this step is to evaluate possible options for those business solutions and applications - packaged, in-house or hosted or custom development – that were flagged for replacement, now or in the future.

This is a high-level evaluation and sense-check that possible solution options including both products and custom development are likely to meet key requirements. The focus should be on products where possible.

The scope of this step is to not conduct a full procurement process. It is concerned with identifying sources of possible sets of product information and preparing vendor contact approaches including technical and business questionnaires to understand the suitability of their products. For public sector organisations, a different and more limited approach to vendor contacts may apply.

Define the high-level functional requirements based on functionality provided by current solutions targeted for replacement and likely future business requirements not currently provided.

Define the high-level operational and solution delivery requirements such as capacity, throughput, number of users, volume of data, availability, resilience and other quality characteristics – see 4.6.4.7 on page 251 for more information on this.

The vendor contact questionnaire should include at least the following points:

- Vendor details – company size, duration in business, product details, numbers of installations of product, maturity of product
- Compliance with functional requirements
- Compliance with operational requirements
- Security model
- Product delivery options
- Customer satisfaction scores
- Implementation project resources and timescale
- Service management and support
- Outline financial analysis – initial cost, maintenance, cost of ownership

At the end of this, summarise the information gathered from vendors, comparing solutions across key requirement and evaluation factors.

4.6.1.6 Business Engagement Activity 2. Define Vision, Business Principles And System Principles

The possible steps for activity *Define Vision, Business Principles And System Principles* are:

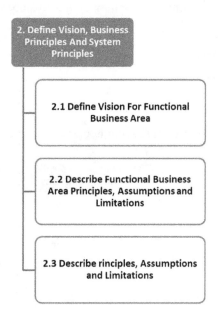

Figure 117 – Steps Within Business Engagement Activity *2. Define Vision, Business Principles And System Principles*

These steps are documented in more detail below:

> 2.1 Define Vision For Functional Business Area
> 2.2 Describe Functional Business Area Principles, Assumptions and Limitations
> 2.3 Describe System Principles, Assumptions and Limitations

4.6.1.6.1 Step 2.1 Define Vision For Functional Business Area

The vision is a high-level description of the desired future architecture and operating structure of the organisation or business function. It is concerned with the desired future state and not, at this stage, how that state can be achieved. It represents an ideal view of what the future should be. There can be more than one vision or alternative versions of the same vision.

The vision is defined, refined and enhanced iterate using various activities:

- Create initial vision based on information known so far – this forms the basis for discussions
- Tools such as the Business Model Canvas
- Key stakeholder interviews
- Vision workshop
- Rich pictures

It is then communicated to participants.

The vision is the means for articulating the target of the architecture engagement. It can be used externally (outside the engagement team) to communicate what the engagement is concerned with and internally (within the team) it can be used to organise and focus work effort and to define the boundaries of the work.

Create a starting vision based on consolidated information collected and analysed. Separate the *What* of the vision from the *How* of its realisation.

The vision should contain the following elements.

- The expected environment in which the organisation or business function operates

    o   Products and services provided
    o   Customer segments supplied
    o   Physical distribution
    o   Competitors
    o   Economy

- The business function operating model in terms of its future core business process groups and constituent business processes

    o   Structure of the business function core operating domains
    o   Organisation structure and operation
    o   Supporting and enabling technology

Use scenarios and process journeys to walk through the internal and external operations for key business activities and detail their flow. Develop inventory of key scenarios and process journeys. The approach breathes life into the operating model and can be used to determine its validity and to identify potential inconsistencies. Describe alternatives and options where relevant. Identify differences and divergences in the information collected. Define the choices and decisions to be made to clarify the vision.

The following table lists some factors to be considered when developing the initial vision:

Factor	Questions
Products and Services	<ul><li>What products and services do we supply</li><li>How many types do we supply?</li><li>How are they different from those of other organisations?</li><li>How do we deliver the products and services?</li><li>How do we develop and enhance them?</li></ul>
Customers	<ul><li>Who do we provide products and services to?</li><li>How broad is the range of customers?</li><li>Why do customers acquire our products and services?</li></ul>

Suppliers and Partners	• Who are our suppliers and partners? • How do we work with them? • How many are there?
Competition	• Who do we compete with? • How do we compete? • How well do we compete? • How are we different from our competitors? • How is competition changing?
Regulatory Landscape	• What is the regulatory landscape? • How compliant are we with regulations? • How is it changing?
Business Processes	• How well defined are our business processes? • How optimised, integrated, efficient and automated are they? • How well do they work in terms of cost and time to operate? • How do we measure performance?
Organisation	• What is our organisation structure? • Who does what? • What does it cost to operate? • How is the organisation operated and managed? • How do we recognise and reward talent and performance?
Locations and Facilities	• Where do we operate from? • How many types of locations do we have?
Solutions, Systems, Data and Technology	• What are the key business systems? • How well do they meet the needs of the organisation? • How well integrated are they? • What is the state of the organisation's technology infrastructure? • Can customers and suppliers interact with the organisations using technology? • How well do we manage data?

Table 39 – Vision Development Factors

Consider using the Business Model Canvass[38] approach to describe the vision for the functional business area. This consists of a structure that expresses the core principles and value proposition of a business in nine elements that are contained in four groups:

1. *Infrastructure*
    o *Key Partners* - the key partners and suppliers needed to achieve the business model
    o *Key Activities* - the most important activities the business must perform to ensure the business model works
    o *Key Resources* - the most important assets to make the business model work
2. *Offering*
    o *Value Propositions* - the value, products and services provided to the customer
3. *Customers*
    o *Customer Relationships* - the customer relationships that need to be created
    o *Channels* - the channels through which the business reaches its customers
    o *Customer Segments* - the types of customers being targeted by the business model
4. *Finances*
    o *Cost Structure* - the most important costs incurred by the business model
    o *Revenue Streams* - the sources through which the business model gets revenue from customers

---

[38] The Business Model Canvas was developed by Alexander Osterwalder. The concept was originally published at https://nonlinearthinking.typepad.com/nonlinear_thinking/2008/07/the-business-model-canvas.html. It followed on from his earlier work ***The Business Model Ontology - A Proposition In A Design Science Approach*** http://www.hec.unil.ch/aosterwa/PhD/Osterwalder_PhD_BM_Ontology.pdf.

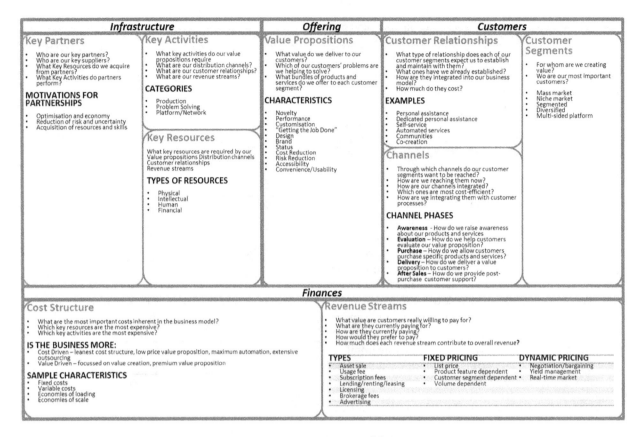

Figure 118 – Business Model Canvass

Identify the key stakeholders who are important to the achievement of the target from the architecture engagement or who know about the business environment. These can be:

- Business executives and heads of business functions
- Those involved in developing business strategy
- Those involved in analysing business and market trends

Prepare structured interview notes using previously documented vision factors and tools such as the business model canvas. Gather information from key stakeholders using structured one-to-one interviews. These will provide hard and soft information:

- Hard – facts, numbers, detail
- Soft – stakeholder level of interest, engagement, commitment and enthusiasm, possible resistance, amount and quality of information provided

Collect information from multiple stakeholders to get different perspectives. Document the information collected and circulate to the stakeholders for review and comments.

Conduct one or more vision workshops. Their purpose is to present the initial consolidated vision, alternatives, differences and decisions for review and elaboration.

Again, separate the *What* of the vision from the *How* of its actualisation. The *How* is a constraint that can be addressed later.

At this stage, a detailed analysis and discussion can be counter-productive. The goal is to achieve (some) consensus on the vision and to create a netted list of disagreements and differences.

Present the information collected using the previous structures and frameworks:

- Scenarios and process journeys
- Vision factors and business model canvas
- Use pictures and diagrams

The topic of rich pictures is discussed in section 4.6.4.6 on page 249. They are (more or less) detailed visualisations that represent information more effectively than lengthy narrative text. Pictures are more easily understood and engaged with and are better tools to elicit information from people. They assist informed discussions. The show relationships and interactions between key entities. They provide a more concise illustration of operations.

Evolve and refine rich picture representations of as-in and to-be situations throughout the engagement exercise.

Rich pictures are not systematic views (yet). They do not contain solution and system-related components such as IT applications, infrastructure and data flows at this stage. These are resolution and implementation-related elements. Resist the temptation to include systematic parts at the investigation stage and pre-judge options for resolution and transformation. We are looking at transformation with a small "t" here. Jumping to conclusions at this stage will limit the scope of information gathered and prejudge resolution options.

Recall that one of the solution component types that comprise the complete solution picture described in section 2.4 on page 33 is Organisational Changes. Any solution will involve some changes to the organisation such as new personnel required to operate the solution and the associated new or changed business processes, deployed existing personnel, changes in business function structure and new skills and experience required.

The exploratory and consulting nature of the architecture engagement means that organisational changes will have a greater part in the target architecture than a pure solution design engagement where a solution is being specified. Achieving the ultimate target architecture is likely to involve some form of organisation change. The required changes may be resisted by some affected stakeholders and other individuals or the organisation itself may be unable to accommodate change. It is important to identify potential blockers early in the business architecture engagement and to continue this throughout the engagement. The recommended actions to address these blockers in order to enable the required change to occur need to be defined. This may be outside the normal skills and experience of the solution architecture function. The solution architect should define the options for these changes. Their achievement can be left to others.

The solution architect can assist with these actions:

- Supporting those that in favour of change
- Identifying and addressing the objections of those who resist change
- Articulating the new culture that will facilitate change
- Defining the change message and communicating the need for change
- Assembling suitable business representatives into a change forum to whom the progress of the engagement and the benefits of change
- Collecting, co-ordinating and responding to feedback
- Creating a communications portal with information that affirms the need for change

The performance of these actions should be led by the engagement sponsor.

4.6.1.6.2 Step 2.2 Describe Functional Business Area Principles, Assumptions and Limitations

This step is concerned with defining the principles, assumptions and limitations for the overall business function and for each of the core business domains. The use of the words *Principles*, *Assumptions* and *Limitations* is interchangeable. Their definitive categorisation is not important at this stage. Just capture them for now.

Principles are values, core beliefs, standards, guidelines, rules, regulations, laws and directions that underpin and govern the overall organisation or business function. Assumptions are used as the basis for decisions. Assumptions need to be validated because they can be incorrect. Limitations are constraints that narrow the range of resolution options and the scope of actions that can be taken.

Figure 119 – Principles, Limitations and Assumptions Across Core Business Domains.

There will also be principles, assumptions and limitations for the extended business domains described in section 4.6.1.1 on page 161 that should be captured.

Principles, assumptions and limitations affect the target vision. Understanding them is important to creating a realistic and achievable vision that meets the needs of the organisation. Information on principles, assumptions and limitations can be initially gathered through a focussed and dedicated workshop. They should be refined and expanded on throughout the engagement.

4.6.1.6.3 Step 2.3 Describe System Principles, Assumptions and Limitations

The step is concerned with describing the usage of solution, applications and systems, technology and data and not the detail of their construction and underlying technologies. It is about describing an external rather than internal view.

- Applications and Systems

  - Current application and system selection, design, operation principles – rules that define usage and actions
  - User interfaces and interaction
  - Integration
  - Constraints that limit operation and use
  - Assumptions on the applications and systems – extendibility, growth, deployment and usage in different ways
  - Who manages and supports

- Information and Data

    - Who and how acquires, owns, uses, manages
    - Limitations
    - Assumptions on data – quality, integration, redundancy

- Technology and Infrastructure

    - Current technology and infrastructure organisation, selection, design, operation principles – rules that define usage and actions
    - Security
    - Standards and compliance
    - Limitations
    - Assumptions on technology and infrastructure – suitability, capacity, growth, adaptability
    - Who manages and supports

Describe the current and target business process principles, assumptions and limitations using a structure along the following lines:

- Principles

    - Process optimisation through compression of work and collapse of roles
    - Include parallel processing
    - Automation as much as possible
    - Decision by exception rather included in the normal processing path than in all cases
    - Cross-functional teams
    - Process information gathering, reporting, analysis and optimisation

- Assumptions

    - Number of people available to process work
    - Number of work items

- Limitations

    - Volumes and levels of process workload
    - Temporal variation in workload
    - Skills required

Describe the current and target organisation and structure principles, assumptions and limitations using a structure along the following lines:

- Principles

    - Organisation structure, hierarchy, reporting
    - Allocation and handling of work
    - How do we want to interact with partners, suppliers, customers

- Assumptions

    - Number of people in each function and role
    - Skills and experience required

- Limitations

    - Numbers of new staff, retraining

- o What limitations apply to organisation change
- o What is the regulatory environment

Describe the current and target locations and offices principles, assumptions and limitations using a structure along the following lines:

- Principles

  - o Number and type of locations and offices
  - o Consolidation of locations and offices as required
  - o Location of work processing

- Assumptions

  - o Size and quality of locations and offices
  - o Costs of locations and offices

- Limitations

  - o Restrictions on options to consolidate locations and offices
  - o Restrictions on options to relocate staff
  - o Restrictions on availability of suitable locations and offices

Present the previously defined vision and information collected during business review across the core six business domains:

- Location and Offices
- Business Processes
- Organisation and Structure
- Technology, Infrastructure and Communications
- Applications and Systems
- Information and Data

Use these structures to validate and refine these principles, assumptions and limitations.

Refer also to the extended business domains if necessary.

4.6.1.7 Business Engagement Activity 3. Document Business Processes, Entity Model, Capacity Planning And Solution Approach

The possible steps for activity *Document Business Processes, Entity Model, Capacity Planning And Solution Approach* are:

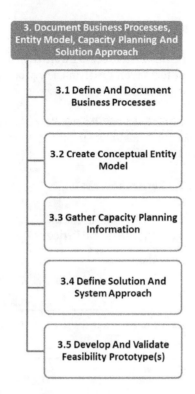

Figure 120 – Steps Within Business Engagement Activity *3. Document Business Processes, Entity Model, Capacity Planning And Solution Approach*

These steps are documented in more detail below:

> 3.1 Define And Document Business Processes
> 3.2 Create Conceptual Entity Model
> 3.3 Gather Capacity Planning Information
> 3.4 Define Solution And System Approach
> 3.5 Develop And Validate Feasibility Prototype(s)

4.6.1.7.1 Step 3.1 Define And Document Business Processes

The objective of this step is the design of the target business processes. Processes are important because they reflect and represent what the organisation does and how it does it. This can be based on the redesign of existing processes to make them more efficient and effective or it can involve the definition of entirely new business processes that replace existing ones.

The importance of business processes to solution design is discussed in section 4.4.2 on page 134. The information contained in that section and the approach to business process analysis can be used here.

This step can be quite lengthy, depending on the extent of the engagement and the number and complexity of existing and new business processes involved. It covers the following work:

- Create business process change/design inventory
- Define process attributes
- Identify existing process enhancements and improvements
- Define the core set of business processes required to operate the target architecture
- Define the target architecture process model
- Create extended process definition
- Define and validate the projected performance characteristics

- Identify and describe the management and support processes

Redesign of existing processes is usually termed ***Business Process Improvement (BPI)***. This is concerned with designing a new process to achieve the desired outputs. The focus is on specifying new processes to replace existing ones so less detail on existing processes needs to be collected.

Design of new business processes is usually termed ***Business Process Redesign (BPR)***. This is concerned with modifying existing process to identify, reduce or eliminate problems and to improve performance. The focus is on collecting detailed information on existing processes so they can be improved.

The two approaches can be used in tandem for different processes.

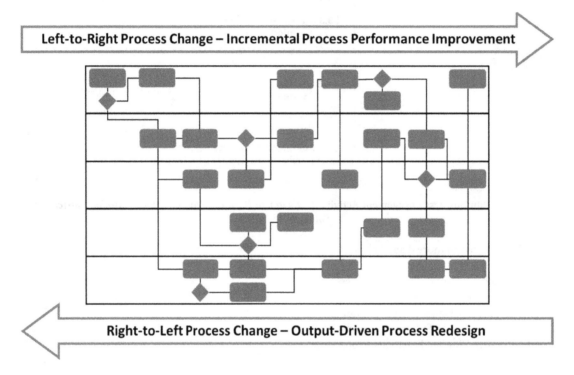

Figure 121 – Right-to-Left BPI and Left-to-Right BPR

BPI can be viewed as left-to-right business process changes. You are working through the operation of existing processes, identifying opportunities and options for changes and improvements.

BPR can be viewed as right-to-left process changes. You are starting with a set of outputs, results and deliverables and are defining the optimum new business process to achieve them.

This section will not cover business process design in detail. The importance of business processes to the design of a complete solution and the approach to business process analysis are discussed in section 4.4.2 on page 134. That section should be read in conjunction with this section.

This step in the architecture engagement is not concerned with detailed process analysis and the design of new processes. It is concerned with documenting processes in sufficient detail to allow problems and resolution to be identified.

Processes can be described to ever more levels of detail.

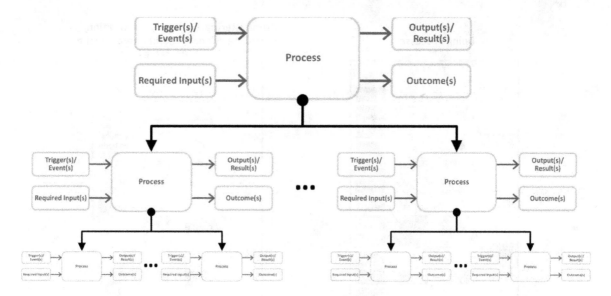

Figure 122 – Process Decomposition

Processes should be decomposed to an appropriate level of detail to gather the required information, and no more.

The focus here is to create and agree an inventory of triggers and events to which the business function reacts and responds and the identification of any new triggers and events required by new/changed processes.

Create and agree an inventory of outputs and results generated in response to triggers and events by process activities. Identify any new outputs and results required by new/changed processes

Create and agree an inventory of outcomes influenced, achieved or desired in response to triggers and events by process activities. Identify any new outcomes desired by new/changed processes.

Create and agree an inventory of key process activities. Identify any new activities required by new/changed processes Decompose large monolithic activities into smaller more granular representations of key process activities

In any organisation and business function, there will be two sets of processes:

1. The processes that do the value-adding work

2. The processes that relate to management and administration of the doing processes and of the business function operations

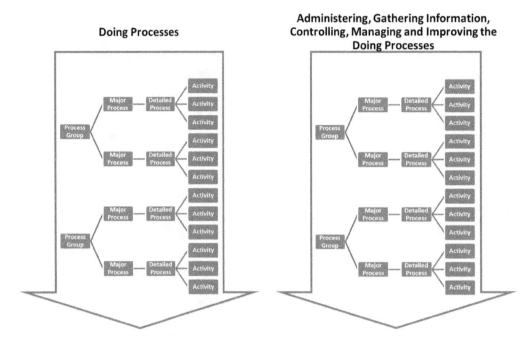

Figure 123 – Doing and Managing Processes

The analysis should focus on the doing processes. The management and support processes can be left to one side for now.

For each of the current key processes, create a process flow description/map at enough detail to ensure it can be understood. Describe the existing process at sufficient level to allow problems, issues and opportunities for improvement to be identified. Existing process analysis is more important for BPI than for BPR exercises. Create an inventory of key processes and the associated issues and opportunities for improvement.

Describe the current and future target process activity performance attributes. Not all process activities will share all performance attributes. For example, some processes that result in the supply of products may require an inventory level to be available and some form of re-ordering trigger when the inventory falls below a threshold. Performance attribute is one that has a cost, direct or indirect. Detail the current and future targeted/desired/expected performance characteristics.

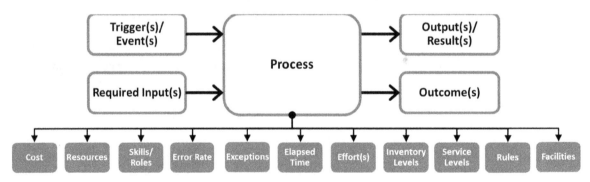

Figure 124 – Process Attributes

The types of process attributes to be defined include:

- *Cost* – how much does the process cost to operate
- *Resources* – what resources/operators are required to operate the process and its steps? What resources are involved in the process?
- *Skills/Roles* – what skills and experience are required to operate the process and its steps? What roles are associated with the process?

- *Exceptions* – what exceptions occur to normal, straight-through processing? How are exceptions identified and handled?
- *Error Rate* – how many errors occur during processing? What are the error types and causes?
- *Elapsed Time* – what is the elapsed time from process start to end?
- *Effort(s)* – how much work of what types is required to operate the process?
- *Inventory Levels* – does the process require any product inventory and, if so, what?
- *Service Levels* – what service levels, if any, apply to the operation of the process?
- *Rules* – what rules does the process implement?
- *Facilities* – what facilities does the process require?

Some of these process attributes may not be known or easily discovered. For example, many organisations do not know the cost of their processes. Where this information is not available, it should be estimated quickly rather than effort and time being expended to extract it.

Identify the roles required for the target processes and the associated skills, experience, education, training and competencies needed to perform them. Include hard and soft skills. This information will be used to design the target organisation structure.

Define the business function location types required to operate the new target processes, if relevant.

Analyse the performance of the existing processes and determine the value they create. Extend the previous business process flow analysis by adding performance and value dimensions.

Provides a target list for enhancements:

- Longest process and process step elapsed time
- Longest process and process step elapsed time relative to processing time
- Greatest number of handoffs
- Processes and process steps with largest number of steps
- Processes and process steps crossing organisation functional boundaries
- Processes and process steps with data quality issues
- Processes and process steps with errors and rework
- Processes and process steps that do not add value
- Processes and process steps experiencing delays in getting responses to requests, internal or external

Use the list of types of wastes (see section 4.4.2 on page 134) to identify most wasteful processes and process steps and thus the top opportunities for improvement.

Define the core set of business processes required to achieve the desired results and outputs for the target architecture. At this stage assume there are no constraints in skills, resources, technology, external interactions or locations. These can be added later. Create an inventory of these core business processes.

Define the target architecture process model. Define the new/redesigned target processes and process steps. There can be many options when defining the new/changed processes. These options can involve organisation change such as:

- Case management approach with assigned case workers
- Team-based processing
- Upskilling teams
- Elimination of cross-functional handoffs
- Automation and technology changes
- Personnel relocation
- Outsourcing
- Integration with external parties

Other changes can include:

- Introduction of parallel processing
- Work prioritisation
- Automated decision making
- Compression of steps
- Collapsing of roles
- Eliminating unnecessary inspections
- Removal of unnecessary steps added for historical reasons to address exceptions and complexity

The focus here is on ensuring that processes add value and on reducing unnecessary process cost.

Then extend the definition of the new/redesigned target processes and process steps with details on:

- The roles that perform them
- When the work is performed
- What supporting solutions and technology are used or required to perform the work

Create a matrix of this extended process definition.

Role	Role 1						Role 2						Role 3					
Technology	Technology 1			Technology 2			Technology 1			Technology 2			Technology 1			Technology 2		
Location	Loc 1	Loc 2	Loc 3	Loc 1	Loc 2	Loc 3	Loc 1	Loc 2	Loc 3	Loc 1	Loc 2	Loc 3	Loc 1	Loc 2	Loc 3	Loc 1	Loc 2	Loc 3
Process Step 1																		
Process Step 2																		
Process Step 3																		
Process Step 4																		
...																		
Process Step N																		

Figure 125 – Extended Process Definition

Define the projected performance characteristics of the future process state. Validate the performance by walking through the processes.

There may be more than one set of future state process options. If so, each needs to be considered with respect to characteristics such as:

- Time to implement
- Likely cost
- Resources required
- Probability of success and risk of failure
- Degree of organisation change and expected amount of disruption caused
- Degree to which the improvement objectives will be achieved

Use these factors to determine the most suitable option or subset of options.

Identify the management processes required to administer, manage and assess the performance of the target future state processes using the steps:

- Collect, analyse and take action on process performance information.
- Measure the satisfaction of the process beneficiary
- Assess process quality, rework and error rate
- Review process cost

There will be general management processes across all operational processes and specific management processes for specific operational processes.

4.6.1.7.2 Step 3.2 Create Conceptual Entity Model

Create an inventory of entities involved the operation of the business function covered by the engagement and how it can deliver its products and services.

Entities are objects about which data is stored and processed. They are people, functions, events, products and can include:

- Business roles and organisation functions involved in the work
- External parties contributing to the products and services
- Products and services
- Beneficiaries of the work done by the business function
- Offices and locations

The conceptual entity model is effectively an Entity Relationship Diagram (ERD). This results in a picture of data flows and interactions within the business function.

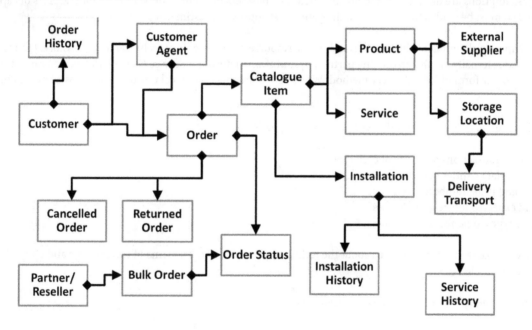

Figure 126 – Sample Entity Relationship Diagram for Conceptual Model

The tasks involved in creating the ERD are:

- Identify the types and groups of entities and the individual entities of each type
- Describe each entity briefly and identify its main characteristic
- Define the interactions and relationships between the entities
- Define the direction and number of interactions and relationships
- Quantify the volumes of interactions
- Identify the major business rules associated with the interactions and relationships

4.6.1.7.3 Step 3.3 Gather Capacity Planning Information

The capacity requirements of a solution affect the design options. Solutions that must handle large volumes of work have very different design characteristics than those of solutions with much smaller throughput.

Capacity planning covers all aspects of business volumetric information such as:

- Technology
- Personnel
- Location
- Physical product production capacity
- Physical product storage capacity
- Physical product transportation capacity

Capacity and resource requirements can also vary according to various cycles and patterns of usage: daily, weekly, monthly and seasonally. Solutions should be sized to handle peak workloads. The required elasticity of the solution resources needs to be identified. This can be an influencing factor when considering a hosted solution or service where resource elasticity is much less expensive.

Capacity and resource usage information will affect overall system(s) performance and the choice of technology and ultimately the solution options. It is important that capacity planning information is reasonably accurate and that the underlying assumptions are understood and documented. The business may not understand technical aspects of capacity planning and so must be guided to an understanding and must approve the estimates produced.

Technology capacity planning involves understanding the resource requirements of technical infrastructure. Ultimately, this can be provided internally, by an outsourcing partner, by an Infrastructure as a Service (IaaS platform, by a hosted service provider some other form of XaaS delivery method. Whatever the method, technical resource usage costs and will be charged for.

Capacity planning metrics depend on the type of work being performed:

- Number of transactions or events of each type
- Number of data entities of each type
- Average and peak numbers
- Past and expected future growth rates
- Resource types to perform work types

Understand or make realistic assumptions about the technology resource requirements of transactions and entity data so the cost model can be understood.

Operation requirements will affect capacity requirements:

- Availability
- Response times
- Service levels
- Acceptable failure rate
- Recovery time

High operational requirements – highly available systems with very good and consistent response times – will affect resource requirements and cost. Therefore, you must understand the resource requirement impact of operational requirements.

Different elements of the overall operation of the business function will have different operational requirements. Externally facing applications will need to be more highly available than internal systems.

The business may not understand technical aspects of operational requirements and so must be guided to an understanding of the consequence of their requirements and must approve the estimates produced.

The business function will operate across different locations and location types, such as:

- Call centre
- Service centre
- Front office processing
- Middle office processing
- Back office processing
- Physical product storage and delivery

Each of these will also have different resource requirements and operational characteristics. You should look to create a resource entity model to understand the structure and volumes of resource consuming entities.

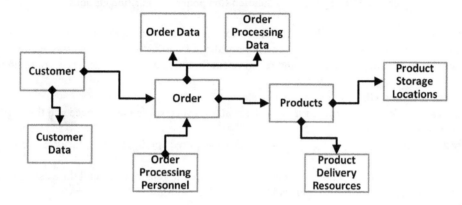

Figure 127 – Sample Resource Entity Model

Create a structured capacity planning model that captures inputs in terms of resource types and volumes and defines the rules used to translate inputs into system resources. Explicitly define assumptions in terms of:

- Growth in volumes of resource utilisation
- Operational requirements and their resource implications

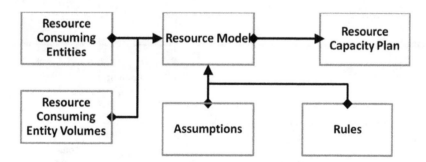

Figure 128 – Sample Capacity Planning Model View

The capacity planning model can be created as a spreadsheet.

Finally, review and agree the capacity plan with the business stakeholders.

4.6.1.7.4 Step 3.4 Define Solution And System Approach

Consider and decide on whether to include a solution product evaluation and determination activity at this stage. You may want to determine the characteristics of the software and system components of the overall solution in more detail before seeking to identify possible suitable products or there may be an overriding requirement to identify likely solutions to meet urgent requirements now.

Agree the approach to solution selection. Decide on whether to perform a parallel product and solution selection exercise.

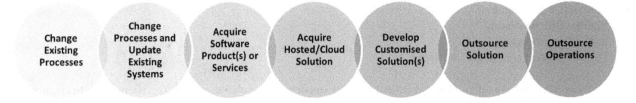

Figure 129 – Spectrum of Solution Component Acquisition Options

There is a spectrum of (not necessarily mutually exclusive) options available for acquiring the product and system components of the overall solution. Separate options can be considered for different components of the overall business function solution, subject to the integration issues and requirements being understood. These types of options include:

- *Change Existing Processes* – the way in which the systems are used can be changed
- *Change Processes and Update Existing Systems* – the business processes can be changed and the existing systems can be modified to provide new functions
- *Acquire Software Product(s) or Services* – a product can be acquired and installed on the organisation's technology infrastructure to replace or extend the existing systems
- *Acquire Hosted/Cloud Solution* – a hosted system can be acquired to replace or extend the existing systems
- *Develop Customised Solution(s)* – the organisation can develop new customised systems
- *Outsource Solution* – the provision of the solution can be outsourced to a service provider
- *Outsource Operations* – the entire set of business operations supported by the systems can be outsourced to a service provider who can use their own systems to deliver the service

Within these option types, there can be several realistic options:

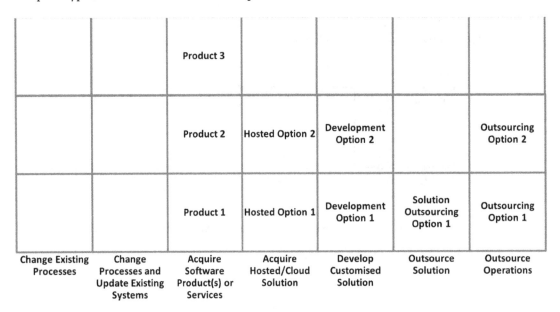

Change Existing Processes	Change Processes and Update Existing Systems	Acquire Software Product(s) or Services	Acquire Hosted/Cloud Solution	Develop Customised Solution	Outsource Solution	Outsource Operations
		Product 3				
		Product 2	Hosted Option 2	Development Option 2		Outsourcing Option 2
		Product 1	Hosted Option 1	Development Option 1	Solution Outsourcing Option 1	Outsourcing Option 1

Figure 130 – Combinations of Options

You need to keep the number of options to a small number.

One of the objectives of the architecture engagement is to reduce the set of options to a small number that are:

- Practical

- Realistic
- Achievable
- Affordable
- Usable
- Compliant with organisation strategy and principles
- Compliant with organisation's enterprise architecture
- Compliant with organisation's appetite for risk

The buy rather than build option affects financial estimates. Remember that the product or service acquisition, either product installed on premises or provided by a hosted service, cost is just one (small) component of the overall solution acquisition and implementation cost. The sources for cost estimates for product or service buy include:

- Issuing formal or informal RFP/RFS (request for proposal/request for solution)
- Previous experiences, either within the organisation or elsewhere
- Vendor contacts

Use indicative estimates if available. Do not spend too much time getting detailed costs at this stage. The issue of cost estimates is described in section 2.4.6 on page 44. There are lots of reasons for poor and inaccurate cost estimates. The topic of organisation biases and how they affect solution estimates including costs is detailed in section 3.1 on page 57.

There are techniques such as Reference Class Forecasting that can be used to improve accuracy in plans and projections by basing them on actual performance in a reference class of comparable solutions. Compare the proposed solution with the reference class distribution to establish the most likely outcome.

Cost estimation can be a painful process. There can be a tendency not to include all cost items. This does not make the costs go away. Accurate cost analysis and estimation are very important as they affect decision-making. You need to avoid problems with inaccurate cost forecasting such as:

- ***Strategic Misrepresentation*** – Deliberate misrepresentation in budgeting caused by distorted incentives
- ***Planning Fallacy*** – Systematic tendency to underestimate how long it will take to complete a task even when there is past experience of similar tasks over-running
- ***Optimism Bias*** – Systematic tendency to be overly optimistic about the outcome of actions

The key sets of factors in any decision include:

- Overall lifetime cost
- Risks associated with solution option
- Resources and time to implement
- Compliance with organisation's business strategy, IT strategy and enterprise architecture

Create a cost model that can be reviewed and updated during the engagement. The structure and detail of the cost model is as important as the cost values themselves. A good cost model reflects the source and structure of costs. It allows the costs to be known and understood. The amounts of each element within the cost model can be changed as more accurate information becomes known. Completely accurate information may not be available at this stage but the model can be created and partially populated. Identify the gaps and repeat the analysis when more certain information is available.

The following outlines the phases and steps of a generalised cost estimation process that can be used to create structured and evidence-based estimates for the system components of the solution.

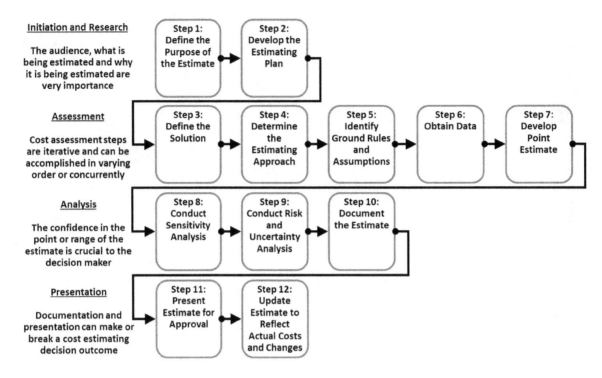

Figure 131 – Cost Estimation Process

This generalised process can be used as a structure to create good quality estimates. The steps in this process are:

Initiation and Research Phase

- Step 1: Define the Purpose of the Estimate

    o   Determine the estimate's purpose
    o   Determine the level of detail required
    o   Determine who will receive the estimate
    o   Determine the overall scope of the estimate

- Step 2: Develop the Estimating Plan

    o   Determine the cost estimating team
    o   Outline the cost estimating approach
    o   Develop the estimate timeline
    o   Determine who will do the independent cost estimate
    o   Develop the schedule

Assessment Phase

- Step 3: Define the Solution

    o   Identify in a technical baseline description document
    o   The purpose of the project
    o   Its system and performance characteristics
    o   Any technology implications
    o   Solution acquisition schedule
    o   Acquisition approach
    o   Relationship to other existing system components
    o   Support (resources, training, etc.) and security needs

- o Risks
- o Assumptions
- o System quantities for development, test, and production
- o Deployment and maintenance plans
- o Predecessor or similar legacy systems

- Step 4: Determine the Estimating Approach

  - o Define work breakdown structure (WBS) and describe each element
  - o Choose the estimating method best suited for each WBS element
  - o Identify potential cross-checks for likely cost and schedule drivers
  - o Develop a cost estimating checklist

- Step 5: Identify Ground Rules and Assumptions

  - o Clearly define what is included and excluded from the estimate
  - o Identify global and program specific assumptions such as:
    - The estimate's timescale, including time-phasing and life cycle
    - Program schedule information by phase
    - Program acquisition strategy
    - Any schedule or budget constraints
    - Inflation assumptions
    - Costs such as travel and other expenses
    - Equipment the organisation is to furnish
    - Prime contractor and major subcontractors
    - Use of existing facilities or new modifications or developments
    - Technology refresh cycles
    - Technology assumptions and new technology to be developed
    - Commonality with legacy systems and assumed heritage savings
    - Effects of new ways of doing business

- Step 6: Obtain Data

  - o Create a data collection plan with emphasis on collecting current and relevant technical, programmatic, cost, and risk data.
  - o Investigate possible data sources
  - o Collect data and normalise them for cost accounting, inflation, learning, and quantity adjustments
  - o Analyse the data to look for cost drivers, trends, and outliers compare results against rules of thumb and standard factors derived from historical data
  - o Interview data sources and document all relevant information including an assessment of data reliability and accuracy

- Step 7: Develop Point Estimate

  - o Develop the cost model by estimating each WBS element, using the best methodology from the data collected
  - o Include all estimating assumptions in the cost model
  - o Express costs in constant year currency
  - o Sum the WBS elements to develop the overall point estimate
  - o Validate the estimate by looking for errors like double counting and omitting costs
  - o Compare estimate against the independent cost estimate and examine w here and why there are differences
  - o Perform cross-checks on cost drivers to see if results are similar
  - o Update the model as more data become available or as changes occur and compare results against previous estimates

Analysis Phase

- Step 8: Conduct Sensitivity Analysis

    o   Test the sensitivity of cost elements to changes in estimating input values and key assumptions
    o   Identify effects of changing the program schedule or quantities on the overall estimate
    o   Determine which assumptions are key cost drivers and which cost elements are affected most by changes

- Step 9: Conduct Risk and Uncertainty Analysis

    o   Determine the level of cost, schedule, and technical risk associated with each WBS element and discuss with technical experts
    o   Analyse each risk for its severity and probability of occurrence
    o   Develop minimum, most likely, and maximum ranges for each element of risk
    o   Use an acceptable statistical analysis methodology to develop a confidence interval around the point estimate
    o   Determine type of risk distributions and reason for their use
    o   Identify the confidence level of the point estimate
    o   Identify the amount of contingency funding and add this to the point estimate to determine the risk-adjusted cost estimate

- Step 10: Document the Estimate

    o   Document all steps used to develop the estimate so that it can be recreated quickly by a cost analyst unfamiliar with the program and produce the same result
    o   Document the purpose of the estimate, the team that prepared it, and who approved the estimate and on what date
    o   Describe the program, including the schedule and technical baseline used to create the estimate
    o   Present the time-phased life-cycle cost of the program
    o   Discuss all ground rules and assumptions
    o   Include auditable and traceable data sources for each cost element
    o   Document for all data sources how the data were normalised
    o   Describe the results of the risk, uncertainty, and sensitivity analyses and whether any contingency funds were identified
    o   Document how the estimate compares to the funding profile
    o   Track how this estimate compares to previous estimates, if applicable

Presentation Phase

- Step 11: Present Estimate for Approval

    o   Develop a briefing that presents the documented life-cycle cost estimate for management approval, including
        ▪   An explanation of the technical and programmatic baseline and any uncertainties
        ▪   A comparison to an independent cost estimate (ICE) with explanations of any differences
        ▪   A comparison of the estimate (life-cycle cost estimate (LCCE) or independent cost estimate to the budget
        ▪   Enough detail so the presenter can easily defend the estimate by showing how it is accurate, complete, and high in quality
    o   Focus the briefing, in a logical manner, on the largest cost elements and drivers of cost
    o   Make the content concise and complete so that those who are unfamiliar with it can easily comprehend the competence that underlies the estimate results
    o   Have more detailed available to respond to more searching questions
    o   Act on and document feedback from management
    o   The cost estimating team should request acceptance of the estimate

- Step 12: Update Estimate to Reflect Actual Costs and Changes

○ Update the estimate to
  ▪ Reflect any changes in technical or program assumptions
  ▪ Keep it current as the program passes through new phases

4.6.1.7.5 Step 3.5 Develop And Validate Feasibility Prototype(s)

Developing a prototype may useful in demonstrating and presenting options or concepts for components of the solution. They can be of use to validate approaches, demonstrate behaviours or algorithms or prove that a solution component can handle the required workload or illustrate the potential solution to the business. Prototypes are not intended to be complete solutions. They are intended to be throwaway developments. They may evolve into production components but where this happens care needs to be taken.

Prototyping is concerned with producing a working model of elements of the solution more quickly than standard approaches. Prototypes bypass functionality such as detailed error checking.

Prototyping is most suitable where the requirements or the design of the solution component is not well defined or understood or when some form of exploratory effort is justified to draw out aspects of the solution.

Prototypes have a cost in terms of resources to implement as well as affecting the engagement schedule.

4.6.1.8 Business Engagement Activity 4. Document Solutions, Applications And Functions

The possible steps for activity *Document Systems, Applications And Functions* are:

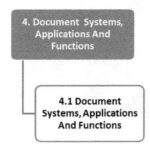

Figure 132 – Steps Within Business Engagement Activity *4. Document Systems, Applications And Functions*

These steps are documented in more detail below:

4.1 Document Systems, Applications And Functions

4.6.1.8.1 Step 4.1 Document Systems, Applications And Functions

The objective of this activity is to define the set of solutions and applications that comprise the overall solution required as part of the target business architecture. It may not be possible at this stage to identify the precise set of applications and their boundaries. The purpose of the applications is to operate the required business processes and support business activities. Applications can perform multiple functions or a single function. The set of applications can include existing legacy applications that will be retained.

The possible set of tasks in this step is:

- Analyse industry-specific applications
- Analyse existing application landscape
- Determine application integration, linkages and interfaces
- Determine business processing applications
- Determine data access approach and applications
- Determine management approach and applications
- Validate applications and previously-defined processes

There may be standard products available for the industry in which the organisation operates that are relevant to the requirements of the business function within the scope of the business architecture engagement. Review such products and applications. Review industry-specific standards to determine applicability to the organisation's requirements. Analyse and classify the suitability of products and the applicability of the standards as:

- Definitely suitable
- Potentially suitable
- Definitely unsuitable

Create an inventory of standard products and industry-specific standards and their classification.

Review the entire existing suite of applications in use to determine which should be retained and which are candidates for replacement:

- Include customisations
- Include reporting and analytics tools

Classify the type of application:

- User productivity
- Reporting and analysis
- Package
- Custom developed
- Information sharing
- Transaction processing

Analyse and classify the suitability of these existing applications:

- Definitely retain
- Potentially retain
- Definitely replace

Create an inventory of such applications and their classification.

Determine application integration, linkages and interfaces. Identify the external applications that interface with the previously identified existing suite of applications and the interfaces between the existing applications. Describe the nature of the interface: frequency, direction, protocol, security, volume, method of interface and exchange. Describe the data that is exchanged in sufficient detail so the effort to implement with new systems can be accurately estimated. The topic of data integration is covered in more detail in section 4.8.5 on page 339.

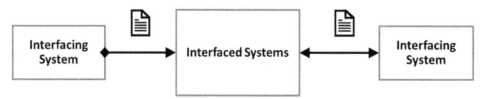

Figure 133 – Inventory of Interfaces, Exchanges and Transfers

Create inventory of integrations, interfaces and exchanges, completing a set of information along the following lines:

Transfer Mechanism	Protocol	Direction	Data Format	Data Content	Encryption	Batch/ Realtime	Source	Target	Frequency
File transfer	HTTP	In	CSV		Yes				Hourly
Mail	HTTPS	Out	XML		No				Daily
Web service	FTP	Bidirectional	JSON						Weekly
Message Queueing			XBRL						On demand
Manual transfer	SFTP		XLSX						
Replication	TLS		Proprietary						
Proprietary	SSH								
API									

Table 40 – Inventory of Interfaces, Exchanges and Transfers

Analyse business processing applications. Business applications are those that process business transactions. These are central to the successful operation of the business function and need to be analysed in more detail. For each application, list the key transactions. List the data entities created or updated by these transactions. List the business processes that use the transactions within the applications.

Describe the architecture of the business transaction processing systems:

• Modular, componentised applications that are loosely integrated
• Monolithic applications with tightly coupled components

The architecture of these systems determines the usefulness of the applications in the future architecture. Monolithic applications may not be part of the future architecture. The options for their replacement include

• Some functions may be outsourced
• Some functions may be provided by hosted applications
• Separate applications may be implemented for some sets of functions

Determine data access approach and applications. Analyse these approaches and applications used to provide access to data. List the data sources. List the data access, extraction and staging approaches.

Determine management approach and applications. List the service management and administration processes and applications that support the operation and use of the business systems.

Consolidate and validate the previously collected and analysed information:

• Inventory of industry-specific standards and the applicability
• Application landscape inventory and their potential future suitability
• Inventory of application integrations, interfaces and exchanges
• Transaction processing applications and their transaction types
• Inventory of data entities created or updated by these transactions
• Inventory of business processes that use the transactions within the applications
• Description of the architecture of the business transaction processing systems
• Inventory of approaches and applications used to provide access to data
• Inventory of service management and administration processes and applications

4.6.1.9 Business Engagement Activity 5. Define Organisation, Infrastructure And Data

The possible steps for activity *Define Organisation, Infrastructure And Data* are:

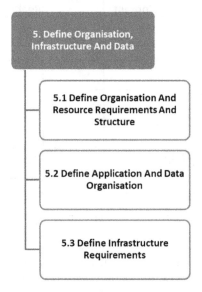

Figure 134 – Steps Within Business Engagement Activity 5. Define Organisation, Infrastructure And Data

These steps are documented in more detail below:

> 5.1 Define Organisation And Resource Requirements And Structure
> 5.2 Define Application And Data Organisation
> 5.3 Define Infrastructure Requirements

4.6.1.9.1 Step 5.1 Define Organisation And Resource Requirements And Structure

Create a high-level future state organisation structure options with details on the roles, staffing levels and locations. Define the high-level structures for allocation and performing work and making decisions. Define the work groups structure and their interactions. Define the management, administration and escalation processes. Create a target organisation chart. Define the differences between the current and future state organisation structures.

Define the target state staffing structures. Map existing roles and structures to the proposed new staffing structure. Create a high-level plan to transition from the existing to the proposed new staffing structure. Staff transitions and organisation changes can be problematic – such change can be resisted or its achievement ineffective. Prepare for and address such resistance to change or reasons why change is not achieved to reduce potential problems.

Review possible resistance to staffing structures and organisation changes. Resistance to change or reasons why change fails can be explicit or concealed. Explicit resistance or reasons can take forms such as:

- Insufficient numbers of appropriate staff to handle workload
- Lack of personnel skill, experience, knowledge
- Lack of effective communication
- Inadequate organisation structures
- Ineffective management structures

Identify hidden resistance factors to change. There are many causes and ways in which organisations and personnel demonstrate resistance to change:

- Fear of job losses
- Fear of loss of status or authority after change
- Bypassing or circumventing new technologies
- Passive aggressive behaviours
- Passive sabotage
- Focussing on existing ways of working and the past rather than the future
- Questioning the need for and the basis of the proposed changes
- Lack of co-operation
- Insistence in involving HR function in organisation change

Examine ways of handling resistance to organisation change such as:

- Remove obvious obstacles
- Allocate sufficient resources
- Communication
- Design organisation interventions to address concerns that give rise to resistance to change

4.6.1.9.2 Step 5.2 Define Application And Data Organisation

Section 4.8 on page 321 contains information on a detailed approach to analysing and defining the data aspects of the architecture of a solution. This section summarises the approach to be taken and the information to be collected in the context of a business engagement.

The tasks to be performed during this step are:

- Define application and data organisation
- Map processing points and connections
- Map application and data usage to processing points
- Analyse service level for applications and data
- Describe options for application and data organisation
- Review options to minimise risks
- Create final application and data organisation options and recommendations

Logical application and data distribution and organisation needs to take place before any physical and technical design can take place. Decide on the optimum location, organisation and distribution of business processing applications and data elements based on factors such as:

- Work types and volumes
- Data types and volumes
- Location(s) of internal users
- Location(s) of population external access users
- Agreed service levels for work types
- Business processes used to perform work
- Number of work locations
- Technical constraints
- Risks
- Cost
- Use of service and outsourcing partners
- Availability of existing infrastructure
- Legal and regulatory restrictions
- Information technology architecture design principles

This ensures there is rational basis for options, recommendations and decisions. The following is a set of tasks to perform to assist with this decision:

- Map processing points and connections
- Map application and data usage to processing points
- Analyse service level for applications and data
- Describe options for application and data organisation
- Review options to minimise risks and cost
- Create final application and data organisation options and recommendations

Identify the options for the location of work processing and the connections between them. These locations can include some of all of:

- Sales
- Middle office
- Service
- Support
- Warehouse
- Delivery
- Outsourced service providers and partners
- Other external users

Not all organisations will have all location types.

Define the processes, activities within processes and the associated data performed at each location, Identify the allocation of work and the movement of work between them. Identify the work processing roles in each location. The goal here is to identify logical and function distribution before defining physical technology design.

Map application and data usage to processing points. Define the systems and applications and the associated data required for the previously defined processing points. Describe how data is used for processing.

Analyse service level for applications and data. Describe the usage factors that will determine the service level requirements of the applications and data, such as:

- Security, privacy, confidentiality
- Frequency of use
- Volume of activity – read, update
- Performance, response time and throughput
- Availability, resilience, recoverability, reliability

Define the similar service requirements of applications, such as:

- Availability, resilience, recoverability, reliability
- Performance, response time and throughput

Define options and recommendations for the locations of applications and data based on processing factor and service requirements. Use the previously gathered information on application options to map specific product and solution options to application and data requirements. The order of priorities is:

- Business processes and their operation and use
- Data
- Important work types and functionality
- Reduction of risk

Consider operational systems, administration, support and management systems and reporting/analysis/decision-support systems.

Review the options to minimise risks. Analyse the previously gathered information and options and consider other non-technical and business options. Consider overall IT architecture principles and standards and organisation IT strategy. Evaluate the risks. Avoid data redundancy. Consider the operational/non-functional requirements and constraints such as:

- Usable
- Affordable
- Deliverable
- Operable
- Supportable
- Maintainable
- Flexible
- Adaptable
- Capable
- Scalable
- Reliable
- Securable
- Available
- Auditable
- Recoverable
- Stable
- Testable
- Accessible

Create the final application and data organisation options and recommendations. Create formal application and data model(s) that consolidates previous information showing:

- Locations
- Applications
- Processing
- Data

4.6.1.9.3 Step 5.3 Define Infrastructure Requirements

Technology includes equipment, communications infrastructure and supporting systems needed to allow the implementation, operation and use of the applications that allow the business processes to function. This includes communications and security infrastructure to allow access to externally hosted applications and to enable data integration, transfer and exchange. It also includes any technology required to enable interactions with outsourced service partners and formal communications with regulators and other such reporting arrangements.

The requirements need to be formally identified and validated to form an input to the technology design activity. These requirements define the features, functions and capabilities to be provided. They do not specify how they are to be provided. This comes later. Technology requirements should be defined using categories such as:

- Reuse of and extension of existing technology
- Financial and affordability constraints and limitations
- Enterprise architecture and IT strategy constraints, limitations and principles
- Operational business process requirements – functional and data

Technology requirements are impacted by characteristics such as locations and connectivity, functionality, work teams, outsourcing and regulation.

Technology will be required at various levels:

- Individual users

- Work groups
- External users
- Office locations
- Centralised application functionality facilities, hosted internally or externally
- Centralised data facilities
- Decision support, reporting, analysis
- Communications and network access and connectivity
- Externally hosted XaaS services and facilities
- Security, identification, authentication, intrusion detection and prevention, load balancing
- Support, service, monitoring
- External mobile access to internally hosted applications

The individual solutions should be able to inherit and reuse much of this infrastructure from existing facilities.

Review the previously created inventory of business processes and their constituent activities and the roles that perform them at each location. Identify the technology functionality needed to allow the process activities to be performed. Consider the operational dimension and its impact on technology requirements such as:

- Performance/throughput/workload – capacity planning and management across static and dynamic elements of the solution
- Availability
- Security
- Reliability

Verify that the technology requirements can address:

- Realtime transaction processing
- Batch processes and processing
- Data storage, access, movement
- Interfaces and data exchanges of all types
    - Internal
        - Existing interfaces
        - Proposed new interfaces
    - External
        - Existing interfaces
        - Proposed new interfaces

Identify any inconsistencies and address these through revision of requirements.

4.6.1.10 Business Engagement Activity 6. Conduct Solution And Product Evaluation And Selection

The possible steps for activity *Conduct Solution And Product Evaluation And Selection* are:

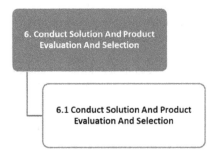

Figure 135 – Steps Within Business Engagement Activity *6. Conduct Solution And Product Evaluation And Selection*

These steps are documented in more detail below:

6.1 Conduct Solution And Product Evaluation And Selection

4.6.1.10.1 Step 6.1 Conduct Solution And Product Evaluation And Selection

The step may take too long in the content of the architecture engagement. Chapter 7 on page 447 covers the topic of solution architecture and solution component acquisition in more detail and should be read with this section.

The approaches to solution evaluation and selection will differ for public and private sector organisations.

The decision to be made when the engagement is being planned and the initial scoping work is being done is whether to conduct one or more evaluation and possible selection exercises of possible product or service options, including outsourcing during the engagement.

Product or service evaluation or selection can take a long time and will therefore affect the duration of the architecture engagement. Evaluation and selection can consist of one or more of:

- A product to be installed in-house on the organisation's infrastructure and that may need to be
- A hosted service, effectively a product supplied through an as-a-service model
- A customised development performed by a supplier
- An outsourced service

The organisation may have a preference for one or more of these options. For example, complete service outsourcing may not be considered. Similarly, the organisation may not be mature in its use of externally hosted XaaS services. The organisation's posture with respect to these options must be understood before an evaluation exercise is started. You need to decide what is and is not acceptable in advance to avoid wasting time.

These are all forms of acquisition of one or more components of the overall solution. These components must fit into the overall solution landscape and be able to work together to deliver the entire solution.

Determine the rigour and structure of the approach to identifying suitable products and services:

- Formal tender, either one or two stage with a possible first stage pre-qualification process to create a short-list of suppliers to engage with during the more thorough and time and resource consuming second stage
- Request for solution
- Direct contact with suitable vendors

It is always best to have some form of structured and formal approach to acquisition ensure the most suitable products or services are successfully identified. Many organisations will have a procurement function and a procurement process that the architecture engagement can deal with to handle the housekeeping elements of the evaluation and possible selection exercise. However, the solution architect must take responsibility for the functional and operational characteristics of the product or service.

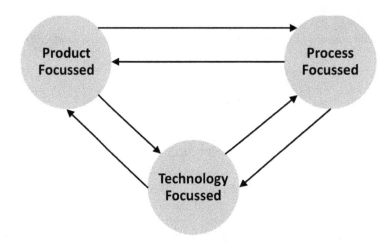

Figure 136 – Approaches To Product and Service Evaluation And Selection

Broadly, there are three approaches to product and service evaluation and selection

1. ***Product Focussed*** - Focus of identifying the functional product or service and change the business processes to those contained in the product

2. ***Process Focussed*** - Focus on the required business processes and identify those products and services that can allow them to be implemented

3. ***Technology Focussed*** - Focus on technology and infrastructure requirements and constraints and identify products and services that can comply with them

These approaches are not necessarily mutually exclusive and they can be mixed. However, there should be a preferred or dominant acquisition focus.

For each of these approaches, you should define and agree the important characteristics and pre-requisites.

The product focussed approach may have the following characteristics and pre-requisites:

- Ideally looking for one rather than multiple components
- The organisation has decided that a product (either installed or hosted) is the best approach to meeting its needs
- The organisation is willing to adapt its processes to those of a product or service
- The organisation accepts the technology, data, deployment and operational model of the selected product or service
- The organisation will allow the product or service define the technology and data architectures, development and release and service management approaches
- The finance required for a product or service acquisition is understood and recognised
- The organisation will accept entering into some form of partnership with the product vendor

The process focussed approach may have the following characteristics and pre-requisites:

- The organisation understands that it wants to implement a process or service that enables its business processes
- The organisation understands that this approach will limit the process or service options
- This approach may mean longer development/customisation and implementation effort, cost and schedule
- The required business processes are understood and have been defined and documented
- The transaction volumes associated with the business processes have been defined

The technology focussed approach may have the following characteristics and pre-requisites:

- The organisation has or is defining a new technical architecture and wants all products and services to comply with these standards

- The organisation understands that this approach will limit the product and service options

The objectives of the evaluation and selection process are:

- To select the most appropriate products or service that meets the specified requirements
- To create an evaluation audit trail and set of supporting documentation that will support the evaluation process and final decision

The output from the process will be a formal product or solution and supplier evaluation and selection recommendation report. Any evaluation process is liable to subjectivity in areas such as:

- The selection of the evaluation factors and the relative weights assigned
- The scores assigned to each product and vendor

The purposes of a formal evaluation process are:

- To eliminate subjectivity as much as possible from the evaluation process
- To provide transparency in the evaluation process
- To ensure that all product and solution options are evaluated in the same way

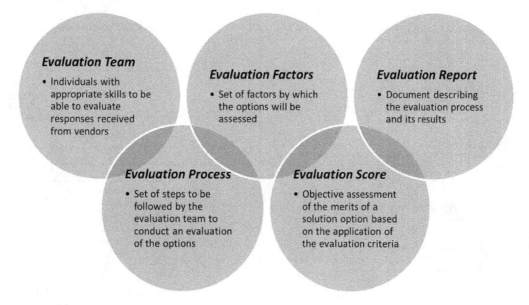

Figure 137 – Core Elements of the Product and Service Evaluation And Selection Process

The core elements of the evaluation and selection process are:

- *Evaluation Team* - Individuals with appropriate skills to be able to evaluate responses received from vendors
- *Evaluation Process* - Set of steps to be followed by the evaluation team to conduct an evaluation of the options
- *Evaluation Factors* - Set of factors by which the options will be assessed
- *Evaluation Score* - Objective assessment of the merits of a solution option based on the application of the evaluation criteria
- *Evaluation Report* - Document describing the evaluation process and its results

A formal structured report provides an audit trail for the conclusions and recommendations. It should contain information along the following lines:

    1. Overview
        a. Executive Summary

2. Statement of Need, Purpose and Scope
3. Short List Selection
   a. List of Vendors Contacted
   b. Product/Service Decision Model
   c. Vendor Supplied Information Summary
   d. Summary of Conclusions and Recommendation
4. Qualifier Selection
   a. Reference Checks and Site Visits
   b. Functional Demonstration Findings
   c. Technical Review Findings
   d. Solution Demonstration Planning Lab Findings
   e. Summary of Qualifier Recommendation
5. Optional Appendices Containing Supporting Material

The high-level set of steps involved in performing a product/service and associated supplier selection are:

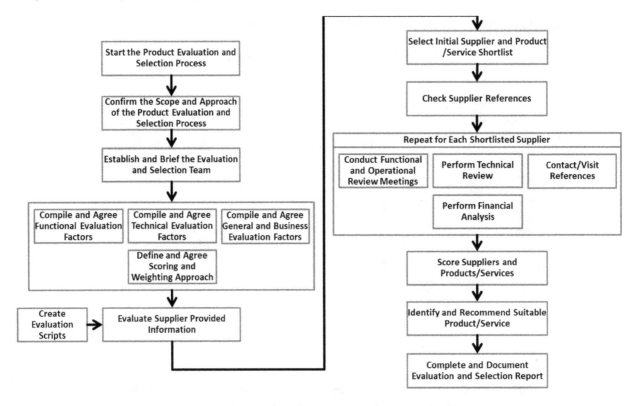

Figure 138 – High Level Steps of Product/Service Evaluation And Selection Process

Step	Description
Start the Product Evaluation and Selection Process	The amount of effort involved in starting the product/service and supplier evaluation and selection activity depends on: • How recently you made any scope and direction decisions on selection options and approaches • Whether the team has already been selected • How familiar each team member is with the functional area within which the application is to be deployed, and the systems currently in use • How experienced the team is with product/service and supplier evaluation and selection
Confirm the Scope and Approach of the Product	Review previous decisions made about the scope of the project. Discuss any scope changes and adjust the work plan to reflect approved changes

Step	Description
Evaluation and Selection Process	Consider the urgency of the need and determine how it impacts the selection strategy
	Determine the timing and general strategy for contract negotiation
	Determine what parties to involve in defining acquisition/procurement procedures, handling legal questions, and negotiating the contract so that the right people can be involved at appropriate points
Establish and Brief the Evaluation and Selection Team	Assemble and organise a solution evaluation and selection team:
	• Include technical personnel who understand the systems management and support processes that are being implemented
	• Include business personnel who understand the operational objectives, business processes and needs of Executive stakeholders and sponsors of the project.
	• Include experts who understand the market context within which the vendors operate so as to ensure an understanding of:
	o The capability and capacity of service providers on the local market where resources will be required
	o The extent to which the vendors' products or services will need to be customised to meet the requirements identified
	o The market for services-based activities (consulting/training/customisation/application development etc.)
	• Provide for a workshop facilitator with a solid background in the subject area if you plan to use facilitated workshops as part of the evaluation and selection process.
	• Keep the core group small but representative of the functional areas the product most affects.
	• Include as support members anyone involved in defining procurement procedures, handling legal questions, and negotiating the contract.
	• Include management personnel responsible for approving the selection
	Once you have established the evaluation and selection team, designate team members to be the supplier contacts. These individuals represent the interests of the client and the systems integrator, answer questions about the solution evaluation and selection process, discuss details with the supplier, arrange supplier contact with other members of the team and are empowered to make informal commitments
	Next, designate a team administrator to administer the supplier scheduling, handle vendor requests, record all vendor contact, obtain and distribute vendor materials and maintain a recording system for supplier materials
	Walk through the evaluation and selection activities with team members to familiarise them with the general process. If the team is relatively inexperienced with solution evaluation and selection, consider using a team-building exercise to preview the process
	Discuss the objectives and principles of the evaluation and selection process with the team to ensure that everyone has a consistent understanding
Compile and Agree Functional Evaluation Factors	Compiling evaluation factors when selecting a product/service involves:
	• Developing or gathering evaluation factors appropriate to the evaluation method
	• Avoiding too much precision
	• Keeping the focus on business priorities
	• Designing a scoring approach that facilitates getting and analysing supplier responses
	• Incorporating the criteria into the scoring approach

Step	Description
	These evaluation factors will be taken from the request for information sent to the suppliers In this step, define the functional evaluation factors - the requirements as seen from the business user's point of view. These requirements represent the business processes the solution needs to accommodate Design functional evaluation factors and group them as follows: • Business processes • Data • External system interfaces • Business performance measurement Collate the functional evaluation factors into a single source
Compile and Agree Technical Evaluation Factors	Define technical evaluation factors to represent the product/service design and its technical infrastructure aspects. The technical requirements concern the operation and infrastructure of the product/service To enhance readability and minimise gaps, develop categories of technical evaluation factors in the areas of: • Systems management and support process • Operational interface • Technical infrastructure • Volume and technical performance Assemble the technical evaluation factors into a single source These evaluation factors will be taken from the request information sent to the suppliers
Compile and Agree General and Business Evaluation Factors	The buyer of a product/service is developing a medium to long-term relationship with the supplier and will expect some, if not all, of the following: • Initial transition, configuration and implementation services • Customisation, configuration and enhancement services • Consulting services • Future changes and releases • Customer support and maintenance services, such as a support line, web portal and a user group General factors include supplier and other miscellaneous factors. These are factors that influence the product/service purchase decision but are not functional or technical in nature Concentrate on factors that would eliminate vendors from the short list. Consult with legal and purchasing personnel to extract general criteria that can quickly narrow the solution selection Add evaluation factors to ensure the team understands the vendor's decision-making and delivery processes, schedules and organisation before making a final product/service selection and developing a delivery plan With functional and technical factors, you are usually looking for a specific response. With general factors questions, you are looking for potential risks and information needed for

Step	Description
	deployment and operation. Collect responses to these factors by asking the vendor directly, by asking references who use the product/service and by conducting your own research
Define and Agree Scoring Approach	To narrow product/service options to a reasonable number, design an overall selection framework to communicate and summarise the results of the supplier reviews. Use weightings to reflect the relative importance of the evaluation factors. Use scoring to indicate how well a supplier's product/service meets the requirements Weighting and scoring are often represented numerically, giving the appearance of objectivity. Keep in mind that these numbers are really just a quick means to communicate subjective judgments. When making the product/service decision, check that the scoring results are consistent with the conclusions of the team
Evaluate Supplier Provided Information	The objective of this activity is to obtain and evaluate the information provided by product/service suppliers that explain how their product/service meet the specific requirements and at what estimated cost. The request for information sent to suppliers should look for a formal and structured response. Suppliers are compared uniformly as to how well they meet the requirements and present their product/service
Create Evaluation Scripts	During the product/service meetings suppliers, the team needs to compare products/services fairly and consistently, even though different products/services are being proposed and discussed. This may be difficult for the team achieve if each supplier is allowed to determine the meeting's sequence, contents and focus. By prescribing that all suppliers follow a planned sequence of requirements, or scripts, you: • Ensure consistency of material addressed across suppliers • Ensure the supplier is presenting those features most important to you and not just those the supplier puts forward as strong points • Can more easily spot features and functions that do not quite match expectations or requirements • Can more easily differentiate how the features and functions differ among products/services You can also use this material when checking supplier references and making reference site visits or contacts
Select Initial Supplier and Product /Service Shortlist	Conduct a workshop to obtain team agreement on whether or not to proceed with product/service evaluation and to reduce the list of suppliers under consideration to a reasonable number such as three or fewer. Use the workshop approach for large products/services or those with a high impact
Check Supplier References	Checking supplier references as another way to confirm that the supplier's product/service and associated implementation services could meet the requirements. Develop a questionnaire to record reference responses. Include questions covering relevant functional, technical and general requirements. Involve members of the team in reference checking. This distributes the work, counteracts individual partiality and provides experience useful in subsequent evaluation activities
Conduct Functional and Operational Review Meetings	Have the shortlisted suppliers conduct functional and operation reviews using the script provided so you can: • Confirm that the product/service can process operate to your required level • Determine, based on your own examination, which product/service provides the best response to needs
Perform Technical Review	Conduct a technical review of the product/service with the supplier's technical personnel. They are usually involved in the provision of the product/service and its underlying technical components. They are not as oriented as the sales staff toward selling the product/service. They usually provide a more realistic view of the product/service and the supplier's ability to deliver and support it. They can also confirm technical infrastructure

Step	Description
	details about operating and using the product/service. The technical review typically has several components: • Demonstration of technical facilities and elements • Review of remaining questions on technical and general evaluation factor responses • Support and operational model comparison • Performance investigation • Review of product/service architecture • Conceptual technical infrastructure design • Review of service delivery and quality • Review the release and patching strategy the supplier applies During the technical review, each team member updates the relevant factor scores. At the end of the technical review, the team meets to reach agreement on the technical review findings.
Contact/Visit References	Decide whether to visit or contact supplier references Plan the approach, contact or visit the sites and then consolidate the findings.
Perform Financial Analysis	This activity is very important for confirming the supplier's financial quotations Ensure the supplier's cost estimates are as accurate as possible by confirming the preliminary cost estimates
Score Suppliers and Products/Services	Review and summarise the scores of all the shortlisted products/services and suppliers Update the scores if necessary based on additional information and any clarification sought from or provided by suppliers
Identify and Recommend Suitable Product/Service	The team is now in a position to select a product/service and supplier to recommend Review the decision to confirm that the product/service approach should still be pursued Determine contract negotiation timing and approach if relevant Conduct a workshop or a work session to select the recommended product/service finalist In general, use a workshop for a large or high-impact product/service
Complete and Document Evaluation and Selection Report	Complete the evaluation process Complete the evaluation documentation Finalise the evaluation report Notify the suppliers that have not been selected or recommended Prepare for any meetings with these suppliers Assess the overall approval with the fulfilment with the evaluation work Summarise the work results and the lessons learned Review and recognise the team performance Close out the evaluation documentation

Table 41 – High Level Steps of Product/Service Evaluation And Selection Process

The outcome of the product/service evaluation and selection exercise may cause changes in the expected solution costs and timescales.

These may need to be reviewed and updated.

4.6.1.11 Business Engagement Activity 7. Design Model Architecture

The possible steps for activity Design Model Architecture are:

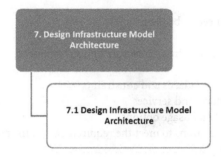

Figure 139 – Steps Within Business Engagement Activity *7. Design Model Architecture*

These steps are documented in more detail below:

7.1 Design Infrastructure Model Architecture

4.6.1.11.1 Step 7.1 Design Infrastructure Model Architecture

Design the architecture options for the product and service components to be implemented as part of the target architecture.

Architecture here includes technical, security and hardware, software, hosted service and communications infrastructure. It does not at this stage include detailed solution architecture.

It will translate the information gathered in the following engagement steps into architecture options:

- *Business Engagement Activity 4. Document Solutions, Applications And Functions* – section 4.6.1.8 on page 205
- *Business Engagement Activity 6. Conduct Solution And Product Evaluation And Selection* – section 4.6.1.10 on page 212

It may not be possible or desirable to define the detailed architecture at this stage. This will depend on the set of components being implemented and whether they are based on available or packaged products/services or are being developed. There also may be a single architecture option or there may be multiple options. The purpose of this activity is to document architecture options to be included in the final business engagement output.

The tasks to be performed here are:

- Decide on those factors that affect the architecture options and designs
- Define the options available
- Review and identify the realistic and achievable target architecture options
- Perform a detailed evaluation of the selected realistic and achievable target architecture options
- Select the preferred target architecture

- Verify the implementability, operability, feasibility and affordability of the preferred target architecture
- Document the architecture

There will be multiple components or layers to the target architecture:

- Communications
- Infrastructure
- Data storage
- Infrastructural/management/administration applications
- Business applications
- Integration
- Security

These components and their options will need to be identified.

Define and elaborate on those factors that affect the architecture options and designs, such as:

- Organisation (enterprise architecture) standards and constraints
- Options available from available products and services
- Available product/service deployment and usage options
- Use and enhancement of existing applications to meet the requirements of the target solution components
- Products and service acquisition policy
- Compliance with relevant and important industry-specific standards
- Performance, throughput, capacity, transaction, user and data volumes
- Scalability along performance dimensions
- Availability, reliability, fault-tolerance
- Security, privacy, data protection
- Locations
- Approaches to interfaces with existing systems and applications and integration
- Cost
- Organisation appetite for risk and new technologies

Determine the appropriateness and the importance of each of the factors and assign some form of weighting. Decide on the approach to evaluating each of the factors.

Identify the set of options to be considered. Review each option with respect to the previously agreed factors that affect the architecture options and designs. There may be multiple combinations of options for each major technical infrastructure component.

There may be existing technical infrastructure including systems, applications and data that need to be considered as part of the future architecture. Evaluate the options for each element of the existing technical infrastructure in terms of four options:

1. *Replace Partially Or Completely* - Replace the existing technical infrastructure with new set. Note that this may require data migration
2. *Encapsulate* - Encapsulate the existing technical infrastructure elements within the proposed new technical infrastructure
3. *Operate in Parallel* - The new and existing technical infrastructure elements will operate in parallel with possibly some form of integration or interface between them
4. *Incorporate* - Incorporate the existing new technical infrastructure elements into the new technical infrastructure elements into a single infrastructure, ensuring the two sets of elements are mutually compatible

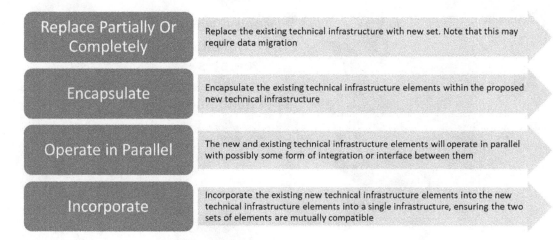

Figure 140 – Options for Existing Technical Infrastructure

Analyse the longlist of possible options and create a shortlist based on those options that most closely match the key architecture factors. Eliminate options that are not feasible or realistic or too expensive.

For each of the shortlisted options create a detailed design showing how it can be implemented, operated, supported, used and its likely cost and time and resources required to implement. Evaluate the impact of the option against the six core business domains and the extended domains, if relevant.

Determine how the solution components comply with the principles defined in *Business Engagement Activity 2. Define Vision, Business Principles And System Principles* – see section 4.6.1.6 on page 183.

Assess and score each of the short-listed architecture options. Where the scores of options are similar, recheck scores assigned to ensure they are valid. Select the preferred architecture option based on the analysis and scoring. If there is no clear option, then consider adding extra evaluation factors to further differentiate options.

Verify the implementability, operability, feasibility and affordability of the preferred target architecture along the three dimensions of:

1. What It Does, How It Operates – the Functionality
2. Cost/Time/Risk To Implement
3. The "xAbles"

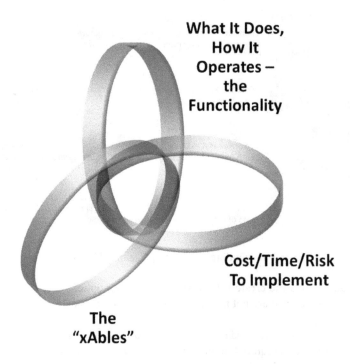

Figure 141 – Dimensions of Verification of Target Architecture

The xAbles are the solution quality factors identified in section 4.6.4.7 on page 251, so called because they all invariably end in "able". These are very important operational requirements that may not be articulated by business users and stakeholders. They are essential to the success of the set of solutions that comprise the target business architecture and its enduring operation and use. Evaluate the solution set with respect to each of these factors.

Walk through the preferred solution with respect to the key processes and processing loads. If necessary, conduct trials on key elements of the preferred target architecture. Consider implementing proof of concept prototypes to validate key design elements.

Document the architecture design. Create summary presentation material. Present and review the architecture with the key business representatives. Update and finalise the material based on feedback at these presentations.

4.6.1.12 Business Engagement Activity 8. Consolidate, Finalise And Review Design

The possible steps for activity *Consolidate, Finalise And Review Design* are:

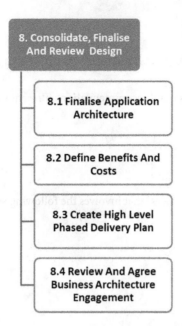

Figure 142 – Steps Within Business Engagement Activity *8. Consolidate, Finalise And Review Design*

The possible steps for activity *Consolidate, Finalise And Review Design* are:

> 8.1 Finalise Application Architecture
> 8.2 Define Benefits And Costs
> 8.3 Create High Level Phased Delivery Plan
> 8.4 Review And Agree Business Architecture Engagement

4.6.1.12.1 Step 8.1 Finalise Application Architecture

This step brings all the information gathered in the previous activities to create a consolidated analysis with a set of recommendations.

Finalise the application architecture based on the technical infrastructure design selected. Finalise the data model. Finalise the list of interfaces. Complete the documentation agreed in Business Engagement Activity 0. Define And Agree Engagement Scope contained in section 4.6.1.4 on page 168.

Circulate with the engagement team for review and feedback and update accordingly

4.6.1.12.2 Step 8.2 Define Benefits And Costs

Validate and update the detailed cost model described in section 4.6.1.7.4 on page 199 with any additional financial information obtained since then such as costing details provided by suppliers in section 4.6.1.10 on page 212.

You can use the solution and benefits validation approach described in section 4.11 on page 381.

4.6.1.12.3 Step 8.3 Create High Level Phased Delivery Plan

Create a plan for the delivery of the solution defined during the architecture engagement. Create a work breakdown structure for the delivery of the changes across the core and extended business domains. Use this work breakdown to create a realistic project schedule.

4.6.1.12.4 Step 8.4 Review And Agree Business Architecture Engagement

Create a draft presentation of the final analysis and recommendations. Present the material to key business representatives. Update and finalise based on feedback.

4.6.2 Solution Design Process

This describes a generalised solution design process that involves the following sequence of activities:

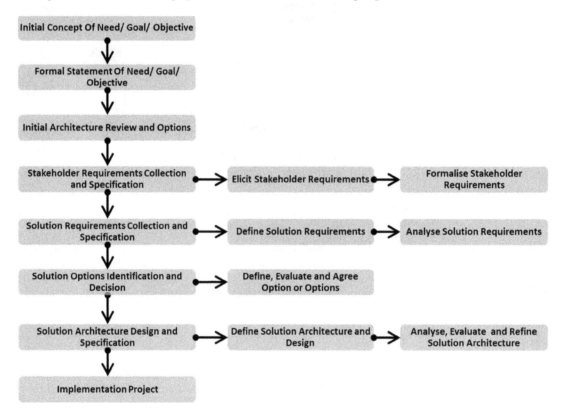

Figure 143 – Generalised Solution Design Process

This solution design process demonstrates the importance of embedding the gathering of business requirements and solution requirements (described in section 4.4 on page 124) in the solution design process rather than being a separate siloed process handed-off to the solution architecture function.

This generalised process maps to the three engagement types shown below.

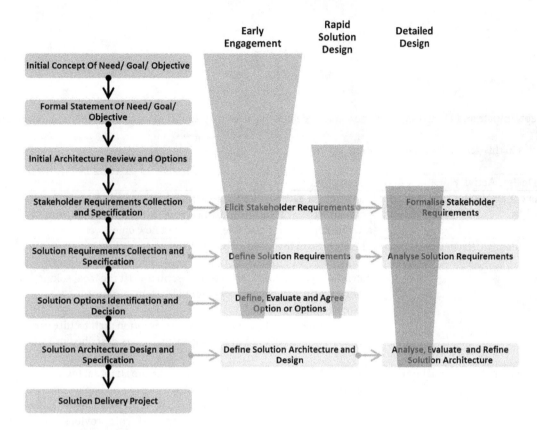

Figure 144 – Generalised Solution Design Process Mapped to Engagement Types

This solution design process can use some or all of the techniques and approaches contained in these engagement types as the design progresses.

- *Early Engagement* – this is business consulting exercise designed to take a not very well describe problematic situation and to define a set of solution options. It is described in section 4.6.4 on page 235. Early engagement starts with a broad undefined situation and narrows it to a set of not formally systematised solutions.

- *Rapid Solution Design* – this is a quick solution scoping exercise. It is narrowly focussed. It is not designed to perform a deep analysis of the problem. It is focussed on identifying systematic solutions. It is described in section 4.6.5 on page 257.

- *Detailed Design* – this is a formal structured solution design process designed to create an information technology solution design specification. It is described in section 4.6.6 on page 276.

The business engagement process described in detail in section 4.6.1 on page 161 does not map to the solution design process as this is a different and more generalised type of solution architecture engagement.

This solution design process is a subset of the wider generalised solution delivery process that is described in section 4.3 on page 112. This solution design process includes the activities involved in creating the design. It does not include the management stream involved in the planning and allocation of resources and budget for the design activities.

Processes are good because they provide predictability in what has to be done, in how long the work will take and in the resources required. They provide certainty that the work will include all the necessary activities to produce a usable output.

Methodologising the solution design process introduces repeatability into the work. However, these processes should be used as an indicator of the work to be done and can be knowingly modified to suit the circumstances of each engagement.

The generalised solution delivery process has the four initial stages of:

1. Concept
2. Initiate
3. Plan
4. Design

The Concept, Initiate and Design stages of the solution delivery process map to this more detailed solution design process.

The activities in this generalised solution design process are:

Solution Design Activity	Description
Initial Concept Of Need/ Goal/ Objective	The business have an idea for a solution based on an apparent need to solve a problem, to do what is currently not possible, to react or respond to an external demand or to be able to achieve a new objective.
Formal Statement Of Need/ Goal/ Objective	This formalises the initial concept to introduce greater consistency and detail. It serves to understand the business, objectives, purposes and potential organisational impacts. It describes what the ideal solution will do. It also identifies the high-level potential system impacts. The business can do this work on its own. Solution architecture can assist by offering a version of the early engagement process described in section 4.6.4 on page 235.
Initial Architecture Review and Options	This uses the formal statement of need to create an initial high-level view of the overall solution, its new and existing systems and applications components, the required functionality, their interfaces, the required processes and the business functions impacted. This provides a container for the requirements and a vision for the solution. This identifies the breadth of the end-to-end solution landscape without defining its depth in detail. The rapid solution design engagement process described in section 4.6.5 on page 257 could be used or adapted for this work.
Stakeholder Requirements Collection and Specification	This uses this initial architectural review output in a structured way to elicit and formalise the set of stakeholder requirements across all the dimensions of functionality, processes and organisation structures and change.
Solution Requirements Collection and Specification	The solution requirements specification is a fuller, more detailed and elaborated set of solution requirements encompassing all the solution components. This includes the requirements explicitly identified by stakeholders and the implied requirements.
Solution Options Identification and Decision	The subset of realistic and achievable solution design options is created. These are evaluated and a decision is made on the most suitable option (or small number of options) to define in detail.
Solution Architecture Design and Specification	This is the detailed solution specification derived from the stakeholder and solution requirements and the selected solution option or options. The detailed design process, or a version of it, described in section 4.6.6 on page 276 can be used here.
Implementation Project	This uses the detailed solution specification to act as an input to solution delivery project definition and to create a realistic implementation plan, schedule, set of costs and required resources.

Table 42 – Generalised Solution Design Process Steps

The design process spans several organisation functions – business, solution architecture and business analysis – that do work or are involved in work at different stages. There may be other functions that are also involved as the solution design is refined such as the other architecture functions described in section 3.3.1 on page 75.

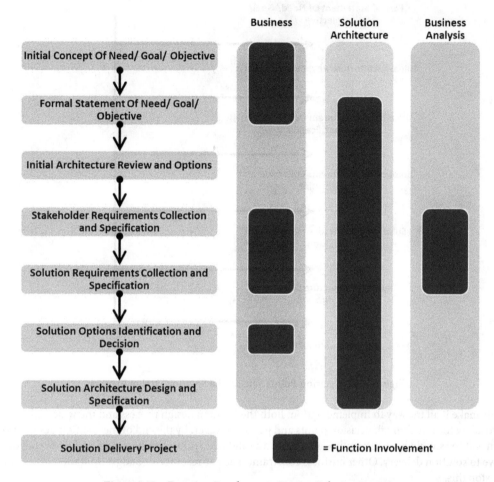

Figure 145 – Function Involvement During Solution Design

The topic of the interface between the solution architecture function and the business analysis function is discussed in more detail in section 4.4 on page 124.

Requirements documentation is one part of the solution design process. The subject of requirements gathering is analysed in more detail in section 4.4 on page 124.

This proposed level and indicative schedule for the involvement of the teams involved in creating a solution design.

Within the solution design process, there is (or should be) a decision point after each stage where a decision is made if it is worthwhile to proceed to the next stage.

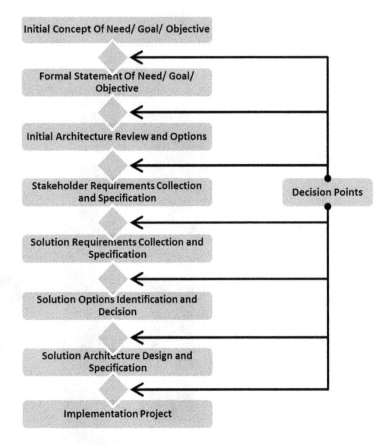

Figure 146 – Decision Points Within the Solution Design Process

Not all concepts make it all the way to implementation. Both the solution design process and the wider solution delivery process need to allow for this through decision points and gates. However, by the end of the solution design process, the solution design will (or should be) sufficiently elaborated and validated against business need and its overall deliverability to allow it to move to solution delivery. Other business constraints such as resource or budget limitation or other business priorities may stop this.

The general rule is to do as little as possible to achieve as much as possible to make an informed decision on whether and how to proceed to the next stage in the solution journey.

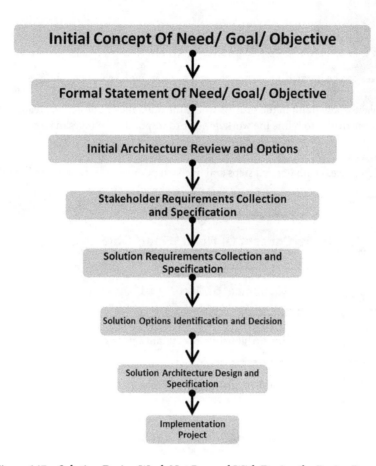

Figure 147 – Solution Design Work Not Proceed With During the Design Process

Finally, the solution design process is not necessarily sequential.

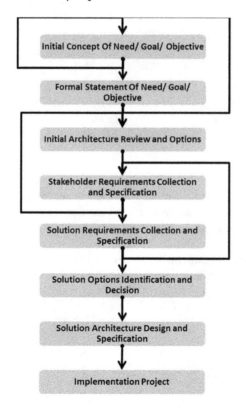

Figure 148 – Iterations During Solution Design Process

The solution design activities can be iterated a number of times to different levels of detail.

These iterations can take place at any point in the process where the outcome of one activity leads to a decision to repeat that activity or a number of prior activities to refine the work done or to respond to changes in circumstances or additional information.

So, the entire solution design process with iterated steps and decision points can be represented as follows:

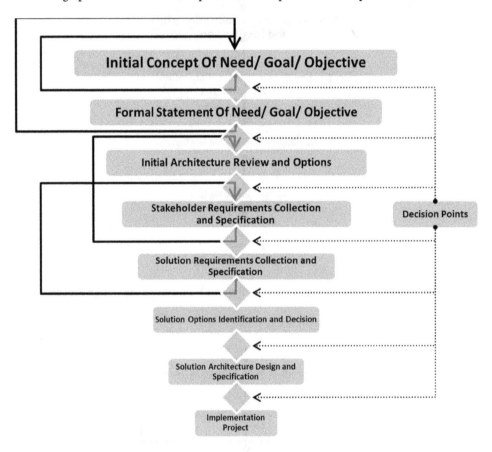

Figure 149 – Representation of Complete Generalised Solution Design Process

However, you need to avoid:

- *Analysis Looping* – where analysis never finished and you never escape the analysis stage. Either or both of the analysis and design function or the business do not want to let go and are always looking for perfection and want to retain ownership. They fear that once analysis ends and delivery starts they will have lost control.

- *Decision/Analysis Looping* – where decision making is deferred because of requests for more analysis. The fear of decision-making is masked by endless requests for more information, additional options and more clarification

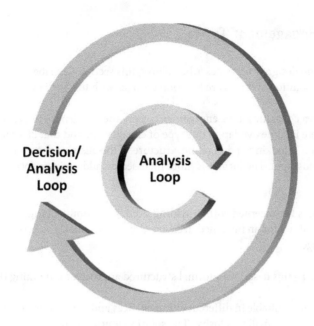

Figure 150 – Analysis and Decision Loops

The subject of knowledge acquisition is covered in section 4.2.1 on page 95.

You need to look for and address the issue of decision avoidance when gathering information and creating solution design options.

Figure 151 – Analysis Paralysis And Decision Avoidance

The solution architect needs to provide leadership in decision making during solution analysis and design. The solution architect needs to focus business needs on solution options and lead the business through the decision-making process. The architect should mediate between business and solution provider, either internal or external. This makes the transition from problem/need to solution implementation and operation easier. The solution architect needs to engage with the complexities of the problem at an early stage.

Section 4.6 on page 161 describes the various engagement types proposed in this book. These provide a structures approach to solution design and thus to making decisions.

4.6.3 Solution Design Engagement Types

Within the context of the solution design process described above, this section describes three different approaches to solution design and the way the solution architecture function engages with the business organisation:

1. ***Early Engagement*** – this is a consulting-type engagement where the problem to be resolved or the opportunity to be addressed is uncertain. There is some overlap in this type of engagement and that of a business architecture engagement. The latter is broader in that it is looking to design the structure of the business function (including any information technology and solution landscape). The former is more focussed on addressing a specific but currently undefined potential solution area.

2. ***Rapid Solution Design*** – this is concerned with providing a quick solution scoping result for a reasonably well-defined solution requirement. This allows for an informed decision to be made quickly to proceed or not to proceed to a more detailed solution design stage.

3. ***Structured Solution Design*** – this describes a formal structured approach for defining the detail of a solution.

Each of these types of engagement is suitable in different circumstances and at different stages in the solution acquisition journey. These engagements are not mutually exclusive. The solution journey could encompass all three at different times. In the context of the conceptual solution delivery processes detailed in section 4.3 on page 112, these three engagement types can be mapped as follows.

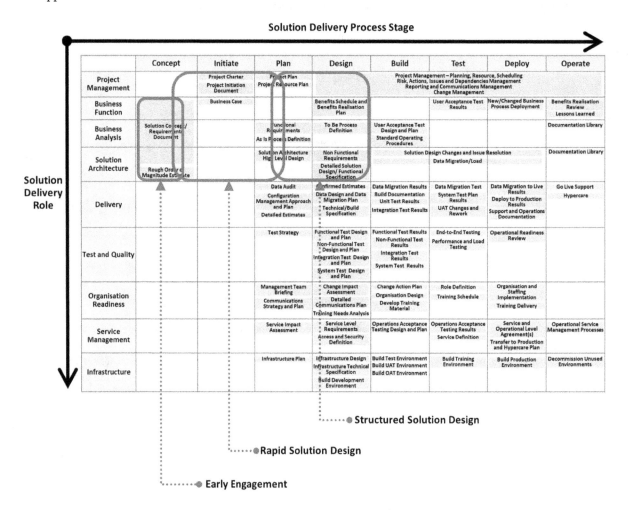

Figure 152 – Solution Design Journey and Solution Architecture Engagement Types

The business engagement process does not map to the solution delivery process as it is a different type of solution architecture engagement and occurs before specific solution design or delivery starts.

Early engagement starts at the earliest stage when the problem and its resolution options are least well-defined and least understood. The early engagement process can be divided into two stages:

1. Where the problem is understood and an approach to its resolution is arrived at
2. Where the resolution is then systematised – converted into a systematic solution design

The rapid solution design engagement creates solution-on-a-page view of the solution options. It can occur after the early engagement or instead of it, if the scope of the problem is reasonably well-defined and accepted by the business stakeholders. The rapid solution design technique can be used as part of the early engagement process to systematise – create a solution system specification – for the problem resolutions identified during early engagement.

The structured solution design engagement creates a detailed solution specification.

Each of these engagements creates outputs or artefacts that perform two functions:

1. Describe the work done and provide an audit trail and a support for any conclusions or recommendations

2. Describe the design of the solution to an appropriate level of detail

The solution design artefact does not necessarily have to be a single monolithic specification that is frozen in time once created.

The core purpose of the solution design artefact that is to allows the work programme to create that solution to be defined and to specify the work in sufficient detail. The solution design process is a journey and the solution design artefact is just one step along that journey. The solution design artefact has to be appropriate for the subsequent solution delivery stages and no more. The topic of solution design artefacts is described in more detail in section 4.10 on page 377.

4.6.4 Early Engagement

4.6.4.1 Introduction

The early engagement process[39] in the solution design and implementation journey is intended to allow the exploration of an as yet undefined solution that resolves a problem or addresses an opportunity. The work is done from both a business and information technology perspective. The objective is to understand the scope, requirements, objectives, approach, options for the resolution and to get a high-level understanding of the likely resources, timescale and cost required before starting the solution implementation.

Early engagement is essentially about problem solving within a systems-thinking framework. However, it is not a generalised approach to problem solving and systems thinking. The problem, its resolution and the translation of the resolution into a systematised solution occurs within the context of an organisation and within the context of the at least tacit acceptance of the need for a solution and indeed for an information technology solution. This adds a specificity to the nature of the problem-solving work being done which narrows its scope and reduces some of the applicability of these more general techniques. There is a great deal of material available on the related subjects of problem solving and systems thinking that can be applied in the more general and wider context.

---

[39] This section is derived from the Soft Systems Methodology originally developed by Peter Checkland. I have modified the approach and extended it to the essentially systematising inherent in solution architecture. See *Checkland, P 1999, Soft Systems Methodology in Action. John Wiley and Sons Ltd, Chichester* ISBN 978-0471986058.

In the following, what is being analysed can be termed a problematic situation. This is used to convey the level of doubt and uncertainty about exactly what the problem is. Similarly, what solves this problematic situation is called a resolution rather than a solution. In the context of this book and of solution architecture in general, solution means the systematised set of components that deliverables an operational solution. Resolution involves moving from the as-is problematic situation to the to-be resolved situation. The resolution is achieved through the creation of solution designs and their subsequent implementation.

There is no merit in identifying a problem if a resolution to that problem is not also identified.

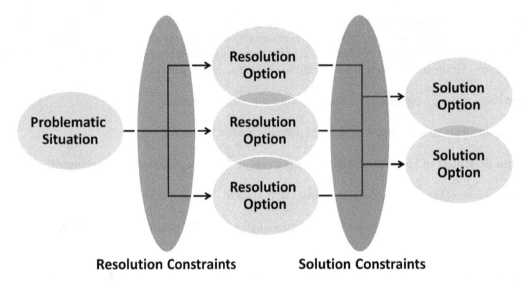

Figure 153 – Path from Problematic Situation to Solution

In the context of solution architecture – the design of a specific solution or set of solutions – the early engagement process is aimed at defining a solution that accomplishes a resolution that resolves a problematic situation. As mentioned above, the early engagement process can be viewed as consisting of two stages:

1. Where the situation requiring a resolution is understood and resolution options or options are agreed by the situation stakeholders
2. Where the resolution is then translated into a solution design with its various solution components

The resolution can be regarded as theoretical answer and the solution as its tangible actualisation in terms of technology and other work and changes.

The problem and resolution analysis may require that the IT function and the solution architecture function in particular look outside their core capabilities and their comfort zones to be able to perform the work.

The early engagement process is not a requirements gathering exercise. Traditional requirements gathering requires substantial initial effort, resources and cost and for the business to commit without doubts, uncertainties and ambiguities being known or resolved. The early engagement process is a problem solving and solution definition exercise. It defines and validates resolution hypotheses at an early stage. This reduces (but not necessarily completely eliminates) doubts, uncertainties and ambiguities in the problem and its resolution, thereby reduces the risk associated with any subsequent solution implementation.

The early engagement process focusses on understanding the overall problem and determining realistic options for viable resolutions. It seeks to address the end-to-end resolution experience.

The early engagement process involves taking a not necessarily well-defined request from the business organisation, defining a resolution and then creating a sufficiently unambiguous set of solution options, including their delivery and operation, quickly and accurately.

The solution design aspect of the engagement process involving aligning the resolution with the current and new or changed organisation structure, processes and systems.

It is a consulting engagement performed by solution architecture. It focusses on understanding the overall problem and determining realistic options for viable resolutions. To be effective, the solution architecture function must have the skills and experience to perform such an engagement and must be trusted by the business to have those capabilities.

The engagement process involves acquiring knowledge and learning about the situation in order to:

- Be able to offer improvements and possible solution options
- Understand the complexity and confusion that exists in the current condition and situation
- Understand the external complexities - economic, business, social, legal, regulatory, partner, competitor, technologies
- Understand how different participants and stakeholders view the current condition and situation and their view what is needed to achieve a resolution

There will be human dimensions to the early engagement process that cannot be ignored and that must be borne in mind throughout the engagement. The engagement exists because a person or group of people have requested the engagement or have been compelled to accept the engagement by their organisational superior. There may be resistance to the engagement. There may be unwillingness to accept the engagement being conducted by the solution architecture function. There will be direct participants – those involved in the engagement – and indirect participants – stakeholders who have delegated direct participation but who will be involved in reviewing the output from the engagement and any recommendations. Each of the parties involved in the engagement will have different motivations. Those leading the engagement process must be aware of these personal aspects and a lack of awareness of them may cause the engagement to fail. The business engagement participants will be involved in the current problem state. They will be affected by changes to the current state proposed by the resolution. There may be conflicting views and opinions between the different participants, direct and indirect.

The benefits of an early engagement exercise include

- It ensures that the business and IT invest in the right solutions in the right way and at the right time
- Assumptions about the problem to be resolved and the resolution options are validated early in the solution design process
- The amount of problem and solution knowledge available will be increased
- It provides for evidence-based decision making
- Participants are brought together to gain a common understanding of and agreement about the situation requiring a resolution and the resolution options
- The accuracy of the subsequent solution implementation planning and forecasting will be improved and any solution delivery will be optimised

There are many principles that underpin the early engagement activities. The most important of these ae:

- Look to understand and tackle the entire problematic situation, from start to end
- Identify the participants, both internal and external, involved in the current operations
- Identify the business processes or, if they do not exist or are not well-defined, the modes and methods of usage and interaction of participants with the current problematic situation
- Understand what participants need and are looking to achieve and experience
- Collect and use data to make decisions in order to make those decisions as evidence-based as possible
- Seek to maximise simplicity of resolution subject to the constraints of necessary complexity
- Keep the engagement team small, skilled, experienced and focussed
- Automate the components of the problematic situation resolution as much as possible

In any engagement, there will be two scopes that govern and define the extent of the work:

- *Scope of the Engagement* – who is involved, the number of participants, their expected involvement, how long it is expected to take, what outputs are expected?

- *Scope Of Situation To Be Resolved* – what are we trying to resolve, what is the core problem or opportunity, what are the secondary or extended or dependent problems or opportunities and are these in scope?

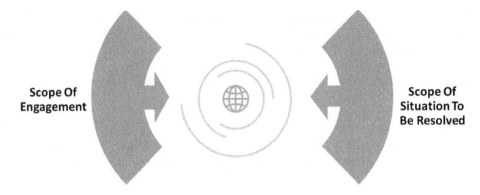

Figure 154 – Getting the Scope of the Early Engagement Right

If the two scopes are uncertain or undefined or not agreed effort will be wasted in clarifying the scope. Uncertain scope tends to indicate a lack of commitment by those looking for the engagement.

If the scope is too wide there will be too much work to be done that will take a long time before results can be obtained and presented. If the scope is too narrow the underlying problematic situation may not be resolved. Getting the scope right means understanding and accepting what the core problematic situation or opportunity to be resolved is and understanding and accepting what needs to be done to arrive at a likely resolution and associated solution design.

The identification of resolution to the problematic solution can be difficult for a variety of reasons. There can be uncertain, undefined or multiple mixed and contradictory objectives among the various stakeholders and the parties in the organisation and outside the organisation that will be impacted by the changes associated with the resolution. There can be a lack of coherence and clarity among stakeholders on what needs to be achieved. Some of the stakeholder needs may not be articulated or expressed. This can be further complicated by factors affecting complexity such as a large number of parties involved in problem and its resolution, large number of interactions and connections between these parties, undefined or partially defined processes.

The challenges can be added to by opposition from some stakeholders and affected parties to the need for a resolution and its associated change. There can be unpredictability and uncertainty in what the problematic situation being analysed and this can change during the analysis. Finally, there can be time and cost constraints on the analysis and resolution definition exercise.

These difficulties represent obstacles to both defining the resolution and then implementing the solution to operationalise the resolution.

Many of these problems cannot be fixed during the engagement. They can represent quite fundamental differences of view. At best they can only be mitigated through limited consensus. The solution architecture will be aware of the difficulties during the early engagement exercise. He or she may not be able to resolve them. But the awareness of them will ensure that they are taken account of when defining the resolution and solution options.

The outputs from the early engagement process should include:

- Statement of the problematic situation to be resolved
- Identification of the parties involved directly with the problematic situation and their interactions
- Identification of the stakeholders of the problematic situation
- Statement of understanding of the business need and drivers for a resolution
- Definition of the scope of the resolution option(s) and identification of their benefits
- Definition of the scope of the solution option(s) and identification of their benefits
- Documentation of the likely scope of solution delivery effort – cost, time, resources, locations

- Definition of organisation impact of solution operation – organisation change, staffing
- Understanding of the overall complexity of delivery and operation
- Definition of possible delivery options

The outcomes of an effective early engagement process include

- Reduced probability of creating poor solution designs – components not included, solution not meeting the requirements of the business function, solution complexity not understood, organisational impact of solution operation not understood, solution implementation cost, time and resources unclear
- Improved business case for investment in solution implementation – greater detail, greater accuracy and greater confidence in the stated costs and benefits
- Increase probability of effective design and reduced subsequent rework and change
- Increased likelihood user satisfaction with the solution that is ultimately delivered

Resolution options are scenarios of the to-be condition/situation/state that resolve or improve the initial problematic situation. There will always be multiple resolution options, each of which will have a different solution component profile. Each resolution option will have a different set of characteristics in terms of suitability, degree of improvement achieved, scope, cost and complexity

All resolution options have impacts and will involve changes: people, organisation and its structure, processes, technology, data and information technology infrastructure. The resolution changes do not necessarily need, or need to be limited to, IT systems. While the achievement of a resolution will always consist of a solution the solution may not always have to consist of IT systems and applications. Even if the solution has IT systems and applications components, these may not always be at the core of the solution: they may be peripheral and exist to support organisation and process changes.

The resolution and its associated solution need to be a staged transition from the as-is situation to the to-be transformed situation from where we are to where we want or need to be

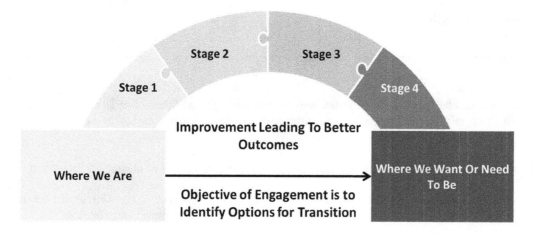

Figure 155 – Resolution Needs To Be Bridge From the As-Is Problematic Situation to a To-Be Improved Situation

The core early engagement process, after which resolution options are identified but solutions are not necessarily defined, involves five main streams of activities that are performed in parallel. The focus moves between each stream as work progresses.

1. *Investigation, Information Gathering* – meeting with business function stakeholders to understand different views of current problem state and desired/idealised future state – this activity is continuous through the engagement
2. *Building Activity Models* – describe views of as-is and desired or planned to-be actions and their sequence – this activity starts after initial information gathering. As the models are built they are expanded on and updated as more information becomes available
3. *Questioning, Verification, Validation, Elaboration* – review activity models with business function stakeholders
4. *Defining Actions* – define actions to implement target to-be activity model

5. *Defining Implementation* – define implementation activities to actualise target to-be activity model

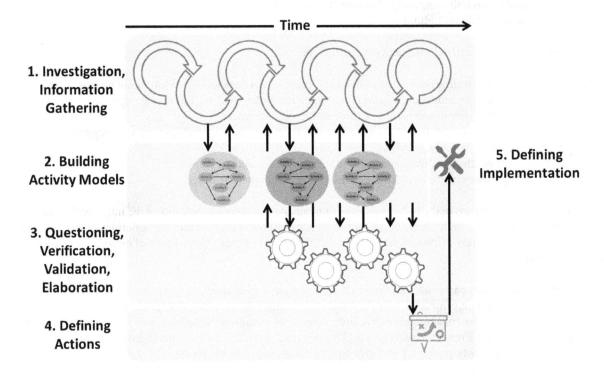

Figure 156 – Core Early Engagement Process

4.6.4.2 What Is A Problem?

There may be concerns about the nature of the problematic situation and the set of circumstances that cause it or give rise to in the first place.

The perception that a problem or problematic situation exists may not be shared or agreed by all stakeholders and participants in the early engagement process or in the stages that precede the acceptance that the early engagement process is the correct approach to take.

The agreement that a problem exists and that its nature is certain may not be definite or unequivocal among this group.

It may be that the problem is such that it does not have a resolution. Or it may be that the set of circumstances that cause the problematic situation can only at best be mitigated or partially circumvented rather than being resolved.

It may be that the problem determination and resolution process that is early engagement does not derive the best resolution. It may be that the early engagement process focuses too quickly on one or a subset of potential resolutions to the exclusion of better resolutions.

It may be that the early engagement process is not suitable because of the nature of the problem.

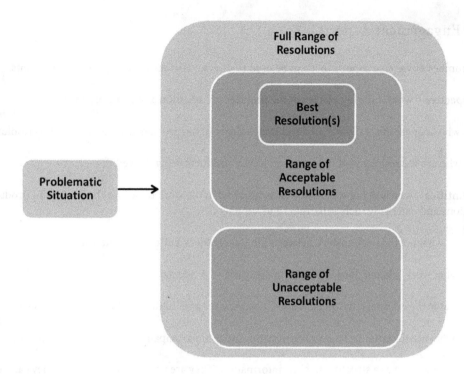

Figure 157 – Problem and Resolution Options

There may be more than one acceptable resolution to the problem.

Before the resolution definition process can start, the problem has to be studied and agreed. We have to understand what renders the situation problematic and then define the underlying problem.

It may be useful to categorise the problem to be resolved along the lines of:

- **Simple** – these are problems whose nature is agreed without difficulty, that are well-structured and whose resolution can be identified quickly without needing significant effort.

- **Intermediate** – these are problems whose nature requires some time to agree but that can be agreed, that that are well-structured and that a resolution can be identified after some time and after exploring a number of resolution options.

- **Difficult** – these are problems that take some time to agree before any resolution identification can take place, that are poorly structured and ill-defined and that require significant effort and the analysis of multiple resolution options before a not necessarily optimal resolution can be agreed.

- **Highly Complex** – these are problems where the causative factors are not known or understood or agreed so the nature of the problem is itself problematic, very poorly structured and not defined and that requires significant effort and the analysis of multiple resolution options and before a not necessarily optimal resolution can be agreed or where no real resolution exists.

The act of categorising the problem may in itself be difficult and there may not be any agreement or consensus on how difficult the problematic situation is. This lack of agreement by stakeholders and engagement participants may in itself be an indicator of difficulty in the problem. Some people may not accept there is a problem or may over and underestimate its severity or impact.

The relates to and overlaps with the topic of problem and solution knowledge and complexity and the approaches that have to be adopted that is discussed in section 4.2 on page 95.

4.6.4.3 Early Engagement Aspects

This describes a number of views or aspects that can be used to direct questions to engagement participants.

- **Overall Perspective** – what is the big picture of the problematic situation and its resolution?

- **Proprietor** – who is or are the real owners of and stakeholders in the problematic situation and its resolution?

- **End Users** – who are the recipients of the set of services or products being delivered?

- **Actors and Entities** – who is doing what and who is involved in the work to deliver the services or products, both within the organisations and externally such as partners and suppliers?

- **Relationships** – what are the relationships between the stakeholders, entities and end users?

- **Processing** – what work is being done to deliver the services or products?

- **Backdrop** – what is the external environment and its constraints and limitations in which the operations occur?

- **Boundaries** – what are the boundaries between and groupings of participants?

These views are intended to act as a structure to elicit information. They are not fixed or absolute. They can be modified and added to in order to gather more relevant details.

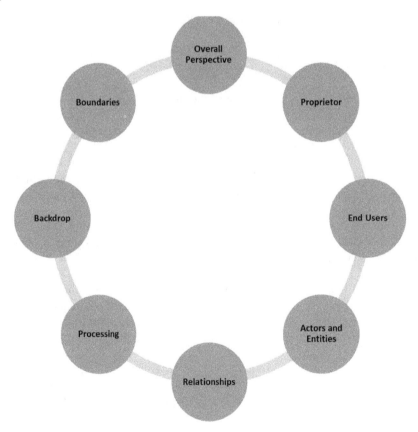

Figure 158 – Early Engagement Information Gathering Aspects

For each of these aspects of view, these are some questions to ask of participants in the engagement or to otherwise get answers to in order to gather information in a structured manner or to prompt discussion. This is not an exhaustive or prescriptive list.

Aspect	Sample Questions To Ask Engagement Participants Or To Get Answers To
Overall Perspective	What is the wider environment – business function, organisational, operating landscape, external entities – in which the problematic situation and any resolution exists? What is the real problem to be resolved? How serious is this problem? What will be the core impact of any resolution? Will this impact be limited or far-reaching? What will be the wider impact of any resolution? Will this impact be limited or far-reaching?
Proprietor	Who are the primary owners of the problematic situation that may be changed as a consequence of the engagement and its associated business functions and business processes? Who are the secondary owners? Who are the other stakeholders? What are the relationships between the primary and secondary owners and stakeholders? What are their roles in the organisation? Do they understand and agree with the need for a change? Will they be part of the resolution? How positively or negatively do they view the likelihood of change? What can be done to get more positively engaged in the resolution definition and agreement process? Are there conflicts or disagreements between the proprietors?
End Users	Who buys/uses/receives the product or service being supplied in the environment where the problematic situation exists? How many different types or groups of users are there? What are the profiles of these end users? Who are the more important and less important end users and why are they so classified? What problems/issues/challenges do these end users experience in buying/using/receiving the product or service? Which are the more important/more frequent/higher impact problems? How will the end users react to the proposed changes? Who will benefit and who will lose out as a consequence of the proposed changes?
Actors and Entities	Who are the actors and entities, both internal and external, who are involved in creating and delivering the product or service being supplied in the environment where the problematic situation exists?

Aspect	Sample Questions To Ask Engagement Participants Or To Get Answers To
	How many different types or groups of actors and entities are there? What are the profiles of these actors and entities? What are their roles?
	Why are the external actors involved in the way they are?
	What problems/issues/challenges do these actors and entities experience in creating and delivering the product or service?
	How will the actors and entities react to the proposed changes?
	Which actors and entities will benefit and who will lose out as a consequence of the proposed changes?
Relationships	What are the relationships between stakeholders, actors and entities? Who are the participants in the relationships?
	What is the nature of these relationships such as are they permanent or temporary, direct or indirect, strong or weak, collaborative or adversarial?
	Which are the more important relationships in terms of operating the set of arrangements that create and deliver the product or service?
	How are the relationships perceived?
	What processes are performed or enabled by these relationships?
	How well do the relationships work? What are their problems and issues?
	What changes are needed in the relationships to achieve or that will be caused by the proposed changes?
	What will the reaction be to these relationship changes?
Processing	What processing is performed to transforming inputs into the products or services being supplied? How many different sets and types of processing are there?
	What are the inputs to these processes? Who supplies the inputs? What issues and problems exist with the supply of these inputs?
	What are the products or services created by these processes? What issues and problems exist with the creation of these products or services?
	What are the steps in these processes?
	What waste occurs in the processes?
	How variable is process performance? What factors affect variability?
	How predictable is process performance?
	How well do the processes work? What are their problems and issues? What happens when the processes fail? In what way do the current processes fail?
	Who knows the processes?
	How are the processes managed? Who managed them? Are they optimised?

Aspect	Sample Questions To Ask Engagement Participants Or To Get Answers To
	What changes are needed in the processes to achieve or that will be caused by the proposed changes?
	What will the reaction be to these process changes?
Backdrop	What are the wider constraints in the operating environment and landscape, such as legislative, regulatory, financial, resource, personnel, time, competitive, safety, health, technological and ethical that impact on the problematic situation?
	How are these constraints currently handled?
	How do these constraints impact the problematic situation?
	How do these constraints impact the resolution?
	In what way can the impacts of these constraints by limited or mitigated?
Boundaries	What barriers exist within the problematic situation? What would you like to do but currently cannot do?
	Where are we fixing the boundary to the problematic situation? Is this too confined or too extreme?
	Are there different views on the problematic situation boundary? If so, how can we reconcile these?
	What is the extent of the problematic situation? Is this view too broad or too narrow?
	Are we looking to resolve problems that do not exist?

Table 43 – Early Engagement Aspect Sample Questions

4.6.4.4 Early Engagement Questions

In addition to the aspect questions, this is non-exhaustive list of other questions that can be asked of participants during information gathering. Like the aspect related questions, the objective is to elicit information and to initiate discussions in order to understand the problematic situation.

- What controls and affects the way in which information, work and resources flow through the situation? What affects do these controls have on throughput and performance? Why are the controls in place? How did they arise? How did they subsequently change?

- Where can the current problematic situation be leveraged to create improvements?

- Are processes and performance monitored and managed? If so, where does process feedback and resulting actions take place and by whom?

- What do we need to do and/or stop doing to have a positive effect on the problematic situation?

- What are the factors and variables affect performance and what impact does each variable have?

- How can these variables and factors be controlled? How linked are these variables?

- What can or needs to be done to change the behaviour of key stakeholders?

- What happens if the proposed resolution does not happen or is only partially implemented?

- What assumptions are being made about the analysis? How valid are these assumptions?

- What assumptions are being made about the resolution? How valid are these assumptions?

- Who makes decisions? What controls do we have over these decision makers? What decisions do we need them to make?

- What interventions will affect the problematic situation? What effects will then have? How can these interventions be achieved?

- What can stop us achieving a resolution? What can be done to prevent these?

- How does strategy development and policy-making task take place in the organisation of the function that is the subject of the engagement? What influence do we need from strategy development and policy-making to achieve a resolution?

- What is needed to ensure that the resolution is successful in solving the problematic situation? What control and influence do we have over their achievement?

- Are the right resources available to the right people at the right time to enable processes to work? If not, what are the problems and how can they be resolved?

- What is the network that links actors and entities?

- How does information flow through the network?

- How does work flow through the network?

- How do resources flow through the network?

- What motivates actors and entities to achieve their objectives?

- What controls do we have over these motivations?

- How are motivations linked to achievements?

- What stresses and circumstances will affect the resolution and cause it to fail or perform sub-optimally? How can we avoid or limit the impact of these circumstances?

The early engagement process is not about asking a long list of questions of participants. It is not an interrogation. It is concerned with gathering information to achieve an objective of defining and agreeing a resolution and a solution design to achieve that resolution. The questions are just a means to that ultimate goal. They are a guide to gathering evidence and stimulating discussion and getting participants to contribute and make their knowledge available.

4.6.4.5 Building Activity Model Stream

The activity involves the definition of initial high-level as-is and to-be activity models. These are generic model consists of three sets of concentric activities:

- **Operational** – what gets done, in what sequence, with what dependencies, with what resources
- **Monitoring, Management, Administration, Control** – control of flow, allocation and reallocation, reporting on throughput, respond to change
- **Improvement, Optimisation** – ensure activities are fit for purpose, delivering benefits, achieving expected outcomes, activity modification and enhancement

Start initially with the as-is activity models to understand the current problematic situation and identify where problems are occurring. These are not and nor are they intended to be detailed process maps.

Activity models are not full business process (re)designs at this stage. The intention at this stage is just capture, initially at a high-level and in more detail as the analysis proceeds, the key activities and their flows.

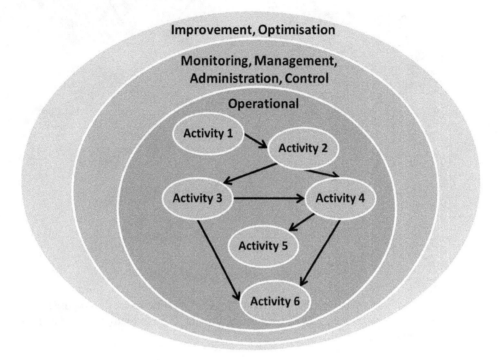

Figure 159 – Activity Model Layers

The operational activity model will define the activities that are performed, their flow and the sequence in which they are performed based on the outcome of previous activities.

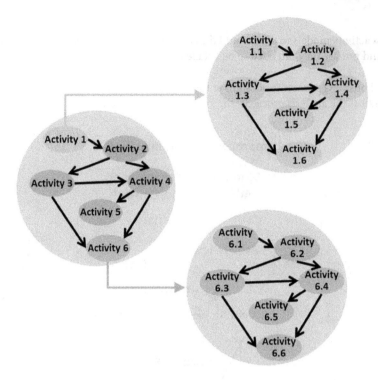

Figure 160 – Layers of Detail in Activity Models

There will be layers of activity models as detail is expanded on and high-level activities are decomposed into lower level activities. This is similar to identifying sub-processes with a process. Initially, keep the activity model definition at a high-level. Detail and refinements can be added later.

The activity models derived from investigations can be used to create a structured set of questions to allow activity details be elaborated, explored, understood and refined. Use the model as a framework to ask informed questions and gather information.

Activity	Trigger(s)	Dependencies	Required Input(s)	Expected Output(s)	Next Step(s)	Expected Outcome(s)	Who and How Performed	What Skills Required	How Monitored	How Quality Maintained
Activity 1										
Activity 2										
Activity 3										
Activity 4										
Activity 5										
Activity 6										

Table 44 – Activity Model Details

Different resolution participants may have different views of the activity models of the current as-is and desired to-be situation.

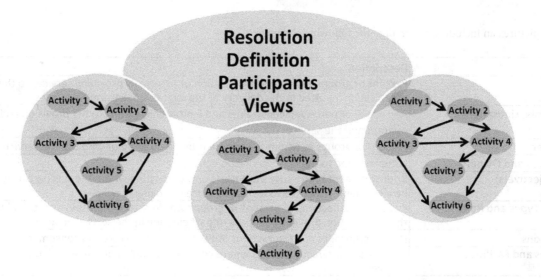

Figure 161 – Different Activity Views by Different Engagement Business Participants

This ambiguity is to be expected. Different participants will have different levels of knowledge of the complexity and the nuances of current activities. Similarly, they will have different views of what the desired to-be set of activities are to resolve the problem.

Live with this ambiguity at the early stages of the analysis and look to create a consensus during later stages. You may need to create several activity models initially and combine them later.

Models are essentially simplifications of the underlying real-world situation and the interactions between participants. This simplification is necessary to capture information. Complexity can be added during refinement and enhancement performed as the engagement proceeds.

4.6.4.6 Rich Pictures

The next stage in the engagement involves the creation of rich pictures, initially of the as-is situation and then of the to-be resolution option or options. These pictures are used to explore, validate and improve the view of the as-in situation.

Rich pictures can be viewed as conceptual or hybrid models of situations combining different views in a single picture. Models are invariably simplifications of the real-world situation they represent. They do not capture all the complexity of the situation. As such these models are wrong. It is important they are not too wrong. Errors relating to not enough detail are tolerable. Fundamental errors relating to entities and their interactions are not tolerable.

These are detailed visualisations that represent information considerably more effectively than lengthy narrative text. The show relationships and interactions between entities. The visual format provides a more concise illustration of the situation. It is a far better tool to elicit information from engagement participants than a text description. Gaps, errors and omissions are more easily identified. Participants can be walked through the situation and its activities and interactions. It assists informed and involved discussions.

Rich pictures can be viewed as a form of organisation and problematic situation mindmap.

Rich pictures can be developed on whiteboards or flipcharts. They should be converted to a printed form that can be accommodated on a page size such as A3.

You can evolve and refine the rich picture representations of as-in and to-be situations throughout the engagement exercise. You cannot expect to capture every piece of information. It is important to focus on the important elements and the key entities and their interactions.

The rich picture can include some or all of the following elements:

Element	Description
Actor	Persons or groups within the organisation or externally providing services to the organisation involved in the delivery of the overall service and their roles
Constraints, Limitations	Any actual or perceived constraints and limitations relating to the provision and operation of the service
Consumer	Persons or groups at whom the service is being directed or who use the service
Core Issues and Owners	Issues relating to the core service objectives
Core Objective(s)	Brief statement of the core purpose(s) of the situation where there is perceived to be a problem – what the associated service is looking to achieve
Entities, Types and Roles	Functional collections of persons or groups within the organisation or external to the organisation providing services or participating in the service delivery
Interactions	Dealings, linkages and interactions between entities, actors and consumers
Locations and Facilities	Locations or interaction points where consumers avail of or are provided with services
Obligations	Obligations of actors and entities, relating to the core service objectives
Options	Options relating to the core service objectives
Processes	Processes that are used to deliver service or support its delivery
Questions	Outstanding questions relating to the core service objectives
Relationships and Dependencies	Relationships and dependencies between other elements of the rich picture This could include details on the nature of the relationship such as permanent or temporary, direct or indirect, strong or weak, collaborative or adversarial
Requirements	Requirements of actors and entities, relating to the core service objectives
Rules	Rules apply to the delivery or provision of the service and to whom the rules apply
Viewpoints	Views or opinions of actors on the provision and operation of the service

Table 45 – Elements of a Rich Picture

A formal tool such as Archimate (see section 8.3.5.1.2 on page 518) could be used to create rich pictures. This would require all parties to be familiar with the Archimate symbol vocabulary.

There is no solution, system or application element in this list. You are not looking at solutions, systems or applications at this stage. There may be some solutions, systems or applications involved in the current problematic situation. They are just enablers of interactions and activities. These solutions may also be contributing to the problem. Introducing solutions and systems now may lead to restricting the resolution to improvements in the operations of these systems. Taking a solutions and systems view will means that interactions will be described in an organised way. We want to understand disorganised connections during this early stage of information gathering and analysis.

Rich pictures do not have a time dimension. The pictures are time-independent representations and show all activities and interactions happening at the same time.

The rich picture can be built-up over time as knowledge is acquired and uncertainty resolved. The key elements to start with are the consumers, actors, entities and relationships.

There can be multiple rich pictures representing the views of different participants. These differences can help understanding and expressing differences in perspective among participants. This in turn can help in clarifying and prioritising requirements.

The following shows a very simplistic example of a logical rich picture. It can be made far more visual than this simple example. The elements can be replaced with icons that more closely represent them.

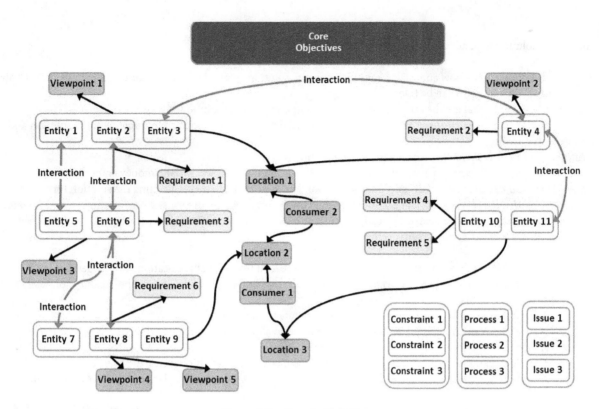

Figure 162 – Sample Rich Picture

In this very simple example, the constraints, processes and issues are listed in a key to the picture.

Rich pictures that represent resolution options are not systematised views of the solution at this stage of the analysis. They do not contain system-related components such as IT applications, infrastructure and data flows at this stage. They link entities, relationships, activities and interactions. Resist the temptation to include systematic parts at the investigation stage and pre-judge options for resolution and transformation. Jumping to conclusions at this stage will limit the scope of information gathered. Rich pictures are information gathering and validation and consensus building tools at this stage.

The rich picture can be used to identify opportunities for changes.

4.6.4.7 Resolution Options

Each resolution option can be evaluated in terms of attributes such as:

- *Achievable* – can it be implemented?
- *Realistic* – is the resolution practical?
- *Desirable* – is the resolution required and suitable?
- *Affordable* – can the organisation afford the likely cost of the resolution
- *Operable* – is the resolution workable?
- *Usable* – can the resolution be used by its participants?
- *Effective* – is the resolution delivering what is expected and required?
- *Efficient* – can the resolution be implemented and operated with a minimum of resources?

These attributes can be used as a checklist to assess each resolution option.

There will be two dimensions to any resolution:

1. Target resolution and transformation scenarios/options – what gets done
2. Options for implementing target scenarios/options – how it gets done – by whom, over how long, in what order

The choice of resolution depends on multiple options such as:

- *Degree of Automation* – how automated should the overall solution be and how much manual intervention and how many manual workarounds can be tolerated?
- *Sourcing Options* – what are the options for sourcing components of the solution?
- *Resources and their Availability* – what internal and external resources are required to implement the solution and how available are they?
- *Timescale and Urgency of Solution* – when is the solution required?
- *Cost and Available Finance* – what is the likely cost of the solution and where will the money come from?
- *Likely Duration of Solution* – how long will the solution last, how long are we architecting the solution for?
- *Organisational Impact* – what is the resolution's impact on the organisation in terms of organisation change: personnel and structure changes, new and existing locations, new business process and changes to existing business processes
- *Solution Quality Factors* – the quality factors include:

  - *Accessible* – is the solution accessible across the proposed user domain – locations, languages and abilities?
  - *Adaptable* – can the solution be applied in different ways and to different areas of the organisation easily and quickly and at low or no cost?
  - *Affordable* – can we afford to implement and operate the solution?
  - *Auditable* – does the solution maintain information to allow its operation be audited?
  - *Available* – can the solution delivery the required availability through resilience and continuity?
  - *Capable* – can the solution accomplish what is intended without additional effort?
  - *Deliverable* – can the solution be delivered for the expected cost using the planned resources and in the planned time?
  - *Flexible* – can the solution be changed easily and quickly or is the solution rigid and inflexible?
  - *Learnable* – can knowledge about how to use the solution be acquired easily and quickly without unnecessary training and documentation?
  - *Maintainable* – can the solution be maintained, changes and new releases and upgrades applied without requiring significant effort or time?
  - *Manageable* – can the system be managed and administered where user, configuration and reference data changes can be made easily and quickly?
  - *Operable* – can the solution be operated without complex and resource-intensive interventions? How automated will its operation be?
  - *Recoverable* – in the event of failure, can the solution be recovered easily, quickly and with the minimum of losses?
  - *Reliable* – will the solution operate reliably, without errors, maintaining quality and generating consistent results without requiring rework?
  - *Scalable* – can the solution accommodate changes in workload, numbers of users, numbers of transactions without significant redesign or change? Is scalability incorporated into the solution?
  - *Securable* – can the solution be secured across all its operations from access to data?
  - *Stable* – is the solution inherently stable or is it fragile so unintended uses or small unallowed for event cause problems?
  - *Suitable* – is the solution fit for its proposed purpose?
  - *Supportable* – can the solution be supported without requiring substantial resources and effort?
  - *Testable* – can the operation of the solution and the results generated from inputs be tested and validated?
  - *Upgradeable* – can the solution be upgraded and enhanced in the future?
  - *Usable* – can the solution be used easily?

Again, these factors can be used as a checklist to assess each resolution option.

The engagement needs to consider both the resolution and the options for its achievement.

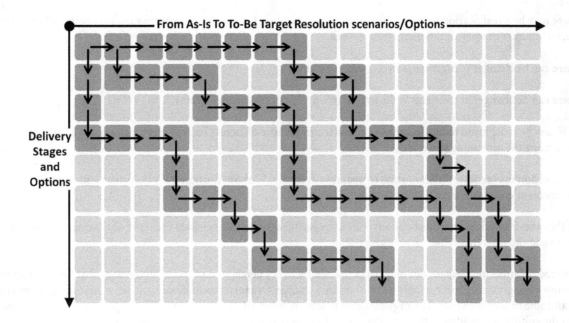

Figure 163 – Resolutions and Their Paths to Implementation

4.6.4.8 Problem Resolution and Organisation Change

Solutions introduce change into organisations. While the management of organisation change is outside the role of the solution architect, the architect should nonetheless be aware of the change implications of the solution options. Resistance to the changes required to operate a solution are a frequent cause of solution delivery being challenged. Similarly, failure to make the necessary organisation changes to allow the solution to operate is also a cause of such problems. In a strict sense the solution may be correct but it may not work or being allowed to work because of lack of involvement or interest in the business solution consumers or hostility to the solution or lack of knowledge in how to use the solution effectively.

- The middle-management layer within the business solution consumer population may view the solution as a threat to their role as, for example, it may automate their roles or move decision-making abilities. This group may seek to sabotage the solution or interfere with its introduction and operation.

- The solution can simply be ignored and the previous approach or solution may continue to be used.

- The solution may not be usable – see section 4.7 on page 311 for more details in solution usability.

New solutions can introduce different types of change into the organisation, such as:

- The solution may introduce a rigidity and lack of flexibility that was present in the operations the solution replaces in areas such as work allocation and the application of rules relating to work processing. This greater rule-based operations may not be accepted. Similarly, the solution can introduce checks and controls that were previously not present or were present to a lesser extent.

- The solution can introduce greater concentration of responsibilities and the removal of previously present local responsibility and decision-making.

- The solution may require more and different data to be entered and to be processed differently.

- The solution can be perceived as introducing more monitoring than was present previously and lead to resistance from the affected workforce.

- There may be a reallocation of work within the affected business teams with some team members being asked to handle greater volumes of work or different types of work.

- There can be changes in organisation reporting structures.

- There can be changes in roles and in the overall role profile of the business teams.

- Staff may be redeployed or lost from the business teams because of factors such as greater automation. This can lead to fear among the remaining personnel.

- The solution may require different skills to operate effectively. Without the necessary transition and support arrangement and structures this can lead to staff frustration.

As part the overall solution view this book advocates, the architect should understand the types of changes the solution introduces and the risks these changes may give rise to.

The required organisation changes can only happen when there is a perception of and an acceptance that there is a problem or challenge or opportunity that can only be resolved by a change. Organisation and business functions impacted must be willing and able to accept change. The organisation's management must support change. The engagement process must be aware of the culture and politics of the organisation and the impacted business functions. Identifying issues around and resistance to change needs to be a part of the engagement process.

Each resolution option will have a different organisation change profile. The implementation of any resolution will depend on the ability of the organisation to change.

Figure 164 – Dimensions of Internal Organisation Change

There are six dimensions of internal organisation change divided into two groups:

1. *Business Oriented Dimensions Of Change*
    1. *Location and Offices* – existing and new locations and facilities of the organisation, their types and functions and the principles that govern the selection of new locations
    2. *Business Processes* – current and future business process definitions, requirements, characteristics, performance
    3. *Organisation and Structure* – organisation resources and arrangement, business unit, function and team structures and composition, relationships, reporting and management, roles and skills

2. *Technology Oriented Dimensions Of Change*
   4. *Technology, Infrastructure and Communications* – current and future technical infrastructure including security, constraints, standards, technology trends, characteristics, performance requirements
   5. *Applications and Systems* – current and future applications and systems, characteristics, constraints, assumptions, requirements, design principles, interface standards, connectivity to business processes
   6. *Information and Data* – data and information architecture, data integration, master and reference data, data access and management

These are internal dimensions of organisation change. If the resolution involves external parties, then they may also experience change. While the organisation has control over changes within its own boundaries, it has much less control, if any, outside these confines. Within the context of externally facing solutions aimed at a consumer population outside the direct control of the organisation, the solution can be rejected, ignored or bypassed. If the external parties who are experiencing changes are entities such as partners or suppliers, then you have some control. If the parties are customers, then you have no real control over how they react to changes.

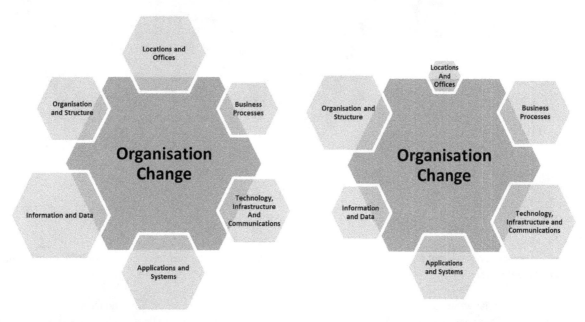

Figure 165 – Different Profiles of Organisation Changes for Different Resolution Options

Every resolution that solves a problem also causes new problems, however small. The resolution value equation is that the value and savings delivered by the resolution and the value of resolving the problem must be greater than the cost of the changes plus the cost of the solution components plus the cost of operating the solution.

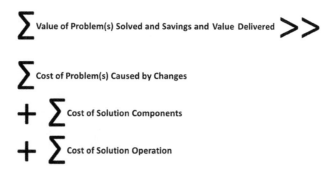

Figure 166 – Solution Value Equation

Ultimately, the success of the resolution can be measured by three fundamental factors:

- *Efficacy* – is it working and delivering the required results?
- *Efficiency* – can it be delivered and operated with the minimum or an acceptable level of resources?
- *Effectiveness* – is the resolution/transformation contributing to a wider, longer-term or greater success or improvement?

Figure 167 – Resolution Success Factors

4.6.4.9 Bringing It All Together And Presenting The Results

The early engagement process is not just about gathering information. The output must be a set of resolution options and how they can be implemented.

The resolutions must exist within a real-world context with all its constraints, limitations and boundaries. Where the resolution includes IT changes, in addition to solution options there will be organisation IT restrictions based on the organisation's enterprise architecture standards. The output from the early engagement process must include delivery and operation options to allow informed decision to be made on the true scope of the resolution.

The various constraints describe in the previous sections - resolution qualities, resolution attributes, resolution paths to implementation, resolution organisation change profile and the organisation's enterprise architecture – will reduce the number of resolution options.

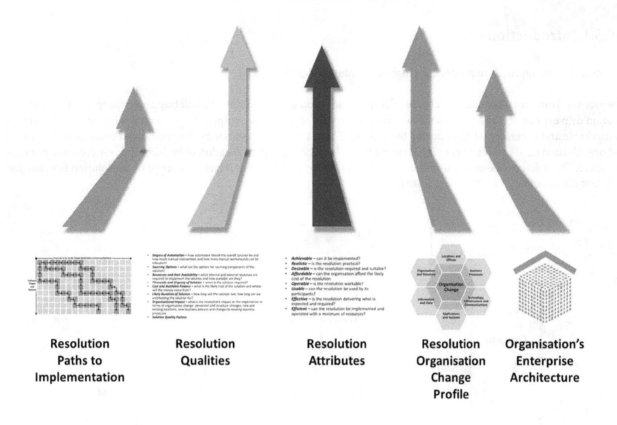

Figure 168 – Superset Of Constraints Sets Will Narrow Range Of Available, Realistic And Achievable Resolution Options

The goal of the engagement process is to describe the resolved situation and the options for achieving the transformation.

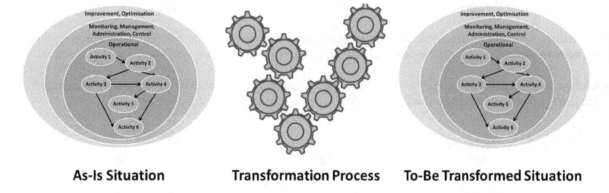

Figure 169 – Moving From The As-Is To The Target To-Be Situation

Ultimately the resolution needs to be translated into an implementable and operable solution. The engagement process should present systematised solutions options that can form the basis for decisions.

The rapid solution design process described later can be used to translate the resolution into a solution design.

4.6.5 Rapid Solution Design Option Engagement

4.6.5.1 Introduction

This describes an approach to producing a high-level solution design quickly.

The journey from initial business concept to operational solution is rarely simple. Not all business concepts progress to solution delivery projects and not all solution delivery projects advance to a completed operational solution. There is always an inevitable and necessary attrition during the process. There are many reasons why this should and could happen. Business and organisation needs and the operational environment both change. The allocation of budgets and resources are prioritised elsewhere. The delivery of other solutions on which this solution is dependent is late. The scope of the solution has changed such that it will not be cost-effective to justify.

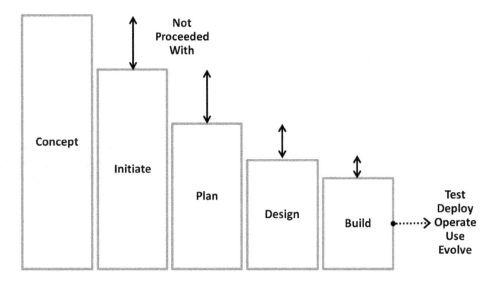

Figure 170 – Attrition from Initial Business Concept to Operational Solution

The cancelation of solutions during their development is not always bad. Solutions that will not deliver business value or that do not address a business need should be cancelled or at least deferred while the business justification is re-evaluated.

The solution design and delivery journey involves making decisions. Progress is achieved through decision making. A solution journey that is not moving towards a resolution is in some form of analysis/decision loop.

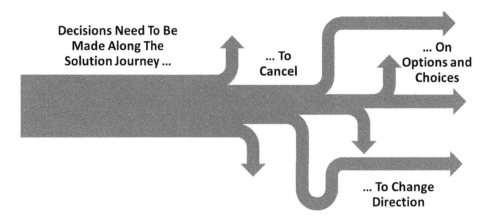

Figure 171 – Decision Making During the Solution Design Journey

Easy decisions have characteristics such as:

• Routine and frequent

- Low cost
- Low impact and few negative and serious consequences
- High level of comfort with decision context and background – comfort zone
- High level of confidence in the outcome

Hard decisions have traits such as:

- Not routine and infrequent
- High degrees of ambiguity, uncertainty and risk
- Potentially high cost
- High impact and potentially large negative and serious consequences
- Low level of comfort with decision context and background – outside the decision maker's comfort zone
- Low level of confidence in the outcome

Easy decisions are easy to make and have few negative consequences. Hard decisions are not easy to make and have potentially greater negative consequences.

Effective decision-making in the solution design process requires knowledge, both about the problem and the solution. (This is covered in section 4.2.1 on page 95.)

In this light, there is a need for a rapid solution concept development process that generates results quickly. There is a need to identify feasible, worthwhile, justifiable concepts that merit proceeding to implementation and to eliminate those that are not cost-effective. The solution architecture function plays an important role in identifying solutions worth implementing and in providing sufficient information to allow an informed decision to be made. This involves creating initial high-level solution architecture that can be expanded on if the solution is being proceeded with. This approach minimises the work done and the effort expended obtained while maximising the information gathered and processed and results and knowledge obtained.

The objective here is to quickly create a solution overview that is sufficiently comprehensive to allow the cost and resources required to out the solution into operation with sufficient accuracy as these estimates are realistic.

The key elements of this initial rapid solution scope and design are:

- *Systems/Applications* – these are existing systems and applications that will participate in the operation of the solution and which may need to be changed and new systems and applications that will have to be delivered as part of the solution

- *System Interfaces* – these are links between systems for the transfer and exchange of data

- *Actors* – these are individuals, groups or business functions who will be involved in the operation and use of the solution

- *Actor-System Interactions* – interactions between Actors and Systems/Applications

- *Actor-Actor Interactions* – interactions between Actors

- *Functions* – these are activities that are performed by actors using facilities and functionality provided by systems

- *Processes* – business processes required to operate the solution and the business processes enabled by the solution, including new business processes and changes to existing business processes

- *Journey* – standard journey through processes/functions and exceptions/deviations from "happy path"

- *Logical Data View* – data elements required

- *Data Exchanges* – movement of data between Systems/Applications

This set of information combines to provide a comprehensive view of the potential solution at an early stage.

This information is divided into two sets: a core and an extended set.

Core Definition Elements	Extended Definition Elements
Processes	System Interfaces
Functions	Actor-System Interactions
Actors	Actor-Actor Interactions
Systems/Applications	Solution Usage Journeys
	Logical Data View
	Data Exchange

Table 46 – Rapid Solution Design Core and Extended Design Elements

This initial scoping approach allows:

- System changes and developments required to be defined
- Potential options for reuse of existing systems to be determined
- Options for manual or automated operation to be pinpointed
- Effort to be estimated
- Organisational impact to be quantified including staffing, training, support, cutover, parallel run, hypercare and documentation
- Dependencies to be identified
- Informed decision to proceed to be made

It provides a worklist or a table of contents of further work if decision to continue is made. Only sufficient work is done at this initial stage to allow a well-informed decision to be made.

4.6.5.2 Step 1 – Identify New and Impacted Existing Business Processes

The first step in the rapid solution scoping exercise is to identify the main existing business processes that will be used in the operation of the solution and any new business processes. Existing business may be able to be used without modification. Others may require modification.

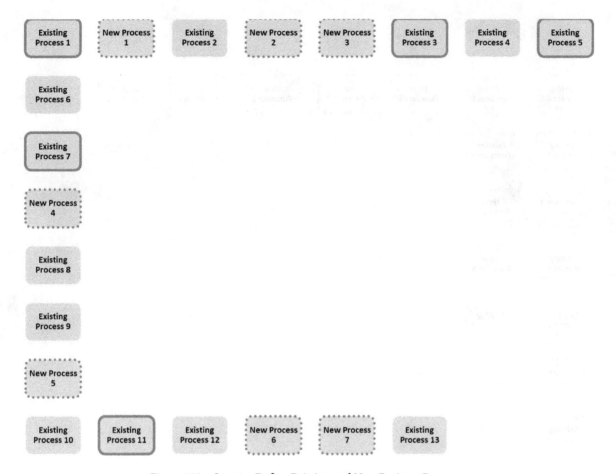

Figure 172 – Step 1 – Define Existing and New Business Processes

Determining the business processes will require the solution design team to engage with the business function that are looking to have the new solution implemented. Processes are important because they reflect and represent what the organisation does and how it does it.

The goal here is not to document the existing business processes or to define the new processes in detail. That work will come later. At this stage it is the inventory of processes and a brief description of their purpose, scope, operation and use that needs to be created and agreed.

Describe the current process landscape in enough detail to allow business rules to be understood and for the issues, problems and improvements required to operate the proposed solution to be identified

Identify and (re)design the theoretical minimum set of core processes required to achieve the required outcomes and results using the proposed new solution assuming there are no constraints.

4.6.5.3 Step 2 – Identify Key Functions

The second step is to identify the functions, abilities and facilities required to enable and operate the processes. These functions represent specific activities that are performed within business processes.

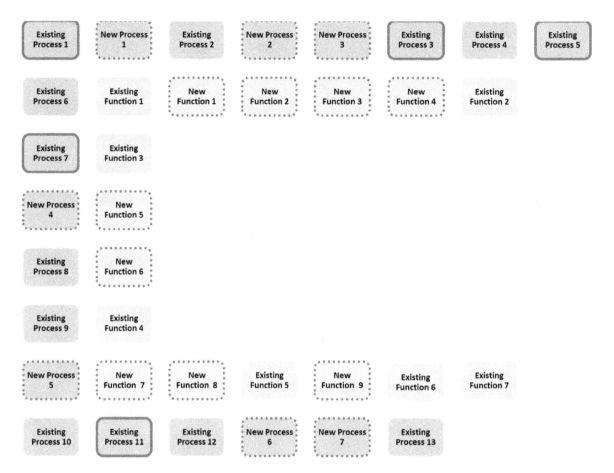

Figure 173 – Step 2 – Define New and Existing Functions

The following is an example of how functions relate to processes. It shows a sample process to buy a product or service. The process can be decomposed into multiple levels and the individual activities.

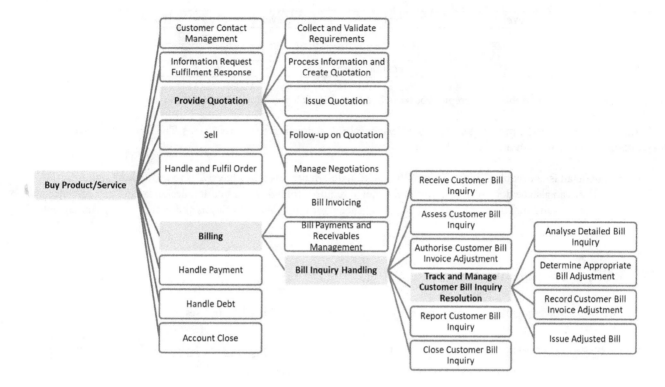

Figure 174 – Sample Process and Function Breakdown – Buy a Product or Service

Level 1	Level 2	Level 3	Level 4	Level 5
Buy Product/Service	Customer Contact Management			
	Information Request Fulfilment Response			
	Provide Quotation	Collect and Validate Requirements		
		Process Information and Create Quotation		
		Issue Quotation		
		Follow-up on Quotation		
		Manage Negotiations		
	Sell			
	Handle and Fulfil Order			
	Billing	Bill Invoicing		
		Bill Payments and Receivables Management		
		Bill Inquiry Handling	Receive Customer Bill Inquiry	
			Assess Customer Bill Inquiry	
			Authorise Customer Bill Invoice Adjustment	
			Track and Manage Customer Bill Inquiry Resolution	Analyse Detailed Bill Inquiry
				Determine Appropriate Bill Adjustment
				Record Customer Bill Invoice Adjustment
				Issue Adjusted Bill
			Report Customer Bill Inquiry	
			Close Customer Bill Inquiry	

Level 1	Level 2	Level 3	Level 4	Level 5
		Handle Payment		
		Handle Debt		
		Account Close		

Table 47 – Sample Process and Function Breakdown – Buy a Product or Service

In this example, the level 1 process ***Buy Product/Service*** is broken down into six level 2 steps. The level 2 step ***Provide Quotation*** is broken down into five level 3 steps.

This level of detail is not required at this stage of the solution design process. The objective is to identify the significant functions. They can also be documented at the level of detail required for a detailed solution design later. Their presence in the list of processes and functions will act as a high-level task list for more detailed analysis and design during subsequent work.

4.6.5.4 Step 3 – Identify Actors

This third step involves identifying actors who will use functions and participate in processes.

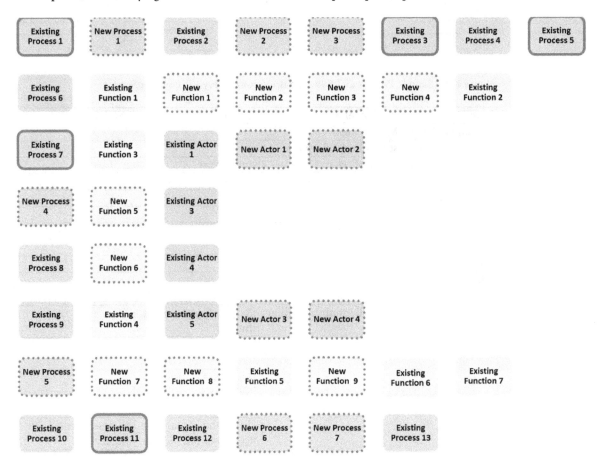

Figure 175 – Step 3 – Define New and Existing Actors

Identify the roles - individuals, groups or business functions - required for the target (existing unchanged, existing changed or new) processes. The list of roles can be used to design the target organisation structure. In the follow-on analysis the skills, experience, education, training and competencies of the actors will be identified.

4.6.5.5 Step 4 – Identify New and Existing Applications

The fourth step is to identify the new systems or applications and changes to existing systems or applications required to provide the previously identified functions.

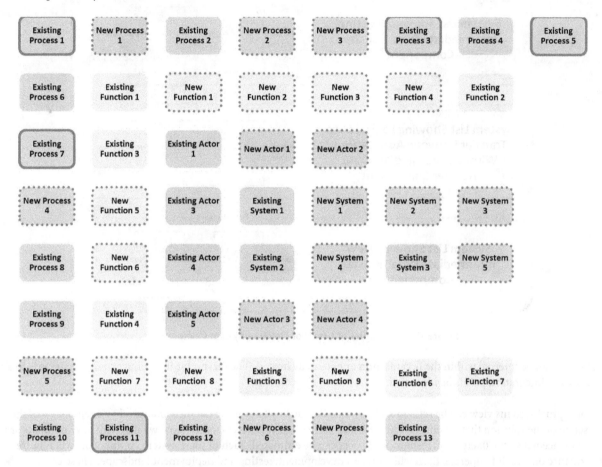

Figure 176 – Step 4 – Existing or New Systems and Applications

This view needs to identify the major solution system components, both new and existing systems that either to continue to operate unchanged or that will require changes. This can be a logical view of what is required that may be different from the final set of system components implemented. It is important to identify the conceptual systems required needed as part of the overall solution. These conceptual systems can be translated later into actual solution

The information accompanying the solution view should identify the business processes each system component enables the operation of and the functions each system component provides. This information could be represented graphically but it might add too much clutter and detail to the diagram that might confuse rather than assisting understanding.

This following shows examples of levels of detail of system components. In the first *System List Showing Existing Intermediate Data Transfer* Component, the intermediate data exchange infrastructural component (such as SFTP or managed file transfer or message queueing facility) is explicitly shown. This is an existing component that is being used as part of the solution. This level of detail is not necessary at the overview design stage. It can be included. But as long as the interfaces between the two functional components are known, its inclusion does not really add much value.

In the second *System List Showing Logical Data Transfer Between Applications Without Intermediate Data Transfer Component*, the existing intermediate data exchange infrastructural component is not shown. The interfaces between the systems ae shown.

In the third *System List Showing New Intermediate Data Transfer Component*, the new intermediate data exchange infrastructural component is explicitly shown. This is useful because this represents a new component that is being implemented as part of the solution.

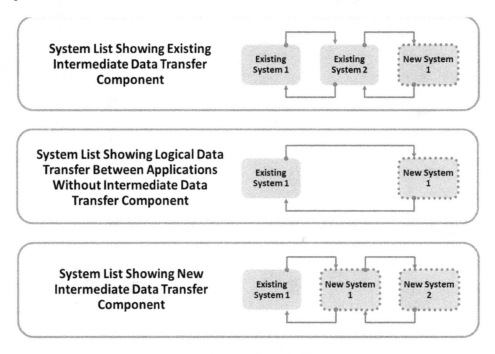

Figure 177 – Examples of Levels of Detail of System Components

The systems can be internal within the organisation or externally hosted. The reason for including external systems is to allow interfaces and integration points be identified.

This conceptual systems view can be refined and expanded on during later more detailed analysis. For a rapid view of the likely scope of the solution that is being produced at this early stage, it is necessary to know what system developments are likely to be needed so the likely time, resources and cost can be estimated. Each of these system components will require infrastructure on which to operate. Each will require a development, testing and deployment landscape. These costs can be quantified that will feed into a wider solution cost and resource model that will be realistic.

4.6.5.6 Step 5 – Identify Data Integrations, Transfers and Exchanges

The fifth step involves the specification of the integrations and data exchanges between the system components that will take place as part of the operation of the solution. Each system to system interface should be identified.

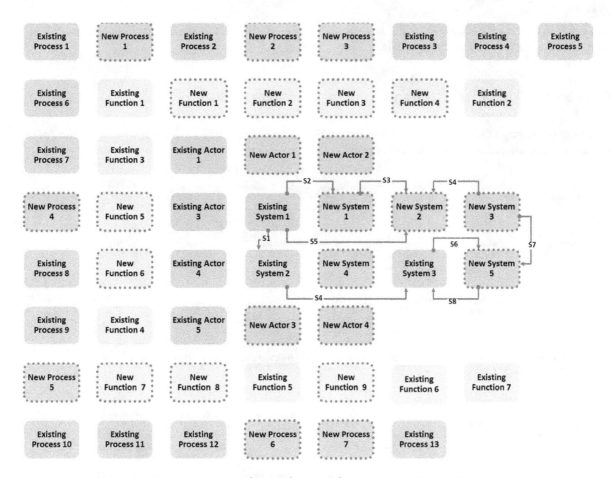

Figure 178 – Step 5 – List Interfaces and Data Exchanges Between System Components

Quantifying data exchanges is valuable because these represent work to be done. For each interface, describe the nature of the interface: frequency, batch or realtime, security and use of encryption, direction, protocol, volume and method of interface and exchange. Detail the data that is exchanged in sufficient detail so the effort to implement with new systems can be accurately estimated.

Number	Source System	Destination System	Description
S1	Existing System 1	Existing System 2	
S2	Existing System 1	New System 1	
S3	New System 1	New System 2	
S4	New System 2	New System 3	
S5	Existing System 1	New System 2	
S6	Existing System 3	New System 5	
S7	New System 3	New System 5	
S8	New System 5	Existing System 3	

Table 48 – List of System Interactions

One output of this step is an inventory of data exchanges involved in the new solution. Data interfaces and exchanges give rise to many problems during solution implementation, testing and cutover to production. Their complexity is frequently overlooked during solution design. Also, the need for interfaces and their monitoring, administration and management and the consequent impact on service management is all too commonly disregarded.

Interfaces give rise to data that must be validated, errors handled, data quality maintained and loaded into a data store. If the data volumes (frequency or amount of both) are large, then this can give rise to performance and throughput problems. A poorly designed data store and data loading can mean that while the data interface works functionality, it is not scalable. Data quality needs to start at the earliest stage of the data pipeline. This means the data interface must include data validation against data rules and reference and master data.

4.6.5.7 Step 6 – Identify Actor and Application Interactions

This sixth step consists of listing interactions actors have with systems and applications that will take place as part of the operation of the solution. Each actor to system interaction should be identified.

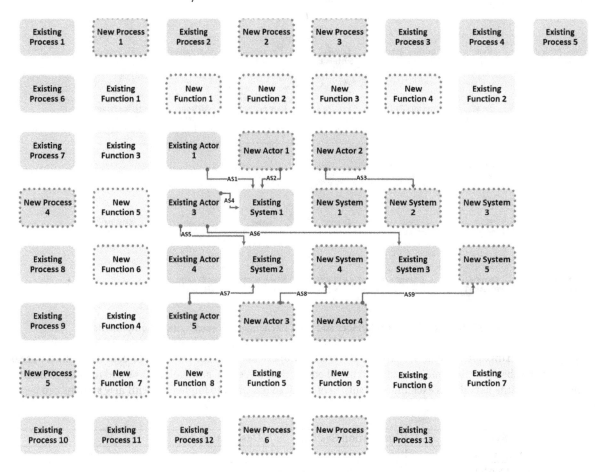

Figure 179 – Step 6 – Identify Actor System Interactions

This step should describe each system or application component each actor accesses or interfaces with, the system functions performed and the information accessed.

Number	Actor	System	Description
AS1	Existing Actor 1	Existing System 1	
AS2	New Actor 1	Existing System 1	
AS3	New Actor 1	New System 2	
AS4	Existing Actor 3	Existing System 1	
AS5	Existing Actor 3	Existing System 2	
AS6	Existing Actor 3	Existing System 3	
AS7	Existing Actor 5	Existing System 2	
AS8	New Actor 1	New System 4	
AS9	New Actor 4	New System 5	

Table 49 – Actor System Interactions

The types of interactions should be listed with details on expected or proposed number and frequency.

4.6.5.8 Step 7 – Identify Actor/Actor Interactions

The seventh step consists of listing interactions actors have with other actor that will take place as part of the operation of the solution. Each actor to actor interaction should be coded.

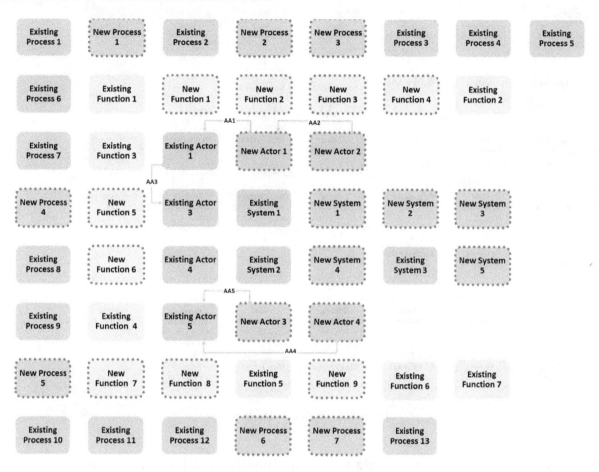

Figure 180 – Step 7 – Identify Actor Actor Interactions

The purpose of this step is to identify new roles and organisation structures required to operate the solution and to list any external users to whom the solution is being presented, if applicable.

Number	Actor	System	Description
AA1	Existing Actor 1	New Actor 1	
AA2	New Actor 1	New Actor 2	
AA3	Existing Actor 1	Existing Actor 3	
AA4	New Actor 3	Existing Actor 5	
AA5	New Actor 4	Existing Actor 5	

Table 50 – Actor Actor Interactions

The nature of the interactions should be listed with details on expected or proposed number and frequency.

4.6.5.9 Steps 1-7 – Solution on a Page

When you bring the results of steps one to seven together the result is a solution view that represents a ***Solution on a Page***. This lists all the key solution components and their interactions

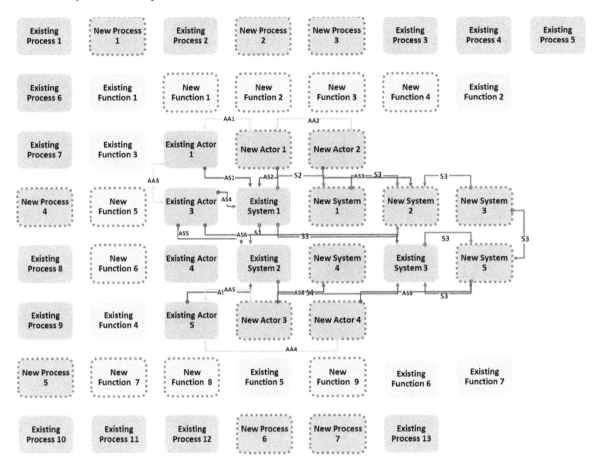

Figure 181 – Basic Solution on a Page

4.6.5.10 Steps 8 and 9 – Identify Data Sets, Data Impacts and Data Movements

Steps 8 and 9 consists of creating the logical data view. This lists the possible data impacts to existing and new systems and data exchanges between systems.

The information on the data aspects of solution architecture contained in section 4.8 on page 321 can be used here.

This view expands on and extends the system interaction view described in step 5. The data impacts on existing and new systems relate to potentially new information that must be generated and/or stored. Some of the data elements will already be catered for in existing systems. They are listed here to ensure they are not omitted from detailed analysis, design and planning. The data exchanges relate to transfers of data between systems. Some of the data exchanges will already exist for existing types of data that are being used to implement the new solution.

Step 8 lists the data impacts. These are sets or groups of related data that will be used within the operation of the solution. At this stage, the individual data fields and their content and format need not be described. It is enough to identify the data sets.

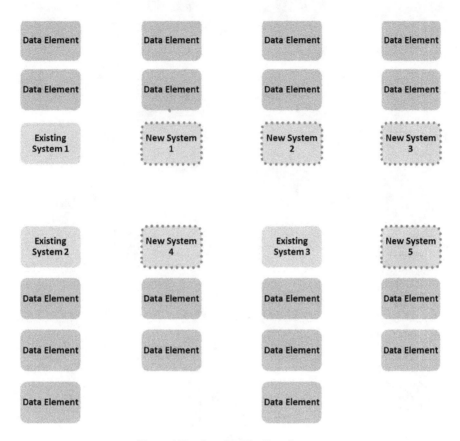

Figure 182 – Step 8 – List Data Impacts

New system components may reuse data that already exists or may create and use new sets of data.

Step 9 shows the data exchanges and movements between systems in the context of the data sets identified in step 8.

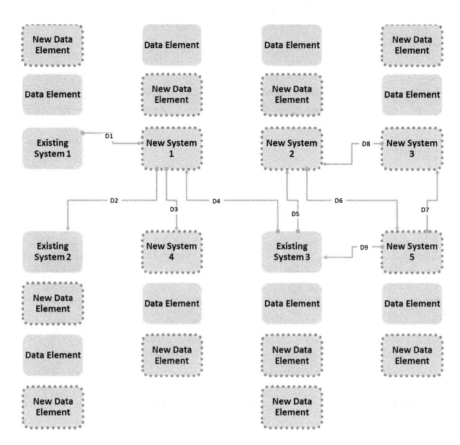

Figure 183 – Step 9 – Data Exchanges Required Between Systems

This view should correspond to the data exchanges listed in step 5.

Number	From System	To System	Data Element	Description
D1	Existing System 1	New System 1		
D2	New System 1	Existing System 2		
D3	New System 1	New System 4		
D4	Existing System 3	New System 1		
D5	Existing System 3	New System 2		
D6	New System 2	New System 5		
D7	New System 5	New System 3		
D8	New System 3	New System 2		
D9	New System 5	Existing System 3		

Table 51 – Data Exchanges Between Systems

4.6.5.11 Step 10 – Create Inventory of Solution Usage Journeys

Step 10 is concerned with creating an inventory of solution usage journeys and documenting them. The journey is the set of steps performed by the user from initiation to completion. This journey is the external representation of the tasks and actions performed by the systems and actors. This step should look at primary solution usage journeys, that it, those that are initiated and performed by primary solution users. A primary solution will give rise to activities that are assigned to and performed by other solution users. These secondary usage journeys are not the major concern of this step.

The solution usage journeys may be regarded as solution use cases but they are intended to be more comprehensive. They describe the entire solution usage experience rather than just a specific set of activities.

Having an inventory of solution usage journeys is valuable as it enables the solution to be validated against the way it is intended to be used. They can be used to discover potential problems with the solution and the interactions between components that occur during the journeys.

Internally, from a solution component and business process view, the journey steps may cross several internal business processes and the work done at those individual steps may be performed by separate business functions using different systems.

For every solution there will be one or more "happy paths" – standard paths through the solution without exception/problem/deviation handling. Exceptions may occur at each step in these happy paths. This high-level solution design should identify solution usage journeys and their possible exceptions.

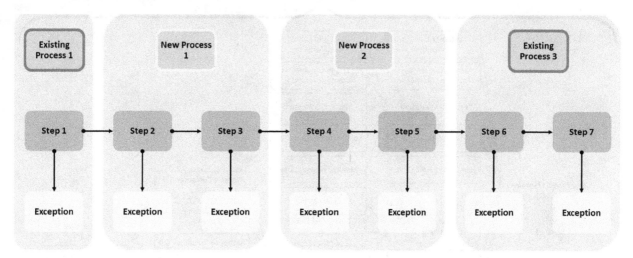

Figure 184 – Step 10 – Solution Usage Journeys

The following shows the possible set of steps involved in the customer journey of buying and using a product or service that is billed based on usage. This is the external representation of the journey that is experienced by the customer.

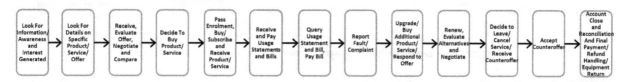

Figure 185 – Sample Solution Usage Journey

The steps in this sample journey are:

1. Look For Information/Awareness and Interest Generated
2. Look For Details on Specific Product/ Service/ Offer
3. Receive, Evaluate Offer, Negotiate and Compare
4. Decide To Buy Product/ Service
5. Pass Enrolment, Buy/ Subscribe and Receive Product/ Service
6. Receive and Pay Usage Statements and Bills
7. Query Usage Statement and Bill, Pay Bill
8. Report Fault/Complaint
9. Upgrade/ Buy Additional Product/Service/Respond to Offer
10. Renew, Evaluate Alternatives and Negotiate
11. Decide to Leave/Cancel Service/Receive Counteroffer
12. Accept Counteroffer

13. Account Close and Reconciliation and Final Payment/Refund Handling/Equipment Return

This sample set of steps will not be experienced by all customers.

This external journey maps to a set of internal business processes such as those contained in the business process breakdown described in Figure 174 on page 263. The external journey represents a cross-functional view of the flow of the solution.

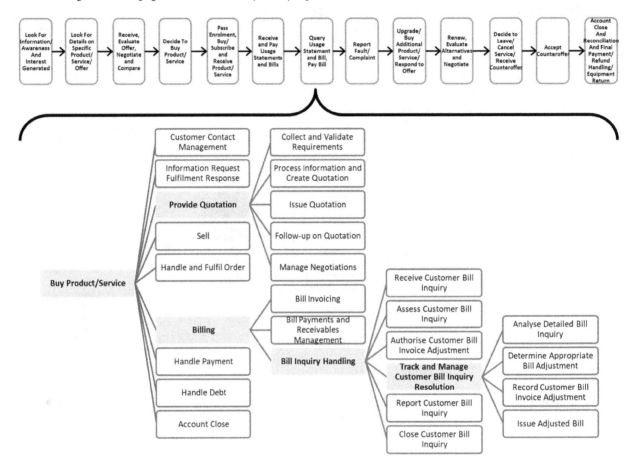

Figure 186 – Sample Solution Usage Journey Mapped to Business Processes

These internal business processes will be performed by different organisation functions. So, the external customer cross-functional journey will map to multiple internal business processes and business functions.

The sample solution usage journey listed above could be modified and enhanced with the addition of exceptions along the following lines.

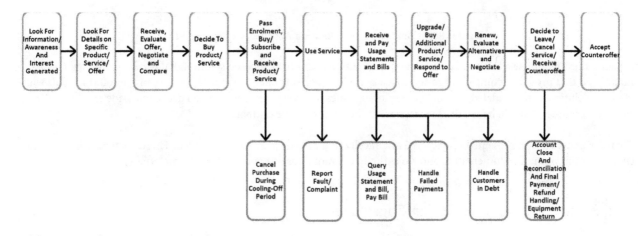

Figure 187 – Sample Solution Usage Journey with Exceptions

4.6.5.12 Summary

This rapid solution scoping approach creates potentially three deliverables, depending on whether all the steps have been followed:

1. Solution Business Processes, Functions, Actors and Systems and Interfaces view
2. Data Impact and Exchanges view
3. Solution Usage Journeys view

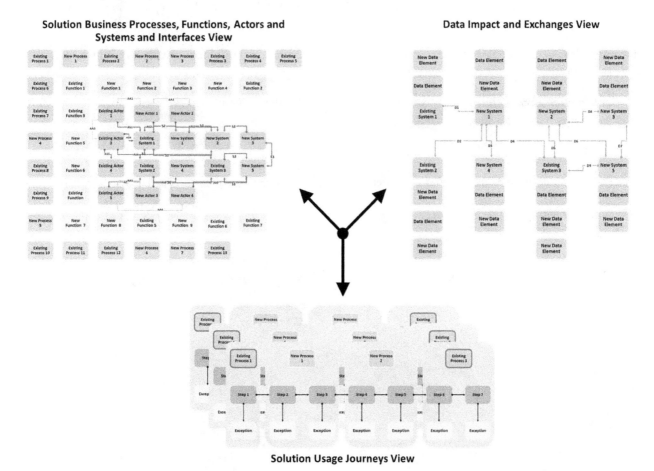

Figure 188 – Combined Rapid Solution Architecture Scoping Views

Together these comprise a substantial amount of information about the proposed solution that can be assembled reasonably quickly and that provide a complete high-level view of the components of and operation and use of the solution. This will allow the solution to be validated, alternatives explored, issues uncovered, evidence-based decisions made and for the cost, time and resources that will be required to implement the solution to be estimated.

The information can be presented visually and graphically so it can be easily comprehended. There is supporting narrative. There is a minimum of documentation and a maximum of amount usable and informative material.

4.6.6 Structured Solution Design Engagement

4.6.6.1 Introduction

The objective of a structured and detailed approach to developing a thorough solution design is to ensure consistency in solution designs and in the solution design process. A structured process allows expectations to be managed in terms of the scope and content of the solution design effort and artefacts and in the time, effort and approach to create that design.

This is a very comprehensive engagement that can take some time and can generate a large amount of documentation and artefacts. You may therefore look to use this as a template for a design process and engagement that can be adapted to specific circumstances and business needs.

This detailed approach provides a checklist that can be used to validate that the solution design option or options are complete.

This approach to solution design is based on using six views as a structure to gather information and to create the design. These six views are divided into two groups:

- *Core Solution Architecture Views* – concerned with the kernel of the solution:
  - Business
  - Functional
  - Data

- *Extended Solution Architecture Views* – concerned with solution implementation and operation:
  - Technical
  - Implementation
  - Management and Operation

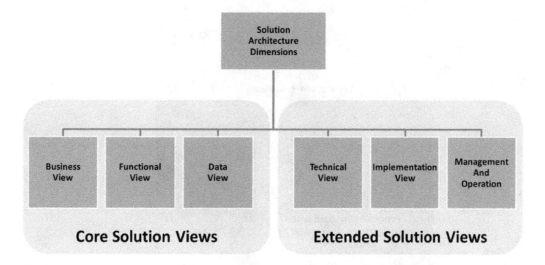

Figure 189 – Core and Extended Solution Views

These solution design dimensions or views are structured sets of requirements, conditions, specifications, provisions, concerns and fundamental principles for each dimension of the overall solution. The views are used to walk through the view-specific aspects of the solution design.

The documentation of these views may contain repeated information. But this engagement is concerned with creating detailed design specifications.

The core dimensions/views define what the solution must do, how it must operate and the results expected. The extended dimensions/views define how the solution must or should be implemented, managed and operated. They describe factors that affect, drive and support decisions made during the solution design process. Many of these factors will have been defined as requirements of the solution and so their delivery will be included in the solution design.

Together these core and extended views describe the end-to-end solution design comprehensively.

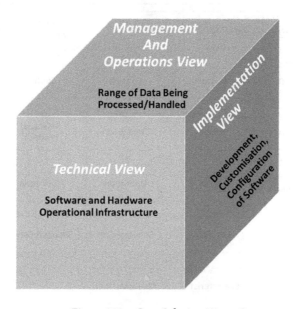

Figure 190 – Core Solution Views Contents

Figure 191 – Extended Solution Views Contents

The *Data View* describes the range of data being handled and processed and the processing being performed.

The *Business and Process View* describes the organisation or business function and the business processes implemented by the solution.

The *Functional and Results View* describes the functions being performed and the results they generate.

The information collected and described in each of the solution views can be summarised as follows.

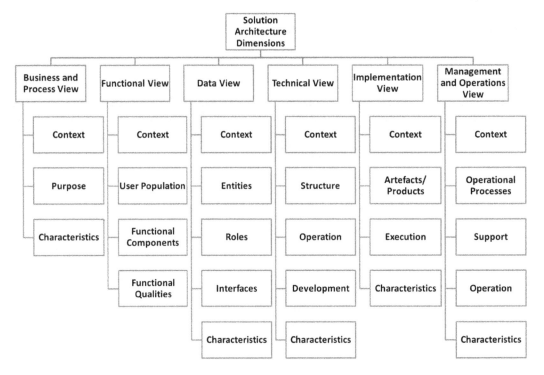

Figure 192 – High-Level Structure of Information Collected from Views

These two sets of views provide a detailed solution design.

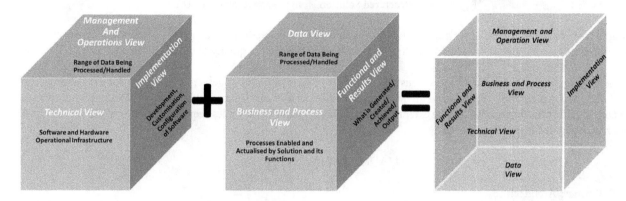

Figure 193 – Combined Core and Extended Solution Views

These are the outputs created from this engagement. For each of these outputs there will be a corresponding information gathering and analysis activity.

This is a potentially very comprehensive set of information. Not all this may be required in all cases. For a new solution design engagement with a new organisation, the information is useful. For an existing organisation with an existing portfolio of solutions that are been expanded and extended, some of the information such as that contained in the business view need not be described.

This structure can then be used as a checklist to validate that the solution design is complete and that the level of detail in the design is sufficient to meet the needs of the solution implementation project.

4.6.6.2 Structured Solution Design Approach and TOGAF

Elements of the structured solution design process described here can be mapped to the TOGAF[40] enterprise architecture framework.

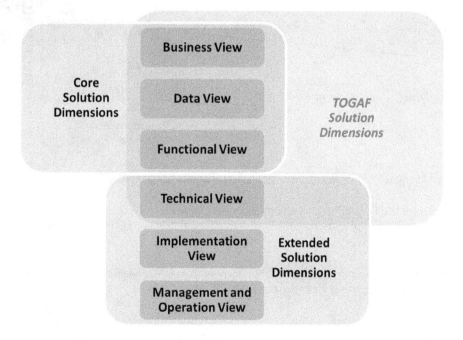

---

[40] See http://www.opengroup.org/togaf.

Figure 194 – Structured Solution Design Approach and TOGAF

Using the existing TOGAF framework allows the existing information collection and analysis structure and approach to be suitably reused to add value to the solution design process and to improve the quality of the deliverables.

TOGAF is a substantial framework that is focussed on enterprise architecture engagements. Its use for solution architecture and design engagements will require adjustment. The amount of the TOGAF framework to be applied will depend on the size and complexity of the target solution, the extent and type of engagement deliverables required and the amount of time and resources available for the engagement.

The TOGAF Architecture Development Method (ADM) contains three phases:

1.   B: Business Architecture
2.   C: Information Systems Architecture
3.   D: Technology Architecture

that can be mapped to the solution design views. In the following I have divided the TOGAF ADM Phase C: Information Systems Architecture into two sub-phases:

1.   TOGAF Phase C1: Data Architecture
2.   TOGAF Phase C2: Solutions and Application Architecture

This allows for a more granular specification of the solution.

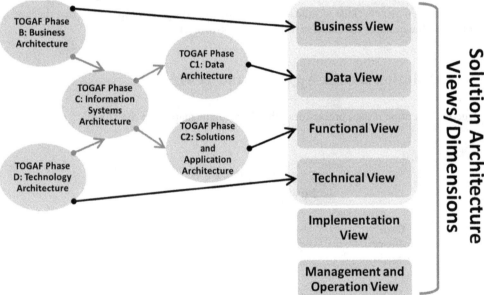

Figure 195 – Mapping TOGAF Architecture Development Method (ADM) Phases to Solution Design Views

This mapping allows parts of the TOGAF architecture framework to be used to create the structured set of activities involved in gathering and analysing information and to create the structured set of deliverables for these views of the solution design process.

The TOGAF ADM framework does not have either an Implementation or a Management and Operation View. However, the same structure that exists for the other four views can be adapted for these.

The TOGAF ADM framework has a common set of steps for each of the architecture phases. These can be adapted for use during the solution design process.

TOGAF ADM Generalised Phase Step	Adaptation to Solution Design Process
1. Select reference models, viewpoints and tools	Determine the governing principles, drivers and the stakeholders and their concerns. Analyse the solution from the viewpoints of business or technical areas such as operations, management, technology and finance, support, operations. Agree on the approach to capturing information, its level of detail and granularity and on the tools and techniques to be used. Determine the building blocks of the solution with respect to the specific view. Describe the entities involved in the solution with respect to the specific view and their relationships.
2. Develop baseline architecture description	Describe the current solution or individual solution component with respect to the specific view, if there is an existing solution or if the new solution will involve existing solution components in as much detail as is useful to define the target solution.
3. Develop target architecture description	Describe the solution from the viewpoint of the solution design view in sufficient detail to allow the solution and its components that are relevant to the view to be defined.
4. Perform gap analysis	Pinpoint any gaps that exist between the baseline and target architecture descriptions previously created, if relevant.
5. Define roadmap components	Create a plan of activities based on the previously created baseline, target and gap analyses.
6. Understand and resolve impacts across the architecture landscape	Analyse the impact of the solution design with respect to the specific view on the solution architecture, identify any conflicts and determine the approach to their resolution.
7. Conduct formal stakeholder review	Review the results of the analysis with the relevant stakeholders.
8. Finalise the architecture	Define the standards to be applied and used for each relevant solution component design with respect to the specific view. Document each relevant solution component design with respect to the specific view. Ensure that the requirements of the solution and traceable to the solution design. Validate that the solution component design meets the previously agreed goals and objectives.
9. Create architecture definition document	Document the view-specific solution design elements.

Table 52 – Mapping TOGAF Architecture Development Method (ADM) Steps to Solution Design

The specific adaptations of each of the TOGAF ADM phases and their activities to the solution design business views are included in the sections on those views. This information is provided so it can contribute to the development of a solution design workplan and to provide visibility to the stakeholders of the solution design process and the level of detail that is being collected.

The following sections describe the information to be collected for each of the six solution views.

4.6.6.3 Business and Process View

This view contains business-level information on the approach being taken to address the requirements of the business drivers for the solution.

This view will work through various viewpoint scenarios to analysis the business and process interactions with the solution to elaborate its design.

The structure of the information collected and analysed within the Business View is:

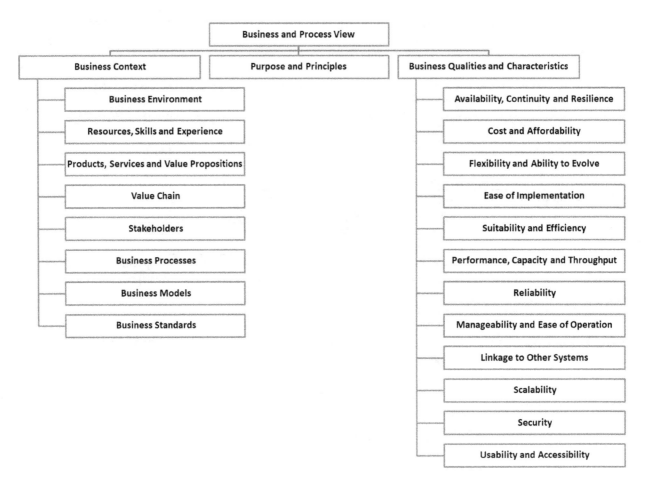

Figure 196 – Business and Process View Information Structure

Business and Process View Subject Area	Business View Topic	Description
Business Context	Business Environment	This contains information on the industry sector or business area in which the organisation operates, the products and services provided, the market into which products and services are provides, the organisation's competitors, the legal and regulatory framework that affects the organisation, the organisation's partners, suppliers and service providers and any political, economic social, geographical, cultural opportunities, challenges and threats. This information can be generic to the entire organisation or specific to the business area where the proposed solution will

Business and Process View Subject Area	Business View Topic	Description
		operate. The information can also be specific to the changing circumstances that give rise to the need for the solution, if any. This background information can be omitted if it does not add value to the solution design.
	Resources, Skills, Experience, Competencies and Capabilities	This details the resources and their skills and experience of the organisation or business function that will use the proposed solution.
	Products, Services and Value Propositions	This describes the products and services provided by the organisation or business function relevant to the solution. It describes the value delivered by these products and services and how the users of the products or services experience that value.
	Value Chain	This details the sets of activities the organisation or business function carries out in order to deliver its products and services. It should describe the inputs to, transformation activities performed and the outputs generated by the organisation or business function in the creation and delivery of products and services.
	Stakeholders	This identifies the internal and external stakeholders relevant to the proposed solution such as customers, employees, organisations and partners.
	Business Processes	This lists the business process that are involved in or affected by the proposed solution area. It identifies the existing business processes that will change and describe the proposed changes. It details the new business processes required to use or enabled by the proposed solution. This should contain an inventory of the business processes. Each process should be described at least to a high level.
	Business Models	This will describe the business operating model for the solution and its use.
	Business Standards	This will describe standards, policies and procedures with which the solution must comply.
Purpose and Principles		For the proposed solution, the describes the vision, business drivers – both internal and external, objectives and strategic intent, specific goals, benefits that will be obtained and metrics and key performance and results indicators that have been identified as part of the solution implementation and operation. This will describe the reason and justification for the solution. It will define the business benefits and areas where savings and greater efficiencies will be obtained from the solution. The principles describe the desired or preferred means for achieving the business purpose.
Characteristics and Qualities	Availability, Continuity and Resilience	This describes the solution characteristics relating to when it will be available and accessible, the continuity and resilience and fault tolerance incorporated into the design and how and from what point it will be recovered and how long recovery will take.

Business and Process View Subject Area	Business View Topic	Description
	Cost and Affordability	This will identify and at least estimate (with a stated accuracy and tolerance) the whole lifetime costs of the solution and its constituent components. It will describe how the solution can be afforded by the organisation or business function. It will estimate the savings that will be generated by the delivery of the defined business benefits.
	Flexibility and Ability to Evolve	This will describe how the solution can be changed to accommodate alterations and variations in its operation and use, volume of workload (numbers of concurrently active users, total user population, volume of work, amount of data), addition of new functionality and incorporation of operations in different areas, potentially in different languages, if applicable. This will describe the overall stability of the solution and its constituent components and their interoperation.
	Ease of Implementation	This will define the attributes of the solution in terms of how it will be tested, validated, implemented, data migrated and loaded and the processes that will be used to accomplish these characteristics.
	Suitability and Efficiency	This will describe how the solution addresses the business need, how efficient its operation and use will be. It also details how accurate the solution's operation will be, how it will be accepted by the population of users, how complete it is and what external and manual work will be required and its overall effectiveness.
	Performance, Capacity and Throughput	This will describe the performance characteristics of the solution across all the processing and capacity dimensions: active users, number of units of work, volume of data. This will include all areas where the solution performs work. It will describe the time taken to perform that work.
	Reliability	This will detail the attributes of the solution in terms of its consistency of operation and use, how bad quality data will be identified and handled and the repeatability of outputs. It will identify any potential weaknesses in the operation of the solution. The approach to logging and auditing of solution use will be described.
	Manageability and Ease of Operation	This will cover the solution attributes relating to the operation and control of the solution, how it is administered and managed, what administration and management functions and activities are required, how it is maintained and serviced, how problems are identified and resolved and the overall stability of the solution.
	Linkage to Other Systems	This will describe the interfaces to and the integrations with other operational systems, the information, including its format and content, being exchanged and the frequency and direction of the exchanges.
	Scalability	This will describe the approach to scaling the solution in response to changes in workload across all solution components.
	Security	This will detail the approach to security across all the solution's components and operations including authentication and nonrepudiation, access controls, audit

Business and Process View Subject Area	Business View Topic	Description
		logging, privacy and confidentiality, encryption and integrity. It will describe how the solution complies with data privacy standards.
	Usability and Accessibility	This will describe how the system will be used by different elements of the user population, how they will interact with it, a view on its ease of use and how it can be understood, the difficulty or intuitiveness of the interfaces and how easy the solution can be learned.

Table 53 – Business and Process View Information Structure

4.6.6.3.1 Adapting TOGAF Business Phase to the Business and Process View

TOGAF ADM Business Architecture Phase Step	Adaptation to Business and Process View Solution Design Process
1. Select reference models, viewpoints and tools	Select the set of business viewpoints or aspects such as operations, financial, management or business user that will form the basis for the business and process views. Select the set of business functions that will be involved in the business and process view based on the proposed scope of the target solution. Identify the business actors in these business functions. Define the business processes and their steps and functions to be included in this view. Define the level of detail and granularity for the viewpoints analysis. Describe the interactions between business functions and actors. Define the artefacts and documentation to be created such as: • Details of the organisation structure, functions and their actors and roles • Use cases and user journeys • Details on business drivers, goals and objectives • Details of processes, triggering events, process flows • Details on products and services provided by processes • Details on metrics and measures currently used • Data structures and flows Define the business-oriented requirements to be collected that will govern the solution to be designed and implemented, including • Requirements, both functional and operational • Principles • Standards and policies • Assumptions • Constraints
2. Develop baseline architecture description	Describe the structure and operation of the current set of solutions from a business and process view that are being targeted for replacement by the new solution, if they exist.

TOGAF ADM Business Architecture Phase Step	Adaptation to Business and Process View Solution Design Process
	If there is no current set of solutions being upgraded or replaced, describe the manual processes and operations that comprise the scope of the target solution and define this as the baseline. If the proposed solution is entirely new, describe the problem or challenge it addresses and define this as the baseline. Gather information on the current architecture only insofar as it will add value to the definition of the target solution. Use the information gathering structures defined in step 1 to organise the information to be collected. Include details on the problems and issues being experienced with the base line solution. Perform this information collection and analysis to the extent that the information collected is needed to define the target solution and how much of the existing solutions will be reused by or integrated into the target solution.
3. Develop target architecture description	Describe the business and process view of the how the target solution should operate using the structures defined in step 1.
4. Perform gap analysis	Compare the baseline and target sets of information to identify gaps between what is currently happening and what will happen using the target solution. The target solution should both be a replacement of and an improvement on the current baseline. Identify the causes of the gaps and differences between the baseline and target business and process views, especially where the target view does not include elements that are in the baseline view and may indicate current items that will be missing from the target. Validate that the target is complete from a business and process view.
5. Define roadmap components	Define the set of business activities that will be required to move from the baseline to the target solutions.
6. Understand and resolve impacts across the architecture landscape	Assess the business and process operations of the target solution against the wider solution and business landscapes. Determine if there are been any changes in either the solution and business landscapes that will impact on the target solution. Determine if there are any initiatives planned or in progress in the wider solution and business landscapes that will impact on the target solution or be impacted by or that can be leveraged by the target solution.
7. Conduct formal stakeholder review	Review the target business and process solution design to establish if it meets the original stated needs. Present the business and process view of the target solution to business stakeholders. Analyse and explain any differences between the target business and process view of the solution and the feedback provided by stakeholders.

TOGAF ADM Business Architecture Phase Step	Adaptation to Business and Process View Solution Design Process
	Consider updating the target business and process solution design if the differences cannot be resolved.
8. Finalise the architecture	Complete the business and process solution aspect of the design. Validate that the defined requirements will be delivered by the design.
9. Create architecture definition document	Document the business justification for the business and process solution aspect of the design describing how the target business structures will be operate the solution. Explain the reasons for the business structures. Document the control, accountability and responsibility aspects of the business and process solution aspect of the design.

Table 54 – Adapting TOGAF Business Phase to the Business and Process View

4.6.6.4 Functional View

This view contains information on the core capabilities of the solution that will address the business drivers, goals and principles.

The structure of the information collected and analysed within the Functional View is:

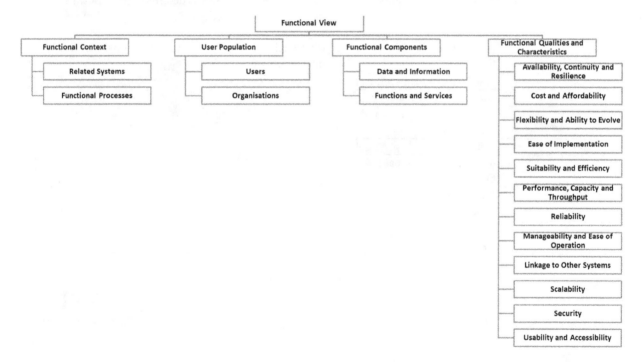

Figure 197 – Functional View Information Structure

Functional View Subject Area	Functional View Topic	Description
Functional Context	Related Systems	This will describe the boundaries between the proposed solution and related systems. It will describe the interactions between them. It will describe the landscape of the related

Functional View Subject Area	Functional View Topic	Description
		systems.
	Functional Processes	This will contain information on the functional and operational processes for administering, supervising and managing the solution. It will describe the reporting included in these processes.
User Population	Users	This will describe the range of user types and roles that will use the solution: internal organisation users, external users, consumers of the solution and suppliers of data to the solution. It will outline the various user interfaces.
	Organisations	This will describe the organisations that interface to and interact with the solution. It will describe these interactions and the modes of interface. The principles to be applied for interacting with these organisations will be described.
Functional Components	Data and Information	This will describe the different types of data, their structures, storage, representations, uses, accesses, data inputs, data output and exchanges
	Functions and Services	This will detail the activities that will be supported by the proposed solution. It will contain an inventory of the solution use cases. The functional processing performed, the data used and generated, and error and exception handling will be defined.
Functional Qualities and Characteristics	Availability, Continuity and Resilience	This uses the same breakdown as described in the Business View in section 4.6.6.3 on page 282.
	Cost and Affordability	
	Flexibility and Ability to Evolve	This will describe these qualities and characteristics from a functional viewpoint.
	Ease of Implementation	
	Suitability and Efficiency	
	Performance, Capacity and Throughput	
	Reliability	
	Manageability and Ease of Operation	
	Linkage to Other Systems	
	Scalability	
	Security	
	Usability and Accessibility	

Table 55 – Functional View Information Structure

4.6.6.4.1 Adapting TOGAF Information Systems Architecture Phase to the Functional View

TOGAF ADM Business Architecture Phase Step	Adaptation to Functional View Solution Design Process
1. Select reference models, viewpoints and tools	Define the central solution design principles, at the target solution level, at the overall solution architecture level and at the enterprise architecture level. Select the set of functional viewpoints or aspects such as integration, solution

TOGAF ADM Business Architecture Phase Step	Adaptation to Functional View Solution Design Process
	operations, implementation or data migration that will form the basis for the functional views and that will be used to work through the functional design aspects of the solution. Select the set of business functions that will be involved in the functional view based on the proposed scope of the target solution. Identify the business actors in these business functions. Define the functional components and their steps and processing to be included in this view. Define the level of detail and granularity for the viewpoints analysis. Describe the interactions between business functions and actors. Define the artefacts and documentation to be created such as: • Functional component interaction • Solution component interaction and interfaces • Solution component operations and management • Solution component implementation dependency • Business and process component usage • Data load and migration • Solution component location Define the functionality-oriented requirements to be collected that will govern the solution to be designed and implemented, including: • Requirements, both functional and operational • Principles • Standards and policies • Assumptions • Constraints
2. Develop application baseline architecture description	Describe the structure and operation of the current set of solutions from a functional view that are being targeted for replacement by the new solution, if they exist. If there is no current set of solutions being upgraded or replaced describe the manual functions being performed that comprise the scope of the target solution and define this as the baseline. If the proposed solution is entirely new, describe the problem or challenge it addresses, the functionality is required and define this as the baseline. Gather information on the current architecture only insofar as it will add value to the definition of the target solution. Use the information gathering structures defined in step 1 to organise the information to be collected. Include details on the problems and issues being experienced with the functionality of the baseline solution.

TOGAF ADM Business Architecture Phase Step	Adaptation to Functional View Solution Design Process
	Perform this information collection and analysis to the extent that the information collected is needed to define the target solution and how much of the existing solutions will be reused by or integrated into the target solution.
3. Develop target architecture description	Describe the functionality of the target solution using the structures defined in step 1. Include in this description references on the data architecture of the target solution and how the business and processes will interact with and use the functionality. Identify any existing function components in the baseline solution that are being reused and incorporated into the target solution and any changes planned for them.
4. Perform gap analysis	Compare the functionality of the current baseline, if relevant and applicable, with that envisaged by the target solution design and identify and explain any gaps or develop an approach for their resolution. Analyse the target functional solution design to ensure it accurately reflects and delivers on the functional requirements and identify and explain any gaps or develop an approach for their resolution. Create an inventory of solution functionality gaps. Create an inventory of solution functional component classifying those that are new and those that are being reused and any changes that are included in the design.
5. Define roadmap components	Define the sequence of activities require to implement the solution functional components.
6. Understand and resolve impacts across the architecture landscape	Assess the functionality and functional components of the target solution against the wider solution and business landscapes to determine if there are any conflicts. Determine if there are been any changes in either the solution functional landscape that will impact on the target solution. Determine if there are any initiatives planned or in progress in the wider solution functional landscape that will impact on the target solution or be impacted by or that can be leveraged by the target solution.
7. Conduct formal stakeholder review	Review the target functionality and functional components of the solution design to establish if it meets the original stated needs. Present the functional view of the target solution with other IT architecture stakeholders to understand if it impacts on or its impacted by application and data architectures. Identify any impact the solution design will have on the infrastructure architecture. Present the functional view of the target solution to business stakeholders. Analyse and explain any differences between the target functional view of the solution and the feedback provided by stakeholders. Consider updating the target functional solution design if the differences cannot be resolved.
8. Finalise the functional architecture	Complete the functional solution aspect of the design.

TOGAF ADM Business Architecture Phase Step	Adaptation to Functional View Solution Design Process
	Itemise the functional components of the solution and describe each. Validate that the defined requirements will be delivered by the design.
9. Create architecture definition document	Document the technical and business justifications for the functional solution component aspects of the design.

Table 56 – Adapting TOGAF Business Phase to the Functional View

4.6.6.5 Data View

This view contains information on the data aspects of the solution. The information on the data aspects of solution architecture contained in section 4.8 on page 321 can be used here.

The structure of the information collected and analysed within the Data View is:

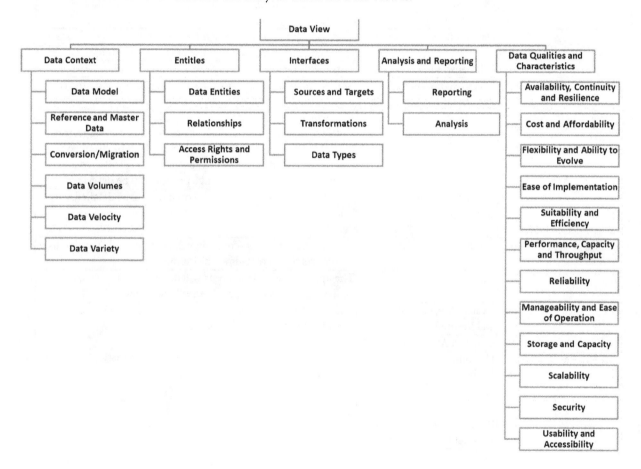

Figure 198 – Data View Information Structure

Data View Subject Area	Data View Topic	Description
Data Context	Data Model	This will describe the overall solution data model. This will define the key data produced and consumed across the organisation by the solution. It will reflect data requirements and designs
	Reference and Master Data	Reference data consists of defined domain values (data

Data View Subject Area	Data View Topic	Description
		vocabularies/dictionaries) including standardised terms, code values and other unique identifiers, business definitions for each value, business relationships within and across domain value lists. Master data is concerned with enabling consistent, shared, contextual use across systems, of the most accurate, timely and relevant version of truth about essential business entities. This will describe reference and master data contained within the solution and the process for its creation, update, and retirement.
	Conversion/Migration	This will define the sources of data to be migrated and the approach to data migration.
	Data Volumes	This will define the data volumes across all data types.
	Data Velocity	This will describe the rate of arrival and change of data.
	Data Variety	This will describe the range of data and the variability with that data.
Entitles	Data Entities	This will define the major types and sources of data necessary to support the operation and use of the application.
	Relationships	This defines the relationships between the entities.
	Access Rights and Permissions	This will define the permissions assigned to data and the roles that have access.
Interfaces	Sources and Targets	This will define the sources and targets for data integrations and exchanges. It will describe the method of exchange, the data flows, the volume of data exchanges and the frequency of exchange. The means by which exchanges are initiated and the security applied to the exchange process will be described.
	Transformations	The transformations performed on data will be detailed.
	Data Types	The source and target data formats and content will be described.
Analysis and Reporting	Reporting	The approach to data reporting will be described. The details on reports to be created will be defined.
	Analysis	The approach to data analysis will be described. The data analysis facilities to be provided will be defined.
Characteristics	Availability, Continuity and Resilience	This uses the same breakdown as described in the Business View in section 4.6.6.3 on page 282.
	Cost and Affordability	
	Flexibility and Ability to Evolve	This will describe these qualities and characteristics from a data viewpoint.
	Ease of Implementation	
	Suitability and Efficiency	
	Performance, Capacity and Throughput	
	Reliability	
	Manageability and Ease of Operation	
	Linkage to Other Systems	
	Scalability	
	Security	
	Usability and Accessibility	

Table 57 – Data View Information Structure

4.6.6.5.1 Adapting TOGAF Information Systems Architecture Phase to the Data View

TOGAF ADM Business Architecture Phase Step	Adaptation to Data View Solution Design Process
1. Select reference models, viewpoints and tools	Define the central solution design principles, at the target solution level, at the overall solution architecture level and at the enterprise architecture level. Select the set of data viewpoints or aspects such as capture, processing, transformation, storage, access and access controls, interface, integration, transfer, initial data load, data migration, operational and historical data, master data, reference data, data reporting and analysis that will form the basis for the data views and that will be used to work through the data design aspects of the solution. Select the set of business functions that will be involved in the data view based on the proposed scope of the target solution. Identify the business actors in these business functions. Define the data components across the viewpoints listed above and their steps and processing to be included in this view. Define the level of detail and granularity for the viewpoints analysis. Describe the interactions between business functions and actors. Define the artefacts and documentation to be created such as: • Data components and their interaction • Data component operations and management • Data component implementation dependency • Data component usage • Data load and migration • Data component location Define the data-oriented requirements to be collected that will govern the solution to be designed and implemented, including: • Requirements, both functional and operational • Principles • Standards and policies • Assumptions • Constraints
2. Develop application baseline architecture description	Describe the structure and operation of the current set of solutions from a data view that are being targeted for replacement by the new solution, if they exist. If there is no current set of solutions being upgraded or replaced describe how the data is currently being handled that comprises the scope of the target solution and define this as the baseline. If the proposed solution is entirely new, describe the data-related aspects of the problem or challenge it addresses, the data that is required and define this as the baseline. Gather information on the current architecture only insofar as it will add value to the definition of the target solution.

TOGAF ADM Business Architecture Phase Step	Adaptation to Data View Solution Design Process
	Use the information gathering structures defined in step 1 to organise the information to be collected. Include details on the problems and issues being experienced with the data of the baseline solution. Perform this information collection and analysis to the extent that the information collected is needed to define the target solution and how much of the existing solutions will be reused by or integrated into the target solution.
3. Develop target architecture description	Describe the data aspects of the target solution using the structures and viewpoints defined in step 1. Include in this description references on the data architecture of the target solution and how the business and processes will interact with and use the data. Identify any existing data components in the baseline solution that are being reused and incorporated into the target solution and any changes planned for them.
4. Perform gap analysis	Compare the data aspects of the current baseline, if relevant and applicable, with that envisaged by the target solution design and identify and explain any gaps or develop an approach for their resolution. Analyse the target data aspects of the solution design to ensure it accurately reflects and delivers on the data requirements and identify and explain any gaps or develop an approach for their resolution. Create an inventory of solution data gaps. Create an inventory of solution data components classifying those that are new and those that are being reused and any changes that are included in the design.
5. Define roadmap components	Define the sequence of activities require to implement the solution data components.
6. Understand and resolve impacts across the architecture landscape	Assess the data components of the target solution against the wider solution and business landscapes to determine if there are any conflicts. Determine if there are been any changes in either the solution data landscape that will impact on the target solution. Determine if there are any initiatives planned or in progress in the wider solution data landscape that will impact on the target solution or be impacted by or that can be leveraged by the target solution.
7. Conduct formal stakeholder review	Review the target data components of the solution design to establish if it meets the original stated needs. Present the data view of the target solution with other IT architecture stakeholders to understand if it impacts on or its impacted by application and data architectures. Identify any impact the solution design will have on the infrastructure architecture. Present the data view of the target solution to business stakeholders. Analyse and explain any differences between the target data view of the solution and the feedback provided by stakeholders.

TOGAF ADM Business Architecture Phase Step	Adaptation to Data View Solution Design Process
	Consider updating the target data solution design if the differences cannot be resolved.
8. Finalise the data architecture	Complete the data solution aspect of the design. Itemise the data components of the solution and describe each. Validate that the defined requirements will be delivered by the design.
9. Create architecture definition document	Document the technical and business justifications for the data solution component aspects of the design.

Table 58 – Adapting TOGAF Business Phase to the Data View

4.6.6.6 Technical View

This view typically defines how to structure the solution and its components and defines the key application components, data, technical hardware and software infrastructure, constraints and limitations, interfaces, standards and development and operation toolsets used. This information will be provided for each software component of the overall solution, including new custom developed software, changes to existing custom developed software and existing or new products that are configured or customised.

The structure of the information collected and analysed within the Technical View is:

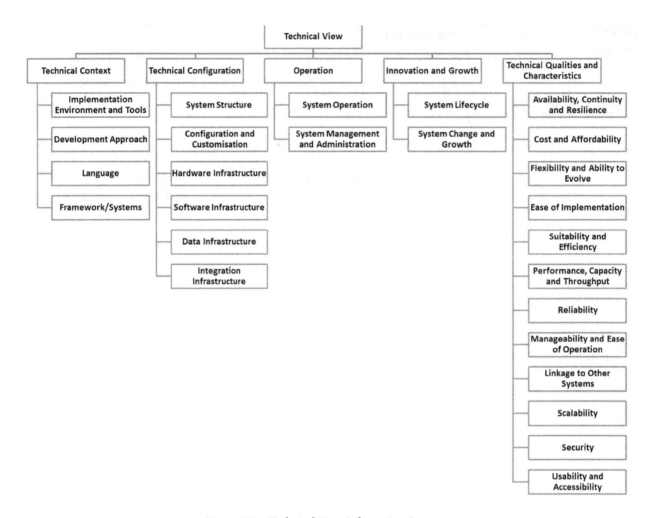

Figure 199 – Technical View Information Structure

Technical View Subject Area	Technical View Topic	Description
Technical Context	Implementation Environment and Tools	The will describe the development/ deployment/runtime/management approach, toolsets, versions and licences required, either in the internal or external hosted environment.
	Development Approach	This will detail the approach to custom software development, if applicable
	Language	This will describe the development languages and versions used. It will reference any style guides that apply.
	Framework/Systems	This will describe any frameworks used in the development.
Technical Configuration	System Structure	This will describe the structure of the solution component including application tiers/layers, subsystems, modules and components, object classes, methods and relationships, data schemas, application services, APIs and protocols used.
	Configuration and Customisation	This will describe the configuration and customisations made to packaged software solution components.
	Hardware Infrastructure	This will detail the hardware infrastructure including servers, communication used across the various development, testing, pre-production and production landscapes.
	Software Infrastructure	This will detail the software infrastructure including application servers, middleware and messaging used across the

Technical View Subject Area	Technical View Topic	Description
		various development, testing, pre-production and production landscapes.
	Data Infrastructure	This will detail the data storage infrastructure including hardware and software used across the various development, testing, pre-production and production landscapes.
	Integration Infrastructure	This will define the integration infrastructure such as service bus across the various development, testing, pre-production and production landscapes.
Operation	System Operation	This will describe details on the solution component operating states, control processes, data flows, interactions and integration points, algorithms, data management, error and exception handling and management and system administration.
	System Management and Administration	This will describe the set of processes that will be used to administer and manage the solution component including: • Alert and Event Management • Access Management • Change Management • Release Management • Configuration Management • Service Level Management • Performance Management • Availability Management • Capacity Management • Service Continuity Management • People Management • Security Management
Innovation and Growth	System Lifecycle	This will detail how the expected lifecycle of the solution.
	System Change and Growth	This will describe how the system can be changed, enhanced, upgraded, configured and modified.
Characteristics	Availability, Continuity and Resilience	This uses the same breakdown as described in the Business View in section 4.6.6.3 on page 282.
	Cost and Affordability	
	Flexibility and Ability to Evolve	This will describe these qualities and characteristics from a technical viewpoint.
	Ease of Implementation	
	Suitability and Efficiency	
	Performance, Capacity and Throughput	
	Reliability	
	Manageability and Ease of Operation	
	Linkage to Other Systems	
	Scalability	
	Security	
	Usability and Accessibility	

Table 59 – Technical View Information Structure

4.6.6.6.1 Adapting TOGAF Technology Architecture Phase to the Technical View

TOGAF ADM Business Architecture Phase Step	Adaptation to Technical View Solution Design Process
1. Select reference models, viewpoints and tools	Define the central solution design principles, at the target solution level, at the overall solution architecture level and at the enterprise architecture level. Select the set of technical viewpoints or aspects such as hardware and software infrastructure, communications, external hosting, access devices and service management that will form the basis for the technology views and that will be used to work through the technical design aspects of the solution. Select the set of information technology functions that will be involved in the technology view based on the proposed scope of the target solution. Identify the information technology actors in these functions. Define the technical components and their location, configuration and interactions to be included in this view. Define the level of detail and granularity for the viewpoints analysis. Describe the interactions between information technology functions and actors. Define the artefacts and documentation to be created such as: • Technical component interaction and interfaces • Technical component operations and management • Technical component implementation dependency • Technical component location Define the technical-oriented requirements to be collected that will govern the solution to be designed and implemented, including: • Requirements, both functional and operational • Principles • Standards and policies • Assumptions • Constraints
2. Develop application baseline architecture description	Describe the structure and operation of the current set of technology components from a technical view that are being targeted for replacement by the new solution, if they exist. If there is no current set of technology components being upgraded or replaced describe the manual functions being performed that comprise the scope of the target solution and define this as the baseline. If the proposed solution is entirely new, describe the problem or challenge it addresses, the technology components is required and define this as the baseline. Gather information on the current technical architecture only insofar as it will add value to the definition of the target solution. Use the information gathering structures defined in step 1 to organise the information to be collected.

TOGAF ADM Business Architecture Phase Step	Adaptation to Technical View Solution Design Process
	Include details on the problems and issues being experienced with the technical aspects of the baseline solution. Perform this information collection and analysis to the extent that the information collected is needed to define the target solution and how much of the existing solutions will be reused by or integrated into the target solution.
3. Develop target architecture description	Describe the technology components of the target solution using the structures defined in step 1. Include in this description references on the technical architecture of the target solution and how the management and support will interact with and use the technical components. Identify any existing technical components in the baseline solution that are being reused and incorporated into the target solution and any changes planned for them.
4. Perform gap analysis	Compare the technical components of the current baseline, if relevant and applicable, with that envisaged by the target solution design and identify and explain any gaps or develop an approach for their resolution. Analyse the target technical solution design to ensure it accurately reflects and delivers on the technical and operational requirements and identify and explain any gaps or develop an approach for their resolution. Create an inventory of solution technical gaps. Create an inventory of solution technical component classifying those that are new and those that are being reused and any changes that are included in the design.
5. Define roadmap components	Define the sequence of activities require to implement the solution technical components.
6. Understand and resolve impacts across the architecture landscape	Assess the technology and technical components of the target solution against the wider solution and business landscapes to determine if there are any conflicts. Determine if there are been any changes in either the solution technical landscape that will impact on the target solution. Determine if there are any initiatives planned or in progress in the wider solution technical landscape that will impact on the target solution or be impacted by or that can be leveraged by the target solution.
7. Conduct formal stakeholder review	Review the target technology and technical components of the solution design to establish if it meets the original stated needs. Present the technical view of the target solution with other IT architecture stakeholders to understand if it impacts on or its impacted by application and data architectures. Identify any impact the solution design will have on the infrastructure architecture. Present the technical view of the target solution to information technology stakeholders. Analyse and explain any differences between the target technical view of the solution and the feedback provided by stakeholders.

TOGAF ADM Business Architecture Phase Step	Adaptation to Technical View Solution Design Process
	Consider updating the target technical solution design if the differences cannot be resolved.
8. Finalise the technical architecture	Complete the technical solution aspect of the design. Itemise the technical components of the solution and describe each. Validate that the defined requirements will be delivered by the design.
9. Create architecture definition document	Document the technical and business justifications for the technical solution component aspects of the design.

Table 60 – Adapting TOGAF Business Phase to the Technical View

4.6.6.7 Implementation View

This view focuses on the specifics of the implementation of customised software and configured or customised software products and on the environments, products, processes, people, and plan required to create the solution.

The structure of the information collected and analysed within the Implementation View is:

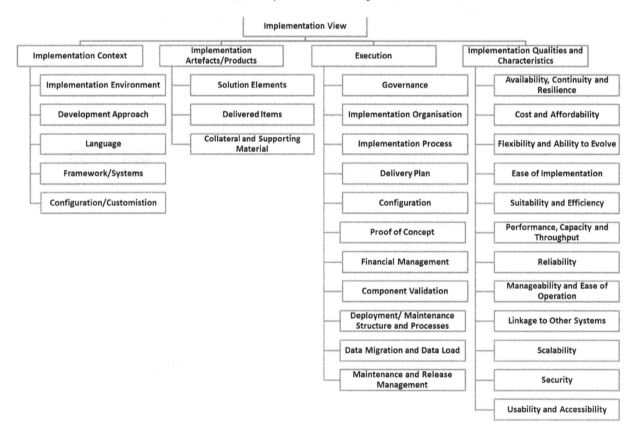

Figure 200 – Implementation View Information Structure

Implementation View Subject Area	Implementation View Topic	Description
Implementation Context	Implementation Environment	This describes the implementation environment.

Implementation View Subject Area	Implementation View Topic	Description
	Development Approach	This describes the approach that will be taken to development, configuration and customisation, including the management of the process.
	Language	This describes the development languages that will be used, including versions.
	Framework/Systems	This describes the development frameworks that will be used.
	Configuration/ Customisation	This describes any configurations and customisations applied to any based product and the approach to making and maintaining these changes
Implementation Artefacts/Products	Solution Elements	This describes the detail of the solution components that will be developed or acquired and configured including its structure.
	Delivered Items	This describes the set of items that will be delivered as part of the component.
	Collateral and Supporting Material	This details any collateral and other material that will be delivered as part of the development of the component.
Execution	Governance	This will describe the process for making decisions, resolving and escalating issues and development.
	Implementation Organisation	This will detail the development organisation structure, roles and responsibilities, capabilities, skills and approach to training in any new skills needed.
	Implementation Process	The will describe the development lifecycle model, the approach to quality assurance and testing. It will also describe the approach to vendor management if relevant.
	Delivery Plan	The will specify the proposed development, configuration and customisation deliverables, stages and phase, milestones, dependencies, schedule, resources. It will also contain a feasibility analysis and a risk model and management plan. It will detail the completion criteria and the reporting procedures.
	Configuration	This will detail the approach to version management, concurrent development, configuration control. It will contain topology map of the component.
	Proof of Concept	This will contain details on any proofs of concept that will be developed during implementation.
	Financial Management	This will contain the implementation cost and approaches to funding model.
	Component Validation	This will define the approach to validating that the developed component meets the requirements of the solution and that the component work individually and together
	Deployment/ Maintenance Structure and Processes	This will describe the user support model, the approach incident reporting and problem management and backup and recovery processes. It will also detail the approach to change control, event logging, monitoring and reporting of service levels and management reporting.
	Data Migration and Data Load	The will identify the initial data to be loaded into the solution data stores and existing data to be migrated into new data structures.
	Maintenance and Release Management	This will describe the approach to applying maintenance fixes and to making available and implementing new releases
Characteristics	Availability, Continuity	This uses the same breakdown as described in the Business

Implementation View Subject Area	Implementation View Topic	Description
	and Resilience	View in section 4.6.6.3 on page 282.
	Cost and Affordability	
	Flexibility and Ability to Evolve	This will describe these qualities and characteristics from an implementation viewpoint.
	Ease of Implementation	
	Suitability and Efficiency	
	Performance, Capacity and Throughput	
	Reliability	
	Manageability and Ease of Operation	
	Linkage to Other Systems	
	Scalability	
	Security	
	Usability and Accessibility	

Table 61 – Implementation View Information Structure

4.6.6.7.1 Adapting TOGAF Technology Architecture Phase to the Implementation View

TOGAF does not have an implementation view. However, the structure for the other views can be used.

TOGAF ADM Business Architecture Phase Step	Adaptation to Implementation View Solution Design Process
1. Select reference models, viewpoints and tools	Define the central solution design principles, at the target solution level, at the overall solution architecture level and at the enterprise architecture level. Select the set of implementation viewpoints or aspects such as hardware and software infrastructure, communications, external hosting, development, component acquisition and configuration, testing, release management and deployment, data load and migration and transition to production that will form the basis for the implementation views and that will be used to work through the implementation design aspects of the solution. Select the set of information technology functions that will be involved in the implementation view based on the proposed scope of the target solution. Identify the information technology actors in these functions. Define the implementation components and their location, configuration and interactions to be included in this view. Define the level of detail and granularity for the viewpoints analysis. Describe the interactions between information technology functions and actors. Define the artefacts and documentation to be created such as: • Implementation component interaction and interfaces • Implementation component operations and management • Implementation component implementation dependency

TOGAF ADM Business Architecture Phase Step	Adaptation to Implementation View Solution Design Process
	• Implementation component location Define the implementation -oriented requirements to be collected that will govern the solution to be designed and implemented, including • Requirements, both functional and operational • Principles • Standards and policies • Assumptions • Constraints
2. Develop application baseline architecture description	Describe the structure and operation of the current set of technology components from an implementation view that are being targeted for replacement by the new solution, if they exist. If there is no current set of technology components being upgraded or replaced describe the manual functions being performed that comprise the scope of the target solution and define this as the baseline. If the proposed solution is entirely new, describe the problem or challenge it addresses, the implementation components is required and define this as the baseline. Gather information on the current technical architecture only insofar as it will add value to the definition of the target solution. Use the information gathering structures defined in step 1 to organise the information to be collected. Include details on the problems and issues being experienced with the implementation aspects of the baseline solution. Perform this information collection and analysis to the extent that the information collected is needed to define the target solution and how much of the existing solutions will be reused by or integrated into the target solution.
3. Develop target architecture description	Describe the implementation components of the target solution using the structures defined in step 1. Include in this description references on the technical architecture of the target solution and how the management and support will interact with and use the implementation components. Identify any existing implementation components in the baseline solution that are being reused and incorporated into the target solution and any changes planned for them.
4. Perform gap analysis	Compare the implementation components of the current baseline, if relevant and applicable, with that envisaged by the target solution design and identify and explain any gaps or develop an approach for their resolution. Analyse the target implementation solution design to ensure it accurately reflects and delivers on the technical and operational requirements and identify and explain any gaps or develop an approach for their resolution. Create an inventory of solution implementation gaps.

TOGAF ADM Business Architecture Phase Step	Adaptation to Implementation View Solution Design Process
	Create an inventory of solution implementation component classifying those that are new and those that are being reused and any changes that are included in the design.
5. Define roadmap components	Define the sequence of activities require to put in place the solution implementation components.
6. Understand and resolve impacts across the architecture landscape	Assess the implementation components of the target solution against the wider solution and business landscapes to determine if there are any conflicts. Determine if there are been any changes in either the solution implementation landscape that will impact on the target solution. Determine if there are any initiatives planned or in progress in the wider solution implementation landscape that will impact on the target solution or be impacted by or that can be leveraged by the target solution.
7. Conduct formal stakeholder review	Review the target implementation components of the solution design to establish if it meets the original stated needs. Present the implementation view of the target solution with other IT architecture stakeholders to understand if it impacts on or its impacted by application and data architectures. Identify any impact the solution design will have on the infrastructure architecture. Present the implementation view of the target solution to information technology stakeholders. Analyse and explain any differences between the target implementation view of the solution and the feedback provided by stakeholders. Consider updating the target implementation solution design if the differences cannot be resolved.
8. Finalise the technical architecture	Complete the implementation solution aspect of the design. Itemise the implementation components of the solution and describe each. Validate that the defined requirements will be delivered by the design.
9. Create architecture definition document	Document the implementation and business justifications for the implementation solution component aspects of the design.

Table 62 – Adapting TOGAF Business Phase to the Implementation View

4.6.6.8 Management and Operations View

This view defines the structures needed to operate the solution after it has been transition to the support function.

The structure of the information collected and analysed within the Management and Operations View is:

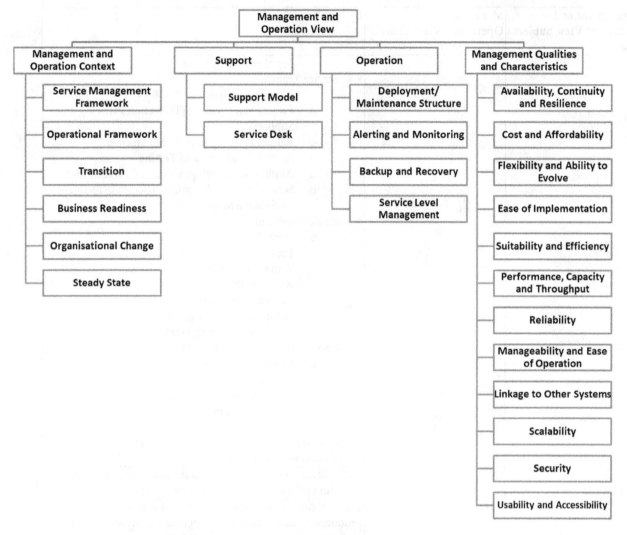

Figure 201 – Management and Operations View Information Structure

Management and Operations View Subject Area	Management and Operations View Topic	Description
Management and Operation Context	Service Management Framework	This describes the overall service management framework across the relevant aspects of service that apply to the organisation: • Service Strategy o Service Portfolio Management o Financial Management • Service Design o Service Catalogue Management o Service Level Management o Risk Management o Capacity Management o Availability Management o IT Service Continuity Management o IT Security Management o Compliance Management o IT Architecture Management

Management and Operations View Subject Area	Management and Operations View Topic	Description

		o Supplier Management
		• Service Transition
		    o Change Management
		    o Project Management (Transition Planning and Support)
		    o Release and Deployment Management
		    o Service Validation and Testing
		    o Application Development and Customisation
		    o Service Asset and Configuration Management
		    o Knowledge Management
		• Service Operation
		    o Event Management
		    o Incident Management
		    o Request Fulfilment
		    o Access Management
		    o Problem Management
		    o IT Operations Management
		    o IT Facilities Management
		• Continual Service Improvement
		    o Service Evaluation
		    o Process Evaluation
		    o Definition of CSI Initiatives
		    o CSI Monitoring
		
		The specific operational processes in these areas that apply to the solution will be described.

	Operational Framework	This will describe the approach to the operating the solution including solution management across all the components,
	Transition	This will detail the approach to solution transition to production, including any parallel runs and hypercare period and approach to support during this interval.
	Business Readiness	This will describe the approach to organisation readiness to accept and use the solution across all the solution dimensions of: • Business process changes • Organisation structure changes • Data migration and load • Data integrations and interfaces • Solution implementation including infrastructure • User testing • Operational acceptance testing • Transition to support • Parallel runs, go live and hypercare
	Organisational Change	This will define the approach to handling organisation change and any organisation changes being implemented as part of the overall solution.
	Steady State	This will describe the steady state operation of the solution.
Support	Support Model	This will detail the specific support model that will be applied to the operation and use of the solution and its components, especially those involving software and data interfaces.
	Service Desk	This will define how the service desk will be trained in the

Management and Operations View Subject Area	Management and Operations View Topic	Description
		support of the application and the supporting documentation.
Operation	Deployment/ Maintenance Structure	This will describe the process for deploying and maintaining the software and infrastructure components of the solution
	Alerting and Monitoring	This will describe the specific alerts generated by the components of the solution and how those alerts are handled.
	Backup and Recovery	This will detail the approach to the backup and recovery of the software and data components of the application, including frequency of backup, replication and failover, recovery procedures, time to recover and any data loss that may occur at a result of recovery.
	Service Level Management	This will describe the service levels that will apply to the components of the solution and how those service levels are monitored and managed.
Characteristics	Availability, Continuity and Resilience	This uses the same breakdown as described in the Business View in section 4.6.6.3 on page 282.
	Cost and Affordability	
	Flexibility and Ability to Evolve	This will describe these qualities and characteristics from a management and operations viewpoint.
	Ease of Implementation	
	Suitability and Efficiency	
	Performance, Capacity and Throughput	
	Reliability	
	Manageability and Ease of Operation	
	Linkage to Other Systems	
	Scalability	
	Security	
	Usability and Accessibility	

Table 63 – Management and Operations View Information Structure

You can use an information technology service management framework such as ITIL[41] to define the structure of the specific service management elements of the management and operations view.

---

[41] See:
https://www.axelos.com/best-practice-solutions/itil

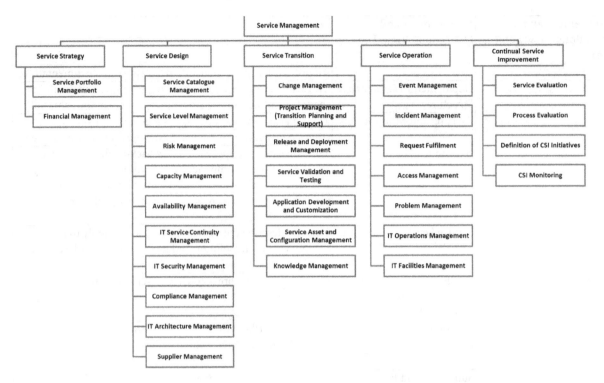

Figure 202 – Information Technology Service Management Framework

While there are criticisms of ITIL in its pure service management viewpoint such as:

- It is very comprehensive which results in many partial implementations and usages that focus on just the areas of incident, problem and change management

- It does not easily fit into a vendor management framework where components of solutions are outsourced or delivered through XaaS models

- It does not expand its viewpoint take into account how the solution components are designed and implemented to make transition to service management easier

- It is poor at handling the end of the life of services and solutions and their transition to new solutions or suppliers

it is still a structure that allows the serviceability (in its widest meaning) of a solution to be assessed.

4.6.6.8.1 Adapting TOGAF Technology Architecture Phase to the Management and Operations View

TOGAF does not have a Management and Operations view. However, the structure for the other views can be used.

TOGAF ADM Business Architecture Phase Step	Adaptation to Management and Operations View Solution Design Process
1. Select reference models, viewpoints and tools	Define the central solution design principles, at the target solution level, at the overall solution architecture level and at the enterprise architecture level. Select the set of management and operations viewpoints or aspects such as service management across all its important dimensions including monitoring and alerting, recovery and availability, capacity planning and management and others that will form the basis for the technology views and that will be used to work through the

TOGAF ADM Business Architecture Phase Step	Adaptation to Management and Operations View Solution Design Process
	management and operations design aspects of the solution. Select the set of information technology functions that will be involved in the management and operations view based on the proposed scope of the target solution. Identify the information technology actors in these functions. Define the management and operations components and their location, configuration and interaction to be included in this view. Define the level of detail and granularity for the viewpoints analysis. Describe the interactions between information technology functions and actors. Define the artefacts and documentation to be created such as: • Management and operations component interaction and interfaces • Management and operations component operations and management • Management and operations component implementation dependency • Management and operations component location Define the management and operations -oriented requirements to be collected that will govern the solution to be designed and implemented, including: • Requirements, both functional and operational • Principles • Standards and policies • Assumptions • Constraints
2. Develop application baseline architecture description	Describe the structure and operation of the current set of management and operations components from a technical view that are being targeted for replacement by the new solution, if they exist. If there is no current set of management and operations components being upgraded or replaced describe the manual functions being performed that comprise the scope of the target solution and define this as the baseline. If the proposed solution is entirely new, describe the problem or challenge it addresses, the management and operations components is required and define this as the baseline. Gather information on the current management and operations architecture only insofar as it will add value to the definition of the target solution. Use the information gathering structures defined in step 1 to organise the information to be collected. Include details on the problems and issues being experienced with the management and operations of the baseline solution. Perform this information collection and analysis to the extent that the information collected is needed to define the target solution and how much of the existing

TOGAF ADM Business Architecture Phase Step	Adaptation to Management and Operations View Solution Design Process
	solutions will be reused by or integrated into the target solution.
3. Develop target architecture description	Describe the management and operations components of the target solution using the structures defined in step 1. Include in this description references on the management and operations architecture of the target solution and how the management and support will interact with and use the management and operations components. Identify any existing management and operations components in the baseline solution that are being reused and incorporated into the target solution and any changes planned for them.
4. Perform gap analysis	Compare the management and operations components of the current baseline, if relevant and applicable, with that envisaged by the target solution design and identify and explain any gaps or develop an approach for their resolution. Analyse the target management and operations solution design to ensure it accurately reflects and delivers on the technical and operational requirements and identify and explain any gaps or develop an approach for their resolution. Create an inventory of solution management and operations gaps. Create an inventory of solution management and operations components classifying those that are new and those that are being reused and any changes that are included in the design.
5. Define roadmap components	Define the sequence of activities require to implement the solution management and operations components.
6. Understand and resolve impacts across the architecture landscape	Assess the management and operations components of the target solution against the wider solution and business landscapes to determine if there are any conflicts. Determine if there are been any changes in either the solution management and operations landscape that will impact on the target solution. Determine if there are any initiatives planned or in progress in the wider solution management and operations landscape that will impact on the target solution or be impacted by or that can be leveraged by the target solution.
7. Conduct formal stakeholder review	Review the target management and operations components of the solution design to establish if it meets the original stated needs. Present the management and operations view of the target solution with other IT architecture stakeholders to understand if it impacts on or its impacted by application and data architectures . Identify any impact the solution design will have on the infrastructure architecture. Present the management and operations view of the target solution to information technology stakeholders. Analyse and explain any differences between the target management and operations view of the solution and the feedback provided by stakeholders. Consider updating the target management and operations solution design if the differences cannot be resolved.
8. Finalise the technical	Complete the management and operations solution aspect of the design.

TOGAF ADM Business Architecture Phase Step	Adaptation to Management and Operations View Solution Design Process
architecture	Itemise the management and operations components of the solution and describe each. Validate that the defined requirements will be delivered by the design.
9. Create architecture definition document	Document the management and operations and business justifications for the technical solution component aspects of the design.

Table 64 – Adapting TOGAF Business Phase to the Management and Operations View

4.7 Solution Architecture and Solution Experience and Usability

The solutions designed by the solution architecture must have a number of quality attributes such as those listed in section 4.6.4.7 on page 251, one of which is that the solution must be usable by and useful to the solution consumers. Solution usability across the solution components takes different forms and has different characteristics. The broader view of usability is greater than the appearance and navigation of the user interface software components of the solution. It encompasses solution quality and accuracy, reliability, consistency of performance and availability.

Section 2.4 on page 33 introduced the concept of a solution as being the sum of a set of components across a range of component types.

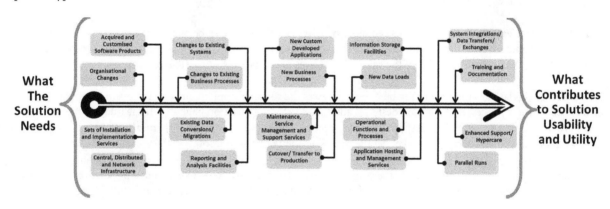

Figure 203 – End to End View of Solution Usability

Solution consumers experience the complete operational solution across its entire scope and experience both its functional and quality properties. Without the complete solution view there will be gaps in the usability of the solution.

Consumers are part of the solution. The solution design should match the consumers' knowledge understanding, expectations and view how the solution should work. One aspect of solution design is the *Principle of Least Astonishment*. This means that the solution should flow and operate as consumers expect it to without unusual behaviours or sudden changes in format, content or sequence.

The solution architect should be an advocate for solution usability. The solution architect should include an evaluation of a solution's usability and the expected experience of the solution consumer in any solution design. The creation of an inventory of solution usage journeys is described in section 4.6.5.11 on page 272.

Solution usability increases the likelihood of solution success. The act of paying attention to usability during solution design means the solution architecture will be aware of the consumer experience and will take action to ensure it is effective. The solution architect therefore needs to take account of user experience as part of the overall solution design process. People are always part of the operation and use of a solution. Solution consumers will interact with the solution in many ways, directly and indirectly. The nature of these interactions should be understood. This is why the rapid solution design engagement described in section 4.6.5 on page 257 includes identifying the solution actors and their interactions with solution components. The solution design needs to deliver on (realistic and fulfillable) consumer expectations and provide an experience that matches these. Solution architects need to be aware of the people and experience aspects of solutions.

Driving business value from information technology solutions depends on matching the technology to the identified solution consumer work practices the solution supports and enables. Solution usability aims to achieve this.

Solution usability is not concerned with promoting form over function. It is about form and function working together.

The consumer experience of a solution is the sum of the experiences across all dimensions of the solutions and the consumer's interaction with it, including both functionality and quality attributes:

- Accuracy
- Ease of interpretation
- Usability
- Utility
- Interoperability
- Integration
- Automation
- Performance
- Consistency
- Reliability
- Availability
- Appearance and navigation

Not all solution usage experiences can be observed directly or are based on experience of consumer-accessed solution functional components. For example, factors such as integration and interoperability are largely hidden from solution consumers but play a part in the usability of the solution and thus the consumer's experience.

Solution usability is related to the underlying business processes the solution implements and the business operates. The importance of business processes to solution design is addressed in section 4.4.2 on page 134. If the underlying business processes are not efficiently defined and especially if the processes are aligned to vertical organisation silos rather than taking a cross-functional end-to-end view, this will affect the overall usability of the solution.

Solution usability is all the more important in the context of digital solutions that are exposed to a population of consumers outside the organisation. See Chapter 5 on page 391 for more details on solution architecture and digital transformation.

Figure 204 – Solution Design and Usability Gulfs

In the consumer's use of a solution, there can be two gulfs – gaps between what the consumer wants and when is provided:

1. *Gulf of Execution* – This is the gap between the desired or required goal of using the solution and the activities and steps required to achieve goal. Execution gulfs can correspond to the multiple steps needed within an application or the need to use multiple applications. They can also be caused by organisational silos and the need for handoffs and a lack of an end-to-end cross-functional application that delivers the associated cross-functional process.

2. *Gulf of Evaluation* – This is the gap between the solution's results and the user's interpretation of or ability to interpret and understand those results. It may not be easy for the consumer to comprehend or evaluate what has happened. The consumer may be unsure if they have been provided with the right information or uncertain if the solution has worked.

To these two gulfs, a third more recent gulf could be added. This is the gap between the experience consumers and organisation employees experience when using social media and other public applications.

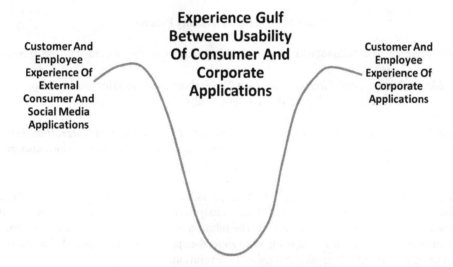

Figure 205 – Gulf Between Corporate and Social Media and Other Consumer Applications

Business organisations tend to be poor at solution usability and design. They also tend to be poor at recognising the existence of these gulfs. The internal IT functions of those businesses tend to view consumer-oriented applications with suspicion and believe that they create risks and costs that must be managed and controlled.

Bridging the experience and expectation gulfs requires attention throughout the solution design and delivery function.

The stages and components of solution usability can be viewed as a pyramid:

Figure 206 – Solution Usability Pyramid

This solution usability hierarchy is as follows, with each level adding to the usability provided by the previous one:

- *Basic, Serviceable And Functional, Limited Attention To Usability* – the solution works. It can be used. It incorporates the required functionality. It provides the right results.

- *Efficient, Consistent, Available, Dependable And Reliable, Error Detection And Correction, Error Tolerance And Handling* – the solution handles data and other consumer errors. It delivers consistent performance and response times. It provides guaranteed availability during the agreed usage intervals.

- *Intuitive And Easy To Use And Understand, Searchable, Navigable, Learnable* – the solution has a natural interface that is easy to learn. Results are presented in a format that is easy to comprehend. Information held in the solution can be searched and results are presented in a usable format. The solution is easy to control and to move through its functions. There is sufficient training and help material available to allow the application to be learned. There are consistent appearance and navigation standards applied throughout the solution.

- *Flexible And Adaptable* – the solution provides facilities to allow it to be used in a variety of ways by consumers. The solution can be adapted to be used in different ways.

- *Common, Shared And Integrated, Guiding, Predicting* – the solution understands the needs of its consumers and navigates them through it. The solution anticipates the needs of consumers and reacts appropriately. The solution operates within a wider solution landscape and provides a consistent experience across this.

Not all solutions need to incorporate the highest level of usability.

The solution design process should include the following characteristics and activities to ensure that solution usability is considered when designing the solution

- Standardised approach to assessing user requirements
- Assessment of requirements used to develop a wider understanding of user needs
- Evaluation includes feedback on quality and delivery of user expectation
- Usability and experience evaluations collected and analysed centrally
- Multiple different approaches to evaluation used
- Assessments performed over wide user group
- Approach to assessment and evaluation updated by previous analyses and experience
- Assessment and evaluation information made available to all project teams
- Evaluations of needs identifies user technical and business capabilities and skills

- Evaluation feedback prioritised and used to define usability for not just current solution but also potential future solutions
- Users are included in design team
- Design team include cognitive frameworks in the solution design process
- Prototyping techniques used widely including prototyping of conceptual and physical design
- Prototyping techniques used to ensure complexity and issues around usability are identified during solution design

Broadly, there are three dimensions of solution usability

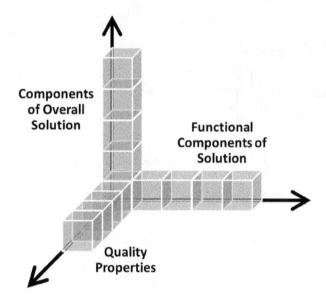

Figure 207 – Dimensions of Solution Usability

These dimensions are:

- **Components of Overall Solution** – the solution consumer will experience directly or indirectly all the components of the solution. For example, with the new data load and existing data migration components, the solution will be pre-loaded with existing data making it more usable. Without any such data load and migration, the solution consumer will not see existing data. So, while the solution will be functionally usable, it actual usability will be diminished.

- **Functional Components of Solution** – solution consumers interact directly with the functional components through their user interfaces. This directly affects the solution usability and impacts the solution consumer's experience.

- **Quality Properties** – the quality properties of a solution (listed in section 4.6.4.7 on page 251) affect its usability indirectly.

Solutions can be viewed the windows into the underlying business processes. Solutions cannot, in themselves, resolve problems with underlying business processes without a process redesign component. The topic of the importance of business processes in solution design is covered in section 4.4.2 on page 134.

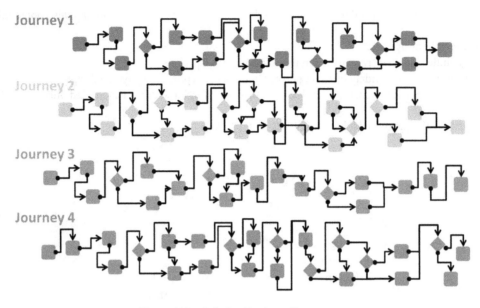

Figure 208 – Solution Business Processes

Taking an end-to-end solution view and understanding how internal solution component interactions impact usability and experience will assist with designing usable solution.

Solution interaction paths will correspond to business processes. Business processes will be (partially) implemented or supported by solutions. There will be many organisation interaction paths with your organisation, depending on:

- Type of interacting party
- Number of interactions

Creating an inventory of interaction journeys and walking through these solution journeys allows you to understand how solution consumers interact with and experience the organisation's solutions:

- Enable problems to be identified
- Use as a basis for a measurement and action framework
- Journeys inventory should be prioritised

Solutions should have the following characteristics:

- Optimise self-service and associated automation and orchestration
- Have a consistent, seamless, continuous experience and appearance across all channels
- Ensure underlying data is consistent across all applications and usage points
- Measure usage and implement processes to analyse and take improvement actions

There is a wider context to the usability of individual solutions as shown below.

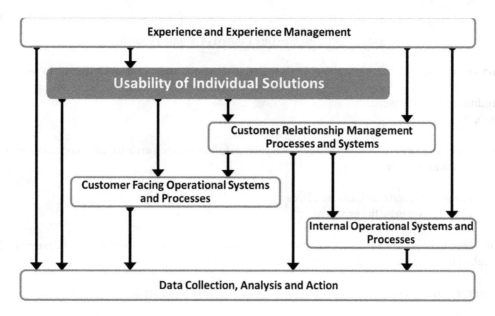

Figure 209 – Wider Context of Solution Usability

The elements of this wider context are:

- *Experience and Experience Management* – constructing overall set of interactions, their aggregation into an overall experience and defining framework to manage these
- *Customer Relationship Management Processes and Systems* – applications and processes to manage operational customer interactions
- *Customer Facing Operational Systems and Processes* – operational systems and their associated processes that support organisation delivery with which customer direct interacts
- *Internal Operational Systems and Processes* – internal systems and their associated processes that support organisation delivery with which customer indirect interacts through interactions with employees and agents
- *Data Collection, Analysis and Action* – framework for gathering information on usage, perform analysis, identifying problems, generating feedback and ensuring actions are taken

Ideally, the solution architecture function should be able to inherit and reuse a solution usability and experience framework already defined and implemented by the organisation.

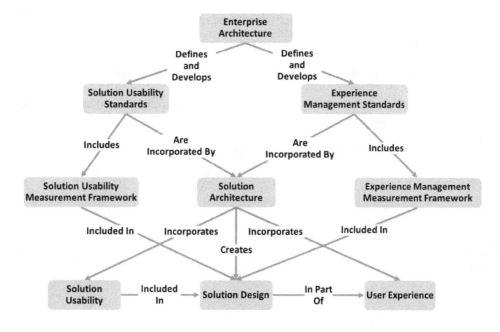

Figure 210 – IT Architecture Context of Solution Usability

The organisation's enterprise architecture function needs to define standards and associated frameworks for:

- Overall solution consumer experience
- Solution usability

Each of these needs to include measurement and analysis framework. The solution architecture needs to incorporate both these standards into solution designs:

- Individual solutions incorporate usability standards
- Overall set of solutions comprise the experience

In the absence of a top-down set of such standards, the solution architecture function should look to develop and roll-out its own. It should embed usability and experience into solution architecture and design.

The set of experiences of the customers of the organisation comprises three main areas:

1. Their direct experience as consumers of externally facing solutions

2. The indirect experience through dealing with organisation employees who are consumers of internal applications

3. Their experience of the products and services provided by the organisation

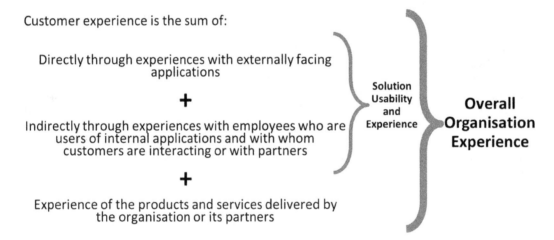

Figure 211 – Solutions and Customer Experiences of the Organisation

High level of employee satisfaction contributes to higher levels of customer satisfaction. Good user experience of internal solutions contributes to good external user experience.

Solution architecture has no influence over the third area. But it can impact the first two.

Figure 212 – Design, Usability and Experience

Design and Usability and Experience represent two sides of the same coin. Design and usability drives experience. Poor usability and experience negatively influence outcomes:

- Frustration and reduced efficiency
- Abandonment of interaction
- Seeking uncosted peer support
- Errors requiring subsequent resolution

Poor solution usability and experience are very difficult to resolve after the solution has been implemented. Retrofitting the necessary usability features is time-consuming and expensive. Organisations almost always do not include user experience in solution architecture and design. They lack the understanding or appreciation of what solution usability is, its relationship to experience and the impact of poor solution usability. This can be caused by factors such as:

- Fear of the scope of usability and its impact on solution design and delivery schedule and cost
- The focus of solution architecture is on meeting stated business requirements and not perceived intangibles such as usability

Lack of solution consumer satisfaction increases cost along the spectrum of solution operation and solution usage outcomes. This leads to greater support, slowness of usage, bypassing systems, rework and abandonment by external users who go elsewhere. Poor usability is not a support issue: by then it is too late.

Section 8.3.4.1 on page 505 discusses the impact of Conway's Law on the solution architecture function. There is, I believe, a corollary to Conway's Law relating to solution usability:

> *Externally presented solutions and experiences tend replicate siloed internal organisation processes, limitations, constraints and structures. Solution usability and solution experience of external solutions replicates the designs of internal solutions.*

This means that organisations tend to be prisoners of their own corporate experiences and structures. That experience constrains choices and produces limitations. Good solution usability and overall experience is frequently outside the knowledge and understanding of organisations.

There are tangible and measurable benefits to good solution usability in terms of:

- Increased productivity
- Reduced results errors and reduced effort to resolve
- Reduced costs on training
- Reduced reliance on help desks
- Decreased data errors, reduced effort to resolve and improved data quality
- Increased conversion rate (for external solution consumers)

- Decreased drop-off rate (for external solution consumers)

There are also costs of poor solution usability.[42]

There are (too) many standards and approaches application usability. The following is a partial list. Many of these are old, partially developed, incomplete and are no longer being maintained, supported or enhanced. Like many such attempts at standards they arise from an academic context. They all largely focus on software application usability rather than looking at the end-to-end solution. This information is presented here without any comments on its applicability or validity in the context of solution architecture.

- *Agile and User Centred Design Integration (AUCDI)* – this is not a fully developed framework. For further information, see documents such as https://ewic.bcs.org/upload/pdf/ewic_hci14_full_paper11.pdf and https://pdfs.semanticscholar.org/d6d2/f500ad75489a0ab69ed770bf1278044aab42.pdf.

- **DATech Standard Usability Test** – the development of this was funded by the German Federal Institute for Occupational Safety and Health (BAuA - Startseite - Bundesanstalt für Arbeitsschutz und Arbeitsmedizin https://www.baua.de/). The original handbook is available in German at https://wiki.qualifizierung.com/lib/exe/fetch.php/fh:pruefhandbuch_iso_9241.pdf.

- *HCD-PCM Visioning HCD-PCM-V* – the Human Centred Design-Process Capability Model (this was developed jointly by Mitsubishi Research Institute, NTT and Otaru University of Commerce in 2002.

- *HIMSS Usability Maturity Model (UMM)* – see https://www.himss.org/himss-usability-maturity-model-umm.

- *Human Factors Integration Process Risk Assessment HFIPRA* – see http://www.processforusability.co.uk/HFIPRA/.

- *Humanware Process Improvement (HPI) Framework* - This dates from 1996 – see http://ash-consulting.com/Humanware.pdf and http://ash-consulting.com/SPI-96-paper.pdf .

- *ISO 18152 Ergonomics of human-system interaction - Specification for the process assessment of human-system issues* – This specifies human-systems model for use in ISO/IEC 15504 (https://www.iso.org/standard/54175.html) Information technology process assessment standard (evaluating the maturity of an organisation in performing the processes that make a system usable, healthy and safe. see https://www.iso.org/standard/56174.html.

- *ISO 18529 - Ergonomics of human-system interaction -Human-centred lifecycle process descriptions* – see https://www.iso.org/standard/33499.html.

- *ISO 9241 Ergonomics of human-system interaction* – see https://www.iso.org/standard/52075.html.

- *Kano model product development and customer satisfaction* – see https://en.wikipedia.org/wiki/Kano_model.

- *KESSU UCD (User-Centred Design) performance assessment (UPA)* – see https://pdfs.semanticscholar.org/81d4/499834857a4fdb2a5d88dad883b3236db236.pdf.

- *Microsoft Solution Framework (MSF)* – see https://www.microsoft.com/en-us/download/details.aspx?id=3214. This includes a solution usability and user readiness element.

- *Nielsen Norman Corporate Usability Maturity Model* – see https://www.nngroup.com/articles/ux-maturity-stages-1-4/.

- *Open Source Usability Maturity Model (OS-UMM)* – see https://ir.lib.uwo.ca/electricalpub/155/.

---

[42] As an example see: https://www.informationweek.com/software/enterprise-applications/avon-pulls-plug-on-$125-million-sap-project/d/d-id/1113061. Avon Products halted on a four-year, $125 million SAP ERP implementation after a test of the system revealed that it was so burdensome and complex to use that many sales representatives quit the company.

- *Oracle Fusion Applications User Experience Patterns and Guidelines* – see
  http://www.oracle.com/us/products/applications/fusion/fusion-apps-user-experience-173408.pdf.

- *Quality Attribute-oriented Software ARchitecture design method (QASAR)* – This is documented in J. Bosch,
  Design and Use of Software Architectures: Adopting and Evolving a Product Line Approach, Pearson Education
  (Addison-Wesley and ACM Press).

- *SAAM: A Method for Analyzing the Properties of Software Architectures* – see
  http://citeseerx.ist.psu.edu/viewdoc/download?doi=10.1.1.127.65&rep=rep1&type=pdf.

- *SALUTA Scenario based Architecture Level UsabiliTy Assessment* – see
  https://pdfs.semanticscholar.org/145a/8b80880359fde2035c134386186184b1e7a7.pdf.

- *Software Engineering Institute (SEI) Architecture Tradeoff Analysis Method (ATAM)* – see
  https://resources.sei.cmu.edu/library/asset-view.cfm?assetid=513908.

- *System Usability Scale (SUS)* – See https://www.usability.gov/how-to-and-tools/methods/system-usability-scale.html.

- *Trillium Model* – see https://web.archive.org/web/20120324210510/http://www.sqi.gu.edu.au/trillium/trillium.html.

- *Usability Leadership Maturity Model ULMM (IBM)*

- *Usability Maturity Model: Human-Centredness Scale UMM-HCS* – see
  http://www.idemployee.id.tue.nl/g.w.m.rauterberg/lecturenotes/usability-maturity-model[1].pdf.

- *Usability Maturity Model: Processes UMM-P* – see
  http://www.idemployee.id.tue.nl/g.w.m.rauterberg/lecturenotes/Usability-Maturity-Model%5B2%5D.PDF.

- *User Centred Design Maturity UCDM* – see https://hal.inria.fr/hal-01405068/document.

4.8 Data Architectural Aspects of Solution Architecture

The detail of the data aspects of solution design is often neglected by the solution architecture function during the solution design process. Data breathes life into a solution. The solution is intrinsically concerned with processing data of potentially many different types and in different ways and generating different data outputs.

Solutions that cannot handle the expected data types, data volumes, data integrations and exchanges, data throughputs or that fail to maintain data quality will inevitably fail. These problems will have to be resolved through rework or additional external activities that become part of the operational solution, often manual, processing or both.

The organisation will (or should) have a data architecture function that defines data management, governance, technology and data processing standards that individual solution designs can inherit without have to perform these basic data design activities from the start for each solution.

Similarly, the organisation will (or should) have implemented infrastructural and backbone data technology solutions – the organisation data plumbing – across the data landscape that solution designs can include, use and reuse without having to implement them for each new solution design.

4.8.1 Data Management Book of Knowledge (DMBOK) Data Architecture Framework

The Data Management Book of Knowledge (DMBOK)[43] can be a useful data architecture and management framework to assist with getting the data aspects of the solution right. There are other data architecture frameworks that can assist such as TOGAF where Phase C: Information Systems Architectures — Data Architecture of the Architecture Development Method covers the topic of data. This is covered in more detail in section 4.6.6.5 on page 291. COBIT (Control Objectives for Information and Related Technologies)[44] can be used to develop information governance and controls but is less useful in the solution architecture domain.

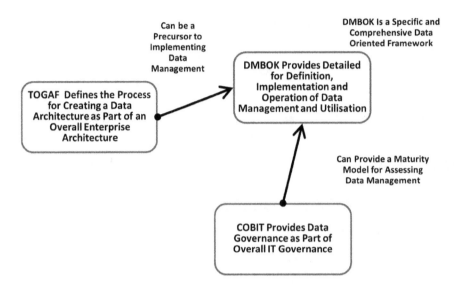

Figure 213 – COBIT, TOGAF and DMBOK Data Management Frameworks

The following diagram illustrates the data management scope of these three frameworks:

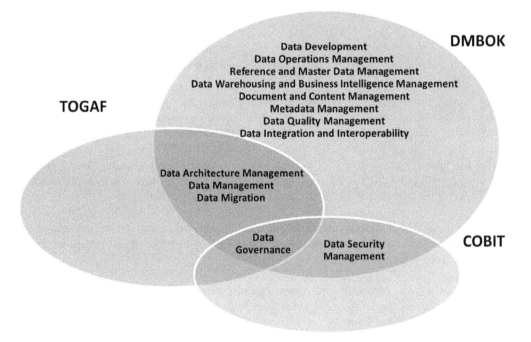

Figure 214 – Data Management Scope of DMBOK, TOGAF and COBIT Frameworks

---

[43] See:
https://dama.org/content/body-knowledge.
[44] See
http://www.isaca.org/Cobit/pages/default.aspx

The DMBOK framework is the more comprehensive and therefore the most useful when analysing the data aspects of solution design.

The DMBOK framework consists of 11 subject areas:

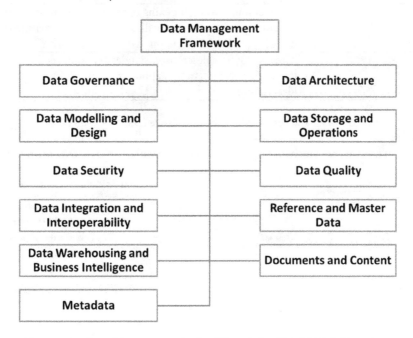

Figure 215 – Data Management Book of Knowledge (DMBOK) Subject Areas

The subject areas of the DMBOK data framework are:

Data Management Book of Knowledge (DMBOK) Subject Areas	Description and Scope
Data Governance	Standards and their enforcement, planning, supervision, control and usage of data resources and the design and implementation of data management processes, data ownership.
Data Architecture	Overall data architecture and data technology standards and design and implement data infrastructural technology solutions.
Data Modelling and Design	Analysis, design, implementation, testing, deployment, maintenance.
Data Storage and Operations	Support physical data assets across the spectrum of data activities from data acquisition to storage to backup, recovery, availability, continuity, retention and purging, capacity planning and management.
Data Security	Data resource security, privacy, confidentiality and access control. The topic of data privacy is covered in more details in section 4.9.2 on page 363. This is becoming ever more important in the context of data privacy initiatives such as GDPR.
Data Quality	Define, monitor, maintain and improve data quality and ensuring data integrity.
Data Integration and Interoperability	Data resource integration, extraction, transformation, movement, delivery, replication, transfer, sharing, federation, virtualisation and operational support.
Reference and Master Data	Manage master versions of shared data resources to reduce redundancy and maintain data quality through standardised data definitions and use

Data Management Book of Knowledge (DMBOK) Subject Areas	Description and Scope
	of common data values.
Data Warehousing and Business Intelligence	Enabling data reporting and analysis, decision support, visualisation and supporting technologies.
Documents and Content	Acquisition, storage, indexing of and access to unstructured data resources such as electronic files and paper records and the integration of these resources with structured data resources.
Metadata	Creation of data description standards and the collection, categorisation, maintenance, integration, application, use and management of data descriptions.

Table 65 – Data Management Book of Knowledge (DMBOK) Subject Areas

This data framework can be used to validate that the solution is complete with respect to data processing.

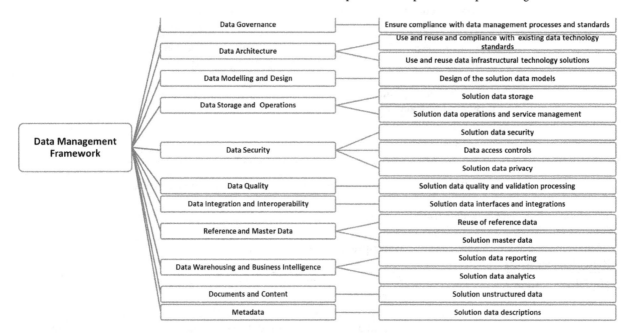

Figure 216 – Using the DMBOK Framework to Ensure the Data Completeness of the Solution Design

In summary, these solution design data completeness checks are:

Data Management Book of Knowledge (DMBOK) Subject Areas	Solution Design Data Completeness Check
Data Governance	• Ensure compliance with data management processes and standards
Data Architecture	• Use and reuse and compliance with existing data technology standards • Use and reuse data infrastructural technology solutions
Data Modelling and Design	• Design of the solution data models
Data Storage and Operations	• Solution data storage • Solution data operations and service management
Data Security	• Solution data security • Data access controls • Solution data privacy
Data Quality	• Solution data quality and validation processing
Data Integration and Interoperability	• Solution data interfaces and integrations
Reference and Master Data	• Reuse of reference data

Data Management Book of Knowledge (DMBOK) Subject Areas	Solution Design Data Completeness Check
	• Solution master data
Data Warehousing and Business Intelligence	• Solution data reporting • Solution data analytics
Documents and Content	• Solution unstructured data
Metadata	• Solution data descriptions

Table 66 – Solution Design Data Completeness Checks

The solution design considerations across these data management subject areas are listed in the following table. As stated above, the organisation should have standards across all these areas that the solution has to comply with rather than the solution having to develop and implement them.

Data Management Book of Knowledge (DMBOK) Subject Areas	Solution Design Consideration
Data Governance	Agree who owns the data Agree what data management standards and policies apply to the data assets Agree and data management reporting standards and metrics
Data Architecture	Ensure the solution complies with enterprise data architecture standards across the elements of data technology, quality, integration, data warehousing and business intelligence, metadata, reference and master data
Data Modelling and Design	Create a comprehensive solution data model to validate that the solution can handle data types, volumes and usage Define the approach to testing and validating the data model
Data Storage and Operations	Specify the data storage hardware and software technology Specify data management policies for data housekeeping activities such as backup and recovery Specify data retention policies Specify data capacity planning details Specify availability and continuity
Data Security	Define data security Define how the solution complies with data privacy regulations such as GDPR (General Data Privacy Regulation)[45], local jurisdiction-specific data privacy and protection legislation, ePrivacy Regulation[46] and any other industry-specific legislation specific to the solution
Data Quality	Specify the approach to data quality including data error identification, handling and notification This should occur at the points where data enters the solution
Data Integration and	Specify the data integrations for the solution across all types: message queue,

---

[45] See:
http://eur-lex.europa.eu/legal-content/en/TXT/?uri=CELEX%3A32016R0679
[46] See:
http://eur-lex.europa.eu/legal-content/EN/TXT/?uri=CELEX%3A52017PC0010

Data Management Book of Knowledge (DMBOK) Subject Areas	Solution Design Consideration
Interoperability	service, API, file transfer, manual data import and extract, email, mail box processing Specify the APIs used by the solution Specify the APIs made available by the solution Specify the security and access control Specify any data transformation, enrichment Specify any data validation, error identification, handling, notification and resolution Specific any collection of audit information
Reference and Master Data	Specify the master data used by the solution Specify the master data created by the solution Specify the reference used by the solution Specify the reference created by the solution
Data Warehousing and Business Intelligence	Specify the approach to data reporting and analysis Specify the approach to reporting on and analysing operational data including data extract, creation of data warehouse or data mart
Documents and Content	Specify any unstructured or document-type data assets the solution uses including its capture, storage, application of index or meta data, access control and data retention
Metadata	Specify the details of metadata linked to unstructured or document-type data assets used by the solution including its storage and management

Table 67 – Data Management Book of Knowledge (DMBOK) Subject Areas Solution Design Considerations

4.8.2 Solution Data Landscape

Every solution design will have a data landscape across which data is generated or acquired, transferred, processed, stored, managed and ultimately deleted. These components of the solution design may use or reuse existing infrastructural data solutions or new facilities may be required.

The following shows a conceptual view of this solution data landscape in terms of data component types. Not all solutions will require all these components. This conceptual view can be used as a checklist to elaborate and validate the solution design and to understand the work that is required to complete the total solution design.

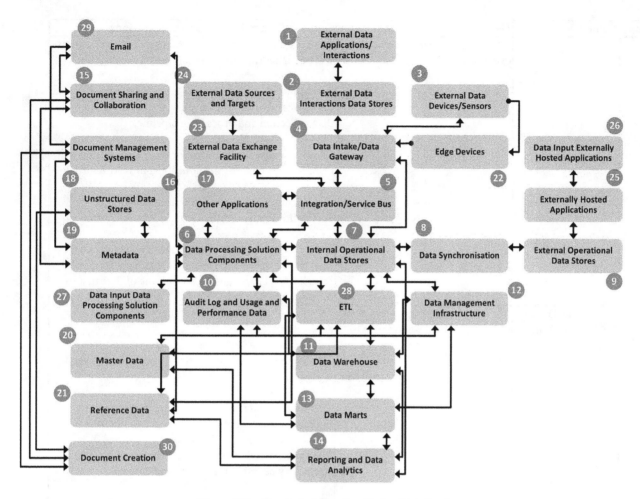

Figure 217 – Conceptual Solution Design Data Landscape

This is a generic and perhaps clumsy and cluttered way of representing all the data sources and targets that can exist for a solution. It can be even more complex and tangled in that there can be several instances of many of these data component types. There can be multiple applications in the solution, both internal and external, each with one or more operational data stores. The solution can interface with several other applications and their data stores. There can be several data exchanges and transfers.

This view does not show any data storage infrastructure. I have assumed that specifying details on physical data infrastructure is outside the scope of solution architecture. The solution architect should state operational requirements for data infrastructure and leave its provision up to the data and infrastructure architecture teams to translate these into physical infrastructure components.

The components of the conceptual solution design data landscape and their solution design considerations are:

Item	Name	Description	Solution Design and Data Considerations
1	External Data Applications/ Interactions	These are the set of applications and data interface and exchange points provided specifically to the range of external parties that supply data to and access data from the enterprise to allow them supply data to and access data from the enterprise.	These applications will either be deployed outside the organisation's core IT infrastructure, hosted by service providers, be cloud-based applications or the organisation will expose an internal application to external access.

These applications will have far higher security requirements than internal use only applications. |

Item	Name	Description	Solution Design and Data Considerations
		These can be hosted internally or externally or a mix of both.	Application interface design and usability expectations will be higher than for internal use only applications. Any application that collects data must ensure that data quality standards are enforced at the earliest step in the data collection and processing pipeline. The availability expectations for these applications will be high. This may require additional infrastructure. The capacity and resource requirements of the applications may be difficult to assess and control. If the applications provide a programmatic interface then this needs to be rigorously controlled in terms of security, level of usage and the volume of data that can be input or extracted.
2	External Data Interactions Data Stores	These are applications and sets of data created by the enterprise to be externally facing where external parties can access information and interact with the enterprise.	These are the data stores associated with the external applications. As with the external applications, they will have very high security requirements. The range of data being stored here should be limited to the minimum necessary. The capacity and resource requirements of the data stores may be difficult to assess and control. The availability expectations for these data stores will be high. This may require additional infrastructure.
3	External Data Devices/Sensors	Sources of remote data measurements (such as RTU - Remote Terminal Unit) and devices connected with services offered by the enterprise (such as ATMs and Kiosks).	These devices can involve: • *Telemetry* - remote measurement including sensing, data transmission, data receipt, reporting, analysis and storage – read-only • *Telecommand* - sending commands to remote devices and systems The means by which data is transferred from the remote decides and the central facility will need to be secure.
4	Data Intake/Data Gateway	This is the set of facilities for handling data supplied to the enterprise including validation and transformation including a possible integration or service bus. This can be hosted internally or externally or a mix of both.	This will have very high security requirements. If the gateway provides a programmatic interface that is exposed publicly then this needs to be rigorously controlled in terms of security, level of usage and the volume of data that can be input or extracted. As a data source the gateway must ensure data quality standards are enforced at the earliest step in the data collection and processing pipeline.
5	Integration/ Service	This is an integration facility or	The standards used by communicating applications

Item	Name	Description	Solution Design and Data Considerations
	Bus	service bus that enables communication between mutually interacting applications.	must be agreed. The range of communication types must be defined. The expectations by the communicating applications must be described. The implementation and operation of the integration/service bus for the solution being design should be described for the following elements: • Information queueing, routing, sequencing and control • Data transformation, enrichment • Security and access control • Maintenance of quality • Validation, error identification, handling, notification and resolution • Management and deployment of changes • Process management, if relevant • Collection of audit information
6	Data Processing Solution Components	This represents the core of the solution consisting of the set of line of business applications deployed on enterprise owned and managed infrastructure or hosted outside the organisation and used by business functions to operate their business processes.	The data storage model(s) of the data processing components should be described in the solution design. These models can include data structures and data storage software and hardware. Many solution architects omit this level of detail from their solution designs, leaving this level of detail to be specified at the technical design or development stages. This frequently leads to errors that can be very difficult to resolve or problems such as performance and throughput. The solution designer needs to understand the data requirements of the solution in terms of data types, data structures, primary data processing, second data processing in terms of reporting and analysis, data volumes and throughput. The technical designers or developers may not have this broad level of appreciation of the data requirements any may therefore implement sub-optimal or even non-functional components. Creating a comprehensive data model at the solution design stage avoids these problems and ensure the solution can handle the required data across all its usage dimensions.
7	Internal Operational Data Stores	These are the various operational data stores used by the Data Processing applications.	The data store must be able to handle the volume of data and the volume of transactions. Data must be appropriately secure. Data models of the stored data assets should be included in the solution design.
8	Data Synchronisation	This is a facility to synchronise internally and externally stored	The facility must manage the movement of data from external to internal data stores. The frequency of data

Item	Name	Description	Solution Design and Data Considerations
		data.	movement and the data being moved should be identified. The synchronisation must be secure.
9	External Operational Data Stores	These are the various operational data stores used by the Data Processing applications used by Data Processing applications hosted outside the organisation.	The data store must be able to handle the volume of data and the volume of transactions. Data must be appropriately secure. These components will typically be provided by third-parties and changing them will commonly not be possible. The solution should specify the operational service types and levels expected of these components rather than looking to control any underlying technology or implementation.
10	Audit Log and Usage and Performance Data	This represents logging, usage and performance data generated by the solution components.	Various components in the solution data landscape will generate data on activities, events, performance or throughput. This must be stored and made available for reporting and analysis. This may need to integrate with existing organisation standards and framework for information and event management. Different solution components may generate different types of audit data. The volume of audit data should be specified. The approach to its retention and management should be detailed.
11	Data Warehouse	These are facilities to create and manage master data and data extracted from operational data to create a data warehouse and data extracts for reporting and analysis. This includes an extract, transformation and load facility. These can be hosted internally or externally or a mix of both.	The approach to reporting and analysis and the types of reporting and analysis facilities provided by the solution should be included in the solution. Reports and analyses can be generated from operational data or from a copy of the operational data that is retained with an additional time dimension added.
12	Data Management Infrastructure	This represents the set of infrastructural applications and facilities used to manage data resources, such as backup and recovery and availability and continuity.	The solution should include details on how the data is managed and the expected levels of service. This should include time to recovery and recovery point.
13	Data Marts	These are extracts from the Data Warehouse for specific reporting purposes.	The approach to reporting and analysis and the types of reporting and analysis facilities provided by the solution should be included in the solution. Data marts may be used to create function-specific reporting and analysis facilities.
14	Reporting and Data Analytics	This represents the range of tools and facilities to report on, analyse, mine and model data. These can be hosted internally or externally or a mix of both.	The range of reports and analyses made available by the solution and the approach to their delivery should be defined.

Item	Name	Description	Solution Design and Data Considerations
15	Document Sharing and Collaboration	These are tools used within the enterprise to share and collaborate on the authoring of documents.	If the solution accepts or creates document type data assets these may be stored in some form of informal document sharing facility where they can be accessed and collaborated on. The volume of document data and the size of the document types should be specified.
16	Document Management Systems	These are systems used to manage transactional and ad hoc structured and unstructured documents in a formal and controlled manner.	If the solution accepts or creates document type data assets these may be formally stored in a structured document management system. The volume of document data and the size of the document types should be specified. The workflows associated with document processing, if any, should be identified.
17	Other Applications	These are existing applications with which the solution data processing components have interfaces for data exchanges.	The data processing solution components may interface with other applications. The solution design should enumerate the interfaces and the nature of data being exchanged and the frequency of exchange.
18	Unstructured Data Stores	These are storage locations for enterprise documentation.	Unstructured document-type data may be held in some form of data store.
19	Metadata	This is the metadata assigned to documents and other unstructured information and the facilities and tolls used to store and manage this metadata.	The metadata to be applied to documents-type data assets should be specified. This should include details on data values and data quality.
20	Master Data	This is the master data maintained by the organisation and the facilities and tools used to store and manage this master data. The organisation may abstract master data from operational systems or may hold master data commonly where it can be used by all data applications.	The solution may create new master data or use existing organisation master data. Changes to the existing master data model should be specified.
21	Reference Data	This is the reference data maintained by the organisation and the facilities and tolls used to store and manage this reference data.	The solution may create new reference data or use existing reference data. Changes to the existing reference data should be specified.
22	Edge Devices	External sensor data sources may connect to edge devices that act as front-end data concentrators, collectors and processors.	The solution may implement edge devices if there is a high volume of data being supplied by sources such as telemetry.
23	External Data Exchange Facilities	These represent data exchanges such as those handled by a managed file transfer facility or messaging queueing. These could be represented separately. They can also be included in the component *External Data Applications/ Interactions* but I	In this conceptual data landscape the external data exchange facilities are where batch type data exchanges and message queueing exchanged are handled. If the solution involves the exchange of files or messages in this way, it will (access to) need some form of such facility

Item	Name	Description	Solution Design and Data Considerations
		have listed this component separately.	
24	External Data Sources and Targets	These are the external entities to which data is sent and from which data is received.	External data entities to which batch data or messages are sent and from which batch data or messages are received should be listed in a manner such as that described in section 4.6.1.8.1 on page 205. While not strictly part of the core solution data landscape, they should be identified as they are sources and targets of data that is part of the data landscape.
25	Externally Hosted Applications	These are line of business externally hosted applications whose data is stored in the component *External Operational Data Stores.*	These applications receive, process and store organisation data. If the overall solution contains any externally hosted applications, they are part of the extended data landscape.
26	Data Input Externally Hosted Applications	This is data entered into the externally hosted application components that comprise the solution.	Details of the data to be entered needs to be defined in the solution design. The design needs to define the data formats and approaches to validation and data quality.
27	Data Input Data Processing Solution Components	This is data entered into the internal application components that comprise the solution.	Details of the data to be entered needs to be defined in the solution design. The design needs to define the data formats and approaches to validation and data quality. The data model(s) used in the internal application components needs to be defined.
28	ETL	This extracts data from operational data stores, perhaps performs some operations on it to transform it and the loads the resulting data into time-oriented data warehouse for reporting and analysis.	The extract, transformation and load operations need to be defined. The source data needs to be specified. The nature of the transformations needs to be described. The target data stores need to be defined.
29	Email	Email plays a part in many applications to perform functions such as send alerts and notifications to users, send confirmation of actions performed or to exchange data.	Any email interactions need to be described.

Table 68 – Components of Conceptual Solution Design Data Landscape

The high-level linkages and flows between these data landscape components are listed below. These interfaces can be one-way or two-way. This list is not exhaustive.

Item	From		To	Linkage
1	External Data Applications/ Interactions	2	External Data Interactions Data Stores	The applications will store data in the data stores.
2	External Data Interactions Data Stores	4	Data Intake/Data Gateway	The external data stores may transfer data to the organisation by way of the data gateway.
3	External Data Devices/Sensors	4	Data Intake/Data Gateway	The external devices and sensors may transfer data to the organisation by way of the data gateway.
		22	Edge Devices	The data sensors may transmit data to edge devices that act as front-end data concentrators, offloading initial data processing from core

Item	From		To	Linkage
				components.
4	Data Intake/Data Gateway	5	Integration/Service Bus	The data intake or data gateway component can supply data that will be passed to the integration bus for processing and onward transmission to other data components.
		7	Internal Operational Data Stores	The data intake or data gateway component can send data directly to or take data directly from one of the operational data store components.
5	Integration/Service Bus	6	Data Processing Solution Components	The integration bus can pass data to and receive data from the data processing components of the solution data landscape.
		7	Internal Operational Data Stores	The integration bus can send data to or receive data from operational data stores.
		17	Other Applications	The integration bus can send data to or receive data from other applications outside the scope of the solution data landscape.
6	Data Processing Solution Components	7	Internal Operational Data Stores	The data processing components of the solution will send data to and receive data from various operational data storage components.
		10	Audit Log and Usage and Performance Data	The data related activities of the data processing components of the solution will generate different types of audit data.
		20	Master Data	The data processing components will read from and might update organisational master data.
		21	Reference Data	The data processing components will read from and might update organisational reference data.
		28	ETL	The ETL component might interface with operational processing components for data processing or the operation of the ETL component might be initiated by the processing components.
7	Internal Operational Data Stores	8	Data Synchronisation	Data held in data stores associated with externally hosted solution components may be transferred via the data synchronisation component.
		11	Data Warehouse	Operational data may be sent to the data warehouse directly or via an extract/transformation/load component.
		12	Data Management Infrastructure	Operational data stores will be managed by elements of the data management infrastructure.
		14	Reporting and Data Analytics	The reporting and data analytics components of the solution may read data directly from the operational data stores.
		28	ETL	The ETL component can read data from data stores, operate on it and store the results in the data warehouse.
8	Data Synchronisation	9	External Operational Data Stores	The data synchronisation component may take data from data stores used by externally hosted or located application components.
10	Audit Log and Usage and Performance Data	11	Data Warehouse	Audit data may be stored in the data warehouse and/or audit data may be collected about data warehouse usage and performance.
		12	Data Management Infrastructure	The data management components may use the audit log data.

Item	From		To	Linkage
11	Data Warehouse	12	Data Management Infrastructure	The data management components may manage the data warehouse.
		13	Data Marts	The data warehouse may send data to data marts for specific reporting applications.
		14	Reporting and Data Analytics	The reporting and analytics components will use the data warehouse.
		28	ETL	The ETL component can write data to the data warehouse.
12	Data Management Infrastructure	13	Data Marts	The data management components may manage the data marts.
13	Data Marts	14	Reporting and Data Analytics	The reporting and analytics components will use the data marts.
14	Reporting and Data Analytics	20	Master Data	The reporting and analytics components may use the master data.
		21	Reference Data	The reporting and analytics components may use the reference data.
15	Document Sharing and Collaboration	19	Metadata	The document sharing components will store metadata relate to documents.
16	Document Management Systems	19	Metadata	The document management components will store metadata relate to documents.
18	Unstructured Data Stores	19	Metadata	The unstructured data storage components may store metadata relate to documents.
24	External Data Sources and Targets	23	External Data Exchange Facility	Data being sent to or received from external data sources and targets will be handled by the data exchange facility.
26	Data Input Externally Hosted Applications	25	Externally Hosted Applications	Data will be input into externally hosted applications.
27	Data Input Data Processing Solution Components	6	Data Processing Solution Components	Data will be input into internally hosted applications.
28	ETL	20	Master Data	The ETL component can update the master data or refer to it when updating the data warehouse.
		21	Reference Data	The ETL component can update the reference data or refer to it when updating the data warehouse.
29	Email	15	Document Sharing and Collaboration	Emails can be stored in the document sharing component.
		18	Document Management Systems	Emails can be stored in the document management system component.
		6	Data Processing Solution Components	The data processing component can generate mails.

Table 69 – Solution Data Landscape Component Linkages

One simple classification of data components is to look at the data-related actions they perform:

1. ***Data Generation*** – it can act as a source for new data that enters the data landscape

2. ***Data Transportation*** – it moves data from one location to another, perhaps performing data transformation on the way

3. ***Data Processing*** – it operates on or processes data according. This may also give rise to new data.

4. ***Data Retention*** – it accepts data for storage and provides data in response to requests for existing stored data

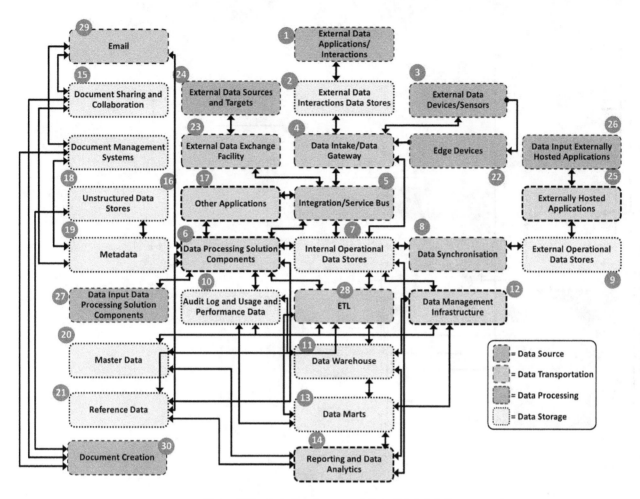

Figure 218 – Data Landscape and Data Related Actions

As mentioned above, not all solution designs will include all the components in the theoretical data landscape. The following shows the components for a fairly conventional solution deployed within the organisation without any externally hosted applications.

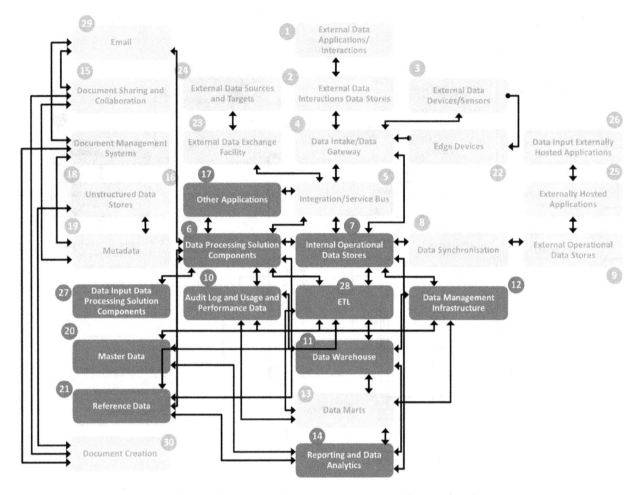

Figure 219 – Data Landscape Components Used by Sample Solution

In this example, the solution design only needs to include the data components:

- Data Processing Solution Components
- Internal Operational Data Stores
- Audit Log and Usage and Performance Data
- Data Warehouse
- Data Management Infrastructure
- Reporting and Data Analytics
- Other Applications
- Master Data
- Reference Data

4.8.3 Solution Data Quality

I am briefly referring to the topic of data quality separately because of its importance. Solutions processes data – receive it, use it, transform it, generate derived data. Data is strategic organisation resource that needs to be managed. So, the data has to be of a consistently high quality. Such high-quality data is necessary for regulatory compliance. It is also essential for business intelligence, reporting and analysis functions.

Data is effectively the foundation of the organisation. It penetrates and infiltrates into every aspect of organisation operation. Good quality data is needed to achieve and maintain operational excellence.

Data quality begins with the originating solution. If poor quality data is allowed to enter the organisation's data landscape, that poor quality data will persist and cause problems thereafter. So, the application needs to be concerned with enforcing data quality rules.

Data quality is not just a matter of data cleanliness. It is also not about fixing poor quality data. It is concerned with data consistency across the organisation's data landscape to ensure that data is stored once and used everywhere thereafter.

Data quality is related to the subjects of reference and master data management. These golden data values represent the most accurate, current, and relevant data values for data types. Reference data is concerned with the classification or categorisation of other data. Traditionally, reference data is stored in tables that are linked via foreign keys to other database tables. The referential integrity functionality of the database management system ensures only valid values from these reference tables are used in these other tables.

Master data is data about the business entities – such as customers, suppliers, partners, products, locations and finance - that provide context for business transactions. These are entities that are referenced repeatedly by the organisation as it transacts business. They can be used by many applications. Master data needs to be the authoritative and most accurate data available about these business entities. It is used to establish the context for subsequent transactions that concern or reference those entities. Master data needs to be stored once, centrally with no data redundancy. Data standards need to be defined and maintained for reference and master data.

Again, while the individual solution design cannot fix the wider organisational data quality, reference and master data problems, the solution architect should not contribute to them. Solution designs should incorporate data quality into their data processing specification. The solution needs to be aware of the reference and master data it uses and should source them centrally.

4.8.4 Data Lifecycle

Data has a generalised lifecycle and passes through a series of stages throughout this lifecycle:

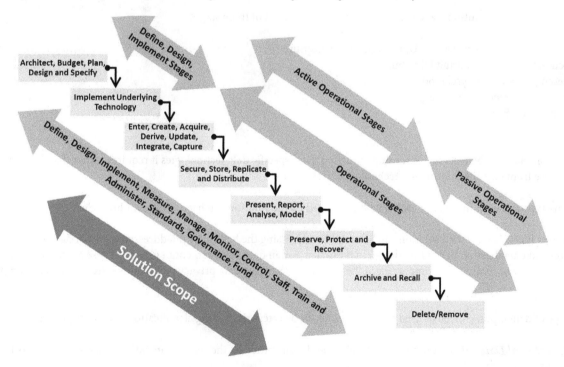

Figure 220 – Generalised Data Lifecycle

These data life stages are:

- *Architect, Budget, Plan, Design and Specify* - This relates to the design and specification of the data storage and management and their supporting processes. This establishes the data management framework

- *Implement Underlying Technology* - This is concerned with implementing the data-related hardware and software technology components. This relates to database components, data storage hardware, backup and recovery software, monitoring and control software and other items

- *Enter, Create, Acquire, Derive, Update, Integrate, Capture* – This stage is where data originated, such as data entry or data capture and acquired from other systems or sources

- *Secure, Store, Replicate and Distribute* – Data is stored with appropriate security and access controls including data access and update audit. It may be replicated to other applications and distributed

- *Present, Report, Analyse, Model* – Concerned with the presentation of information, the generation of reports and analysis and the created of derived information

- *Preserve, Protect and Recover* – Relates to the management of data in terms of backup, recovery and retention/preservation

- *Archive and Recall* – Where information that is no longer active but still required in archived to secondary data storage platforms and from which the information can be recovered if required

- *Delete/Remove* – Concerned with the deletion of data that cannot or does not need to be retained any longer

- *Define, Design, Implement, Measure, Manage, Monitor, Control, Staff, Train and Administer, Standards, Governance, Fund* - This is not a single stage but a set of processes and procedures that cross all stages and is concerned with ensuring that the processes associated with each of the lifestyle stages are operated correctly and that data assurance, quality and governance procedures exist and are operated

Within an individual solution, data will pass through only a subset of these stages:

- Enter, Create, Acquire, Derive, Update, Integrate, Capture
- Secure, Store, Replicate and Distribute
- Present, Report, Analyse, Model
- Preserve, Protect and Recover
- Archive and Recall
- Delete/Remove

The solution may also be responsible for implementing these specific data technologies it requires rather than being able to inherit these from existing information technology infrastructure.

Each data type and each instance of each data type created by the solution can have a different lifecycle.

A data asset lifecycle view for a solution can be useful in addressing the habitually unaddressed topics of data archival, data retention and data deletion in solution design in particular and in data management in general. These aspects of data management are becoming more important in the context of changing data privacy regulations – see section 4.9.2 on page 363.

Each type of data input, created or used by the solution can be categorised using classification approach such as:

- *Operational Data* – this is the core data received and transmitted by the solution in various ways (input, import, exchange, transfer, API)

- *Master and Reference Data* – this refers to shared data used to improve data quality and reduce data redundancy. Components of the solution may update existing or create new master and reference data. This needs to be done in a controlled manner as this data is shared between other solutions

- *Analytic Data and Derived Data* – this is data derived from operational data such as data extracts, reports, analyses and data held in data warehouses and data marts

- *Metadata* – this refers to two separate types of data: names and meanings of information stored in operational data stored and data attached to documents held in a document store

- *Unstructured Data* – this refers to document-type data containing either unstructured text or images of scanned documents

The solution can involve many instances of each of these data types.

	Operational Data	Master and Reference Data	Analytic and Derived Data	Metadata	Unstructured Data
Enter, Create, Acquire, Derive, Update, Integrate, Capture					
Secure, Store, Replicate and Distribute					
Present, Report, Analyse, Model					
Preserve, Protect and Recover					
Archive and Recall					
Delete/Remove					

Figure 221 – Data Asset Lifecycle for Different Data Types

Each operational system may have sets of data across each of these data types.

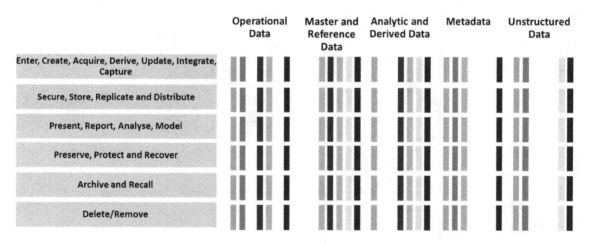

Figure 222 – Data Assets for Different Solution Components Across

The solution design should include an inventory of data types for each solution component.

4.8.5 Data Integration

In the context of solution architecture and design, data integration has multiple meanings and multiple ways of being used such as:

1. Integration in terms of migrating data from a source to a target system and/or loading data into a target system

2. Integration in terms of aggregating data from multiple sources and creating one source, with possibly date and time dimensions added to the integrated data

3. Integration in terms of handling data transfers, exchanges, requests for information using a variety of information movement technologies

4. Integration in terms of synchronising two data sources or regularly extracting data from one data sources to update a target

5. Integration in terms of service orientation and API management

The first four of these are pure data integration requirements. Service orientation can implicitly involve data integration as the results of the service invocation may involve the generation of data results.

Data integration is (or should be) an enterprise-level capability that a solution design can (or should be able to) inherit. The organisation's data fabric should include infrastructural components that deliver these data integration facilities. The solution should not have to create (additional) point-to-point custom integrations.

There may not be a single tool that provides all these functions.

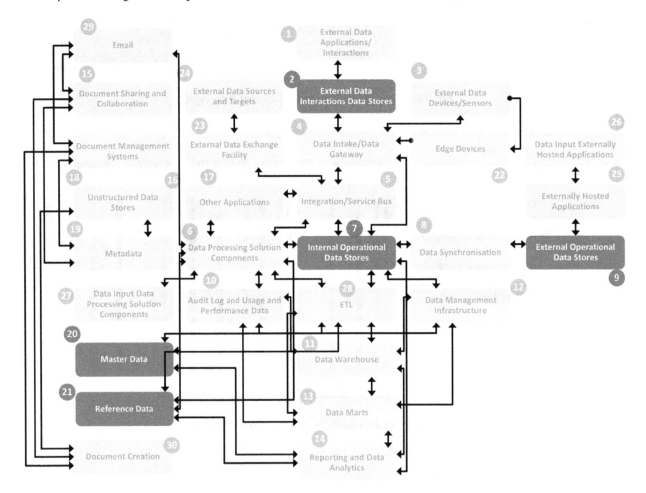

Figure 223 – Data Integration – Possible Scope of Data Migration

The scope of data integration for migration can include the following data landscape components:

- *Internal Operational Data Stores* – the data stores associated with the data processing solution components may need to be loaded with new data or existing data may need to be migrated

- *Master Data* – new master data may need to be created

- *Reference Data* – new reference data may need to be created

- *External Operational Data Stores* – the data stores associated with externally hosted data processing solution components may need to be loaded with new data or existing data may need to be migrated

- *External Data Interactions Data Stores* – the data stores associated with the external interaction data processing solution components may need to be loaded with new data or existing data may need to be migrated

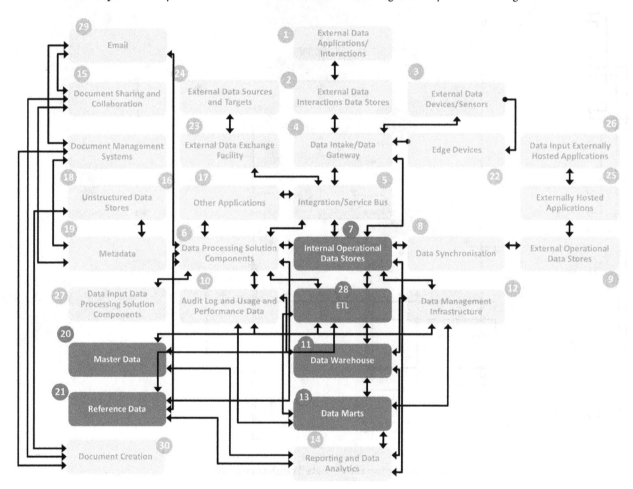

Figure 224 – Data Integration – Data Aggregation

The scope of data integration for data aggregation can include the following data landscape components:

- *Internal Operational Data Stores* – the data stores associated with the data processing solution components will be the source for the data aggregation

- *ETL* – facilities to extract data from operational systems, operate on it if necessary and store the resulting transformed data into the data warehouse may be needed

- *Data Warehouse* – an aggregated data schema will need to be created or expanded. The processes for extracting data from operational data stores and combining it to populate the data warehouse will need to be defined

- *Data Marts* – subsets of aggregated data may be further processes into subject-oriented or business function-oriented data marts

- *Master Data* – master data may be used when aggregating the operational data

- *Reference Data* – reference data may be used when aggregating the operational data

Data aggregation may also involve extracting and combining data from other data sources such as External Operational Data Store, External Data Interactions Data Stores and others.

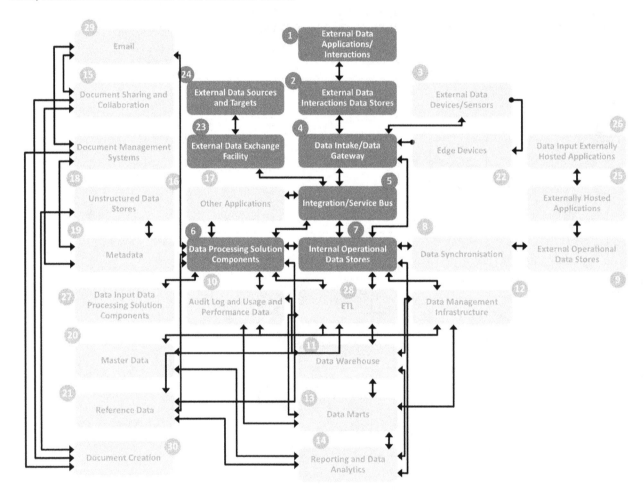

Figure 225 – Data Integration – Data Transfers and Exchanges

The scope of data integration for data transfers and exchanges can include the following data landscape components:

- *Internal Operational Data Stores* – data from the data stores may be extracted and transferred out of the solution or data may be received and be stored

- *Data Processing Solution Components* – the data processing components will need to process data transmission and receipt requests

- *Integration/Service Bus* – the service bus may be involved in mediating the exchanges

- *Data Intake/Data Gateway* – the data gateway may be involved in handling the transmission and receipt of data

- *External Data Exchange Facility* – the exchange facility will handle data transfers

- *External Data Interactions Data Stores* – data held in the data stores associated with the external interaction zone applications may be extracted and transferred

- *External Data Sources and Targets* – data will be sent to and received from these external entities

- *External Data Applications/ Interactions* – external interaction zone applications may receive and transmit data

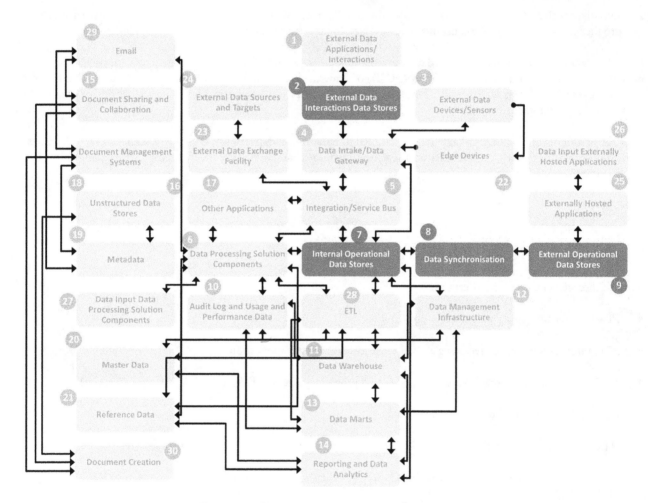

Figure 226 – Data Integration – Data Synchronisation

The scope of data integration for data synchronisation can include the following data landscape components:

- *External Operational Data Stores* – data held in the data stores associated with externally hosted applications may need to be synchronised with internally held data

- *Data Synchronisation* – this component will have the synchronisation of data

- *Internal Operational Data Stores* – internal data may need to be synchronised with external data

- *External Data Interactions Data Stores* – data held in the data stores associated with the external interaction zone applications may need to be synchronised with internally held data

The solution architect must be aware of data integration requirements of the solution.

There are two related technology and business trends that are increasing the need for a comprehensive and joined-up approach to data integration:

1. The movement of applications to cloud or hosted service providers and the adoption of a cloud-first principle by many organisations mean that data integration becoming more important as data and applications are spread across multiple data stores in multiple locations

2. Initiatives such as digital transformation mean that a unified view of data across multiple applications is needed to produce the single view of the consumer needed which in turn leads to greater data integration requirements

Logically, data integrations consist of two data transmission or receipt halves: an incoming data extraction (PULL) or provision (PUSH) half and an outgoing supply (PUSH) or draw-down (PULL) half. There may be a transformation between the two halves where data is reformatted. This integration algebra approach can be used to create generic descriptions of the data exchange requirements.

There are a number of data integration patterns that need to be accommodated by any data integration facility (or facilities). At its most basic, the pattern is a combination a specification of the characteristics of the incoming and outgoing halves of the transfer and the transfer type:

```
{<Integration Pattern>,
<Incoming Location>,
<Incoming Request>,
<Outgoing Location>,
<Outgoing Request>}
```

Some of these data integration patterns are:

- FT – transfer a file using a file transfer protocol

- API –information is requested using an API made available by the application

- MSG – information is exchanged using a messaging protocol (such as SMTP, AMQP, MSMQ or MQSeries)

- ETL – data is exchanged using an ETL process

- HTTP – data is exchanged using HTTP GET/PUT

This list can be extended to cover other data integration approaches such as SOAP and JMS or they can be included as options for integration patterns such as HTTP or MSG.

The location portions of the integration specification will include a specification of access approach and access rights.

The following table summarises some of the possible extended integration patterns

Integration Pattern	INCOMING HALF		OUTGOING HALF		Description
	Location	Request (Push or Pull)	Location	Request (Push or Pull)	
FT	External	PUSH	Internal	PUSH	This specifies a file transfer data integration where a file is sent from an external source and is then transmitted onwards to an internal target or destination

Integration Pattern	INCOMING HALF		OUTGOING HALF		Description
	Location	Request (Push or Pull)	Location	Request (Push or Pull)	
					`{FT,EXT,PUSH,INT,PUSH}`
FT	External	PULL	Internal	PUSH	This specifies a file transfer data integration where a file is retrieved from an external source and is then transmitted onwards to an internal target or destination `{FT,EXT,PULL,INT,PUSH}`
FT	External	PUSH	Internal	PULL	This specifies a file transfer data integration where a file is sent from an external source and then remains there from where it is retrieved by the internal target or destination `{FT,EXT,PUSH,INT,PULL}`
FT	External	PULL	Internal	PULL	This specifies a file transfer data integration where a file is sent from an external source and then then remains there from where it is retrieved by the internal target or destination `{FT,EXT,PULL,INT,PULL}`
API	External	PULL	Internal	PULL	This specifies an API data integration where a data is retrieved from an external source and then remains there from where it is retrieved by the internal target or destination `{API,EXT,PULL,INT,PULL}`
API	Internal	PULL	Internal	PULL	This specifies an API data integration where a data is retrieved from an internal source and then remains there from where it is retrieved by the internal target or destination `{API,INT,PULL,INT,PULL}`
MSG	External	PULL	Internal	PULL	This specifies a message-based data integration where a data is retrieved from an external source and then remains there from where it is retrieved by the internal target or destination `{MSG,EXT,PULL,INT,PUSH}`
MSG	Internal	PULL	Internal	PULL	This specifies a message-based data integration where a data is retrieved from an internal source and then remains there from where it is retrieved by the internal target or destination `{MSG,INT,PULL,INT,PUSH}`
MSG	Internal	PULL	External	PULL	This specifies a message-based data integration where a data is retrieved from an internal source and then remains there from where it is retrieved by the external target or destination `{MSG,INT,PULL,EXT,PUSH}`
ETL	Internal	PULL	Internal	PUSH	This specifies an ETL data integration where a data is retrieved from an internal source and is then transmitted onwards to an internal target or destination `{ETL,INT,PULL,INT,PUSH}`

Integration Pattern	INCOMING HALF		OUTGOING HALF		Description
	Location	Request (Push or Pull)	Location	Request (Push or Pull)	
HTTP	Internal	PULL	Internal	PUSH	This specifies a HTTP-based data integration where a data is retrieved from an internal source and is then transmitted onwards to an internal target or destination {HTTP,INT,PULL,INT,PUSH}
HTTP	External	PULL	Internal	PUSH	This specifies a HTTP-based data integration where a data is retrieved from an external source and is then transmitted onwards to an internal target or destination {HTTP,EXT,PULL,INT,PUSH}
HTTP	Internal	PULL	External	PUSH	This specifies a HTTP-based data integration where a data is retrieved from an internal source and is then transmitted onwards to an external target or destination {HTTP,INT,PULL,EXT,PUSH}
MSG	Internal	PULL			This could specify a broadcast data integration where a message is retrieved from an internal source then remains there where is it is retrieved by any target {MSG,INT,PULL,,}

Table 70 – Data Integration Patterns

The following diagram illustrates the approach to high-level data integration specification:

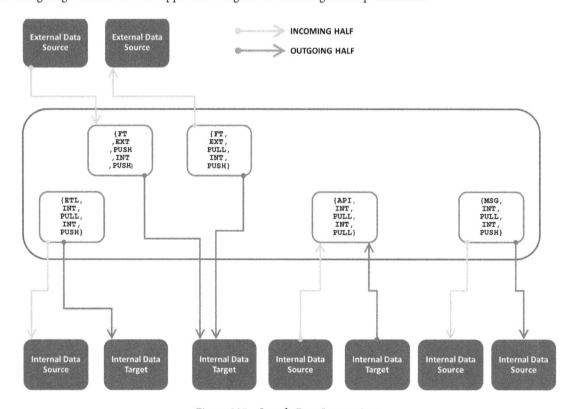

Figure 227 – Sample Data Integrations

This integration algebra approach can be extended by one or more of the following:

- Specifying the formats on the incoming and outgoing messages
- Explicitly identifying the data transformation specification by means of a reference
- Explicitly identifying the data integration with a reference that links to its precise definition

The specification could then be:

```
{<Integration Reference>,

    {
    <Incoming Integration Pattern>,
    <Incoming Location>,
    <Incoming Request>
    <Incoming Data Type>
    }

    <Transformation Specification>

    {
    <Outgoing Integration Pattern>,
    <Outgoing Location>,
    <Outgoing Request>
    <Outgoing Data Type>
    }

}
```

Some of these extended integration attributes could be viewed as redundant.

The following table contains some examples of this extended integration specifications.

Reference	Integration Pattern	Location	Request (Push or Pull)	Data Type	Transformation	Location	Request (Push or Pull)	Data Type	Specification
INTFT001	FT	EXT	PUSH	FILE	TRX001	INT	PUSH	FILE	{INTFT001, {FT,EXT,PUSH,FILE} ,TRX001, {INT,PUSH,FILE} }
INTFT002	FT	EXT	PULL	FILE	TRX002	INT	PUSH	FILE	{INTFT002, {FT,EXT,PULL,FILE} ,TRX002, {INT,PUSH,FILE} }
INTFT003	FT	EXT	PUSH	FILE	TRX003	INT	PULL	FILE	{INTFT003, {FT,EXT,PUSH,FILE} ,TRX003, {INT,PULL,FILE} }
INTFT004	FT	EXT	PULL	FILE	TRX004	INT	PULL	FILE	{INTFT004, {FT,EXT,PULL,FILE} ,TRX004, {INT,PULL,FILE} }
INTAPI005	API	EXT	PULL	XML	TRX005	INT	PULL	JSON	{INTAPI005, {API,EXT,PULL,XML} ,TRX005, {INT,PULL,JSON} }
INTAPI006	API	INT	PULL	JSON	TRX006	INT	PULL	JSON	{INTAPI006, {API,INT,PULL,JSON} ,TRX006, {INT,PULL,JSON} }
INTMSG007	MSG	EXT	PULL	EDI	TRX007	INT	PUSH	XML	{INTMSG007, {MSG,EXT,PULL,EDI} ,TRX007, {INT,PUSH,XML} }
INTMSG00	MSG	INT	PULL	DFDL	TRX008	INT	PUSH	XML	{INTMSG008, {MSG,INT,PULL,DFDL}

Reference	Integration Pattern	Location	Request (Push or Pull)	Data Type	Transformation	Location	Request (Push or Pull)	Data Type	Specification

8									`, TRX008,`
									`{INT, PUSH, XML}`
									`}`

INTMSG009	MSG	INT	PULL	XML	TRX009	EXT	PUSH	JSON	`{INTMSG009,`
									`{MSG, INT, PULL, XML}`
									`, TRX009,`
									`{EXT, PUSH, JSON}`
									`}`

INTETL010	ETL	INT	PULL	DB	TRX010	INT	PUSH	DB	`{INTETL010,`
									`{ETL, INT, PULL, DB}`
									`, TRX010,`
									`{INT, PUSH, DB}`
									`}`

INTHTTP011	HTTP	INT	PULL	XML	TRX011	INT	PUSH	JSON	`{INTHTTP011,`
									`{HTTP, INT, PULL, XML}`
									`, TRX011,`
									`{INT, PUSH, JSON}`
									`}`

INTHTTP012	HTTP	EXT	PULL	JSOM	TRX012	INT	PUSH	DFDL	`{INTHTTP012,`
									`{HTTP, EXT, PULL, JSOM}`
									`, TRX012,`
									`{INT, PUSH, DFDL}`
									`}`

INTHTTP013	HTTP	INT	PULL	SOAP	TRX013	EXT	PUSH	SOAP	`{INTHTTP013,`
									`{HTTP, INT, PULL, SOAP}`
									`, TRX013,`
									`{EXT, PUSH, SOAP}`
									`}`

INTMSG014	MSG	INT	PULL	XML					`{INTMSG014,`
									`{MSG, INT, PULL, XML}`
									`, ,`
									`{, , }`
									`}`

Table 71 – Sample Extended Integration Specifications

The message transformation can consist of multiple processing steps. These should be specified in the definition of the transformation.

Message transformations do not have to occur during data integration. The source data can be passed through as is to the destination. Alternatively, the transformation can occur after the data has been passed through its destination.

It has been the traditional approach to have data transformation being performed during integration by the integration layer or component. This has given rise to problems such as:

- Integration processing is added to and becomes very complex without being properly documented. Frequently it is all too easy to change integration processing such as adding more steps without understanding their impact. The overall application increases in complexity as the transformations defined in the integration layer becomes an extension to the application.

- The integration layer becomes a data store in its own right rather than just being an interim store-and-forward mechanism. Very large amounts of integration data are stored leading to performance problems as well as increased resource requirements.

- There is an expectation that integration data can be recovered from the integration layer as it persistently stores data. This leads to support complexity.

This is not a primary concern of an individual solution design. The principles of and approaches to data integration and transformation need to be define at the data architecture and enterprise architecture levels. But the solution architect needs to be aware of the concerns associated with complex in-flight integration transformations.

The transferred data will generally require some form of transformation to make it usable by the recipient. The recipient could perform this transformation (similar to the Extract, Load and Transform (ELT) approach to data transfer to a data warehouse).

The integration specification could then be:

```
{<Integration Reference>,

    {
    <Incoming Integration Pattern>,
    <Incoming Location>,
    <Incoming Request>
    <Incoming Data Type>
    }

    <In Flight Transformation Specification>

    {
    <Outgoing Integration Pattern>,
    <Outgoing Location>,
    <Outgoing Request>
    <Outgoing Data Type>
    }

    <Final Transformation Specification>

}
```

The following shows some integration patters.

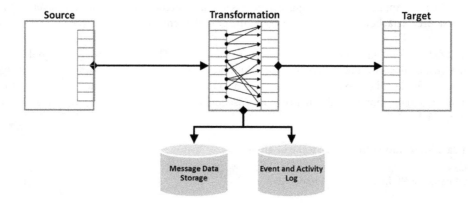

Figure 228 – Data Integration With Integration Layer Transformation

The first is the more traditional where the data source to target format and structure transformation occurs in the integration layer. This data transformation then becomes part of the overall solution.

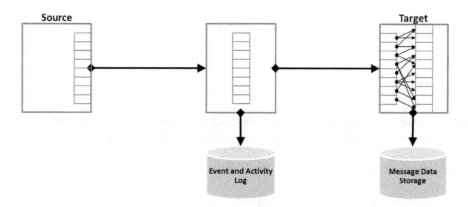

Figure 229 – Data Integration with Transformation at Target

The second integration pattern is where the data is passed through the integration layer unchanged and sent to the target where it is then transformed.

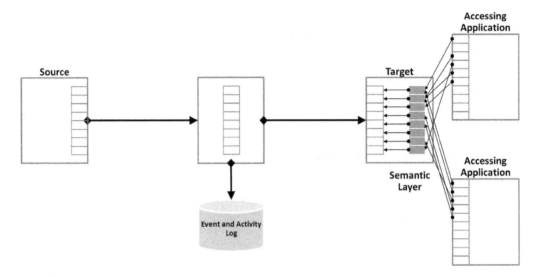

Figure 230 – Data Integration with Preservation of the Original Data Format Content

The third integration pattern is where the data is passed through the integration layer unchanged and sent to the target where it remains it is source format. Applications that require to access the data interact using a semantic layer that maps their access requests to the source data, both the data instance and the data elements within the instance.

The organisation will define its integration standards, approaches and tools. The solution architect should adopt these when creating solution designs. Unless absolutely necessary, the solution architect should avoid point-to-point integrations. The solution architect should also avoid complex integration-layer data transformations. These add complexity to the solution and its subsequent maintenance, support and enhancement. Also, once implemented, these transformations tend to accrete complexity, frequently undocumented.

The attributes of a data integration can include some or all of:

- *Trigger* – what causes a PULL integration to occur

- *Schedule* – what is the schedule or polling interval for a PULL integration

- *Security and Authorisation* – how is data integration authentication and security handled

- *Validation and Error Handling* – what validation should be performed and how should errors be handled and notified

The data integration facility will need to incorporate many other elements and sets of functionality such as:

- *Integration Registry* - this will contain a list of all data integrations

- *Key Store* – this will hold keys used in authentication and access to data sources and targets

- *Usage and Performance Management, Auditing* – usage and performance information will be collected and made available for reporting and analysis. A log of all data integrations will be maintained

- *Load Balancing* – load can be distributed across multiple nodes if necessary

- *Management and Administration* – there will be a facility to manage operation and use

- ***Release, Deployment and Version Management*** – new integrations can be tested, released and deployed to production. Versions of integrations can be maintained and reverted to if necessary

- ***Security*** – there will be security across all accesses to data integration

- ***Data Store*** – there will be a data store to hold data integrations where the outgoing half is accessed by a PULL request

4.8.6 Data Audit and Data Profiling

The information provided in the previous sections can be used to perform a solution data audit to evaluate the data requirements of the solution. The objectives of the data audit are to understand the current and possibly new data management components, systems, structures, infrastructural applications and processes required that are related to the solution being designed. This will then feed into the development of the approach to managing the solution's data and the identification of gaps. The data audit creates a number of data views:

- Data landscape view
- Data supply chain view
- Data model view
- Data lifecycle view
- Current information and data architecture and data strategy view
- Current data management view

4.8.6.1 Data Landscape View

The purpose of the Data Landscape View is to describe the entities and functional units within and outside the organisation with which the solution will interact and to describe the interactions in terms of data flows. This will show the participants in data flows and the data that is passes. The entities can be business units, partners, service providers, regulators, external interacting entitles and others. This is described in section 4.8.2 on page 326.

The data landscape view can be created at different levels of details:

- ***Level 1 – Main Interactions*** - Main interactions and functions associated with the overall solution

- ***Level 2 – Data Exchanges*** - Specific data exchanges of the solution – this is described in section 4.8.5 on page 339

- ***Level 3 – Solution Components*** - What is done within each function as a series of activities

- ***Level 4 – Procedure*** - How each activity is carried out through a series of tasks

- ***Level 5 - Sub Procedure*** - Detailed steps which are carried out to complete a task

4.8.6.2 Data Supply Chain View

The data supply chain view looks at in-bound and out-bound data paths within and outside the organisations in terms of the applications and the data that flows along the data paths. It can be a subset or an extension of the Data Landscape View.

4.8.6.3 Data Model View

The data model is a set of data specifications that reflect data requirements and designs and defines the critical data produced and consumed across the components of the solution. The data model view quantifies the status of the development and specification of the overall solution data model.

It can include:

- Data Steward Responsibility Assignments
- Valid Reference Data Values
- Data Quality Specifications
- Entity Life Cycles

4.8.6.4 Data Lifecycle View

When analysing data, what you are really analysing is the state of the processes around its lifecycle: how well defined those processes are, how automated, how risks and controls are defined and managed and what happens data as it passes through each stage of its life. This is discussed in section 4.8.4 on page 337.

4.8.6.5 Solution Data Audit Approach

The steps in performing the solution data audit are:

1. Build a solution landscape view, including internal and external data-related components and third-parties from which data may be obtained and to which data may be supplied. The solution landscape view can be supplemented with a system and infrastructure view that shows the hardware and software components behind a solution component.

2. Layer onto this information capture, storage and flows: where and what types of information is maintained by applications and that is passed between applications. An application is a collection of systems and infrastructure that delivers an integrated set of functions. It may or may not be necessary to document the underlying infrastructure associated with applications. This may be further complicated because the underlying infrastructure may not be isolated but may itself be part of an application - this would be the case where the server infrastructure is virtualised and managed by virtualisation manager.

3. Categorise information by a classification such as: Operational Data, Master and Reference Data, Analytic Data and Unstructured Data.

4. Define the business units/functions and their use of applications.

5. View the information capture, storage and flows identified above across the stages of their lifecycle.

6. Identify how well the processes and their controls associated with the lifecycle stages are defined, documented and operated. This will identify gaps to be remediated. This will then form the basis of a work plan to resolve any data-related process gaps

4.9 Security and Privacy

4.9.1 Solution Security

Security is a pervasive concern for information technology solutions. This is increasing because of trends such as:

- Exposing corporate applications and data to external solution consumers

- Use of externally hosted infrastructure, platforms and applications

- Use of external sensors and edge devices to collect data that will be part of a solution

The solution architect cannot take responsibility for implementing the organisation's information technology. But the solution architect cannot assume that the solution will inherit a perfect set of security standards across all aspects of the solution. The solution architect must take responsibility for and validate the security of the solution being designed across its full extent.

Security functions are frequently divided into a security architecture role and a security operations role. Security architecture defines and maintains overall security standards and policies and the organisation's security tools. The security operations function implements the security tools and security infrastructure and monitors the operation of the organisation's information technology security, identifying and responding to security events and incidents.

At an organisational level, there will be security infrastructure to prevent security incidents such as denial of service attacks. This section will not cover this level of detail.

This section is not intended to be a detailed review of security standards, tools, technologies, principles and standards. The objective of this section is to describe the set of principles the solution architect should apply when designing the security of the solution and to provide checklists for controls that should apply across the solution landscape. The solution architect can verify that the controls exist and are applied by consulting the appropriate IT architecture function such as security architecture, service architecture and infrastructure architecture. The purpose is to ensure that the solution architect explicitly considers security concerns and issues when designing the solution.

The solution architect cannot take it for granted that the solution being designed will operate in a secure environment. The solution architect must perform a due diligence on solution security. Section 4.8 on page 321 refers to the data lifecycle and in particular to the end-of-life stages involving the definition of data retention and data deletion standards. In the context of increasing data privacy standards and regulation, these definitions are important for personal data.

Most organisations will have a separate information technology security function that operates in parallel to other related IT architecture such as enterprise architecture and service architecture.

In designing a solution, the solution architect must incorporate security considerations into the solution design from the start. The solution architect must not either assume that the solution will be deployed in a secure environment and will inherit the all the necessary security facilities provided by the set of security infrastructural applications and services or that security can be included in the design at a later stage.

The solution architect cannot assume that someone else in the organisation is responsible for solution security.

Frequently, there will be few business requirements relating to security. Those security requirements that are specified will be basic and generic and relate to areas such as restricted access, user authentication, confidentiality of information, role-based access and separation of duties. The business stakeholders will assume that security is provided as standard. The solution architect cannot assume that few security explicit security requirements means limited need for security. The solution architect must be proactive in including comprehensive security features and in validating the security of the solution design.

- Include security considerations from the start in solution designs
- Be proactive in security design
- Always limit access to sensitive applications and information
- Always authenticate access to confirm the identity of the solution consumer
- Encrypt data in transit and at rest
- Exclude rather than include access to applications and data

One approach to solution security is to create a set of solution security templates that can be used to confirm the security of a solution design.

The solution should incorporate security checks and controls in the following areas:

1. *Identity Controls* – these relate to enforcing solution consumer identity standards

2. *Access and Authority Controls* – these relate to enforcing application and data access standards

3. *Physical Controls* – these relate to physical controls to limit access to infrastructure

4. *Change, Configuration and Maintenance Controls* – these relate to controls on changes that can be made to the solution landscape and its components

5. *Management and Audit Controls* – these relate to the collection, storage and processing of solution access and usage audit event data

6. *Acquisition Controls* – these relate to standards and controls applied to the acquisition of products and services from third-party service providers

7. *Integrity Controls* – these relate to ensuring the integrity of data as it is stored, accessed, updated and transferred

8. *Communications and Network Controls* – these relate to controls applied to the network over which the solution operates and through which it is accessed

These controls will span different parts of the solution domains:

1. *Core Infrastructure* – this represents the central infrastructure that enable systems and applications to run and include servers and data storage

2. *Data* – this represents the data assets used by and generated by the applications

3. *Integration, Transfer and Exchange* – this relates to the set of data exchanges, transfers and integrated both between applications in the organisation and from outside, including applications hosted externally

4. *Systems and Applications* – these are the sets of applications, both running on the organisation's infrastructure and those hosted externally

5. *Solution Consumers* – this represents the set of consumers of the applications and data, including individuals within and outside the organisation and applications

6. *Perimeter Infrastructure* – this consists of the set of network infrastructure enabling both internal and external access and includes local and global load balancers, routers and firewalls from this layered view of solution security controls and checks.

These can be represented as concentric circles with infrastructure at the core.

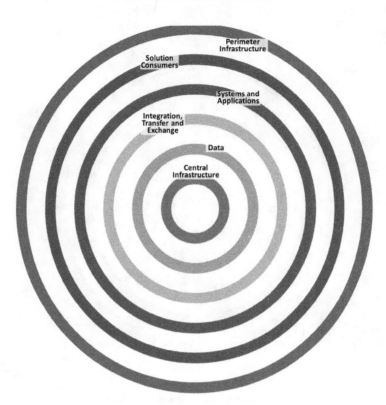

Figure 231 – Solution Domains Impacted by Security Controls

There is a seventh solution domain – the organisation's facilities, offices and locations – that is not included in this list. While identifying organisation changes should be part of the overall solution scope, the security issues relating to them are not really part of the security scope of the solution unless the purpose of the solution is to implement these controls. At some stage, the scope of the solution design and in particular, its security elements, needs to stop and other parts of the organisation need to take responsibility. Physical security for organisation facilities is an example of this.

The sets of controls listed above span these solution domains.

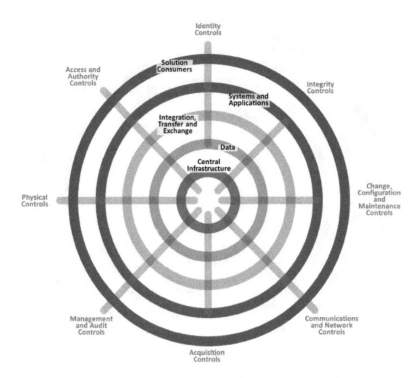

Figure 232 – Security Controls Spanning Solution Domains

1. *Identity Controls* – these apply to the Solution Consumers, Systems and Applications, Integration and Transfer and Exchange and Data domains.

2. *Access and Authority Controls* – these apply to the Perimeter Infrastructure, Solution Consumers, Systems and Applications, Integration, Transfer and Exchange, Data and Central Infrastructure domains.

3. *Physical Controls* – these apply to the Perimeter Infrastructure, Solution Consumers, Systems and Applications, Integration, Transfer and Exchange, Data and Central Infrastructure domains.

4. *Change, Configuration and Maintenance Controls* – these apply to the Perimeter Infrastructure, Solution Consumers, Systems and Applications, Integration, Transfer and Exchange, Data and Central Infrastructure domains.

5. *Management and Audit Controls* – these apply to the Perimeter Infrastructure, Solution Consumers, Systems and Applications, Integration, Transfer and Exchange, Data and Central Infrastructure domains.

6. *Acquisition Controls* – these apply to the Perimeter Infrastructure, Solution Consumers and Systems and Applications, domains.

7. *Integrity Controls* – these apply to the Systems and Applications, Integration and Transfer and Exchange, Data and Central Infrastructure domains.

8. *Communications and Network Controls* – these apply to the Perimeter Infrastructure, Solution Consumers, Systems and Applications, Integration, Transfer and Exchange, Data and Central Infrastructure domains.

Within each of the six securable domains of the solution discussed here, there can be multiple separate individual components:

*   Data can be stored in multiple locations, both within and outside the organisation
*   Data can be transferred between external locations and internal locations, between internal and external data stores and between internal and external applications
*   Systems and applications can run on infrastructure both within and outside the organisation

The security of the solution should be validated with respect to each of these components, especially where the components are located outside the organisation such a provided by a cloud or hosting provider.

The following lists individual checks and controls for each of the areas listed above. This list is not exhaustive but using it should allow the security of the solution to be validated to a sufficient level. The organisation security architecture function may have an existing set of control checks that can be used.

Control Code	Control Type	Control	Description
ICSCIAA	Identity Controls	Solution Consumer Identification And Authentication	Solution consumers are individually identified and authenticated across all accesses except for publicly available and accessible information. Authentication of user identities is performed using one or more of, in the case of multifactor authentication, passwords, tokens or biometrics. The strength of the authentication tools is sufficient and appropriate for the types of systems and data being accessed. The initial logon and authentication tools are subsequently used at the system, application and data levels to provide more complete information security. The solution consumer identification and authentication facilities are sufficiently scalable to handle the number of access requests.
ICPDIAA		Physical Device Identification And Authentication	Physical devices performing accesses are identified and authenticated before access is permitted.
ICSOD		Separation Of Duties	The solution implements separation of duties through authorisation allocated at identification and authentication to eliminate conflicts of interest in the responsibilities and duties of solution consumers.
ICLPA		Least Privilege Access	The solution applies the most limited set of access rights required by solution consumers to allow them perform their assigned tasks.
AAACSC	Access and Authority Controls	Solution Consumer Account Management	There are processes to manage solution access accounts and their solution and data access rights and privileges including their creation, activation, application of changes, regular review, disabling them if necessary and their removal.
AAACAE		Access Enforcement	The solution applies the assigned authorisations to solution consumers for limiting access to the solution and data consistently.
AAACUS		Unsuccessful Solution Access Attempts	The solution implements a limit to the number of consecutive invalid access attempts by a solution consumer during a defined interval after which the solution automatically locks the account our or delays next the allowed access,
AAACSA		Simultaneously Active Sessions	The solution limits the number of concurrently active sessions for any solution consumer.
AAACSL		Session Lock	The solution implements a session lock after a defined interval of inactivity after which the solution consumer must re-authenticate.
AAACST		Session Termination	The solution implements a termination lock after a defined interval of inactivity after which the solution consumer must re-authenticate.
AAACRA		Remote Access	The solution implements remote access to the system and

Control Code	Control Type	Control	Description
			data components subject to controls.
PCPAC	Physical Controls	Physical Access Control	The solution has controls to accessing the physical locations where its components reside. There are controls to the people with this access. These accesses are monitored and reviewed. The activities that can be performed during such an access are controlled and work done is monitored.
CCAMCS	Change, Configuration and Maintenance Controls	System Maintenance Procedures	There are defined system maintenance procedures and related system maintenance controls that detail the roles, responsibilities and coordination of changes across the solution landscape, testing and validation and back-out. Changed are logged.

Personnel performing maintenance are appropriately trained. Appropriate and fit-for-purpose tools are used. |
CCAMCS		Scheduled Maintenance	All scheduled and planning maintenance activities that make changes to the solution landscape including routine and scheduled maintenance, changes, fixes and patches are applied in a controlled manner.
CCAMCR		Remote Maintenance	Access to remote maintenance is controlled. Use of maintenance tools remotely is controlled. Activities and changes are logged.
CCAMCM		Maintenance Personnel	Third-party maintenance personnel must be subject to hiring controls appropriate to the sensitivity of the application and data being maintained.
MAACAP	Management and Audit Controls	Audit Procedures	There are defined audit procedures and associated audit controls in relation to auditing solution activity and events.
MAACSU		Solution Use Notification	The solution application and system components display a notification message before granting system access informing users of their access obligations.
MAACAC		Access Control Usage	The solution incorporates review of audit information to detect unusual activities.
MAACAE		Audit Events	The solution creates audit records for a defined and agreed set of system usage and activity events in a consistent format and writes them to a single location.

The audit information contains the necessary information to determine what events occurred, their source and their outcomes. |
MAACAS		Audit Storage Capacity	The solution has enough audit data storage capacity to ensure that the capacity will not be exceeded leading to loss of information and/or solution problems.
MAACAF		Audit Failures	The solution detects and responds to problems with event logging and auditing.
MAACAM		Audit Monitoring And Reporting	The solution incorporates regularly audit information review and analysis to check for unsuitable or strange activity, investigates suspect activity and notifies this to the relevant people who take appropriate actions.
MAACPO		Protection Of Audit Information	Audit and event logs are protected from unauthorised access, modification and deletion.
ACPASA	Acquisition Controls	Product And Services Acquisition Procedures	There are defined audit procedures for acquiring products and services that includes their compliance with security standards.
ACRPAA		Resources Planning	The solution has sufficient resources allocated to it to enable

Control Code	Control Type	Control	Description
		and Allocation	it to be protected adequately.
ACPASD		Product And Services Documentation	The solution is accompanied by sufficient documentation of a sufficient standard to allow its operation and use by understood so it can be secured.
ACEISS		External Information System Service Providers	The security controls of solution components supplied by external information system service providers incorporate required security controls.
ICSADI	Integrity Controls	Solution And Data Integrity Procedures	There are defined procedures to validate the integrity of the solution and its data across all its components.
ICDTET		Data Transmission, Exchange, Transfer and Integration Integrity	The solution ensures and validates the integrity of information that is exchanged between any of its components and external entities.
ICDTET		Data Transmission, Exchange, Transfer and Integration Confidentiality	The solution ensures and validates the confidentiality of information that is exchanged between any of its components and external entities.
ICIEL		Information Entry Limitations	The solution imposes controls on the entry of data into its components.
ICIAQC		Information Accuracy, Quality, Completeness And Authenticity	The solution incorporates controls to check information for accuracy, quality and authenticity at the earliest step in data supply and identifies and handles errors accordingly and in a consistent way.
ICIPHS		Information Production Handling, Storage And Retention	Information produced by solution components is handled, stored and retained as required.
ICSACP	Communications and Network Controls System And Communications Protection Procedures		There are defined procedures to develop, implement, operate and manage security controls relating the communications networks used or access by solution components.
ICDOSP			The solution incorporates denial of service protection controls if necessary.
ICBP	Denial Of Service Protection Boundary Protection and Intrusion Detection and Prevention		The solution incorporates monitoring and control of communications at the external boundaries of the solution and at main internal boundaries within the solution.
ICCKOA			The solution incorporates the use of cryptographic tools and has controls to manage their use if necessary.
ICPKIC	Cryptographic Key Operation and Management		The solution incorporates controls regarding the distribution and use of PKI certificates and has controls to manage their use if necessary.
ICCSA	Public Key Infrastructure Certificates Controls		The solution incorporates controls to protect the authenticity of communications sessions.
ICCESCC	Communications Session Authenticity External Solution Component Connections		The solution ensures that direct connections from the solution to other solution components outside of organisation network boundary are implemented and operated using connection controls, agreements and appropriate communications facilities. There are controls in place to ensure these communications are actively.

The check and controls can then be mapped to solution landscape templates such as:

1. User access internal and external

2. Data integration from internal data sources
3. Data integration from internal external sources
4. Data storage and access
5. Application components located on cloud or hosted service provider

The following is an example of mapping various access checks and controls on an internal and external solution consumer access.

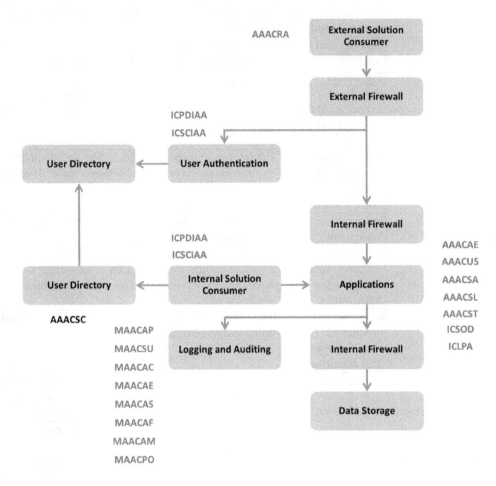

Figure 233 – Security Control Checks for Solution User Access

The following is an example of mapping various access checks and controls on an internal and external data exchange, transfer or integration.

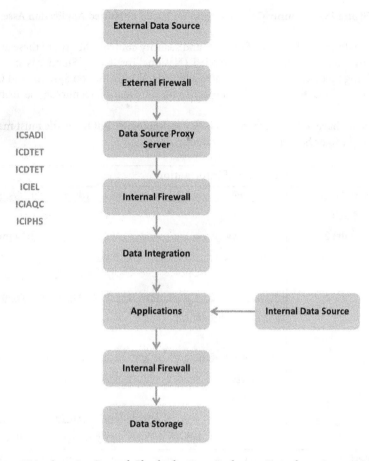

Figure 234 – Security Control Checks for Data Exchange, Transfer or Integration

The following is an example of mapping various access checks and controls where applications are hosted externally.

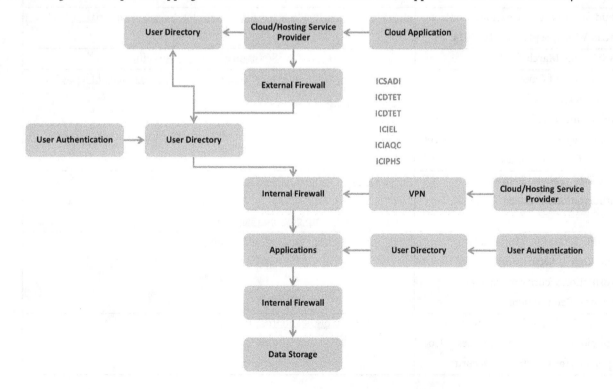

Figure 235 – Security Control Checks for Cloud or Hosted Application Assess

There is a large amount of material on the topic of security and security controls. Many are these are related to or are derived from the catalogue of security controls contained in the NIST (National Institute of Standards and Technology) Special Publication 800-53 - Assessing Security and Privacy Controls in Federal Information Systems and Organizations. The NIST set of security standards have become the accepted best practice for information technology security.

The solution architect does not have to be an expert in security technologies. But he or she must maintain a current awareness of security standards that apply to or have an impact on solution design.

Security Standard	Location of information
AICPA SSAE (Statement Standards Attestation Engagements) 18 SOC (Service Organizations Controls) 2	https://www.aicpa.org/research/standards/auditattest/ssae.html https://www.aicpa.org/content/dam/aicpa/research/standards/auditattest/downloadabledocuments/ssae-no-18.pdf https://www.aicpa.org/interestareas/frc/assuranceadvisoryservices/socforserviceorganizations.html https://www.aicpa.org/content/dam/aicpa/interestareas/frc/assuranceadvisoryservices/downloadabledocuments/dc-200.pdf https://www.aicpa.org/content/dam/aicpa/interestareas/frc/assuranceadvisoryservices/downloadabledocuments/trust-services-criteria.pdf
AICPA Trust Services Criteria for Security, Availability, Processing Integrity, Confidentiality, and Privacy	https://www.aicpa.org/content/dam/aicpa/interestareas/frc/assuranceadvisoryservices/downloadabledocuments/trust-services-criteria.pdf
Cloud Security Alliance Cloud Controls Matrix V3.0.1, September 16, 2014	https://cloudsecurityalliance.org/artifacts/cloud-controls-matrix-v3-0-1/
CNSSI 1253, March 2014	https://www.cnss.gov/CNSS/issuances/Instructions.cfm
Government of Canada CSE (Communications Security Establishment) ITSG-33 (Information Technology Security Guidance) Generic Security Control Profiles	https://cyber.gc.ca/en/guidance/it-security-risk-management-lifecycle-approach-itsg-33
FedRAMP (Federal Risk and Authorization Program) Tailored	https://www.fedramp.gov/documents/ https://www.fedramp.gov/templates/
ISO/IEC 27001:2013 Information technology -- Security techniques -- Information security management systems – Requirements	https://www.iso.org/standard/54534.html
ISO/IEC 27002:2013 Information technology -- Security techniques -- Code of practice for information security	https://www.iso.org/standard/54533.html

Security Standard	Location of information
controls	
NIST Cybersecurity Framework	https://www.nist.gov/cyberframework/
NIST SP 800-171 - Controlled Unclassified Information	
NIST SP 800-53 (R4) - Security and Privacy Controls for Federal Information Systems and Organizations	http://csrc.nist.gov/
PCI DSS 3.2 PCI Security Standards Council	https://www.pcisecuritystandards.org/
US DoD (DISA) Cloud Computing Security Requirements Guide Defense Information Systems Agency (DISA) IASE (Information Security Assurance Environment)	https://iase.disa.mil/cloud_security/Pages/index.aspx https://iasecontent.disa.mil/cloud/Downloads/Cloud_Computing_SRG_v1r3.pdf
European Union Agency for Network and Information Security (ENISA)	https://resilience.enisa.europa.eu/cloud-computing-certification Privacy and Data Protection by Design - https://www.enisa.europa.eu/publications/privacy-and-data-protection-by-design/at_download/fullReport Handbook on Security of Personal Data Processing - https://www.enisa.europa.eu/publications/handbook-on-security-of-personal-data-processing/at_download/fullReport
Leet Security	http://www.leetsecurity.com/ http://www.leetsecurity.com/metodologia/

4.9.2 Solution Data Privacy

4.9.2.1 Overview

The most recent and substantial impact on the topic of solution data privacy have been the European Community's GDPR (General Data Privacy Regulation)[47] and the ePrivacy Regulation[48]. I have included material on this here because the

---

[47] See:
http://eur-lex.europa.eu/legal-content/en/TXT/?uri=CELEX%3A32016R0679
[48] See:
http://eur-lex.europa.eu/legal-content/EN/TXT/?uri=CELEX%3A52017PC0010

processing of personal data is central to many solutions, especially digital solutions (see Chapter 5 on page 391). The solution architect needs to be aware of the growing complexity around data privacy and the processing of personal data.

The data privacy principles that should be incorporated into any solution and its data management processes are:

- *Lawfulness, Fairness and Transparency* - personal data shall be processed lawfully, fairly and in a transparent manner in relation to the data subject

- *Specified, Explicit and Legitimate Purpose* - Personal data must only be collected for specified, explicit and legitimate purposes and not further processed in a manner that is incompatible with those purposes

- *Adequate, Relevant and Limited* - Personal data shall be adequate, relevant and limited to what is necessary in relation to the purposes for which the data is processed

- *Accurate and Up-To-Date* - Personal data shall be accurate, and, where necessary, kept up to date; every reasonable step must be taken to ensure that personal data that is inaccurate, having regard to the purposes for which it is processed, is erased or rectified without undue delay

- *Pseudonymisation/Storage Limits* - Personal data shall be kept in a form which permits identification of data subjects for no longer than is necessary for the purposes for which the personal data is processed

- *Security* - Personal data shall be processed in a manner that ensures appropriate security of personal data, including protection against unauthorised or unauthorised processing and against accidental loss, destruction or damage, using appropriate technical or organisational measures

The operational principle of *Privacy By Design and By Default* requires that data privacy and protection measures are designed and incorporated into the design of business processes and information technology solutions. The solution architect must look to incorporate this principle into the solution design process and into solution designs created.

These impact solution designs directly in two ways:

1. Solutions must ensure that personal data held and processed is identified so it can be managed

2. The solution must allow the set of GDPR-related processes relating to accessing and updating personal data to be easily operated

There are additional indirect impacts on solution design:

1. The solution may require a Data Protection Impact Assessment (DPIA)

2. The solution may incorporate data pseudonymisation

This section is not designed to cover the compete topic of GDPR. It is intended to outline the impact this will have on solution design and the resulting changes that will have to be incorporated into solution designs.

Organisations should have a wider response to data privacy initiatives such as GDPR that the solution architect can inherit and use in solution designs. But, as with other topics such as security, the solution architect cannot take such compliance for granted but must perform a due diligence on such conformity.

4.9.2.2 Personal Information

Personal data is defined in Article 4(1) of the GDPR:

'Personal data' means any information relating to an identified or identifiable natural person ('data subject'); an identifiable natural person is one who can be identified, directly or indirectly, in particular by reference to an identifier such as a name, an identification number, location data, an online identifier or to one or more factors specific to the physical, physiological, genetic, mental, economic, cultural or social identity of that natural person

GDPR applies to personal information. Information is personal if it is:

- Owned by a person
- About a person
- Directed towards a person
- Sent or posted or communicated by a person
- Experienced by a person
- Relevant to a person

The definition of what is personal data is broad and includes all of the following:

Personal Data Type	Personal Data Items
Personal Information	Name, such as full name, maiden name, mother's maiden name, or alias
	Date of birth
	Place of birth
	Full home address
	Country, state, postcode or city of residence
	Marital status
	Telephone numbers, including mobile, business and personal numbers
	Information identifying personally owned property, such as vehicle registration number
	Passport number
	Social insurance or national insurance number
	Residence and geographic records
	Sexual orientation
Biographical Data	Specific age
	Height
	Weight
	Eye colour
	Hair colour
	Photographic image
	Gender
	Racial or ethnic origin
	Any defining physical characteristics
Digital footprint	Digital identities, such as avatars and usernames/handles
	Logon details such as name, screen name, nickname, or handle
	Email address (if private from an association/club membership, etc.)
	IP addresses (in the EU)
	Geo-tracking information and location-based data
	Web usage behaviour or user preferences using persistent cookies
	Asset information, such as Internet Protocol (IP) or Media Access Control (MAC) address
	(MAC) address or other host-specific persistent static identifier that consistently
	Any information that links a particular person to a small, well-defined group
Medical or Heath Data	Patient identifier
	Number of sick days taken from employer and other information relating to any sick leave
	Visits to doctors
	Medical data
	Biological traits including DNA

Personal Data Type	Personal Data Items
	Fitness data
	Medical images such as X-rays, CT scans and ultra sound
	Biometric data such as fingerprints, retinal scans, voice signature or facial geometry
	Medication

Table 72 – Examples of Personal Data

The definition of personal data is very important. It does not just include information a person explicitly supplies. It includes implicit information such as browsing history.

GDPR identifies special categories of personal data for which processing is subject to additional constraints. Processing of personal data revealing racial or ethnic origin, political opinions, religious or philosophical beliefs, or trade union membership and the processing of genetic data, biometric data for the purpose of uniquely identifying a natural person, data concerning health or data concerning a natural person's sex life or sexual orientation shall be prohibited.

4.9.2.3 Personal Data Related Processes and Impact on Solution Design

GDPR requires that organisations implement a number of personal data-related processes. Solutions must track data that is deemed to be personal to allow these processes to be easily and simply operated. The solution architecture function should assist with the development of common responses to these common organisation requirements.

GDPR Process	Description	Impact on Solution Designs
Request Tracking	Individuals can make requests for details of personal information. These requests can be tracked within a separate compliance tracking or within the individual solutions that contain personal data.	Low Requests can be tracked centrally.
Consent and Consent Recording and Tracking	Individual applications that accept personal data should record the individual's compliance with providing that information. Consent management involves: • Identify all points where personal data is collected across all communication channels • Identify the data processing processes where consent is required • Create and publish GDPR consent management notices • Update communication channels such as the organisation web site(s) with GDPR consent notices • If data is collected from children, implement an approach to collect consent from parents or guardians • Update IT systems to record consent details and allow consents to be subsequently updated If there are multiple public-facing applications then each will have to record consent. In this case, such records of consent could be recorded centrally	Low Public-facing applications such as web sites need to be updated to record and store consents. Solution that are exposed to external users will need to comply.
Consent Withdrawal	Persons should have the right to withdraw their previously granted consents. This means they should be able to see what consents they previously granted. The withdrawal of consent should be recorded to establish an audit trail should the need	Low Consent information must be able to be retrieved and

GDPR Process	Description	Impact on Solution Designs
	arise to prove it at some future time. Related systems should be updated to ensure that processing of the person's data is stopped.	updated based on user requests.
Access to Data	Persons have the right to request access to all personal data the organisation stores about them. This implies that there must be a record of all personal data including derived data held across all systems, including manually-maintained and paper records. The data from all these sources must be consolidated and supplied to the requestor. On request, the data controller has to provide: • An overview of the categories of data that are being processed • A copy of the data itself • How it acquired the data • Details on the processing such as the its purposes • With whom the data are shared	Medium Personal data held in solutions must be able to be identified and extracted. This means that personal data must be flagged or otherwise be able to be found.
Data Rectification	Persons have the right to have inaccurate personal data rectified inaccurate personal data.	Medium Personal data held in solutions must be able to be updated (after first being extracted). This means that personal data must be flagged or otherwise be able to be found.
Restriction of Processing	Persons have the right to restriction of processing of their personal data where its accuracy is contested, the processing is unlawful and the person opposes the erasure of the personal data and requests the restriction instead, the data controller no longer needs the personal data for the purposes of the processing or the person has objected to processing and pending the verification of the objection.	Low to Medium The solution that performs processing must be able to identify personal data that is subject to such restrictions. This will not apply to manage organisations.
Data Objection	Persons have the right to object that personal data processing is necessary for the performance of a task. The data controller can no longer process the personal data unless the controller demonstrates compelling legitimate grounds for the processing which override the interests, rights and freedoms of the person.	Medium The solution that performs processing must be able to identify personal data that is subject to such restrictions.
Profiling Objection	Persons have the right not to be subject to a decision based solely on automated processing, including profiling, which produces legal effects concerning him or her or similarly significantly affects him or her.	Medium The solution that performs processing must be able to identify personal data that is subject to such restrictions.
Data Erasure	Persons have the right to have their data erased. This implies	High

GDPR Process	Description	Impact on Solution Designs
	that there must be a record of all personal data including derived data held across all systems, including manually-maintained and paper records. The inventory of personal data must be consulted and the associated personal data for the requesting person deleted. The act of erasing personal data should be recorded. A person has the right to request erasure of and cessation of processing personal data including any copies related to them: • Where the personal data are no longer necessary in relation to the purposes for which they are collected • Where the person has withdrawn their consent • Where the person objects to the processing and there are no overriding legitimate grounds for the processing • Where the processing of the personal data does not otherwise comply with the GDPR	The solution must enable personal data to be deleted and to record the deletion
Data Portability	Persons have the right to have their data transferred to another data controller. As with Access to Data and Data Erasure, this requires that there must be a record of all personal data including derived data and that this can be extracted into a format that can be transferred securely. The data must be provided in a structured and commonly used electronic format. Portability includes the right to have personal data transmitted directly from one controller to another "where technically feasible". The GDPR does not define "technically feasible". Data controllers are encouraged to develop interoperable formats that enable data portability but without there is no obligation for data controllers to adopt or maintain processing systems which are technically compatible with one another. Data controllers are prohibited from establishing barriers to transmission. Requests should be processed within one month of receipt of the request. This one-month period can be extended to a maximum of three months for complex cases as long as the person has been informed about the reasons for such delay within one month of the original request.	Medium The solution must able to export personal data in a format that can be used for subsequent importing the data by another organisation.
Complaint Handling	Persons can complain to their Supervisory Authority that may then forward the complaint to the organisation where it must be handled and responded to.	None A separate complaints handling process and solution can be used.
Personal Data Breach Notification	Organisations must notify their Supervisory Authority of any data breaches.	Medium The solution must be able to identify that a breach has occurred and which sets of personal data have

GDPR Process	Description	Impact on Solution Designs
		been affected.
Person Data Breach Notification	When the data breach is likely to have a high risk to the rights of persons, organisations must notify them of the breach.	Medium The solution must be able to identify that a breach has occurred and which sets of personal data have been affected.
Record of Audits of Third-Party Data Processors	Organisations should regularly audit any third-parties they use for data processing and record the results of the audit.	None These audits can be recorded using a separate solution.

Table 73 – GDPR Processes and Their Impact on Solution Design

Solution designs should be aware of the set of personal data-related processes they must support and enable.

4.9.2.4 GDPR Related Metadata

For each item of personal data collected and held in a solution or stored outside IT systems, there is a need to maintain a set of GDPR-related metadata. The set of metadata will depend on the approach to handling the GDPR compliance processes. It can include some or all of:

GDPR Metadata	Description
Personal Information Flag	Flag indicating that the field contains personal data
Sensitive Information Flag	Flag indicating that the field contains sensitive personal data
Retention Date	The date up to which the information can be retained and after which it must be deleted
Consent Identifier	A link to where consent about the collection and processing of this data is held
Consent Withdrawal Flag	A flag indicating that consent to use the data has been withdrawn
Data Erasure Flag	A flag indicating that the data was erased
GDPR Tracking Identifier	Link to case management facility for activity relating to this field
Restriction of Processing Flag	A flag indicating that the processing of the data is restricted

Table 74 – Personal Data Metadata

The purpose of hold this metadata is to allow personal data held by individual solutions be easily identified. This enables the GDPR processes listed above to be operated.

There are two options with the design of the solution that handles personal data:

1. The solution can store the GDPR related metadata that identifies fields as containing personal data and holds the additional GDPR tracking information such as retention details, consent details and deletion details. This is potentially expensive and time consuming. Each solution would handle its personal data tracking separately. If the data processing components of the solution are sourced from third-parties these organisations may over time update their systems to allow the additional GDPR-related information to be stored.

2. Implement a separate solution that integrates personal data from the operational systems and that creates or maps a single consolidated data store or view of personal data across these operational systems using some form of federated data store. This reduces the impact on existing legacy solutions. This involves developing or sourcing a software system

to provide this consolidated personal data management functionality. One of the issues with having a separate system is that changes that occur in the underlying operational systems have to be reflected in it. This is shown below.

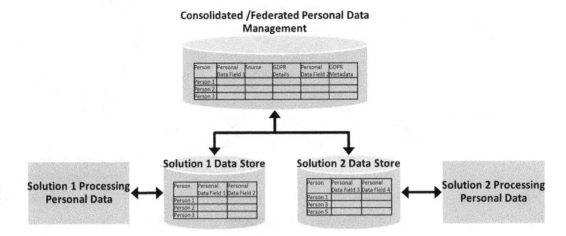

Figure 236 – Consolidated/Federated Personal Data

4.9.2.5 Solution Data Protection Impact Assessment (DPIA)

The design of the solution may be subject to a Data Protection Impact Assessment (DPIA). The solution architect should understand in advance of any formal DPIA being performed of the likely need for such an assessment. If a DPIA is needed the solution architect should design the solution in order that it passes the assessment. The assessment should not be performed and the solution then redesigned to accommodate its findings and requirements.

The use of Privacy Impact Assessments (PIAs) was developed outside the EU, with the UK being the first supervisory authority in the EU to adopt the use of PIAs. In the UK, PIAs have been mandatory for Government departments for several years, as well as being widely used in the privacy sector. The GDPR, in Article 35, introduces mandatory Data Protection Impact Assessments (DPIAs) in respect of high-risk processing, that is, processing that poses a high risk to the rights and freedoms of natural persons.

Article 35(3) of the GDPR designates three specific types of processing as high-risk so that a DPIA is required where one or more of the following is being performed:

1. Processing, including profiling, and on which decisions are based that produce legal effects concerning the natural person or similarly significantly affect the natural person

2. Processing on a large scale of special categories of data referred to in Article 9(1) of the GDPR, or of personal data relating to criminal convictions and offences referred to in Article 10 of the GDPR

3. A systematic monitoring of a publicly accessible area on a large scale

In addition to these three cases in which a DPIA is mandatory, there is a general obligation to conduct a DPIA where there processing is likely to result in a high risk to the rights and freedoms of natural persons as stated in Article 35(1) of the GDPR. Under Article 35(4) of the GDPR, the supervisory authority is required to make public a list of the kind of processing operations that are subject to the requirement for a DPIA under Article 35(1) and will communicate the list to the European Data Protection Board (EDPB)[49]. The supervisory authority may also establish and make public a list of the kind of processing operations for which no data protection impact assessment is required and will communicate that list to the EDPB as stated in Article 35(5) of the GDPR.

---

[49] See:
https://edpb.europa.eu/

A DPIA[50] must address:

- A systematic description of the envisaged processing operations – this should include the flow of personal data through the systems and business processes as business activities are performed

- The purpose of the processing (including, where applicable, the legitimate interest pursued by the controller)

- An assessment of why the processing is being performed and how this is proportional to the underlying need

- An assessment of the risks to the rights and freedoms of the persons affected

- The measures envisaged to address the risks, including safeguards, security measures and mechanisms to ensure the protection of personal data and to demonstrate compliance with GDPR, taking into account the rights and legitimate interests of data subjects concerned

Where the DPIA indicates that the processing remains high risk despite the application of measures to mitigate that risk, the controller must consult the supervisory authority before processing as specified in Article 36(1) of the GDPR. Member States must similarly consult the supervisory authority where they are preparing a proposal for a legislative measure to be adopted by the national parliament or for a regulatory measure based on legislation as specified in Article 36(4) of the GDPR.

4.9.2.6 Data Pseudonymisation

GDPR includes references to data pseudonymisation as gives its benefits as:

As a means of enhancing protection in case of further use of data for research and statistics[51]

As a means of possibly contributing to the compatibility of further use of data[52]

As a means to contribute to "privacy by design" in data applications[53]

The application of pseudonymisation to personal data can reduce the risks to the data subjects concerned and help controllers and processors to meet their data-protection obligations. The explicit introduction of 'pseudonymisation' in this Regulation is not intended to preclude any other measures of data protection.[54]

Pseudonymisation is not anonymisation. Anonymisation means data cannot be attributed to a person. Pseudonymisation means data can be attributed to a person using additional information. It just makes identifying persons from data more difficult, time-consuming and expensive. Pseudonymisation is not a mandatory GDPR requirement. It covered her for completeness.

Most database tools include an encryption option as standard. Data is transparently encrypted as it is written to and decrypted when it is read from the database, sometimes called Transparent Data Encryption (TDE). The solution can use this feature of the underlying solution database(s) to provide personal data pseudonymisation. This reduces the solution design impact. The solution architect still needs to be aware of the approach being taken, if any, to data encryption.

Pseudonymisation means removing the direct link between data and its attribution to a specific individual. Direct data access is replaced with indirect data access that requires some form of key, held separately from the personal data, to translate

---

[50] The Article 29 Working Party - Working Party on the Protection of Individuals with Regard to the Processing of Personal Data, the forerunner of the European Data Protection Board (EDPB) produced guidance on DIPAs - *Guidelines on Data Protection Impact Assessment (DPIA) and determining whether processing is "likely to result in a high risk" for the purposes of Regulation 2016/679* - http://ec.europa.eu/newsroom/document.cfm?doc_id=47711

[51] Article 89 (1) of GDPR

[52] Article 6 (4) of GDPR

[53] Article 25 of GDPR

[54] Recital 28 of GDPR

personal data into a usable format by the accessing application in real time. It adds a layer of complexity, time and expense to person identification. There is still an indirect link so the data is usable. Pseudonymisation provides an extra layer of security. It does not in itself stop personal data being lost. It just reduces the likelihood that lost or leaked personal data can be read – both the encrypted data and the means to decrypt it must be lost or leaked.

Pseudonymisation can encrypt data using approach such as PKI keys, either a single key pair or two key pairs. Each data sender (application) and data receiver (store) gets a pair of keys: Public Key and Private Key. The public keys are published and the private keys are kept secret. Communications between the data sender and the data received involves only public keys and no private key is ever transmitted or shared. Data can be encrypted with the public key. Data can be decrypted with the private key.

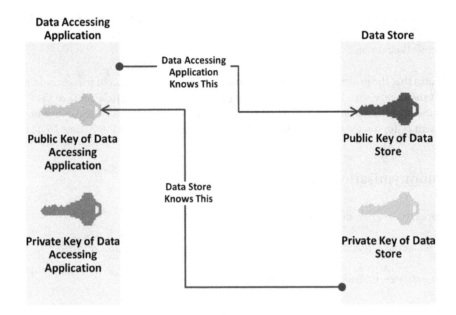

Figure 237 – Data Encryption and Decryption Using Public and Private Keys

With a single key pair, the encryption facility encrypts data using public key and decrypts using private key.

With two key pairs, data is encrypted twice. The encryption facility encrypts data using public key of data store and the private key of data application and decrypts using private keys.

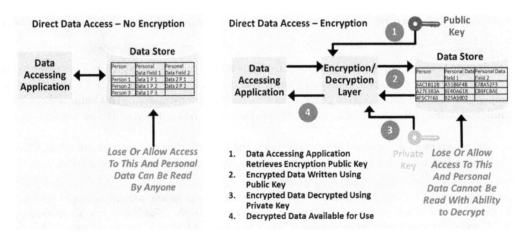

Figure 238 – Reading and Writing Data Using Single Public/Private Key Pair

With two pair encryption, the solution component writing the data encrypts the data with both the public key of the data storage component and its private key.

The data is decrypted for reading on request by the data store decrypting the requested data using the public key of the application that wrote the data and its private key.

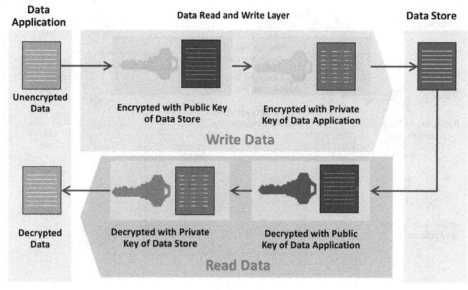

Figure 239 – Reading and Writing Data Using Two Key Pairs

Using two pair encryption can be slow.

Where data is being read by an application different from the one that originally wrote the data, that second application must be able to know the writing application and thus specify that its public key must be used for data retrieval.

Where keys exist at the application level, then all data can be decrypted using the one key. This provides no granularity of data security. Record (or even field) level encryption requires individual keys down to the level of granularity.

In this case, when the record is being written it is encrypted with the public key of the record and then the private key of the application. This needs a separate set of key pairs, one for each record and a way of linking the person to the key that is not simple. This lessens the impact of a data breach but at the cost of complex key management.

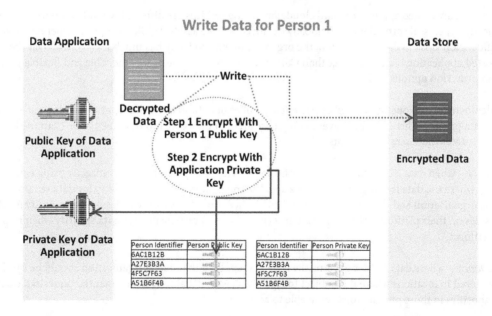

Figure 240 – Granular Data Encryption

The encrypted data can be decrypted using the private key of the record and the applications public key.

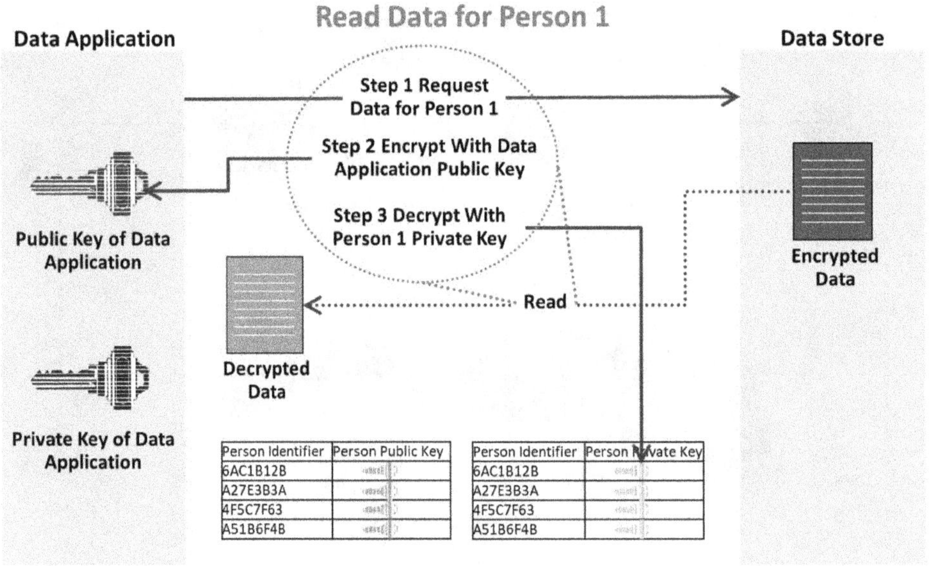

Figure 241 – Granular Data Decryption

4.9.3 Data and Hosted Applications and XaaS/Cloud-Based Services

Externally hosted applications and cloud-based services represent a change in the way information technology services are delivered to the business. The information technology function needs to be ready, capable and prepared to take advantage this solution delivery model suitably and appropriately. This is an example of the IT function acting a lens, focussing business needs on solutions that are acquired or developed that was discussed in section 2.6 on page 50.

The nature of externally hosted applications and cloud computing services results in the organisation having a different and reduced measure control over its data assets.

In this context externally hosted applications and cloud computing services are different. Cloud computing service providers (CSPs) are typically hyper-scale providers with globally deployed service assets. While the option generally exists to have data located a specific region close to the organisation, the organisation has typically has much less control over the service. Providers of hosted applications can be smaller than CSPs and therefore can be more amenable and flexible to service deployment and provision options.

These service deployment and operation models present a number of data–related challenges spanning data control, data protection and data privacy. There are three overlapping core areas of data concern that need to be examined in any solution design that incorporates these service elements

1. ***Data Security*** – when data is moved to a cloud or hosted service of application, either directly using external data storage or indirectly where the data is being managed by a specific application, the responsibility for data security is shared between the organisation and the service provider. The service provider is (more or less) responsibility for data security when it resides on their platform. The organisation is (more or less) responsible for data security when it moved to and from the platform.

2. ***Data Residency*** – where data resides governs the laws that apply to that data. Organisation should be careful that their data is not stored in locations where it is subject to legal frameworks that may have potential undesirable consequences such as authorities in those jurisdictions being able to access it.

3. ***Data Sovereignty*** – irrespective of the physical location of the data storage within the CSP's infrastructure, that stored data may be subject to the laws of other jurisdictions. The CSP with operating entities in other jurisdictions may be obliged to comply with a court order enforcing a data access request. This means that the organisation cannot fully guarantee sovereignty over data held in the cloud. This should govern the sensitivity of the data stored in the cloud.

In the context of data privacy, the ultimate responsibility lies with organisation relying on these third parties.

There are existing standards and approaches that can be adopted for use with data privacy and security compliance. There is no need to develop new standards and approaches. These existing, detailed, well-defined and well-proven frameworks and approaches can and should be used.

Service Organisation Controls (SOC) originally related to auditing of financial transactions performed by third-parties and the controls in place. Over time, these have been extended to cover the operation of the service and its compliance with security, availability, reliability, confidentiality and privacy. This evolution consisted of:

> 1993 – Statement on Auditing Standards (SAS) No. 70, Service Organisations
> 2008 – Trust Services Principles and Criteria for Security, Availability, Processing Integrity, Confidentiality, and Privacy
> 2010 – Standards for Attestation Engagements (SSAE) 16, Reporting on Controls at a Service Organisation
> 2011 – International Auditing and Assurance Standards Board (IAASB) issued International Standard on Assurance Engagements (ISAE) 3402, Assurance Reports on Controls at a Service Organisation
> 2015 – Updated Trust Services Principles and Criteria for Security, Availability, Processing Integrity, Confidentiality, and Privacy
> 2016 – Standards for Attestation Engagements (SSAE) 18, Reporting on Controls at a Service Organisation

These standards have been developed by American Institute of Certified Public Accountants (AICPA - https://www.aicpa.org/) and International Auditing and Assurance Standards Board (IAASB - https://www.iaasb.org/). While they originated from an auditing background, they are more widely and generally applicable.

The material can be reused and applied when drafting service agreements with third-party suppliers and in defining the controls to be applied and audited.

There are five core Trust Services Principles:

1. **Security** - The system is protected against unauthorised access, use, or modification
2. **Availability** - The system is available for operation and use as committed or agreed
3. **Processing Integrity** - System processing is complete, valid, accurate, timely, and authorised
4. **Confidentiality** - Information designated as confidential is protected as committed or agreed
5. **Privacy** – This applies the generally accepted privacy principles (GAPP)

The privacy principle addresses the system's collection, use, retention, disclosure, and disposal of personal information in conformity with the commitments in the entity's privacy notice and with criteria set forth in generally accepted privacy principles (GAPP). This closely mirrors the privacy principles of GDPR.

GAPP consists of 10 principles:

- **Management** - The entity defines documents, communicates, and assigns accountability for its privacy policies and procedures.

- **Notice** - The entity provides notice about its privacy policies and procedures and identifies the purposes for which personal information is collected, used, retained, and disclosed.

- **Choice and Consent** - The entity describes the choices available to the individual and obtains implicit or explicit consent with respect to the collection, use, and disclosure of personal information.

- **Collection** - The entity collects personal information only for the purposes identified in the notice.

- **Use and Retention** - The entity limits the use of personal information to the purposes identified in the notice and for which the individual has provided implicit or explicit consent. The entity retains personal information for only as long as necessary to fulfil the stated purposes or as required by law or regulations and thereafter appropriately disposes of such information.

- **Access** - The entity provides individuals with access to their personal information for re-view and update.

- **Disclosure to Third Parties** - The entity discloses personal information to third parties only for the purposes identified in the notice and with the implicit or explicit consent of the individual.

- **Security for Privacy** - The entity protects personal information against unauthorised access (both physical and logical).

- **Quality** - The entity maintains accurate, complete, and relevant personal information for the purposes identified in the notice.

- **Monitoring and Enforcement** - The entity monitors compliance with its privacy policies and procedures and has procedures to address privacy-related complaints and disputes.

The IAASB[55] (International Auditing and Assurance Standards Board) principles and essential procedures for performing assurance engagements can be found in section INTERNATIONAL STANDARD ON ASSURANCE ENGAGEMENTS 3000 of:

http://www.ifrs.org.ua/wp-content/uploads/2014/11/2014-IAASB-HANDBOOK-VOLUME-2.pdf

The detailed Trust Services Principles and Criteria for Security, Availability, Processing Integrity, Confidentiality, and Privacy document can be found at:

https://www.itm21st.com/Content/Documents/trustservicesprinciples-tsp100.pdf

The Service Organisation Controls (SOC) report is a formal review of the operation of these principles. More details on the SOC report covering Report on Controls at a Service Organisation Relevant to Security, Availability, Processing Integrity, Confidentiality and Privacy can be found at:

https://www.isaca.org/Groups/Professional-English/isae-3402/Documents/SOC2.pdf

The relationship between these standards is:

---

[55] See:
https://www.iaasb.org/

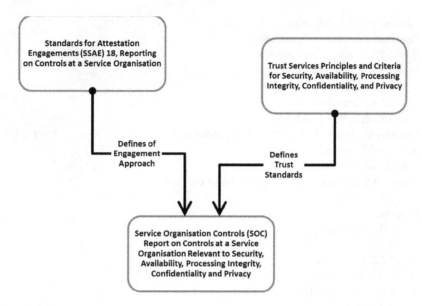

Figure 242 – Relationship Between Data Privacy and Data Security Compliance and Verification Standards

4.10 Solution Architecture and Design Artefacts

The central output from the solution design process is the set of solution design documentation. This can be a single artefact or a set of artefacts. The solution design can be a detailed implementation and operation blueprint or it can exist at higher levels of abstraction. In addition to this final artefact there are potentially many artefacts that are created during the stages of the design process.

Solution design interim artefacts are created for to act as a record of the information gathered, analysis performed, work done and to be available to be used in subsequent solution delivery phases. The act of creating the formal record that is the artefact requires that the information it contains should be organised and correct. This imposes a discipline and a rigour on the creation of the artefacts. This rigour eliminates ambiguity. Creating the artefact requires that the information it contains be organised and articulated clearly.

The artefacts are the basis for an agreement between the solution acquirer and those delivering the solution on what exactly it will do. The complete description of the functions to be performed by the solution detailed in the solution design can be used by the solution acquirer to determine if the solution specified meets their needs.

Artefacts can be used in the delivery estimation process to determine cost, resources required and schedule.

Artefacts are useful as an historical record. Artefacts should only be created when they add value to future stages of solution delivery or when they are needed to act as a proof or record of work done. The artefacts can be useful after the solution is transitions to production for support, maintenance and enhancement purposes. The amount of detail contained in the artefact should only be what is necessary.

Artefacts will allow to solution to be transferred to another service provider or function or for the solution to be reimplemented using different underlying tools and components.

The following is a sample table of contents for a generic idealised solution design document:

1. Introduction, Purpose and Scope
2. Overview and Summary
    2.1. Solution Summary
    2.2. Solution Concepts
    2.3. Application Architecture

This represents the maximum set of information that the solution design should contain. The design document describes the design that has been selected and is complete. The steps that lead to this design, such as the evaluation of other options and alternatives, are best documented elsewhere. The sample table of contents contains information of the service management and service introduction aspects of the solution design. These could be moved to a separate artefact.

This sample table of contents does not include details on approaches to solution implementation or estimates for solution delivery. These can be included in the document but are probably best included elsewhere.

The creation of these artefacts is not an end in itself. The artefacts are created to add value, act as a record or to generate a benefit. If the artefact is not required, it should not be generated.

Artefact creation can go from one extreme to another: from no artefacts, which tends to be associated with agile-type software development, to a large library of artefacts. Artefact creation is not an end in itself. It is a means to an end, which is to deliver operable, usable and supportable solutions and to record work done.

The solution design can be a living artefact that is updated as solution delivery takes place to act as a record of design changes made in response to changes or delivery issues. But at some stage, the design document needs to be closed-off.

The solution architecture function does not exist to create solution design documents and other artefacts. It exists to design solutions that deliver value to the business.

Two of the (many) functions of the Solution Architecture Centre of Excellence described in section 8.3 on page 487 is to develop and maintain a set of artefact templates and to manage solution knowledge generated through maintaining a library of solution artefacts.

There are various sets of artefacts described throughout this book:

- *Solution design and delivery artefacts listed in the solution delivery process* – see section 4.3 on page 112

- *Business engagement* – see section 4.6.1 on page 161

- *Early engagement* – see section 4.6.4 on page 235

- *Rapid solution design* – see section4.6.5 above 4.6.5 on page 257

- *Detailed solution detail* – see section 4.6.6 on page 276

4.11 Solution Assessment and Review

The designed solution should be validated. This validation should cover:

- *Benefits Validation Review* – Validating that the solution design is capable to achieving the stated benefits

- *Overall Solution Design Review* – Validating that the solution is fit for purpose

- *Architectural Compliance Review* – Validating that the solution complies with architectural standards across key architectural areas

- *Implementation Review* – Validating that the solution can be implemented and is affordable

These reviews can be combined. The formality and level of detail of the review effort depend on the size and complexity (see section 4.2.2 on page 100) of the solution. Small, simple solutions do not merit lengthy and time-consuming validations.

The overall solution design should be the subject of a review to validate its suitability for the situation being addressed. The solution design may have evolved during the design process and may have strayed from its original intended use. A review ensures that design decisions are subject to justification and confirmation.

Validating the solution is an important due diligence to perform before implementation starts. It avoids failures.

Solution validation is commonly limited to a form of requirements traceability. This involves verifying that the solution design incorporates the stated requirements. However, this validation can be illusory. As stated in section 4.4 on page 124, requirements tend to be sparse and disconnected and are representations of specific points of functionality that do not aggregate into a defined solution. Verifying that the solution design includes the requirements does not validate the solution.

4.11.1 Solution Benefits Review

The solution has a cost to design, implement and operate. In turn, the solution will be expected to achieve benefits in terms of direct explicitly quantifiable benefits often called tangible or hard and other indeterminate or non-quantifiable benefits, often called intangible or soft. There may be a third set of benefits that can be grouped as strategy realisation and process simplification though these can be included in the second set.

The actual benefits delivered by the solution will only really be known once the solution has been implemented and is operational. But the expected benefits should be stated before the implementation starts. The solution's potential to achieve this can be assessed.

Frequently these benefits are stated in terms of the some or all of the following:

Figure 243 – Solution Potential Benefits

These claimed benefits are:

Benefits Group	Potential Benefit
Quantifiable Benefits	Improved Consumer Service
	Inventory and Work in Progress Reduction
	Staff Reduction
	Productivity Improvement
	Improved Resource Utilisation
	Reduction of Indirect Effort
	Reduced Work Processing Time
	Standardise and Provision Process
	Standardised and Integrated Information
	Improved Performance and Throughput
	Greater Automation

	Cost Reduction through Savings from Old Solutions
	Reduced Management and Administration Costs
	Reduced Quality Assurance Costs
	Reduction in Errors
	Reduction in Waste and Rework
	Increased Revenue and Margin
	Reduction in Solution Maintenance and Operating Costs
Indeterminate Benefits	Improved Cost Structure
	Greater Flexibility and Adaptability
	Process Standardisation
	Improved Management Decision Making Process
	Improved Information Visibility
	More Accurate Information
	Faster Access to Information
	Greater Potential to Use Create Forecasts and Projections
	Enhanced Staff Co-ordination and Co-Operation
	Improved Staff Morale
	Better Staff Career Development
	Increased Consumer Satisfaction
	Greater Integration between Data and Applications

There is overlap between some of these benefits. For example, *Staff Reduction*, *Productivity Improvement* and *Improved Resource Utilisation* are all related, though not identical. Benefits should not be counted twice.

In the same way that solution delivery failure can be classified as *less for more* to some extent (see section 3.1 on page 57), the net benefit of a solution should be determined by *more for less* – how much more will be done for how much less than at present, if the solution replaces one or more existing solutions rather than being completely new.

The solution should be walked through with the inventory of solution usage journeys or uses cases such as described in section 4.6.5.11 on page 272.

Defining the approach to benefits realisation assessment is outside the scope of this book. This topic is covered in greater detail elsewhere. It should be part of the organisation's overall solution delivery methodology.

4.11.2 Solution Design Review

The overall solution design should be the subject of a review to validate its suitability for the situation being addressed. The solution design may have evolved during the design process and may have strayed from its original intended use. A review ensures that design decisions are subject to justification and confirmation.

The ISO/IEC 25010 Quality Model[56] provides a good starting point for the structure of such as review. It can be used to create a structured checklist to assess that the solution is fit for purpose.

---

[56] See:
http://iso25000.com/index.php/en/iso-25000-standards/iso-25010

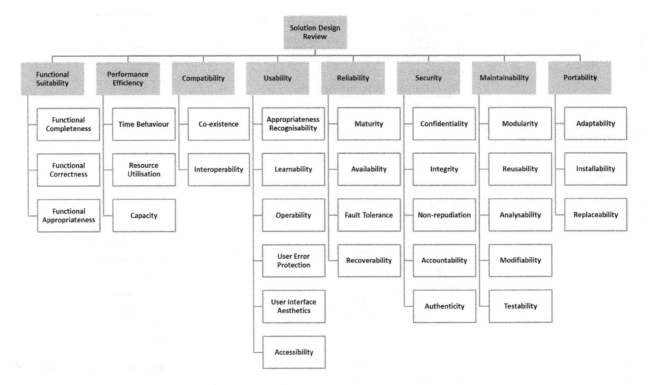

Figure 244 – ISO/IEC 25010 Quality Model

While ISO/IEC 25010 is aimed at evaluating the properties of an individual software product, it can be adapted for more general solution design review purposes where the solution consists of multiple components that must operate together.

Solution Quality Group	Solution Quality	Description
Functional Suitability	Functional Completeness	Does the set of functions provided by the solution components cover all the required tasks and user objectives?
	Functional Correctness	Does the solution generate the required and correct results and outputs with the needed degree of accuracy?
	Functional Appropriateness	By how much does the set of functions provided by the solution components functions enable the accomplishment of the specified tasks and objectives?
Performance Efficiency	Time Behaviour	Do the consumer response times and data processing times and transaction throughput rates of the solution components meet the desired and required objectives for given volumes of workload?
	Resource Utilisation	Do the solution components use the expected and only the expected amounts and types of resources across the various resource types such as processing capacity, data storage, I/O capacity and network communications capacity?
	Capacity	Can the maximum limits of a product in terms of items such as workload throughput, volumes of data, numbers of transactions and data transfers that can be handled by the solution meet the target requirements?
Compatibility	Co-existence	If required, can the solution operate and be used and perform its required functions efficiently while sharing a common environment and set of resources with other solutions or their components without any negative impact on any of the solutions' components?
	Interoperability	Can the solution handle the required data exchanges, transfers and integrations with other components and other solutions with the required accuracy, quality, throughput and timeliness?

Usability	Appropriateness Recognisability	Can solution consumers recognise and understand whether a solution component is appropriate and suitable for their needs?
	Learnability	How easily, quickly and reliably can solution consumers learn how to use the solution components effectively, efficiently, without errors and satisfactorily to perform their work?
	Operability	Do the design characteristics and attributes of the solution components make them easy to operate and control?
	User Error Protection	Do the solution components protect solution consumers against making errors and against the consequences of those errors?
	User Interface Aesthetics	Are the solution consumer interfaces of those user-facing components attractive and satisfying interaction for the user?
	Accessibility	Can the solution be used by consumers with the widest range of characteristics and capabilities to achieve the target solution objectives?
Reliability	Maturity	Do the solution components comply with the reliability targets under standard operation and use?
	Availability	Are the solution components operational, accessible and available for when needed?
	Fault Tolerance	To what extent can the solution and its components continue to operate as intended despite the presence of hardware or software failures?
	Recoverability	In the event of an interruption, error or a failure, in what way and how quickly can the data directly affected be recovered and how quickly will the solution be operational and available?
Security	Confidentiality	Does the solution ensure that its functions and data are accessible only to those authorised and how granular is the access control?
	Integrity	Does the solution prevent unauthorised access to or modification of solution components or their data?
	Non-repudiation	Does the solution ensure that actions or events can be proven to have occurred in order to prevent their subsequent repudiation?
	Accountability	Can the solution trace the actions of a consumer or entity can be traced uniquely to that consumer or entity?
	Authenticity	Can the solution ensure that the identity claimed by a consumer, entity or resource can be proved to be the one asserted?
Maintainability	Modularity	To what extent is the solution composed of separate and distinct components so that change made to one component has little or no impact on the other components?
	Reusability	To what extent can elements or services contained in one solution component can be reused in other systems?
	Analysability	How easily can the impact of potential changes made to one solution component on other solution components be identified and analysed? How easily can problems or failures with the operation of solution components be identified?
	Modifiability	How easily can solution components be modified without introducing defects or degrading existing solution components quality?
	Testability	How easily can solution component test cases and factors be defined and how easily can those tests be performed to determine whether the expected test results and outcomes have been met?
Portability	Adaptability	How easily can the solution components be adapted to accommodate different infrastructural, operational or usage environments?
	Installability	How easily can the solution be successfully installed and/or uninstalled in its various operating environments?

	Replaceability	How easily can solution components be replaced with outer functionality equivalent components in the same environment?

Table 75 – ISO/IEC 25010 Quality Model Applied to Solution Design Reviews

4.11.3 Solution Architectural Review

The solution architectural review should determine the goodness of fit of the solution design to the organisations architecture principles and standards across the architecture domains described in 3.3 on page 75.

- *Enterprise Architecture* – is the solution compliant with the organisation's information technology standards, policies, principles and direction within which the organisation's IT systems are sourced, implemented and operates?

- *Information and Data Architecture* – is the solution compliant with the organisation's standards for the management of data and data-related technologies across the organisation across data types and sources including data management and governance, data quality, data operations and reference and master data management and through its lifecycle?

- *Application Architecture* – is the solution compliant with organisation's approach to information technology applications, their integrations, interactions and data exchanges between applications and the flow of data into and out of applications?

- *Technology Infrastructure Architecture* – is the solution compliant with the organisation information technology infrastructure across the computing, storage and communications landscape, internal and external, including mobile?

- *Service Architecture* – is the solution compliant with the organisation's service management and service operations framework for the operational information technology applications and infrastructure including support, new releases and changes, capacity and performance, events and alerts, service levels, continuity, resilience and availability?

- *Security Architecture* – is the solution compliant with organisation's information technology security standards including hardware, software and data assets from attacks, threats and vulnerabilities that can lead to theft, damage and disruption, both from within and from outside the organisation?

4.11.4 Solution Implementability Review

The implementability of a solution is affected by a number of factors:

1. Is the solution intrinsically capable of being implemented?

2. Is the proposed solution implementation team capable of implementing it?

3. Is the organisation willing to allow it being implemented fully?

The last two of these factors is outside the control of the solution architect. The architect can seek to influence the composition of the solution implementation team to maximise its ability to implement the solution. This can be difficult when the team largely consists of external suppliers and outsourced service providers.

The organisation may look to partially implement the solution, omitting components because of cost, time and resource pressures. As mentioned in section 2.4 on page 33, this descoping removes functionality that is needed for the solution to work fully. The implementation of these components is deferred to (a sometimes non-specific or even non-existent) future stage. The result is a partially completed solution with manual workarounds and with a backlog of rework. Again the solution architect can seek to influence the approach to solution delivery and can work to minimise the impact of such decisions.

The level 3 and 4 solution component breakdown referred to in section 2.4 on page 33 can be used as a checklist to validate that the solution is capable of being implemented.

4.12 Solution Architecture and Estimation

In the context of solution architecture, the topic of estimation arises in two main areas:

1. Estimating the effort required to perform the pure solution architecture business engagement exercises listed in section 4.6 on page 161 and in generating solution designs using the solution design process listed in section 4.6.2 on page 226

2. Assisting with the creation of estimates for the delivery of the designed solution – this can be further divided into two activities

   a) Creating the initial solution delivery estimate using the solution component breakdown created in the solution design

   b) Modifying the initial solution delivery estimate based on an assessment of the solution's complexity

The solution architect must develop a capability in creating accurate and realistic estimates for pure solution design work and in assisting with producing estimates for the wider solution delivery project.

An estimate consists of five core components:

1. Effort to perform the work
2. Elapsed time to perform the work
3. Resources required to perform the work
4. Cost to perform the work derived from resource costs and acquired component costs
5. Schedule of the work based on dependencies between other work elements and availability of resources

In the first of these areas, the estimate can be produced by using the work programme activities and tasks as a work breakdown structure that can be used as a basis to assess the effort. The accuracy of these estimates will improve through experience. They can be validated by reference to previous similar engagements.

The effort to perform a solution design engagement will differ for each organisation, based on factors such as:

- The complexity of the organisation structure and ease or otherwise of performing solution design work
- Level of review and approval that must take place of any work done and solution designs created
- The availability of business resources to participate in the design process
- The structure of the IT function and the number of groups that must be consulted as part of the design process
- The IT architectural standards that must be complied with

The duration and therefore the effort to perform an engagement can be limited in advance in order to guarantee delivery within a defined and agreed interval.

You will know the constraints of you organisation and the impact these have on performing work and creating design deliverable results.

In the second of these estimation areas, the solution architect is just one of many roles that will be involved in creating solution delivery estimates. The individual solution component estimates will be the responsibility of those teams who will be responsible for performing the work. Based on the solution design work, the solution architect should know the scope of the required delivery work and the dependencies that exist between them.

The solution component type breakdown described in section 2.4.2 on page 33 can be used as the basis for a solution scope breakdown (as well as a delivery plan) that is turn can be used to create a structure for solution delivery estimates. This component breakdown is just one example of a work breakdown structure. It is not necessarily the only one. The following table contains a sample breakdown of the components of a solution based on this component type classification.

Solution Component Type	Solution Component
Changes to Existing Systems	Existing System 1 Change
	Existing System 2 Change
New Custom Developed Applications	New Custom Component 1
	New Custom Component 2
	New Custom Component 3
Information Storage Facilities	Information Storage Component 1
	Information Storage Component 2
Acquired and Customised Software Products	Acquired Product 1
	Acquired Product 2
	Acquired Product 3
System Integrations/ Data Transfers/ Exchanges	Integration/Exchange/Transfer 1
	Integration/Exchange/Transfer 2
	Integration/Exchange/Transfer 3
	Integration/Exchange/Transfer 4
Changes to Existing Business Processes	Existing Changed Business Process 1
	Existing Changed Business Process 2
	Existing Changed Business Process 3
New Business Processes	New Business Process 1
	New Business Process 2
Organisational Changes	Organisational Change 1
	Organisational Change 2
Reporting and Analysis Facilities	Reporting Facility 1
	Reporting Facility 2
	Reporting Facility 3
Existing Data Conversions/ Migrations	Data Migration 1
	Data Migration 1
New Data Loads	Data Load 1
	Data Load 2
Training and Documentation	Training Material 1
	Training Material 2
	Documentation 1
	Documentation 2
Central, Distributed and Communications Infrastructure	IT Infrastructure 1
	IT Infrastructure 2
	IT Infrastructure 3
Sets of Installation and Implementation Services	Installation Service 1
	Installation Service 2
	Integration Testing
	System Testing
	User Acceptance Testing
Cutover/ Transfer to Production And Support	Cutover
	Organisation Readiness
Operational Functions and Processes	Operational Process 1
	Operational Process 2
	Operations Acceptance Testing
Parallel Runs	Parallel Run 1
	Parallel Run 2
Enhanced Support/ Hypercare	Hypercare

Solution Component Type	Solution Component
Sets of Maintenance, Service Management and Support Services	Maintenance and Support Service 1
	Maintenance and Support Service 2
	Alerting and Event Management
Application Hosting and Management Services	Hosting/Management Service 1
	Hosting/Management Service 2

Table 76 – Sample Solution Component Type List

These individual components will be delivered at different stages of the project. The solution architect can assist in identifying dependencies between the solution components.

Figure 245 – Sample Solution Components and Their Delivery Scheduling

Each of the components to be delivered as part of the overall solution will require individual implementation and testing. The estimation breakdown structure can broken-down into further levels of details, depending on the accuracy required of the estimates.

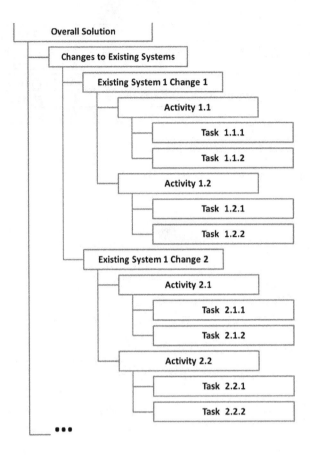

Figure 246 – Granular Solution Delivery Estimate Structure

Using the solution component type structure provides a basis for accurate and traceable estimates. They can be initially produced at a high-level and refined subsequently to greater levels of granularity.

The solution complexity assessment approach described in section 4.2.2 on page 100 can then be used to determine what uplift, if any, should be applied to the initial delivery estimates.

Chapter 5. Solution Architecture and Digital Transformation

5.1 Introduction

As with other topics, a detailed description of digital strategy and transformation is not within the scope of this book. However, the move by organisations to implement digital solutions affects the role of the solution architect in a number of ways:

- It will require the design of solutions of a potentially different type to more conventional solutions

- Digital solutions must operate in a different operational solution framework requiring different design standards and approaches

- More components of digital solutions are more likely to consist of XaaS-deployed applications and services, imposing greater application and data integration requirements and the need for greater solution acquisition due diligence

- The volume and type of data being used and generated by digital solutions in greater than more conventional ones, requiring greater attention to the data architecture aspects of solution design

- Components of digital solutions are more likely to be used by external solution consumers over multiple different access channels and devices requiring greater attention to solution usability and the underlying business processes

- External solution component access imposes greater solution security requirements

- Digital solutions are more likely to process personal data requiring greater attention to data privacy in solution design

This material provides a context for digital solutions the solution architect must design.

The solution architect must be aware of and be able to respond proactively and positively to this digital trend. The solution architect must be aware of its implications and consequences. The architect must be able to add value to and be proactive in the design of the digital solution framework, digital initiatives and to get involved earlier rather than just responding to requests.

However, the terms *digital strategy*, *digital transformation* and *digital solutions* have no consistent definition. They are catch-all terms that have very different meanings to different people. The terms are used with no agreement on their substance, content and purpose.

Figure 247 – Digital Buzzword Bingo

At its most basic, digitalisation involves the conversion of information and process that are currently in a non-digital format into digital form. This is effectively *computerising* what is currently manual, introducing technology-lead change into the organisation, its processes and the way it operates and interacts with external parties.

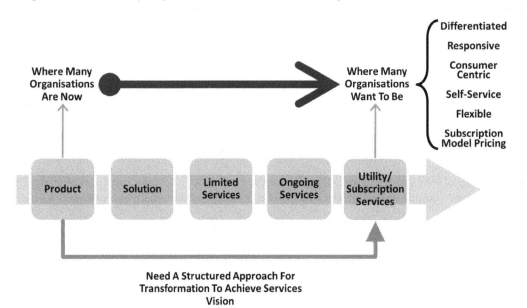

Figure 248 – Organisation Transformation Journey

Frequently digital strategy is used to mean organisation transformation. This involve designing and implementing new organisation structures, processes and supporting and enabling solutions and technologies in order to change the way the organisation operates and interacts with its consumers, suppliers and partners over digital channels. Organisations want to move from just being providers of products to the providers of utility and subscription services. The desired characteristics of the new operating model include differentiated set of services, responsive to the needs of consumers, consumer-centric, greater consumer self-service, flexible operations and subscription model pricing.

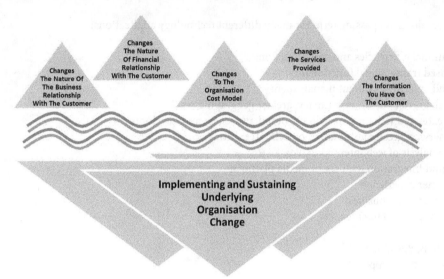

Figure 249 – Digital Transformation Iceberg

Achieving this digital transformation requires a set of changes underpinned and enabled by solutions contained in the digital reference architecture described below. The changes include:

- Changes The Nature Of The Business Relationship With The Customer

- Changes The Nature Of Financial Relationship With The Customer

- Changes To The Organisation Cost Model

- Changes The Services Provided

- Changes The Information You Have On The Customer

Digital strategy is the application of digital technologies – such as the handling and processing large volumes of data, data analysis, and mobile technologies - to the organisation to create new business capabilities. A digital strategy aims to maximise the value and benefits the business derives from its data assets through technology.

So the digital strategy is a statement about the organisation's digital positioning, competitors and customers and collaborators needs and behaviour to achieve a direction for innovation, communication, transaction and promotion.

Digital transformation is concerned with adopting these new technologies and their application. In particular it means extending and exposing business processes to specific parties over specific channels outside the organisation along the dimensions of:

- *External Parties Participating in Digital Interaction/Collaboration* – who of the many parties in your organisation landscape do you interact with digitally

- *Numbers and Types of Interactions/ Collaborations and Business Processes Included in Digital Strategy* – which types of interactions and associated business processes do you digitally implement

- *Channels Included in Digital Strategy* – what digital channels do you interact over

A key aspect of implementing a digital strategy is the extension of internal processes to specific parties over specific channels outside the organisation. This can involve allowing external parties – customers, partners, and suppliers – interact directly with the organisation using, for example, mobile devices.

Digital has become an all-encompassing term for many different technology applications:

- Enabling operational efficiencies and cost reductions
- Greater web-based transactional functionality
- Multi-media and enterprise content management
- Customer portal, greater customer intimacy, greater geographic reach
- Enhanced and extended web presence, digital brand awareness and development
- Customer self-service, greater automation of web interactions
- Collection and analysis of web interaction data
- Greater use of and integration with social media platforms
- Improved customer experience
- Direct sales, ecommerce, ebusiness
- Machine learning/artificial intelligence
- Data analytics
- Mobile selling, B2B, B2C, M2M
- Migration to cloud-based applications
- Multi-channel information access
- Greater enablement of non-PC web access such as mobile technologies

Each person's view of what digital strategy, architecture and transformation means will emphasise a subset of these. It is similar to the parable of the wise men feeling in the dark and identifying an elephant differently based on the just one part of the animal.

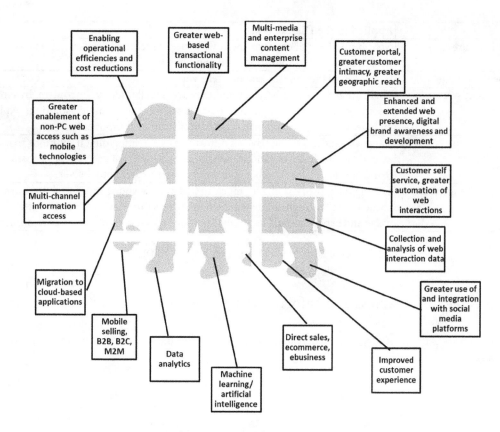

Figure 250 – The Digital Elephant in the Room

So digital is not so much one or more technologies or one of more applications of those technologies in specific areas.

Digital needs to be a platform to allow digital solutions to be designed, implemented and operated. This requires a digital strategy, a digital architecture and a digital operating framework.

The effective use of information technology and an effective information technology function are fundamental to successful digital transformation. This is one area where solution architecture can contribute to the success of digital initiatives.

The fallacies of distributed computing are assumptions made by developers of distributed applications that were identified by Peter Deutsch when working at Sun Microsystems.

The fallacies are assumptions that are false, the consequences of making them include some or all of system failure, increased costs, project delays, reduction in scope or substantial redesign and rework.

These fallacies apply equally to digital initiatives. The solution architect, when involved in designing digital solutions should bear these in mind.

Fallacy	Applied to the Digital World
1.The network is reliable	The external network is outside your control. It is inherently unreliable. It has uncertain performance. Design the solution to identify and handle problems and errors.
2.Latency is zero	Latency is pervasive across network, applications and business processes. Assumptions of zero latency will, at best, lead to failure to meet expectations. Communicate details on processing times to create realistic expectations. Communicate delays.
3.Bandwidth is infinite	Assumptions about bandwidth lead to network-intensive applications that lead to poor and erratic performance. Understand the network traffic the solution gives rise to and the likely impact this will have across the network.

Fallacy	Applied to the Digital World
4.The network is secure	No it is not. Lack of concern about widespread security threats will leads to weaknesses across applications, data and business processes.
5.Topology doesn't change	It changes all the time and no one tells you.
6.There is one administrator	There are many administrators and they are not all under your control. In some cases no one is in control. Ensure that the architecture of digital solutions explicitly includes support, management and administration components.
7.Transport cost is zero	Network bandwidth can have significant costs. Creating digital solutions that are extended outside the organisation will have a significant cost. Create a cost model that identifies all cost and benefits that they are expected to deliver.
8.The network is homogeneous	The digital network is mixed, much of it is outside your control and there are many bottlenecks. The digital consumer population is mixed with different patterns of usage and expectations. Design the solutions to handle this mixed environment.

Table 77 – Fallacies of Distributed Computing Applied to Digital Solutions

5.2 Digital Strategy in Business and Information Technology Context

The organisation context of digital strategy and digital architecture in terms of the solution architecture context described in section 4.1 on page 91 is:

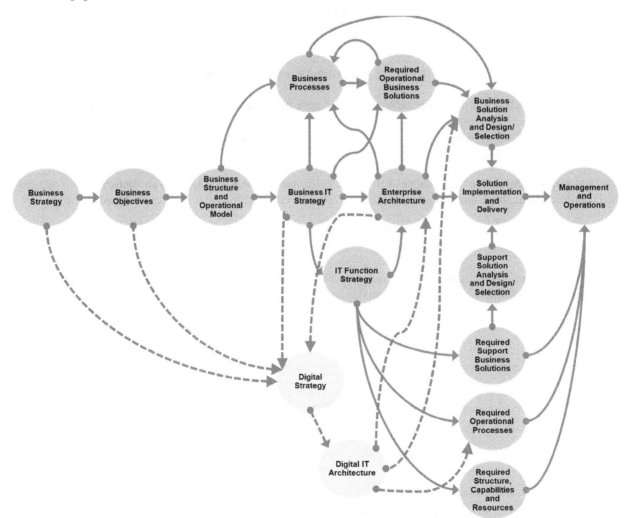

Figure 251 – Organisation Context of Digital Strategy and Digital Architecture

An organisation digital strategy exists in a wider organisation and IT context:

- The organisation will have an overall IT strategy to accomplish the organisation strategy and associated objectives
- The IT function will then need its own internal IT strategy that will structure the function in order to ensure that it can deliver on the wider organisation strategy
- The enterprise digital strategy is connected to the overall IT strategy, the enterprise architecture and the internal IT strategy
- The enterprise digital strategy will be implemented and operated through a digital architecture that is part of the overall enterprise architecture
- This context is important in ensuring that the enterprise digital strategy fits into the overall IT and wider organisational structure
- The enterprise digital strategy exists to ultimately deliver a business benefit and contribute to the achievement of the business strategy
- The strategy must be translated into an operational framework to enable the strategy to be actualised

Like all major organisation transformation programmes, implementing digital initiatives and associated solution will involve changes to the organisation:

- Cross-functional and business process changes
- Technology delivery changes

The domains of change model described throughout this book can be used to identify organisational change impacts.

The organisation must be ready for digital in three ways:

1. Be able to deliver digital initiatives that comprise and achieve the digital strategy
2. Be able to change itself to enable the implementation and operation of digital initiatives
3. Be able to operate digital initiatives

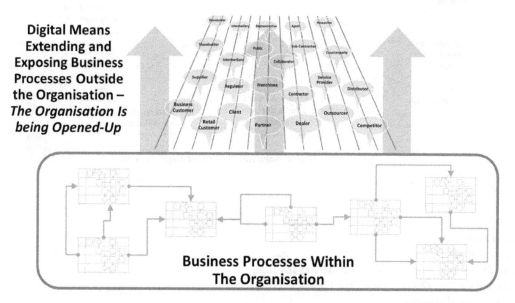

Figure 252 – Digital Strategy And Business Processes – Extending The Organisation's Boundaries

This extension of solutions and their associated business processes outside the organisation means the organisation should implement a digital architecture to allow this to take place easily, quickly, consistently and securely. The importance of business processes to solution design is discussed in section 4.4.2 on page 134.

This extension of solutions exposes the organisation to risks. When you deploy solution outside the organisation, this results in a reduction in the expected and tolerated latency and the asynchronicity of communications between the organisation and external parties. Put simply, this population of external solution consumers expect an always-on and immediate service.

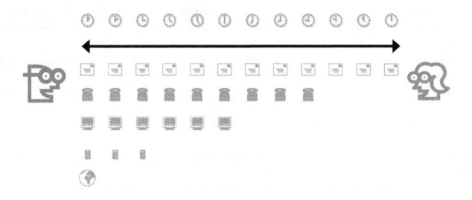

Figure 253 – User Expectations of Response With Digital Platforms

It also leads to a range of expectations from these solution consumers:

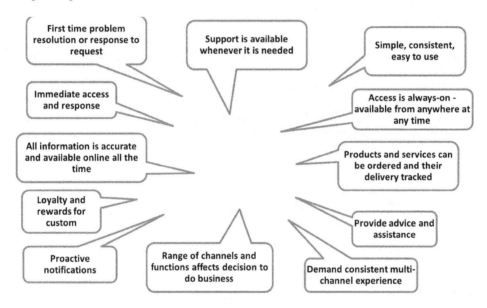

Figure 254 – Digital Solution Consumer Expectations

This list of digital consumer expectations is:

- First time problem resolution or response to request
- Support is available whenever it is needed
- Simple, consistent, easy to use
- Access is always-on - available from anywhere at any time
- Products and services can be ordered and their delivery tracked
- Provide advice and assistance
- Demand consistent multi-channel experience
- Range of channels and functions affects decision to do business
- Proactive notifications
- Loyalty and rewards for custom
- All information is accurate and available online all the time
- Immediate access and response

This affects the way solutions are designed. The solution architect needs to mediate these expectations between solution stakeholders:

- Communicate that the expectations exist and that the solution design needs to incorporate them
- Articulate the impact on solution design of meeting these expectations
- Identify the additional solution components needed to deliver on the expectations

5.3 Digital Target Architecture

In order to design, implement and operate digital solutions, the organisation and its IT architecture functions needs to develop a digital target architecture. This section describes the digital platform that must exist (in some form) to enable the organisation to achieve its digital strategy.

The digital platform represents the framework that the solution architecture must be able to use to design (integrated) digital solutions. These are common building blocks that ensure that digital solution can be deployed and can operate securely and consistently. This allows for reuse of these common components, allowing the focus to be shifted from the solution delivering infrastructural components to concentrating on the functional essence of the solution. This is similar to the data landscape and its constituent components described in section 4.8 on page 321.

Individual digital point solutions represent a waste of resources in their design, implementation and operation.

The complexity of the information technology landscape will increase with the deployment of digital solutions. Unmanaged complexity must be avoided. This leads to greater cost and less flexibility. Some of the issues that can arise include lack of standards, redundant applications, multiple platforms, and inconsistent data. The complexity hinders the organisation's ability to respond to business and economic changes and other external factors. This in turn defeats the reason for implementing a digital strategy in the first place. IT architecture need to define and implement the necessary digital plumbing and infrastructure to allow digital solutions to be provisioned simply, quickly and at low cost.

Solution architecture should not passively accept this digital enablement platform. It needs to contribute to its design and implementation to ensure that solutions designed to operate within it are implementable, operable, supportable and usable. This will make sure that the resulting platform provides a suitable framework for designing solutions and for running those solutions when implemented.

The objectives of this digital target reference architecture are:

- Consistent, personalised and rich user experience across all channels
- Reliable and resilience operation
- Ease of support, management and administration
- Integration of data and services from multiple sources
- Ease of development and deployment of new services
- Ease of change
- Ease of replacement of components
- Collection of usage information for analysis

This provides for:

- Federated operation with support of multiple services
- Standard approach for solution deployment and operation
- Ability to unify services for delivery
- Standard approach to integration
- Management and administration tools
- Data and analytics tools

This digital target reference architecture defines a solution template for the underlying and enabling technology solutions and components required. It defines the target end-state architecture and the set of interim transitional phases required to enable the delivery of a digital strategy and associated roadmap. It needs to reside within the context of the organisation's Enterprise Architecture and other related architectures.

The digital target reference architecture will not exist in isolation. The organisation will have a suite of legacy applications that will need to continue to be operated and may need to the digitally enabled using tools provided by the integration component in the digital target reference architecture.

The level 1 components of this digital platform can include some or all the following groups of components:

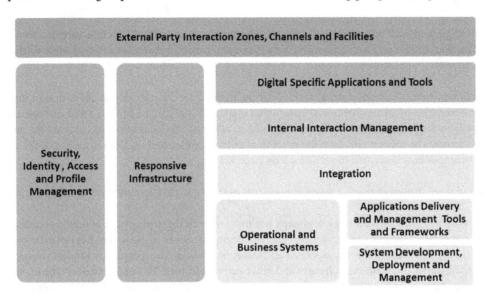

Figure 255 – Digital Platform Level 1 Component Groups

These level 1 component groups are:

- *External Party Interaction Zones, Channels and Facilities* – the set of facilities and applications that are presented to those external parties being interacted with and the channels used – this is the window to the set of products and services offered by the organisation and to the business processes

- *Security, Identity, Access and Profile Management* – internal and external security tools and processes

- *Responsive Infrastructure* – digital application deployment and operating infrastructure

- *Digital Specific Applications and Tools* – the portfolio of specific tools acquired to deliver and operate digital functions

- *Internal Interaction Management* – the set of internal applications that are used to manage external party interactions

- *Integration* – the data, service and process integration layer and associated APIs, including integration catalogue

- *Applications Delivery and Management Tools and Frameworks* – set of tools used to deliver and manage digital applications

- *System Development, Deployment and Management* – the digital application development facility within the organisation

- *Operational and Business Systems* – the existing and new organisation operational and business systems

This is a generalised and indicative view of a digital platform that will enable an organisation design, develop, deploy and operate a range of digital solutions. This can be adapted to the specific needs of the organisation. It can be used to validate that the organisation has the necessary technology facilities in place to facilitate the implementation of a digital strategy. It will allow gaps to be identified and for decisions to be made on exactly what will be implemented.

Many companies have already achieved the status of a platform organisation. Their entire business model is defined around a (logical) information technology platform through which all their products are services are accessed and supplied.

Many other traditional organisations are seeking to transform themselves into platform companies. A banking and financial services organisation becomes a banking platform through which all their financial service-related products and services are delivered. Telecommunications companies are similarly looking to transform themselves into platform companies where there offer an integrated range of services implemented by their telecommunications infrastructure and accessed through a digital platform.

The digital target architecture described above represents an integrated IT platform for the delivery of the organisation's products and services through digital channels. The platform becomes the means for managing interactions between external parties and the organisation. The platform is the logical representation of the organisation as an integrated set of business processes and associated and supporting IT business systems. The platform virtualises legacy applications and business processes. The platform becomes the means to deploy new solutions and to make available new services. The platform is the windows into the organisation.

This digital platform defines the target end-state architecture and the set of interim transitional phases required to enable the delivery of the digital strategy and associated roadmap.

The digital platform defines the overall IT architecture. Solutions must be delivered within this context. Solution architecture must design solutions to fit within this framework. While not all of these framework components need to be in place to implement digital solutions, the framework enables these solutions to be designed and deployed in an integrated manner.

This digital platform is more than a reference architecture. It represents a set of individual infrastructural solutions that must be designed and implemented in order to allow subsequent business solutions to be designed and deployed. It represents the logical (and physical) framework within which solutions must be designed to operate. The platform represents both a set of constraints and a set of standards for solution design.

The reality of the "platform" may be very different from its representation. The platform can (and will be) a mix of existing and new applications. The platform is virtualised view of the digital architecture and the associated digital strategy.

The platform needs to demonstrate the characteristics of:

- Delivering excellent and consistent user experiences
- Reliable, available and delivering appropriate performance, scalability, elasticity
- Secure and trustworthy
- Integrated analytics with processes to ensure continuous improvement
- Integrated solution development and deployment

Across all the component groups, this entire logical platform view consists of a large number of individual components. In this model, there are 82 such logical parts of the platform. These are shown below. There could be more as, for example, the existing set of business systems is represented by groups of application types. Not all organisations will need to implement all components. The decision on what to implement and when to implement it is the role of the digital strategy. From a solution architecture perspective there are two areas of concern:

1. These represent a large number of individual solutions or solution capabilities that must be designed. This represents a considerable workload.

2. The individual solutions must work together closely to create the form of a logical platform. This requires both co-ordination and standards across solution design activities as well as the implementation of infrastructural or plumbing or enabling solutions on which others can be constructed more easily and more quickly.

The actualisation of such a platform requires significant solution design and delivery leadership and capability.

Web Pages and Web Forms	Web Browsers	Mobile Channels	Product and Service Catalogue	Web Chat	Search	Applications
Web Content Management	Call Centre	Preferences	Payments and Transactions	Social Networks	SMS	Data Access and Presentation

User Directory
- Authentication
- Logging
- Single Signon
- Personalisation
- Monitoring
- Access Control
- Identity and Access Management
- Certificate Management

- Resilient and Scalable Firewalls
- Resilient and Scalable Application Servers
- Resilient and Scalable Load Balancers
- Resilient and Scalable Data Storage
- Resilient and Scalable Traffic Management
- Data Security and Encryption
- Resilient and Scalable Web Servers
- Usage and Performance Monitoring

- Web Content Management System
- Multi-Channel Analytics
- Data Collection, Storage and Management
- Product and Service Catalogue Management
- Content Authoring
- Rules Engine/Next Best Action
- Document Management
- Payment Gateway and Merchant Services
- Business Process Management
- Case Management
- Resource Management
- Sales and Marketing
- Customer Relationship Management
- Service Management
- Product Management

- Service Co-ordination and Orchestration
- ETL Services
- Data Management
- Managed File Transfer
- Data Sharing
- Application Integration Services
- Integration Development and Deployment
- Monitoring and Management
- Message Based Data Exchange

- Billing and Assurance
- Partner Relationship Management
- Fulfilment Management
- Legal, Regulatory, Environment, Health and Safety Management
- Customer Information and Relationship Management
- Human Resource Management
- Finance Management
- Facilities Management
- Analytics Facilities

- IT Leadership and Governance
- Programme and Project Management
- Business Process Management
- Capacity Planning, Forecasting, Demand and Supply Management
- Infrastructure, Networks and Communications
- Strategic and Business Planning
- Sourcing and Selection Management
- Benefits Assessment and Realisation
- Organisation Design, Planning and Management
- Security, Continuity and Disaster Recovery
- Solution Architecture and Design
- User Experience Design
- Solution Development and Delivery
- Testing
- Business and Process Analysis and Design
- Service Provisioning, Service Delivery and Service Management
- Change and Change Management
- Data, Information, Knowledge Asset Management

Figure 256 – Digital Platform Component Groups Constituent Items

These groups are not precise. Some of the components represent processes or organisational structures or capabilities rather than technology.

The individual components and their constituent elements represent an integrated whole that must operate together. The linkages between the components will be:

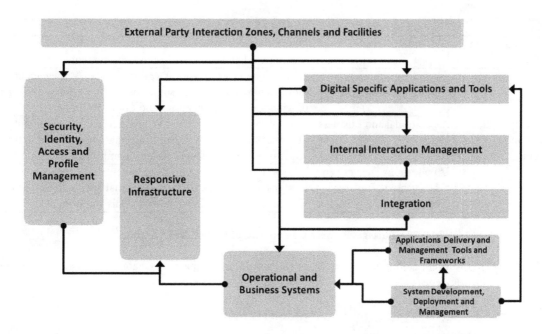

Figure 257 – Linkages Between Components of Digital Target Architecture

These linkages are listed in the table below.

From Component	To Component	Linkage
External Party Interaction Zones, Channels and Facilities	Operational and Business Systems	The External Party Interaction Zones, Channels and Facilities component acts as a front-end too the suite of Operational and Business Systems.
	Security, Identity, Access and Profile Management	The External Party Interaction Zones, Channels and Facilities component uses a common Security, Identity, Access and Profile Management component to authenticate users and access to resources.
	Responsive Infrastructure	The External Party Interaction Zones, Channels and Facilities component uses and relies on a Responsive Infrastructure to deliver good consistent user experience.
	Digital Specific Applications and Tools	The External Party Interaction Zones, Channels and Facilities component uses elements of the Digital Specific Applications and Tools component such as analytics and content management to customise the experience.
	Internal Interaction Management	The External Party Interaction Zones, Channels and Facilities component directs work to the tools contained within the Internal Interaction Management component.
Security, Identity, Access and Profile Management	Responsive Infrastructure	The Security, Identity, Access and Profile Management uses and relies on a Responsive Infrastructure to deliver good consistent performance.
Digital Specific Applications and Tools	Operational and Business Systems	The Digital Specific Applications and Tools component links to the Operational and Business Systems.
Internal Interaction Management	Operational and Business Systems	The Internal Interaction Management component links to the Operational and Business Systems.
Integration	Operational and Business Systems	The Integration component links other applications to the suite of Operational and Business Systems.
Operational and Business Systems	Responsive Infrastructure	The suite of Operational and Business Systems relies on a Responsive Infrastructure to deliver good consistent performance, response time and throughput.
Applications Delivery and	Operational and Business	The Applications Delivery and Management Tools and

From Component	To Component	Linkage
Management Tools and Frameworks	Systems	Frameworks deploys new and updated solutions to the Operational and Business Systems component.
System Development, Deployment and Management	Digital Specific Applications and Tools	The System Development, Deployment and Management designs new and updated solutions that are deployed to the Digital Specific Applications and Tools component.
	Operational and Business Systems	The System Development, Deployment and Management designs new and updated solutions that are deployed to the Operational and Business Systems component.
	Applications Delivery and Management Tools and Frameworks	The System Development, Deployment and Management designs new and updated solutions that are deployed to the Digital Specific Applications and Tools component.

Table 78 – Linkages Between Components of Digital Target Architecture

The level 2 elements of the level 1 component group External Party Interaction Zones, Channels and Facilities can include some or all of the following items:

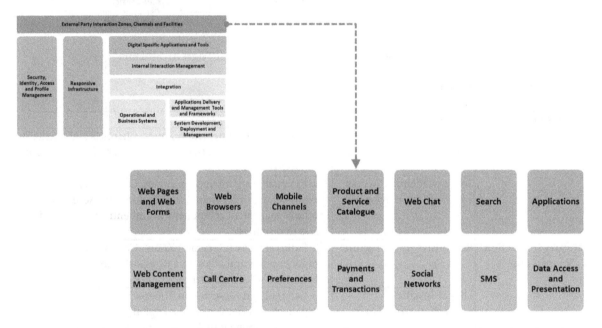

Figure 258 – Level 2 Elements of Level 1 Component Group External Party Interaction Zones, Channels and Facilities

These level 2 elements of External Party Interaction Zones, Channels and Facilities are:

Level 2 Element	Description
Web Pages and Web Forms	This allows the display of web pages using consistent appearance and navigation standards in the web site structure. Web forms allow the capture and validation of information and its onward transmission to the organisation.
Web Content Management	This allows for web content of different types to be created and managed. Content is created once and published to all channels. Content creation can be devolved to multiple content authors. Content is separated from its format. Content can go through an approval workflow prior to its publication. Content can be embargoed until a publication date and time. Content can be flagged for review. Content can have an expiry date. Content is manged using the element Web Content Management in the System Digital Specific Applications and Tools component group and accessed here.

Level 2 Element	Description
Web Browsers	The external interaction zones can be accessed from any supported browser across any device. The content will be formatted and presented for each browser.
Call Centre	There may be a call centre that service consumers contact. The call centre will have access to CRM systems to access consumer details, log calls and interact with consumers.
Mobile Channels	Consumers can interact and access the same content and facilities using mobile devices.
Preferences	Consumer preferences will be stored and used to customise and personalise the access and interaction experience. Consumers can view and update their preferences at any time.
Product and Service Catalogue	There can be a catalogue of products and services consumers can browse and select items from. The catalogue can contain details on items including summary and detailed information, pictures and specification information. Items can have review and expiry dates. The content of the catalogue can be maintained. Packages of offers can be created and priced accordingly. Cross-selling and up-selling rules can be defined. Taxation and delivery cost calculations can be created and maintained. Multiple currencies can be supported.
Payments and Transactions	Payments can be accepted using a variety of cards and other payment types such as vouchers. Multiple merchant acquirers and accounts can be supported. Cards may be able to be stored for recurring and repeat orders. Order history can be stored and viewed by consumers. Customer accounts can be maintained.
Web Chat	This allows consumers select the option to interact with agents over web chat.
Social Networks	This provides interfaces to various social media platforms to allow consumer interactions to be handled and managed and to publish content.
Search	This provides a facility to search all content across all data stores.
SMS	This provides a facility to allow information to be pushed over text messages and for responses to be handled and managed.
Applications	This provides a facility to deploy consumer interaction applications that are more complex than simple web pages and forms. These applications can be deployed to mobile devices as well as being access from standard browsers.
Data Access and Presentation	This enables access to consumer data held in internal data stores and databases to be accessed and presented in a secure manner.

Table 79 – Level 2 Elements of Level 1 Component Group External Party Interaction Zones, Channels and Facilities

The level 2 elements of the level 1 component group Security, Identity, Access and Profile Management will be:

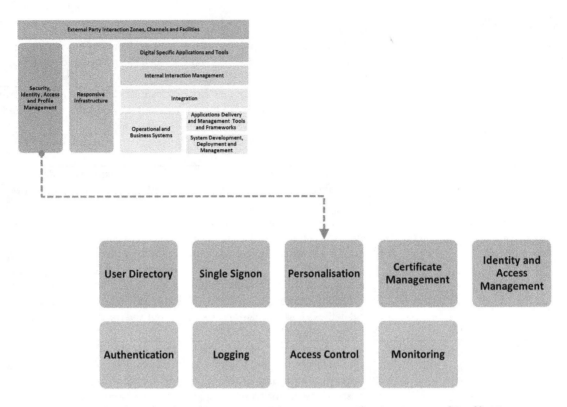

Figure 259 – Level 2 Elements of Level 1 Component Group Security, Identity, Access and Profile Management

These level 2 elements of Security, Identity, Access and Profile Management are:

Level 2 Element	Description
User Directory	This manages a directory of users and their information including access rights and access and usage history.
Authentication	This manages secure user authentication and session management across all channels and devices including multi-factor authentication.
Single Signon	This enables user to authenticate once and have their access rights handled across interactions for that session.
Logging	This logs user authentications and activities.
Personalisation	This enables the personalisation of the consumer experience using previously stored preferences managed by the Preferences element External Party Interaction Zones, Channels and Facilities component group and as well as access and usage history and previous transactions. It includes facilities to make recommendations and offer next best actions.
Access Control	This manages access rights using consumer credentials.
Certificate Management	This contains facilities for managing digital security certificates that are important for establishing trust and conforming to security protocols and includes facilities for certificate creation, issuing, storage, suspension and revocation.
Monitoring	This element allows real time monitoring of activity in order to detect and resolve problems including access breaches.
Identity and Access Management	This provides management facilities to ensure that the right people have the appropriate access to resources including the management of the assignment and removal of access rights.

Table 80 – Level 2 Elements of Level 1 Component Group Security, Identity, Access and Profile Management

The level 2 elements of the level 1 component group Digital Specific Applications and Tools will be:

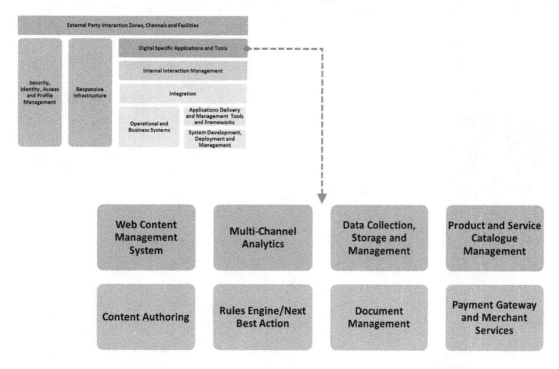

Figure 260 – Level 2 Elements of Level 1 Component Group Digital Specific Applications and Tools

These level 2 elements of Digital Specific Applications and Tools are:

Level 2 Element	Description
Web Content Management System	This is the internal part of the *Web Content Management* element of the *External Party Interaction Zones, Channels and Facilities* component group where content is created and managed before it is made available for presentation to consumers.
Content Authoring	This can provide facilities to create complex context such as multimedia and learning information.
Multi-Channel Analytics	This takes access and usage information from different channels and provides storage and analysis facilities to provide an integrated view across all channels and platforms.
Rules Engine/Next Best Action	The rules engine will allow rules to be created and deployed to manage consumer interactions including the *Product and Service Catalogue* element of the *External Party Interaction Zones, Channels and Facilities* component group. It can, for example, be used to create recommendations and generate next best action advice for consumers.
Data Collection, Storage and Management	This provides facilities to collect, store and manage the range of data associated with digital interactions.
Document Management	This provides services to store and manage documents that may be part of the overall set of digital content. Because of their size, metadata requirements and authoring process documents may be managed separately.
Product and Service Catalogue Management	This provides management facilities for the *Product and Service Catalogue* element of the *External Party Interaction Zones, Channels and Facilities* component group.
Payment Gateway and Merchant Services	This provides the account and merchant acquirer management facilities associated with the *Payments and Transactions* element of the *External Party Interaction Zones, Channels and Facilities* component group.

Table 81 – Level 2 Elements of Level 1 Component Group Digital Specific Applications and Tools

The level 2 elements of the level 1 component group Responsive Infrastructure will be:

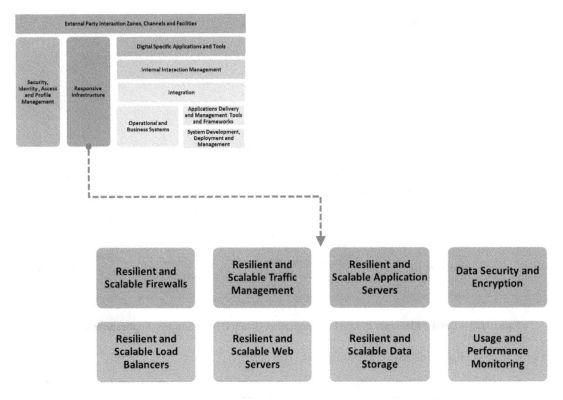

Figure 261 – Level 2 Elements of Level 1 Component Group Responsive Infrastructure

These level 2 elements of Responsive Infrastructure are:

Level 2 Element	Description
Resilient and Scalable Firewalls	This consists of appropriately resilient external and internal firewall infrastructure to handle the expected network load and to provide the necessary security.
Resilient and Scalable Load Balancers	This consists of appropriately resilient global and local network load balancer infrastructure to handle the expected network load and to provide the necessary security.
Resilient and Scalable Traffic Management	This consists of appropriately resilient network traffic management infrastructure to handle the expected network load and to provide the necessary security.
Resilient and Scalable Web Servers	This consists of appropriately resilient web server infrastructure for the set of web services deployed to handle the expected transaction load.
Resilient and Scalable Application Servers	This consists of appropriately resilient applications server infrastructure for the set of applications deployed to handle the expected transaction load.
Resilient and Scalable Data Storage	This consists of appropriately resilient data storage and access infrastructure to handle the expected data storage volumes and access capacity.
Data Security and Encryption	This provides facilities to secure access to data and to encrypt data at it moves throughout and the platform and when it is being stored.
Usage and Performance Monitoring	This allows monitoring of the level of usage of the infrastructure across all components to assess with capacity planning and management and

Level 2 Element	Description
	checking compliance with agreed service levels.

Table 82 – Level 2 Elements of Level 1 Component Group Responsive Infrastructure

The level 2 elements of the level 1 component group Internal Interaction Management will be:

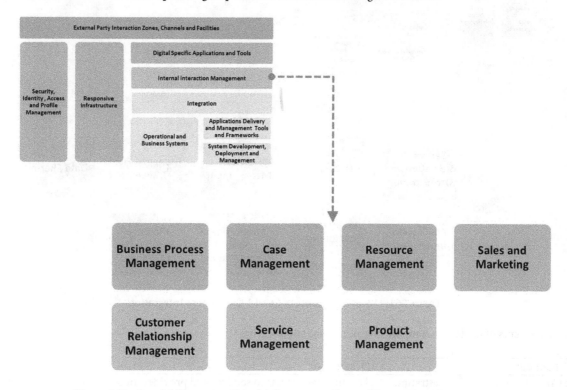

Figure 262 – Level 2 Elements of Level 1 Component Internal Interaction Management

These level 2 elements of Internal Interaction Management are:

Level 2 Element	Description
Business Process Management	This provides facilities to design, execute, document, measure, monitor and control both automated and non-automated business processes.
Customer Relationship Management	This provides facilities to manage customer data and their interaction with the organisation.
Case Management	This allows cases to be created and managed that arise from interactions with the organisation.
Service Management	This provides for the implementation and operation of the service management processes associated with supporting and maintaining the digital platform.
Resource Management	This provides facilities to manage resources and implement and operate the associated processes the resources are allocated across all elements of the digital platform.
Product Management	This provides facilities to manage the product and service lifecycle and to manage the creation of new products and services.
Sales and Marketing	This allows the organisation sales and marketing function interact with the digital platform and generate and manage sales and marketing campaigns.

Table 83 – Level 2 Elements of Level 1 Component Internal Interaction Management

The level 2 elements of the level 1 component group Integration will be:

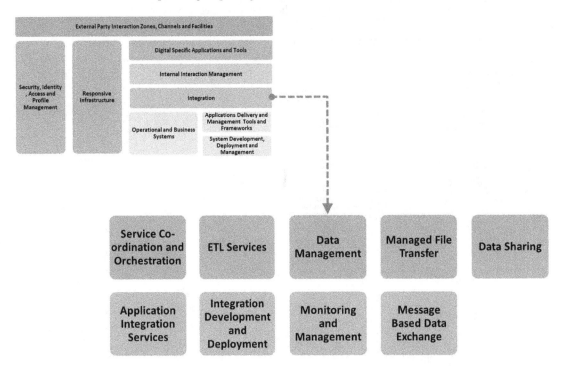

Figure 263 – Level 2 Elements of Level 1 Component Integration

The level 2 elements of the level 1 component group Integration will be:

Level 2 Element	Description
Service Co-ordination and Orchestration	This manages access to services and provides for service communication and integration.
Application Integration Services	This manages the set of application interfaces including their deployment, access and security controls.
ETL Services	This provides facilities to allow data to be extracted from a source, modified and transformed and transmitted to a target.
Integration Development and Deployment	This provides facilities to develop and validate data, application and service integrations and deploy them to into production.
Data Management	This provides data management capabilities including reference and metadata management, managing common business vocabulary, planning, control, and support for data assets across the data lifecycle, from creation and acquisition through archival and purge. It ensures that the data assets are protected and their integrity is assured, manages the availability of assets throughout their lifecycle and optimises data access performance.
Monitoring and Management	This provides for monitoring of the integration suite of components across data, service and application integration and allows the integration environments to be managed.
Managed File Transfer	This component allows for the exchange of file-based data.
Message Based Data Exchange	This component allows for the exchange of message-based data.
Data Sharing	This component allows for data to be securely shared with external parties.

Table 84 – Level 2 Elements of Level 1 Component Integration

The level 2 elements of the level 1 component group Operational and Business Systems will be:

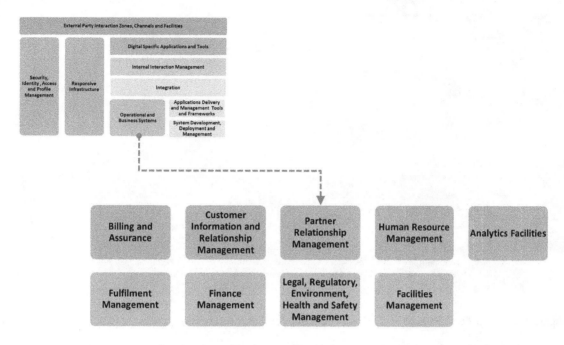

Figure 264 – Level 2 Elements of Level 1 Component Operational and Business Systems

The level 2 elements of the level 1 component group Operational and Business Systems will be:

Level 2 Element	Description
Billing and Assurance	These applications relate to those applications used for product and service billing, credit management, debt collection and related activities.
Fulfilment Management	These applications are used to fulfil the delivery and provision of products and services.
Customer Information and Relationship Management	This provides facilities to manage customer information, maintain a single view of the customer, record details on and manage the customer relationship.
Finance Management	These applications provide financial management including financial planning and analysis and financial consolidation and reporting.
Partner Relationship Management	These are used to manage relationships with partners.
Legal, Regulatory, Environment, Health and Safety Management	These applications manage legal and regulatory compliance across the organisation.
Human Resource Management	These applications enable management of human resources across the range of personnel activities.
Facilities Management	These are used to manage organisation facilities including locations and offices.
Analytics Facilities	These applications provide data reporting and analysis functions and capabilities.

Table 85 – Level 2 Elements of Level 1 Component Operational and Business Systems

The level 2 elements of the level 1 component group Applications Delivery and Management Tools and Frameworks will be:

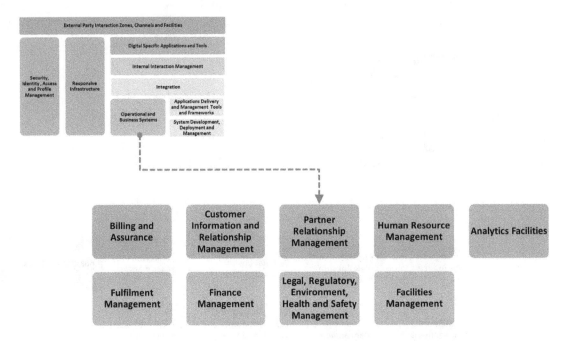

Figure 265 – Level 2 Elements of Level 1 Component Applications Delivery and Management Tools and Frameworks

These describe a set of common processes that should already exist within the organisation. They are listed here as their successful operation and use is required to design, implement and operate the digital platform.

The level 2 elements of the level 1 component group Applications Delivery and Management Tools and Frameworks will be:

Level 2 Element	Description
IT Leadership and Governance	These are processes and structures for the establishment and oversight of the use of information systems and associated technology to meet the needs of the organisation and the achievement of the organisation's goals and objectives and the provision of the required leadership. This includes evaluating current and future needs, directing the planning for supply of these information technology services, service quality and monitoring the compliance with obligations of IT to the organisation's goals and objectives.
Strategic and Business Planning	This relates to the creation and maintenance of the strategy in order to align information systems and technology actions, plans and resources with business objectives and the development of plans to execute that strategy. It involves management of the delivery of the strategy using objectives and accountabilities and of monitoring of its progress.
Programme and Project Management	This is concerned with the definition of standards on and the provision of training, support and guidance on portfolio, programme and project management processes, procedures, tools and techniques. It includes the definition of portfolios, programmes, and projects, delivering them, tracking and reporting of programme and project progress and performance and the maintenance of programme and project artefacts
Sourcing and Selection Management	This is concerned with the definition and operation of standards and advice on the procurement or acquisition or the commissioning of externally supplied products and services. It includes the identification and management of suppliers, selection process definition and operation, procurement governance, conformance to legislation and assurance of information security.
Business Process Management	This provides facilities to design, execute, document, measure, monitor and control both automated and non-automated business processes. It

Level 2 Element	Description
	includes the creation of new approaches to performing business activities, the identification and implementation of improvements to business operations, services and models. It covers the analysis and design of business processes in order to improve business performance and the development of enterprise process management capabilities to increase organisational responsiveness to change.
Benefits Assessment and Realisation	This is concerned with establishing an approach for defining, forecasting, planning, monitoring the realisation of expected benefits and confirming their achievement. It includes identifying and implementing the actions needed to optimise the business benefits.
Capacity Planning, Forecasting, Demand and Supply Management	This is concerned with the analysis and management of business demands for new services or modifications to existing services. It involves working with the business to prioritise demand, analysing patterns of demand, generation of responses to meet both short-term and long-term demand, enabling effective decision making. It also integrates demand analysis and planning with associated strategic, operational and change management processes.
Organisation Design, Planning and Management	This is concerned with the planning, design and implementation of the structure and culture of the information technology function. This includes the workplace environment, locations, role profiles, performance measurements, competencies and skills. It involves enabling the changes needed to adapt to new technologies, new operating models and regulatory and external impacts. It covers identifying key organisational cultural attributes and how these can be implemented and reinforced to deliver improved performance.
Infrastructure, Networks and Communications	This covers the definition, operation and control of the information technology infrastructure including hardware, software, network services and data storage, both internal and external, that is needed to implement, operate and support the information technology needs of the organisation. It includes preparation for the introduction of new or changed services and the monitoring of performance and the use of infrastructure management tools to automate provisioning, testing and deployment.
Security, Continuity and Disaster Recovery	This covers the provision of business and service continuity planning and recovery of information technology services. It includes identifying the systems that are required for supporting critical business processes and the co-ordination of planning, designing, testing and maintenance procedures and contingency plans to address risks and maintain agreed levels of continuity.

Table 86 – Level 2 Elements of Level 1 Component Applications Delivery and Management Tools and Frameworks

The level 2 elements of the level 1 component group System Development, Deployment and Management will be:

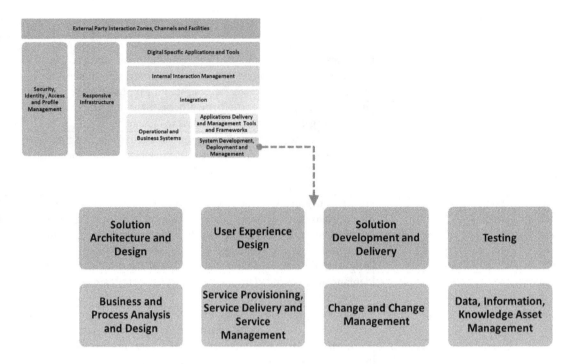

Figure 266 – Level 2 Elements of Level 1 Component System Development, Deployment and Management

The level 2 elements of the level 1 component group System Development, Deployment and Management will be:

Level 2 Element	Description
Solution Architecture and Design	This is the function and process that handles business engagements and creates solution designs to deliver the digital platform.
Business and Process Analysis and Design	This is the function and process that identifies business needs, elicits, analyses, communicates and validates requirements for changes to business processes, policies, and information systems.
User Experience Design	This encompasses solution quality and accuracy, reliability, consistency of performance and availability as well as the appearance, navigation and use of the solution.
Service Provisioning, Service Delivery and Service Management	This is concerned with the introduction of new solutions into the organisation. It involves ensure that the solution operable, usable, supportable and maintainable. It defines the support and maintenance processes. It may include the definition of an initial period of enhanced or hypercare where problems receive special attention to ensure they are resolved quickly. The support function will need to be trained in providing first line support. Second and third level support arrangements will need to be put in place for the operational solution components. The operational and organisational readiness for the solution may need to be assessed and any issues resolved so the organisation is prepared and capable of taking on the solution.
Solution Development and Delivery	This is responsible for implementing the solution and its constituent components, validating their operation, migration data include data reformatting, mapping to new data structures, data enrichment and data cleansing and the implementation of required infrastructure.
Change and Change Management	This includes both the identification, definition and implementation of organisation changes and the management of requested changes during solution implementation.
Testing	This is concerned with the definition of testing standards and the planning, design, management, execution and reporting of tests including test cases, test scripts, test reports and test plans, using testing

Level 2 Element	Description
	tools and techniques. It covers validating that new and changes systems perform as specified and that the risks associated with deployment are understood and documented.
Data, Information, Knowledge Asset Management	This is concerned with the management of solution and information technology knowledge through capturing, sharing, developing and exploiting to support decision making and mitigate risks. It includes the development of collaborative knowledge sharing tools and culture. It also involves understanding the information and data needs of the organisation, the capture, storage and protection of data to ensure the integrity data assets, the improvement of the quality of data and information, including accuracy, integrity, integration, relevance and usefulness of data and maximising the effective use and value of data and information assets. It covers data privacy and confidentiality and security to prevent unauthorised inappropriate use of data and information.

Table 87 – Level 2 Elements of Level 1 Component System Development, Deployment and Management

5.4 Digital and Solution Architecture

As part of the organisation's move to a more digital stance, the solution architecture function needs to design solutions that fit into the target digital architecture framework, if this framework exists. This requires:

- Solution architecture team operating in an integrated manner designing solutions to a set of common standards and that run on the platform
- Solution architecture team leadership ensuring solutions conform to the common standards
- Solution architecture technical leadership to develop and maintain common solution design standards
- Solution architecture updates the digital reference architecture based on solution design experience

These requirements impose a greater rigour on the solution architecture function.

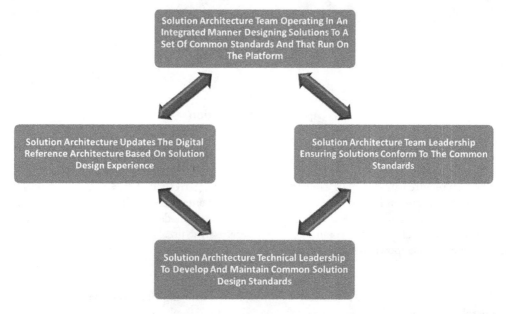

Figure 267 – Solution Architecture and Digital Architecture – Key Solution Design Process Characteristics

The solution architecture function needs to work with the other IT architecture functions to design a set of common infrastructural plumbing solutions that enable the digital business solutions to be designed.

A set of solution architecture standards and their implementation become more important in a digital solution context. These solutions need to encompass common set of standards in areas such as:

- Service orientation
- Microservices
- API service catalogue and API broker
- Cloud and distributed architectures
- Automation
- Standardised data collection and analysis
- Standardised data integration
- Federated security

Solution architecture leadership and management are more important in this operating environment. Solution identification and acquisition skills may need to be improved as many of the solutions will be acquired rather than developed. The speed of solution design or acquisition may need to be improved in order to deploy an operational digital framework quickly. Solution architecture in the context of digital architecture requires greater solution architecture effort.

5.4.1 Digital Solution Integration

Integration is the keyword for successful digital transformation and digital solution design, implementation and operation. It requires the necessary technical integration infrastructure to be in place to enable application, access and data integration.

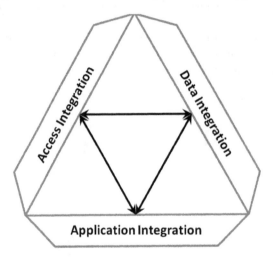

Figure 268 – Access, Application and Data Integration Triad

This triad of integration requirements are quite extensive. They are also interrelated. Access integration means a common identification, validation and authentication foundation. Access rights granted control all subject resource accesses including applications and data. Application integration means individual solutions provide common access to their functionality subject to access rights. This might include a common API and service structure. Data integration means data is integrated across all data sources and generation and creation functions. Data is then commonly accessible including descriptive metadata.

In addition to this functional integration across access, applications and data, digital transformation also means a wider integration across solution designs and integration across architecture and implementation teams.

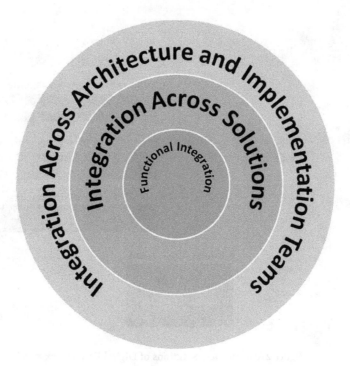

Figure 269 – Wider Integration Across Solution Designs and Other Architecture Teams

Without the necessary technical and business integration and the underlying enabling technology and leadership and organisational support, digital transformation will be just one more failed and abandoned or at best partially successful initiative.

5.4.2 Range of Solutions Within Digital Transformation

Digital transformation involves designing and implementing solutions across a wide range of application and system areas within the context of the digital architecture framework. Two general types of solution will be required:

1. Business function solutions, deployed either as externally facing applications or as operational business systems
2. Internal applications that support the operation of the business systems

In terms of the digital framework described on page 400, the business function solutions can be divided as follows:

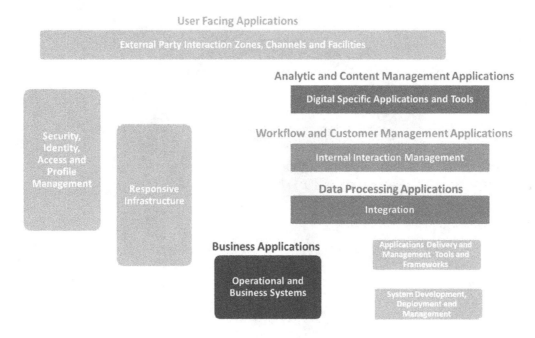

Figure 270 – Business Solutions of Digital Framework

These business solutions include:

- *User Facing Applications in the External Party Interaction Zones, Channels and Facilities group* – these are the set of business applications exposed to external parties

- *Analytic and Content Management Applications in the Digital Specific Applications and Tools group* – these applications provide a range of data management, reporting and analysis facilities to manage data made available to (external) consumers, collect interaction and usage data and enable its reporting and analysis

- *Workflow and Customer Management Applications in the Internal Interaction Management group* – these manage solution consumer interactions

- *Data Processing Applications in the Integration group* – these enable the range of data across the platform to be processed

- *Business Applications in the Operational and Business Systems group* – these are the line of business applications that operate the core business processes

The drivers for digital must be reflected in the approach to solution design and delivery:

- Agility
- Technology
- Response to complexity
- Security
- Need for simplification and automation
- User experience

5.4.3 Digital Design Principles

These are common requirements, characteristics and design principles that need to be included in the design of all solutions. The solution architecture leadership must incorporate these drivers into the of the solution architecture delivery team.

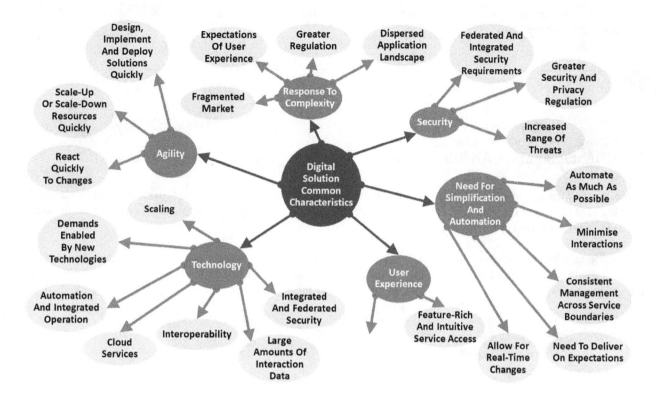

Figure 271 – Digital Solution Common Characteristics

These digital solution common requirements, characteristics and design principles are

Digital Solution Common Characteristics Group	Digital Solution Common Requirement, Characteristic and Design Principle
Agility	Design, implement and deploy solutions that offer complex services quickly.
	Scale-up or scale-down resources quickly and cheaply to meet changes in demand.
	React quickly and cheaply to internal and external market and other changes.
Technology	Scaling of numbers of users, customers, device types and interactions with other organisations.
	Demands for new products and services enabled by new technologies.
	Need for and expectation of automation and integrated operation.
	Cloud services and application deployment and management models.
	Interoperability requirements across multiple applications on dispersed platforms.
	Need to analyse and utilise large amounts of interaction data.
	Need for integrated and federated security across applications.
Response to complexity	Fragmented market with multiple separated specialist service providers with multiple business interactions.
	Expectations of user experience, speed of service delivery.
	Greater regulation.
	Dispersed application landscape.
Security	Federated and integrated security requirements for dispersed application landscape.
	Greater security and privacy regulation.
	Increased range of threats.
Need for simplification and automation	Automate as much as possible to reduce cost, improve accuracy and speed and consistency of service delivery.
	Minimise interactions.
	Consistent management across service boundaries.
	Need to deliver on user and customer expectations.

Digital Solution Common Characteristics Group	Digital Solution Common Requirement, Characteristic and Design Principle
User experience	Feature-rich and intuitive service access, browse and navigation.
	End-to-end product and service lifecycle view.

Table 88 – Digital Solution Common Characteristics

5.4.4 Digital Solution Architecture Interactions With Other Architecture Functions

In the context of designing solutions for digital transformation and the logical digital platform, the solution architecture function needs to ensure that common functional and operational requirements, characteristics and design principles are applied in the solution design process.

In working to deliver the set of solutions that comprise the overall digital framework, the solution architecture function needs to interact with other IT architecture disciplines. These interactions are all the more important in the context of delivering the integrated set of digital solutions that actualise the digital architecture.

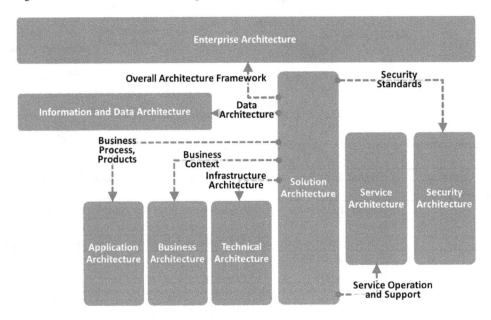

Figure 272 – Solution Architecture Interfaces to Other IT Architecture Functions

The interfaces with the other IT architecture functions are:

- *Enterprise Architecture* – the solutions are designed to be deployed and operated on a coherent and functional digital architecture designed by the enterprise architecture function and for which a set of standards must be defined. The solution architecture function must interface with enterprise architecture to understand the structure of the platform as well as providing feedback on its design and usability.

- *Information and Data Architecture* – the set of digital solutions will generate potentially large amounts of data and data access transactions for which an appropriate data infrastructure will be required. The solution architecture function must understand and be able to specify the data requirements across the data landscape and processing pipeline and work with the information architecture function to ensure its suitability for the data requirements.

- **Application Architecture** – where solutions are developed rather than acquired, there needs to be set of application development standards. The solution architecture function must understand these standards and ensure that those solution components are designed to comply with them.

- **Business Architecture** – the organisation will require business structures, solutions and process changes that will be designed in conjunction with the business architecture function. The solution architecture function must work with the business architecture function to understand the solution requirements and to design those solutions.

- **Technical Architecture** – the set of solutions that comprise the overall digital platform will require a set of infrastructure on which to operate. The solution architecture function must understand and be able to specify the infrastructure requirements and work with the technical architecture function to ensure its suitability for the solution requirements.

- **Service Architecture** – the solutions must be managed, supported, operated and maintained. The solution architecture function must work with the service architecture function to ensure that the designed solution can be transitioned to production.

- **Security Architecture** – the solutions, especially those used by external consumers, and their data must be highly secure. The solution architecture function must ensure that solutions comply with security and privacy requirements.

Digital solution design requires greater discipline to create an integrated set of solutions that operate within the rigour of the digital architecture framework. The solution architecture function must interact with other IT architecture disciplines to ensure the set of solutions that implement the digital framework operates together. This requires greater solution architecture team leadership. This needs to be supplemented and supported by a well-defined set of digital solution design standards.

Chapter 6. Agile Solution Design and Delivery

6.1 Introduction

The topic of solution delivery has already been discussed briefly in section 4.3 on page 112. This section looks at the use of agile solution delivery processes and how they can be applied to the delivery of a solution or some of its constituent components. Section 4.3 on page 112 described the set of components that comprise the complete operational solution. These components are delivered through activities that occur in phases. These phases do not have to occur sequentially. Do not get confused between the *what* of the solution and the *how* of its delivery.

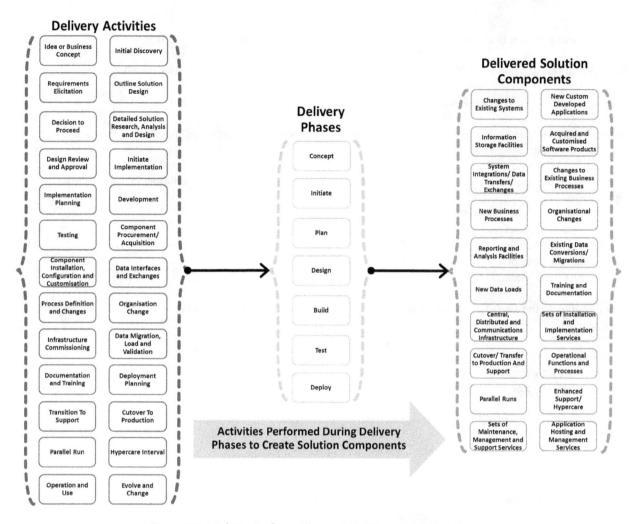

Figure 273 – Solution Delivery Phases, Activities and Solution Components

Section 4.6.4 on page 235 and section 4.6.5 on page 257 describe a solution architecture early engagement and rapid engagement processes respectively. These can be regarded as a form of responsive solution architecture approach that provides results quickly. These engagements can form part of and be used in an agile delivery process – see sections 6.7.1 on page 437 and 6.7.2 on page 438.

The solution architect can determine if the solution or components of it are suitable for an agile delivery approach. The solution architect is best-place to make this assessment.

As I mentioned earlier in this book, the solution architecture function must provide solution leadership and solution subject matter expertise as the solution and its individual components are implemented and integrated. This includes working on the approach to solution delivery and validating that the delivery approach will work. Design guidance is needed throughout the solution delivery and implementation process. The solution architect should take on the role of solution subject matter expert during solution delivery.

6.2 Agile Approach to Solution Delivery

Organisations need to deliver projects to the business in shorter timescales in response to internal and external demands and changes that are occurring more frequently. Solution delivery processes need to be flexible, responsive and agile in order to deliver what the organisation needs when it needs it. Traditionally solutions are delivered in a series of sequential phases designed to create certainty around the solution being delivered. This sequential approach has drawbacks, such as:

- Not sufficiently flexible to accommodate changes in requirements without incurring large costs

- Resources are wasted building features that will not be used or whose actual use has not been validated

- The opportunity to provide feedback is limited until a large part of the solution is delivered

- Solution delivery can take a long time, by when the underlying problematic situation or opportunity being addressed may have changed

An agile approach to solution delivery looks to reduce the risks associated with a sequential solution delivery approach through activities such as:

- Multiple iterations/releases
- Sets of smaller deliveries
- Prioritised requirements
- Greater user involvement

In doing this, it looks to reduce the overall solution delivery cost and accelerate solution delivery and availability. An agile approach tends to be good for projects with inherent uncertainty and volatility such as:

- Transformation and organisational change projects
- Research and development
- Some software development projects

An agile approach to solution delivery is characterised by:

- Driven by user descriptions/scenarios of what is required of the solution
- Seeks constant user feedback
- Recognises that plans are short-lived
- Develops solution iteratively with an emphasis on development activities
- Delivers multiple working solution increments
- Adapts as changes occur

Agile is not suitable for all solution types:

- May not apply to large and complex projects
- May not be suitable to all organisations and people
- Delivered solutions may not be scalable to large volumes of users/transactions/workload/data
- Delivered solutions may not be adaptable to meet future business needs

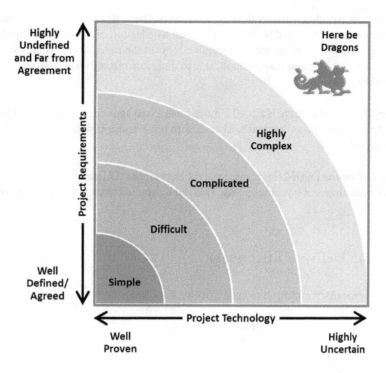

Figure 274 – Classification of Projects and Their Suitability for an Agile Delivery Approach

The fundamental assumption of agile approach to solution delivery is that nothing is built perfectly first time. It is based on the general concept and assumption that of the order of 80% of the solution can be implemented in of the order of 20% of the time that it would take to produce the total solution. The precise percentages are not defined, not the same for all solutions and can be argued over. All deliverables from previous solution delivery project steps can potentially be revisited as part of the iterative approach. Only enough of the current step needs be completed to move to the next step. The approach is designed to address the current and immediate needs of the business. It focuses on the deliver simpler solutions more quickly that are intended to be fit for purpose and easier to maintain and modify after their initial implementation.

Agile has become fashionable without an understanding of the level of effort involved. Agile is all too frequently seen as a magic bullet to resolve solution delivery problems. It is not. ***Agile is hard***. Agile requires commitment, involvement and can be intense and demanding. If you have current solution delivery problems, agile is probably not the solution. You need to fix the underlying organisational issues first.

There are many different agile approaches:

- Adaptive Software Development (ASD)
- Agile Unified Process (AUP)
- Crystal Clear
- DSDM (Dynamic Systems Development Method)
- Essential Unified Process (EssUP)
- FDD (Feature Driven Development)
- Incremental SDLC
- Open Unified Process (OpenUP)
- RAD (Rapid Application Development)
- Scaled Agile Framework
- Scrum Methodology
- Spiral SDLC
- TDD (Test-driven development)
- XP (Extreme programming)

These mainly focus on the narrow aspect of software development. As has been stated many times in the book (see section 2.4.2 on page 33), the complete solution required is rarely, if ever, just a collection of custom-developed software components. Also, the greater acquisition of XaaS components within a solution reduces the need for custom software development. An agile approach suited to software development may be applicable to those custom software components of the solution but not necessarily for the entire solution.

If the entire solution delivery is to be agile, there is a need a more generalised agile approach that can be applied. The remaining sections of this chapter describe an approach. They look to reuse and apply the engagement approaches previously covered in section 4.6 on page 161.

The following approach is based on the DSDM (Dynamic Systems Development Method) approach.[57] It describes a general approach to agile delivery of a solution and its components. This can be applied to the entire solution or to specific components.

6.3 Using Agile Solution Delivery Effectively

The use and applicability of a generalised approach to agile iterative solution delivery consists of four pillars:

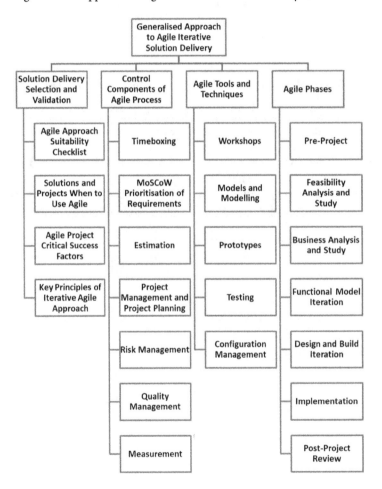

Figure 275 – Pillars of Generalised Approach to Agile Iterative Solution Delivery

These four pillars are:

---

[57] See:
https://www.agilebusiness.org/

Generalised Agile Approach Pillar	Items Within Pillar
Solution Delivery Selection and Validation	• Agile Approach Suitability Checklist • Solutions and Projects When to Use Agile • Agile Project Critical Success Factors • Key Principles of Iterative Agile Approach
Control Components of Agile Process	• Timeboxing • MoSCoW Prioritisation of Requirements • Estimation • Project Management and Project Planning • Risk Management • Quality Management • Measurement
Agile Tools and Techniques	• Workshops • Models and Modelling • Prototypes • Testing • Configuration Management
Agile Solution Delivery Phases	• Pre-Project • Feasibility Analysis and Study • Business Analysis and Study • Functional Model Iteration • Design and Build Iteration • Implementation • Post-Project Review

Table 89 – Pillars of Generalised Approach to Agile Iterative Solution Delivery

The elements in these pillars must be applied and used together for successful agile solution delivery.

6.4 Agile Solution Delivery Pillar One - Solution Delivery Selection and Validation

The elements of the first pillar *Solution Delivery Selection and Validation* consists of four interrelated checks.

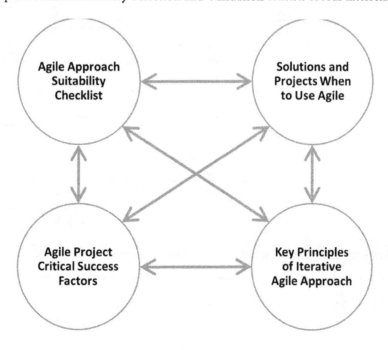

Figure 276 – Using Agile Delivery Approach Effectively

These four sets of checks are described below.

The *Agile Approach Suitability Checklist* check involves getting realistic and truthful answers the following questions:

1. Do the sponsor and management understand and accept the agile philosophy as their buy-in is essential?
2. Will the team members be empowered to make decisions?
3. Is there senior user commitment to provide end user involvement?
4. Can the organisation accommodate the frequent delivery of increments?
5. Will it be possible for the project team to have access to the users throughout the project?
6. Will the project team remain the same throughout the project as stability of the team including the user representatives is important?
7. Will the project team have the appropriate skills including technical skills, knowledge of the business area?
8. Will the individual project teams consist of six people or less?
9. Will the project use technology suitable for prototyping?
10. Is there a highly demonstrable user interface?
11. Is there clear ownership?
12. Will the solution development be computationally non-complex as the more complex the development the greater the risks involved?
13. Can the solution be implemented in increments if required?
14. Has the development a fixed timescale?
15. Can the requirements be prioritised with a mix of Must Haves, Should Haves, Could Haves and Want to Have but Won't Have This Time (MoSCoW rules)?
16. Are the requirements not too detailed and fixed so users can define requirements interactively?

The *Solutions and Projects When to Use Agile* check is characterised as follows:

Solution Type	Solution Type Characteristics
Solution that is interactive, where the functionality is clearly demonstrable at the user interface	• Agile is based on incremental prototyping with close user involvement • User must be able to assess the functionality easily through viewing and operating working prototypes
Solution that has a clearly defined user group	• If the user group is not clearly defined, there may be a danger of driving the solution from a wrong viewpoint or ignoring some important aspect of the project entirely
Solution that is computationally complex and the complexity can be decomposed or isolated	• If the internals of the solution are hard to understand through the user interface then there is a risk • Level of computational complexity is often quite difficult to determine in advance • Interactions between different components that can be difficult to identify up front
Solution that is large, possesses the capability of being split into smaller functional components	• If the proposed solution is large it should be possible to break it down into small, manageable parts, each delivering some clear functionality • These can then be delivered sequentially or in parallel • Each sub-project must be constantly aware of the overall system architecture
Solution that is time-constrained	• There should be a fixed end date by which the project must be completed • If there is no real case for the end date to be fixed, it will be relatively easy to allow schedules to slip and the fundamental benefits of agile approach will be lost
Solution where requirements can be prioritised	• Requirements should be able to be prioritised using the MoSCoW rules

Solution where requirements are unclear or subject to frequent change	• In periods of rapid change, it may be difficult to specify the requirements in detail at the outset of the project making traditional approaches unsuitable • Agile approach is designed specifically to deal with requirements that change and evolve during a project • Applications that are difficult to specify in advance because the users do not know exactly what is needed at the outset

Table 90 – Solutions and Projects When to Use Agile

There are also solutions where agile is not suitable, such as:

- Process control/real-time applications
- Requirements that have to be fully specified before any programs are written
- Safety-critical applications
- Solutions aimed at delivering re-usable components
- Taking an agile can also be difficult where the solution is being acquired from a supplier and/or where the solution is externally hosted

The *Agile Project Critical Success Factors* check includes:

- Acceptance of the agile approach before starting work
- Delegation of decision-making to the business people and developers in the development team
- Commitment of senior business management to provide significant end-user involvement
- Incremental delivery
- Easy access by developers to end-users
- Stability of the team
- Project team should be highly skilled people in terms of both the business area as well as the technical environment
- Size of the project team should be small in order to minimise the overheads of management and communication
- Solution technology that allows iterative development, demonstrable work products and control of versions

The *Key Principles of Iterative Agile Approach* check is as follows:

Agile Principle	Solution Type Characteristics
Active User Involvement Is Essential	• Agile is user-centred • If users are not closely involved throughout the project lifecycle, delays will occur during decisions making • Users may feel that the final solution is imposed by the project team and/or their own management • Users are not outside the project team acting as suppliers of information and reviewers of results but are active participants in the project process • User and thus business commitment are fundamental to success
Collaborative And Co-Operative Approach Between All Stakeholders Is Essential	• The nature of agile projects means that low-level detailed requirements are not necessarily fixed when the team is assembled to perform the work • The short-term direction that a project takes must be quickly decided without the use of restrictive change control procedures • The stakeholders include not only the business and development staff within the project, but also other staff such as service delivery and resource managers • When development is procured from an external supplier, both the vendor and the purchaser organisations should aim for as efficient a process as possible while allowing for flexibility during both the pre-contract phase and when the contracted work is carried out

Agile Project Team Must Be Allowed Make Decisions	• Project teams must be mixed and consist of both IT personnel and users • Project teams must be able to make decisions as requirements are refined and possibly changed • Project teams must be able to agree that defined levels of functionality, usability, etc. are acceptable without frequent need to refer to higher-level management
Focus Is On Frequent Delivery Of Products	• A product-based approach is more flexible than an activity-based one o Products include interim development products, not just delivered solutions • Work of a project team is concentrated on products that can be delivered in an agreed period of time • Enables the team to select the best approach to achieving the products required in the time available • By keeping each period of time short, the team can easily decide which activities are necessary and sufficient to achieve the right products
Fitness For Business Purpose Is The Essential Measure For Acceptance Of Deliverables	• Focus of agile is on delivering the necessary functionality at the required time • Traditional project focus has been on satisfying the contents of a requirements document and conforming to previous deliverables, even though the requirements are often inaccurate, the previous deliverables may be flawed and the business needs may have changed since the start of the project • Solution can be more rigorously engineered subsequently if such an approach is acceptable
Iterative And Incremental Development Is Necessary To Converge On An Accurate Business Solution	• Agile iterative approach allows systems to grow incrementally • Therefore the project team can make full use of feedback from the users • Partial solutions can be delivered to satisfy immediate business needs • Agile approach uses iteration to continuously improve the solution being implemented • When rework is not explicitly recognised in a project lifecycle, the return to previously completed work is surrounded by controlling procedures that slow development down • Rework is built into the agile iterative approach process, the solution can proceed more quickly during iteration
All Changes During Solution Implementation Are Reversible	• To control the evolution of all products (documents, software, test products, etc.), everything must be in a known state at all times • Configuration management must be all-encompassing • Backtracking is a feature of agile iterative approach • Sometimes it may be easier to reconstruct than to backtrack depending on the nature of the change and the environment in which it was made
Requirements Are Baselined At A High Level	• Baselining high-level requirements involves freezing them and agreeing the purpose and scope of the system at a level that allows for detailed investigation of what the requirements imply • More detailed baselines can be established later in the project • The scope should not change significantly • Changing the scope defined in the baselined high-level requirements generally requires escalation
Testing Is Integrated And Performed Throughout The Lifecycle	• Testing is not treated as a separate activity • As the solution is developed incrementally, it is also tested and reviewed by both the project team and users incrementally • Ensures that the project is moving forward not only in the right business direction but is also technically sound • Early in project lifecycle, the testing focus is on validation against the business needs and priorities • Towards the end of the project, the focus is on verifying that the whole system operates effectively – system and integration testing

Table 91 – Key Principles of Iterative Agile Approach

The solution and the delivery function must pass these checks for an agile approach to be considered.

6.5 Agile Solution Delivery Pillar Two - Control Components of Agile Process

The contents of the second pillar *Control Components of Agile Process* are:

Control Components of Agile Process	Details

Timeboxing	• This is a very important aspect of agile iterative process and its use for solution delivery
	• It involves achieving defined objectives at a pre-determined and fixed date through continuous prioritisation and changing of requirements using the MoSCoW control rule
	• The timebox is a fixed interval of time - typically between two and six weeks in length
	• Without the control of timeboxing, project teams can lose their focus and run out of control
	• A timebox must have an agreed scope and clear objectives based on a subset of the prioritised requirements list
	• The objective of a timebox is to make a product - produce something tangible in order for progress and quality to be assessed
	• The team working in the timebox must agree the objectives and must themselves estimate the time required
	• If it appears that deadlines could be missed, the deliverable should be de-scoped dropping the lower priority items
	• The detailed planning of a subsequent timebox containing dependent work cannot be started before the current timebox is complete
	• During each timebox, the team working on the timebox should meet daily to review their progress and to raise issues
	   ○ Provides the team with evidence regarding their progress and the problems they face
	   ○ Highlight risks as they occur
	   ○ Each daily meeting should be limited at 30 minutes and ideally lasts no longer than 15 minutes
	   ○ All team members attend
	• The topics to be covered are:
	   ○ What work has been completed for this timebox since the last daily meeting?
	   ○ What (if anything) got in the way of completing the planned work?
	   ○ What work will be done between now and the next daily meeting?

MoSCoW Prioritisation of Requirements	• *Must Have*
	   ○ Requirements that are fundamental to the system
	   ○ Without them the system will be unworkable and useless
	   ○ Must Haves define the minimum usable subset
	   ○ Agile project guarantees to satisfy all the minimum usable subset
	• *Should Have*
	   ○ Important requirements for which there is a workaround in the short-term and which would normally be classed as mandatory in less time-constrained development, but the system will be useful and usable without them
	• *Could Have*
	   ○ Requirements that can more easily be left out of the increment under development
	• *Want to Have but Won't Have This Time*
	   ○ Requirements that can wait till later development takes place - the Waiting List

Estimation	• Estimation provides the information that is required for two main purposes: 　○ Assess project feasibility by evaluating costs and benefits 　○ Use in project planning, scheduling and control • Estimates should be tight from the outset with frequent deliverables • Estimates that are based on outline business functions provide the closest match with the agile iterative process 　○ The starting point for estimating should be the expected functionality of the end products rather than the activities used to deliver those products • The estimate is a conditional forecast based on the information available at the time 　○ An extrapolation from past and current knowledge to the future 　○ Cannot be done with complete certainty because the future is unknown, therefore the actual effort or cost to deliver will almost always be different to the estimate 　○ Better the quality of the information available for estimating, the closer the estimate is likely to be to the actual figures • Estimation must be based on a defined process so that it is rigorous and repeatable 　○ Whatever process is used, the core information required to estimate is the scope of what is to be delivered and the delivery capability • Contingency must be included in any estimate in order for it to be realistic 　○ Estimates are conditional forecasts that will be affected by future events both internal and external to the project 　○ Events cannot be known with certainty and the estimate must make reasonable allowance for them 　○ Solution development itself is not an exact science 　○ The size of the contingency in an estimate must reflect the degree of uncertainty
Project Management And Project Planning	• The aim of project management is to deliver the right solution on time and on budget using the available resources wisely • The management of traditional projects is about control 　○ Preventing drift from the signed off specification, controlling resources, etc. • Managing an agile project is about enabling constant change while continuously correcting the course of the project in order to maintain its aim at the target - a fixed delivery date for a usable system • To be successful with agile iterative approach, the organisation may have to change organisational and technical elements at the same time • For tradition projects, the project manager has a detailed plan against which to monitor and control activities • In an agile and iterative project, there are typically more activities going on in parallel 　○ Project Manager has a number of distinctive responsibilities to ensure that the project is under control in each phase • Speed of progress can pose some difficulties for managers from a traditional background in IT project management 　○ If problems arise during a timebox then it is often tempting for the traditional manager to renegotiate the end date as that is what they would normally do 　○ In an agile project, the timebox deadline is fixed usually because it is set by the business need 　○ Consequently, the approach is to renegotiate the content of the timebox rather than its duration • In the agile iterative collaborative approach, there is a great deal of interaction between users and implementers in task completion • It is important that communication is clear and concise if rapid development is to be achieved • Agile projects should have an informal but planned communication process • As each timebox is completed, it is the responsibility of the Project Manager to ensure that there is a clear understanding about what is to be delivered in the following timeboxes and to ensure that the relevant requirements are established in detail

Risk Management	• This is an ongoing process throughout the life of a project
	• It is concerned with actively controlling all the risks facing a project or the implementation of the solution it is delivering
	    o Identification of all the risks that may threaten the project for business, systems or technical reasons
	    o Assessment of the impact of those risks on the success of the project should they arise and deciding on the likelihood of the risk occurring and if it happens, on the severity of its impact on the project
	    o Management of those risks through defining specific countermeasures that are aimed at either avoiding the identified risks or accepting them and minimising their detrimental effect on the project
	    o Applying the appropriate countermeasures when a risk materialises
	• Risks must be identified and their impact assessed as early as possible
	• Risks should be continuously reviewed throughout the life of the project, particularly at critical go/no go decision points within the project such as the end of the Business Study and before initiating the development of a new increment
	• All risks should be assessed in terms of their potential impact
	• Risks must be actively managed through countermeasures to minimise their possible impact
	• The emphasis of risk management activities should be on the risks with the highest levels
	• Projects with risks determined as unacceptable by the Executive Sponsor should not be started
	• Projects whose risks rise to an unacceptable level should be stopped

Quality Management	• Quality planning should be an integral part of the project planning activity
	    o Identification of which products are to be produced and which of those warrant specific quality-related activities
	    o How the quality of each type of product is to be checked - for example by review and/or by testing
	    o When quality checks are to be performed; and whether they are they optional or mandatory, whether or not all examples of a particular type of product must be checked or only a sample, and whether items are checked during development or only on completion
	    o Who is responsible for reviewing and testing each product, who has authority to accept the product and what is to happen if such a review or test is unsuccessful
	    o Which criteria are to be used to assess each product's quality - typically by reference to the quality criteria defined in each of the Product Descriptions
	    o Which procedures are to be used to define quality-related processes
	    o Which records are to be kept to document decisions and actions taken
	    o Which standards are to be applied to products (for example, development standards and interface style guides)
	• Audit projects in order to determine their compliance with the organisation's procedures, practices and standards
	• It is important in agile projects that such audits are not allowed to result in unnecessary rework or ineffective effort expenditure
	• The greatest benefit obtained from audits is frequently in causing corporate procedures, practices and standards to be revised in the light of real experience

Measurement	• Measurement is necessary in order to:
	    o Establish a baseline for predicting what will happen in the future
	    o Provide evidence that the process is successful and working
	    o Investigate the process itself in order to highlight and quantify problems
	• Measurement can provide the information to convince management that the introduction of agile iterative approach can provide tangible benefits to the organisation
	• Projects should keep careful records of defects classified by severity and type
	• The success of a project will be whether or not it achieved the stated objectives so these should be described in precise measurable terms
	• Agile approach is focused on satisfying all of the must haves within a fixed elapsed time frame so any measurement of success needs to include all of these

Table 92 – Agile Solution Delivery Pillar Two - Control Components of Agile Process

6.6 Agile Solution Delivery Pillar Three - Agile Tools and Techniques

Agile Tools and Techniques	Details

Workshops	• The topic of workshops has been covered in other sections of this book, especially in relation to Business Engagement in section 4.6.1 on page 161. This workshop material and approach can be reused here
	• A workshop is a structured approach to ensure that a group of people can reach a predetermined objective in a compressed timeframe supported by an impartial facilitator
	• Workshops offer a number of benefits
	    o Rapid, quality decision-making
	        ▪ Because all stakeholders are present at the same time, there is great confidence in the result
	        ▪ Group is focused on the objectives to be achieved in the session so that the information gathering and review cycle is performed at a greater speed
	        ▪ Misunderstandings and disagreements can be worked out at the time
	        ▪ Concerns should therefore have been raised and resolved or noted by the end of the workshop
	    o Greater user buy-in
	        ▪ Workshops, run effectively, lead to participants feeling more involved in the project and decisions being made
	        ▪ Build and maintain enthusiasm
	    o Building team spirit
	        ▪ Controlled way of building rapport as well as delivering
	        ▪ Promotes understanding and co-operation between departments - important when a solution involves many groups
	    o Process redesign by the user community
	        ▪ If practices are reviewed as a result of a workshop, participants can gain a greater understanding of the inputs and implications of their work
	        ▪ Leads to improved efficiencies that are led by the participants themselves, giving greater buy-in and commitment
	        ▪ Greater chance of successful implementation
	    o Clarification of requirements when they are unclear
	        ▪ Business users can be led through their objectives and processes to define what they may require
	        ▪ Participants can explore and model ideas
	        ▪ Successful through a combination of structured discussion and the presence of knowledgeable participants
	• The previously stated agile principles should be applied to the conduct of the workshops

Models and Modelling	<ul><li>Modelling helps the project team gain a good understanding of a business problem, issue or process</li><li>Accurate models reflect the realities of the business world</li><li>Understanding can be gained by analysing the problem from different viewpoints<ul><li>*Business View* - uses a selection of techniques to understand and interpret the business need and to model the business from a future perspective</li><li>*Processing View* - models the system as a set of business processes, or activities, that transform input data items to output data items<ul><li>Processes can be either combined to form higher level processes, which in turn can be combined again to form yet higher-level processes, or decomposed into their constituent sub-processes</li></ul></li><li>*Data View* - models the business information as a set of objects, or entities, and the relationships that exist between these objects</li><li>*Behavioural View* - models the behavioural characteristics of the system in terms of a set of events and states, where events cause changes in the states of the system. Events may be generated within or external to the system</li><li>*User Interface View* - models the interactions and interfaces between the system user and the system itself</li></ul></li></ul>
Prototypes	<ul><li>Prototypes provide a means to allow users ensure that the detail of the requirements is correct</li><li>Demonstration of a prototype broadens the users' awareness of the possibilities for the new system and assists them in giving feedback to the project team</li><li>Accelerates the development process and increases confidence that the right system is being built</li><li>There are various types of prototype:<ul><li>*Business* - demonstrating the business processes and the algorithms being implemented or automated</li><li>*Usability* - investigating aspects of the user interface that do not affect functionality</li><li>*Performance and Capacity* - ensuring that the system will be able to handle full workloads successfully</li><li>*Capability/Technique* – testing a particular design approach or proving a concept</li></ul></li></ul>
Testing	<ul><li>In agile projects testing takes place throughout the project lifecycle and consists of:<ul><li>*Validation* - check that a system is fit for business purpose</li><li>*Benefit-Directed Testing* - testing the parts of the solution that deliver the key business benefits is the highest priority</li><li>*Error-Centric Testing* - objective of designing and running a test is to find an error</li><li>*Testing Throughout the Lifecycle* - performed on all products at all stages of the project</li><li>*Independent Testing* - a product should be tested by someone other than its creator</li><li>*Repeatable Testing* - tests must be repeatable</li></ul></li></ul>
Configuration Management	<ul><li>The dynamic nature of agile projects means good configuration management is required</li><li>Many activities are happening at once and products are being delivered at a very fast pace</li><li>The configuration management strategy and approach must be decided and documented in the Development/Implementation Plan before leaving the Business Study phase</li></ul>

Table 93 – Agile Solution Delivery Pillar Three - Agile Tools and Techniques

6.7 Agile Solution Delivery Pillar Four - Agile Solution Delivery Phases

The characteristics of agile solution delivery are:

- Solution delivery lifecycle is iterative and incremental
- The solution is not be delivered in one go, but in a series of increments, which expand its functionality each time
- Urgent business needs are addressed early while less important functionality is delivered later

- Users see work under construction, review and comment on it and request changes during the development of an increment
- Agile approach provides a generic framework for iterative solution delivery

The agile delivery phases are:

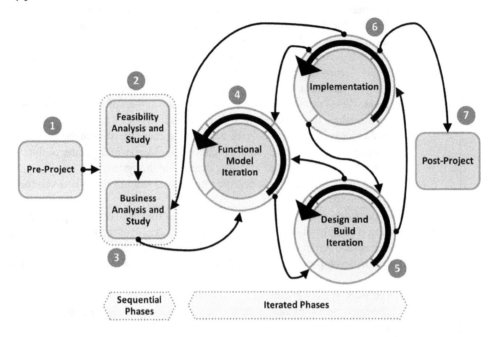

Figure 277 – Agile Delivery Phases and Their Interactions

These phases are:

1. Pre-Project
2. Feasibility Analysis and Study
3. Business Analysis and Study
4. Functional Model Iteration
5. Design and Build Iteration
6. Implementation
7. Post-Project

The three iterated phases within this are:

3. Functional Model Iteration
4. Design and Build Iteration
5. Implementation

The flow within and between these phases is illustrated below.

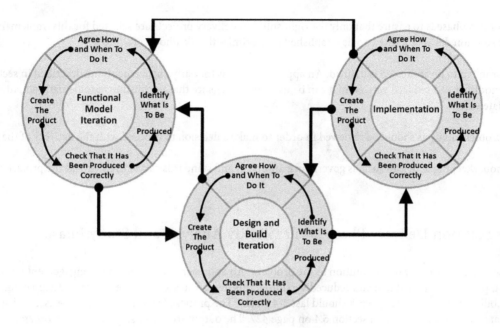

Figure 278 – Iterated Phases Within Agile Solution Delivery

Within each of the iterated phases, there repeated cycles of four activities:

1. Identify what is to be produced
2. Agree how and when to do it
3. Create the product
4. Check that it has been produced correctly by reviewing artefacts, demonstrating a prototype or testing part of the overall solution

Each of the iterated phases delivers increments of work as illustrated below.

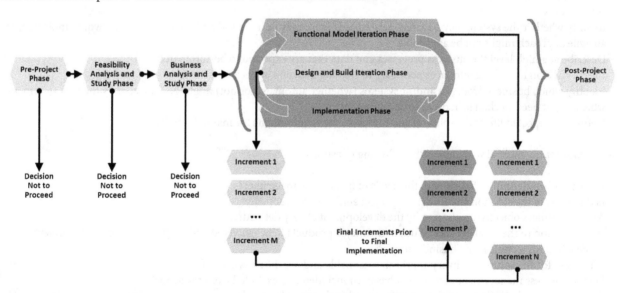

Figure 279 – Increments Delivered Within Agile Delivery Process Iterated Phases

6.7.1 Agile Solution Delivery Phase 1 - Pre-Project Phase

The objective of this phase is to ensure that only the right solution delivery projects are selected for this implementation approach. The solution delivery framework is established to maximise the likelihood of success.

The business problem to be addressed is defined. An approach such as the early engagement one described in section 4.6.4 on page 235 or a modified and reduced version of it can be used here to ensure that the business problematic situation is defined to an appropriate extent.

The business problem analysis should be reviewed in order to make a decision to proceed with the delivery of the solution.

Then project housekeeping activities such as governance approach and standards can be created and the project management team assigned.

6.7.2 Agile Solution Delivery Phase 2 - Feasibility Analysis and Study Phase

This phase assesses the feasibility of the solution to the problem. An approach such as the rapid engagement one detailed in section 4.6.5 on page 257 or a modified and reduced version of this that creates a high-level solution design could be used here. The feasibility analysis and study work should last 2-4 weeks. The proposed solution can then be assessed against the agile appropriateness checklists listed in section 6.4 on page 427. The output from this step in the *Feasibility Report*.

The scope and objectives of the feasibility include:

- Outline the problem to be addressed by the solution
- Define the scope of the solution delivery project
- Give a preliminary indication of any areas within the scope which may be desirable but not essential
- State, at least in outline, the business case for the solution including the expected costs, benefits, assumptions and risks
- Indicate what alternative solutions have been considered
- Define the major products to be delivered by the solution delivery project
- Report on the suitability of an agile approach for use on the solution delivery project
- Document high-level technical and business constraints, e.g. timescale, hardware and software platforms, XaaS components
- Identify whether the system may be safety-related or if there may be any product liability issues that would indicate that an agile approach might not be applicable
- Describe at a high level the business processes and data that are expected to be automated
- Identify at a high level the interfaces necessary to existing data and applications
- Identify which business processes and/or systems (whether automated or not) might be impacted by the new system and which might need to change in order to accommodate it
- Define the expected life of the solution and therefore the requirements for maintainability

The feasibility study must aim to answer the following questions:

1. Is the problem definition in line with the needs of business management?
2. Is the scope of the solution and its deliver project sufficiently clear?
3. Are the business objectives to be met by the development clearly defined?
4. Is the solution to the problem, as laid out in the major products to be delivered and in the objectives of the project, feasible in both technical and business terms?
5. Is the case for the solution delivery approach reasonable and are the risks acceptable?
6. Do the business management accept what has been included and excluded from the scope?
7. Are all associated solutions and their interfaces and exchanges identified?
8. Is any impact on those solutions acceptable?
9. Is the business case for the project to proceed valid?

You may consider developing one or more feasibility prototypes for different solution components during this phase. These can be used to validate the approach or demonstrate the solution interfaces.

Finally, an outline implementation approach should be created during the feasibility phase. This needs to define initial deadlines and milestones for various major phases of work and key deliverables, particularly incremental delivery dates. These deadlines become the major control points and milestones around which the subsequent more detailed lower level plans will be developed.

The purposes of developing this initial plan are:

- To provide business management with initial estimates of the financial and resource requirements of the solution delivery project team and business involvement
- Provide a basis for agreement of timescales for the proposed solution component implementation activities
- Define the high-level acceptance criteria for the proposed deliverables
- Define and agree the approach to the business study phase
- Identify the facilities which the project team will require
- Define the expected path through the agile framework for the solution delivery project
- Identify any currently known issues surrounding the implementation of the solution such a data migration and solution transition to production

Once the initial plan has been developed, it should be validated using the following list of questions:

1. Are the estimates for effort realistic in the light of the details within the feasibility analysis?
2. Are the estimated timescales consistent with the business needs of the solution and its delivery project?
3. Have the business needs been addressed in terms of what is delivered and when?
4. Is business management able to commit to the level of business resources required for the business study and to ongoing user involvement for the proposed duration of the project?
5. Is development management able to commit to the level of development resources required for the business study and to ongoing involvement for the proposed duration of the solution delivery project?
6. Will all necessary facilities be available?
7. Is it clear what the decision factors for acceptance are and are they rigorous enough to define the quality of deliverables while allowing the requirements to vary during development?
8. Are all the currently identified standards and guidelines available and for those that are not yet available, are there sufficient resources to enable their development or procurement?

6.7.3 Agile Solution Delivery Phase 3 - Business Study Phase

The focus is of the business study phase on the business processes affected by the solution and their information and processing needs. The importance of business processes to solution design has been covered already in section 4.4.2 on page 134.

Elements of the business engagement process described in section 4.6.1 on page 161 can be used to perform specific activities during this phase.

To be successful, this phase has to be collaborative. It should use workshops that are attended by knowledgeable and experienced business and solution architecture personnel who can quickly combine their knowledge and gain agreement regarding the priorities of the solution implementation.

The key workshop output is the ***Business Area Definition***. This identifies the business processes and associated information and the groups and types of users who will be affected in any way by the introduction of the solution. The users who will be involved in the implementation of the solution will be identified and agreement reached with their management regarding their involvement.

This phase should create the following outputs:

- Business Area Definition
- Prioritised Requirements List

- Development/Implementation Plan
- Solution Architecture Definition
- Solution Risk Log should be updated

The ***Business Area Definition*** needs to contain a high-level view of the business processes, people and information to be supported by the proposed solution. This developed into the Functional Model during the various iterations of the Functional Model creation. The definition must have sufficient detail to enable to creation of both the implementation plan and a realistic business case.

The approach described in section 4.6.1.6 on page 183 for defining the vision, business and system principles can be applied in creating the Business Area Definition.

The business process analysis performed in this phase can use the method outlined in section 4.6.1.7 on page 190 for documenting business processes, entity model, capacity planning and defining the solution approach.

It needs to identify the business needs that should be supported by the proposed solution. It should refine and extend the previously created business case to include benefits, risks, costs and impact analyses. It should outline the information requirements of the business processes that will be supported. It should name the classes of users impacted by the development and introduction of the proposed system. It should define the business processes and business scenarios that need to change. It should determine all the interfaces, interactions and exchanges with other systems. It should then validate that the proposed solution is still suitable for development using an agile iterative approach.

Generating the ***Prioritised Requirements List*** involves reviewing and prioritising the requirements identified during the Feasibility and Business Studies so that the most important features will be implemented in preference to fewer necessary ones that can be added later, if required and if time and resources are available. This prioritisation will be led by business needs but will also needs to take into account the technical constraints that may cause some requirement to be fulfilled first even though they may be less important in business terms. Operational requirements, such as security, privacy and performance, will affect the prioritisation.

The ***Development/Implementation Plan*** can specify the plans and controls for the whole solution delivery project or just for the next implementation increment. If the latter applies, the plan for the next increment will need added as soon as the current increment is completed. The plan should include the schedule of timeboxes but not their details. Its objectives are:

- Refine and extend the previously create outline plan to provide a more detailed plan for activities within the solution delivery iterations in the next phases
- Provide the development team with an overall approach for implementation
- Define the approach to any proposed prototyping activities and prioritise them
- Define the prototypes that will be developed and when
- Specify how it will be decided when a given prototyping activity should terminate
- Identify the people who will take on the various roles and responsibilities on next phases
- Identify which items are to be subject to configuration management and to outline how and what configuration controls are to be applied
- Define the approach to be taken to testing such as what types of tests are to be run, how they are to be specified and recorded

The plan can be validated using the following checklist:

1. Are the timescales consistent with the business objectives in the Feasibility Report and the Business Area Definition?
2. Does the order of activities within the Development/Implementation Plan reflect the priorities and dependencies in the Prioritised Requirements List?
3. Is the timebox schedule realistic in terms of currently estimated effort and the flow of products?
4. Does the timebox schedule reflect the need to address areas of risk at appropriate times?
5. Are all affected users identified in the Development/Implementation Plan?
6. Is the proposed user effort consistent with the needs of both the existing business processes and the development?
7. Will the necessary effort from all personnel be available when required?
8. Is the selection of the categories of prototypes feasible within the expected implementation environment?

9. Is the method of configuration management appropriate to the environment?
10. Are the proposed extent, depth and formality of testing appropriate?

The ***Solution Architecture Definition*** describes the solution in terms of its constituent components and their interactions. It aims to provide a common understanding of the technical architectures to be used during solution component development, implementation and integration. It contains a description of the any software architectures included in components of the solution such as the major software objects or components and their interactions.

The architecture definition can be validated using the following checklist:

1. Is the solution architecture appropriate for the requirements?
2. Have the risks in the proposed solution architecture been properly considered? In particular, are all components of the proposed solution architecture available and mutually compatible?
3. Will migration from the implementation platform to the production environment platform be able to be performed easily? If not, are all foreseeable problems identified?
4. Is the outline solution architecture sufficiently well-defined to give those involved in implementation a high-level view of the overall solution?
5. Is the solution architecture defined at an appropriate level, so that it will not be too vulnerable to change as the project progresses?
6. Has advantage been taken of any opportunities for reuse of existing components?
7. Can the solution architecture be expected to cope with security, privacy, performance, capacity and resilience requirements?

6.7.4 Agile Solution Delivery Phase 4 - Functional Model Iteration Phase

This phase consists of refining the business-based aspects of the solution and its components, building on the high-level processing and information requirements identified during the Business Study phase.

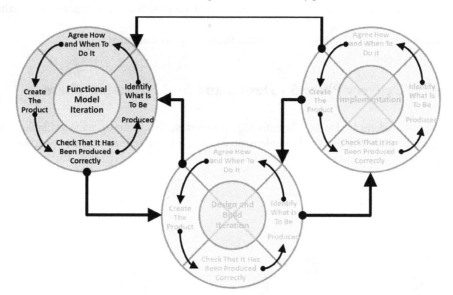

Figure 280 – Agile Solution Delivery Phase 4 - Functional Model Iteration Phase

This phase defines what the solution will do without going into the detail of how non-functional/operational aspects. It develops from and expands and refines the Business Area Definition created during the Business Study phase. It evolves over the life of the solution delivery project expanding in scope and deepening in content with each pass through Functional Model Iteration phase within an increment and with each increment. The artefacts created consist of both documents and tangible deliverables. It provides a concrete demonstration that the functionality and data requirements to be met including all currently known constraints. It demonstrates the feasibility of achieving the non-functional/operational requirements.

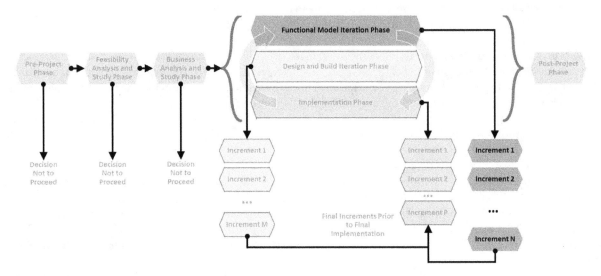

Figure 281 – Iterations During Functional Model Iteration Phase

The work done during this phase can be validated using the following checklist:

1. Does the Functional Model match the needs of the business as documented during discussions and prototyping sessions?
2. Is it within the scope of the development as defined in the Business Area Definition?
3. Are all parts of the Functional Model mutually consistent?
4. Does the model contain the minimum usable subset?
5. Are all essential aspects of integrity and security contained within the Functional Model?
6. Are the requirements for system administration and management visible?
7. Are all static models (such as data storage models) consistent with the Functional Prototype(s) and vice versa?
8. Does the model give confidence that the right levels of security, privacy, performance, capacity and maintainability will be achievable?
9. Is any necessary supporting documentation available and to an adequate standard?

6.7.5 Agile Solution Delivery Phase 5 - Design and Build Iteration Phase

In this phase, the solution is implemented to a sufficiently high standard so that it can be made available to business users with confidence that it can be used. The previously implemented prototypes are refined to meet operational and service management requirements.

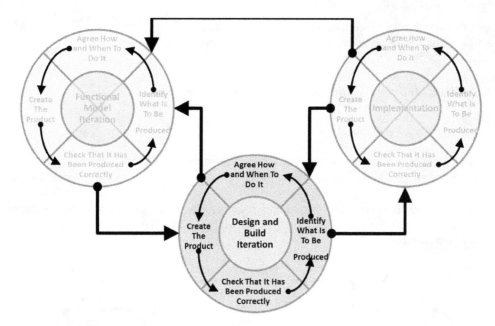

Figure 282 – Agile Solution Delivery Phase 5 - Design and Build Iteration Phase

Operational characteristics of a solution have been covered elsewhere in this book such as section 4.6.4.7 on page 251. These operational and service requirements have significant impact on the degree to which quality controls are applied to solution components. The requirements relating to performance, reliability, security, privacy and maintainability are of particular importance in projects that are trying to deliver a solution quickly. Decisions have to be made by the business as early as possible in the project about what has to be done now and what can be left until later. While functional requirements can be deferred with relative ease, operational requirements tend to be integral to the architecture of the solution and are very difficult to resolve later in solution delivery.

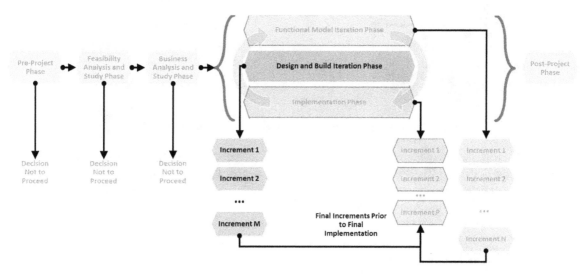

Figure 283 – Iterations During Design and Build Iteration Phase

The work done during this phase can be validated using the following checklist:

1. Are all the operational and service requirements sufficiently quantified and defined?
2. Where operational and service requirements have already been addressed by a Functional Prototype, are these noted as such in the list of operational and service requirements?
3. Have all areas identified in the high-level constraints in the Feasibility Report been considered?
4. Is the set of operational and service requirements complete and consistent both within itself and with the Functional Model?

5. Do all the operational and service requirements add value to the business?
6. Are the operational and service requirements realistic and achievable?

6.7.6 Agile Solution Delivery Phase 6 - Implementation Phase

The purposes of the implementation phases are:

1. To define the detail of how the increment being currently developed will become operational
2. To define the costs and effort in more detail, enabling management to reassess the costs and benefits of the development

This phase defines the activities needed to move the current system increment from the development environment to full operational use. It includes not only the migration of the system itself but also the Training Strategy to ensure that the operational system is used effectively.

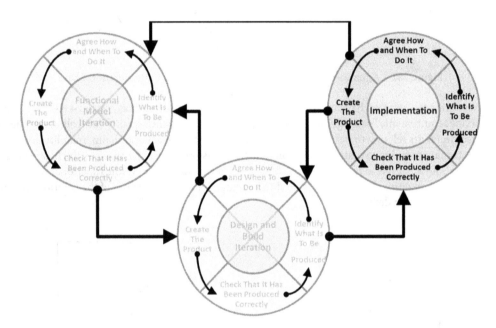

Figure 284 – Agile Solution Delivery Phase 6 - Implementation Phase

The scope of a fully operational system is not just its technical components. Data must be migrated. Users must be trained. A support model must be defined. There may be an initial hypercare period. The implementation increment must be reviewed as soon as possible after delivery of the previous design and build phase so that the next phase of development can be planned and started with as little delay as possible.

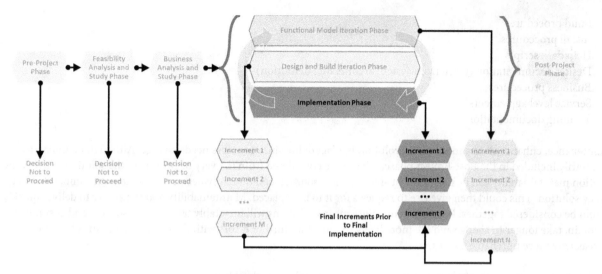

Figure 285 – Iterations During Implementation Phase

The work done during this phase can be validated using the following checklist:
1. Are the plans agreed with the people who will support the increment in operation?
2. Does the schedule still fit in with business needs?
3. Do the cost and effort estimates (both implementation team and user) look realistic for achieving delivery of the solution?
4. Are the necessary resources (both implementation team and user) available to meet this plan?
5. If relevant, are the procedures for handover to maintenance and support staff clear?
6. If relevant, have the requirements for data take-on and/or system cutover been adequately considered?
7. Is the Training Strategy appropriate?
8. Have all changes to the physical environment been adequately considered?
9. Have issues relating to third parties been considered?
10. Has communication (e.g. within the organisation and external solution consumers) been considered?

6.7.7 Agile Solution Delivery Phase 7 - Post-Project Phase

This takes place after the solution has been delivered. It includes support and maintenance activities and, if necessary, a post-implementation review to assess how the solution is being used and how it works. The objectives of this phase include:

- To ensure that the solution is and can be kept operational and to review the way it is actually being used
- To determine whether or not the proposed benefits of the solution as stated during its initial phases have been achieved
- To identify possible improvements is the solution delivery process

The post-implementation review gathers lessons learnt about the system is being used and assesses the benefits achieved.

The deliverables can include:

- User documentation
- Handover documents
- Data load and migration
- Support model
- Hypercare period
- Support guide
- Operating procedures
- Backup and recovery procedures
- Disaster recovery procedures

- Build procedures
- Install procedures
- Help desk scripts
- Design documentation (taken from system architecture definition)
- Business procedures
- Service level agreements
- Training documentation

Maintenance, enhancement and solution evolution is a fact of life since business needs change. Although maintenance is necessarily included in the Post-Project phase, it has to be considered from the very beginning of the solution delivery. Poor solution maintainability can be risk to the business. A new solution could rapidly become a problematic, unmaintainable legacy solution. This could then give rise to requests for it to be replaced. Maintainability and the ability to deliver quickly should be considered together. Poor maintainability means solutions will inevitably take more resources and cost more to maintain, take longer to change and are more likely to introduce further errors with those change and thus become increasingly more unreliable over time.

The work done during this phase can be validated using the following checklist:

1. Does the solution satisfy all the user-defined acceptance criteria?
2. Is the project team satisfied that the solution is sufficiently robust to be put into full operation?
3. Has the solution been tested at an appropriate level, considering its intended use?
4. Is there evidence that all the essential requirements (functional and non-functional) have been tested and, where necessary, demonstrated to the users?
5. Have any and all safety-related and product liability aspects of the system been properly validated, if applicable?
6. Has all functionality that is provided to support implementation been adequately tested (in particular, has account been taken of any need for data conversion/uploading tools)?
7. Are all components of the solution traceable to the Functional Model?
8. Are all components rejected in the design review documents omitted from the solution?
9. Is the solution documentation consistent with the solution?

Chapter 7. Solution Architecture and Solution Acquisition

7.1 Introduction

The complete solution as described in section 2.4 on page 33 may consist of a number of acquired components. The proportion of acquired components in solutions is growing because of a number of factors including:

- The desire by organisations to avoid custom software development and to acquire products that deliver the necessary functionality through configuration and customisation though product customisation is not without risks – see section 3.2 on page 71
- The move to more cloud-based services and hosted applications where the hosted application is configured and customised to suit the needs of the organisation
- Greater outsourcing of services

In its role as the creator of the complete end-to-end solution, the solution architecture function should provide leadership in acquisition process. The solution architect needs to validate that the acquired components will work with the other solution components to deliver a complete solution. The solution architect is not exclusively responsible for the acquisition process. There will (or may) be a procurement function that can handle the mechanics of acquisition.

There are three broad types of acquisition that can be involved in solution architecture and solution design:

1. Acquisition of a product component of the solution that is installed on the organisation's technology infrastructure
2. Acquisition of an externally hosted or cloud-based application or service component of the solution
3. Acquisition of an outsourced service component of the solution

Acquisition types 2 and 3 may be perceived as representing a loss of control by the information technology function. Solutions that were previously developed by the information technology function and run and managed on its technology infrastructure are now sourced elsewhere. However, the trend towards greater use of externally hosted or cloud-based applications and services is a reality. Ignoring it will not make it go away. Rather it may give rise to greater shadow IT as discussed in section 3.3.1 on page 75.

The growth in the use of externally hosted or cloud-based services requires a greater understanding of and emphasis on the acquisition aspects of solution design. This growth requires a methodological approach underpinned by well-defined and accepted principles. The organisation is now relying on an external service to operate its business processes. The nature of that service, what is and is not included and what is possible must be recognised.

Inadequate Preparation = *Problems Start Here*
Flawed Service Provider Selection = *Solution Delivery and Operation Failure Starts Here*
Unclear Contract = *Conflict Begins Here*
Wrong Performance Measurement = *Management Failure Starts Here*
Ineffective Ongoing Management = *Service Delivery Problems Start Here*

The challenges the organisation confronts in the face of this growth in the use externally hosted or cloud-based services are:

- Establishing an appropriate strategy
- Identifying those services that could be delivered use externally hosted or cloud-based services
- Developing appropriate approaches for these sourcing activities
- Managing risks throughout the sourcing activities and lifecycle
- Managing security and privacy, especially of data
- Identifying, selecting and negotiating with service providers
- Conducting service provider governance and performance management
- Managing relationships with their service providers

Many of these challenges are not new. But the dynamic of the information technology product and service supply relationship is changing.

Organisations may find themselves forced to use externally hosted or cloud-based services because on-premises product-based options may simply cease to exist for some solution types.

Most organisations will have an existing procurement function that is responsible for the acquisition of products and services. The purpose of this section is not to define approach to overall solution component sourcing competence or supplier governance competence. The objective is to define the role of solution architecture in the design of solutions where one or more components will be delivered through acquired products installed on the organisation's infrastructure or hosted applications or cloud-based services. The procurement function will handle the general housekeeping activities associated with acquisition. The solution architect will deal with the detailed specifics relating to the solution and its functionality and operation and use.

Competence in solution sourcing is a core skill of the IT function. As mentioned previously in section 2.6 on page 50 the IT function needs to be a lens focussing business needs on solutions. Given that the sourcing activity generally occurs during solution design, it is a key skill of solution architecture. Vendor assessment and validation during the life of the sourcing arrangement is also important. Sourcing should not be a "*fire and forget*" activity.

Product and service procurement activities will be very different for private sector and public sector organisations. The public sector will be governed by various public procurement rules. The private sector can be more flexible and agile though it should still follow a structured approach to ensure that the correct service is procured. Remember that procurement is a means to an end rather than being an end in itself.

Many of the concerns relating to using hosted or cloud-based services are similar across service types: access control, data security, data privacy, data management and data integration. Taking a strategic approach and implementing framework approaches and solution to these common concerns makes the adoption of individual services and the transition from one service provider to another easier and faster.

The solution architect must be able to identify potential options for product and service-based solution components and evaluate their suitability and make recommendations accordingly. The solution architect is in a position to provide the leadership that is necessary in these circumstances. The role of the solution architect can include some or all of the following activities:

1. Specification of the functional solution design to be included in some form of RFQ/RFS/RFP
2. Evaluation of supplier proposals including product and service reviews
3. Assistance with product or service negotiations
4. Assistance with the design of the service arrangements
5. Specification of data migration
6. Specification of data integration
7. Specification of integration with the organisation security and access control environment
8. Specification of product/service configuration and customisation
9. Specification of overall solution design and where the specific hosted product/service fits into it including service operation and management
10. Due diligence of supplier
11. Assistance with transition
12. Assistance with the definition of ongoing service monitoring and performance management processes and structures
13. Assistance with performing the ongoing service monitoring and performance management activities

Section 4.6.1.10 on page 212 already discussed the functional aspects, that is, what the product or service does rather than how it is delivered, of procurement in the context of the business architecture engagement. The information issued to potential suppliers is effectively a functional specification describing what the product or service is required to provide. This specification must be created by the solution architect.

The procurement of externally hosted services and cloud-based services involves, among other issues, data security and privacy concerns. These are referred to in section 4.9.3 on page 374. These relate to the how the service delivery.

It is important to remember that every product and service provision engagement comes to an end. It may happen sooner or later. But it will happen. Ultimately, the product will be replaced or its use will be discontinued. The service will be transitioned to a new service provider. So, every acquisition activity needs to include within it an acknowledgement of and an ability to handle this inevitable termination.

This section is concerned with service acquisition and supplier validation and governance in the context of solution architecture and design. This covers both the analysis and design of the service and assessing the supplier. The amount of effort that should be spent on validating the operation of the service and the suppliers and service providers should be based on the size, cost, importance and type of service being provided. More complex, costly, lengthy solutions/services require greater governance.

As part of the overall solution design the solution architect needs to ascertain the viability of the acquired product or service and to define how it interoperates with the other solution components. There are two overlapping sets of assessment and validation services to be performed:

1. The definition of the service and its onboarding and the transfer of organisation data to it.

2. The assessment of the service provider, especially across the areas of security, availability, processing integrity, confidentiality and privacy. This is especially important for an external service where the organisation relies on a service hosted outside its infrastructure and where organisation data is held outside its boundaries.

There are a number of frameworks that can assist with the structured evaluation of a supplier and of a service and of the onboarding and service transition to that supplier. Their use reduces the effort associated with and improves the quality of such assessments. These include:

- *ITIL*[58] – this is a service delivery management framework that can be used to assess the service framework of the product or service supplier. ITIL is concerned with the set of processes that may be implemented by the service provider to

---

[58] See:
https://www.axelos.com/best-practice-solutions/itil

deliver the contracted services. In the context of service provision, ITIL should be used by the service provider and not by the acquiring organisation.

- *COBIT (Control Objectives for Information and Related Technologies)*[59] – this is a framework for governance and management of the IT function. Again, it can be used to assess the governance framework of the product or service supplier.

- *Service Organisation Controls*[60] – this is an audit approach to supplier and service provider validation. This directly assesses the readiness and ability of the product or service supplier.

- *CMMI eSourcing Capability Model for Client Organisations (eSCM-CL)*[61] – this is capability model for organisations that acquire IT services, especially outsourcing services. It can be readily adapted to the process for planning to move to an externally provided product or service.

- *ISPL (Information Services Procurement Library)*[62] – this is a discontinued development of a set of practices for the management of the acquisition of information technology products and services. It is mentioned here for the sake of completeness.

The solution architect should seek to reuse existing methodologies, approaches and established and proven best practices to reduce the effort associated with performing any given area of work as well as improving quality.

The key aspects of any service are:

---

[59] The current version of COBIT is version 5 – see http://www.isaca.org/COBIT/Pages/COBIT-5.aspx. COBIT 2019 is being introduced – see http://www.isaca.org/cobit/pages/default.aspx.

[60] See: https://www.aicpa.org/interestareas/frc/assuranceadvisoryservices/serviceorganization-smanagement.html. This is also discussed in section 4.9.3 on page 285.

[61] See: http://www.itsqc.org/models/escm-cl/index.html.

[62] ISPL was the main deliverable from the EU SPRITE-S2 (*S*upport and Guidance to the *PR*ocurement of *I*nformation and *TE*lecommunication *S*ystems and *S*ervices) programme – see https://cordis.europa.eu/news/rcn/8049/en. For more details in ISPL see: https://en.wikipedia.org/wiki/Information_Services_Procurement_Library.

Figure 286 – Key Aspects of a Service

These aspects affect how the supplier/service provided should be validated. They are effectively a set of risk factors that dictate the level of supplier governance necessary.

The key service aspects are:

- *Split Between Product And Service* – mix between pure product and services
- *Extent Of Configuration and Customisation* – the amount of configuration and customisation changes needed to the base solution or service to make it usable by the organisation
- *Type Of Engagement* – consulting/ analysis/ implementation and mix of services of these types
- *Expected Duration Of Business Relationship* – how long with the service be provided for or is contracted for
- *Importance of Product/ Service* – sensitivity and importance of product/service to the organisation
- *Expected/ Contracted Cost* – how much the product/service is expected to cost or the contracted cost
- *Size/ Extent Of Product/ Service* – the amount of effort and the number of parties and stakeholders involved in or affected by the product/service
- *Experience And Proven Ability Of Supplier* – how experienced is the supplier in successfully delivering the product/service
- *Novelty Of Product/ Service* – how new or well-proven is the underlying technology and approach of the product/service
- *Complexity Of Product/ Service* – how complex is the product/service – its number of components and interfaces
- *Security, Performance, Reliability, Availability Requirements Of Product/ Service* – are there specific requirements of the product/service in these areas
- *Implementation/ Transition Effort And Time* – what is the estimated or expected effort and time to implement or transition to the product/service
- *Availability Of Skills And Experience With Product/ Service* – how readily available are skills within the organisation

The complexity model discussed in section 4.2.2 on page 100 can be applied here to evaluate the service. These factors can be scored to derive some form of assessment of the riskiness of the service.

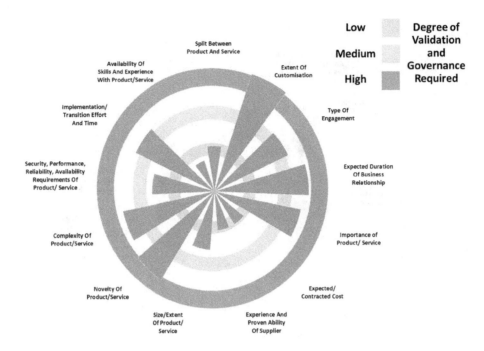

Figure 287 – Sample Assessment of Service

While this assessment is inevitably subjective and the importance of each factor is not identical, this can be used as an indicator of the level of governance to be applied to the service.

7.1.1 Service Planning and Initiation/Transfer Approach

The approach and sets of activities described in this section is based on the CMMI eSourcing Capability Model for Client Organisations described above.

Having an accurate common understanding of the service being provided to the organisation is essential to the successful operation and use of that service.

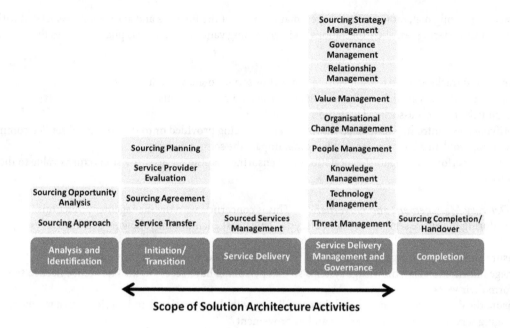

Scope of Solution Architecture Activities

Figure 288 – Sourcing Phases and Activities

The solution and supplier sourcing process consists of five major phases. In the context of a specific solution design, the solution architect should only be involved in phases two to four. The solution architect will not be exclusively involved in these phases. There will be a wider team of which the architect will be a part. The solution architect may be involved in the other phases.

1. ***Analysis and Identification*** – This is concerned with analysing operations and functions to identify those services, processes, or functions that could potentially be provided by an externally hosted product or service. This defines the general principles for this use of this type of service provision and delivery. This phase includes the following activities:

   - Identifying the relevant criteria for selecting externally hosted product or service opportunities
   - Identifying externally hosted product or service opportunities to meet the objectives and criteria
   - Organising options for externally hosted products or services
   - Developing and validating the business case for each externally hosted product or service option
   - Identifying the externally hosted product or service approach and governance model for the proposed service
   - Performing impact and risk analyses of the proposed externally hosted product or service action
   - Making the decision whether or not to implement hosted product or service actions

2. ***Initiation/Transition*** – This is concerned with preparation for and initiation of an externally hosted product or service. This phase includes the following activities:

   - Preparing for service selection by developing the service specification and the factors for selection
   - Soliciting and evaluating potential service providers
   - Preparing for negotiation by having an organisational position on cost, quality and other service aspects that need to be negotiated
   - Defining the formal service level agreements and service provider performance measures
   - Understanding service provider's capabilities by gathering information about the service provider and confirming the assumptions that impact commitments
   - Establishing a formal agreement with the service provider that clearly defines the responsibilities and commitments of the organisation and the and service provider
   - Managing the effective transfer of resources needed for service delivery

3. ***Service Delivery*** – This is concerned with defining the arrangement for and then monitoring the service provider's service delivery capabilities, including the ongoing monitoring of service provider performance to verify that

commitments are being met, monitoring changes, management of the finances and agreements associated with the service provision, fostering realistic expectations and performing value analysis. This phase includes the following activities:

- Planning and tracking the externally hosted product or service management activities
- Ensuring that services are delivered according to the agreed commitments
- Managing the finances associated with the service delivery
- Identifying and controlling modifications to the services being provided or to the associated service commitments
- Facilitating problem resolution for problems that impact the service delivery
- Reconciling performance against expectations and ensuring that the service provision returns value to the organisation

4. ***Service Delivery Management and Governance*** – This is concerned with the management functions that need to be performed during the entire service provision lifecycle. This phase includes the following activities:

- Measure and review the organisation's use of the service and take action to improve it
- Manage information and knowledge systems so that personnel have access to the knowledge needed to effectively perform their work
- Measure the delivery of the service and the compliance with the operational and service level agreement
- Managing service change, enhancement and improvement
- Managing reporting and communications
- Identify and control threats to the organisation's ability to meet its objectives and the requirements of its consumers
- Manage the technology, systems and applications infrastructure used to support delivery of service

5. ***Completion*** – This is concerned with closing down the engagement at the end of the service provision lifecycle and either moving to a new service provider, renewing with the existing service provider or bringing the service within the boundaries of the organisation. This phase includes the following activities:

- Planning for closing down the service and managing the agreement during the close-down period including managing the agreement during termination proceedings, during renewal or during normal completion
- Managing the transfer of resources to the new service provider, whether it is to back to the organisation or to another service provider including the potential transfer of people, technology infrastructure and intellectual property
- Ensuring service continuity during the transfer of responsibilities for service provision
- Identifying and transferring the knowledge capital critical for the delivery of service

These represent general activities to be performed for externally provided services including hosted applications, cloud-based services and outsourcing. They should be used as a starting point to derive a specific set of activities to be performed for a given sourcing action.

In the following, I have separated phases two – Initiation/Transition - and three – Service Delivery - into one group and phase four – Service Delivery Management and Governance - into a separate group. This is because phase four represents an ongoing set of activities performed throughout service delivery. The involvement of the solution architect in this phase can be twofold:

1. Defining the approach to perform these activities
2. Assisting with performing the activities

7.1.1.1 Activities for Initiation/Transition and Service Delivery Phases

The activities for the Initiation and Transition and Service Delivery phases are:

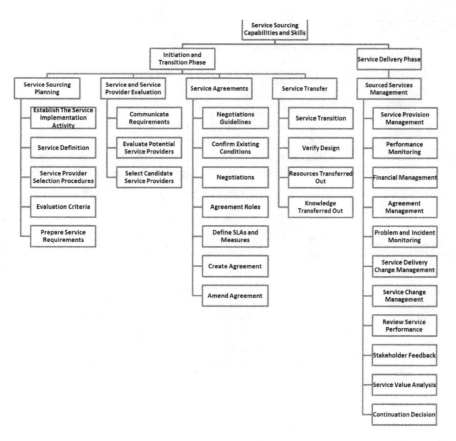

Figure 289 – Possible Solution Architecture Activities During Initiation/Transition and Service Delivery Phases

These are the high-level, indicative and generalised set of activities to be performed for each step. These steps can be applied to all types of service provision. This can be used as a checklist to create a detailed set of service-specific tasks.

Step	Task	Scope and Activities
Service Sourcing Planning	Establish The Service Implementation Activity	• Establish and implement plans for managing the service project for each outsourcing action • Failure to provide appropriate and sufficient governance of service implementation activities can cause difficulties by not having sufficient resources to perform the necessary management activities
	Service Definition	• Define and document the services and service conditions • Set out in specific and measurable terms the services required, how they are to be delivered and the duration that they are required for as well as the performance standards • Document the scope of the service to be performed in service specifications, clearly specifying the desired results and defining the industry standards to be followed • Defining detailed performance measures allow organisation to document the business requirements and rules, service levels and metrics to clarify customer expectations regarding the nature of the relationship, the levels of service to be delivered, the price and how performance will be measured, monitored and reported
	Service Provider Selection Procedures	• Establish and implement procedures to select service providers • Establish detailed procedures that require service providers to answer specific requests in a way that allows responses to be compared • The greater the importance of the potential service, the more attention should be given to the service provider selection procedures
	Evaluation Criteria	• Define the evaluation criteria to be used in selecting service providers

Step	Task	Scope and Activities
		• Main principles for rating should be incorporated in the requests sent to suppliers • Evaluation criteria should provide the basis for evaluating between potential service providers • Documenting the evaluation criteria can minimise the possibility that decisions will be second-guessed or that the reason for making the service selection decision will be forgotten
	Prepare Service Requirements	• Prepare requirements to communicate to prospective service providers • Requirements outline the potential agreement with the service provider • Objective should be to attract the most responses from the most qualified providers • Provide as much information as possible to give service providers a good understanding of what is expected of them
Service and Service Provider Evaluation	Communicate Requirements	• Communicate requirements to prospective service providers • Engaging potential service providers is critical to having a qualified pool of service providers to select from • Failure to follow standard procedures in soliciting prospective service providers can lead to inconsistencies in responses and serve as a potential source of risks or failures in future activities • Consistency in actions with prospective service providers may also be required for compliance with legal requirements of the selection process
	Evaluate Potential Service Providers	• Evaluate potential service providers using documented criteria and selection procedures • Many aspects, including the strategic alignment, reputation, references, experience, financial goals, risk, resource capabilities and information security should be considered while choosing the service provider
	Select Candidate Service Providers	• Select candidate service providers • By following the documented selection procedures, the organisation should be able to use the appropriate evaluation criteria, gather the necessary objective data and guarantee that its overall selection process proceeds in a structured format • This creates a record that can be useful if there is a need to explain how they arrived at a specific selection
Service Agreements	Negotiations Guidelines	• Establish and implement guidelines for negotiations with service providers • Having these guidelines provides a structured approach to negotiation and can improve the internal stakeholder's confidence in the service supplier • Guidelines also help protect the organisation from legal or performance issues by verifying that the necessary aspects of negotiations are covered
	Confirm Existing Conditions	• Establish and implement guidelines to confirm existing conditions • This helps mitigate risk by verifying that the service provider is making its commitments based on a clear understanding of the organisation's current service delivery environment
	Negotiations	• Plan and track negotiations with service providers • Identify and monitor the key topics that require consensus and capture in the formal agreement between the parties • Planning for the negotiation and clearly identifying the key topics reflects a degree of preparation that enhances internal client trust in the capabilities of the organisation which helps in establishing positive relationships • The organisation should be especially concerned with security and intellectual property concerns during negotiations
	Agreement Roles	• Define the roles and responsibilities of the organisation and the service provider under the proposed agreement • Having clearly defined and understood roles and responsibilities helps to guard against mismatched expectations that may result in service delivery

Step	Task	Scope and Activities
		issues
	Define SLAs and Measures	• Define the formal service level agreements and performance measures for the services and service conditions • Performance measures need to be established for each important component of the service provision • Defining the performance measures allows the service provider to rationalise resources to best meet the organisation's needs and allows the organisation to ensure that business requirements are being met • One of the greatest causes of disputes is the gap in understanding between the results expected by the organisation and the level of service the service provider intends to provide
	Create Agreement	• Establish and implement procedures to create agreement • Legal agreements enable all the parties to have a clear understanding of what services will be delivered and at what level of quality • Given the long-term nature of most service provision engagements, implementing procedures for creating well-formed agreements and flexibility in the relationship between the organisation and the service provider are critical to the success of the service
	Amend Agreement	• Establish and implement procedures to amend agreements • Given the long-term nature of most service provision engagements, implementing procedures for amending agreements and flexibility in the relationship between the organisation and the service provider are important to the ongoing success of the service
Service Transfer	Service Transition	• Plan and track the transition of the service • Planning is critical for establishing expectations for both the client and service provider • Forms the basis for tracking transition and deployment tasks and for reviewing and verifying the service design
	Verify Design	• Establish and implement procedures to review and verify the service design • Removing defects early prevents problems during service deployment and enables the service provider to satisfy the client's requirements and meet the service level commitments • Establish an in-depth and rigorous review of the service design
	Resources Transferred Out	• Establish and implement procedures to verify and account for resources transferred to service providers • Track and manage resource transfers in order to facilitate a smooth transfer of responsibilities prior to service delivery • Enables the organisation to verify the transfer of the required resources and to facilitate handling any disputes regarding disposition of resources that might arise at completion
	Knowledge Transferred Out	• Ensure that transfer of knowledge to service providers is planned, supported and verified • Verification that knowledge transfer has successfully occurred can eliminate sources of doubt or confusion as the service moves into delivery • Comprehensive and detailed documentation of transferred knowledge also makes it easier for a client to bring the service delivery back in-house or transition to another service provider
Sourced Services Management	Service Provision Management	• Plan and track services management for the set of services being provided • Well-defined plan for governance and service management is necessary to ensure the organisation's success in managing and monitoring service providers • Planning and tracking are key aspects of service management for the services that occur throughout delivery
	Performance	• Establish and implement procedures to monitor and verify that service

Step	Task	Scope and Activities
	Monitoring	commitments are being met • Verify that the agreed upon service commitments are being met and take appropriate action which may include exercising remedies in the agreement when commitments are not met or are in jeopardy of being missed • The goal of the procedure is to optimise the cost of monitoring and conformance by generating maximum compliance with minimum cost
	Financial Management	• Establish and implement procedures for financial management of the services being provided • Procedures allow the client organisation to develop and maintain cost controls, manage the costs of performing outsourcing management, evaluate financial impact of changes to agreements, clearly understand costs, develop and distribute financial reports and resolve financial issues
	Agreement Management	• Establish and implement procedures for management of agreements governing the services being provided • Manage organisational understanding of key elements of agreements, as appropriate, such as definitions, service activity and task descriptions, service performance levels, problem escalation definitions and service conditions
	Problem and Incident Monitoring	• Participate in problem and incident monitoring and resolution • Monitor the service provider's adherence to problem severity management as well as participating with the service provider in understanding and resolving problems • Establish the need for and implement a reporting process for issues raised by internal stakeholders, such as end users
	Service Delivery Change Management	• Participate in change management activities • Manage modifications of the services in a controlled manner in order to minimise the impact on their delivery, including ensuring that retained services remain synchronised with outsourced services as service changes are implemented • Change management is focused on ensuring that all changes are assessed, approved, implemented and reviewed in a controlled manner
	Service Change Management	• Establish and implement procedures to manage modifications to services • Major business changes, due to growth, business mergers, acquisitions and reorganisations and changing customer requirements, can require service levels to be adjusted, redefined, or even temporarily suspended • Effective service management disciplines help ensure that the effect of changes to one area of the infrastructure or business process are identified prior to the change, that changes are planned and that back out plans are in place
	Review Service Performance	• Establish and implement procedures for reconciling service performance against expectations • Manage the performance of service providers in order to help ensure that the organisation receives the agreed service • Effective management includes identifying deviations in the performance of service providers and taking the appropriate corrective action to assure expected service delivery
	Stakeholder Feedback	• Establish and implement guidelines to collect and organise stakeholder inputs and feedback • Collect, organise and use stakeholder information in order to improve service delivery, service management and relationships with stakeholders
	Service Value Analysis	• Establish and implement procedures for performing value analysis of the services being provided • Expected value propositions for the outsourcing action and their expected outcomes must be well defined and documented

Step	Task	Scope and Activities
		• State value propositions as results that are quantifiable and measurable
	Continuation Decision	• Establish and implement procedures for making decisions about continuing the service • A procedure to reconcile provider performance against expectations as a trend over time will lead to fact-based decisions for fine tuning the services delivered and eventually for future service decisions between options • Service decision may include continued delivery of the service with no changes, identifying necessary amendments to agreements, renewing agreements for an extended duration, or terminating the agreements that are currently in place

Table 94 – Activities During Initiation/Transition and Service Delivery Phases

7.1.1.2 Activities for Ongoing Phases

As referred to above, the ongoing phase represents a set of activities that can be performed during the life of the service arrangement. The potential work for the solution architect in this phase is:

1. Identify the scope of the work and defining the approach to its performance as part of the solution design
2. Assisting in performing some of the work

One of the principles underpinning this approach is that the information technology should seek to get ahead of the curve in establishing a framework for adopting hosted and cloud services rather than having the business function bypass it.

The activities in this phase can be divided into three groups:

1. *Governance Focussed* – these are concerned with how the organisation approaches and implements information technology services that are provided externally

2. *Competency and Change Focussed* – these are concerned with how the organisation changes itself to accommodate the external mode of service provision

3. *Operations Focussed* – these are concerned with the ongoing operation of the service

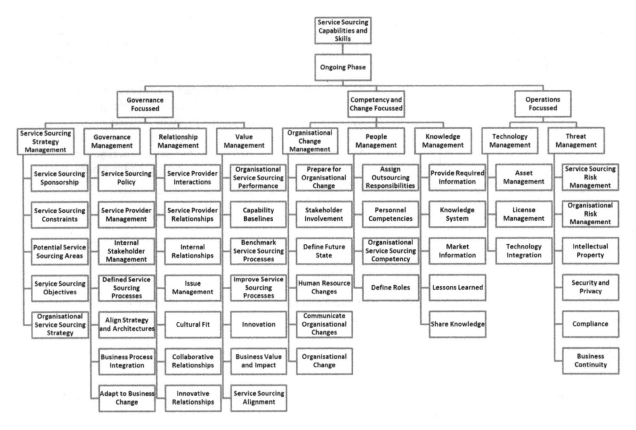

Figure 290 – Possible Solution Architecture Activities During Ongoing Service Phase

The Governance Focussed activities are:

Step	Task	Scope and Activities
Service Sourcing Strategy Management	Service Sourcing Sponsorship	• Establish business and IT management sponsorship for service sourcing • Ensuring that the correct level of senior management supports and is committed to the service sourcing initiatives is critical for the organisation, as service sourcing is often a strategic initiative that crosses functional groups within the organisation • Sponsorship should be established at the appropriate level to have the necessary scope and strategic perspective for the service sourcing activities
	Service Sourcing Constraints	• Identify the constraints that impact the organisation's potential uses of service sourcing • Understand the strategic, administrative and managerial implications of service sourcing
	Potential Service Sourcing Areas	• Decide to what extent service sourcing may be relevant to the organisation's delivery of information technology services • Examine the organisation's business strategies and plans and determine which business processes, skills or competencies are better handled by externally sourced service, leaving the organisation to concentrate on its own core competencies
	Service Sourcing Objectives	• Define, align and document service sourcing objectives • Service sourcing objectives set will reflect the underlying motives for the organisation considering service sourcing as an appropriate part of its information technology strategy • Clearly defined and measurable service sourcing objectives establish the service sourcing principles and enable management to set and attain performance expectations • Service sourcing objectives should be clearly established and supported, aligned with IT and business objectives and support achieving these

Step	Task	Scope and Activities
		business objectives
	Organisational Service Sourcing Strategy	• Define, communicate and maintain the service sourcing strategy of the organisation • Service sourcing strategy should clearly address the organisation's information technology sourcing strategy objectives and be in alignment with the organisation's information technology, business, growth and continuity strategies • Service sourcing objectives set will reflect the underlying motives for the organisation considering service sourcing as an appropriate information technology service provision strategy
Governance Management	Service Sourcing Policy	• Establish and implement the organisational information technology service sourcing policy • Provides the organisational structures, processes and mechanisms needed to manage, assess and improve the organisation's service sourcing initiatives and support the service sourcing strategy • Governance policy should enable effective execution of the key service sourcing activities • Demonstrates leadership and organisational commitment and is a key factor for information technology service sourcing success
	Service Provider Management	• Establish and implement procedures to manage service providers • Having effective relationships with service providers helps the service sourcing organisation expand its capabilities and respond to internal business changing requirements and demands • Includes tracking the performance of service provider • Should be proactive and collaborative, with customers and their service providers working together to resolve issues
	Internal Stakeholder Management	• Establish and implement procedures to manage internal stakeholders • Having procedures to manage the relationships with internal stakeholders helps the outsourcing organisation ensure that externally hosted services meet internal needs and respond to internal business changing demands
	Defined Service Sourcing Processes	• Establish and maintain documented outsourcing processes for use across the organisation • Processes help to ensure mechanisms are in place to manage relationships with service providers while meeting the organisation's service sourcing objectives • Without appropriate service sourcing processes in place, the problems may fail to be identified or managed adequately • Well-developed and implemented service sourcing processes enables the organisation to integrate and institutionalise best practices of planning, organising, acquiring, implementing, delivering, supporting and monitoring outsourcing performance, to ensure that the organisation's service sourcing activities support its business objectives
	Align Strategy and Architectures	• Align strategies and architectures to support service sourcing across the organisation • Engaging in service sourcing activities without ensuring that they are consistent with the organisation's information technology strategy and architectures can lead to significant risk, potential impacts on service delivery and performance and introduce unnecessary issues in service transfer • Continual monitoring of technological advances and regulatory trends will ensure that the organisation's technology architecture remains capable of supporting business process and service sourcing needs
	Business Process Integration	• Establish and implement procedures to manage the integration of business processes with those performed by service providers • IT-enabled service sourcing requires that the client organisation's business processes be integrated with those of the service provider • Processes must be coordinated between all the involved parties to achieve the agreed-to performance and service levels
	Adapt to Business	• Establish and implement guidelines for reviewing and adapting to changes

Step	Task	Scope and Activities
	Change	<ul><li>Processes should be constantly reviewed and refined to ensure that all activities add value appropriately service sourcing In order to achieve the maximum benefits of outsourcing, organisations should review their agreements and rectify any issues that have emerged due to change in business needs or constraints</li></ul>
Relationship Management	Service Provider Interactions	<ul><li>Establish and implement procedures to manage interactions with service providers</li><li>Providing a common point of contact such as a service provider relationship team helps ensure the continuity of communication</li><li>Team should be maintained throughout the service sourcing lifecycle</li></ul>
	Service Provider Relationships	<ul><li>Establish and implement procedures to manage service provider relationships</li><li>Having effective procedures to manage service provider relationships with existing service providers helps the organisation to communicate their changing needs and to proactively determine how to address them while also addressing the organisation's objectives</li><li>Interface between the organisation and its service providers is crucial to successful outcomes</li></ul>
	Internal Relationships	<ul><li>Establish and implement procedures to manage internal business and stakeholder relationships</li><li>Effective collection, analysis and tracking of internal business and stakeholder interactions enables the creation of an extensive record that can provide insight into internal requirements and needs</li><li>Having effective relationships with internal stakeholders helps the service sourcing organisation to understand the internal business and stakeholder changing needs</li></ul>
	Issue Management	<ul><li>Establish and implement procedures to manage issues and their resolution</li><li>Issue management covers identification, documentation, escalation, negotiation and dispute and conflict resolution of issues among the organisation, internal stakeholders and the service provider</li><li>Effective issue management requires that negotiation and resolution techniques between the organisation and service provider organisations be standardised as a common repeatable issue management process</li></ul>
	Cultural Fit	<ul><li>Identify organisational cultural characteristics that could impact the service sourcing relationship and the externally provided services and implement actions to achieve cultural fit</li><li>Addressing cultural differences also improves stakeholder satisfaction and enables all involved personnel to work together effectively</li></ul>
	Collaborative Relationships	<ul><li>Establish and implement guidelines for developing collaborative relationships with service providers</li><li>A key to successfully managing service sourcing during long-term relationships is building trust and collaboration that goes beyond an agreement's legal requirements to explore new ways that clients and service providers can engage in win-win activities</li></ul>
	Innovative Relationships	<ul><li>Develop relationships that focus on value creation through innovation</li><li>Value creation includes identifying opportunities of greater business value for the client, including innovations such as new business arrangements or enhanced technologies and other opportunities for creating value or making improvements</li></ul>
Value Management	Organisational Service Sourcing Performance	<ul><li>Establish and implement procedures to review organisational service sourcing performance</li><li>Organise key performance measurements across the client organisation in order to manage and improve organisational service sourcing performance</li><li>Organisations need to manage their service sourcing activities by identifying and utilising measures or indicators that best represent the factors that lead to improved customer, operational and financial performance</li></ul>
	Capability Baselines	<ul><li>Define capability baselines for the client organisation by organising service sourcing performance data</li></ul>

Step	Task	Scope and Activities
		• Provides a basis for the service sourcing organisation to organise whether performance deviations are within expected ranges or if they represent exceptions that need to be investigated and addressed
	Benchmark Service Sourcing Processes	• Benchmark the organisation's service sourcing -related processes by comparing performance with other organisations involved in similar relationships • Benchmarking allows the organisation to objectively organise its service sourcing processes • Measure the performance of the organisation's processes and compares them to the measured performance of industry best practices • Compare the organisation's processes to industry best practices in order to identify the practices that lead to superior performance • Compare the organisation's processes against standards or models
	Improve Service Sourcing Processes	• Improve service sourcing-related processes based on reviews of organisational outsourcing performance • Use the knowledge gained from performance reviews in order to improve the organisation's service sourcing performance and increase the stakeholders' value
	Innovation	• Establish and implement programs to encourage and deploy innovations through service sourcing relationships and service sourcing services across the organisation • Innovations may spring from many sources: people, markets and service providers, as well as reviews of ongoing service sourcing performance • Major changes that affect the organisation need to be actively managed because of the learning curve and potential impacts associated with the change
	Business Value and Impact	• Organise the business value and impact of organisational service sourcing performance • Evaluate the organisation's service sourcing capability and its contribution to business value and impacts
	Service Sourcing Alignment	• Align the organisation's service sourcing activities and results with its business objectives and strategy • Enhance the alignment of service sourcing results across the organisation and with organisational performance and business objectives • Analyses allow management to align service sourcing performance across the entire organisation and to use their service sourcing activities strategically to achieve organisational business objectives

Table 95 – Ongoing Phase Governance Focussed Activities

The Competency and Change Focussed activities are:

Step	Task	Scope and Activities
Organisational Change Management	Prepare for Organisational Change	• Prepare for changes across the organisation needed to support the organisation's service sourcing actions • Assess the organisation's readiness for change and determine the gaps that need to be closed to ensure a successful transition to a new service delivery and operation model • Service sourcing can have change implications for an organisation depending on the nature and scope of the service
	Stakeholder Involvement	• Identify and involve relevant stakeholders in service sourcing activities
	Define Future State	• Define the future organisational structure and process model to operate and support service sourcing • Organisational structure and its process architecture must be defined in order to establish the business model that will be implemented
	Human Resource	• Establish and implement human resource strategies and plans to support

Step	Task	Scope and Activities
	Changes	the organisation's service sourcing actions • Address the workforce changes that may occur as a result of service sourcing activities • Management should develop effective action plans to deal with personnel issues during its service sourcing activities
	Communicate Organisational Changes	• Establish and implement communications strategies and plans to support the organisation's service sourcing actions • Define and explain the compelling need for a potential service sourcing action • Business and technical justification of a potential service sourcing action should be communicated clearly and early in the process
	Organisational Change	• Manage organisational change to support service sourcing actions • New service delivery and operation model that service sourcing brings to an organisation impacts some of the key stakeholders - employees, users and support functions • Change management captures the impact of service sourcing on various human dimensions of the organisation throughout a service sourcing engagement and then enables addressing these issues
People Management	Assign Outsourcing Responsibilities	• Assign roles and responsibilities to outsourcing personnel based on appropriate personnel competencies • Having qualified personnel helps to ensure that work can be performed • Personnel competency is the combination of knowledge, skills and process abilities that specific personnel in the client organisation possess
	Personnel Competencies	• Develop personnel competencies needed by individuals with service sourcing responsibilities to perform their assignments • Address personnel competency gaps in order to enable personnel to effectively perform their roles and responsibilities • Effective training helps to ensure that personnel can perform their assigned roles and responsibilities • Training requirements must be identified to satisfy the needs of both the service sourcing engagement and the organisation's service sourcing objectives
	Organisational Service Sourcing Competency	• Define and manage a workforce competency focused on service sourcing across the organisation • Organisation must develop a workforce competency in organising, planning, managing and evaluating service sourcing activities • Failure to address the knowledge, skill and competency needs of those involved in service sourcing and governance activities exposes the organisation to risks that could be prevented by having a knowledgeable and competent service sourcing workforce
	Define Roles	• Define and communicate the roles and responsibilities of service sourcing personnel across the organisation • Clearly define the roles, responsibilities and authority of service sourcing personnel, as part of the overall service sourcing process, in order to enable them to effectively perform their assigned work • Aligning outsourcing personnel's roles, responsibilities and authority with organisational objectives should result in improved performance
Knowledge Management	Provide Required Information	• Identify, control and provide the information that personnel need to perform their service sourcing responsibilities • Provide access to the information that is essential for personnel to do their work in order to enable personnel to work efficiently • Easy access to required information enables personnel to be more efficient and effective in the performance of their work
	Knowledge System	• Utilise a knowledge recording and management system or tool to identify,

Step	Task	Scope and Activities
		control and disseminate service sourcing information • A knowledge system is not necessarily a central repository of information but is rather a coordinated method for managing and communicating needed information
	Market Information	• Organise and use information about the service provider market • Information includes the service provider's industry market share, external delivery partners and their existing clients
	Lessons Learned	• Organise and use knowledge gained from service sourcing activities • Effectively organising and using the knowledge gained from prior and current initiatives enables clients to reuse its best practices, to address problems that have occurred and to improve overall value obtained through current and future initiatives
	Share Knowledge	• Establish and implement procedures to share knowledge among stakeholders • Knowledge sharing procedures also clarify the rules by which knowledge can be shared between internal stakeholders, client service sourcing personnel, service providers and their suppliers and partners

Table 96 – Ongoing Phase Competency and Change Focussed Activities

The Operations Focussed activities are:

Step	Task	Scope and Activities
Technology Management	Asset Management	Ensure that technology assets are managed according to documented procedures
	License Management	Ensure that technology licenses are managed according to documented procedures
	Technology Integration	• Establish and implement procedures to manage the organisation's integration of its technology infrastructure with service providers • Integration can range in scope from integrating with a single service sourcing initiative and one service provider to more complex cases of integrating with several initiatives and multiple service providers and their appropriate partners • For the integration of technology infrastructure may be identified during the process of gathering requirements of a service sourcing opportunity
Threat Management	Service Sourcing Risk Management	• Establish and implement procedures to identify, assess and manage service sourcing risks • Effective risk management is particularly critical in the early stages of a service sourcing initiative, where requirements are being organised and service is being designed to meet those requirements • Problems encountered here can impact the success of service delivery and associated business benefits throughout the life of the initiative
	Organisational Risk Management	• Establish and implement procedures to manage risks across multiple sourced services and service providers • Effective identification and assessment of risks enables the organisation to take mitigating actions to lower the impact should a risk event occur • Effective risk management improves the stakeholders' confidence in the organisation's ability to maintain needed services and service levels
	Intellectual Property	• Establish and implement procedures to protect the intellectual property of stakeholders • Inappropriate use or disclosure of intellectual property can damage the relationship with stakeholders, may cause financial loss and make the client organisation vulnerable to disputes or legal action • Organisation should have a formalised policy on the protection of

Step	Task	Scope and Activities
		intellectual property that is used to provide direction for creating the procedures on protection of intellectual property
	Security and Privacy	• Establish and implement procedures to meet security and privacy requirements • Breakdowns, such as security breaches, can impact the organisation's ability to provide business continuity, thereby damaging the relationship and making the involved parties vulnerable to legal action • Effective security is essential for meeting privacy requirements and protecting intellectual property • Security requirements may come from the organisation or statutes and regulations governing the service being delivered
	Compliance	• Establish and implement procedures to comply with applicable standards and statutory and regulatory requirements • Organisation must implement procedures to address governance, risk and compliance • Procedures ensure that they comply with standards, statutes and regulations that impact their service sourcing capability and their services in order to meet statutory, regulatory and stakeholder requirements and to avoid stakeholder dissatisfaction and legal or audit issues
	Business Continuity	• Establish and implement procedures to ensure business continuity of sourced services • Prepare for possible disasters in order to minimise their impact on the client organisation's ability to continue business activities • Preparation covers service delivery, security, the protection of intellectual property, crisis management and the safety of personnel and promotes confidence in the organisation's and service providers' ability to react effectively to adverse situations

Table 97 – Ongoing Phase Operations Focussed Activities

7.1.2 Supplier Assessment and Validation

This section expands on the use of the Service Organisation Controls approach described above for supplier assessment and validation. These are a set of checks to be applied across the areas of the supplier, security, availability, processing integrity, confidentiality and privacy. There are currently 53 controls in total across all topics. This is a generalised and detailed set of checks that can be adapted for each service provision arrangement.

The Service Organisation Controls structure is:

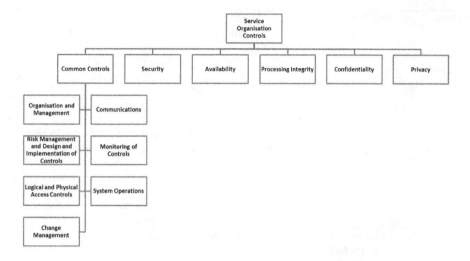

Figure 291 – Service Organisation Controls Structure

The detail of the controls across these topics is listed in the table below. This can be used as a checklist to gauge the service supplier and to identify potential gaps during supplier selection and evaluation. The same validation process can be repeated if necessary during the life of the service supply arrangement.

Number	Control Topic	Control Subtopic	Control Description
1	Common Controls	Organisation and Management	The ***Service Provider/Supplier*** has defined organisational structures, reporting lines, authorities, and responsibilities for the design, development, implementation, operation, maintenance and monitoring of the Solution/Service enabling it to meet its commitments and requirements as they relate to ***Security/Availability/Processing Integrity/Confidentiality***.
2			Responsibility and accountability for designing, developing, implementing, operating, maintaining, monitoring and approving the ***Service Provider/Supplier's Solution/Service*** controls are assigned to individuals within the ***Service Provider/Supplier*** with authority to ensure policies and other solution/service requirements are effectively promulgated and placed in operation.
3			Personnel responsible for designing, developing, implementing, operating, maintaining and monitoring the ***Solution/Service*** affecting ***Security/Availability/Processing Integrity/Confidentiality*** have the qualifications and resources to fulfil their responsibilities.
4			The ***Service Provider/Supplier*** has established workforce conduct standards, implemented workforce candidate background screening procedures and conducts enforcement procedures to enable it to meet its commitments and requirements as they relate to ***Security/Availability/Processing Integrity/Confidentiality***.
			The ***Service Provider/Supplier*** has defined organisational structures, reporting lines, authorities, and responsibilities for the design, development, implementation, operation, maintenance and monitoring of the ***Solution/Service*** enabling it to meet its commitments and requirements as they relate to ***Security/Availability/Processing Integrity/Confidentiality***.
1		Communications	Information regarding the design and operation of the ***Solution/Service*** and its boundaries has been prepared and communicated to authorised internal and external *Solution/Service* users to permit users to understand their role in the ***Solution/Service*** and the results of ***Solution/Service*** operation.
2			The ***Service Provider/Supplier's Security/Availability/Processing Integrity/Confidentiality*** commitments are communicated to external users, as appropriate, and those commitments and the associated *Solution/Service* requirements are communicated to

Number	Control Topic	Control Subtopic	Control Description
			internal **Solution/Service** users to enable them to carry out their responsibilities.
3			The **Service Provider/Supplier** communicates the responsibilities of internal and external users and others whose roles affect **Solution/Service** operation.
4			Internal and external personnel with responsibility for designing, developing, implementing, operating, maintaining and monitoring controls, relevant to the **Security/Availability/Processing Integrity/Confidentiality** of the **Solution/Service** have the information necessary to carry out those responsibilities.
5			Internal and external **Solution/Service** users have been provided with information on how to report **Security/Availability/Processing Integrity/Confidentiality** failures, incidents, concerns, and other complaints to appropriate personnel.
1		Risk Management And Design And Implementation Of Controls	The **Service Provider/Supplier**: 1 - Identifies potential threats that would impair **Solution/Service's Security/Availability/Processing Integrity/Confidentiality** commitments and requirements 2 - Analyses the significance of risks associated with the identified threats 3 - Determines mitigation strategies for those risks (including controls and other mitigation strategies).
2			The **Service Provider/Supplier** designs, develops, and implements controls, including policies and procedures, to implement its risk mitigation strategy.
3			The **Service Provider/Supplier**: 1 - Identifies and assesses changes (for example, environmental, regulatory, and technological changes) that could significantly affect the **Solution/Service** of internal control for **Security/Availability/Processing Integrity/Confidentiality** and reassesses risks and mitigation strategies based on the changes 2 - Reassesses the suitability of the design and deployment of control activities based on the operation and monitoring of those activities and updates them as necessary.
1		Monitoring Of Controls	The design and operating effectiveness of controls are periodically evaluated against **Security/Availability/Processing Integrity/Confidentiality** commitments and requirements, corrections and other necessary actions relating to identified deficiencies are taken in a timely manner.
1		Logical And Physical Access Controls	Logical access security software, infrastructure, and architectures have been implemented to support: 1 - Identification and authentication of authorised users 2 - Restriction of authorised user access to **Solution/Service** components, or portions thereof, authorised by management, including hardware, data, software, mobile devices, output, and offline elements 3 - Prevention and detection of unauthorised access.
2			New internal and external **Solution/Service** users are registered and authorised prior to being issued **Solution/Service** credentials and granted the ability to access the **Solution/Service**. User **Solution/Service** credentials are removed when user access is no longer authorised.
3			Internal and external **Solution/Service** users are identified and authenticated when accessing the **Solution/Service** components (for example, infrastructure, software, and data).
4			Access to data, software, functions, and other IT resources is authorised and is modified or removed based on roles,

Number	Control Topic	Control Subtopic	Control Description
			responsibilities, or the **Solution/Service** design and changes to them.
5			Physical access to facilities housing the **Solution/Service** (for example, data centres, backup media storage, and other sensitive locations as well as sensitive **Solution/Service** components within those locations) is restricted to authorised personnel.
6			Logical access security measures have been implemented to protect against **Security/Availability/Processing Integrity/Confidentiality** threats from sources outside the boundaries of the **Solution/Service**.
7			The transmission, movement, and removal of information is restricted to authorised users and processes, and is protected during transmission, movement, or removal enabling the **Service Provider/Supplier** to meet its commitments and requirements as they relate to **Security/Availability/Processing Integrity/Confidentiality**.
8			Controls have been implemented to prevent or detect and act upon the introduction of unauthorised or malicious software.
1		System Operations	Vulnerabilities of *Solution/Service* components to **Security/Availability/Processing Integrity/Confidentiality** breaches and incidents due to malicious acts, natural disasters, or errors are monitored and evaluated and countermeasures are implemented to compensate for known and new vulnerabilities.
2			**Security/Availability/Processing Integrity/Confidentiality** incidents, including logical and physical security breaches, failures, concerns, and other complaints, are identified, reported to appropriate personnel, and acted on in accordance with established incident response procedures.
1		Change Management	**Security/Availability/Processing Integrity/Confidentiality** commitments and requirements, are addressed, during the **Solution/Service** implementation lifecycle including design, acquisition, implementation, configuration, testing, modification, and maintenance of **Solution/Service** components.
2			Infrastructure, data, software, and procedures are updated as necessary to remain consistent with the **Solution/Service** commitments and requirements as they relate to **Security/Availability/Processing Integrity/Confidentiality**.
3			Change management processes are initiated when deficiencies in the design or operating effectiveness of controls are identified during **Solution/Service** operation and monitoring.
4			Changes to **Solution/Service** components are authorised, designed, developed, configured, documented, tested, approved, and implemented in accordance with **Security/Availability/Processing Integrity/Confidentiality** commitments and requirements.
1	Availability		Current processing capacity and usage are maintained, monitored, and evaluated to manage demand and to enable the implementation of additional capacity to help meet availability commitments and requirements.
2			Environmental protections, software, data backup processes, and recovery infrastructure are designed, developed, implemented, operated, maintained, and monitored to meet availability commitments and requirements.
3			Procedures supporting **Solution/Service** recovery in accordance with recovery plans are periodically tested to help meet availability commitments and requirements.
1	Processing Integrity		Procedures exist to prevent, detect, and correct processing errors to meet processing integrity commitments and requirements.
2			**Solution/Service** inputs are measured and recorded completely, accurately, and timely in accordance with processing integrity commitments and requirements.
3			Data is processed completely, accurately, and timely as authorised in accordance with pro-cessing integrity commitments and

Number	Control Topic	Control Subtopic	Control Description
			requirements.
4			Data is stored and maintained completely and accurately for its specified life span in accordance with processing integrity commitments and requirements.
5			*Solution/Service* output is complete, accurate, distributed, and retained in accordance with processing integrity commitments and requirements.
6			Modification of data is authorised, using authorised procedures in accordance with processing integrity commitments and requirements.
1	Confidentiality		Confidential information is protected during the *Solution/Service* design, development, testing, implementation, and change processes in accordance with confidentiality commitments and requirements.
2			Confidential information within the boundaries of the *Solution/Service* is protected against unauthorised access, use, and disclosure during input, processing, retention, output, and disposition in accordance with confidentiality commitments and requirements.
3			Access to confidential information from outside the boundaries of the *Solution/Service* and disclosure of confidential information is restricted to authorised parties in accordance with confidentiality commitments and requirements.
4			The *Service Provider/Supplier* obtains confidentiality commitments that are consistent with the *Service Provider/Supplier's* confidentiality requirements from vendors and other third parties whose products and services comprise part of the *Solution/Service* and have access to confidential information.
5			Compliance with confidentiality commitments and requirements by vendors and others third parties whose products and services comprise part of the *Solution/Service* is assessed on a periodic and as-needed basis and corrective action is taken, if necessary.
6			Changes to confidentiality commitments and requirements are communicated to internal and external users, vendors, and other third parties whose products and services are included in the *Solution/Service*.
1	Privacy		The *Service Provider/Supplier* defines documents, communicates, and assigns accountability for its privacy policies and procedures.
2			The *Service Provider/Supplier* provides notice about its privacy policies and procedures and identifies the purposes for which personal information is collected, used, retained, and disclosed.
3			The *Service Provider/Supplier* describes the choices available to the individual and obtains implicit or explicit consent with respect to the collection, use, and disclosure of personal information.
4			The *Service Provider/Supplier* collects personal information only for the purposes identified in the notice.
5			The *Service Provider/Supplier* limits the use of personal information to the purposes identified in the notice and for which the individual has provided implicit or explicit consent. The *Service Provider/Supplier* retains personal information for only as long as necessary to fulfil the stated purposes or as required by law or regulations and thereafter appropriately disposes of such information.
6			The *Service Provider/Supplier* provides individuals with access to their personal information for re-view and update.
7			The *Service Provider/Supplier* discloses personal information to third parties only for the purposes identified in the notice and with the implicit or explicit consent of the individual.
8			The *Service Provider/Supplier* protects personal information against unauthorised access (both physical and logical).

Number	Control Topic	Control Subtopic	Control Description
9			The *Service Provider/Supplier* maintains accurate, complete, and relevant personal information for the purposes identified in the notice.
10			The *Service Provider/Supplier* monitors compliance with its privacy policies and procedures and has procedures to address privacy-related complaints and disputes.

Table 98 – Service Organisation Controls

Chapter 8. The Solution Architecture Function

8.1 Introduction

This section looks at the topics of the solution architect and the skills, capabilities, personal characteristics and experience they should have and of the solution architecture function. It describes a solution architect competency model and identifies existing learning and skills frameworks that could be used to assess and improve solution architects.

It introduces the concept of a Solution Architecture Centre of Excellence in the context of the structure of the solution architecture function.

It identifies a range of solution architecture frameworks that can be used to assist in the delivery of services.

8.2 Solution Architecture Skills, Capabilities and Experience

The following is an idealised set of skills, capabilities and experience the solution architect should possess in order to perform the role and deliver value to the information technology function and the wider business.

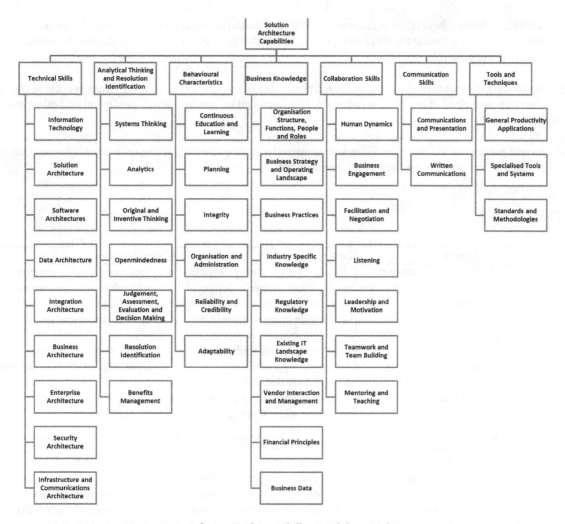

Figure 292 – Solution Architect Skills, Capabilities and Experience

This is a both a broad and deep set of skills. Many of these skills are not unique to solution architecture. Many are basic skills required to work effectively in an organisation. The individual architect may not possess all these skills. The gaps can be identified and filled-in over time. The wider solution architecture function should have access to all these skills.

This is an informal solution architect capability model. Some of these skills will be more important than others. Each organisation will require different sets of skills from its solution architects depending on their roles, the work to be done, the profile of the organisation, the expected programme of work and the area in which the organisation operates. The organisation can use this general capabilities model as a basis for deriving one that is specific to their needs.

These capabilities and characteristics are divided in seven groups:

1. *Technical Skills* – these are skills, knowledge and experience in the application and use of technologies and their incorporation into solution designs
2. *Analytical Thinking and Resolution Identification* – these are skills in the areas of applying knowledge and experience to situations and information and applying creativity to the identification and assessment of solution options
3. *Behavioural Characteristics* – these are personal characteristics, ways of performing work, interacting with others and conducting oneself
4. *Business Knowledge* – these relate to knowledge about the organisation, the specific area in which it operates, partners, suppliers and competitors and the regulatory landscape as well as the wider business environment and business operating principles
5. *Collaboration Skills* – these are skills in working with others, both within the solution architecture function and with the wider business organisation and handling and resolving issues

6. ***Communication Skills*** – these relate to the way in which the solution architect communicates and presents ideas
7. ***Tools and Techniques*** – these are skills in various tools, methodologies, approaches and standards the solution architect will use in performing the role

This capability model can be used to assess the skill levels of member of the solution architecture team in order to create training and development plans. It can be used to identify high-performing individuals and team members with aptitudes in particular areas.

The solution architect can use this model to define a programme to develop their skills. The solution architect can use this framework to discuss their career progression with their manager.

8.2.1 Technical Skills

Capability	Objective	Description	Characteristics
Information Technology	Solution architects must possess a broad knowledge of information technology architectures, principles, deployment and operating models and their application and use in order to design technically effective and efficient solutions.	This requires the ability to apply technical knowledge to design solutions. Solution architects must have a wide range of knowledge across information technology concepts, systems, applications and operating models and patterns. Solution architects must be able to use this knowledge during the solution design process.	• Broad range of information technology and experience including that not currently in use in the organisation • Ability to reuse and apply knowledge to solution designs
Solution Architecture	Solution architects must understand the principles of solution architecture and design and be able to design complete deliverable, operable and usable information technology solutions.	This requires knowledge and experience of solution architecture principles and their application to creating realistic and achievable solutions. Solution architects must understand what comprises a solution and be able to create designs for new solutions that meet the underlying business requirement as well as being technically sound.	• Understanding of what a solution consists of • Be able to create quality solution designs that deliver on the essential business needs • Be able to create solution designs that are deliverable, operable, usable, supportable and maintainable
Software Architectures	Solution architects must understand how the software components of solutions are developed and implemented so solutions incorporating these elements can be optimally designed	This requires knowledge of the principles of software development and operation and what can be realistically achieved during the development process. Solution architects must understand the development approaches and tools used by the organisation so the solution being designed include these standards.	• Knowledge of software development and operation principles and patterns • Knowledge of software development approaches adopted by the organisation
Data Architecture	Solution architects must understand data architectures including data storage, integration, transfer and exchange so the data components of the solution can be optimally	This requires knowledges of data storage and data integration principles across all aspects of the organisation data landscape. Solution architects must be able to design solutions to accommodate the types, movement and storage	• Knowledge of data storage design • Knowledge of data-related capacity planning • Knowledge of data security

Capability	Objective	Description	Characteristics
	designed subject to data security and privacy requirements and principles.	of data and be able to handle the volumes of data and data-related transactions.	and privacy • Knowledge of solution data lifecycle
Integration Architecture	Solution architects must understand how solution components and solutions can integrated and interact with one another and to define and optimise those activities.	This requires a knowledge of integration options, standards, approaches and technologies. Solution architects must be able to define the most suitable approaches and technologies and must be able to analyse performance and throughput.	• Knowledge of integration, interaction and transfer approaches and technologies • Knowledge of integration-related transformation and processing • Knowledge of integration-related capacity planning • Knowledge of integration-related security
Business Architecture	Solution architects must understand how to analyse the operation of an existing business function or entire organisation with a view to improving its operations or developing a new business function, with a strong focus on processes and technology in order to incorporate these components into solution design.	This requires knowledge of business function operations including business function structure, business processes, technologies and applications and systems used and information and data generated and used. Solution architects must be able to design solutions to accommodate business architecture changes.	• Knowledge of business architecture principles • Knowledge of organisation and business function structures • Knowledge of organisation and business function business processes • Knowledge of organisation and business function systems and technology infrastructure • Knowledge of organisation and business function information and data
Enterprise Architecture	Solution architects must understand the principles of enterprise architecture in order to design solutions that incorporate enterprise architecture standards and principles.	This requires a knowledge of enterprise architecture principles and standards and how they affect the design of solutions. The solution architect must work with enterprise architecture to comply with standards and to develop and enhance those standards.	• Knowledge of enterprise architecture principles and standards and its application to and influence on solution design
Security Architecture	Solution architects must understand security across the solution landscape including identity and access control, data security and privacy, integration, transfer and exchange, infrastructure, audit, management and administration security in	This requires a knowledge of the security landscape as it affects the operation and use of solutions from authentication and access control, role-based access rights, data storage and movement security and encryption. The solution architect must work with the security architecture function to understand security standards	• Knowledge of information technology security principles and standards across all aspects of solution design and operation • Knowledge of security risks associated with solution designs

Capability	Objective	Description	Characteristics
	order to ensure that solutions are secure.	and to apply them to solution design.	
Infrastructure and Communications Architecture	Solution architects must under the infrastructure on which the solutions are implemented and operated in order to ensure that the solution infrastructure is sufficient to meet business and operational requirements	This requires a knowledge of infrastructure design principles across processing, storage and communications, both within the organisation and externally provided infrastructure. The solution architect must understand how the solution design impacts on technology infrastructure and what infrastructure requirements the solution will give rise to	• Knowledge of information technology infrastructure principles • Knowledge of the impact solution design and solution operations will have on technology infrastructure

Table 99 – Solution Architect Technical Skills

8.2.2 Analytical Thinking and Resolution Identification

Capability	Objective	Description	Characteristics
Systems Thinking	Solutions architects must understand how people, processes and technology and their properties and characteristics work together as an integrated system in order to design complete solutions that include all components required to work.	Systems thinking is concerned with the system as a whole that arises from the interoperation of its constituent people, processes and technology. The behaviour of the system cannot always be understood by understanding its individual components. Being aware of the systems thinking view means solution architects will design complete solutions rather than individual components.	• Knowledge of systems thinking principles including the likely impacts of changes in individual components and how positive and negative reinforcement works in system operation • Knowledge of how the system reacts to and compensates for changes, internal and external
Analytics	Solution architects must be able to analyse data in a wide variety for formats and types in order to understand characteristics of the problematic situation for which a solution is being designed in order to include information and insights from those analyses into the design.	Analytics is a general set of skills relating to data analysis to derive information and insights from raw information. Analysis of solution-related data can provide solution-related understanding across many arears such as capacity, performance, throughput, growth across the resource dimensions of numbers of users, transactions, data volumes and over time, including time-based patterns of resource-consumption.	• Understanding of the principles of data analysis • Knowledge of solution-related data especially in the areas of capacity planning and forecasting • Knowledge of trend analysis
Original and Inventive Thinking	Solution architects must be able to produce new approaches, alternatives and options for resolving problematic situations for approaches in order to	The ability to generate inventive and creative solution options means that a complete range of solution options is considered. Assumptions and prejudices are questions and not taken for	• Ability to apply inventive and creating thinking in a structured way • Ability to consider all options

Capability	Objective	Description	Characteristics
	generate solution design options	granted. New ideas are accepted or rejected on their merits and value to the solution design.	
Open-mindedness	Solution architects should be open to new concepts, ideas and technologies that may be able to be usefully incorporated into solution designs and be open to the views and opinion of others that may contain suggestion on how solution designs can be improved.	The ability to accept that new concepts, ideas and technologies could contribute to the design of a solution means that a wider range of solution options are considered. The ability of the solution architect to accept feedback and comments on solution designs from other stakeholders and participants in the solution design process means that solutions are subject to validation and assessment throughout the design process.	• Ability to accept new ideas • Ability to accept feedback
Judgement, Assessment, Evaluation and Decision Making	Solution architects must be able to apply judgements when assessing information and solution design options. Solution architects must understand the factors involved in performing structured evaluations and decisions and to apply them to create better solution designs.	The solution design process is concerned with making decisions by evaluating available information, available options and the underlying problematic situation that the solution aims to resolve. The ability to apply structured assessment and decision-making principles based on analysis and evaluation factors means that solution designs are based on evidence. The solution architect must be able to balance options and make appropriate compromises in order to progress the design process. The solution architect must not get cause in an analysis/decision loop constantly looking for more information in order to achieve an unachievable perfection in the solution design.	• Ability to define and apply assessment and decision-making factors • Ability to make decisions based on available information • Ability to limit appropriately the time and effort expended on analysis and option creation based on diminishing value being achieved
Resolution Identification	Solution architects must be able to understand and define the core of the problem to be resolved or the opportunity to be developed in order to define practical, realistic and achievable resolutions that contribute to the overall solution design process.	The ability to define a solution that resolves a problem or addresses a challenges means being able to: • Clearly and accurately define the problem to be resolved in a way that is accepted by all stakeholders, resolving differences and conflicts while doing so • Identifying resolution options using creativity and inventiveness	• Ability to define problems clearly and accurately • Ability to resolve differences and create a common understanding • Ability to articulate the most acceptable and preferred resolution • Ability to accept suggestions and modify the solution design

Capability	Objective	Description	Characteristics
		• Making decisions about options using judgement to define the preferred resolution • Articulating the resolution and gaining acceptable by stakeholders through reasoned justification • Ability to accept feedback and modify the resolution accordingly	
Benefits Management	The solution architect must be able to define the actual benefits the solution will deliver in order to justify the solution design options selected and the cost of implementing and operating the solution.	The designed solution will be expected to achieve benefits in terms of direct explicitly quantifiable benefits and other indeterminate or non-quantifiable benefits. The solution architect must be able to evaluate these stated benefits to validate that they are achievable and to determine how the solution as designed can achieve them. The solution has a cost to design, implement and operate. The total value of all the benefits must be greater than this.	• Ability to assess solution benefits • Ability to value solution benefits • Ability to assess solution cost against the value the benefits delivered • Ability to validate the solution can deliver the expected benefits

Table 100 – Solution Architect Analytical Thinking and Resolution Identification Skills

8.2.3 Behavioural Characteristics

Capability	Objective	Description	Characteristics
Continuous Education and Learning	Solution architects must be able and willing to learn new ideas, technologies and concepts as well as learn about the business areas where solutions will be targeted to address business needs to ensure that solution designs are optimal.	Every solution design process involves learning about the underlying business area where the problem or challenge exists that the solution is intended to address. Similarly, the underlying technologies incorporated into solutions are constantly changing. Being capable of learning new concepts and ideas and then being able to apply that new education to solution designs is a vital part of solution architecture.	• Openness and the ability to acquire knowledge • Ability to apply newly acquired learning
Planning	Solution architects must be able to plan the design process to understand the scope of the work, create a plan to perform the design work and create a solution design. This ensures that	The solution design process must have a beginning and an end. The solution architect must be able to plan the work needed to bring the design process to a successful conclusion and to articulate that plan to stakeholders. The plan	• Ability to plan the solution design process • Ability to manage the solution design plan and process and report of progress and status of work

Capability	Objective	Description	Characteristics
	the design process achieves a conclusion and so can move to the next stages if appropriate.	needs to include the activities that must be performed, the resources required and the schedule for the work. The solution architect must also be able to manage changes during the design process and update the plan. The solution architect must be able to communicate on the progress of the plan.	• Ability to manage changes during solution design
Integrity	Solution architects must demonstrate (and be allowed to demonstrate) integrity. They must be able to win the respect and trust of stakeholders in the solution design process. They must be realistic in what can be achieved and must deliver on the expectations they create. They must be able to articulate when solution designs present problems. They must communicate when problems are occurring with solution design process as early as possible.	In the solution design process, integrity means: • Meeting agreed deadlines and performing assigned actions • Raising potential problems with the resolution being asked for as soon as the architect becomes aware of the situation • Being honest in dealings with stakeholders and other participants in the solution design process • Being honest about mistakes made and taking action to rectify them as soon as practical • Not raising issues unnecessarily without due consideration and assessment • Not overstating the potential seriousness of possible problems	• Ability to identify, evaluate and present potential problems and determine possible resolution options • Ability to manage workload and create and comply with realistic and achievable work schedule
Organisation and Administration	Solution architects must be able to organise their work and the various business engagement and solution design activities. This ensures that work is done to a sufficient quality within the expected time and that the work is documented to ensure there is a record of what was done.	Solution architecture engagements should be organised and performed in an efficient, effective and timely manner. Expectations should be managed and delivered on. The engagements should be administered with information collected and artefacts created stored centrally, effort recorded, meetings planned for and their outcomes recorded. Work should be prioritised. The solution architect must be able to manage the information collection and	• Ability to work efficiently and effectively and to complete work to a sufficient quality within the agreed time • Ability to administer workload • Ability to manage and deliver expectations • Ability to manage and organise information and documentation

Capability	Objective	Description	Characteristics
		analysis process to avoid devoting too much time to it.	
Reliability and Credibility	Solution architects must be able to gain the trust of the business stakeholders and other participants in solution design engagements. The outputs from the engagement must be credible and accepted by stakeholders.	Solution designs must be credible and deserved to be believed and accepted. The underlying work done to create the design must be reliable. The solution architect must be able to be relied on to work effectively and create solution designs that can also be relied on to work and address the problem or challenge. The solution stakeholders will feel confident to share information with and involve the solution architect in making decisions.	• Ability to gain the confidence of stakeholders so they have credibility in the solution design work • The solution stakeholders willingly share information with the solution architect • The solution stakeholders willingly involve the solution architect in making decisions on solution options
Adaptability	Solution architects must be able to work on a wide variety of solution types in a variety of engagements across the full range of functions within the organisations and be able to create solution designs to meet all these circumstances.	The solution architecture function will be called upon to work across the organisation to create solution designs to meet many different needs. The solution architecture team must be adaptable and flexible to work on all these engagements.	• Ability to work across many solution types across all organisation functions • Ability to willingly adapt to different circumstances with ease and speed

Table 101 – Solution Architect Behavioural Characteristics

8.2.4 Business Knowledge

Capability	Objective	Description	Characteristics
Organisation Structure, Functions, People and Roles	The solution architect must understand the structure of the organisation in which they work in order to operate effectively.	The solution architecture function designs solutions to deliver value to the business. To be good at means the solution architects must understand the functional structure of the organisation and the roles and the people who occupy them in order to navigate through the complexities of the solution design process. This knowledge will allow the solution architect identify sources of business expertise when necessary. Organisation and people knowledge means the solution architect will be better able to handle organisational politics.	• Knowledge of the organisation structure, business functions, roles and people
Business Strategy and Operating Landscape	The solution architect must design solutions to meet the needs of the business. To do this successfully, the solution	The solution architect must have a good awareness and appreciation of the strategy of the business and the associated business objectives. This knowledge will govern the	• Knowledge of the business strategy and associated objectives • Knowledge of the business

Capability	Objective	Description	Characteristics
	architect must understand what the business is looking to achieve and the environment in which it operates.	solutions being designed.	operating landscape
Business Practices	The solution architect must understand how businesses function in general and the practices and principles that underpin general business operations. This will ensure that solutions will work in a business context.	There are common practices and principles that apply to most organisations. There is a common operating model. There are common processes and structures across the area of business strategy and management, core business operations and supporting processes. The solution architect must have a good general understanding of these to ensure that solutions will work in this framework.	• Knowledge of the general principles of business operations and practices • Knowledge of common business structures and processes
Industry Specific Knowledge	The solution architect should understand the specific area in which the organisation operates, the products and services it supplies, its consumers and the specific concerns and issues that apply to make certain that solutions incorporate this knowledge.	The specific area in which an organisation operates will have its own challenges. Industry-specific knowledge will ensure that the solution architect can apply experience of solutions that have work successfully with similar organisations. This will increase the value those solutions provide to the organisation. The solution architect must keep up to date with what is happening in the organisation's sector, any trends that are occurring, what solution suppliers in the sector are offering, what industry organisations are promoting and what partner and competitor organisations are doing.	• Knowledge of the specific industry sector in which the organisation operates • Ability to keep current with trends and changes in the sector • Knowledge of suppliers and partners and the solutions they offer or are implementing • Knowledge of competitors and the solutions they are implementing
Regulatory Knowledge	The solution architect must understand the changing regulatory landscape in which the organisation operates. Regulatory changes give rise to may requests for new solutions. This knowledge will ensure that solutions are designed that meet the needs of the business.	Every organisation will be subject to a range of regulations, both industry-specific and general. The set of regulations is constantly changing. Regulatory and compliance demands are a common source of requests for new solutions. Keeping current with the relevant regulations means the solution architect will be able to engage quickly with the business should the requirement for a solution arise.	• Knowledge of regulations that apply to the organisation • Ability to keep current with changes in regulatory and compliance frameworks • Ability to understand the impact regulations and regulatory changes will have on the operations and solutions of the organisation
Existing IT Landscape Knowledge	The solution architect must understand the existing set of solutions and technologies that are	The organisation will have an existing set of technology infrastructure on which existing solutions operate. New solutions	• Knowledge of the existing technology infrastructure • Knowledge of the existing

Capability	Objective	Description	Characteristics
	installed and operate within the organisations as new solutions will have to co-exist and integrate with the existing technology and solution landscape.	will either or both of operate on this landscape and need to integrate with some of the existing solutions. Knowledge about the technologies and solutions in use in the organisations will be necessary to create operable solution designs.	solution infrastructure
Vendor Interaction and Management	The solution architect must be able to work with providers of products and services that are included in solution designs and ensure that the best interests of the organisation are always given priority.	Many solutions will incorporate products or services provided by external suppliers. The solution architect must know how to work with vendors to identify the most appropriate products and services that meet the needs of the organisation and know how to interact with suppliers to the advantage of the organisation.	• Knowledge of procurements standards and procedures • Ability to understand the functions and features of products and services and how they can best serve the needs of the organisation • Ability to understand how external products and services can be integrated into the organisation's solution and technology infrastructure
Financial Principles	The solution architect must know the way the organisation accounts for expenditure on solutions as, for example, capital and operating expenses to understand the costs of solutions in order to determine the most cost-effective solution options.	Solutions cost money to implement and operate. Organisations account for expenditure in different ways with different cost models for different sets of internally and externally supplied products and services. The solution architect must also realise the proportion each of the components of the solution contributes to the overall solution cost. Knowing the financial standards the organisation applies means that the costs of solution options can be defined. This will be one of the factors used to select the most suitable solution.	• Knowledge of organisation financial cost model • Knowledge of the cost of solution components
Business Data	The business will already store and process data, both structured and unstructured, operational, reference and metadata, original and derived data in a range of storage platforms and technologies. New solutions will both generate and use new and data. The solution architect must understand business data structures to create solution designs that work	New solutions will require existing data to be migrated as well as new data to be loaded. This data may need to be transformed to suit the requirements of the solution. The solution may need to integrate with existing business data structures. Data used for reporting and analysis may be derived from operational data. The solution architect must understand existing data structures and technologies to ensure that solution designs	• Knowledge of existing organisation data landscape • Knowledge of existing organisation existing data technology landscape and standards

Capability	Objective	Description	Characteristics
	with them.		

Table 102 – Solution Architect Business Knowledge

8.2.5 Collaboration Skills

Capability	Objective	Description	Characteristics
Human Dynamics	Human dynamics relates to how people, groups and organisations behave, interact and communicate, individually and collectively. Solutions are designed to be used. The solution architect should understand human dynamics in the areas of: • Dealing with individuals and groups when creating the solution design • Incorporating solution usability into the solution design.	The solution architect needs to understand how people and groups that are part of the solution design process and/or who will be consumers of the solution operate. The solution architect needs to look beyond pure information gathered to understand the unspoken factors that affect how people interact with the solution design process and what hidden plans and schemes could be at play. Consumers are part of the solution. The solution design should match the consumers' knowledge understanding, expectations and view how the solution should work.	• Ability to appreciate the human dynamics elements of people and group behaviour, communication and interaction and the impact this may have on the solution design process • Ability to understand the human element of solution usage
Business Engagement	A central part of the solution design process is engaging with the business function where the request or need for the solution arises. The solution architect must be able to conduct different business engagement types and maximise the results generated.	Business engagement is necessary to understand the needs of the business in order to create an optimal solution design. These engagements can occur in varying circumstances from difficult and uncooperative business participants to ones with limited involvement or availability. The solution architect must be able to design a business engagement that suits the set of circumstances in order to create the most effective solution design. The solution architect must be able to identify problems with the engagement that are impacting the solution design and handle or appropriately escalate them.	• Ability to design business engagements to suit different circumstances • Ability to handle problems in business engagements
Facilitation and Negotiation	The solution architect must be able to facilitate discussions between business engagement participants with differing views and assist with negotiating a resolution. Similarly, the solution	Disagreements and differing priorities and emphases will always exist when engaging with solution stakeholders both business and information technology. The solution architect must be able to act as a facilitator enabling business participants	• Ability to facilitate and discussions • Ability to achieve win-win outcomes • Ability to document the outcomes of meetings and

Capability	Objective	Description	Characteristics
	architect must be able to facilitate discussions between information technology solution stakeholders.	express their opinions with a view to each understanding the others' viewpoints. This may necessitate the solution architect understand that the openly stated views and opinions do not necessarily represent the real positions of the participants. The solution architect should not take sides in any disagreements but seek to have the participants reach a common understanding themselves.	workshops • Ability to keep discussions focussed • Ability to understand unspoken positions and to get participants express their real views • Ability to limit the time spent on discussions • Ability allow participants to reach conclusions
Listening	The solution architect must be able to listen to the views and opinions of solution stakeholders without taking a position in order to maximise the amount and accuracy of the information captured so it can be incorporated into the solution design.	The solution architect must be able to actively listen to what solution stakeholder say and be able to confirm understanding of the information provided during discussions. The solution must be able to listen to the messages being articulated, understand how the participants are joining-in the process and how they perceive the solution architect.	• Ability to actively listen • Ability to respond appropriately
Leadership and Motivation	The solution architect may be required to demonstrate leadership in a number of ways during a business engagement or a solution design process: • Lead a team of other solution architects and possibly business analysis • Lead business participants where disagreements need to be resolved • Take control, especially towards the end of the engagement or design process when decisions must be made and conclusions reached.	By virtue of their role in the business engagement or solution design the solution architect will always be in some form of leadership role. Ultimately the solution architect is responsible for taking the information gathered and the requirements provided and creating an effective and efficient solution design. The solution architect must be comfortable in assuming a leadership role, especially where there is a need to make decisions. Leadership is concerned with leading the participants to reach a common conclusion and a shared understanding and agreement. The solution architect must always focus on the desired goal and lead others towards it.	• Ability to focus on the desired end-state and lead others towards it • Ability to lead a technical team and share and allocate work across team members • Ability to show leadership throughout the engagement or solution design process
Teamwork and Team Building	The solution architect must be able to work with the wider solution design and implementation team	There can be several overlapping teams involved in the solution design process:	• Ability to create a team environment where participants co-operate and share

Capability	Objective	Description	Characteristics
	to ensure that the most effective solution is designed and then implemented.	• Team of architect and other technical participants such as business analysis • Team of business participants and stakeholders involved in information provision • Team of other information technology stakeholders who will have technical roles in the solution design • Team of those involved in the implementation and operation of the solution The solution architect must be able to work in these different team environments. Team building can take time and go through different phases of conflict and agreement. Individual team members may have different skill and experience levels that must be catered for. Some team members can be more demanding than others. Disagreements and differences can arise from emotional reasons or because of different levels of understanding. The solution architect needs to be able to recognise and handle both types.	• Ability to recognise the sources of differences and disagreements • Ability to create a view of shared ownership of the solution design or engagement output
Mentoring and Teaching	The solution design team will include participants with differing sets and levels of skills and experience. The solution architect must be able to ensure that participants learn from the process. The solution architect must be able to share knowledge and experience to develop the team to enhance the quality of future work.	Each team member will have a different style of and ability to learn. The learning potential of the engagement or design process must not be wasted, while balancing the need to achieve the objective. The solution architect must share his knowledge and experience with less proficient team members to ensure that they can contribute more in subsequent engagements.	• Ability to ensure that the learning potential of solution design engagements is maximised • Ability to share knowledge, experience and mentor other team members

Table 103 – Solution Architect Collaboration Skills

8.2.6 Communication Skills

Capability	Objective	Description	Characteristics
Communications	The solution architect	Communications occurs	• Ability to communicate

Capability	Objective	Description	Characteristics
and Presentation	must be able to communicate with solution design and engagement participants and to present the results of the work to business and information technology stakeholders clearly and cogently. This ensures the solution design is optimal and is understood by all.	throughout the engagement of solution design process. The solution architect needs to act as a communications hub taking information, transforming it and articulating it to participants. The solution architect must be able to make himself or herself understood and to know that the message has been understood by the audience. The solution architect must be able to create effective communications and presentations to express the message effectively. The message must be adapted to the target audience. In some cases, the message being communicated may be difficult or unpleasant. This must be communicated calmly.	effectively • Ability to present effectively • Ability to create context-sensitive communications and presentations • Ability to communicate bad news calmly
Written Communications	The outputs from any engagement or solution design process is a set of written artefacts that contain a record of what was discussed and considered and what conclusions were reached. The written artefacts will be used during subsequent implementation activities. The ability to create written communications is crucial to the solution design and implementation process.	Written communications are at the core of the solution design process. The communications need to be clear, well-structured, unambiguous, sufficiently detailed to be fit for purpose and easy to understand. While these artefacts are not meant to be perfectly constructed pieces of text, they should be reasonably well-written and free from grammatical and spelling errors. They should also include diagrams and charts as these can communicate concepts considerably more effectively that large sections of text. Different written communications may be aimed at different sets of stakeholders and must be written accordingly.	• Ability to write effectively • Ability to tailor written communications to the target audience and purpose • Ability to create effective and useful diagrams and charts to include in written communications

Table 104 – Solution Architect Communication Skills

8.2.7 Tools and Techniques

Capability	Objective	Description	Characteristics
General Productivity Applications	Most organisation communications are written using a standard set	The available communication, information organisation and analysis tools must be used	• Expert level of knowledge in common communications tools

Capability	Objective	Description	Characteristics
	of tools: Work, Excel, PowerPoint, Outlook and Visio. These can be supplemented by an increased number of web-based messaging, productivity and information sharing tools. The solution architect needs to be very proficient in their use to create well-written and well-presented documents to assist with the solution design process.	appropriately to generate value during the solution design process. After the engagement has ended, these communications will remain as the record of knowledge captured and generated. The documents created by these tools will be constantly updated and contributed to during the design process. Versions of these documents must be maintained as a record.	• Ability to use tools to create effective information • Ability to organise documents and versions
Specialised Tools and Systems	Specialised tools may be used in areas such as requirements generation, traceability and management, process analysis, description and specification, solution description. There will also be specialised tools for data reporting and analysis, data profiling and data storage structure design. The solution architecture must be proficient is using any such specialised tools used by the organisation.	These specialised tools must be used appropriately where they add value to the solution design process.	• Ability to use specialised tools in the solution design process • Ability to manage information held in any specialised tools
Standards and Methodologies	Standard approaches, techniques and methodologies to business engagement and solution design improve quality, reduce effort, allow reuse of other work and provide predictability in the process. The solution architect must be fluent in the application and use of the selected approaches adopted by the organisation.	There can be different structured approaches used by the solution architecture function for different types of engagement. Similarly there can be different methodologies used to elicit, represent and analyse information. The solution architect must be able to apply the most suitable approach to a given process and must understand its use in order to get the best results.	• Knowledge of engagement methodologies and processes in use • Ability to apply methodologies appropriately

Table 105 – Solution Architect Tools and Techniques Skills

8.3 Solution Architecture Function

8.3.1 Solution Architecture Function Context

As discussed in section 3.3.2 on page 80 the size and importance of solution architecture function depends on the size and proportion of the Change the Business function to the organisation. Solution architecture is concerned about designing problem resolutions and solutions to meet the needs of the business. If the desired, required and expected rate of change of the organisation is low then the size of the solution architecture function will be correspondingly low.

Section 4.1 on page 91 described the organisational context of the Solution Architecture function and the organisational components and their linkages needed to make sure than the business gets solutions that meet their needs in order to achieve business and information technology alignment.

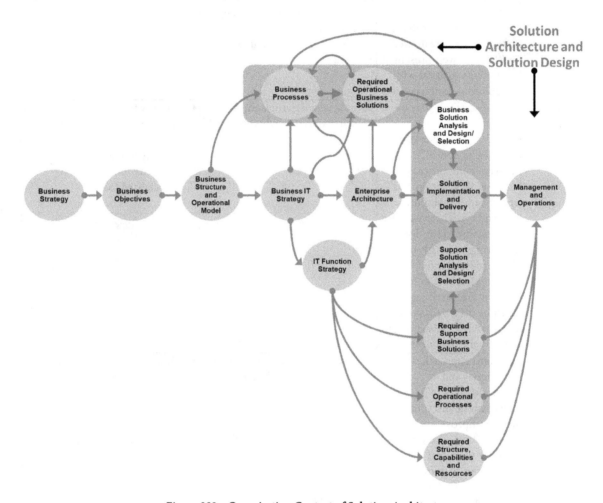

Figure 293 – Organisation Context of Solution Architecture

This is the context within which the Solution Architecture function needs to operate. The Solution Architecture function does not operate in isolation. There is no merit is having a high-performing function if other parts of the information technology function do not demonstrate the same degree of performance. The Solution Architecture function is part of a wider team who all must work together to achieve results and objectives.

Section 3.3.1 on page 75 discussed the linkages that exist between the Solution Architecture function and the other information technology functions and the business functions where the need for problem resolutions and solutions arise.

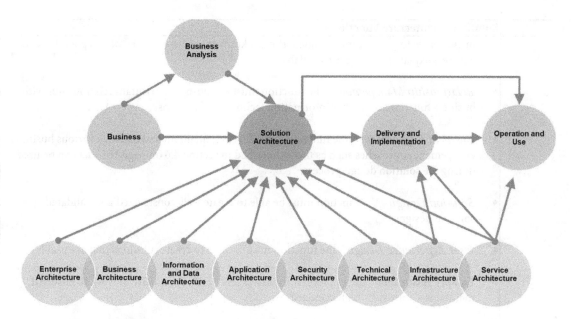

Figure 294 – Solution Architecture – Linkages to Other Information Technology Functions

The solution architecture function should be the glue that joins all these elements together – business, business analysis, other IT architecture disciplines and the teams involved in the delivery of the various solution components – to create usable and used solutions designs that are translated into operable and usable solutions.

Solution architecture both works directly with the business organisation and the business analysis function to understand the requirements for and the background of the desired solution. Solution architecture then incorporates the standards developed by the other architecture areas into the solution design. Solution architecture works with the solution delivery and implementation teams as the solution design is translated into reality.

8.3.2 Solution Architecture Function Structure

The six core domain business function model introduced in section 2.4 on page 33 can be used as a framework to design the target structure of the solution architecture function

Domain	Solution Architecture Function
Location and Offices	The solution architecture function can be located centrally or team members can be located in the business functions to foster and maintain a relationship with the business. However, the function should be managed and controlled centrally. All the solution architects should belong and feel that they belong to a core solution architecture competency function.
Business Processes	The solution architecture function needs to implement and operate the following business processes and capabilities: • *Strategic and Business Planning* – the function needs to understand the overall business strategy, the organisation's information technology strategy and design its own internal vision, strategy and business plans based on enabling the delivery of these. • *Accounting, Funding, Financing, Budgeting and Planning* – the solution needs to deliver business value. This means that it must understand its costs and understand and be able to demonstrate the value it creates. Overall business value means some or all of achieving efficiencies, realising cost savings, increasing consumer satisfaction, reducing time-to-market, increasing revenue and profit and increasing competitive advantage. • *Demand and Supply Management, Capacity Forecasting and Planning* – the function

Domain	Solution Architecture Function
	must be able to plan for its workload. It must know the work expected of it is good time to ensure adequate resources are available. • *Relationship Management* – the function must establish and maintain relationships with business functions and other information technology functions. • *Business Engagement* – the function must develop, maintain and enhance various business engagement approaches such as those described in section 4.6 on page 161 that can be used during the solution design process. • *Solution Design* – the function must be able to create well-constructed and validated solution designs. • *User Experience Design* – the function must be able to create solutions that are usable. • *Quality Assurance* – the function must assess and verify the quality of work to ensure it maintains a consistent high standard. • *Benefits Assessment and Realisation* – the function must be able to identify the benefits that a solution will enable and validate that those benefits have been achieved. • *Change and Change Management* – the function must be able to handle change during business engagement and solution design. • *Service Provisioning, Service Delivery and Service Management* – the function must work with the service management function to ensure that solutions are operable, supportable and maintainable can be transitioned to production. • *Innovation and Research* – the function must constantly keep current with technology, business and regulatory changes that will impact its workload or provide new options for business solutions. The function must devote a portion of its effort to research to maintain this currency.
Organisation and Structure	The function must manage resources, team structures and composition, roles and skills, reporting and management. • *Leadership and Governance* – the management of the function must be able to offer solution architecture leadership, both internally to the team and externally to the information technology function and the wider business organisation. • *Organisation Design and Planning* – the function must be structured and organised to perform the required workload and deliver the required results. • *People Asset Management* – the function must manage the team of solution architects, recruit new staff, manage their careers, manage talent and succession, training and mentoring • *Capability Model* – the function must develop and use a capability model such as the one described in section 8.2 on page 472 to identify gaps in skills and experience and prepare development plans accordingly.
Technology, Infrastructure and Communications	The function must maintain an understanding of the organisation's information technology, infrastructure and communications landscape including security, constraints, standards, technology trends, characteristics, performance requirements and any changes that are made to it.
Applications and Systems	The function must maintain an understanding of the organisation's systems and applications landscape including underlying technology, data, operational processes, support and maintenance and any changes that are made to them.

Domain	Solution Architecture Function
Information and Data	The function must maintain an understanding of the organisation's data landscape including operating data, data stores, master data, reference data, data warehouses and data marts, data reporting and analytics and any changes that are made to them. The function must understand any data integrations, interfaces and transfers and any transformations performed. The function must also implement processes to manage its own data including knowledge assets.

Table 106 – Applying the Business Function Domain Model to the Solution Architecture Function

The management of the Solution Architecture function will involve mediating between three views:

1. *External* – making the skills and capabilities of the function known to the wider business, handling requests from business functions for consulting and solution design engagement, understanding the scope of the work, scheduling work, managing expectations, managing the progress and the quality of the work done and any deliverables created, handling and resolving issues and establishing and maintaining relationships. The management must understand the business strategy and objectives and issues facing the business. The management can also advertise the work and ability of the function and conduct regular showcase events where new technologies and technical capabilities are demonstrated to the business.

2. *Internal* – developing and managing the team, allocating work, overseeing quality reviews, providing assistance with business engagement, recruiting, training and mentoring the team and managing talent and succession.

3. *Information Technology* – developing and maintaining relationships with information technology management to understand and contribute to the development of the information technology strategy, ensuring that the services provided comply with the overall approach agreed by the information technology management. The management must work with other information architecture disciplines such as enterprise, security and data architecture to both understand the standards they are evolving to ensure solutions comply with them and to assist with the development of those standards. The management must also develop and maintain relationships with the solution delivery and service management functions to ensure that there is continuity between design solutions and their subsequent implementation and transition to operation and that the solution architecture function is actively involved during this work.

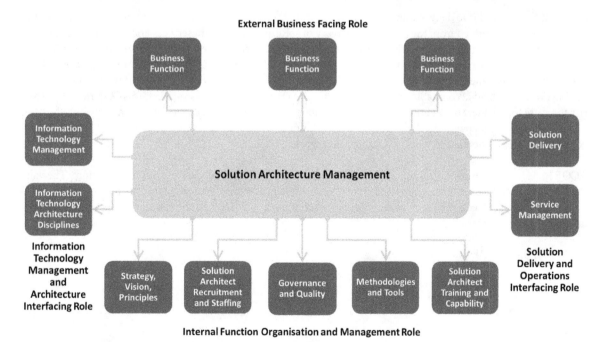

Figure 295 – Solution Architecture Function Management

8.3.3 Solution Architecture Centre of Excellence

The solution architecture function should aspire to be a *Solution Architecture Centre Of Excellence* (SACOE). This is concerned with developing a mature function that is highly-skilled at solution architecture and design and provides solution and consulting leadership to the organisation.

Developing an SACOE requires vision and resources of both the solution architecture function and information technology management.

The solution architecture function has the capability to develop both the business insight and solution and technology expertise to act as the business/technology authority and be the bridge between the business and technology domains of the organisation. The function can thus enable the organisation achieve value and consequences such as:

- Understand, respond to and where appropriate, anticipate external business changes that will affect the organisation
- Enable the organisation to change in response to external demands and trends
- Understand the potential of new technology initiatives and capabilities and determine how the organisation can use these to its advantage
- Ensure that solutions are aligned to the achievement of the business strategy and objectives
- Break the cycle of challenged solution delivery projects
- Differentiate the organisation and enable it to achieve operational and competitive advantage
- Ensure that value flows through the organisation to the consumer

Implementing an SACOE requires:

- A solution architecture function structure along the lines of that described in section 8.3.2 on page 489

- A solution architect capability model such as that described in section 8.2 on page 472 to measure the capabilities of the team and to create training and development plans

- A plan for its implementation and operation and the ongoing measurement of its functioning

The purpose of the SACOE is to deliver value to the organisation, both to the information technology function and to the wider business. Value is derived from the successful delivery of solution architecture services and the impact they have on business operation in terms of greater solution delivery success. But the delivery of solution architecture services in themselves is not a measure of value generated. Services are a necessary but not a sufficient measure of value. Measurements of solution architecture value cannot not be about just the number of engagements completed and the solution designs created. However, to be held accountable and responsible for the creation of business value, the SACOE must have the authority to create that value. Some of the issues and limitations around the design of the solution architecture function are discussed in section 8.3.4 on page 504. The issue of solution failure is examined in section 3.1 on page 57. The solution architecture value proposition has to work and continue to work.

The SACOE is clearly not responsible for generating all the value that the business derives from the solution. The value is generated by the entire delivery team, from the initial business stakeholder involvement to the business using the solution and being supported and operated by the service management and support function and the solution being maintained by the information technology function.

The functions of the SACOE should be:

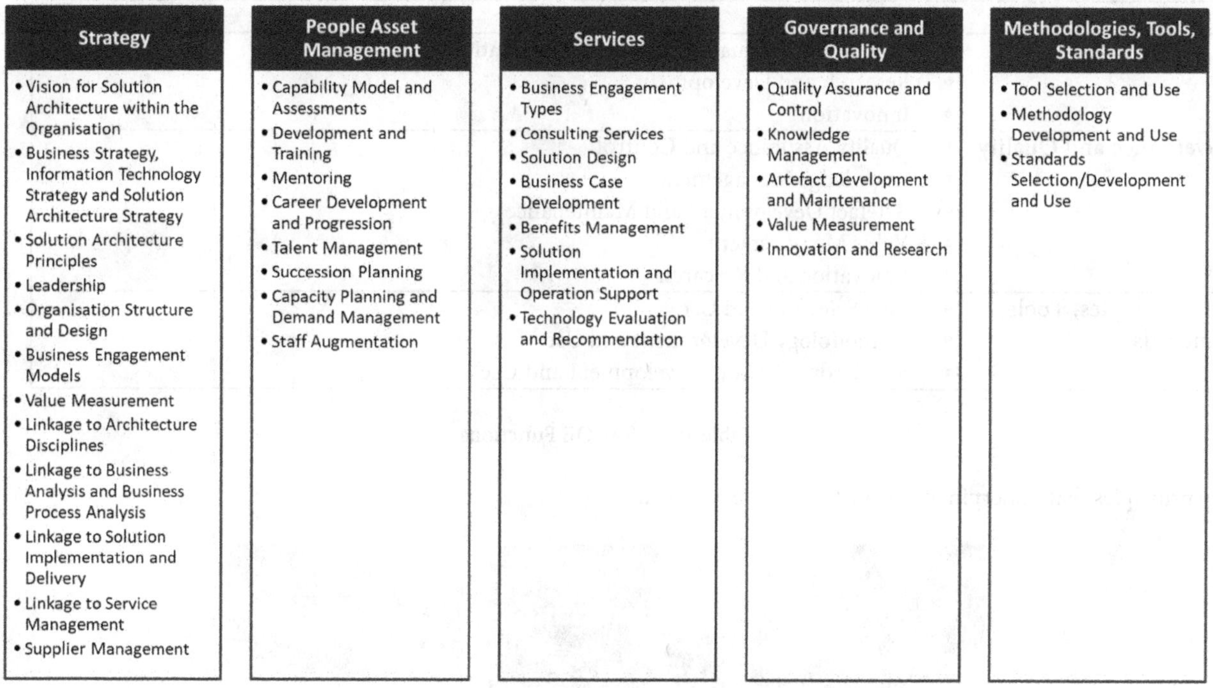

Strategy	People Asset Management	Services	Governance and Quality	Methodologies, Tools, Standards
• Vision for Solution Architecture within the Organisation • Business Strategy, Information Technology Strategy and Solution Architecture Strategy • Solution Architecture Principles • Leadership • Organisation Structure and Design • Business Engagement Models • Value Measurement • Linkage to Architecture Disciplines • Linkage to Business Analysis and Business Process Analysis • Linkage to Solution Implementation and Delivery • Linkage to Service Management • Supplier Management	• Capability Model and Assessments • Development and Training • Mentoring • Career Development and Progression • Talent Management • Succession Planning • Capacity Planning and Demand Management • Staff Augmentation	• Business Engagement Types • Consulting Services • Solution Design • Business Case Development • Benefits Management • Solution Implementation and Operation Support • Technology Evaluation and Recommendation	• Quality Assurance and Control • Knowledge Management • Artefact Development and Maintenance • Value Measurement • Innovation and Research	• Tool Selection and Use • Methodology Development and Use • Standards Selection/Development and Use

Figure 296 – Solution Architecture Centre Of Excellence (SACOE) Functions

These functions are listed in the table below.

Function	Elements
Vision and Strategy	• Vision for Solution Architecture within the Organisation • Business Strategy, Information Technology Strategy and Solution Architecture Strategy • Solution Architecture Principles • Leadership • Organisation Structure and Design • Business Engagement Models • Value Measurement • Linkage to Architecture Disciplines • Linkage to Business Analysis and Business Process Analysis • Linkage to Solution Implementation and Delivery • Linkage to Service Management • Supplier Management
People Asset Management	• Capability Model and Assessments • Development and Training • Mentoring • Career Development and Progression • Talent Management • Succession Planning • Capacity Planning and Demand Management • Staff Augmentation
Services	• Business Engagement Types • Consulting Services • Solution Design • Business Case Development • Benefits Management • Solution Implementation and Operation Support

Function	Elements
	• Technology Evaluation and Recommendation • Research and Development • Innovation
Governance and Quality	• Quality Assurance and Control • Knowledge Management • Artefact Development and Maintenance • Value Measurement • Innovation and Research
Methodologies, Tools, Standards	• Tool Selection and Use • Methodology Development and Use • Standards Selection/Development and Use

Table 107 – SACOE Functions

The principles that underpin the operation of the SACOE are:

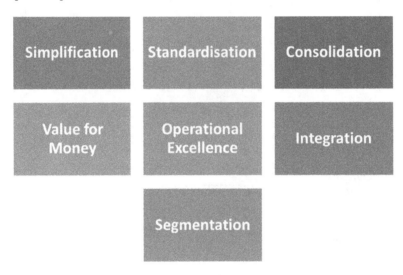

Figure 297 – Solution Architecture Principles

These principles are:

- *Simplification* – Eliminate unnecessary complexity

- *Standardisation* – Define and adhere to standards and research and adopt proven practices that work for other organisations

- *Consolidation* – Reduce the number of individual solution technologies and platforms

- *Value for Money* – Ensure that the solution architecture function delivers business value

- *Operational Excellence* – Deliver consistent high-quality service

- *Integration* – Ensure solutions and their components and operations integrate and interoperate

- *Segmentation* – Create standard, reusable components

Much is made of maturity models and their ability to assess the experience and development of a function or practices. Maturity models do not measure outputs, deliverables, achievements, value realised, outcomes generated or influenced. The maturity model can be regarded as an indirect proxy for these results as the underlying function or practice has to be mature to attain these or there is a correlation between maturity and achievement. However maturity and value are not identical.

Most maturity models lack rigour. There is little of any formal research into the assignment of maturity levels and the correlation of that level to value and benefits achieved.

The following illustrates a simple example of a possible solution architecture maturity model:

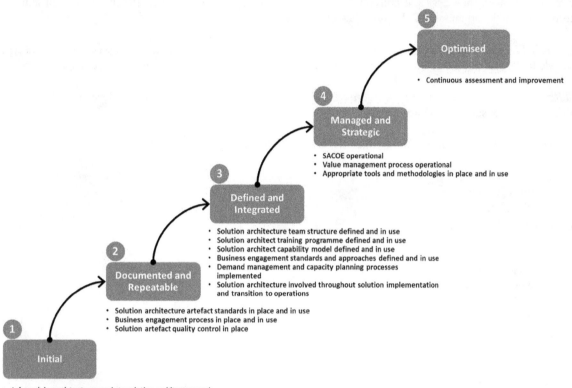

Figure 298 – Possible Solution Architecture Maturity Model

The levels and attributes of this informal maturity model are:

Maturity Level	Characteristics
Initial	• Informal, inconsistent approach to solution architecture and solution design • No functioning solution architecture function with standards • Solution architecture operations siloed and not part of overall solution delivery
Documented and Repeatable	• Solution architecture artefact standards in place and in use • Business engagement process in place and in use • Solution artefact quality control in place
Defined and Integrated	• Solution architecture team structure defined and in use • Solution architect training programme defined and in use • Solution architect capability model defined and in use • Business engagement standards and approaches defined and in use • Demand management and capacity planning processes implemented • Solution architecture involved throughout solution implementation and transition to operations
Managed and	• SACOE operational

Maturity Level	Characteristics
Strategic	• Value management process operational • Appropriate tools and methodologies in place and in use
Optimised	• Continuous assessment and improvement

Table 108 – Possible Solution Architecture Maturity Model

There are other proven knowledge and skills frameworks that can be applied to both assess the current state of solution architecture within the organisation. The following looks at two of these:

1. *Bloom's Taxonomy of Knowledge* – the describes an approach the acquisition of knowledge across different types of knowledge and how this could be used to both measure and improve the solution architecture function

2. *Skills Framework for the Information Age (SFIA)* – this contain role definitions and skill levels and characteristics for different levels of solution architect roles

The revised *Bloom's Taxonomy of Knowledge*[63] defines six levels of knowledge and its use:

1. Remember
   a. Recognising
   b. Recalling
2. Understand
   a. Interpreting
   b. Exemplifying
   c. Classifying
   d. Summarising
   e. Inferring
   f. Comparing
   g. Explaining
3. Apply
   a. Executing
   b. Implementing
4. Analyse
   a. Differentiating
   b. Organising
   c. Attributing
5. Evaluate
   a. Checking
   b. Critiquing
6. Create
   a. Generating
   b. Planning
   c. Producing

across four types of knowledge:

1. Factual Knowledge
   a. Knowledge of terminology
   b. Knowledge of specific details and elements
2. Conceptual Knowledge
   a. Knowledge of classifications and categories

---

[63] This refers to the knowledge model defined in *A taxonomy for learning, teaching, and assessing: a revision of Bloom's taxonomy of educational objectives Anderson, Lorin W.; Krathwohl, David R.; Bloom, Benjamin S.* ISBN 0321084055. Information on this knowledge model is widely available. For an example, see:
https://cft.vanderbilt.edu/guides-sub-pages/blooms-taxonomy/

  b. Knowledge of principles and generalisations
  c. Knowledge of theories, models, and structures
3. Procedural Knowledge
  a. Knowledge of subject-specific skills and algorithms
  b. Knowledge of subject-specific techniques and methods
  c. Knowledge of criteria for determining when to use appropriate procedures
4. Metacognitive Knowledge
  a. Strategic knowledge
  b. Knowledge about cognitive tasks, including appropriate contextual and conditional knowledge
  c. Self-knowledge

While Bloom's Taxonomy of Knowledge is designed for use in the area of education, it can be more widely applied. It is underpinned by substantial academic research.

This results in a 24-cell knowledge application process and knowledge type matrix.

Knowledge Type	Knowledge Application Process					
	Remember	Understand	Apply	Apply	Evaluate	Create
Factual Knowledge						
Conceptual Knowledge						
Procedural Knowledge						
Metacognitive Knowledge						

Table 109 – Knowledge Type and Application Classification

This framework could be adapted to assess the state of the solution architecture function and of individual team members. The four knowledge types as applied to solution architecture could be as follows:

Knowledge Type	Solution Architecture Individual Knowledge	Solution Architecture Function Knowledge
Factual Knowledge	• Basic knowledge of solution design and its use • Knowledge of information technology application and infrastructural components • Basic knowledge of solution design artefacts	• Basic solution architecture function knowledge with Informal approach to solution architecture and solution design • Basic knowledge of wider information technology and business context of solution design
Conceptual Knowledge	• Knowledge of solution design in the wider context of business requirements and solution implementation and operation • Knowledge of solution usability	• Knowledge management and reuse • Basic knowledge of business engagement process • Knowledge of business strategy solution and solution implementation and operation contexts • Knowledge of solution quality control • Knowledge of function costs
Procedural Knowledge	• Knowledge of business engagement processes, tools, techniques and methodologies • Knowledge of benefits identification and validation • Basic knowledge of business value of solutions	• Knowledge of function and team capabilities • Knowledge of business engagement processes, tools, techniques and methodologies • Knowledge of resource demand management and capacity planning processes • Knowledge of relationship management
Metacognitive Knowledge	• Knowledge of business and information	• Knowledge of continuous assessment

Knowledge Type	Solution Architecture Individual Knowledge	Solution Architecture Function Knowledge
	technology strategy • Knowledge of development of methodologies and approaches • Knowledge of value measurement	and improvement • Knowledge of business value process and its measurement

Table 110 – Knowledge Types Applied to Solution Architecture

This approach could be used to assess the current state of knowledge within the solution architecture team and to identify gaps that need to be filled.

One other skills framework that could be adapted to assess the state of the solution architecture function and of individual team members and to develop a plan to address any gaps is the ***Skills Framework for the Information Age (SFIA)***[64]. This is an information technology specific skills and competency framework. It aims to describe the skills and competencies required by information technology professionals across a variety of roles in the areas of:

• Strategy and architecture
• Change and transformation
• Development and implementation
• Delivery and operation
• Skills and quality
• Relationships and engagement

The SFIA is free to use for individual organisations. It is a very broad model and so is not very detailed for specific skills.

The model can be used in a number of organisational roles at various levels. At the organisation level, it can be used to determine current and future strategic capability planning and for aligning organisational capabilities to information technology and business strategies.

At the business function level, it can be used for measuring current skill levels and planning for future capacity requirements, creating role specifications, managing and deploying resources and identifying risks related to teams and developing people management plans.

The model has seven skill levels:

1. Follow
2. Assist
3. Apply
4. Enable
5. Ensure, Advise
6. Initiate, Influence
7. Set Strategy, Inspire, Mobilise

There are five attributes used to classify each skill levels:

1. Autonomy
2. Influence
3. Complexity
4. Knowledge
5. Business Skills

This results in a 35-cell matrix of attributes at various skill levels.

---

[64] See:
http://www.sfia-online.org/

Skill Level	Attributes				
	Autonomy	Influence	Complexity	Knowledge	Business Skills
1. Follow					
2. Assist					
3. Apply					
4. Enable					
5. Ensure, Advise					
6. Initiate, Influence					
7. Set Strategy, Inspire, Mobilise					

Table 111 – Skills Framework for the Information Age (SFIA) Skill Level and Attribute Matrix

The skills contained in the SFIA model are:

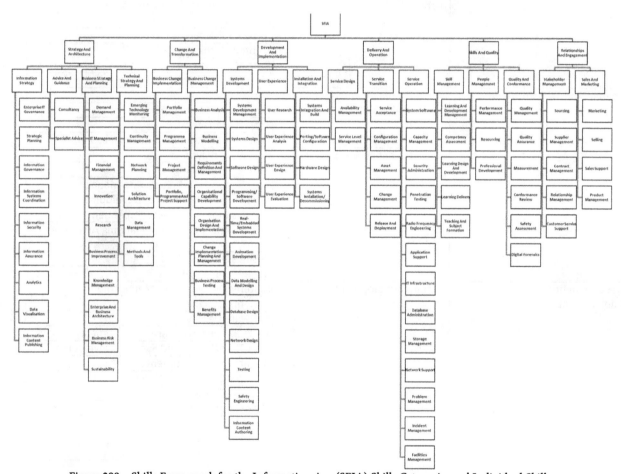

Figure 299 – Skills Framework for the Information Age (SFIA) Skills Categories and Individual Skills

These skills categories and individual skills are:

Skill Category	Skill Sub-Category	Skill
Strategy And Architecture	Information Strategy	Enterprise IT Governance
		Strategic Planning
		Information Governance
		Information Systems Coordination
		Information Security
		Information Assurance
		Analytics

Skill Category	Skill Sub-Category	Skill
		Data Visualisation
		Information Content Publishing
	Advice And Guidance	Consultancy
		Specialist Advice
	Business Strategy And Planning	Demand Management
		IT Management
		Financial Management
		Innovation
		Research
		Business Process Improvement
		Knowledge Management
		Enterprise And Business Architecture
		Business Risk Management
		Sustainability
	Technical Strategy And Planning	Emerging Technology Monitoring
		Continuity Management
		Network Planning
		Solution Architecture
		Data Management
		Methods And Tools
Change And Transformation	Business Change Implementation	Portfolio Management
		Programme Management
		Project Management
		Portfolio, Programme And Project Support
	Business Change Management	Business Analysis
		Business Modelling
		Requirements Definition And Management
		Organisational Capability Development
		Organisation Design And Implementation
		Change Implementation Planning And Management
		Business Process Testing
		Benefits Management
Development And Implementation	Systems Development	Systems Development Management
		Systems Design
		Software Design
		Programming/Software Development
		Real-Time/Embedded Systems Development
		Animation Development
		Data Modelling And Design
		Database Design
		Network Design
		Testing
		Safety Engineering
		Information Content Authoring
	User Experience	User Research
		User Experience Analysis
		User Experience Design
		User Experience Evaluation
	Installation And Integration	Systems Integration And Build
		Porting/Software Configuration
		Hardware Design
		Systems Installation/Decommissioning
Delivery And Operation	Service Design	Availability Management
		Service Level Management
	Service Transition	Service Acceptance
		Configuration Management
		Asset Management

Skill Category	Skill Sub-Category	Skill
		Change Management
		Release And Deployment
	Service Operation	System Software
		Capacity Management
		Security Administration
		Penetration Testing
		Radio Frequency Engineering
		Application Support
		IT Infrastructure
		Database Administration
		Storage Management
		Network Support
		Problem Management
		Incident Management
		Facilities Management
Skills And Quality	Skill Management	Learning And Development Management
		Competency Assessment
		Learning Design And Development
		Learning Delivery
		Teaching And Subject Formation
	People Management	Performance Management
		Resourcing
		Professional Development
	Quality And Conformance	Quality Management
		Quality Assurance
		Measurement
		Conformance Review
		Safety Assessment
		Digital Forensics
Relationships And Engagement	Stakeholder Management	Sourcing
		Supplier Management
		Contract Management
		Relationship Management
		Customer Service Support
	Sales And Marketing	Marketing
		Selling
		Sales Support
		Product Management

Table 112 – SFIA Skills Categories and Individual Skills

Within the SFIA the *Solution Architecture* skill belongs in the *Technical Strategy And Planning* sub-category within the *Strategy And Architecture* category. So the SFIA framework takes quite a narrow view of solution architecture rather than the broader view this book advocates.

It assigns skill levels 4 to 6 to solution architecture with level 4 representing the most junior of the solution architect roles and level 6 representing the most senior in the SFIA skills framework.

Skill Level	Solution Architecture Skill Level Description
4. Enable	<ul><li>Contributes to the development of solution architectures in specific business, infrastructure or functional areas</li><li>Identifies and evaluates alternative architectures and the trade-offs in cost, performance and scalability</li><li>Produces specifications of cloud-based or on-premises components, tiers and interfaces, for translation into detailed designs using selected services and products</li><li>Supports a change programme or project through the preparation of technical plans and application of design principles that comply with enterprise and solution architecture</li></ul>

Skill Level	Solution Architecture Skill Level Description
	standards (including security)
5. **Ensure, Advise**	• Leads the development of solution architectures in specific business, infrastructure or functional areas • Ensures that appropriate tools and methods are available, understood and employed in architecture development • Within a change programme, leads the preparation of technical plans and, in liaison with business assurance and project staff, ensures that appropriate technical resources are made available • Provides advice on technical aspects of solution development and integration (including requests for changes, deviations from specifications, etc.) and ensures that relevant technical strategies, policies, standards and practices (including security) are applied correctly
6. **Initiate, Influence**	• Leads the development of architectures for complex solutions, ensuring consistency with specified requirements agreed with both external, and internal customers • Takes full responsibility for the balance between functional, service quality and systems management requirements within a significant area of the organisation • Establishes policy and strategy for the selection of solution architecture components, and co-ordinates design activities, promoting the discipline to ensure consistency • Ensures that appropriate standards (corporate, industry, national and international) are adhered to • Within a business change programme, manages the target design, policies and standards, working proactively to maintain a stable, viable architecture and ensure consistency of design across projects within the programme

Table 113 – SFIA Skill Levels 4 to 6 Specification for Solution Architecture

The characteristics and behaviour of each of the solution architect skill levels is defined in terms of:

• Autonomy
• Influence
• Complexity
• Knowledge
• Business Skills

The following table defines the characteristics of the level 4 or junior solution architect:

Attribute	Characteristics
Autonomy	• Works under general direction within a clear framework of accountability • Exercises substantial personal responsibility and autonomy Plans own work to meet given objectives and processes
Influence	• Influences customers, suppliers and partners at account level • May have some responsibility for the work of others and for the allocation of resources Participates in external activities related to own specialism • Makes decisions which influence the success of projects and team objectives • Collaborates regularly with team members, users and customers • Engages to ensure that user needs are being met throughout
Complexity	• Work includes a broad range of complex technical or professional activities, in a variety of contexts • Investigates, defines and resolves complex issues
Knowledge	• Has a thorough understanding of recognised generic industry bodies of knowledge and specialist bodies of knowledge as necessary • Has gained a thorough knowledge of the domain of the organisation • Is able to apply the knowledge effectively in unfamiliar situations and actively maintains own knowledge and contributes to the development of others • Rapidly absorbs new information and applies it effectively

Attribute	Characteristics
	• Maintains an awareness of developing practices and their application and takes responsibility for driving own development
Business Skills	• Communicates fluently, orally and in writing, and can present complex information to both technical and non-technical audiences • Plans, schedules and monitors work to meet time and quality targets • Facilitates collaboration between stakeholders who share common objectives • Selects appropriately from applicable standards, methods, tools and applications • Fully understands the importance of security to own work and the operation of the organisation • Seeks specialist security knowledge or advice when required to support own work or work of immediate colleagues

Table 114 – SFIA Skill Attributes for Solution Architecture Skill Level 4

The following table defines the characteristics of the level 5 or mid-range solution architect:

Attribute	Characteristics
Autonomy	• Works under broad direction • Work is often self-initiated • Is fully responsible for meeting allocated technical and/or project/supervisory objectives • Establishes milestones and has a significant role in the assignment of tasks and/or responsibilities.
Influence	• Influences organisation, customers, suppliers, partners and peers on the contribution of own specialism • Builds appropriate and effective business relationships • Makes decisions which impact the success of assigned work, i.e. results, deadlines and budget • Has significant influence over the allocation and management of resources appropriate to given assignments • Leads on user/customer collaboration throughout all stages of work • Ensures users' needs are met consistently through each work stage.
Complexity	• Performs an extensive range and variety of complex technical and/or professional work activities • Undertakes work which requires the application of fundamental principles in a wide and often unpredictable range of contexts • Understands the relationship between own specialism and wider customer/organisational requirements.
Knowledge	• Is fully familiar with recognised industry bodies of knowledge both generic and specific • Actively seeks out new knowledge for own personal development and the mentoring or coaching of others • Develops a wider breadth of knowledge across the industry or business • Applies knowledge to help to define the standards which others will apply.
Business Skills	• Demonstrates leadership • Communicates effectively, both formally and informally • Facilitates collaboration between stakeholders who have diverse objectives • Analyses, designs, plans, executes and evaluates work to time, cost and quality targets • Analyses requirements and advises on scope and options for continuous operational improvement • Takes all requirements into account when making proposals • Demonstrates creativity, innovation and ethical thinking in applying solutions for the benefit of the customer/stakeholder • Advises on the available standards, methods, tools and applications relevant to own specialism and can make appropriate choices from alternatives • Maintains an awareness of developments in the industry • Takes initiative to keep skills up to date

Attribute	Characteristics
	• Mentors colleagues
	• Assesses and evaluates risk.
	• Proactively ensures security is appropriately addressed within their area by self and others
	• Engages or works with security specialists as necessary
	• Contributes to the security culture of the organisation

Table 115 – SFIA Skill Attributes for Solution Architecture Skill Level 5

The following table defines the characteristics of the level 6 or senior solution architect:

Attribute	Characteristics
Autonomy	• Has defined authority and accountability for actions and decisions within a significant area of work, including technical, financial and quality aspects • Establishes organisational objectives and assigns responsibilities
Influence	• Influences policy and strategy formation. Initiates influential relationships with internal and external customers, suppliers and partners at senior management level, including industry leaders • Makes decisions which impact the work of employing organisations, achievement of organisational objectives and financial performance
Complexity	• Has a broad business understanding and deep understanding of own specialism(s) • Performs highly complex work activities covering technical, financial and quality aspects. Contributes to the implementation of policy and strategy • Creatively applies a wide range of technical and/or management principles.
Knowledge	• Promotes the application of generic and specific bodies of knowledge in own organisation • Has developed business knowledge of the activities and practices of own organisation and those of suppliers, partners, competitors and clients.
Business Skills	• Demonstrates clear leadership • Communicates effectively at all levels to both technical and non-technical audiences • Understands the implications of new technologies • Understands and communicates industry developments, and the role and impact of technology in the employing organisation • Absorbs complex information • Promotes compliance with relevant legislation and the need for services, products and working practices to provide equal access and equal opportunity to people with diverse abilities • Takes the initiative to keep both own and colleagues' skills up to date • Manages and mitigates risk • Takes a leading role in promoting security throughout own area of responsibilities and collectively in the organisations

Table 116 – SFIA Skill Attributes for Solution Architecture Skill Level 6

The SFIA framework can be adapted for use in measuring the capabilities of individual solution architects and of the wider solution architecture function.

8.3.4 Some Solution Architecture Function Issues

This section examines some negative issues that can arise with the design and structure of the solution architecture function and how they can be identified and their impact minimised.

8.3.4.1 Conway's Law

As I mentioned earlier, the work of the solution architecture function has to be measured by the value it creates rather than the services it provides and the outputs it produces or contributes to. The former is a direct measure. The latter are at best indirect measures and can give rise to artificial incentives to do unnecessary work.

Dr Melvin Conway wrote a short article in April 1968[65] on the subject of systems design. Over 50 years later it is still as insightful as when it was originally written. It stands as a warning to the solution architecture function on how its designs solutions and how it structures itself. The article gave rise to the concept of Conway's Law:

> The basic thesis of this article is that **organizations which design systems** (in the broad sense used here) **are constrained to produce designs which are copies of the communication structures of these organizations.** We have seen that this fact has important implications for the management of system design. Primarily, we have found a criterion for the structuring of design organizations: a design effort should be organized according to the need for communication.

The core concept is that because many different people in an organisation are involved in the design of a (complex) solution and its components, the structure of the system and the interfaces between its components reflects the way the individuals involved in the design communicate. That communication occurs along the lines of the structure of the organisation.

It is related to the concepts of:

- *Design By Committee* – where the solution is designed by a group where individuals are advocating different viewpoints and where the design incorporates compromises aimed at pacifying individuals rather than for pure solution technical need. It is frequently an example of *Parkinson's Law of Triviality*[66] where a disproportionate effort is expended on minor design elements.

- *Scope or Feature Creep* – where additional features are added to the solution not because they are needed or desirable but are included as a result of compromise.

The article contained some other observations on the solution design process and on the operation of the solution design function:

> Parkinson's Law[67] plays an important role in the overassignment of design effort. As long as the manager's prestige and power are tied to the size of his budget, he will be motivated to expand his organization. This is an inappropriate motive in the management of a system design activity. Once the organization exists, of course, it will be used. Probably the greatest single common factor behind many poorly designed systems now in existence has been the availability of a design organization in need of work.

A solution architecture function grows in size. There is greater prestige to being the manager of a large function. It then must justify its size by producing overcomplicated designs and implementing design processes that are intrinsically time-consuming and not value-adding. The structure of the wider organisation ensures the design function is incentivised to become large. The large design function then creates work for itself to justify its size and existence. Conway's response to this is:

> Ways must be found to reward design managers for keeping their organizations lean and flexible. There is need for a philosophy of system design management which is not based on the assumption that adding manpower simply adds to productivity. The development of such a philosophy promises to unearth basic questions about

---

[65] *How Do Committees Invent? - Design Organization Criteria* http://www.melconway.com/Home/pdf/committees.pdf

[66] "*The time spent on any item of the agenda will be in inverse proportion to the sum involved.*" **Parkinson's Law, and Other Studies in Administration** Cyril Northcote Parkinson and Robert Osborn ISBN 978-8087888919 Houghton Mifflin, 1957.

[67] "*Work expands so as to fill the time available for its completion... The importance of Parkinson's Law lies in the fact that it is a law of growth based upon an analysis of the factors by which that growth is controlled.*" **Parkinson's Law, and Other Studies in Administration** Cyril Northcote Parkinson and Robert Osborn ISBN 978-8087888919 Houghton Mifflin, 1957.

value of resources and techniques of communication which will need to be answered before our system-building technology can proceed with confidence.

The solution design process Conway describes in his article and where organisational problems arise can be described as follows:

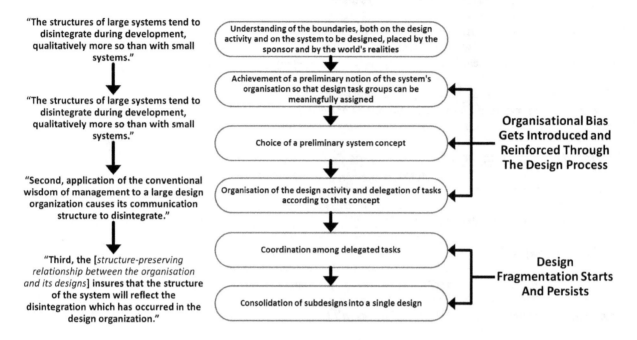

Figure 300 – Solution Delivery Process Failings and Conway's Law

Conway's Law is a warning rather than a prediction. It provides an insight into the solution design problems that can occur if the solution architecture function, the solution design structures, processes and function are not optimised (and continually re-optimised). What it describes does not have to happen, but all too frequently does.

8.3.4.2 Cognitive Diversity

The **Value in Diversity Hypothesis** was introduced by Hong and Scott[68]:

> *The main result of this paper provides conditions under which, in the limit, **a random group of intelligent problem solvers will outperform a group of the best problem solvers**. Our result provides insights into the trade-off between diversity and ability. An ideal group would contain high-ability problem solvers who are diverse.*
>
> *...*
>
> *Our result has implications for organizational forms and management styles, especially for problem-solving firms and organizations. In an environment where competition depends on continuous innovation and introduction of new products, firms with organizational forms that take advantage of the power of functional diversity should perform well. The research we cited earlier by computer scientists and organizational theorists who explore how to best exploit functional diversity becomes even more relevant. Most importantly, though, our result suggests that diversity in perspective and heuristic space should be encouraged. We should do more*

---

[68] **Groups of diverse problem solvers can outperform groups of high-ability problem solvers** Lu Hong and Scott E. Page https://www.pnas.org/content/101/46/16385.
See also: **Teams Solve Problems Faster When They're More Cognitively Diverse** by Alison Reynolds David Lewis https://hbr.org/2017/03/teams-solve-problems-faster-when-theyre-more-cognitively-diverse.

than just exploit our existing diversity. We may want to encourage even greater functional diversity, given its advantages.

One important aspect of solution architecture is problem-solving and the identification of optimum solutions to problems. The concept of cognitive diversity as a contributing factor to solution design can be illustrated using the concept that solutions to problems can be represented as minima on a graph.

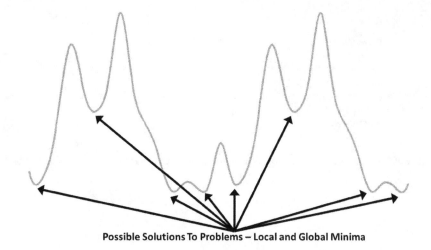

Possible Solutions To Problems – Local and Global Minima

Figure 301 – Solutions To Problems Can Be Represented As Minima On A Graph

When you are on the graph, how do you know that the minimum value you have found represents the absolute lowest value or just a local minimum without navigating through the entire graph?

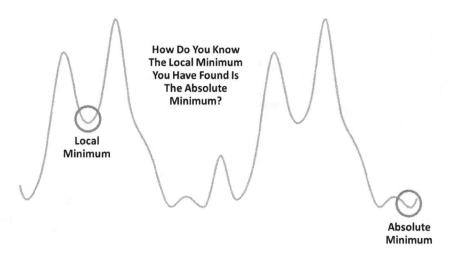

Figure 302 – Solutions To Problems Can Be Represented As Minima In Graph

Where the team has a narrowly focussed set of skills, they will tend to focus on the same (perhaps sub-optimal) solution.

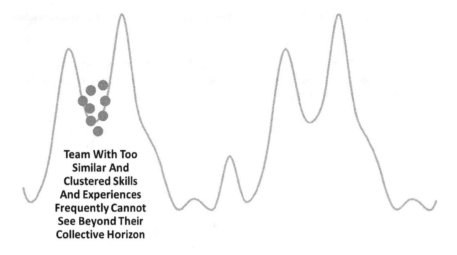

**Team With Too
Similar And
Clustered Skills
And Experiences
Frequently Cannot
See Beyond Their
Collective Horizon**

Figure 303 – Solution Identification Where the Team Has a Narrowly Focussed Set of Skills

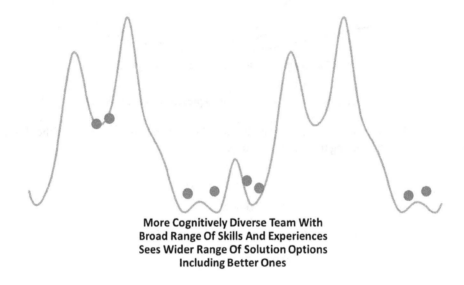

**More Cognitively Diverse Team With
Broad Range Of Skills And Experiences
Sees Wider Range Of Solution Options
Including Better Ones**

Figure 304 – Solution Identification Where the Team Has a Broad Range Of Skills

There are three dimensions to cognitive diversity:

1. *Knowledge/Experience/Skills* – "tangible" diversity – measure of specific skills that are not directly relevant to the domain of the organisation

2. *Mindset/Viewpoint/Attitude/Frame Of Reference* – "intangible" diversity – measure of creativity/ originality/ ingenuity

3. *Extent Of Cognitive Diversity* – Need to find an appropriate level/amount for the organisation to balance benefits and challenges

The abilities of individuals grow slowly over time. Collective organisation diversity can grow more quickly.

It is common for organisations, when hiring, to look for people with specific skills in the domain or industry in which the organisation operates: banks look for people with banking skills, pharmaceutical companies look for pharmaceutical skills and experience and so on. This bias also occurs across the dimensions of age, gender, race and ethnicity.

Organisations and those in them who hire new staff tend to look for people with similar skills and experience, reinforcing bias and ensuring similarity. This is an example of an organisation's comfort zone – where the organisation remains and repeats what it is familiar and comfortable with. Organisations reproduce themselves through unconscious reinforcement and bias. Organisations consequently have difficulty in reacting to change, introducing innovations and achieving necessary transformation. New organisations with new structures perform well initially and overtake established ones until they too become affected by embedded lack of cognitive diversity and are themselves overtaken.

The business processes of most organisations can be generalised into three common groups:

1. *Core Operational Processes* – drive and operate the organisation, deliver value, support external party interactions

2. *Management and Support Processes* – internal processes and associated business functions that enable the operation and delivery of the core operational processes

3. *Vision, Strategy, Business Management* – processes that measure, control and optimise the operational and support processes and set the direction of the organisation

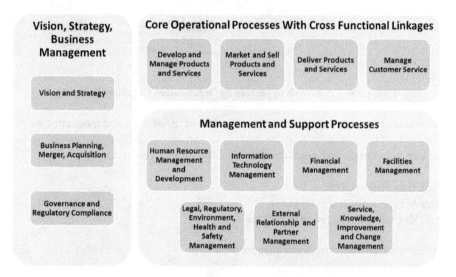

Figure 305 – Generalised Organisation Business Process Structure

Instead of looking for domain-specific skills, organisation can (and should) look for excellence in those process areas that are common to all organisations. This is similar to benchmarking[69] where organisations seek to compare their business processes and performance metrics to industry bests and best practices from other companies and learn from those who achieve superior performance.

---

[69] See:
https://www.globalbenchmarking.org/.

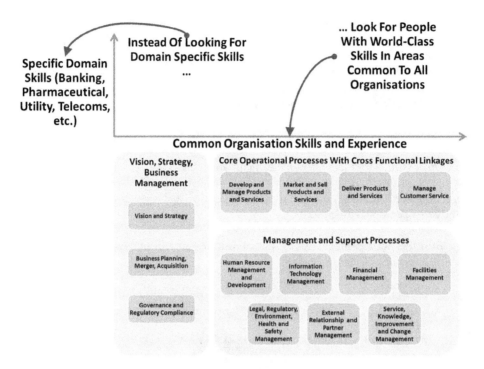

Figure 306 – Approach to Increasing Organisation Cognitive Diversity

Cognitive diversity in the solution architecture function is an enabler of innovation and more effective problem resolution.

However, there is a balance to be struck with cognitive diversity. Too little can result in:

- Lack of range of solution design options
- Lack of broad range of experience and perspective
- Rushed decision making with no evaluation of options

But too much diversity can also have negative consequences such as:

- Too many solution design options with no decision
- High overhead of managing very diverse teams
- Too much time spent on research and analysis

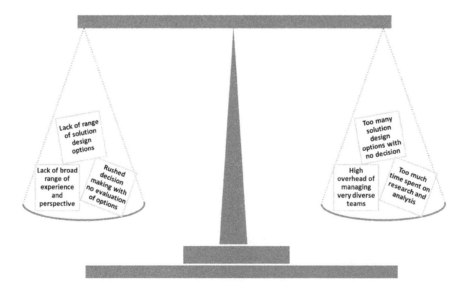

Figure 307 – Cognitive Diversity Balancing Act

There are no simple and objective cognitive diversity metrics. There are attempts to develop complex measures based on cognitive distance of members of the group and to quantify the cognitive synergy of the group[70]. These measures can be quite subjective. Any subjective measure of cognitive diversity may itself be biased and may not represent actual and effective cognitive diversity that delivers successful outcomes.

The right balance of cognitive diversity for any solution architecture function involves a balance of the three factors listed above:

1. *Knowledge/Experience/Skills* – "tangible" diversity – measure of specific skills that are not directly relevant to the domain of the organisation

2. *Mindset/Viewpoint/Attitude/Frame Of Reference* – "intangible" diversity – measure of creativity/ originality/ ingenuity

3. *Extent Of Cognitive Diversity* – Need to find an appropriate level/amount for the organisation to balance benefits and challenges

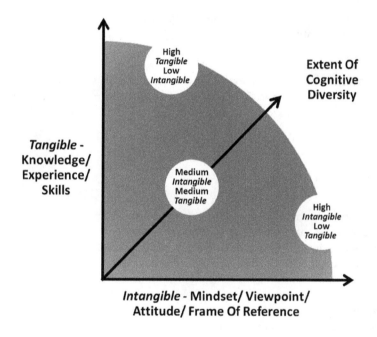

Figure 308 – Finding The Right Balance Of Cognitive Diversity

The value of cognitive diversity to organisations is greatest in the thinking areas such as solution architecture. Achieving cognitive diversity can be painful and challenging. Managing diverse teams can be difficult.

8.3.5 Solution Architecture Tools

---

[70] For an example, see *Cognitive Distance, Absorptive Capacity and Group Rationality: A Simulation Study* Petru Lucian Curşeu, Oleh Krehel, Joep H. M. Evers, Adrian Muntean https://www.ncbi.nlm.nih.gov/pmc/articles/PMC4196901/.

Solution architecture tools and techniques can be useful in increasing productivity, expanding reuse of previous work and introducing precision and rigour into the solution design and business engagement processes and the subsequent solution implementation. Tools can augment the solution design process and assist with the creation of business value.

This section contains information on three sets of tools:

- Solution architecture description language

- Enterprise architecture description languages

- Other tools and techniques that can be useful to the solution architecture in the solution design process

The use of tools has a cost in terms overhead, training, enforcement of standards, building-up a repository of solutions to make the tool usable and management of the environment. The tools should delivery benefits that exceed their usage costs.

There is a tendency to see the tool as a panacea that will resolve all problems. The reality is that a tool offers some benefits but imposes operating constraints, overheads, burdens and requirements that make the benefits of the use less than clear-cut. Repository-based tools generally require more, in some cases, considerably more input effort. In return they give you the ability to generate more outputs, views and reports. They also make long-term maintenance of the input information easier. But they also require that the information repository is kept current which involves a maintenance effort.

The tool is ultimately only as good and as useful as the people using it and the effort expended in become fluent in its use. The value from a tool is derived from its continued and widespread use. Expecting a tool to magically solve all your problems is simply irrational.

Tools also tend to incorporate their own representation and display language. This must be learned both by the users of the tool and the consumers of the outputs of the tool. If the language is complex this may not offer any benefits. The use of representation languages is covered in other sections – Archimate in section 8.3.5.1.2 on page 518 and BPMN in section 4.4.2.1 on page 151.

8.3.5.1 Solution Architecture Design Tools

There are two competing sets of requirements of any solution representational language or approach relating to simplicity and complexity. Simplicity is good for communication where a simple message can be expressed and understood quickly. Complexity is needed to include all the solution detail needed both to understand the scope of the solution to create accurate resource estimates and then to itemise the work to be done. The ideal approach supports both and can easily move from one to the other.

The representational language or approach needs to enable participation and sharing between the solution designers, the business solution stakeholders and the delivery and service introduction functions. This ensures that the business knows what the solution will do and how it will operate, eliminating surprises during later solution delivery.

The characteristics of a good representational language or approach include:

- The approach allows the solution to be represented at different levels of complexity. Solutions that are complex consist of multiple interacting components. So, the understanding the entire scope (its breadth) of the solution is more important than understanding the detail (its depth). The representation approach needs to be able to handle complexity to enable the solution and its components and options to be analysed. The decomposition of the solution to different levels of detail allows information appropriate to that level to be considered. The analysis of lower levels of detail can be deferred.

- The approach needs to handle to analysis of data and the processing or functional elements of the solution. As I mentioned throughout this book, data breathes life into a solution and cannot be ignored in all its states – creation, transportation, processing and retention - during solution design. Data is not a consideration after the solution has been designed. It is a principal solution design factor.

- The approach should include at its heart a visualisation and graphical representation of solution structure and its constituent parts, solution boundaries, component relationships, interactions and integrations, data flows and processing with drill-down and drill-up to the levels of solution design complexity referred to above. Pictures communicate understanding and meaning with far greater ease than long sections of narrative. The approach can include a formal graphical notation but this must be easy to create and to understand. The requirement to use separate tools to create the representation or to learn the representation notation militates against its usability and utility.

- The approach should emphasise simplicity over complexity. Complexity is acceptable when information is being exchanged between technical staff. Ease of understanding and use is more important when communicating concepts to business stakeholders and non-technical solution design participants.

- The approach should allow related sets of functions to be partitioned and examined separate from other solution components. This allows the areas of concern of different sets of business solution stakeholders to be isolated and analysed without reference to the complexity of the entire solution.

A common and consistent approach allows all participants to become fluent in its use and to derive value.

The characteristics of a tool that supports the design process include:

- Solution entities and elements are created once and can be maintained thereafter so information is consistent. This means the tool includes some form of entity data store. Entities should be uniquely identified and this identification should appear of all .

- The tool should maintain a library of entities and interaction types with pre-defined characteristics.

- Entities created for different solution designs should be able to be reused.

- The tool should be easy to use and to update information.

- The tools should allow the creation of solution implementation detailed outputs that can be passed to the delivery team.

- Manage versions of solution designs and the differences between them.

- Create multiple solution design options to allow their differences to be analysed to understand the optimum solution.

- Allow prototypes of solution components to be generated.

- Support simulation of solution operation and use to analyse and validate performance, throughput and usage.

- Link to requirements to allow mapping of requirements space to solutions space.

The core objectives of solution architecture design tools are:

- To make the solution design process easier, faster, more repeatable, to ensure quality, to enforce standards and to allow sharing and reuse.

- To specify the solution design clearly.

- To enable better management of the solution design process across all solution designs and across the solution architecture function.

- To allow the unambiguous communication of solution designs to solution stakeholders: consumers, implementers, delivery managers.

The tools should embody a solution design engagement process that allows their application as designs are being evolved.

Ideally there would be a standard solution architecture description language (SADL) that could be used across the solution design and delivery process. In reality, there are a large number of partially developed SADLs. As with the solution usability standards listed in section 4.7 on page 311 many of these are old, partially developed, incomplete and are no longer being enhanced. Many arose from an academic context and never transitioned to be being used in a commercial environment. They also tend to focus largely on software development rather than on wider solution design. The state of solution architecture description language development and use is poor.

The following table lists a small subset of the available SADL and related toolsets. There are far too many to list here. Such a list would largely pointless. There is a longer list available from http://www.di.univaq.it/malavolta/al/.

Architectural Description Language	Description	Links	Status
AADL	Architecture Analysis and Design Language It is aimed at the design of real-time performance-critical distributed computer systems, This was developed by the SAE International (initially the Society of Automotive Engineers - https://www.sae.org/) There is a range of AADL publications available at: https://wiki.sei.cmu.edu/aadl/index.php/Publications_arranged_by_year	http://www.aadl.info/aadl/currentsite/ There is a commercial tool called STOOD that implements AADL - https://www.ellidiss.com/products/stood/	Not being developed actively This is not suitable for general solution design activities
ABACUS	This is aimed at enterprise architecture rather than solution architecture	https://www.avolutionsoftware.com/abacus/	Commercial product
Acme Project	This is a very basic tool for describing components of a solution and their interactions	http://www.cs.cmu.edu/~acme/	Not being developed
ADML	Architecture Description Markup Language It is an XML-based representation language for architecture management rather than solution architecture	https://www.opengroup.org/architecture/adml/adml_home.htm	
Archimate	ArchiMate is developed by The Open Group. It is aimed enterprise architecture modelling to support the description, analysis and visualisation of enterprise architectures across business areas. It can be applied to generating high-level solution designs ArchiMate is supported by a number of commercial tools Section 8.3.5.1.2 on page 518 contains more details on Archimate	http://www.opengroup.org/subjectareas/enterprise/archimate There is a variety of Archimate-related publications available from The Open Group: https://publications.opengroup.org/ There are commercial tools that support Archimate such as: https://www.archimatetool.com/ https://bizzdesign.com/	Current

Architectural Description Language	Description	Links	Status
		https://www.softwareag.com/be/products/aris_alfabet/eam/default https://erwin.com/products/enterprise-architecture/	
byADL	Build Your ADL This is aimed at developing ADLs for use in software rather than solution architecture	http://byadl.di.univaq.it/	Not being developed
ISO/IEC/ IEEE 42010	Systems and software engineering - Architecture description This specifies the how architecture descriptions of systems are organised and expressed. It includes details on architecture viewpoints, architecture frameworks and architecture description languages for use in architecture descriptions. This is a very high-level approach to solution design. It is not a tool but a document that describes an approach	https://www.iso.org/standard/50508.html	Current
Rapide	This is aimed at designing large distributed systems	http://complexevents.com/stanford/rapide/	Not being developed
SSADM	Structured Systems Analysis and Design Methodology (SSADM) is an approach to the analysis and design of information technology solutions. It dates from 1980. Section 8.3.5.1.1 on page 516 contains more details on SSADM.		Not being developed
Stratus Modeling Language	StratusML is a modelling framework for cloud applications. It allows cloud providers, developers and administrators, to define their application services and estimate the their performance and cost under different sets of circumstances	http://www.stargroup.uwaterloo.ca/~mhamdaqa/stratusml/index.html	Not being developed
SysML	Systems Modeling Language SysML is a generalised modelling language for large and complex engineering systems. It evolved from and generalises UML outside its pure software area of focus. ISO/IEC 19514:2017 specifies SysML	https://www.iso.org/standard/65231.html)	Current
UML	Unified Modeling Language This is a development-oriented software engineering modelling language. UML is a large and complex set of software description techniques. The UML-based model of the software product is visualised through a number of diagrams: static or structural that show entities and dynamic or behavioural that show collaborations, flows and interactions. Elements of UML can be useful in describing a solution. But the overhead in creating a	https://www.omg.org/spec/NIEM-UML/About-NIEM-UML/	Current

Architectural Description Language	Description	Links	Status
	full UML description of a software product is substantial		
USL	Universal Systems Language This is a modelling language and method for specifying and designing software and other systems. It is developed by Hamilton Technologies.	http://htius.com/	Current

Table 117 – Partial List of Solution Architecture Description Languages

8.3.5.1.1 Structured Systems Analysis and Design Methodology (SSADM)

SSADM belongs to the era of systems analysis and the systems analyst role as discussed in section 2.3 on page 30. While it is a very old methodology and design technique, its principles can be easily applied to solution architecture. There is much to recommend in the SSADM approach to solution design.

As it was designed and used, SSADM took a very sequential (waterfall) approach to solution design and placed substantial emphasis on the creation of documentation. However, the approach can be used without adhering rigidly to these usage characteristics.

SSADM involves the application of a sequence of analysis, documentation and system design tasks. It uses a combination of narrative and diagrams throughout the life cycle of the design of a system from the initial design idea to its actual physical design.

SSADM uses a combination of three core solution design and operation techniques:

- **Logical Data Modelling** – This is the static view of the solution. This involves identifying, modelling and describing the data elements and requirements of the system under design. This is described in an Entity Relationship Diagram (ERD). The output is a data model containing entities (units about which the solution needs to hold information), attributes (data characteristics of the entities) and relationships (links between entities).

- **Data Flow Modelling** – This is the dynamic view of the solution. This involves identifying, modelling and describing how data flows around the system. This is described in a Data Flow Diagram (DFD). Data Flow Modeling involves defining the following data elements

  - **Data Processes** – these tasks and activities that transform source data to target data

  - **Data Stores** – this is where data is held with differing degrees of persistence

  - **External Data Source/Target Entities** –these are entities that transmit data to the system or receive data from the system)

  - Data Flows – these describe how data is transmitted between

- **Entity Life History (ELH)** – This is a time-oriented view of the solution. This shows the solution from the viewpoint of how the entities and data in the solution changes over time. The ELH aims to show the complete full set of changes that can occur to the entities and data with the context of each change. An ELH is a diagrammatic representation of the life of a single entity, from its creation to its deletion. The life is expressed as the permitted sequence of events that can cause the entity to change. An event may be thought of as whatever brings a process into action to change entities, so although it is a process that changes the entity, it is the event that is the cause of the change.

The SSADM solution design approach consists of six steps:

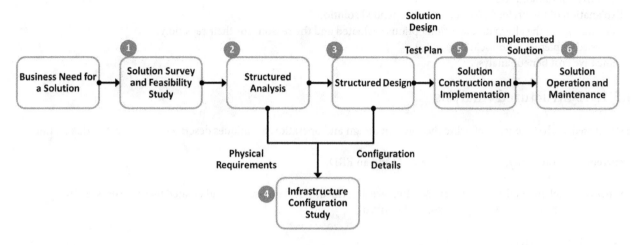

Figure 309 – SSADM Design Approach

These steps are:

1. Solution Survey and Feasibility Study
2. Structured Analysis
3. Structured Design
4. Infrastructure Configuration Study
5. Solution Construction and Implementation
6. Solution Operation and Maintenance

8.3.5.1.1.1 Solution Survey and Feasibility Study

The scope of this depends on whether there is an existing, possibly deficient, solution that is to be replaced or whether what is envisaged is a new solution. Underpinning each of these alternatives will be an initial set of business requirements.

If there is an existing solution, the scope of is operation and use is described.

The flaws in the current solution with respect to the business requirements will be identified.

The objectives and constraints of the proposed new solution will be defined.

This step will also determine the feasibility of the solution. A set of high-level solution options will be identified and analysed in terms of their:

- Financial feasibility – how much will the solution cost and what benefits will it generate?

- Technical feasibility – can the solution be implemented and can the operational requirements be delivered?

- Service feasibility – can the solution be introduced into the organisation and can it be operated and used? Can the required organisation changes be achieved?

There are other types of solution feasibility headings such as Legal/Regulatory/Compliance and Security.

The output from this step is a solution feasibility report that covers:

- The work done

- Summary of business requirements
- Objectives of the solution
- Explanation of the preferred/selected/recommended solution
- Information on the alternative solution options evaluated and the reasons for their rejection
- Proposed implementation schedule
- Indicative cost benefit analysis

8.3.5.1.1.2 Structured Analysis

The structured analysis consists of using the solution design and operation techniques described at the start of this section.

The current solution, if any, is described by a DFD and an ERD.

The processes implemented by the current solution are described. The data used by and created by the processes are described. The performance of the processes is described.

8.3.5.1.1.3 Structured Design

The proposed solution is described in a DFD and ERD. The ELH for the solution is created.

The consumer interfaces to the solution are described.

The approach to testing is described

8.3.5.1.1.4 Infrastructure Configuration Study

The infrastructure configuration required for solution implementation and operation are described.

8.3.5.1.1.5 Solution Construction and Implementation

The solution is implemented. This can include:

- Component acquisition
- Component development
- Unit, integration and system testing
- User acceptance testing
- Data migration and load
- Solution documentation and training
- Transition to production and support

8.3.5.1.1.6 Solution Operation and Maintenance

This represents the ongoing solution maintenance, operation and use phase. It can include ongoing enhancement, correction of problems and improvements.

8.3.5.1.2 Archimate

I am including a separate brief section on the Archimate visual model representation format because it can be of use in solution architecture engagements where business-level and high-level solution and technical capabilities and associated processes are to be described visually. It is not meant to be used for detailed modelling.

Even though Archimate is intended to be applied in an enterprise architecture context, it can be just as easily applied to solution architecture.

Archimate is a model representation language. It has its own set of symbols, grammar and syntax. It has the potential to provide a common language between IT and business to describe in a (reasonably) unambiguous and rigorous way. However, to be useful, both parties must understand the language and trust that it can be used to represent their needs.

Archimate can be viewed as an inflected entity relationship representational language where language elements are represented by adding symbols to the basic entity. The successful use of Archimate depends on all those involved knowing the vocabulary of inflections.

Like any other descriptive approach, Archimate is only useful if it can generate value, that is, if the cost of adopting and using it is less than the benefits it creates. There are many tools including open source ones[71] that implement Archimate. Once the organisation and architecture information is entered into the model, it can be viewed graphically.

The high-level structure of Archimate is shown below.

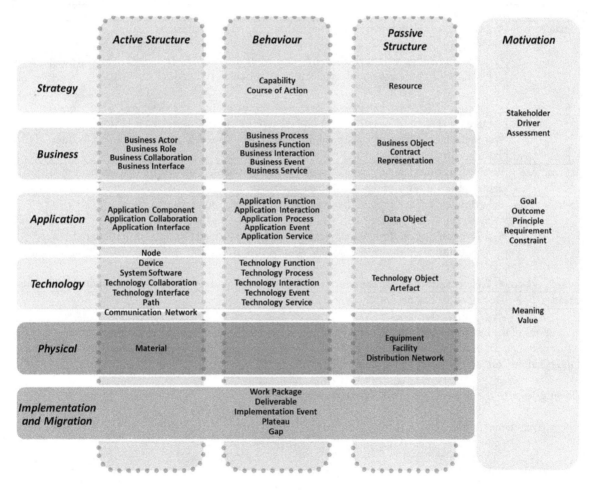

Figure 310 – Archimate Structure

The horizontal bars represent layers of the Archimate representation language. They are levels at which the organisation can be modelled or described.

Layers	Description

---

[71] See:
https://www.archimatetool.com/

Layers	Description
Strategy	Establish high-level business goals, architecture principles and initial business requirements
Business	Describes the business architecture of an enterprise - structure and interaction between the business strategy, organisation, functions, business processes and information needs
Application	Describes the information systems architectures of the enterprise - structure and interaction of the applications
Technology	Describes the technology architecture of the enterprise - structure and interaction of the platform services and logical and physical technology components
Physical	Describes physical facilities and equipment, distribution networks and materials
Implementation and Migration	Describes the support of implementation and migration through the opportunities and solutions identification, migration planning and implementation governance

Table 118 – Archimate Layers

The vertical bars represent aspects. These represent characteristics related to the concerns of different stakeholders.

Aspect	Description
Active Structure	Active structure elements are the subjects that can perform behaviour • *Internal active structure element* - represents entities that are capable of performing behaviour - business actors, application components and nodes • *External active structure element* - represents a point of access where one or more services are provided to the environment and the interfaces that expose this behaviour to the environment. The interface provides an external view of the service and hides its internal structure
Passive Structure	Passive structure elements are accessed by behaviour elements. They are frequently information or data objects but can also represent physical objects
Behaviour	Behaviour elements represent the dynamic aspects of the enterprise: • *Internal behaviour element* - unit of activity performed by one or more active structure elements • *External behaviour element* – service representing an explicitly defined exposed behaviour
Motivation	Describes the business motivation elements

The intersections of the horizontal aspects and the vertical layers contain elements that describe the constituent parts of the architecture and their set of characteristics. These elements are components that are used to construct the architecture model. Not all intersections contain elements.

The following describe the elements of each of the Archimate layers.

The strategy layer elements are:

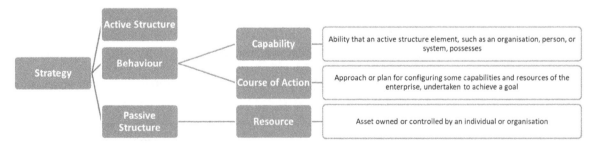

Figure 311 – Archimate Strategy Layer Elements

The symbols for these elements are:

Element	Symbol	Description
Capability		Ability that an active structure element, such as an organisation, person, or system, possesses
Course of Action		Approach or plan for configuring some capabilities and resources of the enterprise, undertaken to achieve a goal
Resource		Asset owned or controlled by an individual or organisation

Table 119 – Archimate Strategy Layer Elements

The business layer elements are:

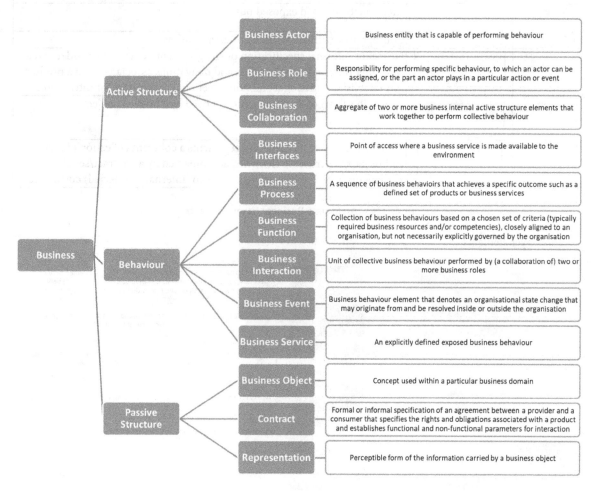

Figure 312 – Archimate Business Layer Elements

The symbols for these elements are:

Element	Symbol	Description
Business Actor		Business entity that is capable of performing behaviour
Business Role		Responsibility for performing specific behaviour, to which an actor can be assigned, or the part an actor plays in a particular action or event

Element	Symbol	Description
Business Collaboration		Aggregate of two or more business internal active structure elements that work together to perform collective behaviour
Business Interfaces		Point of access where a business service is made available to the environment
Business Process		A sequence of business behaviours that achieves a specific outcome such as a defined set of products or business services
Business Function		Collection of business behaviours based on a chosen set of criteria (typically required business resources and/or competencies), closely aligned to an organisation, but not necessarily explicitly governed by the organisation
Business Interaction		Unit of collective business behaviour performed by (a collaboration of) two or more business roles
Business Event		Business behaviour element that denotes an organisational state change that may originate from and be resolved inside or outside the organisation
Business Service		An explicitly defined exposed business behaviour
Business Object		Concept used within a particular business domain
Contract		Formal or informal specification of an agreement between a provider and a consumer that specifies the rights and obligations associated with a product and establishes functional and non-functional parameters for interaction
Representation		Perceptible form of the information carried by a business object
Product		This is a composite element and represents a coherent collection of services and/or passive structure elements, accompanied by a contract/set of agreements, which is offered as a whole to (internal or external) customers

Table 120 – Archimate Business Layer Elements

The application layer elements are:

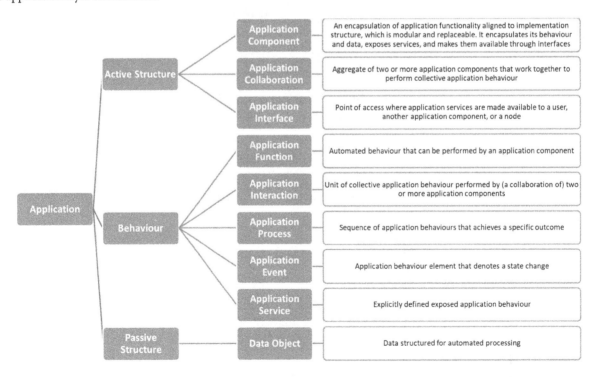

Figure 313 – Archimate Application Layer Elements

The symbols for these elements are:

Element	Symbol	Description
Application Component		An encapsulation of application functionality aligned to implementation structure, which is modular and replaceable. It encapsulates its behaviour and data, exposes services, and makes them available through interfaces
Application Collaboration		Aggregate of two or more application components that work together to perform collective application behaviour
Application Interface		Point of access where application services are made available to a user, another application component, or a node
Application Function		Automated behaviour that can be performed by an application component
Application Interaction		Unit of collective application behaviour performed by (a collaboration of) two or more application components
Application Process		Sequence of application behaviours that achieves a specific outcome
Application Event		Application behaviour element that denotes a state change
Application Service		Explicitly defined exposed application behaviour
Data Object		Data structured for automated processing

Table 121 – Archimate Application Layer Elements

The technology layer elements are:

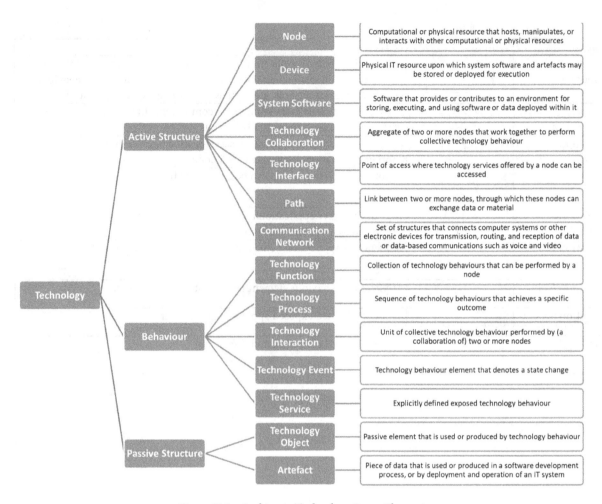

Figure 314 – Archimate Technology Layer Elements

The symbols for these elements are:

Element	Symbol	Description
Node		Computational or physical resource that hosts, manipulates, or interacts with other computational or physical resources
Device		Physical IT resource upon which system software and artefacts may be stored or deployed for execution
System Software		Software that provides or contributes to an environment for storing, executing, and using software or data deployed within it
Technology Collaboration		Aggregate of two or more nodes that work together to perform collective technology behaviour
Technology Interface		Point of access where technology services offered by a node can be accessed
Path		Link between two or more nodes, through which these nodes can exchange data or material
Communication Network		Set of structures that connects computer systems or other electronic devices for transmission, routing, and reception of data or data-based communications such as voice and video
Technology Function		Collection of technology behaviours that can be performed by a node
Technology Process		Sequence of technology behaviours that achieves a specific outcome

Element	Symbol	Description
Technology Interaction		Unit of collective technology behaviour performed by (a collaboration of) two or more nodes
Technology Event		Technology behaviour element that denotes a state change
Technology Service		Explicitly defined exposed technology behaviour
Technology Object		Passive element that is used or produced by technology behaviour
Artefact		Piece of data that is used or produced in a software development process, or by deployment and operation of an IT system

Table 122 – Archimate Technology Layer Elements

The physical layer elements are:

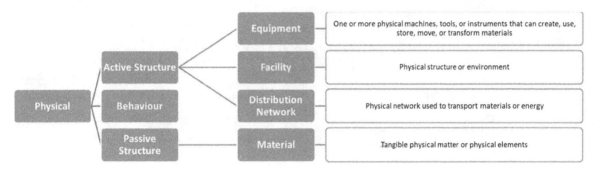

Figure 315 – Archimate Physical Layer Elements

The symbols for these elements are:

Element	Symbol	Description
Equipment		One or more physical machines, tools, or instruments that can create, use, store, move, or transform materials
Facility		Physical structure or environment
Distribution Network		Physical network used to transport materials or energy
Material		Tangible physical matter or physical elements

Table 123 – Archimate Physical Layer Elements

The motivation aspect elements are:

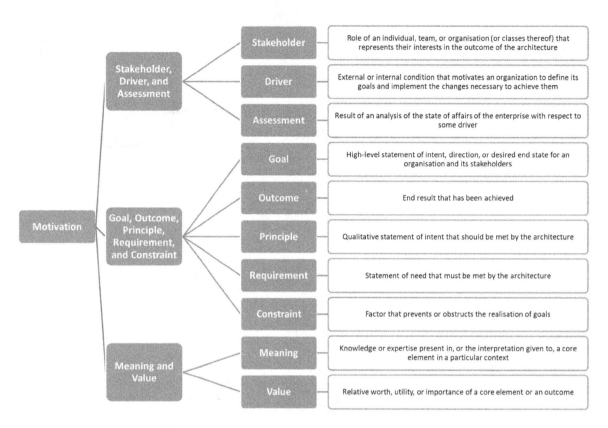

Figure 316 – Archimate Motivation Aspect Elements

Element	Symbol	Description
Stakeholder		Role of an individual, team, or organisation (or classes thereof) that represents their interests in the outcome of the architecture
Driver		External or internal condition that motivates an organisation to define its goals and implement the changes necessary to achieve them
Assessment		Result of an analysis of the state of affairs of the enterprise with respect to some driver
Goal		High-level statement of intent, direction, or desired end state for an organisation and its stakeholders
Outcome		End result that has been achieved
Principle		Qualitative statement of intent that should be met by the architecture
Requirement		Statement of need that must be met by the architecture
Constraint		Factor that prevents or obstructs the realisation of goals
Meaning		Knowledge or expertise present in, or the interpretation given to, a core element in a particular context
Value		Relative worth, utility, or importance of a core element or an outcome

Table 124 – Archimate Motivation Aspect Elements

Simplistically, the Solution on a Page representation described in section Steps 1-7 – Solution on a Page on page 270 could be represented in Archimate as follows:

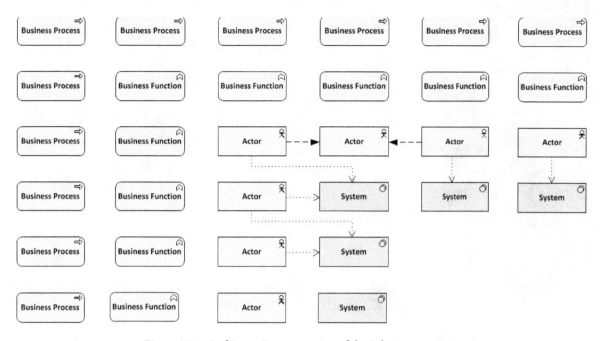

Figure 317 – Archimate Representation of the Solution on a Page

The data integration options described in section 4.8.5 on page 339 could be represented in Archimate as:

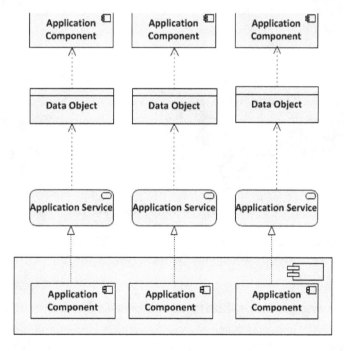

Figure 318 – Archimate Representation of Sample Data Integration and Exchange Options

The solution data landscape described in section 4.8.2 on page 326 could be represented in Archimate as:

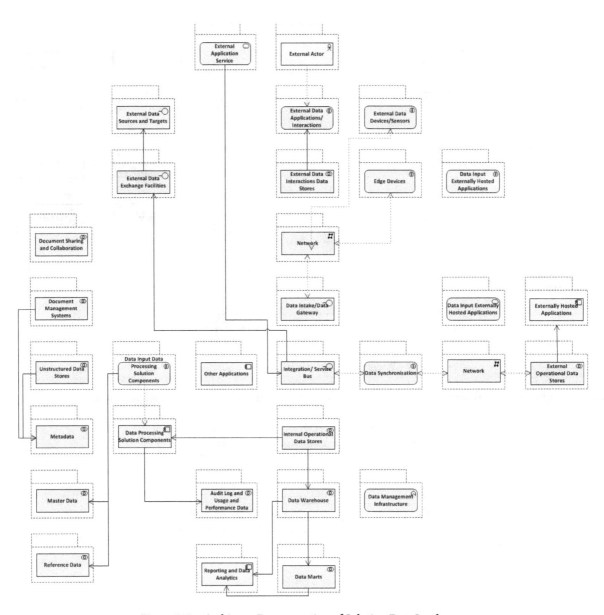

Figure 319 – Archimate Representation of Solution Data Landscape

Clearly there is greater rigour in formal representations of solution designs. This is achieved at the expense of greater complexity. I will leave the reader to decide if this approach has merit.

8.3.5.2 IT Architecture Frameworks, Methodologies and Description Languages

The following table lists some information technology architecture - encompassing some or all of enterprise architecture, business architecture and solution architecture - methodologies, languages, tools, frameworks and approaches. Some of these can be adapted to be used for solution architecture and the solution design process.

The enterprise architecture area is well-served with tools and frameworks.

Name	Description	Links	Status
ABACUS	This is aimed at enterprise architecture rather than solution architecture. It is a tool to allow enterprise architectures to be defined and modelled.	https://www.avolutionsoftware.com/abacus/	Commercial product

Name	Description	Links	Status
			Current
ArchiMate	ArchiMate is developed by The Open Group. It is aimed enterprise architecture modelling to support the description, analysis and visualisation of enterprise architectures across business areas. It can be applied to generating high-level solution designs

ArchiMate is supported by a number of commercial tools. | https://www.archimatetool.com/

http://www.opengroup.org/subjectareas/enterprise/archimate | |
| *Australian Defence Architecture Framework* | This describes a framework for acquiring capabilities from initial need to requirements specification to acquisition. | http://www.defence.gov.au/publications/docs/Defence%20Capability%20Development%20Handbook%20(DCDH)%202014%20-%20internet%20copy.pdf | Current |
| *Australian Government Architecture Reference Models* | This describes the Australian Government Architecture (AGA) and the Enterprise Architecture Principles. | https://www.finance.gov.au/archive/policy-guides-procurement/australian-government-architecture-aga/

https://www.finance.gov.au/sites/default/files/aga-ref-models.pdf | Archived |
| *Business Process Framework (eTOM)/ Frameworx* | The TM Forum is a telecommunications industry association. Its Frameworx Architecture includes Application (TAM), Business Process (eTOM) and Information (SID) frameworks. While aimed at telecommunications companies, it can be more widely applied to other utility-type organisations. | https://www.tmforum.org/business-process-framework/

https://www.tmforum.org/collaboration/frameworx-project/ | Proprietary and current |
Common Approach to Federal Enterprise Architecture		https://obamawhitehouse.archives.gov/sites/default/files/omb/assets/egov_docs/common_approach_to_federal_ea.pdf	Archived
CORA Model for IT Application Reference Architecture	CORA describes a Common Reference Architecture for implementing solutions, managing complexity and risk and introducing innovation.	http://www.coramodel.com/	Current
Data Management Book of Knowledge	This is aimed at data architectures. It is described in more details in section 4.8 on page 321.	https://www.dama.org/content/body-knowledge	Current
Department of National Defence/Canadian Armed Forces Architecture Framework	Department of National Defence / Canadian Armed Forces Architecture Framework (DNDAF).

This describes an enterprise architecture lifecycle management approach that includes governance, design, building, analysis and change management. | http://www.forces.gc.ca/en/about-policies-standards/dndaf.page | Current |
| *Dragon1* | This is a visualisation tool for representing and analysing an organisation's enterprise architecture. | https://www.dragon1.com/enterprise-architecture- | Current |

Name	Description	Links	Status
		tool	
Dynamic Architecture	This was developed by Sogeti until 2012. It consisted of five modules: 1. Infrastructure architecture 2. Software architecture 3. Business architecture 4. Governance IT governance, 5. Principles about the development of architectural principles	https://www.sogeti.nl/expertises/dya (In Dutch)	Archived
EAM Pattern Catalog	This is a library of Enterprise Architecture Management pattern. It aims to describe possible solutions for recurring problems. These can be adapted to a specific enterprise context.	http://eam-initiative.org/pages/1dgrgdhvpv2y2/Enterprise-Architecture-Management-Pattern-Catalog	Current
Enterprise Architecture Body of Knowledge	This aims to be a reference of ready-to-use knowledge concerning enterprise architecture.	http://eabok.org/	Current
ESS Enterprise Architecture Reference Framework	This is the European Statistical System Enterprise Architecture Reference Framework (ESS EARF). More information is available from: https://ec.europa.eu/eurostat/cros/system/files/ESS Reference_architecture_v1.0_29.09.2015.pdf	https://ec.europa.eu/eurostat/cros/content/ess-enterprise-architecture-reference-framework_en	Archived
Essential Architecture Framework	This relates to the Essential enterprise architecture tool. This is a commercial product.	https://www.enterprise-architecture.org/	Current
European Space Agency Architecture Framework	ESA-AF aims to describe a basis for enterprise architecture and systems of systems engineering by defining a common architecture definition language and processes. It is tailored to ESA's needs but can be applied elsewhere.	https://essr.esa.int/project/esa-architecture-framework	Current
Extreme Architecture Framework	This is based on the book Handbook of Enterprise Systems Architecture in Practice.	http://lonsdalesystems.com/post/extreme-architecture-framework-a-canvas-for-agile-enterprise-architecture	Current
Gartner's Enterprise Architecture Framework	Gartner acquired this when the acquired the Meta Group in 2005. It is not being developed.	https://www.gartner.com/doc/486650/gartners-enterprise-architecture-process-framework	Archived
IASA	Information Technology Architecture Body of Knowledge (ITABoK) 3.0 Global Business Technology Architecture contains a range of tools and resources aimed at IT architects.	https://iasaglobal.org/itabok3_0/	Current
Leading Enterprise Architecture Development (LEAD)ing Practice	This is a commercially available set of Enterprise Architecture Standards.	https://www.leadingpractice.com/enterprise-standards/enterprise-architecture/	Current
MEGAF	MEGAF is a generic meta model for software architecture meta models that aims to provide	http://megaf.di.univaq.it/	Archived

Name	Description	Links	Status
	infrastructure for realising architecture frameworks focussing on reusing viewpoints and languages and considering stakeholders and their concerns as part of the framework.		
Method for an Integrated Knowledge Environment	MIKE 2.0 is focussed on data and aims to define an information supply chain within the organisation from how data is created, accessed, presented and used in decision making to how it is kept secure, stored and destroyed.	http://mike2.openmethodology.org/	Current
National Association of State Chief Information Officers (NASCIO)	While NASCIO is focussed on US state and local, their enterprise architecture toolkit is a comprehensive framework for that combines structure, processes and templates to document the target architecture in a systematic and ordered way. It is a very good point to start any work on developing an EA practice, especially for public service organisations. The toolkit dates from 2004 and so is quite old, pre-dating the move to cloud-based services and platforms but the core principles remain current. It covers the architectural areas of: • Business Architecture • Information Architecture • Technology Architecture • Solution Architecture and thus can contribute to the design of solution architecture policies, standards and practices.	https://www.nascio.org/EA https://www.nascio.org/portals/0/EAToolKit/NASCIO-AEADTool-Kitv3.pdf	Current
National Enterprise Architecture Framework	This is produced by the government of the Kingdom of Bahrain. It contains a basic EA maturity model. It is a simple EA framework but one that can be used to assist with the development of EA. It is less applicable to solution architecture.	http://www.nea.gov.bh/	Current
NATO Architecture Framework	This defines a methodology for developing an EA practice. It is well structured. It is less applicable to solution architecture.	https://www.nato.int/cps/en/natohq/topics_157575.htm https://www.nato.int/nato_static_fl2014/assets/pdf/pdf_2018_08/20180801_180801-ac322-d_2018_0002_naf_final.pdf	Current
NIST Enterprise Architecture Model	The NIST EA Model is a reference framework for EA defining the relationships between of enterprise business, information and technology environments.	https://bigdatawg.nist.gov/_uploadfiles/M0197_v1_3201181507.pdf	Archived
OIO Enterprise Architecture Method	The OIO Architecture is developed by the Danish Agency for Digitisation (DAD) within the Ministry of Finance.	http://arkitekturguiden.digitaliser.dk/introduction-national-enterprise-	Current

Name	Description	Links	Status
	Most of the material is available only in Danish. Some of the documents are in English. It is less applicable to solution architecture.	architecture-denmark	
Pragmatic Enterprise Architecture Framework	This defines an EA implementation framework. It is less applicable to solution architecture.	http://www.pragmaticea.com/	Current
Rozanski and Woods	This is aimed at addressing the issue of designing and implementing effective software architectures for information systems. It dates from 2013.	https://www.viewpoints-and-perspectives.info/	Current
The Open Group Architecture Framework	TOGAF is the most widely referenced enterprise architecture framework. Elements can be applied to the solution architecture domain.	http://www.opengroup.org/subjectareas/enterprise/togaf	Current
UK Ministry of Defence Architecture Framework	While aimed supporting defence planning and change management activities, it is a well-recognised enterprise architecture framework. It contains views which are rules and templates aimed at providing a visualisation of the business area being analysed: • Strategic views (StVs) • Operational views (OVs) • Service oriented views (SOVs) • Systems views (SVs) • Acquisition views (AcVs) • Technical views (TVs) It is can be applied to the solution architecture domain.	https://www.gov.uk/guidance/mod-architecture-framework	Current
US Department of Defense Architecture Framework	This is a comprehensive architecture framework aimed at enabling the development of information technology architectures to allow information sharing. It is similar to the UK Ministry of Defence Architecture Framework. It incorporates a range of viewpoints and models to describe architectures: • Capability Viewpoint • Data and Information Viewpoint • Operational Viewpoint • Project Viewpoint • Services Viewpoint • Standards Viewpoint • Systems Viewpoint • Conceptual Data Model • Logical Data Model • Physical Data Model • Operational Activity Model • Operational Rules Model	https://dodcio.defense.gov/Library/DoD-Architecture-Framework/	Current

Name	Description	Links	Status
	• Services Rules Model • Systems Rules Model It is can be applied to the solution architecture domain.		

Table 125 – Enterprise Architecture Frameworks and Languages

Chapter 9. Solution Architecture and Innovation

The topic of innovation is covered in greater detail in other publications. The purpose of this brief section is to discuss innovation within the context of the solution architecture function and the contribution it can make.

The word *Innovation* is being used and misused pervasively without a clear definition, meaning or understanding of what is really meant. Innovation is not just about having ideas. Innovation is about driving the generation of good ideas and ensuring their appropriate adoption. Innovation is about generating business value: an idea without implementation has little merit.

Innovation =

Good Idea That is Defined and Validated

+ Appropriate Implementation and Adoption

+ Generation of Value

Figure 320 – Innovation Formula

Innovation needs to be a complete process from idea to operation,

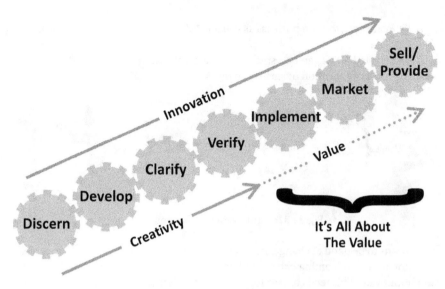

Figure 321 – Complete Innovation Process

Given the potentially large number of innovation ideas, organisations can waste resources and effort in evaluating ideas that will have little business impact. The innovation process needs to link innovation ideas to business objectives so their potential business impact and value can be assessed quickly.

Innovation can involve a new idea or an existing idea or process that is improved or an existing idea or process that is implemented or applied elsewhere in the organisation. Innovation extends creativity to the implementation of ideas and the generation of value.

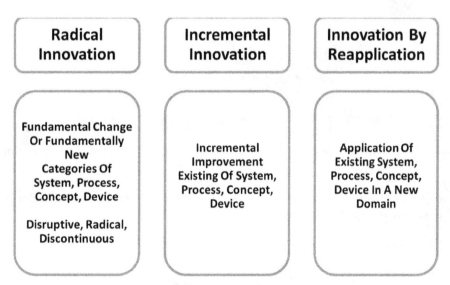

Figure 322 – Types of Innovation

The types of innovation are:

- *Radical Innovation* - Fundamental Change Or Fundamentally New Categories Of System, Process, Concept, Device, Disruptive, Radical, Discontinuous

- *Incremental Innovation* - Incremental Improvement Existing Of System, Process, Concept, Device

- *Innovation By Reapplication* - Application Of Existing System, Process, Concept, Device In A New Domain

Some regard *Innovation By Reapplication* as a business as usual function rather than pure innovation.

Innovation is not necessarily one big idea. It can be a small idea or a combination of smaller ideas. Greater value sometimes can be obtained more quickly by the application of smaller changes.

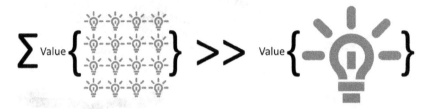

Figure 323 – Innovation Value Equation

To be good at innovation means to be good at change. Innovation implies and requires change. It exposes an organisation to change. Successful innovation means welcoming change and being able to successfully deliver change. Simply put, if you cannot change, you cannot innovate. This tends to be a forgotten dimension of innovation. However, once the organisation becomes good at innovation and change, this reinforces the culture of innovation, creating a *virtuous circle*.

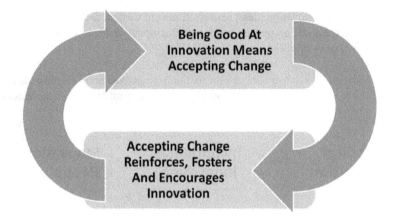

Figure 324 – Being Good At Innovation Means Being Good At Change

Section 3.3.1 on page 75 referred to the ways in which the IT architecture disciplines should and can contribute to the success of the business:

1. By taking the needs of the business for business solutions and supporting and enabling technologies into an information technology infrastructure and a portfolio of business solutions

2. By identifying potential uses for new technologies to enable the business to operate more effectively

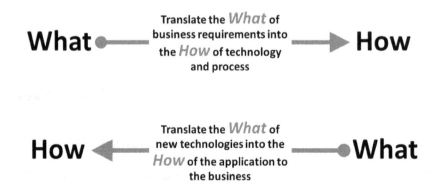

Figure 325 – Solution Architecture and Innovation

This is a two-way model of innovation where the information technology function is well-placed to offer innovation services, skills and expertise to the business organisation. Most business innovations will have a technology dimension or will require technology to being achieved. However, for the information technology function to do this, it must be able to offer these services and must be regarded by the business as a credible supplier of those services.

The topic of innovation was examined briefly in the topic on digital architecture and organisation transformation in Chapter 5 on page 391. Digital architecture is implicitly concerned with changing the way the organisation interacts with its consumers, suppliers and partners using information technology. This means there is a need to innovate in order to successfully implement initiatives such as digital transformation. However, digital transformation is not synonymous with innovation. Innovation is a much more general organisational capability.

Section 3.3.2 on page 80 referred to the run-the-business/change-the-business profile of the organisation. Innovation needs to be balanced against run-the-business activities. Too much innovation and associated organisation change can be disruptive and inefficient. Within the information technology function, solution architecture and the solution designs it creates are the primary means by which information technology solution changes are introduced into to the organisation. So just as the information technology function is well-placed to offer innovation services, the solution architecture function within information technology is best-placed to offer these services.

Any innovation process needs to include a fast, light-touch stage for validating and filtering innovation concepts, including their rejection if there is not sufficient value. The engagement section of this book (section 4.6 on page 161) describes a number of different engagement types that can be used as part of the innovation process to quickly evaluate the solution-related aspects of a business problem or challenge:

- The early engagement process (section 4.6.4 on page 235) can be used to explore the innovation concept in a structured way

- The rapid solution design process (section 4.6.5 on page 257) can be applied to define the specific of the solution required to achieve the innovation to allow the innovation concept to be assessed

An effective innovation process also requires greater openness, sponsoring of research and development initiatives including the allocation of time and resources to do this work and tolerance of the ambiguity intrinsic in this work.

To this end, the solution architecture function should include within its resource allocation and work programme a defined amount of time for each team member to research, explore and experiment with new technologies and capabilities. This research can be incorporated into a Technology Radar view of the potential impact the technology could have on the organisation and a view of its current usage by other organisations, its maturity and an estimate of its cost to implement. The impact could be rated on a scale of:

- *Adopt/Implement* – the technology is worth adopting by the organisation as it will deliver definite benefits
- *Trial/Pilot* – the organisation should invest more resources in installing the technology to determine its usefulness
- *Assess/Research* – the organisation should invest more resources in further research on the technology
- *Hold/Watch* – the organisation should maintain an awareness of the technology but not pursue it any further

These Technology Radar can be published regularly to the wider organisation.

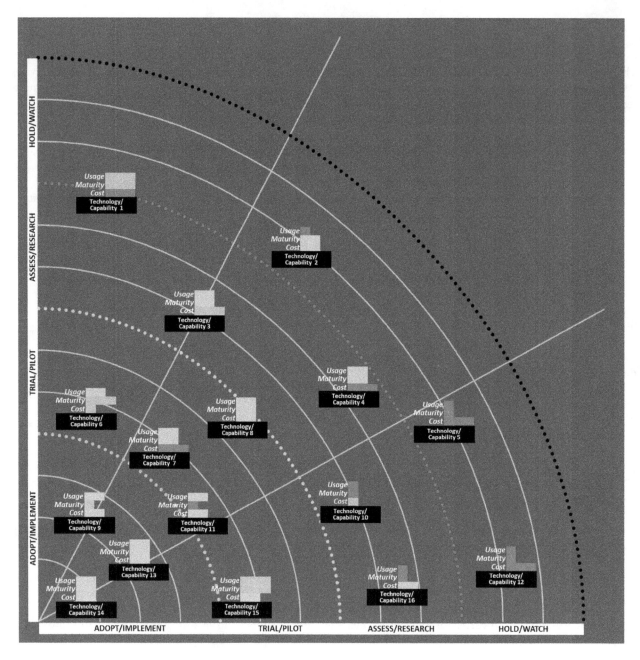

Figure 326 – Sample Technology Radar

Innovation can be found across all parts of the organisation. Opportunities for innovation can exist everywhere.

	Business Model	How Do You Make Money?
Finance	Networking and Alliances	How Do You Work With Other Organisations For Mutual Benefit?
Processes	Core Processes	How Do You Create and Add Value To Your Products And Services?
	Enabling Processes	How Are Core Processes Supported And Enabled?
Products and Services	Product Performance	How Do You Design Your Core Products And Services?
	Product System	How Do You Connect Or Provide A Common Platform For Your Products And Services?
	Service	How Do You Provide Value To Your Consumers Beyond Your Core Products And Services?
Provision and	Channels	How Do You Get Core Products And Services to Market?

Delivery	Brand	How Do You Communicate Your Core Products And Services?
	Customer Experience	How Do Consumers Feel When They Interact With Your Organisation And Your Products And Services?

Table 126 – Areas To Look For Innovation

Traditional research and development areas have tended to dominate innovation resources. Innovation investment is typically skewed in favour of products.

The following chart illustrates the typical innovation investment profile across the innovation areas listed above.

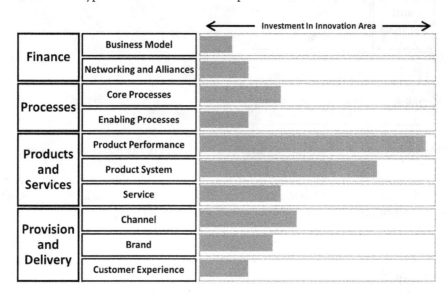

Figure 327 – Profile Of Investment In Innovation Across Innovation Areas

Innovation within the areas of processes and business models is limited while product and service investment is considerably higher.

The following chart profiles the return on investment achieved in the same areas of innovation.

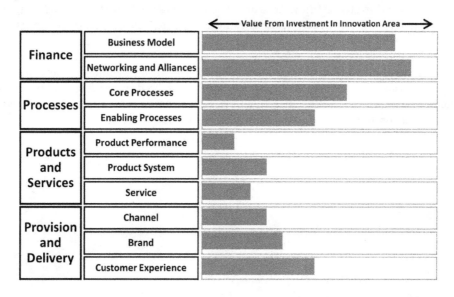

Figure 328 – Profile Of Return on Investment In Innovation Across Innovation Areas

The following chart overlays the investment and return on investment profiles in the innovation areas, highlighting the differences.

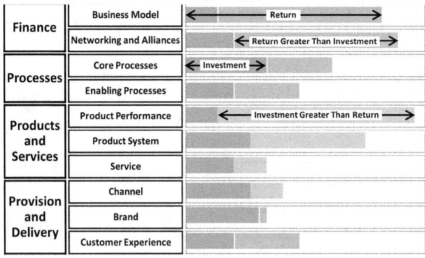

Figure 329 – Comparison of Investment and Return on Investment In Innovation Across Innovation Areas

There are large gaps in returns across innovation areas. Small investments in non-traditional areas yield significant returns. Large investments in traditional research and development areas yield small returns. This is the concept of the breakthrough innovation which seems very attractive but which can be very difficult to achieve.

Product and service investment can give a poor return. Investment is these areas is risky with a high reward potential but with a corresponding high risk. Product and service innovation can be seductive. It can be seen by managers in those areas as a source of prestige (see section 8.3.4.1 on page 505 that discusses Conway's Law and on the greater prestige that attaches to being the manager of a large function). But it can take a long time. Many product and service developments fail or are cancelled before delivery.

It may be that there is a failure in the innovation process in relation to products and services. Too much time and money may be spent without reaching a conclusion quickly.

Frequently simpler innovation in the areas of processes and business models can generate much better returns and do so more quickly with lower risk and greater certainty. Some of this can be explained by sustained pattern of investment in traditional research and development and history of low investment in improvements outside these areas. So latent available improvements can be achieved more easily and quickly in the areas of processes and business models.

Nonetheless this demonstrates that innovation can be successfully applied outside traditional product and service-oriented areas to yield value to the organisation. At best the organisation needs a balanced approach to innovation. The solution architecture function should be enabled to offer innovation services as part of its wider portfolio of business engagement and solution design services. The function needs to be capable of offering these services.